The Chronicle of

for the Crusading Period

from

al-Kāmil fī'l-ta'rīkh

The Chronicle of Ibn al-Athīr for the Crusading Period

from

al-Kāmil fī'l-ta'rīkh

Part 1

The Years 491-541/1097-1146

The Coming of the Franks and The Muslim Response

Translated by

D.S. Richards

ASHGATE

First published in paperback 2010.

Published by
Ashgate Publishing Limited
Wey Court East
Union Road
Farnham
Surrey, GU9 7PT
England

Ashgate Publishing Company
Suite 420
101 Cherry Street
Burlington
VT 05401-4405
USA

www.ashgate.com

British Library Cataloguing in Publication Data
Ibn al-Athir, Izz al-Din, 1160–1233
The Chronicle of Ibn al-Athir for the Crusading Period from al-Kamil i'l-Ta'rikh
Part 1: The Years 541–589/1146–1193: The Age of Nur al-Din and Saladin. –
(Crusade Texts in Translation; 13)
1. Crusades – Early works to 1800. I. Title II. Richards, D. S. (Donald Sidney), 1935–.
940.1'82

Library of Congress Control Number: 2006926785

ISBN 9780754640776 (hbk)
ISBN 9780754669500 (pbk)

Mixed Sources
Product group from well-managed forests and other controlled sources
www.fsc.org Cert no. SA-COC-1565
© 1996 Forest Stewardship Council
FSC

Printed and bound in Great Britain by
MPG Books Group, UK

Contents

Preface

Ibn al-Athīr's chronicle, *al-Kāmil fi'l-ta'rīkh*, which one could translate as *The Perfect* or *Complete Work of History*, is an impressive achievement. Within the wide chronological and geographical scope of its pages it presents a narrative that starts with Creation, passes through those areas of pre-Islamic history that Muslims were aware of, that is, accounts of Persian, Roman and Jewish history and the traditions of the Arabs before Islam, and then traces in a broadly annalistic fashion the history of the caliphate and the various dynasties that succeeded one another in the Islamic world from Spain to the borders of central Asia.

His narrative ends abruptly towards the end of the second decade of the thirteenth century just a little before his death. The standard nineteenth-century edition reproduces from the manuscripts the rubric that announced the year 629/1231-2 but was never followed by any further text. Other, mainly minor, indications within the text indicate that the work did not ever receive a final revision.

In the manuscript age the relative paucity of books and the fragility of stored knowledge meant that there was a continual reprocessing of previous writings. Especially in the field of historiography, as time passed and history's tale grew longer, there was a strong tendency to reduce previous material to manageable proportions and then append an account of one's own times. This is clearly what Ibn al-Athīr was about over the whole range of his work. For the first centuries of Islam his main source was the chronicle of al-Ṭabarī. The introduction to the *Kāmil* that Ibn al-Athīr wrote makes it clear that his aim was to produce a discrete work which would enable students of history to dispense with the need to consult a variety of works. This may well be described as an undertaking of abbreviation but the result is a work of considerable dimensions. The edition used for this translation amounts to twelve substantial volumes. It is the comprehensiveness of his narrative that gives this work its value, as does the fact that, following on from those parts that are based on al-Ṭabarī, this chronicle preserves sources that have not otherwise survived. That these sources are not always explicitly identified is regrettable. However, it is a generally held opinion that the study of Islamic history would be much the poorer without Ibn al-Athīr's *Kāmil*.

This volume appears in the series Crusader Texts in Translation. Ibn al-Athīr's account of the Muslim struggle with the Crusaders is, of course, the justification for its inclusion and this translation starts from the point at which Ibn al-Athīr introduces into his narrative reference to the background and initial progress of the First Crusade, that is, the year 491/1097-8, which comes in the tenth volume of the Beirut edition. This translation ends with the death of Zankī in 541/1146, which may be understood to mark the end of a stage in the response of Islam to the phenomenon of the Crusades.

However, the wide scope of this chronicle takes it well beyond the events in Syria and Palestine. The fortunes of the Abbasid caliphate at Baghdad and the rivalries for power within the Saljuq sultanate loom large in this account. We read of the renewed inroads of Turkish nomads and of other invaders into Transoxania at one end of the Islamic world and at the other we read of the decline of the Almoravid dynasty in the Maghrib, the rise of the Almohads (*al-Muwaḥḥidūn*) and events in Spain. Inevitably some matters are dealt with in a more summary fashion than others. Ibn al-Athīr was aware (and not alone in this) of the widespread threat from Europe, the advance of Christian power in Spain and the expansionism of Norman Sicily, in addition to the invasion of the Holy Land and the establishment of Christian states there. The space devoted to the confrontation with the Crusaders is significant, and rightly so, of course, because the Crusades affected the inhabitants of the areas of direct contact in ways that cannot be overestimated. However, from the wide-ranging contents of this volume one may acknowledge that this matter was not all-consuming for Muslims, at least, not in the mind of one thirteenth-century Mesopotamian historian.

I am grateful to the editors of this series for their willingness to add this volume and the sequels that are planned and in preparation to their growing list of translated sources for the history of the Crusades. My thanks go to my former colleagues and to the library staff of the Oriental Institute at Oxford for their continued welcome and support. In particular I owe much to the help of Professor Geert Jan van Gelder and Dr Emilie Savage-Smith, respectively for the elucidation of problematic verses and for enlightenment on matters medical and astrological. I thank Dr Peter Jackson of the University of Keele for reading this in draft, correcting my slips and making valuable suggestions. As always my debt to my wife Pamela for unfailing support is immeasurable.

Introduction

The author, Ibn al-Athīr

The family of Ibn al-Athīr was associated with the Zankid dynasty, especially the branch centred on Mosul. His father administered the *dīwān*, the central bureau in the Mesopotamian town of Jazīrat ibn 'Umar, the modern Cizre on the Tigris above Mosul, and was a protégé of the influential vizier, Jamāl al-Dīn Muḥammad al-Isfahānī. The family owned orchards (*basātīn*) at a place called al-'Aqīma across the Tigris from Jazīrat Ibn 'Umar. There was a family house in their village of Qaṣr Ḥarb. In Rajab 579/October-November 1183 his father moved to Mosul.

Ibn al-Athīr's two brothers, one older and one younger, also had noteworthy careers in the administrative and scholarly fields. The older one was Majd al-Dīn Mubārak, who was born in 544/1149 and died in 606/1210. His bureaucratic career was entirely in the service of the Zankid house and he wrote works of a philological and religious character. The younger brother, Ḍiyā' al-Dīn Naṣr Allāh, who was born in 558/1163, followed a more brilliant career, but one with more political hazards. He served Saladin towards the end of his reign and was vizier for the wayward son of Saladin, al-Afḍal 'Alī. His official correspondence was collected and preserved as a model of prose style and he was also the author of influential works on literary criticism. He died in 637/1239 when in Baghdad on an embassy from Mosul.[1]

Our historian, Ibn al-Athīr, was born on 4 Jumādā I 555/13 May 1160 at Jazīrat Ibn 'Umar. Hence the adjective expressing affiliation, al-Jazarī, which is added to his full name, that is, 'Izz al-Dīn Abū'l-Ḥasan 'Alī ibn Muḥammad al-Jazarī. We gain mere glimpses of his life from the random remarks in his own writings and from the biographical notice that Ibn Khallikān put in his well-known biographical dictionary. After early studies at home, Ibn al-Athīr performed a pilgrimage to Mecca in 576/1181. On his return via Baghdad he continued his studies there but was again in Mosul by 581/1185-6 in time for Saladin's second siege of that city. In 584/1188-9 he was in Syria with the aim of visiting Jerusalem after Saladin's great victories and possibly may have met him at the siege of Krak des Chevaliers, although he does not positively say so.

At no stage is there any indication that Ibn al-Athīr had the sort of direct involvement with any regime that his father and two brothers had. There is no mention of any regular employment in the bureaucracy. When mentioning his

---

[1] For the careers and literary output of Majd al-Dīn and Ḍiyā' al-Dīn, see *EI(2)*, iii, 723–5.

great predecessor, the historian al-Ṭabarī, Ibn al-Athīr comments that he was content with the income from a village in Ṭabaristān which his father had left him.[2] One wonders whether something of the same sort might have been true of Ibn al-Athīr himself. Towards the end of his life he enjoyed the patronage of Shihāb al-Dīn Ṭughril, the Atabeg of Aleppo, and it was in Aleppo that Ibn Khallikān met him and described him as 'perfect in accomplishments, of generous character and very modest.' Another patron at this period was Badr al-Dīn Lu'lu', an emir of the Zankids who made himself independent ruler of Mosul. At the age of seventy-three, Ibn al-Athīr died at Mosul in Sha'bān 630/June 1233.

The writings of Ibn al-Athīr

In addition to his major chronicle, which will be separately dealt with below, Ibn al-Athīr produced three other works, one in the field of *'ilm*, religious learning, one specialist reference work and one historical monograph.

His contribution to the Islamic religious sciences was a large alphabetically-arranged compendium of the Companions of the Prophet who transmitted Prophetic Tradition (*Ḥadīth*). The title he gave this work, which was begun in Jerusalem and completed in Mosul, is *The Lions of the Thicket concerning Knowledge of the Companions* (*Usd al-ghāba fī ma'rifat al-ṣaḥāba*). There are three modern editions, the most recent of which is a Beirut, 1997 edition by Khalīl Shīḥa. The section on the Prophet Muḥammad was extracted from this work and published separately as *al-Sīra al-nabawiyya* (*The Life of the Prophet*) by the Beirut house Dār al-Wirāqa in 1391/1971.

The reference work is a revision of an earlier work by al-Sam'ānī,[3] who died in 562/1166 and made an alphabetical list of *nisba*s, the adjectives that express an affiliation of some sort (for example, al-Jazarī mentioned above), and provided explanations and identifications for them. This work was called simply *The Book of Nisbas* (*Kitāb al-ansāb*). Ibn al-Athīr entitled his 'successful, improved' version[4] *The Quintessence concerning the Correction of Nisbas* (*al-Lubāb fī tahdhīb al-ansāb*). Towards the end of the Mamluke period al-Suyūṭī produced an abbreviated version of Ibn al-Athīr's work which he called *The Essence of the Quintessence* (*Lubb al-lubāb*).[5]

His historical monograph was expressly written to celebrate the Zankid dynasty and to record the author's deep sense of obligation both on his own account and on behalf of his family for the favour shown them. It is in this work that Ibn al-Athīr's

---

2 *Kāmil*, viii, 136.

3 See *Encyclopedia of Arabic Literature*, ii, 684.

4 *EI(2)*, iii, 724. There is a Cairo edition in three volumes, 1356-60/1937-40 and a partial edition by F. Wüstenfeld, Göttingen, 1835. More recently it has been edited by 'Abd al-Laṭīf Ḥasan 'Abd al-Raḥmān, Beirut, 2000.

5 Ed. P.J. Veth, Leiden, 1851.

often noted partiality for the Zankid house is at its most obvious. This monograph is written with a greater striving for literary effect and a more frequent use of elevated language and rhymed prose.

The monograph has the title *The Resplendent History of the Atabeg Dynasty* (*al-Ta'rīkh al-bāhir fī'l-dawla al-atābakiyya*). It was probably written in the period 609-15/1212-18 and its narrative ends with the death of Nūr al-Dīn Arslān in Rajab 607/January 1211.[6] The text was first published in *Receuil des Historiens des Croisades, Historiens orientaux*, ii, part 1, Paris, 1876, edited by de Slane and de Meynard. A more recent edition is that of A.A. Tolaymat (Cairo, 1963).

The chronicle, *al-Kāmil fī'l-ta'rīkh*

Exactly when Ibn al-Athīr began to write his major chronicle cannot be known. He himself says that he wrote much of it in the family house in the village of Qaṣr Ḥarb below Mosul, where the family built a hospice for Sufis and endowed it with the rents from the village. The ruins of the palace of Ḥarb ibn 'Abd Allāh, one of the Abbasid al-Manṣūr's generals, were visible there.[7] To suppose that Ibn al-Athīr's imagination might have been stirred by the sight of them, as was the imagination of Gibbon when he sat among the ruins of the Forum at Rome, is perhaps to attribute to him an anachronistic sensibility. However that might be, Ibn al-Athīr wrote large sections of his chronicle before he embarked on the *Bāhir* monograph. It has been argued[8] that he brought the narrative of his first version of the chronicle, which is what he refers to as *al-Mustaqṣā fī'l-ta'rīkh* (*The Comprehensive Account of History*), down to the year 595/1198-9 at least, before putting it aside (as he himself says in the introduction subsequently provided for the full work) and taking up the writing of the *Bāhir*. Before 620/1223 Ibn al-Athīr returned to his major work, revised it, brought it up to date, gave it its new title, *al-Kāmil fī'l-ta'rīkh*, and included cross references to the *Bāhir*. The Paris Ms 1499 preserves this stage of the work. His patron, Badr al-Dīn Lu'lu', encouraged and urged him to engage with his magnum opus again. Probably a further revision and bringing up to date took place in 625/1228. After that his writing remained more or less up to date with events until the work ended suddenly at the close of 628/late 1231.

In the period covered by this translation there are several instances of Ibn al-Athīr's practice of covering at a convenient point a number of connected developments that stretch over several years. In other words one should note examples of his breaking what would be a strict annalistic arrangement of the

---

6 For the composition date and relationship with the *Kāmil*, see Richards, 'Ibn al-Athīr', 78-80, and Richards, 'Some consideration'.

7 *Kāmil*, v, 572.

8 See Richards, 'Ibn al-Athīr', 78-83.

material. A significant example of this is the extended passage on the rise of the Almohads in the Maghrib, which is given under the year 514/1120-21 but looks backwards and forwards, taking the narrative down to 544/1149-50.

If this readiness to ignore the annalistic format is considered a merit of his writing, the deficiency regularly pointed out is his failure to identify his sources, by which the main supporting texts for his narrative are meant. Nobody can deny that here and there specific sources are mentioned, literary or oral, but they are generally for incidental comment or material or to attribute an illustrative anecdote. Authors mentioned, apart from the poets that are quoted, include al-Ṣūlī, Ibn 'Asākir and 'Imād al-Dīn al-Isfahānī. However, there are two historians whose works, apart from any incidental reference, provide the solid bulk of Ibn al-Athīr's material in this volume, although without explicit acknowledgment. They are Ibn al-Jawzī, who died in 597/1200, and Ibn al-Qalānisī, who died the year Ibn al-Athīr was born, 555/1160. The former was above all his source for events in Baghdad, Iraq and Persia, while the latter predominately provided material for Syria and the region to the north of Syria. Ibn al-Athīr's use of his sources for Muslim relations with the Crusading states has been examined in detail and found wanting by H.A.R. Gibb.[9] However, it must remain an open question, and by its nature an unanswerable one, whether the apparent distortions of Ibn al-Athīr's sources are the result of conscious intent or the result of inaccurate and muddled abbreviating or conflation. To provide a balance, the generous view of Gabrieli may be quoted here:

> One man stands out as a true historian from the ranks of more or less diligent chroniclers: Ibn al-Athīr. His reputation among Orientalists has recently diminished, because of the free and tendentious use he makes of his sources, but the qualities that reduce his reliability as documentary evidence are those of an original thinker, outstanding among so many passive compilers of facts.[10]

Ibn al-Athīr's own family, his father and brothers, were a direct channel of information because of their close contact with the Zankid regime. This is perhaps more strikingly obvious in the material of the *Bāhir* than it is in the *Kāmil*. Only occasionally does Ibn al-Athīr mention that he personally had had access to archival material, for example when he reports that he had seen the document (a *manshūr*) in which Sultan Sanjar, as overlord, granted an *iqṭā'* to Sultan Mahmūd.[11]

A question that arises is whether Ibn al-Athīr had access to, and used, historical works written in Persian. Claude Cahen believed that he had no Persian, although it is not clear on what basis. As an addition to the previous discussion of this point, one might point to three other explanations or interpretations of Persian names and

---

[9] H.A.R. Gibb, 'Notes on the Arabic Materials for the History of the Early Crusades,' *Bulletin of the School of Oriental and African Studies*, vol. vii, 1935, 739–54.

[10] Gabrieli, *Arab Historians*, xix–xx.

[11] *Bāhir*, 21.

one expression found early in his chronicle.[12] These explanations could, of course, have been borrowed from an Arabic source. They cannot themselves prove any understanding of Persian. For what it is worth, Ibn al-Athīr records[13] that his father did not understand what a mamluke said to Zankī in *al-'ajamiyya*, which could have been either Persian or Turkish.

One interesting feature of the *Kāmil* is the relatively extensive introduction which Ibn al-Athīr provided for his chronicle. A little of this may be sampled in English translation provided by F. Rosenthal.[14] In this introduction the author defends the discipline of history, which was still regarded with suspicion by some of the ulema, and gives his views on the nature and purposes of history. His views are typical of historians, both Islamic and European, in the Middle Ages. History is above all a mine of exempla, practical and moral lessons that teach the wise man what he should aim to imitate and what he ought to avoid. This belief that history has a positive use, that its lessons may change people for the better and bring them to choose better ways, cannot easily be reconciled with the opposing notion that the progress of human affairs is governed by a pre-ordained plan of God. In Ibn al-Athīr's chronicle the divine plan is indeed frequently put forward as the explanation of events, while Ibn al-Athīr also gives explanations for events in terms of an individual's desires and interests or of wider political or strategic considerations. Unless we accept that the expression of the fatalistic view is merely conventional, we must recognise the contradiction in the author's thinking. However, when Ibn al-Athīr's writes 'the reason for this was that ...', he not infrequently provides not what one would now accept as a logical reason but rather an expository narrative of events. The semantic range of the Arabic *sabab* is such that it can mean 'cause' but also 'means, way.' Hence the translation 'this came about because ...', followed by an account of the particular course of events.

One might note in passing that in a short extract from the introduction translated by Rosenthal[15] Ibn al-Athīr condemns the recording by historians of certain trivial details, in which he includes appointments of minor officials, changes in prices for foodstuffs and such like. Even a casual reading of this chronicle will show that Ibn al-Athīr's own work was far from innocent of such items. In particular, he, like any mediaeval historian, cannot resist strange natural events and prodigies. The reader might well find odd the practice of giving the often rather jejune obituary notices under the various years. They appear to be selected somewhat arbitrarily from available sources and generally tell one very little. However, Ibn al-Athīr is making a nod, even though a rather mechanical one, towards the notion of the importance of the continuity of scholarship and the on-going transmission of religious knowledge.

---

[12] Richards, 'Some consideration', 88; and see *Kāmil*, i, 58, 64, 76.

[13] *Bāhir*, 78.

[14] Rosenthal, *Historiography*, 298–300, 336–7.

[15] See previous note.

Editions and previous translations of *al-Kāmil*

Relevant extracts from Ibn al-Athīr's *al-Kāmil*, accompanied by a French translation, were published as part of the monumental series of sources for the Crusades, the *Receuil des Historiens des Croisades*. The text which covered the years 491-585/1098-1190 was published in the first volume of the set designated *Historiens Orientaux*, pages 189-744, by De Slane in 1872. Extracts from the remainder, covering the years 585-628/1190-1231, followed in volume ii, part 1, pages 3-180, published in 1887.

The whole text of the chronicle was edited for the first time by C.J. Thornberg and published at Leiden in fourteen volumes, the last two of which are volumes of indices, between the years 1851-76. In 1301-2/1884-5 and in 1303/1886 two editions, both of twelve volumes, were issued at Cairo. Thornberg's edition was used as a basis for a new edition from the Beirut publishing house of Dār Ṣādir in 1965-7. This edition appeared in thirteen volumes, the last being an index volume, and reproduced the apparatus criticus in Latin of its predecessor and added some further notes of its own. The text itself was not reproduced photomechanically but was reset in type. Certain new errors resulted from this, although the Beirut edition also repeated some errors, and sometimes the omissions, of its model.

In recent years two further editions have appeared from Beirut. One prepared by ʻUmar Tadmurī was issued in 1417/1997 by the publishing house Dār al-Kitāb al-ʻArabī. It has an apparatus criticus and is in eleven volumes, the last of which is a volume of indices. The other, again in eleven volumes, appeared in 1418/1998 from Dār al-Kutub al-ʻIlmiyya, edited by Abū'l-Fida' ʻAbd Allāh al-Qāḍī. It has no introduction and hardly any annotation. The last volume contains indices prepared by Ibrahīm Shams al-Dīn.

The French version of the extracts in the *Receuil* series seems to have been the main source of knowledge of Ibn al-Athīr's work for those without access to the Arabic original. Edmond Fagnan published a French translation of passages from the *Kāmil* relevant to North African and Spanish affairs.[16] Other extracts dealing with Crusading history were translated by Francesco Gabrieli into Italian and are also available in English.[17] Amin Maalouf interspersed his narrative with many scattered passages, translated from Ibn al-Athīr, in his *Les Croisades vues par les Arabes*, of which there is an English version.[18]

---

[16] The passages that correspond to the matter of this volume are in Fagnan, *Annales*, 510-59.

[17] For the relevant passages for this volume, see Gabrieli, *Arab Historians*, 3-23, 41-3, 50-55.

[18] Amin Maalouf, *The Crusades through Arab Eyes*, trans. Jon Rothschild, London, 1984.

The present translation

The Dār Ṣādir edition has been used as the basis for this translation and is generally referred to in the footnotes as 'the text' or 'the edition'. For ease of reference to the original Arabic the page numbers of this edition have been given in bold type within square brackets. These page numbers have also been used for any cross-references. Frequent recourse has been made to the edition of Thornberg and the variant readings that are recorded in its notes. When a reading from that source has been adopted, it will be mentioned in the translation's footnotes. Square brackets have also been used to correct omissions in the text or for clarification when extra wording is felt to be necessary in the English. In addition I have consulted the Bodleian Ms. Pococke 346, which appears to offer a few good readings and obvious corrections that were not utilised by Thornberg.

Dates according to the Ḥijrī calendar within the text have been converted according to the tables provided by G.S.P. Grenville[19] and the equivalent placed within square brackets in the text. As the Muslim calendar uses lunar months and the beginning of each month depended on the sighting of the new moon, converted dates are subject to an error of plus or minus a few days. If the day of the week is not stated in the original, then the equivalent Christian date given is not absolutely secure. When the day of the week is given, then it may be understood that the correspondence is correct in all details. If an 'equals' sign is added (=), this indicates that a necessary adjustment has been made in the conversion.

Ibn al-Athīr's prose style in the Kāmil is for the most part straightforward. It might even be argued that it is somewhat pedestrian and repetitive. Every translator's aim is to be accurate and readable - in that order. When translating Arabic it is highly desirable to vary the syntax and rhythm of the original. An English version would be intolerable, if this were not done. Since some effort to add variation has, unashamedly, been made, one can only trust that the 'enlivening' has not been excessive. At times one is aware of an ambiguity in Arabic prose narrative over the precise application of third-person pronouns, particularly in the absence of any reflexive pronoun or pronominal adjective. In addition, one feels the occasional need in an English version to spell out the identity of a person rather than maintain the original's pronominal approach, all for the sake of clarity. Whenever I have made a change on the basis of such considerations it has not been especially noted and the hope is that the interpretation has been correct in all cases.

There is the thorny matter of transliteration. Some place names and some terms are given in an English garb where such exist or are attested in dictionaries, such as Homs, Mosul, Edessa, Kaabah, khutbah, cadi and madrasah. Otherwise, a generally accepted transliteration style has been adopted, similar to that used by

---

[19] See G.S.P. Grenville, *The Muslim and Christian Calendars being tables for the conversion of Muslim and Christian dates from the Hijra to the year A.D. 2000*, Oxford, 1963.

the *Encyclopaedia of Islam*, although 'j' replaces 'dj' and 'q' replaces 'ḳ'. However, no fetishistic concern for consistency should be expected from this translator. This is particularly so when Persian or Turkish elements are concerned.

A more serious problem is what to do with a term which has not gained a place in English dictionaries and which it is entirely certain that no native English term can quite replace. For example, *iqṭā'* has been translated as 'fief' although no exact correspondence exists between the two institutions. I fear that the reader can only be urged to inform himself about the *iqṭā'* in mediaeval Muslim society and bring that understanding to 'fief'.[20]

Some explanatory comments will follow, which, it is hoped, will shed some light on similar points in the translation, in addition to whatever the annotation may suggest. This is how certain items have been dealt with:

1. *Malik* in modern terms means 'king', but here is normally given as 'prince', because it was used as a title for younger or lesser members of the Saljuq house, who might rule over a particular area as an appanage.

2. A *malik* was often assigned an *aṭābeg*, a term derived from two Turkish elements, meaning 'father' and 'lord' and signifying a cross between a regent and a guardian. The office of atabeg was often a step to fully independent rule.

3. 'Emir' (from Arabic *amīr*) denotes a member of the military elite, a member of the officer class which, granted the nature of society, wielded wide authority and jurisdiction.

4. The *shiḥna* was a military man, who controlled the garrison of a town or area and also had a policing, public order role. I have translated it as 'prefect'.

5. The *naqīb* was a representative of either the Abbasid family or of the Alids, responsible for keeping genealogical records and administering any charitable trusts in their favour. I have used the traditional term 'syndic' for this office and 'chief syndic' for *naqīb al-nuqabā'*.

6. 'Headman' translates the Arabic *ra'īs*, a civilian official who represents the interests of a given urban centre and also mediates those of the central regime.

7. 'Hospice' translates *ribāṭ*, an endowed institution where Sufis (members of the mystic orders of Islam) lodged, studied and practised their rites.

8. 'Mamluke' has been adopted rather than the strictly transliterated *mamlūk* ('owned'), denoting a slave, but most often a Turk of relatively privileged status, trained for a military career. 'Mamluke' also translates *ghulām*, the term with the same significance, used more frequently in the eastern Islamic world.

9. 'Vizier' is the first minister of the civilian bureaucracy.

10. It is difficult to avoid 'chamberlain' as the translation for *ḥājib*, the official primarily involved in the ordering of the court. As this office came to be held by military men, its duties expanded to the commanding and disciplining of troops. The composite term that recognises this, that is *amīr ḥājib*, has been rendered unimaginatively, but unexceptionably, as 'emir-chamberlain'.

---

[20] See, e.g., Lambton, 'Reflections'; *eadem*, *Continuity and Change*, chapter 3.

11. The Arabic term '*Ḥadīth*' has been used for what is often called in English the Tradition of the Prophet, the vast body of material which records (with chains of authorities) the sayings, doings and opinions of Muḥammad. Each record preserved is an 'ḥadīth'.

12. The Shiite sectarians, the offshoot of the Ismā'īlīs often called the Assassins, appear under their indigenous name as Bāṭinīs. This is derived from their concept of the *bāṭin*, their esoteric learning.

13. The Dīwān denotes the totality of the caliphal court and administration. With lower case it means a department of a regime's civilian bureaucracy.

14. '*Faqīh*', an expert on fiqh, Islamic law and jurisprudence, has been translated as 'lawyer'.

15. The '*ayyārūn*', whom I have called 'the urban gangs', were a complicated urban phenomenon. They resembled brigand guilds with residual religious commitment and cooperative welfare ideals and could, according to the times, either support or threaten the regime.[21]

16. The sizeable province of al-Jibāl, which stretches in a diagonal across north-western Iran and is centred on Hamadhān, is translated as 'the Uplands'.

---

[21] See C. Cahen, 'Mouvements populaires et autonomisme urbain dans l'Asie musulmane de Moyen Age,' *Arabica*, v, 1958, 225-50; vi, 1959, 25-56, 223-65.

The Chronicle of Ibn al-Athīr

The Coming of the Franks
and
the Muslim Response

[272] The Year 491 [1097-1098]

How the Franks took the city of Antioch

The power of the Franks and their increased importance were first manifested by their invasion of the lands of Islam and their conquest of part of them in the year 478 [1085-6], for [that was when] they took the city of Toledo and other cities of Spain, as we have already mentioned.[1]

Then in the year 484 [1091-2] they attacked and conquered the island of Sicily, as we have also mentioned.[2] They descended on the coasts of Ifrīqiya[3] and seized some part, which was then taken back from them. Later they took other parts, as you shall see.

When it was the year 490 [1096-7] they invaded Syria. The reason for their invasion was that their ruler, Baldwin, a relative of Roger the Frank who had conquered Sicily, gathered a great host of Franks and sent to Roger saying, 'I have gathered a great host and I am coming to you. I shall proceed to Ifrīqiya to take it and I shall be a neighbour of yours.' Roger assembled his men and consulted them about this. They said, 'By the truth of the Gospel, this is excellent for us and them. The lands will become Christian lands.' Roger raised his leg and gave a loud fart. 'By the truth of my religion,' he said, 'there is more use in that than in what you have to say!' 'How so?' they asked. 'If they come to me,' he replied, 'I shall require vast expenditure and ships to convey them to Ifrīqiya and troops [**273**] of mine also. If they take the territory it will be theirs and resources from Sicily will go to them. I shall be deprived of the money that comes in every year from agricultural revenues. If they do not succeed, they will return to my lands and I shall suffer from them. Tamīm[4] will say, "You have betrayed me and broken the agreement I have [with you]." Our mutual contacts and visits will be interrupted. The land of Ifrīqiya will be waiting for us. Whenever we find the strength we will take it.'

He summoned Baldwin's envoy and said to him, 'If you are determined to wage holy war on the Muslims, then the best way is to conquer Jerusalem. You will free it from their hands and have glory. Between me and the people of Ifrīqiya, however, are oaths and treaties.' They therefore made their preparations and marched forth to Syria.

It has been said that the Alid rulers of Egypt[5] became fearful when they saw the

[1] See *Kāmil*, x, 142-3.

[2] See *Kāmil*, x, 193-8.

[3] The loose term for the eastern part of the Maghrib (see *EI(2)*, iii, 1047-50).

[4] See below p. [**279**].

[5] i.e. the Fatimid caliphs.

strength and power of the Saljuq state, that it had gained control of Syrian lands as far as Gaza, leaving no buffer state between the Saljuqs and Egypt to protect them, and that Aqsīs[6] had entered Egypt and blockaded it. They therefore sent to the Franks to invite them to invade Syria, to conquer it and separate them and the [other] Muslims, but God knows best.

After they had decided to march to Syria, they went to Constantinople to cross the straits into Muslim lands, to travel on by land, for that would be easier for them. When they arrived, the Byzantine emperor refused them passage through his territory. He said, 'I will not allow you to cross into the lands of Islam until you swear to me that you will surrender Antioch to me.' His aim was to urge them to move into Islamic lands, assuming that Turks would not spare a single one of them, because he had seen how fierce they were and their control of the lands. [**274**] They agreed to that and crossed the Bosphorus at Constantinople in the year 490 [1096-7].

They reached the lands of Qilij Arslān ibn Sulaymān ibn Qutlumish,[7] namely Konya and other cities. Having arrived there, they were met by Qilij Arslān with his hosts, who resisted them. They put him to flight in Rajab 490 [July 1097] after a battle[8] and then traversed his lands into those of the son of the Armenian[9] which they marched through before emerging at Antioch and putting it under siege.

When the ruler Yaghī Siyān[10] heard of their coming, he feared the Christians in the city. He sent out the Muslim inhabitants by themselves and ordered them to dig the moat. Then the next day he sent out the Christians also to dig the moat, unaccompanied by any Muslim. They laboured on it until the evening but when they wished to enter the city he prevented them and said, 'You can give me Antioch until I see how things will be with us and the Franks.' They asked, 'Who will look after our sons and our wives?' 'I will look after them in your place,' he replied. So they held back and took up residence in the Frankish camp. The Franks besieged the city for nine months. Yaghī Siyān displayed such courage, excellent counsel, resolution and careful planning as had never been seen from anyone else. Most of the Franks perished. Had they remained in the numbers they set out with, they would have overwhelmed the lands of Islam. Yaghī Siyān protected the families of those Christians of Antioch, whom he had expelled, and restrained the hands that would do them harm.

After their siege of Antioch had lasted long, the Franks made contact with one of the men garrisoning the towers, who was an armourer, known as Rūzbah,[11] and

---

6 Alternative name for Atsiz ibn Uvak, a Turkoman chief who attacked Egypt in 1077 (see *EI(2)*, i, 750-51).

7 Saljuq sultan of Asia Minor (Rūm), died 1107 (see *EI(2)*, v, 103-4).

8 This is the battle of Dorylaeum, fought, according to Ibn Qal., 134, 'ten days left of Rajab [3 July]'. The accepted date is 1 July.

9 Perhaps Constantine I, son of Rupen I (1095-1102) is intended.

10 Turkish emir, given Aleppo as fief by Sultan Malikshāh.

11 According to Ibn Qal., 136, he was an Armenian named Nayrūz (Fayrūz?).

offered him money and grants of land. He was in charge of a tower next to the valley, which was built with a window overlooking the valley. After they had made an arrangement with this cursed armourer, they came to the window, which they opened and through which they entered. A large number climbed up on ropes. When they numbered more than five hundred, they blew the trumpet. That was [**275**] at dawn. The defenders were already tired from many sleepless nights on guard. Yaghī Siyān awoke and asked what was happening. He was told, 'That trumpet is from the citadel. No doubt it has already been taken.' However, it was not from the citadel but merely from that tower. He was seized with fear, opened the city gate and left in headlong flight with thirty retainers. His deputy as governor of the city came and asked after him. He was told that he had fled, so he himself fled by another gate. That was a boon for the Franks. Had he held firm for a while, they would have perished. The Franks entered the city through the gate and sacked it, killing the Muslims that were there. This was in Jumada I [April-May 1098].[12]

When the next day dawned, Yaghī Siyān came to his senses again. He had been like one distraught. He looked at himself after he had covered several leagues and said to those with him, 'Where am I?' 'Four leagues from Antioch,' he was told. He then regretted his flight to safety and his failure to fight until he either drove them from the city or was himself killed. He started to lament and bewail having abandoned his wife, his children and the Muslim population. Because of the violence of what afflicted him he fell from his horse in a faint. When he fell to the ground, his followers went to remount him but he could not hold on, for he was close to death. They therefore left him and rode away. An Armenian, who was cutting firewood and came across him when he was at his last gasp, killed him, cut off his head and took it to the Franks at Antioch.[13]

The Franks had written to the ruler of Aleppo and of Damascus, saying that they had no designs on lands other than those which had been in the hands of the Byzantines, that they had no other ambitions. This was a ruse and a trick on their part to stop aid being given to the ruler of Antioch.

[276] How the Muslims marched against the Franks and what befell them

When Qiwām al-Dawla Karbughā[14] heard of the Franks' doings and their conquest

---

[12] The city fell in fact in early June 1098. The sources give varying days and dates, but according to Ibn Qal., 136, it fell on the eve of Friday 1 Rajab/4 June. The citadel surrendered a week later.

[13] For the background and events leading to the fall of Antioch, see Asbridge, *Principality of Antioch*, 15-38.

[13] Governor of Mosul and other Mesopotamian towns, supporter of Barkyāruq and patron of Zankī. He died either at Marāgha in 494/1101 (Ibn Qal., 140; *Bāhir*, 16) or near Khoy in 495/1102 (see below pp. [**341-2**]).

of Antioch, he gathered his forces and marched to Syria. He camped at Marj Dābiq,[15] where the troops of Syria, both Turks and Arabs, rallied to him, apart from those who were in Aleppo. There assembled with him Duqāq ibn Tutush,[16] Tughtakīn the Atabeg,[17] Janāḥ al-Dawla the lord of Homs,[18] Arslān Tāsh the lord of Sinjār, Suqmān ibn Artuq[19] and other emirs, the likes of whom are not to be found. Hearing of this, the Franks' misfortunes increased and they were fearful because of their weakness and their shortage of provisions. The Muslims came and besieged them in Antioch, but Karbughā behaved badly towards the Muslims with him. He angered the emirs and lorded it over them, imagining that they would stay with him despite that. However, infuriated by this, they secretly planned to betray him, if there should be a battle, and they determined to give him up when the armies clashed.

The Franks, after they had taken Antioch, were left there for twelve days with nothing to eat. The powerful fed on their horses, while the wretched poor ate carrion and leaves. In view of this, they sent to Karbughā, asking him for terms to leave the city, but he did not grant what they sought. He said, 'My sword alone will eject you.'

The following princes were with them: Baldwin,[20] [Raymond of] St. Gilles,[21] Count Godfrey, the Count **[277]** lord of Edessa[22] and Bohemond the lord of Antioch, their leader. There was a monk there, of influence amongst them, who was a cunning man. He said to them, 'The Messiah (blessings be upon Him) had a lance which was buried in the church at Antioch, which was a great building.[23] If you find it, you will prevail, but if you do not find it, then destruction is assured.' He had previously buried a lance in a place there and removed the traces [of his digging]. He commanded them to fast and repent, which they did for three days. On the fourth day he took them all into the place, accompanied by the common people and workmen. They dug everywhere and found it as he had said. 'Rejoice

---

[15] The 'plain' near Dābiq in North Syria (see *EI(2)*, vi, 544).

[16] Saljuq prince of Damascus, died 497/1104.

[17] Ẓāhir al-Dīn Abū Manṣūr Ṭughtakīn, freedman of Tutush and atabeg (i.e. regent/guardian) of Duqāq. Founder of the short-lived Būrid dynasty in Damascus, he died in 522/1128 (see *EI(2)*, x, 600).

[18] Atabeg of Riḍwān ibn Tutush, ruled independently in Homs from 490/1097 and was assassinated in 496/1103.

[19] Correct 'Sulayman' in the text. Suqmān (died *c*.1104) was a member of the Turkoman Artuqid dynasty, for which see *EI(2)*, i, 662-7.

[20] In the original 'Bardwīl', which, as a variant for 'Baghdawīn', represents Baldwin (cf. *Bāhir*, 18). Baldwin of Le Bourg, subsequently count of Edessa and then King Baldwin II, is intended. In the comparable list in *Zubdat al-ḥalab*, ii, 134, he appears as 'Baghdawīn'. Cf. the list in Eddé, *Description*, 246.

[21] Count of Toulouse. The text has 'Ṣanjīl'.

[22] Baldwin of Boulogne, count of Edessa and future Baldwin I, is meant, although he was not present at Antioch. *Zubdat al-ḥalab*, ii, 134, mentions him as 'his [Godfrey's] brother, the count', as does Eddé, *Description*, 246.

in your coming victory', he said to them.[24]

On the fifth day they went out of the gate in scattered groups of five or six or so. The Muslims said to Karbughā, 'You ought to stand at the gate and kill all that come out, because now, when they are scattered, it is easy to deal with them.' He replied, 'No, do not do that. Leave them alone until they have all come out and then we can kill them.' He did not allow his men to engage them. However, one group of Muslims did kill several that had come out but he came in person and ordered them to desist.

When the Franks had all come out and not one of them remained within, they drew up a great battle line. At that, the Muslims turned their backs in flight, firstly because of the contempt and the scorn with which Karbughā had treated them and secondly because he had prevented them from killing the Franks. Their flight was complete. Not one of them struck a blow with a sword, thrust with a spear or shot an arrow. The last to flee were Suqmān ibn Artuq and Janāḥ al-Dawla because they were stationed in ambush. Karbughā fled with them. When the Franks observed this, they thought that it was a trick, since there had been no battle such as to cause a flight [**278**] and they feared to pursue them. A company of warriors for the faith[25] stood firm and fought zealously, seeking martyrdom. The Franks slew thousands of them and seized as booty the provisions, money, furnishings, horses and weapons that were in the camp. Their situation was restored and their strength returned.

Account of the Franks' conquest of Ma'arrat al-Nu'mān

After the Franks had dealt with the Muslims as they did, they marched to Ma'arrat al-Nu'mān[26] and camped around it for a siege. The inhabitants fought them fiercely and the Franks experienced hardship and trouble, as they met with serious resistance and hard-fought opposition. They then constructed a wooden tower to come alongside the city wall. The battle waged around it but with no harm to the Muslims. When it was night some of the Muslims became fearful and were overcome with defeatism and dismay. They thought that, if they fortified themselves in some of the large houses, they could hold out there, so they went down from the wall and abandoned the place they had been defending. Another group saw them and did as they did, so that their place on the wall was also abandoned. Group after group followed their neighbours in descending from the wall until it was quite deserted. The Franks climbed on to it with ladders. When

---

[23] This is the cathedral of St Peter, called al-Qusyān (Eddé, *Description*, 224, note 4; 231-2).

[24] This lance, claimed to be the one used to pierce Jesus' side, was found in the Church of St Peter by a Provencal, Peter Bartholomew.

[25] *Mujāhidīn.* Quite probably volunteer auxiliaries were intended, rather than regular troops.

they were up there, the Muslims were quite at a loss and entered their houses. For three days the Franks put them to the sword and killed more than one hundred thousand. They enslaved many and took possession of the town.[27]

They remained for forty days and then marched to ʻArqa,[28] which they besieged for four months. They mined the wall in several places but could not take the place. Munqidh,[29] the ruler of Shayzar, sent envoys and reached an agreement with them. They marched on to Homs, which they besieged, until the ruler, Janāḥ al-Dawla, came to terms with them. Then by way of the Nāqūra Pass[30] they left for Acre but were unable to take it.

[279] Account of the war between Sanjar and Dawlatshāh

Dawlatshāh was a descendant of the Saljuq rulers. A number of the troops of Yabghu, the brother of Tughril Beg, who were in Tukhāristān,[31] gathered to him and they took Walwālij[32] and Kamanj.[33] The Sultan Sanjar and his army marched against them. He came to Balkh which he entered in Rajab of this year [June 1098], and then left the town to give battle to Dawlatshāh, who did not have sufficient troops to stand against his army. Dawlatshāh's troops fought a little and then fled. Dawlatshāh was taken prisoner and brought before Sanjar, who spared his life but imprisoned him, and later on blinded him. Sanjar sent an army to the city of Tirmidh, which he conquered and handed over to Tughriltakīn.

Miscellaneous events

During this year Tamīm[34] ibn al-Muʻizz ibn Bādīs, the ruler of Ifrīqiya, conquered the island of Jerba, the island of Kerkenna[35] and the city of Tunis. There was in Ifrīqiya a severe famine in which many people perished.

---

[26] Town in North Syria, two days' journey south of Aleppo (*EI (2)*, v, 922–7).

[27] For events at Maʻarrat al-Nuʻmān, see Asbridge, *Principality of Antioch*, 39–40.

[28] Situated at the western end of the Homs-Tripoli gap, about 15 miles from the latter place.

[29] At this date the ruling member of the Munqidh clan at Shayzar (on the Orontes) was Naṣr ibn ʻAlī ibn Muqallad (ruled 475–92/1082–98). See *EI(2)*, vii, 577–80, s.v. Munḳidh.

[30] i.e. the Ladder of Tyre, on the coast between Tyre and Acre.

[31] The region along the southern banks of the middle and upper Oxus River (*EI(2)*, x, 600–602).

[32] Yāqūt, iv, 940, simply says 'town in Badakhshān.' It was south of the Oxus and four days' journey east of Balkh, near the site of the more recent Qunduz (see Barthold, *Turkestan*, 67; Krawulsky, 107, and cf. Le Strange, *Eastern Caliphate*, 428).

[33] Unidentified. Is it perhaps identical with K.m.n.j.th, 'village in Transoxania' (Yāqūt, iv, 305)?

[34] Fifth ruler of the Zīrid dynasty, born 422/1031, died 501/1108. See *EI(2)*, x, 172.

[35] The name of an archipelago, and its main island, off the eastern coast of Tunisia, see

This year the caliph sent an envoy to Sultan Barkyāruq to seek aid against the Franks, stressing the importance of this matter and the need to deal with it before it became more serious.

This year the following died:

In Sha'bān [July 1098] Abū'l-Ḥasan Aḥmad ibn 'Abd al-Qādir ibn Muḥammad ibn Yūsuf, who was born in the year 412 [1021-2] and was an excellent scholar of Ḥadīth.

Abū'l-Faḍl 'Abd al-Wahhāb ibn Abī Muḥammad al-Tamīmī al-Ḥanbalī. He was [**280**] a learned and eloquent scholar.

In Shawwāl [September 1098] Ṭirād ibn Muḥammad al-Zaynabī.[36] For Ḥadīth his chains of transmission had high authority. The office of syndic of the Abbasids was held after him by his son, Sharaf al-Dīn 'Alī ibn Ṭirād.

In Dhū'l-Qa'da [October 1098] Abū'l-Fatḥ al-Muẓaffar ibn Ra'īs al-Ru'asā' Abī'l-Qāsim ibn al-Muslima.[37] His house was a gathering place of scholars and divines. One of those who frequented it until his death was the Shaykh Abū Isḥāq al-Shīrāzī.

Abū'l-Faraj Sahl ibn Bishr ibn Aḥmad al-Isfarā'īnī, one of the leading scholars of Ḥadīth.

EI(2), iv, 650-52.

36 See Makdisi, *Ibn 'Aqīl*, 183-4.

37 i.e. the son of the caliph's vizier put to death by al-Basāsīrī (Richards, *Annals*, 121-4).

The Year 492 [1098–1099]

Account of the rebellion and murder of Emir Unur

When Sultan Barkyāruq went to Khurasan, he put Emir Unur in charge of all the lands of Fars. The Shabankara had come to dominate there despite the variety of their clans and tribes. They sought the help of the lord of Kirman, Īrān Shāh ibn Qāwurt.[1] Having joined forces, they met Emir Unur in battle and defeated him, so that he retired in disarray to Isfahan. He sent to the sultan asking for permission to join him in Khurasan, but he ordered him to remain in the region of the Uplands, gave him command over Iraq, and wrote to the troops in the vicinity that they should obey him. He stayed at Isfahan, then left to go to his fief in Azerbayjan. When he returned the influence of the Bāṭinīs[2] had spread in Isfahan. He took it upon himself to fight them and besieged a fortress on the mountain at Isfahan.

Mu'ayyad al-Mulk, the son of Niẓām al-Mulk, who was in Baghdad, made contact with Unur and left to go to al-Ḥilla. He was well received by Ṣadaqa and moved on from his court to Emir Unur. Having joined Unur, he and others warned him against Sultan Barkyāruq, stressed the dangers of meeting with him and advised him to keep far away. They suggested he should write to Ghiyāth al-Dīn Muḥammad ibn Mālik Shāh, who was at that time in Ganja. Unur determined to break with the sultan and discussed that step. This became public, so he became more fearful **[282]** of the sultan. He assembled about 10,000 mounted troops, known for their bravery, and he marched from Isfahan to Rayy. He sent to the sultan, to say that he was his humble and obedient servant, if he surrendered Majd al-Mulk al-Balāsānī[3] to him, but if he did not, then he would rebel and cast off his allegiance.

While he was breaking his fast, for it was his custom to fast several days a week, and when he was close to finishing his meal, three half-breed Turks from Khwarazm, who belonged to his cavalry, attacked him. One collided with the torch and knocked it over, the second ran into the lamp and extinguished it, but the third struck him with a dagger and killed him. His bodyguard was killed with him. In the darkness all were in confusion. They ransacked his treasure chests and the army scattered and broke up. He was left lying on the ground, as nothing could be found to carry him on. Later he was taken to his residence at Isfahan and there buried.

---

1 The Saljūq prince, Bahā' al-Dawla, who ruled 490–95/1097–1101.

2 The Ismā'īlī Shiite sect (the Assassins), so called from their belief in the esoteric teaching of their Imams (*al-bāṭin*).

3 i.e. Abū'l-Faḍl As'ad ibn Muḥammad, a Shiite and senior administrator of Barkyāruq.

News of his death reached Sultan Barkyāruq at Khuwar al-Rayy,[4] after he had left Khurasan intending to wage war on him, although he was extremely apprehensive about fighting him and about the outcome of the affair. Majd al-Mulk al-Balāsānī rejoiced at his death, although a like fate soon awaited him. Unur was thirty-seven years old. He fasted and prayed frequently, did much good and loved men of piety.

How the Franks (God curse them) took Jerusalem

Jerusalem had been held by Tāj al-Dawla Tutush who assigned it to Emir Suqmān ibn Artuq the Turkoman. When the Franks defeated the Turks at Antioch and made slaughter amongst them, the power of the Turks weakened [**283**] and they lost cohesion. When the Egyptians saw their weakness, they marched to Jerusalem, led by al-Afḍal ibn Badr al-Jamālī. There they besieged Suqmān and Īlghāzī, the sons of Artuq, and also their cousin Savanj and their nephew Yāqūtī. They set up forty and more trebuchets against the town and demolished parts of its wall. The inhabitants fought back and the fighting and the siege lasted somewhat over forty days, until the Egyptians took the city on terms in Sha'bān 489 [July 1096]. Al-Afḍal treated Suqmān, Īlghāzī and their followers well, gave them generous gifts and sent them on their way to Damascus. Subsequently they crossed the Euphrates. Suqmān took up residence in Edessa but Īlghāzī moved to Iraq.

The Egyptians appointed as deputy in Jerusalem a man called Iftikhār al-Dawla, who remained there until this present time, when the Franks attacked after they had besieged Acre but with no success. After their arrival they erected forty trebuchets or more and they constructed two towers, one on Mount Zion side but the Muslims burnt that one and killed all inside. After they had completely destroyed it by fire, their help was then called for, as the city defences had been overwhelmed on the other side. The Franks did indeed take the city from the north in the forenoon of Friday, seven days remaining of Sha'bān [15 July 1099]. The inhabitants became prey for the sword. For a week the Franks continued to slaughter the Muslims. A group of Muslims took refuge in the Tower of David[5] and defended themselves there. They resisted for three days and then the Franks offered them safe-conduct, so they surrendered the place. The Franks kept faith with them and they departed at night for Ascalon, where they remained.

In the Aqsa Mosque the Franks killed more than 70,000, a large number of them [**284**] being imams, ulema, righteous men and ascetics, Muslims who had left their native lands and come to live a holy life in this august spot. The Franks took forty or more silver candlesticks from the Dome of the Rock, each of which weighed 3,600 dirhams, and also a silver candelabrum weighing forty Syrian rotls. They

---

4 A district in N. Persia, south of Damavand. See *EI(2)*, iv, 1029.

5 i.e. the citadel, in Arabic called the Miḥrāb of David.

removed 150 small candlesticks of silver and twenty or so of gold. The booty they took was beyond counting.

In Ramaḍān [22 July–20 August 1099] men came to Baghdad from Syria seeking assistance, accompanied by the Cadi Abū Sa'd al-Harawī. They recounted in the Diwan a narrative which brought tears to the eye and pained the heart. They demonstrated in the mosque on Friday and cried out for help, weeping and reducing others to tears. A tale was told of the killing of men, the enslavement of women and children and the plundering of property that had fallen upon the Muslims in that revered, august place. Because of the severity of their suffering they did not observe their fast. The caliph ordered the following to be sent on a mission, the Cadi Abū Muḥammad al-Damghānī, Abū Bakr al-Shāshī,[6] Abū'l-Qāsim al-Zanjānī, Abū'l-Wafā ibn 'Aqīl,[7] Abū Sa'd al-Ḥulwānī and Abū'l-Ḥusayn ibn Sammāk. They set out for Ḥulwān but news came to them of the death of Majd al-Mulk al-Balāsānī, as we shall relate, so they returned without achieving any aim or any goal. The rulers were all at variance, as we shall relate, and so the Franks conquered the lands.[8]

[286] Account of warfare between the Franks and the Egyptians

In Ramaḍān of this year [22 July–20 August 1099] there was a battle between Egyptian troops and the Franks. The reason was that al-Afḍal Emir al-Juyūsh,[9] when he heard what had befallen the people of Jerusalem, assembled and mobilised his forces and marched to Ascalon. He sent to the Franks, condemning their actions and threatening them. They sent the envoy back with their reply and, setting out on his tracks, came upon the Egyptians a little after the arrival of the envoy. The Egyptians had no intelligence of their coming or that they had made any move. They were not ready for combat. The cry went up, 'To horse' and they donned their armour but the Franks were too quick for them and put them to flight. Having inflicted losses on them, the Franks took the property, weapons and whatever else was in their camp as booty.

Al-Afḍal fled and entered Ascalon. A number of the routed troops went and hid themselves in a grove of sycamore trees, which were abundant there. The Franks set fire to a part so that some perished within and those that came out were killed. Al-Afḍal returned to Egypt with his close retinue and the Franks besieged Ascalon and pressed it hard. The population offered a tribute of 12,000 dinars, although another report says 20,000. Then the Franks returned to Jerusalem.

---

6 A prominent Shāfi'ī scholar, died 507/1114. See Makdisi, *Ibn 'Aqīl*, 208-10.

7 This is the leading Ḥanbalī, 'Alī ibn 'Aqīl, the subject of Makdisi's *Ibn 'Aqīl et la Résurgence de l'Islam etc.*

8 Twenty-two verses by Abū'l-Muẓaffar al-Abīwardī are omitted at this point.

9 Emir al-Juyūsh (Commander of the Armies) was the title used by the viziers, al-Afḍal Shāhinshāh and his father, Badr al-Jamālī.

[287] Account of the beginning of the career of Sultan Muḥammad ibn Malikshāh

The Sultan Muḥammad and Sanjar were brothers who shared the same mother and father. Their mother was an *umm walad*.[10] At the death of his father Malikshāh, Muḥammad was with him in Baghdad. Along with his brother Maḥmūd and Terken Khātūn, his father's wife, he went to Isfahan. When Barkyāruq besieged Isfahan, Muḥammad left in disguise and went to his mother, who was with the army of his brother Barkyāruq. He sought out the Sultan Barkyāruq and went with him to Baghdad in the year 486 [1093]. Barkyāruq assigned him Ganja and its districts as an appanage and placed with him as an atabeg Emir Qutlugh Takīn, whom Muḥammad, when he became strong enough, put to death. He proceeded to seize control of all the districts of Arran of which Ganja was a part. At that time the ambitious energy of Muḥammad came to be recognised.

Sultan Malikshāh had taken those lands from Faḍlūn ibn Abī'l-Aswar al-Rawādī and handed them over to Sarhank Savtakīn the Eunuch. He assigned Astarābādh to Faḍlūn, who again took on the farm of his lands. Later he rebelled there when he became powerful. The sultan sent Emir Būzān against him, who fought and captured him. His lands were assigned to several persons, including Yaghī Siyān, the lord of Antioch. On the death of Yaghī Siyān his son took over his father's government of these areas. Faḍlūn died in Baghdad in the year 484 [1091] in a state of extreme poverty in a mosque by the Tigris.

We have already mentioned before this the changes of fortune of Mu'ayyad al-Mulk 'Ubayd Allāh, son of Niẓām al-Mulk, how he was with Emir Unur and encouraged him to rebel against Sultan Barkyāruq. When Unur was killed [**288**], Mu'ayyad al-Mulk went to Prince Muḥammad and advised him to break with his brother and strive to win the sultanate, which he did. He stopped the khutbah in Barkyāruq's name throughout his lands and had the prayers said for himself as sultan, having appointed Mu'ayyad al-Mulk as his vizier.

Then followed the killing of Majd al-Mulk al-Balāsānī and the army's alienation from Sultan Barkyāruq. They abandoned him and went over to Sultan Muḥammad, whom they met at Khurraqān and, having joined him, marched towards Rayy.

When Sultan Barkyāruq's troops had left him, he travelled by forced marches to Rayy, where he was joined by Emir Yināl ibn Anūshtakīn al-Ḥusāmī, one of his senior emirs. Bringing considerable forces, 'Izz al-Mulk Manṣūr ibn Niẓām al-Mulk also came to him, accompanied by his mother, the daughter of the Georgian king. News of the arrival of his brother Muḥammad with an army reached him, so he left Rayy to go to Isfahan, but the inhabitants did not open the gates to him. He went on to Khūzistān, as we shall relate.

On 2 Dhū'l-Qa'da [20 September 1099] Sultan Muḥammad arrived at Rayy. He

---

[10] Literally 'mother of a child', the term for a concubine freed on bearing her master a child.

found that Zubayda Khātūn, the mother of his brother Sultan Barkyāruq, had remained behind after her son's departure. Mu'ayyad al-Mulk seized her and imprisoned her in the citadel. He made her sign a document that she would produce 5,000 dinars. His intention was to kill her although his councillors advised him not to do so. He did not accept their advice. They said to him, 'The army loves her son. It's only because of her that they have turned against him. When she is killed, they will veer towards[11] him again. Do not be deceived by these troops. They have betrayed those who were good to them, however much they trusted them.' He did not listen to their words but took her up to the citadel where she was strangled. She was forty-two years old. When the Sultan Barkyāruq took Mu'ayyad al-Mulk prisoner, he saw his signature on his note for 5,000 dinars and this was the main reason for his being executed.

[289] The making of the khutbah in Baghdad for Muḥammad

When Sultan Muḥammad's position had become strong, Sa'd al-Dawla Goharā'īn left Baghdad to join him, having become alienated from Sultan Barkyāruq. He and Karbughā, the lord of Mosul, Jokermish, the lord of Jazīrat [ibn 'Umar],[12] Surkhāb ibn Badr, the lord of Kinkiwar, and others came together and went to Sultan Muḥammad, who met them at Qum. He sent Sa'd al-Dawla back to Baghdad and gave him a robe of honour. Karbughā and Jokermish travelled in his retinue to Isfahan. When Goharā'īn came to Baghdad he requested the caliph to allow the khutbah in the name of Sultan Muḥammad. This was granted and the khutbah was made in his name on Friday 17 Dhū'l-Ḥijja [4 November 1099]. He was given the honorific title Ghiyāth al-Dunyā wa'l-Dīn.[13]

Account of the murder of Majd al-Mulk al-Balāsānī

We have mentioned before how Majd al-Mulk Abū'l-Faḍl As'ad ibn Muḥammad gained a dominant control over the administration of Sultan Barkyāruq. When he had reached the acme beyond which there was nothing more to be gained, he was overwhelmed by disasters and misfortunes from directions he had not reckoned on.

As for the reason for his murder, when the Bāṭinīs carried out a series of assassinations of senior emirs in the sultan's state, this was laid at his door, and it was claimed that he was the person who had incited them to kill those they had killed. The murder of Emir Bursuq aggravated this. His sons, Zankī, Āqbūrī and

---

[11] Following the variant reading *ilayhi*.

[12] The modern Cizre, on the Tigris.

[13] Literally Succour of Worldly Affairs and of Religion.

the others, suspected Majd al-Mulk of killing him, and they broke with the sultan.

The sultan went to Zanjān because he had heard that Sultan Muḥammad had rebelled against him, as [**290**] we have related. The emirs then became ambitious. The Marshal of the Horse, Bilge Beg,[14] Tughāyuruk ibn Ilyazan and others sent to the emirs, the sons of Bursuq, to ask them to join them and to make an agreement with them to demand that the sultan surrender Majd al-Dīn to them so that they could kill him. They met together and sent to the Sultan Barkyāruq, who was in Sujās, a city near Hamadhān, requesting the handing over of Majd al-Dīn. The whole army backed them in that. They said, 'If he is handed over to us, then we shall be your slaves, faithfully serving you. If we are thwarted, we shall leave and take him by force.' The sultan refused to give him up, but Majd al-Dīn sent to the sultan to say, 'It is in your best interest to keep the emirs that serve you. Kill me yourself to avoid my being killed by these people which would weaken your rule.' The sultan could not bring himself to agree to his being put to death. He sent to the emirs to ask them to swear to preserve his life and to imprison him in one of the castles. When they swore this, he surrendered him to them. However, the mamluke troops killed him before he reached the emirs. The discord then quietened down.

It is remarkable that his shroud used to accompany him everywhere at home and abroad. One day his treasurer opened a chest and Majd al-Dīn saw the shroud. He said, 'What am I doing with this? My fate will not end with a shroud. By God, I shall merely be left cast down on the ground.' So it came to pass. Many a saying says to him who utters it, 'Let me be!'

After he was killed, his head was taken to Mu'ayyad al-Mulk, son of Niẓām al-Mulk. Majd al-Dīn was a good man, who prayed much during the night. He gave copious alms, especially to the Alids and the scions of great houses. He disliked the shedding of blood. He had Shiite sympathies, although he spoke well of the Companions and cursed those that spoke ill of them. After his death the emirs sent to the sultan, saying, 'Your best course is to return to Rayy. We will march against your brother to fight him and we shall settle this great matter.' He set out [**291**] after some reluctance. Two hundred horsemen followed him, not more. The army plundered the pavilions of the sultan, his mother and all his companions, then returned to Rayy and marched against Sultan Muḥammad.

Miscellaneous events

In Sha'bān of this year [23 June–21 July 1099] al-Kiyā Abū'l-Ḥasan 'Alī ibn Muḥammad al-Ṭabarī, known as al-Harrās, the Shafi'ī lawyer, whose honorific title was 'Imād al-Dīn Shams al-Islām, arrived with a message from Sultan Barkyāruq for the caliph. He was one of the followers of the Imam of the Two Sanctuaries Abū'l-Ma'ālī al-Juwaynī and had been born in the year 450 [1058].

---

[14] The text has B.l.kābak.

Majd al-Mulk al-Balāsānī had been his patron and the Vizier 'Amīd al-Dawla Ibn Jahīr stood to receive him when he came into his presence.

This year Abū'l-Qāsim, the son of the Imam of the Two Sanctuaries Abū'l-Ma'āli al-Juwaynī, was killed at Nishapur, where he was the preacher (*khaṭīb*). The common people suspected that Abū'l-Barakāt al-Tha'labī had been the one who plotted to have him killed, so they attacked him, killed him and ate his flesh.

There was a great famine in Khurasan, during which provisions were impossible to find. It lasted two years. The reason was that the rain destroyed all the crops and afterwards a virulent epidemic struck the populace. Vast numbers died who could not be buried because they were so many.

The following died this year:

In Sha'bān [23 June–21 July 1099], Abū'l-Ghanā'im al-Fāriqī, a Shāfi'ī lawyer, in Jazīrat Ibn 'Umar. He was an excellent scholar and an ascetic.

In Ṣafar [January 1099] Abū 'Abd Allāh al-Ḥusayn ibn Ṭalḥa al-Na'ālī, who was aged [**292**] about ninety. His status in the transmission of Ḥadīth was high. It is claimed that he died in the year 493 [1099–1100].

In Sha'bān, Abū Ghālib Muḥammad ibn 'Alī ibn al-Ṣabbāgh, a Shāfi'ī lawyer. He studied law with his cousin, Abū Naṣr,[15] and was of a pleasant and modest character.

---

[15] Abū Naṣr 'Abd al-Sayyid ibn Muḥammad (400–477/1009–1084), a leading Shāfi'ī scholar. See Makdisi, *Ibn 'Aqīl*, 206–8.

The Year 493 [1099-1100]

The restoration of the khutbah in the name of Sultan Barkyāruq at Baghdad

This year at Baghdad the khutbah was restored to Sultan Barkyāruq. This came about as follows. In the past year Barkyāruq had gone from Rayy to Khūzistān, which he and all those with him entered in a very poor state. The commander of his army at that time was Yināl ibn Anūshtakīn al-Ḥusāmī. Other emirs came to him and he moved to Wāsiṭ, where his troops treated the populace wickedly and plundered the district. Emir Ṣadaqa ibn Mazyad, the lord of al-Ḥilla, joined him there. Some persons fell upon the sultan in an assassination attempt, but they were seized and brought before him. They confessed that Emir Sarmaz, the prefect of Isfahan, had put them up to kill him. One was executed and the rest were imprisoned. The sultan then went to Baghdad which he entered on 17 Ṣafar [= 1 January 1100], The khutbah was made in his name at Baghdad on Friday, 15 Ṣafar [= 30 December 1099], two days before his arrival.

Sa'd al-Dawla Goharā'īn was in al-Shufay'ī,[1] loyal to Sultan Muḥammad. He went to Dāy Marj[2] with Īlghāzī ibn Artuq and other emirs, and sent to Mu'ayyad al-Mulk and Sultan Muḥammad urging them to join him. They sent Karbughā, lord of Mosul, and Jokermish, lord of Jazīrat Ibn 'Umar, to him. Jokermish requested permission from Goharā'īn to return to his lands. He said that the situation there was disturbed. [**294**] Permission was granted but a number of emirs remained with Goharā'īn and they agreed to act with one mind without dissension. Their decision was to write to Sultan Barkyāruq, saying to him, 'Come out to join us. There is not amongst us one who will fight you.'

The one who advised this was Karbughā. He said to Goharā'īn, 'We have gained no advantage at all from Muḥammad or Mu'ayyad al-Mulk.' This was because he was hostile to the latter. When Barkyāruq came to them they dismounted and kissed the earth, before returning with him to Baghdad. Barkyāruq restored to Gohāra'īn all the weapons, mounts and other things that he had taken from him, and he appointed al-A'azz Abū'l-Maḥāsin 'Abd al-Jalīl ibn 'Alī ibn Muḥammad al-Dihistānī as vizier in Baghdad and arrested 'Amīd al-Dawla Ibn Jahīr, the caliph's vizier, demanding from him all he had acquired from Diyār Bakr and Mosul when he and his father ruled there in the reign of Malikshāh. It was settled that he should pay 160,000 dinars. The caliph bestowed a robe of honour on Sultan Barkyāruq.

---

[1] *Kāmil*, ix, 49, mentions this place in the vicinity of Baghdad. *Kāmil*, xi, 25, has the caliph stopping there after leaving Baghdad (one Ms. reading is al-Sufay'ī). This is how Yāqūt, ii, 665, gives it, placing it on the east bank at Baghdad.

[2] Unidentified.

Account of the battle between the Sultans Barkyāruq and Muḥammad and the restoration of the khutbah for Muḥammad at Baghdad

This year Barkyāruq travelled from Baghdad to Shahrazūr, where he remained for three days and was joined by a great host of Turkomans and others. He marched against his brother, Sultan Muḥammad, to wage war on him. The headman of Hamadhān wrote to him urging him to come there and take the fiefs of the emirs who were with his brother, but he declined. He proceeded against his brother and a battle between them took place on 4 Rajab [14 May 1100]. This was at Isbīdh-rūdh,[3] which means White River, at a distance of several leagues from Hamadhān, the first battle between Barkyāruq and his brother Sultan Muḥammad.

[**295**] With Muḥammad there were about 20,000 soldiers. Muḥammad was in the centre with Emir Sarmaz. On the right wing was the Marshal of the Horse with his son, Ayāz, and on the left Mu'ayyad al-Mulk and the Niẓāmiyya.[4] Sultan Barkyāruq was also in his centre with his vizier al-A'azz Abū'l-Maḥāsin, while Goharā'īn, 'Izz al-Dawla[5] ibn Ṣadaqa ibn Mazyad and Surkhāb ibn Badr were on his right wing and Karbughā and others on his left. Goharā'īn from Barkyāruq's right wing attacked Muḥammad's left, where were Mu'ayyad al-Mulk and the Niẓāmiyya. The latter broke and Barkyāruq's army entered their tents and plundered them. However, Muḥammad's right charged Barkyāruq's left, which was routed. Muḥammad's right wing joined him in the centre to attack Barkyāruq and those with him. Barkyāruq fled and Muḥammad took his position. When Goharā'īn returned from his pursuit of the fugitives he had routed, his horse stumbled and brought him down. A Khurasanian came and killed him, taking his head. Barkyāruq's troops scattered and he himself was left with fifty horsemen.

His vizier, al-A'azz Abū'l-Maḥāsin, was taken prisoner and given honourable treatment by Mu'ayyad al-Mulk ibn Niẓām al-Mulk, who erected tents and a pavilion for him and brought him household effects and clothing. He guaranteed to make him civilian administrator[6] of Baghdad and sent him back there. He ordered him to petition for the restoration of the khutbah for Sultan Muḥammad in Baghdad. On his arrival he made representations about that and it was granted. The khutbah was made in Muḥammad's name on Friday 14 Rajab [25 May 1100].

The death of Sa'd al-Dawla Goharā'īn

This year, in Rajab [May], Sa'd al-Dawla Goharā'īn was killed in the battle we have mentioned before. His career began when he became a eunuch of the Prince

---

[3] The Safīd Rūd (in modern form) flows into the Caspian east of Rasht and is far from Hamadhan.

[4] Here a collective noun denoting the body of mamluke troops raised by Niẓām al-Mulk.

[5] See below p. [**302**].

[6] In Arabic *'imāda* (the office of the *'amīd*).

Abū Kālījār, son of Sulṭān al-Dawla ibn Buwayh, transferred to him from a woman of Qurqūb[7] in Khūzistān. Whenever he went [**296**] to Ahwāz, he would meet with her and review her affairs. Her family gained much benefit from him. Abū Kālījār sent him with his son, Abū Naṣr, to Baghdad. When Sultan Tughril Beg arrested the latter, Abū Kālījār went with him to the castle of Ṭabarak.[8] Upon the death of Abū Naṣr he switched to the service of Sultan Alp Arslān and protected him with his own person when Yūsuf al-Khwārazmī wounded him.[9]

Alp Arslān had assigned him Wāsiṭ and appointed him a prefect of Baghdad. When Alp Arslān was killed, his son Malikshāh sent him to Baghdad and he brought back his robes of honour and investiture diploma. No eunuch before him had ever enjoyed such influence and freedom of action, and such obedience and attention to his service on the part of the great emirs. He was judicious, generous and of upright conduct. He did not extract money from any of those under his authority. His good qualities were many.

Account of Sultan Barkyāruq's position after his defeat and also his flight from his brother Sanjar, and the killing of the Justicer Ḥabashī

After Barkyāruq was defeated by his brother Sultan Muḥammad he travelled for a little, accompanied by fifty mounted men, and then stopped at 'Utuma[10] where he rested. He then set out for Rayy and sent to those he knew wanted him and preferred his rule. He summoned them and a sizeable number assembled around him. He travelled to Isfarā'īn and wrote to summon the Justicer[11] Ḥabashī ibn Altūntāq, who was at Dāmghān. He replied, advising Barkyāruq to remain in Nishapur until he could join him. At that time most of Khurasan, Ṭabaristān and Jurjān was in his hands. When Barkyāruq arrived at Nishapur, he arrested its leading citizens, took them away but released them later. He kept hold of the civil administrator of Khurasan, Abū Muḥammad, and also Abū'l-Qāsim ibn Abī'l-Ma'ālī al-Juwaynī. The latter died, poisoned when under arrest. It has already been said that he was killed in the year 492 [1098-9].[12]

[**297**] Barkyāruq returned and summoned the Justicer, who excused himself because Sultan Sanjar was attacking his lands with the troops of Balkh and he requested Sultan Barkyāruq to come to his help against Sanjar. This he did with a thousand horsemen. Only the senior emirs amongst the followers of Sanjar knew

7 According to Yāqūt, iv, 65, a middle-sized town within the circle of Wāsiṭ, Basra and al-Ahwāz.
8 A hill-top castle near Rayy, destroyed by Sultan Ṭughril III in 588/1192 (Yāqūt, iii, 507).
9 For this incident in 465/1072, see Richards, *Annals*, 176-7.
10 Unidentified. Yāqūt, iii, 612, only names a fort near Zabīd in Yemen.
11 This archaic term is used to render the office of the *amīr-i dād* (officer of justice or of redress of grievances).
12 See above p. [**291**].

of his coming. They did not tell the junior officers to prevent them from fleeing. The Justicer had 20,000 horse and his troops included 5,000 Bāṭinī footsoldiers.

The battle between Barkyāruq and his brother Sanjar took place outside al-Nawshajān.[13] Emir Buzghush was on Sanjar's right wing, Emir Kundkuz on his left and Emir Rustam in the centre. Barkyāruq charged Rustam and slew him with a lance thrust. His men and Sanjar's men fled. While Barkyāruq's troops occupied themselves with plunder, Buzghush and Kundkuz charged and slew them as they fled. The infantry fled towards a pass between two mountains. A flood of water was released against them, which destroyed them. Barkyāruq's men suffered a rout. He himself had seized his brother Sanjar's mother when Sanjar's troops first ran away. She feared that he would kill her in revenge for his mother but he summoned her to him and put her mind at ease. He said, 'I have only taken you until my brother Sanjar releases the prisoners he has. You are not the equal of my mother for me to kill you.' Upon Sanjar's release of his prisoners Barkyāruq freed her.

The Justicer fled to one of the villages and was captured by a Turkoman. He gave him 100,000 dinars to save his life but the man did not release him and took him to Buzghush who killed him.

Barkyāruq went to Jurjān and then to Dāmghān, travelling by the desert. He was sighted in certain places with seventeen horsemen and one dromedary. Later his company grew larger [**298**] and he came to have 3,000 horsemen, with Jāwlī Saqao amongst others. He set out for Isfahan after a communication from the inhabitants, but Sultan Muḥammad heard of this and got there before him, so he withdrew to Sumayram.[14]

The capture of the city of Sfax by Tamīm ibn al-Mu'izz

Tamīm ibn al-Mu'izz captured the city of Sfax this year. Its ruler Ḥammū[15] had returned and taken control. His situation improved greatly through a vizier he had who had taken refuge with him, one of al-Mu'izz's secretaries, an excellent advisor and administrator. Ḥammū's rule flourished because of him and his power increased greatly. Tamīm wrote to this person, asking him to join his service. He made promises to him and went to great lengths to attract him but he did not agree.

Tamīm therefore sent an army to besiege Sfax and ordered the emir whom he made commander of the force to destroy and burn everything around the city and to cut down the trees, except for what belonged to that vizier, which he was not to

---

13 Yāqūt, iv, 823, places it on the Jaxartes.

14 Yāqūt, iii, 151: 'a town half-way between Isfahan and Shiraz.' Cf. Krawulsky, 313, s.v. Šemrom (Šemīrom?).

15 A certain Ḥammū ibn Malīl took Sfax from a weakened Zīrid state in 451/1059, see *EI(2)*, viii, 763, s.v. Safākūs.

touch but make every effort to save. This he did and when Ḥammū saw what he did to the people's property apart from the vizier's, he became suspicious of him and killed him. The order of his state disintegrated and Tamīm's force took over the city. Ḥammū left and took himself to Makan ibn Kāmil al-Dihmānī, with whom he resided. He was well treated by him and remained there until his death.

Account of the dismissal of the caliph's vizier, 'Amīd al-Dawla, and his death

When Mu'ayyad al-Dawla, the vizier of Sultan Muḥammad, freed al-A'azz Abū'l-Maḥāsin, Barkyāruq's vizier, and guaranteed him the office of administrator in Baghdad, he ordered him to petition the caliph for the dismissal of his vizier, 'Amīd [**299**] al-Dawla Ibn Jahīr. He set out from the [royal] camp and when 'Amīd al-Dawla heard this news, he instructed General[16] Ṣabāwa ibn Khumārtakīn to go out to meet al-A'azz on the road and kill him.

The general had been present at the battle with Barkyāruq and when the army had been routed he made for Baghdad. He now went out to meet al-A'azz Abū'l-Maḥāsin on the road and, encountering him close to Ba'qūbā, he fell upon the men with him. Al-A'azz sought refuge and protection in the settlement. Seeing that, General Ṣabāwa sent to him to say, 'You are the vizier of the Sultan Barkyāruq and I am his servant. If you are ready to serve him, come out to us, so that we can travel to Baghdad and establish the khutbah for the sultan and you will be the vizier whose word is not disobeyed. If you do not agree to this, then there is nothing between us but the sword.' Al-A'azz did agree and they met. Ṣabāwa informed him how 'Amīd al-Dawla had commanded him to kill him. That night passed and al-A'azz sent for Emir Īlghāzī ibn Artuq, who had come with him but had left him to go to al-Rādhān. Īlghāzī arrived in the night and at that moment Ṣabāwa's hopes were frustrated and he left him.

Al-A'azz went on to Baghdad and made representations for the dismissal of 'Amīd al-Dawla, who was then dismissed in Ramaḍān [10 July–8 August 1100]. Of his wealth 25,000 dinars were seized and he and his brothers were arrested. He continued out of office until 16 Shawwāl [24 August 1100] and then he died in prison in the Caliphal Palace. He was born in Muḥarram of the year 435 [August 1043] and was an intelligent, generous and judicious man, except that he was very arrogant, and one could almost keep a tally of his words. If ever he addressed a few words to any man, that person would receive congratulations on the conversation.

---

[16] *Iṣbahbudh*, from the Persian *isbāhbud.*

[300] Account of the Muslims' victory over the Franks

In Dhū'l-Qa'da of this year [7 September–6 October 1100] Gumushtakīn[17] ibn al-Dānishmand Ṭaylū, who was only called Ibn al-Dānishmand because his father had been a 'teacher' of the Turkomans and whose fortunes so prospered that he gained power as lord of Malaṭya, Sīwās and other places, met in battle Bohemond the Frank, who was one of the Frankish commanders, near Malaṭya. Its ruler[18] had written to Bohemond and asked him to come. He came to his aid with 5,000 men. Ibn al-Dānishmand met them in battle and Bohemond was defeated and taken prisoner.[19]

Seven Frankish counts came by sea and aimed to free Bohemond. They came to a castle called Ankara, which they took, killing the Muslims there. They then proceeded to another castle in which was Ismā'īl ibn al-Dānishmand. They put it under siege but Ibn al-Dānishmand assembled a large force and confronted the Franks. He laid an ambush and engaged them. The ambushers came forth and not a single one of the 300,000 Franks escaped, apart from 3,000 who fled by night and escaped wounded.[20]

Ibn al-Dānishmand went to Malaṭya and seized it, taking its lord captive. Later the Frankish army marched against him from Antioch. He met and broke them. These events occurred within just a few months.

[301] Miscellaneous events

During this year in Sha'bān [11 June–9 July 1100] the power of the urban gangs[21] grew on the West Bank at Baghdad and the damage they did became serious. The caliph ordered Kamāl al-Dawla Yumn to bring order to the city. He seized several of their leaders and hunted the rest but they fled.

At this time too prices fell in Iraq. A *kurr*[22] of wheat had reached 70 dinars and possibly it was much more at certain times. The rains failed and the rivers dried up. Mortality was high, so much so that it was impossible to bury the dead. At times six corpses were borne on one bier. Medicines and simples were not to be found.

In Rajab of this year [13 May–10 June] the lord of Antioch, Bohemond the

---

[17] The son of the founder of this Turkoman dynasty (*c.*1085-1178) in Asia Minor. See *EI(2)*, ii, 110–11, s.v. Dānishmendids. Ṭaylū is briefly discussed in Cahen, *Pre-Ottoman Turkey*, 83.

[18] The Armenian governor, Gabriel.

[19] For these events, see Asbridge, *Principality of Antioch*, 51.

[20] This paragraph refers to the various Crusading armies that crossed Anatolia in 1101 and met disastrous defeats. See Runciman, ii, 18–29.

[21] In Arabic *al-'ayyārūn*.

[22] A *kurr* ranged from 2,700 to 3,000 kg (see Hinz, 42–3).

Frank, marched to Apamea and besieged it. He fought the inhabitants for several days and destroyed the crops before withdrawing.[23]

In Ramaḍān [10 July-8 August 1100] Emir Bilge Beg Sarmaz was killed at Isfahan in the palace of Sultan Muḥammad. He had been very wary of the Bāṭinīs, never omitting to wear his breastplate and always having an escort. On that particular day he did not wear his breastplate and entered the sultan's palace with just a few men. The Bāṭinīs slew him. One was killed and another got away.

There also died this year:

Abū'l-Ḥasan al-Bisṭāmī the Sufi. His convent on the Tigris west of Baghdad is famous and was built by Abū'l-Ghanā'im ibn al-Muḥallabān.

Abū Naṣr ibn Abī 'Abd Allāh ibn Jarda, who came originally from 'Ukbarā and after whom [**302**] is named the Mosque of Ibn Jarada and the Waste of Ibn Jarada in Baghdad.[24]

Abū 'Alī Yaḥyā ibn Jazla, the doctor. He was a Christian but converted to Islam. He wrote *Kitāb al-Minhāj*.[25]

In Shawwāl [9 August-6 September 1100] 'Abd al-Razzāq the Sufi from Ghazna, who resided in the convent of 'Attāb and went on several pilgrimages as a pious mendicant. He did not leave money for a shroud. His wife said, 'When you die, we shall be disgraced.' 'Why shall we be disgraced?' he asked. She replied, 'Because you do not possess anything to be buried in.' He said, 'I would be disgraced only if I did leave something for my shroud.'

In Ramaḍān [10 July-8 August 1100] 'Izz al-Dawla Abū'l-Makārim Muḥammad ibn Sayf al-Dawla Ṣadaqa ibn Mazyad.[26]

---

23 See Asbridge, *Principality of Antioch*, 50-51.

24 For the mosque and the 'waste' or ruin (*kharāba*), see Makdisi, 'Topography', 293 and references there cited.

25 He was Yaḥyā ibn 'Īsā ibn Jazla, died Sha'bān 493/June 1100 (*GAL*, i, 485). He wrote legal documents for Cadi al-Dāmghānī and treated neighbours and acquaintances without charging a fee (*Muntaẓam*, ix, 119).

26 Cf. *Muntaẓam*, ix, 119.

[303] The Year 494 [1100-1101]

Account of the hostilities between the two sultans, Barkyāruq and Muḥammad, and the death of Mu'ayyad al-Mulk

On 3 Jumādā II this year [5 April 1101] there was the second battle between Sultan Barkyāruq and Sultan Muḥammad. We have already mentioned under the year 493 [1099-1100] how Barkyāruq was defeated by his brother Muḥammad and how he wandered throughout the lands and came to Isfahan but did not enter. From there he went to Khūzistān, to 'Askar Mukram. Emirs Zankī and Ilbakī, sons of Bursuq, came to him and entered his service. He spent two months there and then travelled to Hamadhān. That was where Emir Ayāz joined him.

The reason for this was that the Marshal of Horse had recently died and Ayāz suspected Mu'ayyad al-Mulk of having given him poison. This feeling was strengthened by the fact that the vizier of the Marshal fled just after his death. Ayāz's conviction that he was guilty grew stronger. He seized the vizier and put him to death. The Marshal had adopted Ayāz as a son to whom his troops attached themselves, and he bequeathed to Ayāz all his wealth. When the latter became estranged because of what had happened, he wrote to Barkyāruq and joined him with 5,000 horsemen and became part of his forces.

Muḥammad marched to confront his brother. When the two armies were near to one another, Emir Surkhāb ibn Kaykhusro, lord of Āveh, defected to Sultan Barkyāruq who received him with honour. **[304]** The battle took place on 3 Jumādā II [5 April]. With Barkyāruq were 50,000, while his brother Muḥammad had 15,000. They met and fought all that day. Detachment after detachment of Muḥammad's army defected to Barkyāruq, who rewarded them with largess. A remarkable sign of his coming victory had been that, when Barkyāruq's infantry were in need of shields, on the morning of the day of battle twelve loads of weapons arrived from Isfahan, of which eight contained shields which were distributed to the troops. When they arrived Barkyāruq dismounted and prayed two *rak'as*[1] in gratitude to God Almighty.

The fighting continued until the end of the day and then Sultan Muḥammad and his troops broke. Mu'ayyad al-Mulk was taken prisoner by a mamluke of Majd al-Mulk al-Balāsānī and was brought before Barkyāruq who upbraided him and listed how he had treated him, how he had slandered his mother at one time, accused him of following the Bāṭinī creed at another, urged his brother Muḥammad to rebel against him and himself thrown off his allegiance and other matters. Mu'ayyad al-

[1] A *rak'a* is a fixed series of ritual movements (bows, prostrations, etc.).

Mulk remained silent without a word in response. Barkyāruq slew him with his own hand and for several days he was left lying on the ground until Emir Ayāz asked if he could bury him, which was allowed. He was carried to his father's mausoleum in Isfahan and buried with him. He was a miser and treated the emirs badly. However, he was very cunning and full of guile in improving the authority of the state. At the time he was killed he was about fifty years old.

During Ṣafar [6 December 1100-3 January 1101] Barkyāruq had appointed as his vizier al-A'azz Abū'l-Maḥāsin 'Abd al-Jalīl ibn 'Alī al-Dihistānī. When Mu'ayyad al-Mulk was killed, the Vizier al-A'azz sent Abū Ibrāhīm al-Asadābādhī as an envoy to Baghdad to seize the wealth of Mu'ayyad al-Mulk. In Baghdad he took up residence in Mu'ayyad al-Mulk's house and the latter's cousin, Muḥammad al-Sharābī, was handed over to him, [**305**] from whom the money and jewels were extracted after he had received and suffered some bad treatment and torture. Various treasures of his were seized from other places in the lands of the Persians, such as a ruby gem which weighed forty-one *mithqāls*.[2]

After the conclusion of this battle Barkyāruq went to Rayy, where Qiwām al-Dawla Karbughā, lord of Mosul, and Nūr al-Dawla Dubays ibn Ṣadaqa ibn Mazyad came to him.

What happened to Sultan Muḥammad after the defeat and his meeting with his brother Prince Sanjar

After the defeat Sultan Muḥammad set out for Khurasan, to his brother Sanjar, for they had the same mother. He stopped in Jurjān and wrote to his brother asking for money, clothing and such like. Sanjar sent him what he asked for and their correspondence continued until they swore mutual oaths and came to an agreement.

Only two emirs leading about 300 horsemen remained with Muḥammad. When their alliance was established, Prince Sanjar set out from Khurasan with his forces towards his brother Muḥammad. They met in Jurjān and from there went on to Dāmghān. The Khurasanian army destroyed this place, whose inhabitants fled to the castle of Girdkūh.[3] The army ruined all the lands that they seized and famine affected those regions widely, so that people ate carrion and dogs, and some ate human flesh.

They both moved on to Rayy and, when they arrived there, [**306**] the Niẓāmiyya and others rallied to them, so their following became numerous, their military potential significant, and fear of them mastered all hearts.

---

[2] If the standard *mithqāl* in Iraq was 4.46 g (Hinz, 5), the gem weighed nearly 183 g.

[3] A castle,18 km west of Dāmghān (see Krawulsky, 329-30). It was part of the Justicer Ḥabashī's possessions in Khurasan (see Bundārī, 259-60).

What action Sultan Barkyāruq took and his entry into Baghdad

When Barkyāruq was at Rayy after the defeat of his brother Muḥammad, many troops joined him until he had about 100,000 cavalry. Provisions became in short supply, so the army split up. Dubays ibn Ṣadaqa returned to his father. Then the Prince Mawdūd ibn Ismā'īl ibn Yāqūtī rebelled in Azerbayjan and Barkyāruq sent Qiwām al-Dawla Karbughā against him with 10,000 horse. Emir Ayāz asked leave to go home to Hamadhān to celebrate the Ramaḍān fast there and to return after the end of the fast, which was granted. Thus the army was scattered for reasons like these and Barkyāruq remained with small numbers.

He was informed that his two brothers had gathered forces and mobilised troops and that they, on hearing how few were with him, had set out towards him in forced marches and were pressing on with the stages of their march to catch him before he could concentrate his forces. When they drew near, he abandoned his position. Those who had been in awe of him now had designs on him and those who had hopes for him now despaired. He set out for Hamadhān to join up with Ayāz but he heard that Ayāz had written to Muḥammad to be with him and one of his supporters, fearing for the area he ruled, Hamadhān and elsewhere. Learning of this, Barkyāruq withdrew and made for Khūzistān. When he approached Tustar he wrote to the emirs, the sons of Bursuq, to summon them but they did not present themselves when they knew that Ayāz had not done so and also because they feared Sultan Muḥammad. Barkyāruq now went to Iraq and, after he had reached Ḥulwān, the messenger of Emir Ayāz came to him, asking him to halt so that he could come to him.

[**307**] This was because Ayāz contacted Sultan Muḥammad about joining him and becoming part of his forces, but Muḥammad rejected this and dispatched troops against Hamadhān, so Ayāz fled, abandoning the city, and followed after Sultan Barkyāruq. The latter halted at Ḥulwān where Ayāz joined him and the two then marched to Baghdad.

Muḥammad's army seized the money, mounts, equipment and such like that Ayāz had left behind in Hamadhān, as he had had insufficient time to move it. It included 500 Arab horses, each of which, it was said, was worth between 300 and 500 dinars. They plundered his house and extorted money from several of his followers. The headman of Hamadhān was mulcted of 1,000 dinars.

After Ayāz had come to Barkyāruq, their combined force amounted to 5,000 horse, although they had lost their tents and baggage. Barkyāruq arrived at Baghdad on 17 Dhū'l-Qa'da [13 September 1101] and the caliph sent Amīn al-Dawla ibn Mūsilāyā with a formal retinue to meet him on the road. At the Feast of the Sacrifice [6 October 1101] the caliph sent a minbar to the Sultanian residence and the Sharīf Abū'l-Karam preached from it and led the prayers at the feast. Barkyāruq did not attend because he was ill.

Money was short for Barkyāruq. He did not have anything to spend on himself or his army. He sent to the caliph complaining of hardship and lack of funds and asking for some help to meet his needs. After discussions agreement was reached on 50,000 dinars which the caliph delivered to him. Barkyāruq and his men laid hands on people's property. Many suffered their depredations and the inhabitants longed for them to be removed. Meanwhile, necessity drove them to commit a shameful act. It happened that Abū Muḥammad 'Ubayd Allāh ibn Manṣūr, known as Ibn Ṣulayḥa, arrived, **[308]** the cadi and ruler of Jabala in Syria, as a refugee from the Franks, as we shall relate. He had with him substantial sums of money and they took it all from him.

How Ṣadaqa ibn Mazyad disobeyed Barkyāruq

Emir Ṣadaqa ibn Manṣūr ibn Dubays ibn Mazyad, the lord of al-Ḥilla, cast off his allegiance to Sultan Barkyāruq this year and dropped the khutbah in his name throughout his lands. He transferred it to Sultan Muḥammad.

The reason for this was that the Vizier al-A'azz Abū'l-Maḥāsin al-Dihistānī, Sultan Barkyāruq's vizier, sent to Ṣadaqa, saying to him, 'A million and more dinars remain in your hands belonging to the treasury of the sultan. If you do not send them, we shall dispatch our forces to your lands and take them from you.' When he received this communication, he cancelled the khutbah and made it in Muḥammad's name.

After Barkyāruq came to Baghdad, as described, he sent to Ṣadaqa time after time, summoning him to present himself, but he did not respond. Emir Ayāz sent to him, advising him to come before the sultan and to guarantee to give him all that he wanted. He replied, 'I shall not come and I shall not obey the sultan, unless he surrenders to me his vizier, Abū'l-Maḥāsin. If he does not, then let him not imagine that I shall ever wait upon him and let what will be be. If he hands him to me, I shall be his faithful servant and give him good and loyal service.' This was not acceptable, so the break became complete. Ṣadaqa sent to Kūfa and drove out the sultan's deputy there and annexed it.

[309] Account of Sultan Muḥammad's coming to Baghdad and Sultan Barkyāruq's departure

This year, on 27 Dhū'l-Qa'da [22 September 1101], Sultan Muḥammad and Sanjar came to Baghdad. After his conquest of Hamadhān and elsewhere Muḥammad had set out for Baghdad. When he had reached Ḥulwān, Īlghāzī ibn Artuq joined him with his troops and became a loyal subject. Muḥammad's army now numbered more than 10,000 cavalry, not counting the support personnel.

When news of this arrived, Barkyāruq was seriously ill. Rumours about him were being spread by his close staff morning and evening. They were in turmoil, fearful, agitated and confused. He was carried in a litter across to the West Bank and they halted at Ramla.[4] Only intermittent signs of life remained to Barkyāruq. His followers were convinced that he would die and discussed what he was to be buried in and where.

At that point he said to them, 'I feel myself to be stronger and I can move more.' They were much relieved and so continued their march. The other army now arrived and the two forces were in sight of one another, with the Tigris between them. They exchanged shots and insults. Muḥammad's troops mostly reviled them [with shouts of] 'Bāṭinī [heretics]!' using that as an insult. They plundered the region that lay on their march until they arrived at Wāsiṭ.

After Sultan Muḥammad had come to Baghdad and taken up residence in the Sultanian palace, the Caliph al-Mustaẓhir bi-Allāh issued an official memorandum, which expressed his displeasure at the evil conduct of Barkyāruq and his followers [**310**] and his delight at Muḥammad's arrival. The khutbah was made in his name in the Dīwān. Sanjar lodged in the house of Goharā'īn. After Mu'ayyad al-Mulk, Muḥammad had appointed as his vizier Khaṭīr al-Mulk Abū Manṣūr Muḥammad ibn al-Ḥusayn. In Muḥarram of the year 495 [26 October–25 November 1101] Emir Sayf al-Dīn Ṣadaqa came to Muḥammad and the whole population went out to meet him.

Account of what happened to the Cadi of Jabala

His name was Abū Muḥammad 'Ubayd Allāh ibn Manṣūr, known as Ibn Ṣulayḥa. His father [Manṣūr] was the headman of Jabala when the Byzantines ruled there over the Muslims, and acted as their cadi. When the power of the Byzantines weakened and the Muslims took control, the town came under the authority of Jalāl al-Mulk Abū'l-Ḥasan 'Alī ibn 'Ammār, the lord of Tripoli, and Manṣūr retained his position as judge there. When the latter died, his son Abū Muḥammad succeeded him. He loved the military life and favoured the soldiery. His ambitious energy was clear to see and Ibn 'Ammār wished to arrest him. Aware of this, Abū Muḥammad rebelled and established the khutbah in favour of the Abbasids. Ibn 'Ammār offered money to Duqāq ibn Tutush to attack and besiege him, which he agreed to do but did not have any success. His comrade, Atabeg Ṭughtakīn, was hit by an arrow in his knee which had a lasting effect.

Abū Muḥammad remained in control there until the Franks came (God curse them) and put Jabala under siege. He spread the word that the Sultan Barkyāruq had set out for Syria, which gained wide currency and so the Franks withdrew. When they confirmed that the sultan was occupied elsewhere, they renewed their siege. He then spread the rumour that the Egyptians were coming to confront them,

[4] Al-Ramla here is probably a variant (or a mistake) for al-Ramaliyya (an easy error in Arabic script), an open space on the edge of Ḥarbiyya district towards the Anbār Gate (see Le Strange, *Baghdad*, 134).

so they withdrew a second time, but then returned. He agreed with the local Christians that [**311**] they should communicate with the Franks and promise them the surrender of one of the city's towers and the capture of the city. When the message reached them, they despatched 300 of their leading and bravest men who came to that tower. One by one they continued to climb the ropes, and as each one of them reached where Ibn Ṣulayḥa was on the wall he killed him. Eventually he killed them all, and when morning came he threw the heads down to the Franks, who then departed.

Yet another time they besieged the place and erected a wooden tower to attack it. They broke down a city tower but by the morning Abū Muḥammad had rebuilt it. Then they mined the city wall, so he sallied forth and engaged them, before giving way before them. They pursued him but his men emerged from those mines and came on the Franks from their rear. They fled and their commander, known as the Constable,[5] was captured. He ransomed himself with a large sum.

Abū Muḥammad realised that they would not give up their attacks and that he did not have the manpower to resist. He sent to Atabeg Ṭughtakīn asking him to send someone he trusted to take over the port of Jabala and defend it, so that he himself could come to Damascus with his wealth and his family. His request was granted and Ṭughtakīn sent him his son, Tāj al-Mulūk Būrī. Abū Muḥammad surrendered the town to him and set out for Damascus. He asked to be sent to Baghdad, which was done. He was sent on his way, accompanied by men to guard him until he arrived at Anbār.

After his arrival at Damascus, the lord of Tripoli, Ibn ʿAmmār, had sent to Prince Duqāq, saying, 'Hand over Ibn Ṣulayḥa to me, stripped bare. Take all his possessions, and I shall give you 300,000 dinars,' but this he did not do.

Having arrived at Anbār, Abū Muḥammad remained there for a few days and then travelled on to Baghdad, where Sultan Barkyāruq was. On his arrival the Vizier al-Aʿazz Abū'l-Maḥāsin summoned him [**312**] and said to him, 'The sultan is in need. The troops are asking him for what he does not have. We want 30,000 dinars from you. It will be a great favour to him, which will earn you reward and thanks.' He replied, 'I hear and obey,' and did not ask him to reduce the figure at all. He continued, 'My baggage and possessions are in Anbār in the house I stopped at.' The vizier sent several men to it, where they found much money and precious objects, including 1,100 wonderfully made gold and silver articles and clothes and turbans the like of which is not often to be found.

These events which cover from the defeat of Sultan Muḥammad to this point we should properly relate after the killing of the Bāṭinīs. The events took place towards the end of the year [autumn 1101], while the killing was in Shaʿbān [June 1101]. We put these events first to make them follow consecutively with nothing separating them.

Now when Tāj al-Mulūk Būrī took control of Jabala, he and his men treated the

---

[5] In Arabic *kund iṣṭabl.*

inhabitants badly. They did things to them that the people censured. They wrote to the Cadi Fakhr al-Mulk Abū ʻAlī ʻAmmār ibn Muḥammad ibn ʻAmmār, the lord of Tripoli, and complained of what was being done to them. They asked him to send some of his men to whom they could surrender the town. He agreed and sent a force, which entered Jabala and, uniting with the inhabitants, fought Tāj al-Mulūk and his men. The Turks were defeated and Ibn ʻAmmār's troops took control of Jabala. They made Tāj al-Mulūk a prisoner and took him to Tripoli, where he was well received by Ibn ʻAmmār and treated kindly. Ibn ʻAmmār sent him to his father in Damascus with apologies, explaining the situation to him, how he feared that the Franks would conquer Jabala.

[313] The massacre of the Bāṭinīs

In Shaʻbān of this year [June 1101] Sultan Barkyāruq ordered the massacre of the Bāṭinīs, otherwise known as the Ismāʻīlīs, who were in former times called the Qarāmiṭa. We shall now begin with an account of their origins and then the reason for their massacre.

The earliest anything was known about them, I mean, about this latest movement, which has become notorious as the Bāṭinīs or Ismāʻīlīs, was in the reign of Sultan Malikshāh. Eighteen of them gathered and prayed at the time of the Feast in Sāveh. The city prefect got to hear of them and put them in prison under arrest. Later, after enquiries about them, they were released. This is the first gathering they had.

They preached their message to a muezzin, a man from Sāveh, who was living in Isfahan but he did not respond to their call. Fearing that he might report them, they killed him. He was their first victim. Suspicion [of involvement] fell on a carpenter, called Ṭāhir. He was killed as a warning to the public and dragged by a leg through the markets. He was their first 'martyr'. His father was a preacher who came to Baghdad with Sultan Barkyāruq in the year 486 [1093] and rose in his favour. He later went to Basra and acted as cadi there. Subsequently he went on a mission to Kirmān, where the populace killed him in a riot that took place there. They claimed that he was a Bāṭinī.

[314] The first place they took control of and made into a stronghold was a town near Qā'in. Its headman was of their persuasion, so they gathered and grew strong there. A large caravan going to Qā'in from Kirmān passed by them. Along with his men and the Bāṭinīs he attacked the caravan and killed all in it. Only a single Turkoman escaped and came to Qā'in to tell the tale. The people there hastened, along with Cadi al-Kirmānī, to wage jihad on them but could achieve nothing. Later on, after Niẓām al-Mulk was slain and Sultan Malikshāh died, their power grew and their military might increased, as did their ambitions.

The reason for their power in Isfahan was that, after Sultan Barkyāruq had besieged Isfahan, where his brother Maḥmūd and the latter's mother the Lady

Jalāliyya were, and had withdrawn, the Bāṭinī creed was made public and spread far and wide. They had been scattered in various places but now they came together and began to kidnap all the opponents they could and kill them. They did this with a great number and became a serious danger, so that, if a man was later than his normal time for coming home, people were sure he had been killed and sat to receive condolences. People became cautious and would not go out alone. One day a muezzin was taken. A Bāṭinī neighbour of his seized him. As his family started to bewail his loss, the Bāṭinīs took him on to the roof of his house and showed him how his family were beating their faces and weeping. He was unable to say a word as he was so terrified of them.

Account of how the common people reacted in Isfahan

After this affliction had touched many of the people of Isfahan, God Almighty allowed humiliation and revenge to strike the perpetrators. It came about that a man entered the house of a friend of his and noticed clothes, [**315**] sandals and undergarments he did not recognise. He went out and spoke of this matter, which people then investigated and learnt that they belonged to men who had been killed. The citizens rose in anger, investigating who had been killed and making enquiries. They seized control of the quarters where the Bāṭinīs were. The latter, whenever a man passed by them, would forcibly take him into one of their houses, kill him and then throw him down a pit in the house that had been prepared for that.

A blind man stood at the entrance to a quarter there. When someone came by he would ask him to lead him a few steps to the quarter's gate. The man would do this and as he entered he would be seized and killed. The Shāfi'ī lawyer Abū'l-Qāsim Mas'ūd ibn Muḥammad al-Khujandī devoted himself to taking revenge. He assembled a sizeable mob with weapons and ordered them to dig trenches and light fires in them. The common people commenced to bring Bāṭinīs, singly and in droves, and throw them into the flames. They put a man in charge of the fire pits and called him Mālik.[6] A great multitude of them were massacred.

Account of the fortresses they conquered in Persian lands

The Bāṭinīs conquered several fortresses, including the castle of Isfahan. This was not an ancient one but had been built by Sultan Malikshāh. The reason for its construction was that a Byzantine officer came to him, accepted Islam and joined his service. One day Malikshāh went hunting and a hound, an excellent hunter, ran away and went up [**316**] the hill there. The sultan and the Byzantine followed it

---

[6] The name of the angel who guards Hell.

and found it on the site of the [future] fortress. The Byzantine said to him, 'Had we a hill like this, we would put a castle on it which would prove useful for us.' When the sultan ordered its construction, Niẓam al-Mulk vetoed it but his view was ignored. After it was completed the Byzantine was made fortress commander.

At the end of Malikshāh's reign when Isfahan came into the hands of the Lady, she dismissed the commander and appointed someone else, a man from Daylam called Ziyār. He died and a man from Khūzistān came to the castle who was joined by Aḥmad ibn 'Aṭṭāsh, to whom the Bāṭinīs had given a crown. They had collected money for him and made him their leader despite his lack of learning. His father had been a leader amongst them. He became an associate of the fortress commander and remained with him, trusted and allowed to administer affairs. After the death of the commander Aḥmad ibn 'Aṭṭāsh took control. The Muslims suffered a lot from him, from seizure of their goods, murder, brigandage and constant fear. They used to say, 'A castle led to by a dog and suggested by an infidel inevitably must end in evil!'

Another castle was Alamūt in the district of Qazwīn. It is said that a Daylamī prince, who was fond of hunting, flew an eagle one day and, when he followed it, he saw that it alighted on the site of this [future] castle. He found it to be an impregnable position, so ordered the castle to be built there and called it Aluh Mūt, which in the Daylamī tongue means 'the eagle's teaching'. This place and the vicinity are called Ṭāliqān. There are strong fortresses there, of which the most famous is Alamūt. This region was held as a tax farm by Sharafshāh al-Ja'farī, who appointed as his deputy an Alid, a simple-minded and guileless man.

Al-Ḥasan ibn al-Ṣabbāḥ was an energetic and capable man with a knowledge of geometry, arithmetic, astronomy, magic and other matters. The headman of Rayy was someone called Abū Muslim, who was the son-in-law of Niẓām al-Mulk. He suspected al-Ḥasan ibn al-Ṣabbāḥ of welcoming several Egyptian agents. [**317**] Ibn al-Ṣabbāḥ was wary of him, for Niẓām al-Mulk held him in respect. One day on the basis of his knowledge of physiognomy, Abū Muslim said to him, 'Soon this man will lead the weak common people astray.' When Ibn al-Ṣabbāḥ fled from Abū Muslim, he pursued him but without catching him.

Ibn al-Ṣabbāḥ was a disciple of Ibn 'Aṭṭāsh, the medical man who seized the castle of Isfahan. He went on far-ranging journeys, which brought him to Egypt. He had an audience with the ruler al-Mustanṣir, who received him with honour and gave him money, ordering him to call people to recognise his Imamate. Ibn al-Ṣabbāḥ asked, 'Who is the Imam after you?' and he indicated his son Nizār. After Egypt Ibn al-Ṣabbāḥ went to Syria, Mesopotamia, Diyār Bakr and Anatolia and then returned to Khurasan. He visited Kashghar and Transoxania, wandering amongst peoples and leading them astray.

When he saw Alamūt and got to know the inhabitants of that region, he stayed on amongst them and, eager to mislead them, carried on his preaching in secret. He made a show of asceticism and wore haircloth. Most of the people followed him. The Alid governor of the castle had a good opinion of him and used to hold sessions with him to gain spiritual benefit from him. When Ibn al-Ṣabbāḥ had consolidated his position, he went to the Alid in the castle one day and said to him, 'Leave this castle.' The Alid smiled, as he thought he was joking, but Ibn al-Ṣabbāḥ ordered some of his men to eject the Alid, which they did. He sent him to Dāmghān, having given him his property, and so took control of the castle.

Hearing this news, Niẓām al-Mulk sent an army to the castle of Alamūt. They besieged it and blockaded the roads to it. Ibn al-Ṣabbāḥ suffered from the siege, so sent men to assassinate Niẓām al-Mulk. After he was killed the army withdrew from Alamūt. Later Sultan Muḥammad ibn Malikshāh sent an army in that direction, which besieged the fortress. This will be related, God willing.

[**318**] Another fortress is Ṭabas and part of Quhistān. The reason they ruled there is that in Quhistān there remained survivors of the Sīmjūr family, emirs of Khurasan in the days of the Samanids. One of the survivors of the line was a man called al-Munawwar, who was held in respect by high and low. When Kul-Sārigh controlled Quhistān he treated the people unjustly and tyrannically. He wished to take a sister of al-Munawwar without legal sanctions. This compelled al-Munawwar to seek support from the Ismā'īlīs and to ally with them. Thus they became important in Quhistān, which they came to control, including Khūr, Khūsaf, Zawzan, Qā'in, Tūn and the neighbouring regions.

There was also the castle of Wasnamkūh which they seized, near to Abhar, in the year 484 [1091]. People suffered from it, especially the inhabitants of Abhar who asked for aid from Sultan Barkyāruq. He arranged for men to besiege it. It was invested for eight months and taken in the year 489 [1096]. All within were killed to the very last man.

Another castle was that of Khālanjān, five leagues from Isfahan. It was held by Mu'ayyad al-Mulk, son of Niẓām al-Mulk, and then passed to Jāwulī Saqāo, who put a Turk in position there. A Bāṭinī carpenter made friends with him and gave him a beautiful gift. He cultivated him until he was fully trusted, even given the keys of the castle. He invited the Turk and his men to a feast and served them wine until they were drunk. He then summoned Ibn 'Aṭṭāsh, who arrived with a group of his followers. The castle was handed to him and he killed the garrison apart from the Turk, for he escaped. This increased Ibn 'Aṭṭāsh's power and he acquired many sources of revenue paid by the people of Isfahan.

One of their renowned castles was Ustūnāwand between Rayy and Āmul. They acquired it after Malikshāh. The lord of the place left it, was killed and the castle was taken.

The castle of Ardahnu[7] was taken by Abū'l-Futūḥ, the nephew of al-Ḥasan ibn al-Ṣabbāḥ, [**319**] and there was also Girdkūh, which is famous. Other castles are the Inspector's Castle[8] in Khūzistān and the castle of al-Ṭunbūr two leagues from Arrajān, which was seized by Abū Ḥamza the Cobbler, a citizen of Arrajān. He

7 Given thus in Yāqūt, i, 204, and described as 'a strong castle in the district of Rayy'.

8 i.e. Qal'at al-Nāẓir.

went to Egypt and returned as a leading agent of theirs. The castle of Khaladkhān is between Fars and Khūzistān. It was a home for evil men who preyed on the high road for about 200 years until 'Aḍud al-Dawla ibn Buwayh conquered it and killed its inhabitants. When the power of the state passed to Malikshāh, he assigned it to Emir Unur and made him chatelain. The Bāṭinīs in Arrajān sent to him, asking him to sell it but he refused, so they said to him, 'We shall send you someone to dispute with you until he makes the truth plain to you.' He agreed to that, so they sent him a Daylamī to dispute with him. The chatelain had a mamluke he had raised to whom he entrusted the keys of the castle. The Bāṭinī won him over and he agreed to the arrest of his master and the surrender of the castle. The chatelain was seized (although released later) and the castle surrendered. Afterwards they took control of several castles, but these are the best known of them.

How Jāwulī Saqāo dealt with the Bāṭinīs

During this year Jāwulī Saqāo put a great multitude of them to death. The reason for this was that the area governed by this emir was between Rāmhurmuz and Arrajān. [**320**] When the Bāṭinīs took the castles in Khūzistān and Fars that have been mentioned, increasing their nuisance, for they interrupted travel on the roads in those regions, he concerted a plan with a group of his followers, who gave out that they were at odds with him. They left him and sought out the Bāṭinīs, pretending to be with them and of their views. They remained with them until they were trusted.

Then Jāwulī announced that the emirs, the sons of Bursuq, were planning to attack him and take his lands and that he was determined to leave, because he could not withstand them, and go to Hamadhān. After this became known and he had set out, his followers who were with the Bāṭinīs and in the plot said, 'Let us go to where he will pass and seize him and what property he has with him.' They set out with three hundred of their leaders and champions. When they met, Jāwulī's men in their ranks turned against them and put them to the sword. Only three individuals escaped. They climbed a hill and fled. Jāwulī took their horses, weapons and such like as booty.

The killing of the lord of Kirmān, a Bāṭinī, and the change of ruler

Tīrānshāh ibn Tūrānshāh ibn Qāwurt Beg[9] was the person who killed the Ismā'īlī Turks. They are not to be associated with this Bāṭinī sect. They are merely named

[9] Qāwurt Beg, son of Chaghrī Beg, was killed after opposing his nephew Malikshāh in 465/1073. His descendants formed a separate Saljuq dynasty in Kirmān.

after an emir who was called Ismā'īl, and they were Sunnīs. He killed 2,000 of them in cold blood and cut off the hands of 2,000.

A man called Abū Zur'a, who was a clerk in Khūzistān, came to Tīrānshāh [**321**] and successfully convinced him of the merits of the Bāṭinī doctrine. There was a Ḥanafī lawyer with Tīrānshāh, called Aḥmad ibn al-Ḥusayn al-Balkhī, who was greatly respected by people. He summoned him in the night and held a long session with him. When he left, Tīrānshāh sent men after him to kill him. In the morning people came into his presence, including his army commander, who said to Tīrānshāh, 'O prince, who killed this lawyer?' He replied, 'You are prefect of the town and you ask me who killed him!' 'I know his killer,' he said and rose and left. With three hundred horsemen he left his service and went to Isfahan. Tīrānshāh sent 2,000 horsemen to track him and bring him back but he fought and defeated them. He went on to Isfahan, where were Sultan Muḥammad and Mu'ayyad al-Mulk. The sultan received him with honour and said, 'You are the father of princes.'

After his departure the troops of Kirmān became dissatisfied, united together and fought Tīrānshāh. They expelled him from Bardsīr which is the main city of Kirmān. When he had left it, the cadi and the army agreed to set up Arslānshāh ibn Kirmānshāh ibn Qāwurt Beg. Tīrānshāh went to the city of Bam in Kirmān, whose inhabitants opposed him and denied him entry. They seized the money and jewels that he had. He made for the castle of Sumayram and fortified himself within. An emir known as Muḥammad Bihsutūn was there. Arslānshāh sent an army which besieged the castle. Muḥammad Bihsutūn said to Tīrānshāh, 'Depart from me. I do not hold with betraying you. I am a Muslim, but your being here is harmful to me. You are causing my religion to be called into suspicion.' When Tīrānshāh had decided to leave, Muḥammad Bihsutūn sent to the commander of the forces besieging them to inform him of Tīrānshāh's departure. A detachment of troops was sent to intercept him. They caught and seized him and what he had with him. They also took Abū Zur'a. Arslānshāh dispatched men to kill them both and took over all the the lands of Kirmān.

[322] Why Barkyāruq killed the Bāṭinīs

When the importance of the Bāṭinīs had grown, their military power increased and their numbers greatly multiplied, hatred and rancour arose between them and their opponents. After they had killed several senior emirs, most of whom were loyal to Muḥammad and hostile to Sultan Barkyāruq, such as the prefect of Isfahan, Sarmaz, and Arghush and Kumush, mamlukes of Niẓām al-Mulk, and his son-in-law and others besides, the enemies of Barkyāruq attributed these deeds to him and suspected him of sympathy towards the Bāṭinīs.

When Sultan Barkyāruq had been victorious, routed his brother, Sultan Muhammad, and killed the latter's vizier, Mu'ayyad al-Mulk, a number of Bāṭinīs began to act openly amongst his army and led astray many, introducing them to their doctrine. They became almost dominant in numbers and power. The army came to contain a group of their leaders, so their significance increased and they started to threaten death to those who did not agree with them. Those who opposed them became fearful, with the result that not one of them, neither emir nor under-officer, dared to go from home unprotected but would wear a breastplate under his clothes. Even the Vizier al-A'azz Abū'l-Maḥāsin used to don chain-mail beneath his clothes. His close associates asked Sultan Barkyāruq for permission to come before him with their weapons and told him of their fear of those that might attack them. He gave permission for them to do so.

They advised the sultan to strike at them before he was incapable of repairing the situation and told him how people suspected him of an inclination towards their doctrine, with the result that the troops of his brother Sultan Muḥammad were making that their taunt. On the battlefield they mocked them, saying, 'Bāṭinī [heretics]!' All these incentives coalesced and the sultan gave permission for the Bāṭinīs to be attacked and killed. He rode out **[323]** with the army and hunted them down. They seized several from their tents and only insignificant persons escaped.

One of those suspected of being their leader was Emir Muḥammad ibn Dushmanziyār ibn 'Alā' al-Dawla Abī Ja'far ibn Kākūya, the lord of Yazd. He fled, journeying for a day and a night. On the second day he was found amongst the army, having lost his way and unaware of his whereabouts. He was killed and the following proverb is appropriate here: 'His own legs brought you a traitor'. His tents were plundered and he was found to have a stock of weapons. Some suspects were taken out to the Hippodrome and executed. Several innocent persons were killed who were not of them but who had been falsely accused by their enemies. Amongst those executed was the son of Kayqubād, the governor of Takrīt. His father had not changed Barkyāruq's khutbah but had embarked on repairing and fortifying the citadel. He demolished the town's congregational mosque, which was close to the citadel, so that no attack could be launched from it. He converted a church in the town into a mosque where prayers were held.

A letter was sent to Baghdad for the arrest of Abū Ibrāhīm al-Asadābādhī who was already there as an envoy of Barkyāruq to seize Mu'ayyad al-Mulk's property. He was one of the Bāṭinīs' leading notables. He was arrested and imprisoned. When they were about to execute him, he said, 'Suppose you kill me, can you kill all in the castles and towns?' He was put to death and no funeral prayers were said over him. He was thrown outside the city wall. He had a grown-up son who was killed by the army with the others.

The people of 'Āna had been connected with this doctrine in the past. Their attitude was reported to the Vizier Abū Shujā' during the reign of al-Muqtadī bi-Amr Allāh. He summoned them to Baghdad and questioned their shaykhs concerning what was said about them. They denied and rejected it, so he let them go.

Also suspected of being a Bāṭinī was al-Kiyā al-Harrās,[10] the professor at the Niẓāmiyya. This accusation was brought to Sultan Muḥammad, who ordered his arrest. The Caliph al-Mustaẓhir bi-Allāh sent to have him released and testified to the soundness of his beliefs and his high standing in religious learning. He was allowed to go free.

[324] How Emir Buzghush besieged Quhistān and Ṭabas

This year Emir Buzghush, who was the greatest emir with Sultan Sanjar, assembled many detachments, supplied them with money and weapons and marched into Ismā'īlī territory which he plundered and laid waste. He killed very many of them and put Ṭabas under a close siege. He employed trebuchets against it and demolished much of its wall. The defenders weakened and it only remained to overrun the place when they sent large bribes and persuaded him to give up his aim. He retired and left them. What had been destroyed of the walls was repaired and the stores of weapons and provisions restocked. Later, in the year 497 [1103–4], Buzghush came against them once more with the result that we shall relate, God willing.

Account of the Franks' conquests in Syria

Godfrey, the king of the Franks in Syria and ruler of Jerusalem, marched to Acre on the coast and besieged it. He was hit by an arrow and killed. He had rebuilt the city of Jaffa and handed it over to a Frankish count, called Tancred. After Godfrey was killed, his brother Baldwin went to Jerusalem with 500 horse and foot. This news came to Prince Duqāq, the lord of Damascus, who moved with his army to confront him, accompanied by Emir Janāḥ al-Dawla with his troops. In the battle that followed he won a victory over the Franks.

During this year the Franks took the city of Sarūj in Mesopotamia. The reason for this was that the Franks had already taken the city of Edessa by treaty with its inhabitants, most of whom were Armenians. There were **[325]** few Muslims there. At the present time Suqmān gathered a large force of Turkomans in Sarūj and attacked the Franks. When they met in battle the Franks defeated him in Rabī' I [January 1101] and after the complete rout of the Muslims, they went to Sarūj, which they took over after a siege. They killed many of the inhabitants, enslaved their women and plundered their property. Only those who had left in flight survived.

Also this year the Franks conquered Haifa, which is near Acre on the coast. They took it by force, whereas they took Arsūf by treaty and expelled the

[10] Named as al-Harrāsī (died 504/1110) in Makdisi, *Ibn 'Aqīl*, 216–19.

inhabitants. In Rajab [May 1101] they took Caesarea by the sword, killing its people and plundering what was there.

Miscellaneous events

In the month of Ramaḍān of this year [July 1101] the Caliph al-Mustaẓhir bi-Allāh ordered the opening of the Palace Mosque and that superogatory prayers at this time of fasting should be performed. This had not been customary. He also ordered that 'In the name of God, the Merciful, the Compassionate' should be pronounced plainly. This also had not been the custom, although the clear pronouncement of the *basmalah* had only been abandoned in the Baghdad mosques because the Alids, the rulers of Egypt, used to practise that.[11] It was dropped to be different from them and not to follow the practice of the school of the Imam Aḥmad [ibn Ḥanbal]. He also ordered the practice of *qunūt*[12] according to the Shāfi'ī school. On the twenty-ninth night [28 July] there was a complete recitation of the Koran. A large crowd of people gathered. Za'īm al-Ru'asā' Abū'l-Qāsim 'Alī ibn Fakhr al-Dawla ibn Jahīr, the brother of 'Amīd al-Dawla, had just been released from prison. He mingled with the crowd and left Baghdad by a gap in the city wall. He went to join Sayf al-Dawla Ṣadaqa ibn Mazyad, [**326**] who welcomed him with honour and gave him lodgings.

The following died this year:

In Muḥarram [6 November-6 December 1100] Jamāl al-Dawla Abū Naṣr, son of Ra'īs al-Ru'asā' ibn al-Muslima, the steward (*ustādh*) of the caliphal palace.

The Cadi Aḥmad ibn Muḥammad ibn 'Abd al-Wāḥid, Abū Manṣūr Ibn al-Ṣabbāgh, the Shāfi'ī lawyer. He received his learning from his cousin, the Shaykh Abū Naṣr Ibn al-Ṣabbāgh. He used to fast for extended periods and transmitted Ḥadīth from the Cadi Abū'l-Ṭayyib al-Ṭabarī and others.

Sharaf al-Mulk Abū Sa'd Muḥammad ibn Manṣūr al-Khwārazmī, the Comptroller, in Isfahan. He was comptroller in the bureau of Sultan Malikshāh. He gave 100,000 dinars to be allowed to give up that office. He built a mosque by the tomb of Abū Ḥanīfa (God's mercy on him), a madrasah at the Ṭāq Gate and another in Marv, all for the Ḥanafīs.

In Ṣafar [December 1100] the Cadi Abū'l-Ma'ālī 'Azīzī, who was a Shāfi'ī and an Ash'arī from Jīlān. A pious man, he was the author of many excellent works. There are amusing stories that connect him with the inhabitants of the Azaj Gate, for whom he was cadi although they hated him as he hated them.

---

[11] The status of the formula at the beginning of each Koranic *sūra* is at issue. The Ḥanafīs gave it a lower standing and therefore did not say it out loud in ritual worship. The Shāfi'īs had the opposite view. See *EI(2)*, i, 1984.

[12] A term with manifold definitions concerning attitudes during prayer. It also denoted prayers that 'consisted of prayers and blessings for the Muslims and curses upon the unbelievers' (*EI(2)*, v, 395).

As'ad ibn Mas'ūd ibn 'Alī ibn Muḥammad, Abū Ibrāhīm al-'Utbī, a descendant of 'Utba ibn Ghazwān. He came from Nishapur, born in 404 [1013-14], and transmitted from Abū Bakr al-Ḥīrī and others.

Also in Ṣafar Muḥammad ibn Muḥammad ibn 'Abd al-Bāqī ibn al-Ḥasan ibn Muḥammad ibn Ṭawq, Abū'l-Faḍā'il al-Rab'ī al-Mawṣilī, the Shāfi'ī lawyer, who studied with Abū Isḥāq al-Shīrāzī. [**327**] He heard Ḥadīth from Abū'l-Ṭayyib al-Ṭabarī and others, and was an honest, reliable transmitter.

In Rabī' I [January 1101] Muḥammad ibn 'Alī ibn 'Ubayd Allāh ibn Aḥmad ibn Ṣāliḥ ibn Sulaymān ibn Wad'ān, Abū Naṣr, the Mosul Cadi. He was the author of *The Wad'āniyya Forty*,[13] to which others added supplements. It is said that he plagiarised what had been Zayd ibn Rifā'a al-Hāshimī's composition. The bulk of his ḥadīths are suspect in their content.[14]

Also in Rabī' I [January 1101] Naṣr ibn Aḥmad ibn 'Abd Allāh ibn al-Baṭar al-Qārī, Abū'l-Khaṭṭāb, who was born in the year 398 [1007-8] and heard [Ḥadīth from] Ibn Razquwayh and others. People travelled to meet him because of the high status of his authorities and his transmission was sound.

---

[13] For the author and extant commentaries on this collection of Ḥadīth, apparently named after his ancestor, see *GAL*, i, 355 and Suppl. i, 602.

[14] i.e. *munkar*, a technical term of Ḥadīth scholarship.

[328] The Year 495 [1101–1102]

Account of the death of al-Musta'lī bi-Allāh and the accession of al-Āmir bi-Aḥkām Allāh

There died during this year al-Musta'lī bi-Allāh Abū'l-Qāsim Aḥmad ibn Ma'add al-Mustanṣir bi-Allāh the Alid, the caliph of Egypt, on 17 Ṣafar [11 December 1101]. He was born on 20 Sha'bān in the year 467 [10 April 1075] and his caliphate lasted seven years and about two months. The power behind his reign had been al-Afḍal.

After his death his son Abū 'Alī al-Manṣūr, who was born on 13 Muḥarram in the year 490 [31 December 1096], succeeded him and he was proclaimed as caliph on the day his father died, when he was aged five years, one month and four days. He was given the title al-Āmir bi-Aḥkām Allāh. Among those who were called to be caliph there was never one younger than he or al-Mustanṣir, although al-Mustanṣir was older than this one was. Because of al-Āmir's young age he was unable to ride a horse. Al-Afḍal, son of Emīr al-Juyūsh, undertook the role of regent very competently and continued to administer affairs until he was killed in the year 515 [1121–2].

[329] The conflict between Sultan Barkyāruq and Sultan Muḥammad and the peace that was made

In Ṣafar [25 November–23 December 1101] there was the third battle between the two sultans, Barkyāruq and Muḥammad. Under the year 494 [1100–1101] we have mentioned that Muḥammad came to Baghdad and that Barkyāruq withdrew to Wāsiṭ. Muḥammad remained there until 17 Muḥarram of this year [11 November 1101] and then he and his brother Sultan Sanjar retired to their own lands, Sanjar making for Khurasan and Muḥammad for Hamadhān. After Muḥammad had left Baghdad, news came that Barkyāruq had meddled with the caliph's domain at Wāsiṭ and that he had been heard to say concerning the caliph things that it is indecent to mention. The caliph sent after Sultan Muḥammad and called him back to Baghdad and repeated what had been told to him. He planned to take action with Muḥammad to fight Barkyāruq. Muḥammad said, 'There is no need for the Commander of the Faithful to take action. I shall undertake this quite satisfactorily.' He returned to Baghdad and set up Abū'l-Ma'ālī al-Mufaḍḍal ibn 'Abd al-Razzāq to gather money and Īlghāzī as prefect. When he entered Baghdad, he had left his troops on the Khurasan road. They plundered the area and laid it waste, so Muḥammad took them with him and made a forced march to Rūdhrāwar.

As for Sultan Barkyāruq, it has been said under the year 494 [1100-1101] that he had left Baghdad for Wāsiṭ when Muḥammad arrived. When the troops in Wāsiṭ heard [**330**] of his approach, they were fearful, took their women, children and property, collected all the boats there and went down to al-Zubaydiyya, where they remained.

The sultan arrived extremely ill, being carried in a litter. Many of their mounts had perished and much of their equipment been lost, because they had been forcing their march, fearing that Sultan Muḥammad or Emir Ṣadaqa, lord of al-Ḥilla, would pursue them. Every bridge they crossed they destroyed to prevent any of their pursuers crossing it.

When they came to Wāsiṭ, Barkyāruq recovered. He and his men had no thought other than to cross from the west bank to the east, but they could find no boat. It was winter and very cold. The river was high. The inhabitants, fearful of them, remained fast in the mosque or in their houses. The streets and the markets were devoid of any passer-by. Cadi Abū ʻAlī al-Fāriqī went to the army and met with Emir Ayāz and the vizier and pleaded with them for the sake of the people. He requested the sending of a prefect to put their minds at rest. They agreed to his request and said to him, 'We want you to collect some people for us who will take our mounts across by swimming with them.' He gathered some Wāsiṭ youths and gave them considerble pay, and so they took their mounts across, horses, mules and camels. Emir Ayāz drove the mounts in person and acted like a groom. They had only one boat which had brought the sultan down from Baghdad. They transported their goods and baggage in this. When they were on the east bank they felt secure and the troops plundered the region. The cadi returned and renewed his plead for them to desist. His request was listened to and men were sent with him to stop the plundering.

[**331**] The troops of Wāsiṭ sent to Sultan Barkyāruq asking for a guarantee of safety so that they could offer themselves for his service. This he granted and most of them came to him and travelled with him to the lands of the sons of Bursuq. The latter also joined his service and thus the armies gathered around him.

He heard of his brother's departure from Baghdad and set out to follow him via Nihāwand and caught up with him at Rūdhrāwar. The two armies were well matched in numbers, each of them having 4,000 Turkish horsemen. They stood in their ranks the first day all day long but no fighting occurred between them because of the extreme cold. On the second day they came again and stood face to face in the same way. A man on one side would stand forward and a potential opponent would emerge. However, as they drew close, they would embrace one another, greet and then part.

Emir Baldajī and others from Muḥammad's army went out to meet Emir Ayāz and the Vizier al-Aʻazz. They got together and agreed to make peace because of the suffering, ennui and fatigue that affected everyone. The basis of the agreement was that Barkyāruq should be sultan and Muḥammad a [subordinate] prince, entitled to a thrice-daily military band.[1] The territory he would hold was to be Ganja and its districts, Azerbayjan, Diyār Bakr and Mesopotamia, including Mosul, and the Sultan Barkyāruq would support him with troops to allow him to conquer the lands that held out against him. Each one took an oath to the other. Both parties left the field on 4 Rabīʻ I [27 December 1101]. Barkyāruq went to Qarātakīn's Pasture,[2] making for Sāveh and Sultan Muḥammad to Asadābādh. Both armies broke up and each emir went off to his fief.

[332] Account of the battle between Sultan Barkyāruq and Muḥammad and the collapse of their peace agreement

In Jumādā I [21 February–22 March 1102] the fourth battle between Sultan Barkyāruq and his brother Muḥammad took place. This came about because Sultan Muḥammad left Rūdhrāwar, the site of the above-mentioned clash, to go to Asadābādh and from there to Qazwīn. The emirs who had exerted themselves to bring about the peace he accused of treachery and lack of commitment to himself. He arranged with the headman of Qazwīn to make an approach to himself through those emirs to get him to attend his table. The headman duly made his request to the sultan through them, and he attended his feast, after first refusing. He charged his entourage to carry weapons under their surcoats. He came to the feast, accompanied by Emir Aytakīn and Basmal. The latter, one of his senior emirs, he killed, and he blinded Emir Aytakīn.

Emir Yināl ibn Anūshtakīn al-Ḥusāmī had parted from Barkyāruq and remained waging war on the Bāṭinīs in their castles and mountains. He now sought out Sultan Muḥammad and proceeded with him to Rayy, sounding his military band fives times daily. Troops flocked to him and after he had been there eight days his brother Barkyāruq arrived on the ninth day and a battle ensued at Rayy. The numbers of the two forces were balanced, each army being 10,000 horsemen. When they ranged opposite one another, Emir Surkhāb ibn Kaykhusro the Daylamī, lord of Āveh, charged Emir Yināl and routed him. The whole army of Muḥammad followed him in rout and were scattered. **[333]** Most of them went towards Ṭabaristān. In this battle only one person was killed and that not in the heat of battle. A section of the defeated fled in the direction of Qazwīn. Muḥammad's treasure chests were plundered, while he with a small detachment went to Isfahan, himself carrying his standard so that his men would follow him. Emir Ilbakī ibn Bursuq and Emir Ayāz pursued him as far as Qum and Sultan Barkyāruq went after his brother Muḥammad's men and seized their baggage.

---

1 The *nawba* referred to the performance of military music before the gates of great men. Originally the privilege of the caliph, it was widened to sultans, princes and emirs. Performance at the times of the five daily prayers was more prestigious than three-fold performance and implied superiority. See *EI(2)*, vii, 927ff., s.v. *naḳḳāra-khāna.*

2 In Arabic Marj Qarātakīn. Yāqūt, iv, 489, gives Marj Qarābulīn ('one day's journey from

How Sultan Muḥammad was besieged in Isfahan

After Sultan Muḥammad had fled from the battle we have mentioned at Rayy, he went to Isfahan with seventy horsemen. The city was under his control and he had a lieutenant there. With him were Emir Yināl and other emirs. He entered the city in Rabīʿ I [24 December 1101-22 January 1102] and ordered the repair of those parts of the walls that were in a poor state. This was the wall that ʿAlāʿ al-Dīn ibn Kākūya had built in the year 429 [1037-8] when he was in fear of Ṭughrilbeg. Muḥammad ordered the moat to be made deeper until water rose in it. He entrusted a gate to each emir. He had with him in the city 1,100 horse and 500 foot and he set up trebuchets.

Hearing that his brother Muḥammad had gone to Isfahan, Sultan Barkyāruq followed him and arrived in Jumādā I [21 February-22 March 1102] with his large army, more than 15,000 horse and 100,000 auxiliaries. He put the city under siege and pressed it hard.

Every night Muḥammad patrolled the city wall three times. When there was a worsening **[334]** in the situation of the besieged, he expelled the weak and the poor from the city so that whole quarters were emptied. Provisions became in short supply and people ate horse, camel and the like and money was scarce. Sultan Muḥammad was obliged to borrow from the city notables. He took much money and then the troops made further demands, so he imposed more levies on the inhabitants, which he took by threats and violence. Prices contined to rise, until ten *mann*s of wheat reached a dinar and four rotls of meat also a dinar.[3] Every 100 rotls of straw cost four dinars. Other property became cheap and was disregarded because there were no buyers. Prices among Barkyāruq's army were low.

The siege of the city lasted until 10 Dhū'l-Ḥijja [25 September 1102]. Sultan Muḥammad saw that he was powerless to defend the city. The more his situation weakened the more he was determined to leave and seek some other place where he could gather troops and return to raise his rival's blockade. So he left the city with 150 horse, accompanied by Emir Yināl. He left several of his senior emirs in the city with the rest of his army. When he abandoned his army and the city, none of their mounts was capable of the journey because fodder had been so short, so he halted at a distance of six leagues.

Hearing of his departure, Barkyāruq sent Emir Ayāz after him with a large force, ordering a swift march to pursue him. It is said that Muḥammad outstripped them and they failed to catch him and so returned. It is also said that on the contrary they caught up with him and he sent to Emir Ayāz to say, 'You know that on your head are undertakings and oaths that are still valid. I have done nothing to you to make you strive to harm me', so Ayāz turned back and sent him horses. He

---

Hamadhān in the direction of Isfahan, where the Saljūqs had several battles').

3 In Iraq 1 *mann* was equivalent to 816.5 g., and there were 2 rotls in a *mann*. In cities of Iran the *mann* varied greatly and was usually of heavier weight (see Hinz, 16-17).

took his banner, his ceremonial parasol and three loads of dinars [**335**] and returned to Barkyāruq. He came before him with the banners of his brother Muḥammad reversed. Barkyāruq objected to that and said, 'Although he has behaved badly, it is not right that he should be treated thus.' Ayaz gave a full report and Barkyāruq approved what he had done.

After Muḥammad had left Isfahan, more than 100,000 men, criminals, peasants and plunder-seekers, gathered and assaulted the city with ladders and siege towers. They filled in the moat with straw and came up close to the wall. Some climbed up ladders but the inhabitants fought like men determined to defend their womenfolk and their property, so they retired frustrated. The emirs then advised Barkyāruq to withdraw which he did on 18 Dhū'l-Ḥijja [3 October 1102]. He left in control of the old city, which is called Shahristān, Turshuk al-Ṣawābī with 1,000 horse and his son, Malikshāh. He went to Hamadhān. This is one of the greatest wonders to be recorded that a besieged sultan, whose supplies were cut off, while being acknowledged as ruler in most of the land, should be freed from a serious siege and escape from a numerous army, all of whom had him as the target of their spears and their arrows.

The killing of the Vizier al-A'azz and the appointment of al-Khaṭīr Abū Manṣūr

Barkyāruq's vizier, al-A'azz Abū'l-Maḥāsin 'Abd al-Jalīl ibn Muḥammad al-Dihistānī, was killed on 12 Ṣafar this year [6 December 1101] at Isfahan, while he was besieging it with Barkyāruq. On that day he rode from his tent to wait upon the sultan and a fair-haired youth came to him. It is said that he was a page of Abū Sa'īd al-Ḥaddād, whom the vizier had put to death in the past year. He seized the opportunity to attack. It is also said that he was a Bāṭinī. He wounded him in several places. The vizier's men scattered and ran away. They came back and the man who came closest to him was severely wounded. The attacker returned to [**336**] the vizier and left him at the last gasp of life.

The vizier was generous, big-hearted and of a pleasant disposition. He also built many buildings. People shunned him because he began his period of office when the norms of administration had changed and no income or money remained. Out of necessity he did things that caused people to dread him.

He was good at relations with the merchants and very many became rich because of him. They used to ask him to do business with them. When he was killed, they lost a great amount of money.

It is related that a certain merchant sold him some goods for 1,000 dinars. He said to the merchant, 'Take fifty *kurr*s of wheat from al-Rādhān to pay for them.' The merchant refused to take them and said, 'I only want cash.' The following day, when the merchant came to him, he said, 'Congratulations!' 'What is this about?' he asked. 'It's about your wheat,' he said. 'I do not have any wheat and I do not want any' 'Oh yes,' he continued, 'I have sold each *kurr* for fifty dinars.' 'But I did not accept that,' replied the other. The vizier said, 'I am not the man to break a contract that I have made.' 'I went away,' said the merchant, 'and I received from the sale of the wheat 2,500 dinars. I added a like sum to that and did some business with him, but he was killed and everything was lost.'

He had a high regard for alchemy and formed a close connection with an alchemist who made him promises month after month and year after year. One of his friends said to him, after the alchemist had transferred the cost of a *kurr* of wheat to him and asked for extra, 'If he were genuine in his work, he would not be asking for extra over such a small sum.' The vizier was killed, without seeing any result.

When al-A'azz Abū'l-Maḥāsin was killed, he was succeeded as vizier by al-Khaṭīr Abū Manṣūr al-Maybudhī, who had been vizier for Sultan Muḥammad. The reason why he gave up Muḥammad's vizierate was that he was with him in Isfahan, while Barkyāruq was besieging, [**337**] and Muḥammad had entrusted to him one of the gates to guard. Emir Yināl ibn Anūshtakīn said to him, 'You charged us, when we were in Rayy, to go to Hamadhān, and you said, "I will support the army with my own money and I will supply them with what will sustain them." This must be done.' Al-Khaṭīr said to him, 'I shall do it.' After nightfall he left the city, went out by the gate that was entrusted to him and set out for his town of Maybudh. He remained there, secure in its citadel. Sultan Barkyāruq sent troops to besiege him. He came down as a suppliant and was carried to the army on a mule with a pack-saddle. On the way he heard of the death of the Vizier al-A'azz and he received a letter from the sultan granting him safe-conduct. His mind was put at rest and on arrival at the army he was given a robe of honour and appointed to the vizierate.

A series of events to be taken as a lesson

In the year 493 [1099-1100] the goods and the houses of the Banū Jahīr at the Commoners' Gate were sold. The money raised came to Mu'ayyad al-Mulk but then he was killed in the year 494 [1100-1101] and his property and baggage were sold. All was seized and carried to the Vizier al-A'azz. Then this vizier was killed and his goods sold and his wealth divided up. The sultan and those who succeeded to office after him took most of it and it was scattered to the four winds. This is the result of service to princes.

Discord between Īlghāzī and the Baghdad populace

In Rajab of this year [21 April-20 March 1102] there was a serious disturbance between the troops of Emir Īlghāzī ibn Artuq, the prefect of Baghdad, and the local populace. [**338**] This came about because Īlghāzī, who was on the Khurasan Road, returned to Baghdad. On arrival a group of his men came to the Tigris and called to a boatman to take them across. He was slow, so one of them shot an arrow at him, which hit him in his groin[4] and killed him. The populace seized his killer and made for the Nubian Gate. They were met by a son of Īlghāzī with a detachment of men who rescued the man. In the Tuesday Market the mob stoned them, so he went to his father to seek help. The captain of the gate arrested the ring-leaders but that did not satisfy Īlghāzī, who crossed with his men to the quarter of the boatmen, known as the Cotton Merchants' District, followed by a large crowd who plundered what they could find and carry. The urban gangs (*'ayyārūn*) turned against them and killed most of them.

The survivors embarked on vessels to cross the Tigris. When they had reached the middle of the river the boatmen jumped into the water and left them to drown. More died by drowning than in the fighting. Īlghāzī gathered the Turkomans and wanted to sack the West Bank. However, the caliph sent the Chief Cadi and al-Kiyā al-Harrās, the professor at the Niẓāmiyya, to him to stop him doing that, so he desisted.

The lord of Basra attacks Wāsiṭ and then retires

On 20 Shawwāl [7 August 1102] Emir Ismā'īl, lord of Basra, attacked the town of Wāsiṭ to take possession of it.

Let us begin with mention of Ismā'īl and his changing fortunes until he came to rule Basra. He was Ismā'īl ibn Salānjuq[5] and during the reign of Malikshāh he held the prefecture of Rayy. When he took the post, the inhabitants of Rayy and al-Rustāqiyya had reduced their governors to impotence. They were totally unable to exercise control. He followed a course which improved them by executing a large number of the people, so that they came to heel. The sultan made leading reins and hobbles for horses from their scalps that were sent to him. Later Ismā'īl was dismissed from Rayy.

Sultan Barkyāruq assigned Basra as a fief to Emir Qumāj, who sent this Emir [**339**] Ismā'īl there as his deputy. When Qumāj broke with Barkyāruq and moved to Khurasan, Ismā'īl was tempted to seize Basra for himself. Muhadhdhab al-Dawla ibn Abī'l-Jabr went down from the Marsh to fight him, accompanied by Ma'qal ibn Ṣadaqa ibn Manṣūr ibn al-Ḥusayn al-Asadī, lord of Dubays' 'island'. They advanced with a large assemblage of boats and horses, and came to Maṭārā.

While Ma'qal was fighting close to the castle that Yināl had built at Maṭārā and

---

[4] The meaning of *fī mash'arihi* is doubtful. It may either be a 'noun of place' from *shi'ra* 'pubic hair', hence 'groin', or from the verb *sha'ara* 'to feel, sense', hence 'organ of sense, feeling' – but which? 'Eye', 'heart' ?

[5] See below p. [**402**], s.a. 499, where he is called Ismā'īl ibn Arslānjuq.

Ismā'īl had repaired and strengthened, a random arrow hit and killed him. Ibn Abī'l-Jabr returned to the Marsh while Ismā'īl seized his boats. That was in the year 491 [1097-8]. Ibn Abī'l-Jabr asked for reinforcements from Goharā'īn, who sent Abū'l-Ḥasan al-Harawī and 'Abbās ibn Abī'l-Jabr to support him. These two confronted Ismā'īl but he defeated them and took them both prisoner. He freed 'Abbās in return for money that his father sent and the two made peace. As for al-Harawī, he remained in prison for a while and was then freed for 5,000 dinars, but Ismā'īl did not actually receive anything.

Ismā'īl grew powerul and built a castle at Ubulla and another on the coast opposite Matārā. He became widely feared and the Basrans enjoyed security under him. He abolished some of the non-canonical taxes and his area of rule expanded because the sultans were preoccupied. He took control of Mashān and annexed it to what he held.

During this year some of the troops of Wāsiṭ wrote to him about surrendering to him. His desire for Wāsiṭ was very strong, so he took ship up to Nahrābān and contacted them about surrendering, but they refused. They said, 'We made contact with you but now we have changed our minds.' He therefore went further up the east bank and camped beneath the date palms, with his ships before him and the Wāsit army camped opposite. [**340**] He wrote to them, making promises, but they gave no response.

The populace united with the troops and reviled him in a most ugly manner. Giving up hope, he withdrew towards Basra. The enemy marched opposite him on the other bank until he came to al-'Amar. Above the town Ismā'īl sent a detachment of his men across, thinking that the town was empty and that the inhabitants had left, as he saw the large numbers facing him, and that he would set fire to the town. If the Turks returned he would withdraw from their rear. His thinking was flawed because the populace were on the Tigris bank, their vanguard in the town and their rear with the Turks opposite him.

When his men crossed, the Turks along with the locals fell on them, killing thirty of them and capturing very many. The rest threw themselves into the water. In this way an unexpected disaster came upon him. His leading men had been taken prisoner, so he returned to Basra. It was lucky for him that he returned, for Emir Abū Sa'd Muḥammad ibn Muḍar ibn Maḥmūd had set out for Basra at that time. He possessed extensive lands, including half of 'Umān, Jannāba, Sīrāf and the Island of Banū Nafīs.

The reason for Ismā'īl's attack was that he had been joined by a man called Ja'farak, another whose name was Zanjawayh and a third called Abū'l-Faḍl al-Ubullī, who urged him to build boats to send fighting men by water against Abū Sa'd and others. He built twenty or more vessels and when Abū Sa'd learnt what was happening he sent a large force of his men in about fifty boats, who came to the Basra arm of the Tigris. That was in the previous year. They continued [**341**] hostilities, overwhelmed a detachment of Ismā'īl's men and killed the commander of the Ubulla fortress. They wrote to the sons of Bursuq in Khūzistān to ask them to send an army to help them take Basra. The reply was delayed, so both sides were content to make peace on condition that Ismā'īl would hand over Ja'farak and his companion to his rivals and that he would assign them places in the districts of Basra that they specified.

After their withdrawal he did none of this. Indeed, he seized two boats belonging to some followers of Abū Sa'd. This encouraged the latter to set out in person in many vessels, more than a hundred in number, both large and small, as far as the mouth of the Ubulla river. Ismā'īl's troops came out in a number of boats and a battle took place. The Gulf men[6] were about 10,000 strong and Ismā'īl led 700. The former sailed up the Tigris and burnt several places. Ismā'īl's army dispersed, part in Ubulla, part in Nahr al-Dayr and the rest in other places.

When Ismā'īl was too weak to resist Abū Sa'd, he requested the caliph's agent acting in all the lands dependent on the Dīwān to strive to make a peace. The agent wrote to Abū Sa'd and received a reply recounting how Ismā'īl had treated him badly time after time. Letters went back and forth between them and eventually peace was agreed and made. After a meeting Abū Sa'd returned to his lands and each one carried away a handsome present from the other.

Account of the death of Karbughā and how Mūsā al-Turkomānī took Mosul, then Jokermish after him, and how Suqmān gained Ḥiṣn [Kayfā]

In Dhū'l-Qa'da [17 August–15 September 1102] Qiwām al-Dawla Karbughā died near the city of Khoy. Sultan Barkyāruq had sent him in the previous year to Azerbayjan, as [**342**] we have related, and he took it over. He came to Khoy and fell ill there for thirteen days. With him was the General Ṣabāwa ibn Khumārtakīn and Sunqurjah. He left affairs in the latter's hands and ordered the Turks to obey him, taking an oath for him from the army. He died four leagues from Khoy. He was wrapped in a rug because there was no proper shroud and buried at Khoy.

Sunqurjah with most of the army went to Mosul and took control there. He remained for three days. The notables of Mosul had written to Mūsā al-Turkomānī who was at Ḥiṣn Kayfā acting as Karbughā's deputy. They asked him to hurry so that they could hand the city to him, so he made forced marches. Sunqurjah heard of his coming and thought that he had come to be at his service. He went out to meet him with the citizens. As they drew close, each one dismounted to honour the other. They embraced, wept for Qiwām al-Dawla and then went on together.

Amongst other matters Sunqurjah said to Mūsā, 'Of all that our lord possessed I would like his cushion, his position and the money. The local governorates are yours and at your disposal.' Mūsā replied, 'Who are we to have positions and seats of honour? It is for the sultan to decide. He will appoint the person he wants and

---

6 In Arabic *al-baḥrīyūn*. My conjectural translation in this context is based on the list of Abū Sa'd's possessions just above.

give the position to whomsoever he chooses.' Arguments followed between them and Sunqurjah drew his sword and struck Mūsā's head with the flat of the sword, wounding him. Mūsā threw himself to the ground and dragged Sunqurjah down, bringing him to the ground. With Mūsā there was the son of Manṣūr ibn Marwān whose father had been lord of Diyār Bakr. He pulled a dagger and struck Sunqurjah's head with it, separating it from his body. Mūsā entered the town and gave robes of honour to Sunqurjah's men and eased their minds. Thus authority in the province passed to him.

When the lord of Jazīrat Ibn 'Umar, Shams al-Dawla Jokermish, heard the news, [**343**] he went to Nisibis and took control. Mūsā marched towards Jazīrat [Ibn 'Umar] but when he drew near to Jokermish his army betrayed him and joined Jokermish, so Mūsā returned to Mosul where Jokermish came and besieged him for a long time. Mūsā sought assistance from Emir Suqmān ibn Artuq, who was at that time in Diyār Bakr, and gave him Ḥiṣn Kayfā and 10,000 dinars. Suqmān came to join him and Jokermish withdrew.

Mūsā went out to meet Suqmān and when Mūsā was near a village called Karāthā a number of the mamlukes of Karbughā surprised him and killed him. One of them shot him with an arrow. His followers retired in disorder. He was buried on a hill there which is now known as Mūsā's Hill. Emir Suqmān returned to Ḥiṣn Kayfā and ruled there. It is in the hands of his descendants until today, the year 620 [1223], when its ruler is Ghāzī ibn Qarā Arslān ibn Dā'ūd ibn Suqmān ibn Artuq.

Jokermish marched to Mosul and put it under siege for some days, then received its peaceful surrender. He ruled well there. He arrested the followers of Karbughā who had killed Mūsā and put them to death. Later he gained control of Khābūr and subdued the Arabs and the Kurds who then gave him their allegiance.

Account of [Raymond of] St. Gilles the Frank and what he did at the siege of Tripoli

[Raymond of] St. Gilles the Frank (God curse him!) had met Qilij Arslān ibn Sulaymān ibn Qutlumish, the lord of Konya, when the former led 100,000 warriors and the latter was [**344**] at the head of a small band. They fought and the Franks were defeated. Many were killed and many were taken captive. Qilij Arslān returned with booty and a victory which he had not reckoned on. Defeated, and with 300 men, [Raymond] continued to Syria.[7]

Fakhr al-Mulk Ibn 'Ammār, the lord of Tripoli, sent to Emir Yākhuz, Janāḥ al-Dawla's deputy in charge of Homs, and to Prince Duqāq ibn Tutush, to say, 'Our

---

7 Raymond had, after a visit to Constantinople, joined a Franco-Lombard crusade in spring 1101 which was destroyed by a Saljuq-Danishmand coalition. He escaped back to Constantinople, and later returned by sea to Syria, where he was imprisoned by Tancred (Runciman, ii, 20-31).

best course is to deal quickly with [Raymond] while he has these manageable numbers.' Emir Yākhuz took the field in person and Duqāq sent 2,000 soldiers. Reinforcements from Tripoli joined them and they mustered at the gates of Tripoli and drew up battle lines to confront [Raymond]. He sent one hundred of his men against the men of Tripoli, one hundred against the troops of Damascus and fifty against the troops of Homs, himself remaining with fifty. The troops of Homs broke at first view [of the enemy] and turned their backs in flight. The Damascus force followed them. The men of Tripoli fought the hundred who opposed them. When [Raymond] observed this he charged with the remaining two hundred and shattered the men of Tripoli, killing 7,000 of them. Thereupon [Raymond] settled down to besiege Tripoli.

The inhabitants of the Mountain and likewise those of al-Sawād,[8] of whom most were Christians, came and aided him in the siege. The defenders fought most stoutly and three hundred Franks were killed. [Raymond] made a truce in return for money and horses and withdrew to the town of Anṭarsūs in the district of Tripoli and besieged it. The town fell and the Muslims there were killed. He then proceeded to the fortress of al-Ṭūbān,[9] which is in the vicinity of Rafaniyya and whose commander was called Ibn al-'Arīḍ. He resisted and the garrison of the fort won a victory and took prisoner one of the greatest of the Frankish knights. [Raymond] offered to ransom him for 10,000 dinars and 1,000 captives, but Ibn al-'Arīḍ did not accept this.

[**345**] Account of Frankish deeds

This year the Dānishmand released Bohemond the Frank, the lord of Antioch, whom he had captured, as has already been related.[10] He received from him 100,000 dinars and the promise that he would free the daughter of Yaghī Siyān who had been lord of Antioch. She was a prisoner of Bohemond.

Released from prison, Bohemond returned to Antioch, which greatly strengthened the morale of its people. Hardly had he settled before he sent to the inhabitants of the Marches,[11] Qinnisrīn and neighbouring places demanding tribute. On account of this the Muslims suffered so much that the landmark buildings which the Dānishmand had constructed fell into decay.

[Raymond of] St. Gilles marched to put Ḥiṣn al-Akrād under siege. Janāḥ al-

---

8 The fertile area east of the Jordan and north of 'Ajlūn, known to the Franks as Suhite or Suete.

9 Ṭūbān is N.W. of Homs and south of Rafaniyya.

10 See p. [**300**] above. According to *EI(2)*, ii, 110, Bohemond was released in Sha'bān 496/May 1103. He and the Dānishmand allied against the Byzantines and the Saljuqs of Rūm.

11 In Arabic *al-'Awāṣim*, the inner parts of the northern frontier zone between Syria and Anatolia (*EI(2)*, i, 761–2).

Dawla gathered his forces to make a march to surprise him but a Bāṭinī assassinated him in the Friday mosque. It is said that Riḍwān, his stepson, set his killer on him. After his death [Raymond] arrived before Homs the morning of the following day, invested the town, blockaded the inhabitants and seized the surrounding areas.[12]

The Count descended upon Acre in Jumādā II [23 March-20 April 1102] and began a close siege. He almost took the place, having set up trebuchets and siege towers. He had sixteen ships at sea. The Muslims from all the other coastal regions gathered together, attacked their machines and towers and burnt them. They also burnt the ships. This was a wonderful victory through which God humbled the infidels.

This year the Frankish count, lord of Edessa, came to Beirut on the Syrian coast and besieged it closely. He remained there a long time but did not meet with any success and so withdrew.

In Rajab of this year [21 April-20 March 1102] the forces of Egypt marched to Ascalon to defend the Syrian lands that remained in their hands against the Franks. Baldwin, lord of Jerusalem, heard about them [**346**] and went to meet them with 700 knights. God gave victory to the Muslims in the battle and the Franks fled after many were killed. Baldwin fled and hid in a thicket of reeds which was set on fire. He suffered burns to part of his body but he escaped the fire in the direction of Ramla. The Muslims pursued him and surrounded him. He disguised himself and got away to Jaffa. Many of his men were killed or captured.

The return of the castle of Khuftīdhakān to Surkhāb ibn Badr

This year the castle of Khuftīdhakān was restored to Emir Surkhāb[13] ibn Badr ibn Muhalhil. How it came to be taken from him was as follows. Al-Qarābulī, a member of the tribe of Turkomans called Salghur, had come to the lands of Surkhāb who denied him pasture land and killed several of his followers. Al-Qarābulī went to the Turkomans and enlisted them to raise a large army. Surkhāb met him in battle in which al-Qarābulī killed close on two thousand of his Kurdish followers. Surkhāb fled to one of his mountains with twenty men.

The two officers in the castle of Khuftīdhakān heard this news and were tempted to seize the place. It contained stores and money valued at more than 2,000,000 dinars. They therefore made themselves masters of it. The Sultan

[12] For a general account of Count Raymond's relations with Muslim states, see Richard, *Comté de Tripoli*, 12-25.

[13] Surkhāb, who died in 500/1106, was of the Kurdish dynasty called the 'Annāzids (see *EI(2)*, i, 512–13). In the district of Irbil there were two large castles covered by the name Khuftīdhakān. The one associated especially with Surkhāb was on the Shahrazūr road (Yāqūt, ii, 456).

Barkyāruq passed nearby and they sent him 200,000 dinars. The Turkomans took control of all the lands of Surkhāb ibn Badr, apart from Daqūqā and Shahrazūr.

Now when this present time came, one of the two officers killed the other and sent [**347**] to Surkhāb asking him for guarantees so that he could hand the castle to him. He gave him a guarantee of his life and the property that he had acquired, so the transfer was made and the bargain kept.

The killing of Qadir Khān, the ruler of Samarqand

We have previously mentioned Prince Sanjar's coming to Baghdad with his brother Sultan Muḥammad and his return to Khurasan. On his arrival at Nishapur he made the khutbah for his brother Muḥammad in all of Khurasan. When he was at Baghdad, the ruler of Samarqand, Qadir Khān Jibrīl ibn 'Umar, had designs on Khurasan because of Sanjar's absence. He assembled troops that filled the plains (it was said that they were 100,000 soldiers, both Muslims and unbelievers) and he marched into Sanjar's territory.

One of Sanjar's emirs, called Kundughdī, had written to Qadir Khān with intelligence and now, after Sanjar's return, informed him of Sanjar's illness and that he was at death's door. He encouraged his designs by referring to the current difference between the Sultans Barkyāruq and Muḥammad and the virulent hatred of Barkyāruq for Sanjar. He advised haste while the difference was still a fact, urging that, if he acted quickly, he would win Khurasan and Iraq. So Qadir Khān invaded with speed and boldness. Sanjar heard the news when he had recovered, and hurried towards him to bring him to battle and defend his lands against him. One of those with him was the afore-mentioned Kundughdī, unsuspected of anything that he had done. Sanjar came to Balkh with 6,000 horse, where he was separated from Qadir Khān [**348**] by about five days' journey. Kundughdī fled to Qadir Khān and both swore to each other to act loyally in concert. Kundughdī then went to Tirmidh and seized control there. The motive for his conduct was envy of Emir Buzghush's standing.

Qadir Khān advanced and when the two armies had drawn close, Sanjar sent to remind Qadir Khān of their old treaties and undertakings but his words were disregarded. He sent spies and agents to Qadir Khān, so that nothing he did was hidden from him. Someone brought news that Qadir Khān had camped near Balkh and that he had gone hunting with 300 horsemen. At that, Sanjar ordered Emir Buzghush to seek him out. He came upon him when he was engaged in that pursuit. There was a fight and the men with Qadir Khān did not hold firm but fled. Kundughdī and Qadir Khān were taken and brought to Sanjar. Qadir Khān kissed the ground and apologised. Sanjar said to him, 'Whether you have bowed before us or not, your only recompense is the sword.' He then ordered him to be slain.

When Kundughdī heard this, he escaped and went down into an irrigation tunnel where he walked underground for two leagues, despite the gout he suffered from and the two large snakes he killed there. He got to the exit before his followers and then went with 300 horse to Ghazna.

It is said in a different version that Sanjar gathered large forces and met Qadir Khān in a great battle, in which many were killed. Qadir Khān and his army were defeated, He was taken to Sanjar as a prisoner and executed. Sanjar besieged Tirmidh, where Kundughdī was. The latter asked for terms which Sanjar granted, so he surrendered and handed over Tirmidh. Sanjar ordered him to leave his territory, and he went to Ghazna. When he arrived there, the ruler 'Alā' al-Dawla[14] received him with honour and gave him an important position.

[**349**] It happened that the ruler of Ghazna determined to attack Ūtān, a difficult mountainous area forty leagues from Ghazna. The inhabitants had rebelled against him and fortified themselves behind their castles and their rugged roads. 'Alā' al-Dawla's troops fought them without gaining any advantage. Kundughdī advanced independently and, after a gallant action, won a victory and took booty from them which he carried to 'Alā' al-Dawla, who accepted none of it but bestowed it all on Kundughdī. The army was enraged, envying him for that and also for his being close to their ruler and in such demand. They suggested his arrest and said, 'We cannot be sure that he will not attack some place and do to the state what cannot be remedied.' 'Alā' al-Dawla replied, 'I realise what you intend. But who shall I get to arrest him? I fear to order you to arrest him, for you will incur some dishonour.' They said, 'The right course is for you to appoint him to some region and to have him arrested when he goes there.' So he appointed him to two castles where it was customary for him to imprison people he feared.

Kundughdī set off and when he drew near, he realised what was planned for him. He burnt all his property, slaughtered his camels and travelled on unencumbered with baggage. During his residence at Ghazna he used to enquire about routes and all their branches, for he was sorry that he had come to this region. On his way now, he questioned a shepherd about the route he wanted. He showed him the way but Kundughdī took him with him, fearing that he might have deceived him. He kept going until he arrived near Herat and there he died. He was a mamluke of Tutush ibn Alp Arslān whom Tutush's brother Malikshāh blinded and imprisoned at Takrīt. We have already related his story.[15]

[350] Muḥammad Khān becomes ruler of Samarqand

During this year Sultan Sanjar summoned Muḥammad Arslān Khān ibn Sulaymān ibn Dā'ūd Bughrā Khān from Marv and made him ruler over Samarqand after

---

[14] A member of the Ghaznavid dynasty, Mas'ūd III ibn Ibrāhīm.

[15] This is nowhere in the text. Did Ibn al-Athīr have a confused memory of Malikshāh's blinding and imprisoning (in Takrit) the son of Tekesh ibn Alp Arslān (see Richards, *Annals*, 276).

Qadir Khān. This Muḥammad Khān was a member of the Qarākhānid dynasty in Transoxania.[16] His mother was the daughter of Sultan Malikshāh. He had been driven from the ruling position of his ancestors and went to Marv, where he remained until this present time.

After the death of Qadir Khān, Sanjar put Muḥammad in charge of his lands and sent large forces with him. They crossed the river [Oxus] and the armies in all those regions offered him their allegiance. His position grew great and his armies numerous, except that an emir called Sāghir Beg[17] set himself up as a rival for kingship and was very ambitious. Muḥammad fought battles with him, in some of which he required assistance from Sanjar's troops, as we shall relate later, God willing.

After Muḥammad Khān had become ruler he ruled his subjects well with counsel from Sanjar. He avoided the shedding of blood and his palace became a magnet and his presence a place of sanctuary.

Miscellaneous events

In Rabī' I [24 December 1101–22 January 1102] Tāj al-Ru'asā', the nephew of Amīn al-Dawla Abū Sa'd ibn al-Mūṣilāyā, went out to al-Ḥilla al-Sayfiyya, to seek the protection of Sayf al-Dīn Ṣadaqa. The reason for this was that al-A'azz, the vizier of Sultan Barkyāruq, claimed that he was the person who was influencing the caliph in favour of Sultan Muḥammad. His uncle Amīn al-Dawla kept away from [**351**] the Dīwān and sat at home. After the death of the Vizier al-A'azz, as we have related, Tāj al-Ru'asā' came back from al-Ḥilla to Baghdad and his uncle returned to his office.

Also during this month the civil administrator al-Muhadhdhab Abū'l-Majd, the brother of the Vizier al-A'azz, came to Baghdad, as deputy for his brother, imagining that Īlghāzī would not oppose them, since Barkyāruq and Muḥammad had reached an agreement, as we have mentioned. However, Īlghāzī arrested him, as he had not changed from his allegiance to Muḥammad.

There came to Baghdad in Jumādā I [21 February–22 March 1102] the son of Tekesh ibn Alp Arslān, who had taken control of Mosul but was deceived by the people there, so that he left for Baghdad. After his arrival Īlghāzī ibn Artuq gave him his daughter in marriage.

In the month of Ramaḍān [19 June-18 July 1102] the caliph appointed as vizier

[16] The Turkish Qarakhanids (the Black Khans) ruled in Central Asia from the late tenth to the early thirteenth century. For a list of rulers and an historical summary, see Bosworth, *New Islamic Dynasties*, 181–4.

[17] The text here has Hāghū Beg. In addition to this spelling, this Qarākhānid claimant appears as Sāghir or Sāghū or Sāghun Beg (see Barthold, *Turkestan*, 319; Bosworth, 'The Iranian world', 139).

Sadīd al-Mulk Abū'l-Ma'ālī ibn 'Abd al-Razzāq, who was given the title 'Aḍud al-Dīn.[18]

At Hīt in Ṣafar [25 November-23 December 1101] the Raba'ī clan killed the town cadi, Abū 'Alī ibn al-Muthannā. He was a pious man, a Ḥanafī lawyer and a follower of the Cadi Abū 'Abd Allāh al-Dāmghānī. This cadi followed the local judicial practice of mediating between the tribes. The clan accused him of partiality against them and one of them killed him. The rest regretted his killing when it was too late to do so.

This year Sayf al-Dīn Ṣadaqa ibn Mazyad built two Friday mosques at al-Ḥilla and took it as his place of residence. Previously he and his ancestors had lived only in bedouin tents.

[**352**] On Jumādā I [21 February-22 March 1102] al-Mu'ayyad ibn Sharaf al-Dawla Muslim ibn Quraysh, emir of the Banū 'Uqayl, was killed by the Banū Numayr near Hīt in an act of retaliation.

This year the following died:

Cadi al-Bandanījī, the blind Shāfi'ī lawyer.[19] He had moved to Mecca and lived as a pious scholar there for forty years, studying law, hearing Ḥadīth and engaging in worship.

Abū 'Abd Allāh al-Ḥusayn ibn Muḥammad al-Ṭabarī in Isfahan. He studied Shāfi'ī law in the Niẓāmiyya Madrasah. He was more than ninety years old and one of the followers of Abū Isḥaq [al-Shīrāzī].

Emir Manẓūr ibn 'Umāra al-Ḥusaynī, the emir of Medina (blessings be on the dweller there!), whose son took his place. He was a descendant of al-Muhannā and he killed the architect whom Majd al-Mulk al-Balāsānī had sent to repair the dome over the tomb of al-Ḥasan ibn 'Alī and al-'Abbās[20] (may God be pleased with them both). After al-Balāsānī had been killed, the architect, who was from Qum, was put to death by Manẓūr although he had given him a guarantee of security. He had fled from him to Mecca and Manẓūr had sent him his guarantee.

---

18 That is, Help of the Religion.

19 He was Abū Naṣr Muḥammad ibn Hibat Allāh (*Muntaẓam*, ix, 133).

20 An uncle of the Prophet and the eponym of the Abbasid dynasty of caliphs.

[353] The Year 496 [1102-1103]

How Yināl took control of Rayy and how, when it was taken from him, he came to Baghdad

The khutbah at Rayy was in the name of Sultan Barkyāruq. When Sultan Muḥammad left Isfahan, as we have related, accompanied by Yināl ibn Anūshtakīn al-Ḥusāmī, the latter asked him for permission to go to Rayy and establish the khutbah there in his name. This was granted, so he set out, he and his brother 'Alī ibn Anūshtakīn. They arrived in Ṣafar [14 November-12 December 1102] and Barkyāruq's deputies there submitted to him. The khutbah was made for Muḥammad and Yināl took control of the city. He treated the inhabitants badly and extorted 200,000 dinars from them. He remained there until the middle of Rabī' I [27 December 1102] and then Emir Bursuq ibn Bursuq arrived from Sultan Barkyāruq. Fighting took place between them at the gate of Rayy in which Yināl and the brother 'Alī were put to flight.

'Alī returned to Qazwīn where he was governor but Yināl entered the Uplands where his followers were dispersed and many were killed. He came to Baghdad with 700 men. The caliph received him with honour and he and Īlghāzī and Suqmān, the sons of Artuq, meeting at the shrine of Abū Ḥanīfa, swore to be loyal to Sultan Muḥammad. They went to Sayf al-Dawla Ṣadaqa, who took the same oath before them, and then they returned.

[354] What Yināl did in Iraq

We have mentioned Yināl ibn Anūshtakīn's coming to Baghdad. Once established in Baghdad he tyrannised the inhabitants of the whole city and extorted money from them. His men high-handedly subjected the populace to beatings, murder and illegal taxation. They also extorted money from the financial officials.

The caliph sent the Chief Cadi Abū'l-Ḥasan al-Dāmghānī to him to order him to stop and to get him to see how terrible were the wickedness and violence that he was perpetrating. He also called on Īlghāẓī several times, for Yināl had married his sister at this time, the one who had been the wife of Tāj al-Dawla Tutush. Eventually Īlghāzī acted as intermediary. They went to Yināl and made him swear an oath to be obedient and give up oppressing the populace and to restrain and check his followers. He swore but did not stand by his oath. He broke it and continued his oppression and wicked deeds.

The caliph sent to Sayf al-Dawla Ṣadaqa and informed him how Yināl was plundering property and shedding blood. He asked him to come in person to restrain Yināl. Ṣadaqa left al-Ḥilla in Ramaḍān [June 1103] and arrived in Baghdad on 4 Shawwāl [11 July 1103]. He pitched his tents in al-Najmī and then he, Yināl, Īlghāzī and the officials of the Caliphal Dīwān, all met. It was settled that he should take some money and leave Iraq. Yināl asked for a delay, while Ṣadaqa returned to al-Ḥilla on 19 Shawwāl [26 July] but left his son Dubays in Baghdad to prevent his wrong-doing or his going beyond the limit imposed on him. Yināl remained until the beginning of Dhū'l-Qa'da [6 August] and then went to Awānā, where he plundered and interfered with traffic on the highway. The people suffered greatly, for he outdid himself in wickedness and assigned villages to his followers. The caliph contacted Ṣadaqa on the matter, who sent 1,000 horsemen. Along with some of the caliph's and the prefect of Baghdad Īlghāzī's men they set out towards him. When Yināl heard [**355**] of their approach, he crossed the Tigris and went to Bājisrā, which he left in chaos, and then on to Shahrabān, whose inhabitants resisted him with a show of force. There were some fatalities. He departed and came to Azerbayjan, seeking to join Sultan Muḥammad. Both Dubays ibn Ṣadaqa and Īlghāzī, the prefect of Baghdad, returned to their respective places.

The coming of Kumushtakīn al-Qayṣarī as prefect to Baghdad and the discord between him and Īlghāzī, Suqmān and Ṣadaqa

In the middle of Rabī' I this year [27 December 1102] Kumushtakīn al-Qayṣarī came to Baghdad as prefect, sent by Sultan Barkyāruq. We have mentioned in the previous year Barkyāruq's leaving Isfahan for Hamadhān. When he arrived, he sent Kumushtakīn to Baghdad to act as prefect. Hearing this, Īlghāzī, who was prefect of Baghdad for Sultan Muḥammad, sent to his brother Suqmān ibn Artuq, lord of Ḥiṣn Kayfā, summoning him to help him resist Kumushtakīn. He also went to Sayf al-Dawla Ṣadaqa at al-Ḥilla. He met with him and requested him to make a new treaty to resist anyone who attacks from Barkyāruq's side. Ṣadaqa agreed and gave him his sworn word. Īlghāzī returned [to Baghdad].

Suqmān came with his army and on the way he plundered Takrīt. His seizure of the place came about because he had sent a group of Turkomans to Takrīt who had with them some loads of cheese, clarified butter and honey. They sold what they had and spread the news that Suqmān had given up any idea of going down into Iraq. The populace therefore felt secure but the Turkomans attacked the watch that night, killed them and opened the gates. Suqmān arrived and having entered, he sacked the town. When he then came to Baghdad he camped at Ramla.[1]

[**356**] Kumushtakīn arrived on 1 Rabī' I [13 December 1102] at Qinnisrīn and made contact with all who favoured Barkyāruq, informing them that he was nearby. Several came out to join him and they met at Bandabījīn. They told him how things stood and advised haste. He acted accordingly and reached Baghdad in

---

1 See above p. [**309**].

mid-Rabīʿ I [27 December]. Īlghāzī abandoned his residence, joined his brother Suqmān, and together they went up to Ramla and plundered some of the villages of Dujayl. A detachment of Kumushtakīn's army went after them but turned back.

At Baghdad the khutbah was made in Barkyāruq's name and Kumushtakīn al-Qayṣarī sent [an envoy] to Sayf al-Dawla Ṣadaqa, accompanied by a chamberlain from the caliph's Dīwān, about his giving allegiance to Barkyāruq but he did not respond. Indeed, he unveiled his opposition and moved from al-Ḥilla to Jisr Ṣarṣar. The khutbah for Barkyāruq in Baghdad was interrupted and neither of the sultans was mentioned on the pulpits there. The preachers restricted themselves to praying for the caliph and no one else.

When Sayf al-Dawla arrived at Ṣarṣar he contacted Īlghāzī and Suqmān, who were at Bajrā, to inform them that he had come to help them, so they turned back and plundered Dujayl, not sparing any village, large or small. Property was seized and virgins raped. The Bedouin and Kurds with Sayf al-Dawla Ṣadaqa committed outrages at King's Canal,[2] except that they were not reported to have seized and violated women as the Turkomans did. Nevertheless they stopped at nothing, beating and burning, to take property. People's livelihoods were ruined and prices rose high. Bread which had been at ten rotls for a *qīrāṭ*[3] became three rotls for the same and all other items rose similarly.

The caliph sent to Sayf al-Dawla to try to improve matters but no basis for this was agreed. Īlghāzī and Suqmān, together with Dubays ibn Sayf al-Dawla, returned from Dujayl and camped at Ramla. A large crowd of the common people opposed them and in a battle [**357**] four of their number were killed and several seized but they were released after their weapons were taken away. The situation of the people became yet more dire, so the caliph sent the Chief Cadi Abū'l-Ḥasan ibn al-Dāmghānī and Tāj al-Ru'asā' ibn al-Mūṣilāyā to Sayf al-Dawla, ordering him to refrain from the actions he was associated with, telling him the state of the populace and how serious the situation was. He announced, with much bluster and fulmination, that he would obey the caliph if he expelled Kumushtakīn from Baghdad but otherwise there was nothing for it but the sword.

After the return of the envoy it was settled that Kumushtakīn should be sent out of Baghdad. He departed on 12 Rabīʿ II [23 January 1103] and went to Nahrawān. Sayf al-Dawla returned to his own lands and the khutbah for Sultan Muḥammad was restored at Baghdad. Kumushtakīn went to Wāsiṭ where the populace was frightened of him and wished to leave to seek safety further down river. Kumushtakīn stopped that, made the khutbah for Barkyāruq at Wāsiṭ and ravaged much of its agricultural land.

Hearing of this, Ṣadaqa travelled to Wāsiṭ and after entering the town treated the populace with justice and prevented his troops from harming them. Īlghāzī

---

2 In Arabic Nahr al-Malik (at times it appears as Nahr Malik). The canal begins at al-Fallūja and is one of the four main canals that connect the Euphrates with the Tigris. A town of the same name is on its banks.

3 In Iraq and Persia a *mithqāl* of gold equalled 20 *qīrāṭ*s (Hinz, 2).

joined him there and Kumushtakīn left, fortifying himself in Dijla. Sayf al-Dawla was told that there was a ford there, so he set out with his troops, armed for battle. When Kumushtakīn's troops saw them they abandoned him and he was left with his personal following only, so he requested terms from Sayf al-Dawla. When they were agreed, he came to him and was honourably received. Sayf al-Dawla said to him, 'You have become fat.' He replied, 'Allowed to get fat! By you! You have chased us from Baghdad and then from Wāsiṭ, and we are at our wit's end.'

Ṣadaqa offered guarantees to all the troops of Wāsiṭ and those with Kumushtakīn, apart from two men, who later came back to him and received a safe conduct from him. Kumushtakīn returned to Barkyāruq and the khutbah in Wāsiṭ was restored in Sultan Muḥammad's name with Sayf al-Dawla and Īlghāzī being mentioned after him. Each appointed as his deputy [**358**] there his son and both left on 20 Jumādā I [1 March 1103]. The populace were then safe from what they had feared.

Īlghāzī went up to Baghdad, while Sayf al-Dawla Ṣadaqa returned to al-Ḥilla. He sent his youngest son Manṣūr with Īlghāzī to al-Mustaẓhir bi-Allāh, asking for his good will, for the caliph was displeased because of these events. Manṣūr came to Baghdad and made his representations. His request was granted.

Account of Ṣadaqa's taking control of Hīt

The town of Hīt had belonged to Sharaf al-Dawla Muslim ibn Quraysh to whom it had been assigned by Sultan Alp Arslān, and he continued to hold it until he was killed.[4] The civilian administrators of Baghdad had oversight of it until the death of Malikshāh and then Tutush ibn Alp Arslān took it. When Sultan Barkyāruq came to power, he assigned it to Bahā' al-Dawla Tharwān ibn Wahb ibn Wuhayba. He and his Banū 'Uqayl followers remained allied with Sayf al-Dawla Ṣadaqa. The two of them were close friends and Ṣadaqa used to visit him often but then they fell out.

The reason was that Ṣadaqa married a daughter of his to his cousin. Tharwān had previously sought her hand but had been refused. The 'Uqayl tribesmen who were in the settlement of Sayf al-Dawla took an oath to act as one against him. Sayf al-Dawla disapproved of that. A little later Tharwān went on pilgrimage, returned ill and was put under close guard by Sayf al-Dawla, who said, 'I must have Hīt.' Tharwān sent his chamberlain, having put his hand to a document handing over the town to him.

[**359**] At that time Muḥammad ibn Rāfi' ibn Rifā' ibn Ḍubay'a ibn Mālik ibn al-Muqallad ibn Ja'far was in Hīt. Ṣadaqa sent his son Dubays with the chamberlain to take over the town but Muḥammad refused to surrender it to him. Dubays

---

4 Muslim, a member of the Arab 'Uqaylid dynasty, was assigned Hīt and other places in 458/1065-6 and died in 478/1085 (see Richards, *Annals*, 158, 218–19).

returned to his father. After Ṣadaqa had taken Wāsiṭ on this occasion he marched up to Hīt with his army. Manṣūr ibn Kathīr, Tharwān's nephew, moved against him with a group of his followers. They met Sayf al-Dawla and fought him for a period of the day. Then some of the Raba'ī clan opened the town to Sayf al-Dawla and his men entered. When Manṣūr and his men saw that, they surrendered the town to him, which he therefore gained the same day he arrived. He gave a robe of honour to Manṣūr and some of his leading followers and returned to al-Ḥilla, having left his cousin, Thābit ibn Kāmil, in charge.

The battle between Barkyāruq and Muḥammad

This year on 8 Jumādā II [19 March 1103] the fifth battle between Sultan Barkyāruq and Sultan Muḥammad took place.

Ganja and the lands of Arrān were all held by Sultan Muḥammad, and his army was there, whose commander was Emir Ghuzoghlu. After Muḥammad had remained for a long time besieged in Isfahan, Ghuzoghlu, Emir Manṣūr ibn Niẓām al-Mulk and the latter's nephew Muḥammad ibn Mu'ayyad al-Mulk ibn Niẓām al-Mulk set out intending to go to his aid so that he could see their loyalty. The last place where the khutbah was observed in Muḥammad's name was Zanjān, adjacent to Azerbayjān.

They arrived at Rayy on 20 Dhū'l-Ḥijja in the year 495 [5 October 1102] after it had been abandoned [**360**] by Barkyāruq's troops. They entered and remained there for three days. News reached them that Sultan Muḥammad had left Isfahan and arrived at Sāveh. They set out to join him which they did at Hamadhān, finding Yināl and 'Alī, the two sons of Anūshtakīn al-Ḥusāmī, with him. In all their numbers reached 6,000 and they stayed there until the last days of Muḥarram [mid-November 1102]. Intelligence came that Sultan Barkyāruq had arrived. They had various views about what to do. Yināl and 'Alī went to Rayy, as we have related, while Sultan Muḥammad decided to proceed to Shirwān. He came to Ardabīl, where he received an envoy from Prince Mawdūd ibn Ismā'īl ibn Yāqūtī, the ruler of part of Azerbayjan, which had belonged previously to his father, Ismā'īl. Mawdūd was the maternal uncle of Sultan Barkyāruq and his sister was the wife of Sultan Muḥammad and he was seeking from Barkyāruq blood revenge for his father, who had been killed earlier at the beginning of Barkyāruq's reign. His message was 'It is fitting for you to come to us that we may unite in allegiance to you and fight our enemy.' Muḥammad set out with all haste. On the way he went hunting between Ardabīl and Baylaqān.[5] He became separated from his troops and a leopard leapt on him unawares and wounded him in the arm. He took a dagger and split the leopard's belly, threw it off his horse and escaped.

---

[5] Near modern Shusha in the Nagorno-Karabakh district, Azerbayjan.

In the middle of Rabīʿ I [27 December 1102] Mawdūd ibn Ismāʿīl died, aged twenty-two. Barkyāruq had heard of the union of Sultan Muḥammad and Prince Mawdūd and after a march with no halts, arrived after Mawdūd's death. The latter's army had already agreed to give their allegiance to Muḥammad and had given him their oath, amongst them being Sukmān al-Quṭbī,[6] Muḥammad ibn Yaghī Siyān, whose father had been ruler of Antioch, and Qizil Arslān the Red Lion.[7] [**361**] After Barkyāruq's arrival, there was a battle between them before the gate of Khoy in Azerbayjan at sunset and it lasted until the final nightfall prayer. It happened that Emir Ayāz took with him 500 fresh horsemen and, when the troops of both sides were exhausted, he led them in an attack on Muḥammad's army. He shattered them and they turned their backs in flight, every man looking out for himself.

Sultan Barkyāruq made for a mountain between Marāgha and Tabriz with abundant pasture and water, where he remained for some days, and then went to Zanjān. As for Sultan Muḥammad, he, with a group of his followers, went to Arjīsh in Armenia, forty leagues from the battle and part of the district of Khilāṭ in the fief of Emir Sukmān al-Quṭbī. From there he went to Khilāṭ, where Emir ʿAlī, the lord of Erzerum, joined him, and then on to Ānī, whose lord was Manūchihr, the brother of Faḍlūn al-Rawādī. From there he travelled to Tabriz in Azerbayjan. We shall recount, God willing, the rest of their story under the year 497 [1103-4] when they made peace.

Emir Muḥammad ibn Mu'ayyad al-Mulk ibn Niẓām al-Mulk was with Sultan Muḥammad at this battle. He fled and went into Diyār Bakr and from there went down river to Jazīrat ibn ʿUmar and then on to Baghdad. During the lifetime of his father he used to live at Baghdad in the Madrasah Market. Complaints about him came to his father, who wrote to Goharā'īn ordering his arrest. He sought refuge in the Caliphal Palace. In the year 492 [1098-9] he went to Majd al-Mulk al-Balāsānī, at the time when his father was at Ganja with Sultan Muḥammad before the latter had had his name proclaimed in the khutbah. After the murder of Majd al-Mulk he went to his father, who had become Sultan Muḥammad's vizier and made the khutbah [**362**] for Muḥammad as sultan. He stayed on after his father had been killed and became close to Muḥammad. He was present with him at this battle from which he fled.

---

6 Sukmān (sometimes Suqmān) was the founder of the dynasty of the Shahs of Armenia which ruled from a base in Khilāṭ (493-604/1100-1207), see *EI(2)*, ix, 193, s.v. Shāh-i Arman; Bosworth, *New Islamic Dynasties*, 197.

7 The text mistakenly has 'son of the Red Lion' (*al-sabʿ al-aḥmar*, which is the Arabic version of Qizil Arslān). He ruled lands south of Lake Van with the Artuqid Īlghāzī as his overlord (see al-Fāriqī, 269, 272; Hillenbrand, *Muslim Principality*, 104).

The dismissal of Sadīd al-Mulk, the caliph's vizier, and Abū Sa'd ibn al-Mūṣalāyā's exercise of the vizieral office

In the middle of Rajab this year [24 April 1103] the Vizier Sadīd al-Mulk Abū'l-Ma'ālī, the caliph's vizier, was arrested and imprisoned in the Caliphal Palace. His family had joined him from Isfahan and they were brought to be with him. He was held in comfortable confinement.

The reason for his dismissal was his ignorance of the system of the caliph's administration. He had spent his life on the affairs of the sultans and they did not have this system. After his arrest, Amīn al-Dawla ibn al-Mūṣilāyā resumed control of the Dīwān.

There was a remarkable conversation that presaged what happened some days later. Sadīd al-Mulk was residing in the house of 'Amīd al-Dawla ibn Jahīr. He held an open session there that people attended for the preaching of [Abū]'l-Mu'ayyad 'Īsā al-Ghaznawī.[8] They recited some verses that the latter had extemporized.

O Sadīd al-Mulk, you have reached high office but waded into a sea
Whose billows are deep. Guard well your soul there!
Revive the landmarks of good deeds and make
The tongue of truth your victory in this world.
There is a lesson to be learnt from past men. Saddle up
Your placid mount in safety or your headstrong one.

Thereupon Sadīd al-Mulk said, 'Whoever drinks the sultan's soup burns his lips, even if [**363**] sometime later.' He gestured towards the palace and recited, 'You dwelt in the houses of those who wronged their own souls and you saw plainly how We treated them.'[9] The vizier was arrested a few days afterwards.

How Prince Duqāq took the town of Raḥba

During Sha'bān [10 May–7 June 1103] Duqāq ibn Tutush, the lord of Damascus, took Raḥba, which had been in the hands of a man called Qaymāz, a mamluke of Sultan Alp Arslān, who had taken control of it after the killing of Karbughā.

Duqāq, along with Tughtakīn, his atabeg, marched against him and besieged him, but later withdrew. However, in Ṣafar [14 November–12 December 1102] Qaymāz died and his place was taken by a Turkish mamluke named Ḥasan. He dismissed many of his troops, made the khutbah in his own name and, wary of Duqāq, took defensive measures. Several of the officers whom he feared he arrested and executed several town notables and imprisoned and mulcted others. Duqāq again marched to besiege him and the populace delivered the town into his

---

8 An Ash'arite preacher and poet, died 498/1104–5 (see below p. [**397**]). For notices on him, see *Muntaẓam*, ix, 145, and Makdisi, *Ibn 'Aqīl*, 375.

9 Koran, xiv, 45.

hands. Ḥasan took refuge in the citadel but surrendered it after Duqāq had given him guarantees and assigned him a large fief in Syria. Duqāq reorganised the affairs of Raḥba and treated the inhabitants well. Having stationed a garrison there, he departed for Damascus.

[364] Account of the Franks' deeds in Syria

In Egypt al-Afḍal Emir al-Juyūsh had sent a mamluke of his father's, called Sa'd al-Dawla and known as al-Ṭawāshī, to Syria to fight the Franks. He met them between Ramla and Jaffa. The commander of the Franks was known as Baldwin (God curse him). They drew up their battle lines and when the battle began the Franks made a whole-hearted charge and the Muslims fled the field.

Astrologers had been predicting to Sa'd al-Dawla that he would die through a fall from a horse, so he was cautious about riding. He became governor of Beirut where the ground was furnished with paving-stones. He had the paving removed for fear that his horse would slip or stumble and give him a fall. Caution did not help him when fate struck. During this battle he fled but his horse lost its footing and he died in the fall. The Franks seized his tents and all that the Muslims had.

After this al-Afḍal sent his son, Sharaf al-Ma'ālī, at the head of a large force. They and the Franks met at Yāzūr near Ramla. The Franks suffered a defeat and there was great slaughter amongst them. Their survivors returned exhausted. When Baldwin saw how serious things were, he feared death or captivity, so threw himself into the grass and hid. Once the Muslims were some distance away, he emerged and went to Ramla. Sharaf al-Ma'ālī ibn Afḍal left the battle-field and besieged a castle at Ramla where were 700 Frankish nobles, including Baldwin, who left in disguise for Jaffa.[10] Al-Afḍal's son fought those that remained for fifteen days and then captured them. He killed 400 of them in cold blood and sent 300 as prisoners to Egypt.

His followers disagreed about their next objective. Some said, 'Let us attack Jerusalem **[365]** and conquer it.' Others said, 'Let us attack Jaffa and take it.' While they disagreed in this way, a large host of Franks arrived by sea, intending a pilgrimage to Jerusalem. Baldwin directed them to join him on an expedition. They marched to Ascalon, where Sharaf al-Ma'ālī was. He was not strong enough to resist them but God was kind to the Muslims. The Franks from overseas saw how strong Ascalon was and feared a night attack, so they withdrew to Jaffa. Al-Afḍal's son returned to his father, who sent another person, called Tāj al-'Ajam, one of the greatest of his father's mamlukes, by land with 4,000 horsemen and by sea sent a man called Cadi Ibn Qādūs with the fleet. The fleet blockaded Jaffa while Tāj al-'Ajam came to Ascalon. Ibn Qādūs summoned Tāj al-'Ajam to him to unite their military action against the Franks, but he said, 'I cannot join you except

[10] Cf. the account already given under the previous year.

by order of al-Afḍal,' so he made no move to help him. Ibn Qādūs sent to the cadi of Ascalon, the notaries and local notables and took their signed statements that he had remained twenty days at Jaffa and summoned Tāj al-'Ajam, who neither came to him nor sent any man. When al-Afḍal became aware of what had happened, he sent people who arrested Tāj al-'Ajam and he sent another man, called Jamāl al-Mulk, whom he placed in Ascalon and made commander of the Syrian troops.

By the end of this year the Franks (God curse them) held Jerusalem, Palestine except for Ascalon, and also Jaffa, Arsūf, Caesarea, Haifa, Tiberias, Lattakia and Antioch. In Mesopotamia they had Edessa and Sarūj.

[Raymond of] St. Gilles was besieging the city of Tripoli, although provisions were getting through to it. It was held by Fakhr al-Mulk **[366]** Ibn 'Ammār, who was sending his men in ships to raid the lands in Frankish hands and kill anyone they found. His aim in this was to empty the countryside of people who could farm it, to make the Franks short of provisions so that they would go away.

Miscellaneous events

On 6 Muḥarram [20 October 1102] the daughter of the Commander of the Faithful al-Qā'im bi-Allāh, the widow of Sultan Tughril Beg, died. She was known for her piety and abundant almsgiving. The Caliph al-Mustaẓhir bi-Allāh had confined her to her residence because it was rumoured that she was working to depose him.

In the month of Sha'bān [10 May–7 June 1103] al-Mustaẓhir bi-Allāh appointed Za'īm al-Ru'asā' Abū'l-Qāsim ibn Jahīr as vizier, summoning him from al-Ḥilla, from Sayf al-Dawla Ṣadaqa. Under the previous year we have mentioned the reason why he went there. On his arrival at Baghdad all the officials of state went out to greet him. He received a full set of robes of honour and was given his seat in the Dīwān and the title Qiwām al-Dīn.[11]

In the same month Abū'l-Muẓaffar ibn al-Khujandī, who used to give sermons, was killed at Rayy. As he descended from his dias he was killed by an Alid, who was killed in his turn. Al-Khujandī was buried in the mosque. His family came originally from Khujand in Transoxania and could be traced back to al-Muhallab ibn Abī Ṣufra.[12] Niẓām al-Mulk, who heard Abū Bakr Muḥammad ibn Thābit al-Khujandī preach at Marv, was delighted by his discourse and recognised his standing in law and religious learning. He took him to Isfahan, where he became professor at Niẓām al-Mulk's madrasah and gained an extensive reputation **[367]** and abundant worldly reward.

In Transoxania Sāghir Beg, a descendant of the Qarākhānids, gathered large forces and attacked Muḥammad Khān, whom Sultan Sanjar had made ruler of

---

[11] i.e. Support of the Religion.

[12] A chief of the Azd tribe who fought the Khārijite schismatics and governed Khurasan for the Umayyads in the late seventh century.

Samarqand, and challenged him for his kingdom. Muḥammad Khān was too weak for him, so sent to Sanjar asking for aid. The latter marched to Samarqand and drove Sāghir Beg away, who, fearful and seeking refuge, sent asking for terms and pardon from Sanjar. This was granted and Sāghir Beg presented himself before Sanjar. Peace was made between him and Muḥammad Khān, each one swearing an oath to the other. Sanjar returned to Khurasan and arrived at Marv in Rabīʿ I of the year 497 [December 1103].

This present year Abū'l-Maʿālī al-Ṣāliḥ died. He lived at the Arcade Gate as an ascetic; he was credited with manifest prodigies.[13]

[13] He was buried in Baghdad near the tomb of Ibn Ḥanbal (*Muntaẓam*, ix, 136–7).

Balak ibn Bahrām ibn Artuq's capture of the town of 'Āna

In Muḥarram of this year [October 1103] Balak ibn Bahrām ibn Artuq, who was the nephew of Īlghāzī ibn Artuq, took control of the town of 'Āna and of al-Ḥadītha. He had held Sarūj but the Franks took it from him, so he went and took 'Āna from the Banū Ya'īsh ibn 'Īsā ibn Khilāṭ. They sought out Sayf al-Dawla Ṣadaqa ibn Mazyad, accompanied by their shaykhs, and asked him to go up to 'Āna and receive it from them. He agreed and travelled up with them.

The Turkomans and Balak[1] withdrew and Ṣadaqa took hostages from them before returning to al-Ḥilla. Then Balak with 2,000 Turkomans came back but was resisted for a while by Ṣadaqa's men. He sought a guide for a place to ford to attack 'Āna, crossed over and won a victory, plundered them, and captured all their womenfolk. He then passed downstream towards Hīt on the Syrian bank but, having arrived near that town, he retired the same day. When he had heard of this, Ṣadaqa dispatched some troops but recalled them when Balak retired.

[369] The Franks raid Raqqa and Qal'at Ja'bar

In this year during Ṣafar [November 1103] the Franks from Edessa raided the plain of Raqqa and Qal'at Ja'bar. When they left Edessa they divided into two parties and travelled from their base for one day during which their raid on the two towns was to take place. They carried out the raid as they planned and drove off the cattle. They made prisoners of all the Muslims who fell into their hands. The two towns were held by Sālim ibn Mālik ibn Badrān ibn al-Muqallad ibn al-Musayyib, to whom Malikshāh had given them in the year 479 [1086-7], as we have mentioned under that year.[2]

Account of the peace made between Sultan Barkyāruq and Muḥammad

Peace was made between the two sultans, Barkyāruq and Muḥammad, the sons of Malikshāh, in Rabī' II of this year [January 1104].

The reason was that the war had been long-lasting between them and ruin was widespread. Wealth was now plundered, blood shed, cities destroyed and villages

---

1 The edition has Bahrām.

2 See Richards, *Annals*, 225-6,

burnt. The sultanate had become a prize for ambitious men and an office without authority, the rulers being the dominated after having been the dominators. This was something the great emirs preferred and were in favour of, so that their own sway, their insubordination and their arrogance might continue.

[370] Sultan Barkyāruq at that time was in Rayy, where the khutbah was in his name, as it was also in the Uplands, Ṭabaristān, Khūzistān, Fars, Diyār Bakr, the Jazīra and the Two Noble Sanctuaries.[3] Sultan Muḥammad was in Azerbayjan, where the khutbah was made for him, and also in Arrāniyya, Armenia, Isfahan and the whole of Iraq except for Takrīt. As for the region of the Marshes, in one part the khutbah was for Barkyāruq and in another for Muḥammad. However, in Basra the khutbah was in both their names. Throughout the whole of Khurasan, that is to say, from the frontiers of Jurjān to Transoxania, the khutbah was in the name of Sanjar and his brother Muḥammad.

When Sultan Barkyāruq saw his lack of money and the increasing greed of his soldiers, he sent the Cadi Abū'l-Muẓaffar al-Jurjānī al-Ḥanafī and Abū'l-Faraj Aḥmad ibn 'Abd al-Ghaffār al-Hamadhānī, known as Qarātakīn's man, to his brother Muḥammad about settling terms of peace. They came to him when he was in the vicinity of Marāgha and told him of their mission. They urged him to accept peace and its benefits, while recalling the destruction that prevailed throughout the lands and the ambitions of the enemies of Islam on the confines of its world. He agreed and sent some envoys to negotiate. The matter was settled and each prince swore an oath to the other. The treaty stipulated that Barkyāruq should not oppose his brother Muḥammad over his entitlement to the royal salute,[4] that his name should not be mentioned with his brother's in any of the lands that became Muḥammad's, that they should not correspond with one another but that any correspondence should be between their viziers, that no soldier should be prevented from joining whichever of the two he wished, that Sultan Muḥammad should have from the river known as the White River (Isbīdh Rūd) to Bāb al-Abwāb, and Diyār Bakr, the Jazīra, Mosul and Syria, and that in Iraq he should be suzerain over the lands of Sayf al-Dawla Ṣadaqa.

[371] Barkyāruq accepted this and disagreement and strife came to an end. Muḥammad sent to his men in Isfahan ordering them to leave the town and to surrender it to his brother's men. Barkyāruq went to Isfahan and after his brother's men had handed the place over to him, he invited them to join him in his service but they refused and thought it right to persevere in the service of their lord. The members of both armies called them 'the loyal ones'. They departed from Isfahan, taking with them to Sultan Muḥammad his womenfolk. Barkyāruq treated these men with honour and conveyed to his brother's family much money and 300 camels and 120 mules to carry their heavy baggage. He also sent troops with them to be at their service.

---

3 i.e. Mecca and Medina.

4 Literally 'not oppose ... concerning the drum.'

When the envoys of Barkyāruq came to the Caliph al-Mustaẓhir bi-Allāh with news of the peace and the terms agreed upon, Īlghāzī attended the Dīwān and requested the establishment of the khutbah for Barkyāruq. This was agreed and his name was mentioned in the khutbah in the Dīwān on Thursday 19 Jumādā I [Thursday 18 February 1104]. The next day his name was proclaimed in the mosques and this was also done in Wāsiṭ.

After Īlghāzī had made the khutbah for Barkyāruq in Baghdad and became one of his party, Emir Ṣadaqa sent to the caliph, saying, 'The Commander of the Faithful used to attribute to me all the violations of the duty of service and the obligations of allegiance and the lack of God-fearingness that Īlghāzī was responsible for, but now he has turned his face against the sultan who appointed him. I cannot endure that, but rather I shall march to expel him from Baghdad.'

[**372**] Having heard of this, Īlghāzī began to gather Turkomans. Ṣadaqa came to Baghdad and stopped opposite the Tāj. He kissed the earth in obeisance and camped in his tent on the West Bank. Īlghāzī left Baghdad for Ba'qūbā and sent to Ṣadaqa pleading as an excuse for his allegiance to Barkyāruq the peace that had come about and that his fief, Ḥulwān and other places, were part of Barkyāruq's lands and that Baghdad where he was prefect had passed into his hands. This is what had brought him into Barkyāruq's allegiance. Ṣadaqa was satisfied with this explanation and returned to al-Ḥilla.

In Dhū'l-Qa'da [26 July–24 August 1104] robes of honour were sent from the caliph to Sultan Barkyāruq and to Emir Ayāz and Barkyāruq's vizier, namely al-Khaṭīr, and also the sultanian investiture diploma. All swore oaths to the caliph and [the envoys] returned.

The Franks' conquest of Jubayl and Acre in Syria

This year there arrived at the city of Lattakia from the lands of the Franks ships carrying merchants, troops and pilgrims and others. [Raymond of] St. Gilles the Frank sought their aid for the siege of Tripoli, so they besieged it with him by land and sea. They pressed their assault for several days but saw no encouraging result, so they marched away to Jubayl which they besieged and attacked fiercely. After the inhabitants had seen that they could not withstand the Franks, they accepted terms and surrendered the city to them. However, the Franks did not remain faithful to the terms but seized their property which they extracted using punishments and all sorts of torture.

[**373**] When they had finished with Jubayl, they came to Acre where Baldwin, king of the Franks and ruler of Jerusalem, called on their services in the siege. They descended upon the place and besieged it by land and sea. The governor there was named Banā,[5] known as Zahr al-Dawla al-Juyūshī, indicating his

[5] This name of dubious vocalisation is given by Ibn Qal., 144, as B.n.' which is read by

affiliation to Emir al-Juyūsh al-Afḍal. He resisted them stoutly while they attacked time after time. Eventually he was incapable of holding the city and left, so that the Franks took it forcibly by the sword, perpetrating vile deeds on the inhabitants. The governor went to Damascus where he stayed until he returned to Egypt. He made his excuses to al-Afḍal who accepted his plea.

How Suqmān and Jokermish attacked the Franks

When the Franks (may God Almighty forsake them) vaunted their conquests of Islamic territory and, luckily for them, the armies and princes of Islam were distracted by fighting one another, then the Muslims were divided in their opinions, their aspirations were at variance and their wealth dissipated.

Ḥarrān was in the hands of a mamluke of Malikshāh, whose name was Qarājā, who in the previous year appointed as his deputy there a man called Muḥammad al-Isfahānī and then went away. Al-Isfahānī rebelled against Qarājā and was helped by the inhabitants because of Qarājā's oppression. Al-Isfahānī was firm and bold. He allowed no followers of Qarājā to remain in Ḥarran other than a Turkish mamluke known as Jāwulī, whom he made commander-in-chief of his army. He became friendly with him and one day joined him in a drinking session. Jāwulī had planned with a servant of his to kill him. They slew him while he was drunk. [**374**] At that juncture the Franks marched to Ḥarrān and put it under siege.

Between Mu'īn al-Dawla Suqmān and Shams al-Dawla Jokermish there were hostilities, since Suqmān was seeking revenge for the killing of his nephew (the reason for Jokermish's killing him I shall relate, God willing) and both were preparing to confront the other. When they heard this news, they each sent to the other calling for unity to rescue the situation at Ḥarrān and announcing that he had offered himself to God's service in return for His reward to come. Each accepted what the other wanted and so they set out and met at al-Khābūr, where they swore mutual oaths and marched on to meet the Franks.

With Suqmān were 7,000 Turkoman horse, while Jokermish had 3,000 Turkish, Arab and Kurdish horse. They met at the River Balīkh, where their pitched battle took place.[6] The Muslims feigned flight and were pursued by the Franks for about two leagues. The Muslims then turned about and killed them at will. The Turkomans' hands were filled with booty and they acquired great wealth, because the Frankish camp followers were close by. Bohemond, lord of Antioch, and Tancred, lord of the Coast, had drawn apart behind a hill to attack the Muslims from their rear when the battle was fully engaged. When they did emerge, they saw

---

Gibb, *Damascus Chronicle*, 61, as Bannā'. Cf. Ibn Shaddād, *Liban*, 174: N.bā (B.nā in the Ms.); Yāqūt, iii, 708: N.bā.'.

6 According to Ibn Qal., 143, on 9 Sha'bān/7 May 1104. For the effects of this Frankish defeat, see Asbridge, *Principality of Antioch*, 55-6.

the Franks already in retreat and their camp followers plundered. They both waited until nightfall and then fled. The Muslims pursued them and killed many of their followers and took a like number of prisoners. The two escaped with six knights.

Count Baldwin, the lord of Edessa, escaped with several of their nobles. They waded into the River Balīkh but their horses became stuck in the mud. One of Suqmān's men, a Turkoman, came **[375]** and captured them. He took Baldwin to his master's tents who had set out with some of his men to pursue Bohemond. The followers of Jokermish saw that Suqmān's men had seized the Franks' property and that they would go back with no gain of booty. They said to Jokermish, 'What will our standing be with our peers and with the Turkomans if the latter depart with the booty and we have no share?' They convinced him to seize the Count, so he sent men who took the Count from Suqmān's tents. When the latter returned he was outraged and his men mounted for a fight but he restrained them, saying, 'Let not the Muslims' joy at this expedition be replaced by despair because of our disagreements. I prefer not to assuage my wrath through our enemies' enjoyment of Muslim troubles.' He departed immediately, taking the Franks' weapons and standards. He gave his men the Frankish apparel to wear and their horses to ride. He then came to several castles of Shayḥān,[7] held by Franks, who came out, in the belief that their comrades had been victorious, only to be killed and have their castle taken. This happened at a number of castles.

Jokermish, on the other hand, went to Ḥarrān and received its surrender. Having arranged for his man to be in charge there, he left for Edessa, which he besieged for fifteen days. Then he returned to Mosul, taking with him the Count whom he had seized from Suqmān's tents. The Count ransomed himself for thirty-five dinars and 160 Muslim captives. The number of the Franks who had been killed was close to 12,000.

The death of Duqāq and the accession of his brother

In the month of Ramaḍān [June 1104] the lord of Damascus, Prince Duqāq, son of Tutush ibn Alp Arslān, died. His Atabeg Ṭughtakīn proclaimed a young son of Duqāq, who was one year old, **[376]** and made him the nominal ruler. Later he cancelled the khutbah in his name and made it for Baktāsh ibn Tutush, this infant's uncle, in Dhū'l-Ḥijja [September 1104]. He was twelve years of age.[8]

Ṭughtakīn suggested that he attack Raḥba. He duly went there, took it and

---

7 Not identified. It is tempting to amend to Sayḥān, the river in the Cilician plain, but this moves this action far to the west. Is it possible that Jayḥān, which flows just west of Mar'ash, could have been intended?

8 Duqāq died 12 Ramaḍān/8 June. The infant was called Tutush and he also 'died during these days.' The uncle, that is, brother of Duqāq, whose name is given as Muḥyi al-Dīn Ertāsh, was proclaimed on Saturday 24 Dhū'l-Ḥijja/17 September, according to Ibn Qal., 144–5.

returned. However, Ṭughtakīn prevented him from entering the city, so he proceeded to some castles of his, while Ṭughtakīn restored the khutbah for the infant son of Duqāq.[9]

The reason why Baktāsh became estranged from Ṭughtakīn was that his mother warned him to be fearful of him. She said, 'He is the husband of Duqāq's mother and she will not leave him alone until she has you killed and established her [grand]son as ruler.' He was fearful therefore and some people who envied Ṭughtakīn proposed as his best course that he leave Damascus, go to Baalbek, gather men, seek military aid from the Franks, return to Damascus and take it from Ṭughtakīn. Secretly he left Damascus in Ṣafar of the year 498 [22 October–19 November 1104] and was joined by Emir Aytakīn al-Ḥalabī, lord of Buṣrā, one of those who had made this plan with Baktāsh. They both ravaged the district of Ḥawrān and were joined by men intent on lawlessness. They made contact with Baldwin, king of the Franks, to ask for his military support. He responded to this and went to join them and they settled the terms of their agreement with him. They remained for a few days with him but on his part they saw only incitement to trouble-making and destruction in the Damascus region. When they despaired of his aid, they left him and set out through the desert to Raḥba. Baktāsh took it but then left.

[**377**] Ṭughtakīn became well established in Damascus and gained a monopoly of power. He treated the inhabitants well and spread justice among them, so that they were greatly delighted with him.

How Ṣadaqa took control of Wāsiṭ

In Shawwāl of this year [27 June–25 July 1104] Sayf al-Dawla Ṣadaqa ibn Mazyad went down river from al-Ḥilla to Wāsiṭ with a large army. On his instructions the following announcement was made among the Turks there: 'If anyone remains, we will no longer be responsible for him.' One group of them left to go to Barkyāruq and another to go to Baghdad. Yet another joined with Ṣadaqa. He summoned Muhadhdhab al-Dawla ibn Abī'l-Jabr, the lord of the Marsh, and assigned him the financial administration of the town for a period to end with the ending of the year, in return for 50,000 dinars. He then returned to al-Ḥilla and Muhadhdhab al-Dawla stayed in Wāsiṭ until 6 Dhū'l-Qa'da [31 July] before going back down to his own area.

Miscellaneous events

Sadīd al-Mulk Abū'l-Ma'ālī, who had been the caliph's vizier, was freed from

---

[9] This paragraph is not supported by the text of Ibn Qal.

prison in Rabī‘ I [December 1103]. On his release he fled to Sayf al-Dīn's settlement and from there to the Sultan Barkyāruq, who invested him with the general oversight of his realm.

This year there died suddenly Amīn al-Dawla Abū Sa‘d al-‘Alā’ ibn al-Ḥasan ibn al-Mūṣilāyā, who had gone blind. He was eloquent, with an excellent command of correct Arabic. He began his service for al-Qā’im bi-Amr Allāh [**378**] in the year 432 [1040–41], and then served the caliphs for 65 years, every day with increasing standing, until he renounced the vizierate. He was a Christian who converted to Islam in the year 484 [1091]. He gave alms abundantly and was of handsome presence and honest purpose. He gave his property in trust for charitable aims. His letters are famous and excellent. After his death, his nephew Abū Naṣr was given a robe of honour and the title Niẓām al-Ḥaḍratayn and entrusted with the Chancery.

This year there were many commotions amongst the common people in Baghdad and the urban gangs became widespread.

Abū Nu‘aym ibn Sāwa, the Wāsiṭī doctor, was killed. He was one of those skilled in medical practice with many excellent successes to his credit.

Sultan Sanjar dismissed his vizier al-Mujīr Abū'l-Fatḥ al-Ṭughrā’ī this year. This came about because Emir Buzghush, the commander-in-chief of Sanjar's army, had a note thrown to him which said, ‘You will not prosper with this sultan.’ Another came to Sanjar: ‘You will not prosper with Emir Buzghush and the size of his following.’ Buzghush assembled the turbanned officials and showed them the two missives. They agreed that al-Ṭughrā’ī's clerk was suspect. Evidence against him was forthcoming and he was executed. Sanjar arrested al-Ṭughrā’ī and intended to put him to death but Buzghush stopped him and said, ‘He is owed something for some service!’ Sanjar exiled him to Ghazna.

In this year Buzghush gathered many troops from Khurasan and was joined by many volunteers. He marched to fight the Ismā‘īlīs. He attacked Ṭabas which was in their hands. His troops reduced it and the neighbouring castles and villages to ruin. Many were killed or taken into captivity and much plundered. Horrible things were done to them. Sanjar's officials advised that they should be granted guarantees of security and that it should be stipulated that they build no castle, purchase no arms and call no one [**379**] to accept their beliefs. Many people were displeased with these terms and this peace. They held it against Sanjar. Then, after his return from this expedition, Buzghush died. The closing act of his career was this Jihad expedition (may God have mercy on him!).

The following died this year:

Abū Bakr ‘Alī ibn Aḥmad ibn Zakarīyā’ al-Ṭuraythīthī, who was a celebrated sufi and scholar of Ḥadīth.[10]

---

[10] Ibn al-Jawzī calls him Aḥmad ibn ‘Alī ibn al-Ḥusayn ibn Zakarīyā’ (born 412/1021–2, died Jumādā II 497/March 1104) and reports critically on his scholarship (*Muntaẓam*, ix, 138–9).

Cadi Abū'l-Ḥusayn Aḥmad ibn Muḥammad al-Thaqafī, the cadi of Kufa, in Rajab [April 1104]. He was born in Rabī' I of the year 422 [March 1031]. He was a descendant of 'Urwa ibn Mas'ūd and a pupil of Cadi al-Dāmghānī. He was succeeded in his office after his death by his son, Abū'l-Barakāt.

In Rabī' II [January 1104] Abū 'Abd Allāh al-Ḥusayn ibn 'Alī ibn al-Busarī, the merchant and Ḥadīth scholar. He was born in the year 404 [1013-14].[11]

---

[11] In *Muntaẓam*, ix, 140: the year 410/1019-20.

The Year 498 [1104-1105]

Account of the death of Sultan Barkyāruq

On 2 Rabīʿ II [21 December 1104] Sultan Barkyāruq ibn Malikshāh died. He had fallen ill with wasting and haemorrhoids in Isfahan. From there he travelled in a litter to Baghdad. Having reached Barūjird he became too weak to be moved. For forty days he stayed there. Then his illness intensified and when he despaired of his life he invested his son Malikshāh, who was at that time aged four years and eight months. He bestowed a robe of honour on Emir Ayāz and summoned a number of emirs whom he informed that he had appointed his son his successor to the sultanate and had made Emir Ayāz his atabeg. He ordered them to obey them both and to cooperate with them to defend the sultanate and preserve it for his son. All responded that they would hear and obey and give their lives and wealth to preserve his son and his position as sultan. He asked for their oath to that, which they gave. Then he ordered them to proceed to Baghdad. On their way, when they were twelve leagues from Barūjird, news of his death came to them. Barkyāruq had remained behind intending to return to Isfahan but his fate forestalled him.

After Emir Ayāz had heard of his death, he commanded his vizier al-Khaṭīr al-Maybudhī and others to convey his coffin to Isfahan. This was done and he was buried in the mausoleum which his concubine had built for him. She died a few days afterwards and was buried opposite him. Ayāz brought the pavilions, tents, parasol, sunshade[1] and all that was required for a sultan and put it at the disposal of his son Malikshāh.

[381] Account of Barkyāruq's age and a little about his life

When Barkyāruq died he was twenty-five years old. He had borne the title of sultan for twelve years and four months. He had endured more wars and vagaries of fate than anyone. His career vacillated between ease and hardship, possession of power and loss of it. On numerous occasions, after giving up his material comforts, he was on the point of losing his life. Just at this moment, when his position had become strong and his opponents had submitted to him and become obedient, death overtook him. In his wars he was defeated only once. His emirs were ambitious to replace him because of the widespread dissension. They even sought to kill his lieutenants and he was unable to defend them. At the time when

[1] Amongst the rulers' regalia *al-shamsa* (or *al-shamsiyya*), here translated 'sunshade,' has the same function as *al-jitr* ('parasol'). See *EI(2)*, vii, 191-5, s.v. *miẓalla*.

he was mentioned in the khutbah at Baghdad a famine occurred and business and commerce came to a halt. Despite that he was loved by the people and they preferred him as sultan.

We have mentioned already what we have learnt about how he was the plaything of circumstances. One of the most astonishing examples is his entry into Isfahan, fleeing from his uncle Tutush, when the army of his brother Muḥammad, its ruler, allowed him to enter with the intention of seizing him. However, it chanced that his brother Muḥammad died and the troops were obliged to make Barkyāruq ruler. This is one of the best cases of 'Deliverance after Adversity.'[2]

He was forbearing, generous, patient, intelligent, very affable and of excellent aptitude. He used not to punish excessively. Indeed, he forgave more often than he punished.

[382] How the khutbah was made for Malikshāh ibn Barkyāruq

The khutbah was made for Malikshāh ibn Barkyarūq in the Dīwān this year on Thursday, the last day of Rabī' II [=19 January 1105], and in the mosques of Baghdad on the following day, the Friday.

The reason for this was that in Muḥarram [21 September-21 October 1104] Īlghāzī, the prefect of Baghdad, travelled to Sultan Barkyāruq when he was at Isfahan, to urge him to come to Baghdad. He set out with Barkyāruq and after the latter had died he continued with his son Malikshāh and Emir Ayāz to Baghdad. They arrived on 17 Rabī' II [5 January 1105]. On the way they met with severe cold, the like of which they had never seen, so much so that they were unable to get water because it was frozen solid.

The Vizier Abū'l-Qāsim 'Alī ibn Jahīr came out and met them in Diyālā. They numbered 5,000 horse. Īlghāzī and Emir Ṭughāyuruk came to the Dīwān and made representations for the establishing of the khutbah for Malikshāh ibn Barkyāruq. This was granted and the khutbah duly made. He was given the titles of his grandfather Malikshāh, that is to say, Jalāl al-Dawla and others. The making of the khutbah in his name was accompanied by a scattering of dinars.

Sultan Muḥammad's siege of Jokermish in Mosul

After the Sultans Barkyāruq and Muḥammad had made peace, as we related under the previous year, and Muḥammad had surrendered the city of Isfahan to Barkyāruq, the latter travelled there and Muḥammad remained in Tabrīz in Azerbayjan until his men who were in Isfahan joined him. After their arrival he

[2] In Arabic *al-Faraj ba'd al-Shidda*, a literary genre and also the title of its most famous example, the collection of anecdotes illustrating that theme by al-Tanūkhī (329-34/940-94).

appointed as vizier Sa'd al-Mulk Abū'l-Maḥāsin because of his excellent work in guarding Isfahan. He remained until Ṣafar [22 October–19 November 1104] [**383**] and went to Marāgha, then to Irbil, intending to attack Jokermish, the lord of Mosul, and take his lands.

Having heard of his march against him, Jokermish restored the walls of Mosul and repaired whatever was in need of repair. He ordered the countryfolk around to enter the city and allowed his men to plunder those who did not.

Muḥammad put the city under siege and Jokermish sent to him, reminding him that there was peace between him and his brother and that part of the agreement had been that Mosul and the lands of the Jazīra should be his own. He showed him the document to that effect from Barkyāruq and the sworn declaration that Mosul would be handed over to him. Muḥammad said to him, 'If you submit, I shall not take it from you, but I shall confirm your possession of it and the khutbah there shall be in my name.' Jokermish replied, 'Since the peace I have received letters of the sultan ordering me not to give up the city to anyone but him.'

When Muḥammad saw that he resisted, he began the battle and attacked with sappers and siege towers. The garrison fought fiercely and killed many because of their love for Jokermish on account of his good rule over them. Jokermish ordered the opening of small gates in the wall from which foot-soldiers could make sallies. They inflicted many losses on the besiegers. Muḥammad made another assault and his men mined the wall but night intervened and by the morning the garrison had repaired it and manned it with soldiers. During the siege prices remained low. Wheat was sold at thirty *makkūk*[3] for a dinar and barley at fifty for a dinar.

Some of Jokermish's troops had assembled at Tell Ya'far from where they were raiding the fringes of the [besieging] army and preventing provisions from reaching it. The hostilities continued until 10 Jumādā I [27 January 1105] and then news of Sultan Barkyāruq's death came to Jokermish. He summoned the inhabitants [**384**] and consulted them about what to do now that the sultan had died. They said, 'Our wealth and our lives are at your disposal. You know better your own situation. Consult the troops for they understand this better.' So he consulted his emirs, who said, 'When the sultan was alive, we were secure and no one could invade our territory. Since he is dead, the people now have only this one sultan and the best course is to enter under his allegiance.'

Jokermish therefore sent to Muḥammad offering allegiance and requesting the presence of his vizier, Sa'd al-Mulk. The latter came and, taking his hand, said, 'The politic thing for you would be to present yourself now before the sultan, for he will not oppose you in anything that you request.' He took his hand and stood up, so Jokermish left with him. When the people of Mosul saw that he had gone to the sultan, they began to weep and wail and heap dust on to their heads. When Jokermish came before Sultan Muḥammad, he received him with kindness and

---

[3] In tenth-century Baghdad 1 *makkūk* was approximately 6 kg or 7.5 litres of wheat. In thirteenth-century Mosul it was more than twice as much (see Hinz, 44).

respect. He embraced him and did not allow him to take a seat, but said, 'Go back to your people, for their hearts are with you and they are watching for your return.' Jokermish kissed the ground and returned along with several of the sultan's personal staff. He asked the sultan the next day to enter the city to be given a ceremonial reception but he declined, so Jokermish laid on a great banquet outside Mosul and brought presents and gifts for the sultan, and for his vizier items of great value.

The sultan comes to Baghdad and makes peace with his nephew and Emir Ayāz

When news of Sultan Barkyāruq's demise came to his brother Sultan Muḥammad during his siege of Mosul, he held a session of condolence and came to terms with Jokermish, the ruler of Mosul, as we have mentioned. He then went to Baghdad, accompanied by Sukmān al-Quṭbī, who is so named after Quṭb al-Dawla Ismā'īl [**385**] ibn Yāqūtī ibn Da'ūd, Ismā'īl being the cousin of Malikshāh. With him went Jokermish and other emirs.

Sayf al-Dawla Ṣadaqa, the lord of al-Ḥilla, had gathered a large body of troops, whose number reached 15,000 horse and 10,000 foot, and he sent his two sons, Badrān and Dubays, to Sultan Muḥammad to urge him to come to Baghdad. The sultan took them both with him to Baghdad. When Emir Ayāz heard of his coming, he and his troops left their quarters and set up tents in al-Zāhir, outside Baghdad. He assembled the emirs and consulted them about what to do. They offered him their allegiance and swore to fight and do battle for him. They would defend him against the sultan and act together with him in obedience to Malikshāh ibn Barkyāruq. The most committed to that were Yināl and Ṣabāwa, for they had gone to great lengths to stir up opposition to Muḥammad and to deny him the sultanate. After they had dispersed, Ayāz's vizier, Ṣafī al-Dīn Abū'l-Maḥāsin, said to him, 'My master, my life is linked to the stability of your good fortune and your power. I am more closely bound to you than these men. The right course is not what they advise. Each one of them[4] intends, using you, to follow a path and gain a profit for himself. Most of them are your rivals for position. It is only their shortage of men and money that prevents them from opposing you. The correct thing to do is to make terms with Sultan Muḥammad and give him allegiance. He will confirm you in your fief and add to it whatever you wish.'

Emir Ayāz's opinion fluctuated between peace and conflict, although his moves towards conflict were plain to see. He collected together the boats that were at Baghdad and secured the streets against any sudden attack on his troops or the city.

[**386**] Sultan Muḥammad arrived at Baghdad on Friday eight days left of Jumādā I [=10 February 1105] and camped on the West Bank in upper Baghdad.

---

4 Reading *kullan min-hum* and emending *kalāma-hum* of the edition.

The khutbah was made for him on the West Bank and for Malikshāh ibn Barkyāruq on the East Bank. In the Mosque of al-Manṣūr, however, the preacher said, 'O God, prosper the Sultan of the World!' and then fell silent.

The population feared that trouble and looting would be widespread. Ayāz rode out with his troops, who were determined to fight. He proceeded until he was in sight of Muḥammad's army and then retired to his tents. He called upon his emirs to swear a second time to be loyal to Malikshāh. Some agreed but others hung back and said, 'We have sworn once. There is nothing to be gained in renewing our oath. If we are faithful to the first, we shall be to the second, and if we are not faithful to the first, then we shall not keep the second.'

Thereupon Ayāz ordered his vizier Ṣafī al-Dīn Abū'l-Maḥāsin to cross over to Sultan Muḥammad to propose peace, recognition of his sultanate and the cessation of opposition to him. He crossed to Muḥammad's army on Saturday seven days left of the same month [=11 February] and met with his vizier, Sa'd al-Mulk Abū'l-Maḥāsin Sa'd ibn Muḥammad. He told him of his purpose and they both came before Sultan Muḥammad. Ṣafī al-Dīn delivered the message of his master Ayāz and his excuses for his deeds during the reign of Barkyāruq. Muḥammad gave a kind answer, which calmed and satisfied his mind, and agreed to swear the oath that was requested of him.

On the morrow the Chief Cadi, the two Syndics and Ṣafī al-Dīn appeared before Sultan Muḥammad. His vizier Sa'd al-Mulk said to him, 'Ayāz is fearful because of his past actions [**387**] and he requests a written guarantee for Malikshāh, your nephew, and for himself and for the emirs with him.' The sultan replied, 'Malikshāh is my son. There is no distinction between me and my brother. As for Ayāz and the emirs, I shall swear an oath to them, except for Yināl al-Ḥusāmī and Ṣabāwa.' Al-Kiyā al-Harrās, the professor at the Niẓāmiyya, administered the oath to that effect in the presence of the company. The next day Emir Ayāz attended on the sultan. He was met by the sultan's vizier and all the notables. At that time Sayf al-Dawla Ṣadaqa arrived and both entered the presence of the sultan together, who honoured them and showed them his kindness. It is said that, on the contrary, the sultan rode out and welcomed them and that one halted on his right hand and the other on his left. The sultan remained in Baghdad until Sha'bān [began 17 April 1105], then went to Isfahan, where he did what we shall relate, God willing.

Account of the killing of Emir Ayāz

This year on 13 Jumādā II [1 April 1105] Emir Ayāz was killed by Sultan Muḥammad. This came about because, when Ayāz conceded that Muḥammad was sultan, he became one of his men and secured an oath from the sultan. On 8 Jumādā II [24 February 1105] he prepared a great banquet in his house, the residence of Goharā'īn, to which he invited the sultan and presented him with a lot of items, including the ruby 'mountain', which had been taken from the estate of Mu'ayyad al-Mulk ibn Niẓām al-Mulk. Mention of this has already been made.[5] Sayf al-Dawla Ṣadaqa ibn Mazyad was present with the sultan.

[**388**] By ill fate Ayāz instructed his mamlukes to wear armour from his arsenal to have them inspected by the sultan. A man from Abhar joined them, joking with them and making them laugh, despite his being a Sufi. They said to him, 'We must put a breastplate on you and have you inspected.' They put the breastplate under his shirt and seized hold of him, although he was begging them to desist, but they did not. Because of their rough treatment, he ran away from them and went in among the sultan's special guard to take refuge with them. The sultan saw that he was scared and wearing bulky clothing. His suspicions aroused, he told a mamluke of his in Turkish to feel him without anyone knowing. This he did and became aware of the breastplate under his shirt. He informed the sultan, who became apprehensive and said, 'If the turbanned classes have donned armour, what about the soldiers!' His apprehension increased because he was in Ayāz's house and in his power. He rose and left the house and returned to his own residence.

On 13th of the month [1 April] the sultan summoned Emir Ṣadaqa, Ayāz and Jokermish and other emirs. He sent to them when they had assembled: 'We have heard that Qilij Arslān ibn Sulaymān ibn Qutlumish has attacked Diyār Bakr to conquer it and has sent [troops] from there to the Jazīra. It is necessary that you agree on whom to send to resist him in battle.' The gathering said, 'The only man for this is Emir Ayāz,' to which Ayāz said, 'Sayf al-Dawla Ṣadaqa ibn Mazyad and I ought to unite for this matter and repel this invader.' This was reported to the sultan who replied with a summons for Ayāz, Ṣadaqa and the Vizier Sa'd al-Mulk, to arrange the matter at his court. They rose to go to him.

The sultan had prepared a group of his guard to kill Ayāz when he entered his presence. As he came in, one of them struck his head and separated it from his body. Ṣadaqa covered his face with his sleeve and [**389**] the vizier fainted. Ayāz was wrapped in some sacking and thrown into the street near the Royal Palace. His troops rode out and plundered what they could from his house. The sultan sent men to protect it from being sacked, and Ayāz's followers dispersed straightaway. This great wealth and mighty power faded away in a moment because of some levity and joking. The following day some volunteer fighters provided a shroud and buried him in the cemetery adjacent to the tomb of Abū Ḥanīfa (God have mercy on him).

He had passed forty years of age and was one of the mamlukes of Sultan Malikshāh, after whose death he passed into the troop of another emir who adopted him as a son. He was abundant in manly virtue, brave and of excellent judgment in warfare. His vizier Ṣafī al-Dīn went into hiding but was later taken and carried to the house of the Vizier Sa'd al-Mulk. In Ramaḍān [16 May–13 June 1105] he

---

5 See above p. [**305**]. The variant reading *al-jabal* (mountain) has been adopted rather than *al-ḥabl* (rope), as the previous passage refers to a single item (*qiṭ'a*).

was put to death at the age of thirty-six. He was from a house of municipal headship in Hamadhān.

The death of Suqmān ibn Artuq

Fakhr al-Mulk Ibn ʻAmmār, the ruler of Tripoli, had written to Suqmān inviting him to aid him against the Franks. He offered him help with money and men. While he was preparing to march, a letter from Ṭughtakīn, lord of Damascus, came informing him that he was ill and on the point of death and that he feared, if he died without anyone to defend Damascus, that the Franks would conquer it. He urged him to come so that he could make him his successor and enjoin what he should do to guard the city. Made aware if this, Suqmān hastened [**390**] his departure, aiming to acquire Damascus and to attack the Franks at Tripoli and drive them away.

He came to al-Qaryatayn and intelligence of this reached Ṭughtakīn, who now feared the result of what he had done. So great was his anxiety that his illness worsened. His men blamed him for the shortcomings of his planning and warned him of the result of what he had done. They said to him, 'You have seen your master Tāj al-Dīn when he called him to Damascus for his defense, how he killed him when he set eyes on him.' While they were pondering by what means they could change his mind, they heard that Suqmān had reached al-Qaryatayn and then died. His men carried him home and so a deliverance came which they had not reckoned on.

Suqmān's fatal illness was diphtheria which had afflicted him often. His followers advised him to return to Ḥiṣn Kayfā but he refused. He said, 'No, I shall go on. If I recover I shall fulfil what I have planned. God shall not see me unwilling to shoulder the burden of battling the Franks for fear of my death. If my fate overtakes me, I shall be a martyr marching to the Jihad.' So they went on. He lost the use of his tongue for two days and expired in Ṣafar [22 October–19 November 1104], leaving his son Ibrāhīm with his men. He was placed in a coffin and carried back to Ḥiṣn Kayfā. He was resolute and crafty, a man of good sense and many good works. We have related how he came to take Ḥiṣn Kayfā.

As for his conquest of Mārdīn, Karbughā had left Mosul and attacked Āmid, waging war on its ruler, a Turkoman, who asked for aid from Suqmān. He arrived and faced Karbughā in battle. ʻImād al-Dīn Zankī ibn Āqsunqur, at that time still a child, was present with Karbughā, accompanied by a large body of his father's men. When the fighting was at its fiercest and Suqmān had the upper hand, [**391**] Āqsunqur's men threw Zankī, their master's son, among the hooves of the horses and said, 'Fight for your master's child!' They then fought very fiercely and Suqmān was defeated. They took his nephew, Yāqūtī [ibn Alpyārūk][6] ibn Artuq,

6 See the Artuqid dynastic table in *EI(2)*, i, 663.

prisoner and he was held by Karbughā in the citadel of Mārdīn. The ruler there was a singer of Sultan Barkyāruq's who had asked him for Mārdīn and its district and had received it as a fief. Yāqūtī remained in prison for a while and then the wife of Artuq went to Karbughā and asked for his release. He was released and settled in Mārdīn which he had come to like. He stayed there to work towards gaining the place and taking control there.

The Kurds at Mārdīn had plans to remove the ruler, the singer. Several times they raided the district. Yaqūtī made contact with him to say, 'A love and friendship has grown between us. I wish to make your town prosperous by defending it against the Kurds. I shall raid some places and take money which I shall spend on your town, while dwelling in the suburbs.' Given permission for this, he began to raid from the gates of Khilāṭ to Baghdad. Some of the troops of the citadel started to join him, eager for gain. He received them generously and did not interfere with them, so they came to trust him.

It came about that on a certain occasion most of them joined him and on returning from the raid he ordered them to be arrested and fettered. He came quickly to the citadel and announced to their families within, 'Open the gate or otherwise I shall cut off their heads.' They refused, so he killed one man. Then those within surrendered the citadel to him and he took up residence there.

Later he gathered a host and marched to Nisibis and raided the town of Jazīrat ibn 'Umar, which belonged to Jokermish. When his men returned with their booty, Jokermish came against them. Yāqūtī was afflicted by an illness which made him unable to wear armour or ride a horse. However, he was carried to his horse [**392**] and put in the saddle. An arrow hit him and he fell from the horse. Jokermish came up to him, as he was giving up the ghost, wept to see him and said, 'What brought you to do what you have done, O Yāqūtī?' He gave no reply and expired. Artuq's wife went to her son Suqmān, gathered the Turkomans and demanded revenge for her grandson. Suqmān besieged Nisibis, which was Jokermish's. The latter sent a large sum of money secretly to Suqmān, who took it and was satisfied. He said, 'He was killed in battle and his killer is unknown.'

After Yāqūtī, his brother 'Alī ruled Mārdīn and became subject to Jokermish. He appointed as his lieutenant there an emir also called 'Alī. 'Alī, the governor in Mārdīn, sent to Suqmān, saying, 'Your nephew intends to surrender Mārdīn to Jokermish.' So Suqmān went there in person and took it over. 'Alī, his nephew, came to him and asked for the citadel to be restored to him. Suqmān replied, 'I have taken it simply to prevent the destruction of our house.' He assigned him Jabal Jūr as a fief and transferred him there.

Every year Jokermish was giving 'Alī 20,000 dinars. When his uncle Suqmān took Mārdīn from him, 'Alī sent to Jokermish asking him for money. Jokermish responded, 'I gave you money only out of respect for Mārdīn and because I feared you as a neighbour. But now do whatever you want. You have no power over me.'

The state of the Bāṭinīs this year in Khurasan

This year a large group of Ismā'īlīs set out from Ṭuraythīth, one of the districts of Bayhaq. They raided far and wide in those parts and killed large numbers of the inhabitants. [**393**] They plundered their property and took their women into captivity, failing to hold to the previous truce.

This year their cause strengthened and their power increased. They did not restrain their hands from those they wished to kill because the sultans were distracted. This is one of the things they did. A pilgrim caravan assembled this year from Transoxania, Khurasan, India and elsewhere. When they reached Khuwār al-Rayy, the Bāṭinīs attacked them at dawn and put them to the sword. They slew them at will and took their goods and their herds as booty, leaving nothing.

They killed Abū Ja'far ibn al-Mushāṭ, one of the leading Shāfi'ī scholars, this year. He learnt his law from al-Khujandī and used to teach and give sermons in Rayy. As he got down from his teaching stool, a Bāṭinī came up to him and killed him.

How the Franks stood this year in relation to the Muslims in Syria

In Sha'bān of this year [April 1105] there was a battle between Tancred the Frank, lord of Antioch, and Prince Riḍwān, lord of Aleppo, in which Riḍwān was defeated.[7]

This came about because Tancred besieged the castle of Artāḥ, where there was a lieutenant of Prince Riḍwān. The Franks pressed the Muslims hard, so his lieutenant sent to Riḍwān to inform him of the siege he was undergoing, which had weakened him, and to ask for help. Riḍwān set out with a large force of cavalry and 7,000 foot-soldiers, 3,000 of whom were jihad volunteers. They came to Qinnisrīn, only a little distance from the Franks. When Tancred saw the great number of the Muslims, he sent to Riḍwān, seeking to make peace. The latter wished to agree but General Ṣabāwa, who had sought him out and entered his service after the death of Ayāz, argued against it. He therefore declined to make peace [**394**] and the battle lines were drawn up. The Franks retreated without a fight, but then they said, 'Let us return and make one charge. Then either we succeed or we lose!' They therefore charged the Muslims who did not hold firm but were broken. Many were killed and many taken prisoner.

The infantry had already entered the Franks' camp after their initial retreat and they were busy with plunder. The Franks killed them. Only the odd fugitive

---

7 For events around this battle, dated 20 April 1105, see Asbridge, *Principality of Antioch*, 57–8.

escaped, to be taken prisoner later. Those in Artāḥ fled to Aleppo, leaving it to be taken by the Franks (God curse them). General Ṣabāwa fled to Ṭughtakīn, the atabeg of Damascus, and became one of his followers.

A battle between the Franks and the Egyptians

This year in Dhū'l-Ḥijja [13 August-10 September 1105] there was a battle between the Franks and the Egyptians in which neither side gained an advantage. It occurred thus. Al-Afḍal, the vizier of the ruler of Egypt, had sent his son Sharaf al-Ma'ālī against the Franks in the previous year. He had beaten them and taken Ramla from them. However, the Egyptians and the Bedouin had a disagreement. Each party claimed the victory was its. When a detachment of Franks came against them, each party neglected to support the other, so that the Franks were likely to gain the upper hand. At that, Sharaf al-Ma'ālī departed to go to his father in Egypt, who dispatched his other son, that is, Sanā' al-Mulk Ḥusayn, with several emirs, including Jamāl al-Mulk, the Egyptians' governor in Ascalon. They sent to Ṭughtakīn, atabeg of Damascus, asking him for troops. He sent General Ṣabāwa to them with 1,300 cavalry. The Egyptians were 5,000 strong.

Baldwin the Frank, lord [**395**] of Jerusalem, Acre and Jaffa, moved against them with 1,300 cavalry and 8,000 foot. The encounter took place between Ascalon and Jaffa. Neither side gained a victory over the other. On the Muslim side 1,200 were killed and on the Frankish the same. One of the slain was Jamāl al-Mulk, emir of Ascalon.

When the Muslims saw that equal damage had been done by both sides, they broke off the battle and returned to Ascalon. Ṣabāwa returned to Damascus. Several Muslims had been with the Franks, including Baktāsh ibn Tutush. Ṭughtakīn had transferred sovereign rule to his nephew, Duqāq's son, still a young child, as we have related.[8] This is what motivated Baktāsh to go to the Franks and join them.

Miscellaneous events

During this year the Turkomans caused much trouble on the Khurasan road in the districts of Iraq. Previously they had been seizing property and interrupting traffic but they had some self-imposed limits. When this year came they cast off all restraint and committed abominable acts. Īlghāzī ibn Artuq, the prefect of Iraq, appointed over that region his nephew, Balak ibn Bahrām ibn Artuq, and ordered him to control and guard it and prevent disturbances there. He undertook this in

---

[8] See above pp. [**375-6**].

exemplary fashion, protecting the area and restraining high-handedness. Balak went to the castle of Khānījār, part of the territory of Surkhāb ibn Badr, besieged and conquered it.

In Sha'bān [17 April–15 May 1105] Sultan Muḥammad appointed Qasīm al-Dawla Sunqur al-Bursuqī prefect [**396**] in Iraq. He was known for his goodness, his piety and good faith. He never once abandoned Muḥammad in all his wars.

This year Sultan Muḥammad assigned Kufa as a fief to Emir Qaymāz and instructed Ṣadaqa to protect his officials from the Khafāja tribe, which he agreed to do.

In the month of Ramaḍān [16 May–13 June 1105] Sultan Muḥammad came to Isfahan and guaranteed the security of the inhabitants. They trusted that the disorder, violence and extortion that had been overwhelming them would cease. What a difference between his departure in secret flight and his return as all-powerful sultan! He dispensed justice to the people, removed what they hated and restrained the harmful hands of the soldiery and others. The word of a common citizen became stronger than the word of a soldier and a soldier's hand weaker than a citizen's on account of the awe felt for the sultan and his justice.

In many of the countries smallpox was widespread this year, especially in Iraq, where it was found in every part. An untold number of children died. It was followed by much sickness and great loss of life.

The following died this year:

In Shawwāl [15 June–13 July 1105] Aḥmad ibn Muḥammad ibn Aḥmad, Abū 'Alī al-Bardānī, the Koran scholar. He was born in the year 426 [1034–5]. He heard Ḥadīth from Ibn Ghaylān, al-Barmakī, al-'Ushārī and others.

Abū'l-Ma'ālī Thābit ibn Bandār ibn Ibrāhīm al-Baqqāl, born in the year 416 [1025–6]. He heard Ḥadīth from Abū Bakr al-Burqānī and Abū 'Alī ibn Shādhān. His death occurred in Jumādā II [17 February–17 March 1105].

On 4 Jumādā I [21 January 1105] Abū'l-Ḥasan Muḥammad ibn 'Alī ibn Abī'l-Ṣaqar, [**397**] the Shāfi'ī lawyer, who was born in the year 409 [1018–19]. He was a literary man and a poet. Some of his verses are:

> Anyone who says, 'I have respect and gravity
> And our lord thinks highly of me,'
> Without that being of use to his friend,
> May he be a nobody!

Abū Naṣr, the nephew of Ibn al-Mūṣilāyā, who was a secretary of outstanding competence for the caliph, aged seventy. He left no heir because he had converted to Islam and his family was Christian, so they did not inherit. He was careful with his money, although he gave much in alms.

Abū'l-Mu'ayyad 'Īsā ibn 'Abd Allāh ibn al-Qāsim al-Ghaznawī. He was a preacher, a poet and a clerk. He came to Baghdad and delivered sermons there. He supported the school of al-Ash‘arī and was held in very great regard. He left Baghdad and died in Isfarā’īn.

[398] The Year 499 [1105-1106]

Mankūbars' rebellion against Sultan Muḥammad

In Muḥarram of this year [13 September-13 October 1105] Mankūbars, son of Prince Būribars ibn Alp Arslān, the cousin of Sultan Muḥammad, openly rebelled and revealed his opposition to the sultan. This came about because he was residing in Isfahan and severe hardship overtook him. His supplies were cut off, so he left and went to Nihāwand. A group of the army joined him there and several emirs backed him in his project. He seized control of Nihāwand and made the khutbah in his own name. He also wrote to the emirs, the sons of Bursuq, to invite them to give him their allegiance and support.

Sultan Muḥammad had arrested Zankī, son of Bursuq, who wrote to his brothers and warned them against giving allegiance to Mankūbars and about the harm and danger that would follow. He ordered them so to contrive matters as to be able to arrest him. When their brother's letter came to them with this message they sent to Mankūbars, offering allegiance and cooperation. He and they travelled to a meeting, where, near their own lands, that is to say, Khūzistān, they seized hold of him. His men scattered and he was taken to Isfahan, where the sultan imprisoned him with the sons of his uncle Tekesh. Zankī ibn Bursuq was freed and restored to his position but the sultan relieved him and his brothers of their fiefs, Līshtar, Sābūr Khwāst[1] [399] and elsewhere, between Ahwāz and Hamadhān, and assigned them in exchange Dīnawar and other places.

It happened this year that there appeared, also in Nihāwand, a man from the countryside who claimed to be a prophet. A great host of the country folk gave him their obedience and followed him. They sold their properties and gave him the money they received for them, all of which he proceeded to disburse. He named four of his followers Abū Bakr, 'Umar, 'Uthmān and 'Alī.[2] He was eventually killed at Nihāwand and the inhabitants said, 'In the space of two months two men appeared amongst us, one claimed prophethood and the other sovereignty. The cause of neither succeeded.'

Account of a battle between Ṭughtakīn and the Franks

This year in Ṣafar [14 October-10 November 1105] there was a battle between

---

[1] In Luristān, south of Khurramabād (Krawulsky, 365-6). Līshtar (or Alīshar) is between Nihāwand and Sābūr Khwāst (Krawulsky, 358-9).

[2] The names of the first four 'rightly-guided' caliphs.

Atabeg Ṭughtakīn, lord of Damascus, and one of the mighty counts of the Franks.[3] It happened like this. There was a series of battles and raids between the army of Damascus and Baldwin, with victory now to the former and now to the latter. In the end Baldwin built a castle about two days' journey from Damascus. Ṭughtakīn was fearful of what would result from this and the harm that would ensue. He gathered his forces and marched out to fight them. Baldwin, king of Jerusalem, Acre and elsewhere, came to this count to support him and aid him against the Muslims. The count told him that he did not need him and that he was capable of facing the Muslims, if they attacked him, so Baldwin returned to Acre.

[400] Ṭughtakīn advanced towards the Franks and a fierce battle was joined. Two emirs of the army of Damascus fled and Ṭughtakīn pursued and killed them. The Franks retired to their castle and took refuge within it. Ṭughtakīn said, 'If anyone fights them well and makes a request from me, I shall meet it for him. To anyone who brings me a stone from the castle I shall give five dinars.' The foot-soldiers risked their lives and climbed up to the castle and brought it to ruin. They carried its stones to Ṭughtakīn, who fulfilled the promise he had made them. He ordered the stones to be thrown into the valley. Of the garrison he had taken he ordered all to be killed, but he spared the knights, who were two hundred in number, as captives. Of those who were in the fortress only a few escaped.

Ṭughtakīn returned victorious to Damascus and for four days the city was *en fête*. He then left for Rafaniyya, one of the fortresses of Syria, which the Franks had conquered. The ruler there was the nephew[4] of [Raymond of] St. Gilles, who himself was still besieging Tripoli. Ṭughtakīn began a siege and then took the fortress, killing 500 Franks there.

A battle between 'Ubāda and Khafāja

This year there was a fierce battle between the 'Ubāda and Khafāja. The reason was that a group of Khafāja had taken two camels from a man of 'Ubāda. He came to them and demanded their return but they gave him nothing. So on a raid he took eleven camels from them. Khafāja caught up with him **[401]** and killed one of his companions and cut off the hand of another. This happened at a site in the settlement of Sayf al-Dawla, whose inhabitants separated them.

'Ubāda heard the news and, having agreed a rendezvous, they went down to Iraq to take vengeance. They set out with several of their emirs and they were as many as 7,000 horse in all. Khafāja, who were inferior in numbers, made contact with them to offer blood-money and to make peace. This was not accepted by 'Ubāda. Sayf al-Dawla Ṣadaqa advised them to do so but they did not agree. They met in battle near Kufa. 'Ubāda had camels and sheep among their tents. Khafāja stationed 300 horsemen in ambush and skirmished without any serious

3 This was Hugh of Tiberias, who was killed at this time (Stevenson, *Crusaders*, 48).

4 William Jordan, count of Cerdagne.

engagement. They kept this up for three days but the fighting intensified and they came to close quarters, abandoning lances and exchanging sword blows. As this continued, although both sides were exhausted, Khafāja's fresh ambushers suddenly appeared. 'Ubāda fled and Khafāja were victorious. Twelve 'Ubāda chiefs were slain and several men of Khafāja. The latter seized booty, that is, horses, camels, sheep and slaves of both sexes.

Emir Ṣadaqa ibn Mazyad had secretly aided Khafāja. When the defeated came to him, he congratulated them on their escape but one of them said to him, 'I continued to fight and give blow for blow, eager to defeat them, until I saw your gray horse carrying one of them. I realised that they [**402**] had brought your horses and your men against us and that we could not deal with them. They were victorious over us with your help and subdued us with your weapons.' Ṣadaqa gave no reply.

How Ṣadaqa took Basra

In Jumādā I this year [January 1106] Sayf al-Dawla went down from al-Ḥilla to Basra and took control of it. We have mentioned previously that Isma'īl ibn Arslānjuq had taken Basra and its surroundings and remained in authority there for ten years,[5] with increasing power and influence because of the continuing dispute between the sultans. He seized sultanian properties and had contacted Ṣadaqa, claiming that he was his subject and obedient to him. Sultan Muḥammad planned, when his position had become firmly established, to send a fief holder to Basra to take it from Ismā'īl. Ṣadaqa proposed himself to effect this and so Basra was conferred upon him. The sultan deputed a civilian administrator to be in charge of what belonged to the sultan there. Isma'īl opposed him and did not allow him to function. His actions gave up any pretence of polite relations, so the sultan ordered Ṣadaqa to attack him and take Basra from him. Ṣadaqa made moves to that end.

However, it happened that Mankūbars rebelled, opposed the sultan and made to attack Wāsiṭ. Ismā'īl was delighted and his high-handedness increased. Ṣadaqa sent a chamberlain of his, who had previously served his father and grandfather, to Ismā'īl ordering him to give up the prefecture and its functions to Muhadhdhab al-Dawla ibn Abī'l-Jabr because it had been his responsibility. The latter came to the office of the prefect and took from it four hundred [**403**] dinars. Ismā'īl summoned him and put him in prison, taking back the money. Seeing this open opposition, Ṣadaqa left al-Ḥilla, declaring that he was going to Raḥba but then made all speed to Basra. He was in the vicinity before Ismā'īl was aware of it. The latter distributed his men throughout the forts that he had built at Maṭārā, Nahr Ma'qal and elsewhere, and he imprisoned the leading Abbasids and Alids, the cadi of Basra, the professor of the madrasah and the local notables.

---

[5] See above p. [**338**], s.a. 495, where he is called Ismā'īl ibn Salānjuq.

Ṣadaqa moved against Basra and a battle took place between a detachment of his army and a detachment of the Basrans in which was killed Abū'l-Najm ibn Abī'l-Qāsim al-Warrāmī, the nephew of Sayf al-Dawla Ṣadaqa. Someone wrote the following verses, a panegyric for Sayf al-Dawla and an elegy for Abū'l-Najm:

Rejoice, O best of those who protect the sacred sanctuary,
At a victory with which you have succoured worldly affairs as well as religion.
You rode to Basra the Noble with a select company
Of heroes like 'Alī's army on the day of Ṣiffīn.
Abū'l-Najm fell there like a bright star [*najm*],
But was a missile against the devils.[6]

Ṣadaqa remained besieging Ismā'īl at Basra but some of his men advised him to retire and told him that they would gain no advantage. He urged them to stay. They said, 'If he makes us retire, it will be a defeat.' Sayf al-Dawla was of the opinion that they should stay and he said, 'If we are unable to take Basra, no one will obey me and people will think that I am powerless.'

Then Ismā'īl sallied from the town and gave battle. Some of Ṣadaqa's men went to another part of the town and gained entrance. They killed a great number of the countryfolk whom Ismā'īl had gathered. Ismā'īl fled towards his castle on the Island[7] but he was overtaken by a follower of Ṣadaqa who was about to kill him when one of his mamlukes sacrificed himself to save his life. The fatal blow fell on him. Basra was sacked and the Bedouin of the surrounding country, who were with Ṣadaqa, and others looted everything in it. [**404**] Only the quarter that was neighbour to the tomb of Ṭalḥa and the Mirbad Market was spared. The resident Abbasids entered the Niẓāmiyya Madrasah, where they resisted strongly, and they protected the Mirbad. The disaster fell upon all the inhabitants of the town, apart from those mentioned. Ismā'īl took refuge in his castle.

It chanced that Muhadhdhab al-Dawla ibn Abī'l-Jabr came down river in many ships and took the fort belonging to Ismā'īl at Maṭārā. He killed a host of Ismā'īl's men there and took many to Ṣadaqa who set them free.

Hearing of this, Ismā'īl sent to Ṣadaqa asking for guarantees for himself, his family and his property. Ṣadaqa agreed and gave him seven days' grace. Ismā'īl took all he could of what he held precious, and what he could not transport he destroyed by throwing it into the water and by other means. He then presented himself to Ṣadaqa, who guaranteed the inhabitants of Basra against all harm and appointed a prefect over them. On 3 Jumādā II [10 February 1106] he returned to al-Ḥilla after having remained at Basra for sixteen days.

Now Ismā'īl, after Ṣadaqa had gone to al-Ḥilla, himself made for al-Bāsiyān[8]

---

6 A reference here to Koran, lxvii, 5: 'We have decked the lower heaven with lamps. We have placed them as missiles against the devils.'

7 In Arabic *al-jazīra*. It is not clear what is referred to. Perhaps in this context it means the 'island' between the final reaches of the Tigris and the Dujayl.

until his property arrived by ship. He then went to Fārs and began to fall out with his followers and his wife. He arrested several of his intimates, saying to them, 'You gave my son Afrāsiyāb poison that caused his death.' He had died in Ṣafar of this year [13 October–10 November 1105]. Many of them abandoned Ismā'īl. Even his wife abandoned him and travelled to Baghdad.

Ismā'īl was seized by a fever which quite overcame him. When he had reached Rāmhurmuz, he retired alone to his tent and did not appear to his men for a day and a night. They realised that he had died, so plundered his property and scattered. The emir in Rāmhurmuz sent after them, brought them back and recovered his property they had taken. He was buried near [**405**] Īdhāj, past fifty years of age. He had ruled well over the people of Basra in recent times.

How Riḍwān besieged Nisibis and then withdrew

In the month of Ramaḍān [7 May–5 June 1106] Prince Riḍwān ibn Tutush besieged Nisibis. This came about because he planned to wage war on the Franks. The following emirs assembled with him, Īlghāzī ibn Artuq, who was prefect of Baghdad, General Ṣabāwa and Alpī ibn Arslān Tāsh, lord of Sinjār and son-in-law of Jokermish, lord of Mosul. Īlghāzī proposed, 'Our best course is to attack the lands of Jokermish and those adjacent to take control there and increase our strength with their troops and resources.' Alpī agreed. He marched to Nisibis with 10,000 cavalry on the first day of Ramaḍān [7 May], having previously stationed there two emirs, men of his, with a troop of soldiers. They established a strong position in the town and engaged those within the walls. Alpī ibn Arslān Tāsh was hit by an arrow and badly wounded. He returned to Sinjār.

Jokermish heard that they had descended upon Nisibis, while he was at al-Ḥāmma, which is close to Ṭanza, taking a cure from an illness with its waters. He set out for Mosul, where the surrounding country folk had fled for refuge. He camped at the city gate, planning to go to war with Riḍwān. However, he employed guile and wrote to the leaders of Riḍwān's army, offering bribes which undermined their loyalty. He ordered his men in Nisibis to give their respects to Riḍwān and to send provisions out to him, while taking all precautions. He himself sent to Riḍwān offering his respects and acceptance of [**406**] his authority, saying 'Sultan Muḥammad besieged me and achieved nothing. He withdrew on terms. If you arrest Īlghāzī, of whose wickedness and evil you and others are well aware, then I shall be with you and shall aid you with my men, my money and my weapons.'

This happened when Riḍwān's attitude towards Īlghāzī had already changed

[8] The modern Qarye-ye Būzī, situated on the coast of Khūzistān, near the border with Fārs (see Le Strange, *Caliphate*, 242–3; Krawulsky, 347).

and become worse and worse, so that he had formed a plan to arrest him. He summoned him one day and said, 'This is a strong city. The Franks may perhaps take Aleppo. The politic course is to make peace with Jokermish and bring him into our company, for he will take the field with numerous, outstandingly equipped troops. Let us return to fight the Franks, for that is something that will again unite the Muslims.' Īlghāzī replied, 'You came under your own command but now you are under my command. I cannot permit you to leave without taking this town. Either you remain or I shall be the first to fight you.'

Īlghāzī had become very self-confident because of the large number of Turkomans who had flocked to him. Meanwhile, Riḍwān had plotted with some of his followers to arrest him. When the situation that we have mentioned arose, Riḍwān commanded them to seize him and put him in chains. Hearing how things were, the Turkomans declared their opposition and displeasure. They broke with Riḍwān and sought refuge within the walls of the town. Īlghāzī was taken up into its fortress and the troops in Nisibis came out and gave Riḍwān their help. When the Turkomans saw this they dispersed and plundered the cattle and whatever else they could. Straightaway Riḍwān departed and travelled to Aleppo.

Jokermish had left Mosul intending to fight these men. When he had gone as far as Tell Ya'far messengers brought him the good news that Riḍwān had withdrawn in dissension and disarray. At that, he set out for Sinjār and Riḍwān's envoys came to him, appealing for aid and claiming credit for his treatment of Īlghāzī. Jokermish agreed but only to deceive him and did not fulfil what he promised him. He descended on Sinjār to assuage his wrath against his son-in-law Alpī ibn Arslān Tāsh for his hostile intentions and his aid [**407**] for his enemies. Alpī was gravely ill because of the arrow that had hit him at Nisibis. When Jokermish camped before Sinjār, Alpī ordered his men to carry him to him. They bore him on a litter into his presence and he began to excuse himself for what he had done, saying 'I have come as a sinner. Do with me what you will.' Jokermish softened towards him and restored him to his lands but he expired after his return. After his death the men in Sinjār rebelled against Jokermish and seized the town. During the rest of Ramaḍān and then Shawwāl [June 1106] he fought them but without gaining any success. Tamīrak, the brother of Arslān Tāsh and uncle of Alpī, came and reached an agreement with Jokermish and offered him his allegiance. Jokermish returned to Mosul.

Account of Ṭughtakīn's conquest of Buṣrā

Under the year 497 [1103-4] we have mentioned the circumstances of Baktāsh ibn Tutush, his departure from Damascus and his joining the Franks, along with Aytakīn al-Ḥalabī, lord of Buṣrā, how they both went to Raḥba and then returned. When their situation became weak, Ṭughtakīn marched to Buṣrā and put it under siege, while it was held by men of Aytakīn. They made contact with Ṭughtakīn and offered to surrender to him after a delay which they fixed between them. He accepted this and retired to Damascus. When the fixed period elapsed during this year, he received the surrender of the place and treated the men there well and kept faith with the promises given them. He treated them with great respect and they were loud in his praises and blessings upon him. Their hearts inclined to him and they came to love him.

[**408**] Account of the Franks' taking of the fortress of Apamea

This year the Franks took the fortress of Apamea in Syria. This came about in the following way. Khalaf ibn Mulā'ib al-Kilābī had seized power in Homs and caused much harm. His men were waylaying travellers and many outlaws had joined him. So Tutush ibn Alp Arslān took Homs from him[9] and sent him far away. Vicissitudes of fortune led to his entering Egypt. He received no attention from anyone there and yet he stayed.

It happened that the governor on behalf of Prince Riḍwān in Apamea, sent to the ruler of Egypt, for he was inclined to their beliefs, asking them for someone to whom he could surrender the castle, a very strong fortress. Ibn Mulā'ib petitioned that he be the resident there, saying 'I am very eager to fight the Franks and I am dedicated to the Jihad.' They therefore gave it to him but took hostages from him. Once he had power there, he cast off his allegiance and did not observe what was due to them. They sent threats of what they would do to his son whom they held, but he replied, 'I shall not give up my place. Send me one of my son's limbs and I shall eat it!' They then despaired of his return to obedience, and so he remained in Apamea, terrifying travellers and disrupting traffic. Many evil-doers flocked to him and he became very wealthy.

Then the Franks captured Sarmīn, one of the dependencies of Aleppo, whose inhabitants were extreme Shiites. After the Frankish conquest the inhabitants were scattered. The cadi there went to Ibn Mulā'ib and dwelt with him, honoured, loved and trusted. However, the cadi worked a deceitful plan against him. He wrote [**409**] to Abū Ṭāhir, known as al-Ṣā'igh (the Goldsmith), a leading man of Prince Riḍwān, a chief Bāṭinī and one of their agents, and agreed a plan to assassinate Ibn Mulā'ib and hand Apamea to Riḍwān. Some of this became known. His sons came to Ibn Mulā'ib, for they had slipped out of Egypt, and said, 'We have heard such and such about this cadi. The best plan is for you to deal with him and watch out for yourself. The matter is public knowledge.' Ibn Mulā'ib summoned him and he came with a Koran copy in his sleeve because he saw the signs of trouble. Ibn Mulā'ib told him what had come to his ears, to which he replied, 'O Emir, everyone knows that I came to you fearful and hungry. You gave me security, enriched me

---

9 Tutush, Sultan Malikshāh's brother, took Homs from Khalaf in 485/1092-3 (Richards, *Annals*, 251-2).

and held me in esteem, so I became wealthy and influential. If some of those who envy me my position with you and your favour lavished on me have slandered me to you, then I beseech you to take all I have and I shall leave as I came.' He swore to be true and loyal, so Ibn Mulā'ib accepted his plea and gave him his protection.

The cadi renewed his correspondence with Abū Ṭāhir al-Ṣā'igh and advised him to agree with Riḍwān to send 300 men of Sarmīn. He should send with them some Frankish horses, some of their weapons and some Frankish heads, and they should go to Ibn Mulā'ib and pretend that they were warriors for the faith, who complained of their bad treatment from Ridwān and his men, which had led them to leave him, and that they had met with a detachment of Franks and defeated them and were now bringing all they had to Ibn Mulā'ib. Then when he allowed them to stay they would agree on a plan to outsmart him. Abū Ṭāhir did [**410**] this and the men arrived at Apamea and came to Ibn Mulā'ib with the horses and other things. He accepted them and ordered them to stay with him, lodging them in Apamea's suburb.

On a certain night when the guard had gone to sleep in the castle, the cadi and those men of Sarmīn in the fortress rose and let down ropes. All those recently come climbed up and sought out Ibn Mulā'ib's sons and also his cousins and his followers whom they killed. The cadi and some others went to Ibn Mulā'ib who was with his emirs. He heard them approach and said, 'Who are you?' 'The angel of death come to seize your soul,' was the reply. Ibn Mulā'ib pleaded with him in God's name but with no hesitation he gave him a fatal wound and also killed his companions. His two sons fled. One was killed but the other reached Abū'l-Ḥasan ibn Munqidh, the lord of Shayzar, who gave him protection because of a pact between them.

Hearing the news from Apamea, al-Ṣā'igh travelled there, not doubting that it was now his, but the cadi said to him, 'If you come to an agreement and remain with me, then you are right welcome and we shall be under your command, but otherwise return from where you have come.' Al-Ṣā'igh's hopes were dashed.

Now one of the sons of Ibn Mulā'ib, who had fallen out with his father, was in Damascus with Ṭughtakīn. Ṭughtakīn had put him in charge of a castle and he had undertaken to guard the highway. However, he failed to do so and took to brigandage, seizing the caravans. They appealed to Ṭughtakīn for help, who sent people to hunt him down. He therefore fled to the Franks and urged them to attack the fortress of Apamea. He said, 'It has only provisions for a month.' The Franks besieged it and when the inhabitants faced starvation it fell to them.[10] They slew the cadi who acted the despot there and also took and put to death al-Ṣā'igh, who was the person who brought the beliefs of the Bāṭinīs to the fore in Syria.

This is what a source has related, namely that Abū Ṭāhir al-Ṣā'igh was killed by

---

[10] After Apamea fell in August 1106 Tancred gave land in the area to the sons [sic] of Khalaf ibn Mulā'ib (Asbridge, *Principality of Antioch*, 60).

the Franks at Apamea. However, it has been said that Ibn Badī', the headman of Aleppo, killed him in the year 507 [1113–14] after the death of Riḍwān and we have mentioned that there.[11] God knows best!

[411] How the Bedouin sacked Basra

We have mentioned that the Emir Ṣadaqa gained control of Basra and appointed as his deputy there a mamluke who had belonged to his grandfather Dubays ibn Mazyad, named Altūntāsh, and stationed 120 cavalry with him. The Rabī'a and al-Muntafiq Bedouin and other Arabs allied to them gathered together and attacked Basra in large numbers. Altūntāsh resisted but was taken prisoner and his men fled. The garrison was unable to hold the town. The Bedouin entered by force of arms towards the end of Dhū'l-Ḥijja [ended 1 September 1106] and pillaged whatever they could. They continued to sack and burn for thirty-two days. The population fled as refugees into the country. An endowed library, which had been established by Cadi Abū'l-Faraj ibn Abī'l-Baqā', was ransacked.

The news came to Ṣadaqa and he despatched a force which arrived when the Bedouin had already left. Sultan Muḥammad then sent a prefect and a civilian administrator to Basra and took it away from Ṣadaqa. The population returned and commenced its reconstruction.

The state of Syrian Tripoli in relation to the Franks

[Raymond of] St. Gilles the Frank (God curse him) took Jabala and continued with his siege of Tripoli. Seeing that he was unable to capture the place, he built a fortress[12] in the vicinity and built a settlement below it. [**412**] He kept a watchful eye on the town and awaited the arrival of an opportunity to attack.

Fakhr al-Mulk Abū 'Alī ibn 'Ammār, lord of Tripoli, sallied forth and burned his settlement. [Raymond] stood on one of the burning roofs, with several of his counts and knights, and it collapsed under him. Because of this [Raymond] was ill for ten days and then he died. He was carried to Jerusalem and buried there.

The Byzantine emperor ordered his men in Lattakia to transport provisions to the Franks at Tripoli. They were taken by sea. Fakhr al-Mulk ibn 'Ammār sent a fleet to sea to intercept. A fierce battle ensued between the Muslims and the Byzantines in which the Muslims boarded and captured a ship. They took the crew prisoner and returned.

For five years until this present time the conflict continued between the people

---

[11] See below p. [**499**].

[12] The castle known as Mount Pilgrim, which Count Raymond had completed by the spring of 1104 (Runciman, ii, 60).

of Tripoli and the Franks. Provisions became short and the population feared for their lives, their children and their womenfolk. The poor left and the rich were impoverished. Ibn 'Ammār showed great endurance, courage and sound policy.

One of the things that damaged the Muslims was that the ruler of Tripoli sought the aid of Suqmān ibn Artuq, who assembled his forces and set out but died on the way, as we have related. If God wills a course he provides for it to happen!

Ibn 'Ammār supplied payments for the troops and the indigent. When his money dwindled, he began to levy from people what he would expend under the heading of Jihad. From two rich men he took money and from others too. The two went out to the Franks and said, 'Our lord has extorted money from us. We have come out to join you.' They mentioned to the Franks that provisions were coming from 'Arqa and the Mountain, so the Franks posted a body of men on that side to stop anything entering the town. Ibn 'Ammār sent to offer the Franks a lot of money to surrender the two men. They refused, but Ibn 'Ammār arranged for people to assassinate them.

[**413**] Tripoli was one of the greatest cities of Islam and one of the most handsome and rich. The inhabitants sold an unaccountable amount of jewellery and rare vessels. Silver bullion was sold at every hundred dirhams for a dinar. What a great difference between this situation and the state of the Byzantines in the days of Sultan Alp Arslān! We have related how he defeated them in the year 463 [1071].[13] One of his men, namely Kumushtakīn, the secretary of 'Amīd al-Mulk, had fled from him in fear when his master 'Amīd al-Mulk was arrested. He went to Raqqa, took it and was joined by many Turkomans, including al-Afshīn and Aḥmad Shāh. They, however, killed him and sent his money to Alp Arslān. Al-Afshīn entered Byzantine territory and fought against Philaretos,[14] lord of Antioch, whom he defeated, killing a large host of Byzantines. The Byzantine emperor marched from Constantinople to Malaṭya. Al-Afshīn entered his lands and reached as far as Amorium. On this raid he killed 100,000 souls. After he had returned to Islamic lands and those with him had dispersed, he was attacked by the troops of Edessa, which was then in Byzantine hands, and also by the Bedouin of the Banū Numayr. With two hundred cavalry he met and defeated them, plundering them and the Byzantine lands. The emperor sent an envoy to al-Qā'im bi-Amr Allāh asking for peace. The latter sent to Alp Arslān concerning this and peace was made with the Byzantines for 100,000 dinars, 4,000 garments of different sorts and 300 head of mule. What a difference between these two situations!

What a difference, I say, between the situation of these wretched men whom I dismiss as incapable and the situation of people in this age of ours, that is the year 616 [1219-20], faced again by the Franks and by the Tatars. You will see this fully explained, God willing, so that you can understand the difference. We beseech God Almighty [**414**] to provide for Islam and the Muslims someone who will

---

[13] For his account of the defeat of Romanus IV Diogenes, see Richards, *Annals*, 170-72.

[14] In the text al-Firdaws.

undertake to bring them victory and to defend them with those of His creatures whom He loves. 'That is not difficult for God.'[15]

Miscellaneous events

During this year there came to Baghdad one of the Veiled Ones, the princes of the Maghrib, with the intention of visiting the Caliphal Palace. He was received with honour. With him was a man called the Lawyer, also one of the Veiled Ones. The Lawyer gave a sermon in the palace mosque to a great crowd that assembled. He preached while veiled, so that only his eyes could be seen. This Veiled One had been present with the son of al-Afḍal Emīr al-Juyūsh in Egypt, at his battle with the Franks, when he showed great valour.

The reason for his coming to Baghdad was that the people of the Maghrib held bad beliefs about the Alids, the rulers of Egypt. Whenever they wished to go on pilgrimage they avoided Egypt. Emīr al-Juyūsh Badr, the father of al-Afḍal, wished to establish good relations with them but they showed no inclination for that nor any desire for rapprochement. Badr ordered those who were taken to be killed. When his son al-Afḍal came to power, he treated them well and sought the aid of those who accepted his overtures to fight the Franks. This man was one of those who fought alongside him. After his association with the Egyptians he feared to return to his own country, so came to Baghdad. Then later he returned to Damascus. The Egyptians had not a single battle with the Franks that he did not participate in. In one of them he met a martyr's death. He was brave, a deadly and bold fighter.

In Rabīʿ II [11 December 1105–8 January 1106] a tailed comet appeared in the sky, like the rainbow, [**415**] tracking from the west towards the middle of the sky. It could be seen close to the sun before its night-time appearance. It continued to appear for several nights and then it disappeared.

This year the Prince Qilij Arslān ibn Sulaymān ibn Qutlumish, the ruler of Anatolia, came to Edessa to besiege it. The Franks held it. The followers of Jokermish stationed in Ḥarrān contacted him to surrender to him. He went there and took over the town. The inhabitants were delighted with his coming for the sake of the Jihad against the Franks. He remained in Ḥarrān for some days but then fell seriously ill which necessitated his return to Malaṭya. He went back in his ill state while his men stayed in Ḥarrān.

The following died this year:

The Shaykh Abū Manṣūr al-Khayyāṭ al-Muqrī, the imam of the Mosque of Ibn Jurda. He was charitable and pious.

The Cadi Abū al-ʿAlāʾ Ṣāʿid ibn Abī Muḥammad al-Nīsābūrī al-Ḥanafī, killed in the mosque of Isfahan by a Bāṭinī assassin.

---

[15] Koran, xiv, 20.

At the age of fifty Abū'l-Fawāris al-Ḥusayn ibn 'Alī ibn al-Ḥusayn ibn al-Khāzin, the possessor of an excellent hand, who is said to have written five hundred copies of the Koran.[16]

In Muḥarram [13 September-13 October 1105] the Cadi Abū'l-Faraj 'Ubayd Allāh ibn al-Ḥasan, the cadi of Basra, aged eighty-three years. He was one of the renowned Shāfi'ī lawyers who studied under al-Māwardī and Abū Isḥāq. He learnt grammar with al-Raqqī, al-Dahhān and Ibn Burhān. He was virtuous and esteemed by caliphs and sultans.

Also in Muḥarram [13 September-13 October 1105] Sahl ibn Aḥmad ibn 'Alī al-Arghayānī, Abū'l-Fatḥ the Judge. He studied law under al-Juwaynī and excelled. He later gave up legal disputation and built a hospice (*ribāṭ*), where he concerned himself [**416**] with worship and recitation of the Koran.

In Ṣafar [14 October-10 November 1105] the Emir Muhārish ibn Mujallī, about eighty years old. He is the person with whom the Caliph al-Qā'im stayed at Ḥadītha.[17] He prayed and fasted much and loved goodness and those that did good. When he died, his son Sulaymān succeeded him as ruler of Ḥadītha.

---

16 This person (with a variation is his name) is also listed under the year 502, see below p. [**474**].

17 This was while the Emir Basāsīrī held Baghdad in 450-51/1058-9 before Ṭughril Beg reinstated the caliph. See Richards, *Annals*, 123, 125-6.

[**417**]

The Year 500 [1106-1107]

The death of Yūsuf ibn Tāshfīn and the succession of his son 'Alī

The ruler of the Maghrib and Andalusia, the Commander of the Muslims Yūsuf ibn Tāshfīn died this year. He was a good ruler, charitable and just, who favoured the men of religion and religious learning, honoured them and followed their ideas. When he conquered Andalusia, as we have related, he assembled the lawyers and treated them very well. They said to him, 'It is proper that your authority should come from the caliph to make obedience to you incumbent on all and sundry.' So he sent an envoy to the Caliph al-Mustaẓhir bi-Allāh, the Commander of the Faithful, with a large gift and sent a letter, in which he mentioned the Frankish territories that God had conquered [at his hands] and his efforts to bring victory to Islam, and also requested investiture with rule over his lands. A diploma granting him what he wished was issued from the caliphal chancery and he was given the title 'Commander of the Muslims'. Robes of honour were also sent to him and he was greatly delighted with this.

He it was who built the city of Marrakech for the Almoravids and remained ruler until the year 500 [1106-7]. After his death his son 'Alī ibn Yūsuf succeeded him and also took the title 'Commander of the Muslims'. Even more did he honour the ulema and pay attention to their advice. Whenever one of them preached, he humbly listened to the sermon and it would soften his heart, as was quite plain to see.

Yūsuf ibn Tāshfīn was forbearing, generous, pious and charitable. He loved the men of religion and religious learning and gave them authority in his lands. He loved to show mercy and forgive great offences. Here is an illustration of this. Three men met together. One of them desired a thousand dinars as trading capital. The wish [**418**] of the second man was for a post in which he could serve the Commander of the Muslims. The third man desired the latter's wife, the woman from al-Nafzāwa.[1] She was one of the most beautiful of women and held authority in his lands. Yūsuf heard this story and summoned them. He gave the one who wanted capital a thousand dinars, he employed the second and said to the one who desired his wife, 'O foolish one, what induced you to seek what you will never attain?' He then sent him to her and she left him in a tent for three days, every day having the same food brought to him. She then summoned him and said, 'What have you eaten during these days?' He answered, 'Just the one sort.' She then said, 'All women are just the same too,' ordered money and clothes for him and sent him away.

---

[1] i.e. al-Nafzāwiyya. Her personal name was Zaynab.

The killing of Fakhr al-Mulk ibn Niẓām al-Mulk

On the day of ʿĀshūrāʾ this year [11 September 1106] Fakhr al-Mulk Abūʾl-Muẓaffar ʿAlī ibn Niẓām al-Mulk was killed, the oldest of Niẓām al-Mulk's sons. Under the year 488 [1095-6] we have mentioned how he became vizier for Sultan Barkyāruq. When he gave up being his vizier he went to Nishapur and remained with Prince Sanjar ibn Malikshāh, as *his* vizier. On the day of ʿĀshūrāʾ he awoke and before breaking his fast he said to his followers, 'During the night I saw al-Ḥusayn ibn ʿAlī (on him be peace) in my dream, saying to me, "Hasten to us and let the breaking of your fast be with us." My thoughts have been busy with this, but there is no avoiding God's decision and what He decrees.' They said to him, 'God protect you! The best course is not to leave your residence today or tonight.' He passed that day praying and reciting the Koran and he gave a great amount in alms.

[419] When the time for evening prayer came, he left the palace he was in to go to the women's residence. He heard the cries of a petitioner, extremely agonized, who was saying, 'The Muslims have all departed. There is no-one left to investigate a grievance or take the hand of a troubled man.' Fakhr al-Mulk called him over, out of pity for him, and said, 'What is your situation?' The man handed him a petition and while Fakhr al-Mulk was perusing it, he stabbed him with a dagger and killed him. The Bāṭinī was taken to Sanjar, who put him to torture. He made a false confession, implicating several of the sultan's men. He said, 'They incited me to kill him,' wishing to kill both by his own hand and by his calumny. Those whom he named were put to death, though falsely accused. After them the Bāṭinī was executed. Fakhr al-Mulk was sixty-six years old.

How Ṣadaqa ibn Mazyad took Takrit

In Ṣafar of this year [October 1106] the Emir Sayf al-Dawla Ṣadaqa ibn Manṣūr ibn Mazyad took over the fortress of Takrit. We have mentioned previously that it belonged to the Banū Maqin of the ʿUqaylids. Until the end of the year 427 [autumn 1036] it was in the hands of Rāfiʿ ibn al-Ḥusayn ibn Maqin. He died and rule there passed to his nephew Abū Manʿa Khamīs ibn Taghlib ibn Ḥammād, who found there 500,000 dinars apart from gold and silver items. He died in the year 435 [1043-4] and was succeeded by his son Abū Ghashshām.

In the year 444 [1052-3] he was seized and imprisoned by ʿĪsā who took control of the fortress and its treasures. When Ṭughril Beg passed by in the year 448 [1056-7] ʿĪsā came to terms with him on payment of some money and so Ṭughril Beg moved on.

[420] After ʿĪsā's death, his wife Amīra feared that Abū Ghashshām would return and take power in the fortress, so she killed him, after he had been kept in prison for four years. She appointed as her deputy in the fortress Abūʾl-Ghanāʾim ibn al-Muḥallabān but he surrendered it to the followers of Sultan Ṭughril Beg. She went to Mosul where the son of Abū Ghashshām slew her in revenge for his father and Sharaf al-Dawla ibn Quraysh appropriated her wealth. Ṭughril Beg handed control of the fortress to a man called Abū'l-'Abbās al-Rāzī but he died there after six months. It was then taken by the *Mihrbāṭ*,[2] that is, Abū Ja'far Muḥammad ibn Aḥmad ibn Khushnām from the town of al-Thughr. He remained for twenty-one years and after his death was succeeded by his son for two years until Terken Khātūn took it from him. Goharā'īn ruled there on her behalf.

After the death of Malikshāh, Qasīm al-Dawla Āqsunqur, the lord of Aleppo, was in charge there. When he was killed, it passed to Emir Kumushtakīn al-Jāndār, who placed there a man called Abū'l-Maṣāri'. Then it reverted to Goharā'īn as a fief until Majd al-Mulk al-Balāsānī took it from him and it came under the authority of Kayqubād ibn Hazārasb al-Daylamī, who remained there for twelve years. He tyrannised the population and ruled badly. When Suqmān ibn Artuq passed by in 496 [1102-3] and plundered the town, Kayqubād was plundering the place by night and Suqmān by day!

When Sultan Muḥammad became established after the death of his brother Barkyāruq, he gave it as a fief to Emir Āqsunqur al-Bursuqī, the prefect of Baghdad. He went and besieged it for a period longer than seven months until the situation became difficult for Kayqubād. The latter made contact with Ṣadaqa ibn Mazyad to surrender the town to him. Ṣadaqa made his way there in Ṣafar of this year [October 1106] and took it over. Al-Bursuqī came south but was unable to take it.

Eight days after leaving the citadel Kayqubād died, aged sixty. Ṣadaqa appointed as his deputy there Warrām ibn Abī Firās ibn Warrām. Kayqubād was said to be associated with the Bāṭinīs. His death was fortunate for Ṣadaqa, for, had Kayqubād remained in his service, Ṣadaqa would have been exposed to people's suspicions about his beliefs and his religious orientation.

[421] Account of hostilites between 'Ubāda and Khafāja

In Rabī' I this year [November 1106] there was a battle between 'Ubāda and Khafāja, in which the former were victorious and took their revenge on the Khafāja.

This came about because Sayf al-Dawla Ṣadaqa sent his son Badrān with an army to the edge of his lands near the Marsh to protect them from the Khafāja because they were causing trouble to the inhabitants of those regions. The Khafāja

[2] The text has *al-m.h.r.bāṭ* and Bundārī, 72, *al-m.h.r.yāṭ*, apparently a title but unidentified. It is unlikely to be a corruption of the old (fourth- and fifth-century) title *mardpet*, not attested as late as this. See Garsoïan, *Epic Histories*, 542–3. Could it just be a corruption of *vardapet*?

drew near to him and threatened the inhabitants, so he wrote to his father complaining about them and informing him of their doings. Ṣadaqa summoned the 'Ubāda, to whom the Khafāja had done in the past year what we have already related.[3] When they came, he told them to prepare themselves for a campaign with his troops to revenge themselves on the Khafāja. They marched in the vanguard of his army and came upon an encampment of the Khafāja, the Banū Kulayb, taking them by surprise at night before they were aware. They said, 'Who are you?' "Ubāda,' they replied, 'We have scores to settle.' Having realised that they were 'Ubāda, in the fight that followed, the Khafāja held firm. Then, while the battle was proceeding, the drums of the army were heard and they broke. The 'Ubāda killed several of them, including ten of their chiefs, and they abandoned their womenfolk. Ṣadaqa ordered that they be guarded and protected and he also ordered that the 'Ubāda be given a preferential share of the booty taken from the Khafāja to recompense them for what had been taken from them in the past year.

The Khafāja suffered greatly in leaving their lands, having their flocks plundered and losing their men. They withdrew to the region of Basra while the 'Ubāda took up residence in the Khafāja's lands.

After the defeat of the Khafāja, their dispersal and the plunder of their flocks, one of their women came to Emir **[422]** Ṣadaqa and said to him, 'You have enslaved us, stripped us of our power, banished us and deprived us of respect. May God requite you in your person! May He make your family a replica of ours.' Ṣadaqa suppressed his anger and put up with her words; indeed, he gave her forty camels. Only a little time passed before God requited Ṣadaqa in his own person and in his children. The entreaties of the aggrieved are highly regarded by God.

How Jāwulī Saqāo went towards Mosul and took its ruler Jokermish captive

This year in Muḥarram [September 1106] Sultan Muḥammad gave Mosul and its districts, which were held by Jokermish, to Jāwulī Saqāo as a fief. Previously Jāwulī had governed the lands between Khūzistān and Fars, where he remained for two years and repaired and fortified their castles. He ruled the people wickedly, cutting off hands and noses and blinding eyes.

After Muḥammad became well established in the sultanate, Jāwulī was fearful of him. The sultan sent Emir Mawdūd ibn Altūntakīn to him but Jāwulī resisted him behind his walls. Mawdūd besieged him for eight months and then Jāwulī sent to the sultan, saying, 'I will not submit myself to Mawdūd but if you send someone else I shall give up.' The sultan sent him his ring by the Marshal of Horse, so Jāwulī submitted and came to pay his respects at Isfahan. He met with all that he could wish for and was ordered by the sultan to march against the Franks to take

---

[3] See above pp. [**400–402**].

their territory from them and was given Mosul, Diyār Bakr and all of the Jazīra as his fief.

When Jokermish had returned from the sultan's presence to his lands, as we have recounted, he promised personal service and payment of tribute. However, once firmly settled in his lands, he did not carry out what he had said and found service and payment of tribute burdensome. The sultan therefore assigned his lands to Jāwulī, who came to Baghdad, remained there until [**423**] the beginning of Rabī' I [31 October 1106], and then marched against Mosul. He took a route by al-Bawāzīj, which he captured and sacked for four days, after he had given guarantees to the populace and promised that he would protect them. After taking it he moved on to Irbil.

As for Jokermish, when he heard of his coming, he sent out orders for his troops to muster. He received a letter from Abū'l-Hayjā' ibn Mūsak, the Hadhbānī Kurd, lord of Irbil, telling of Jāwulī's conquest of al-Bawāzīj and saying, 'If you do not hasten your coming so that we may unite and resist him, I shall be forced to come to terms with him and join him.' Jokermish therefore made all haste, crossed to the east of the Tigris and marched with the army of Mosul before all his troops had gathered. Abū'l-Hayjā' sent him his army with his sons. They met at the village of Bākalbā in the district of Irbil.

Jāwulī encountered them with 1,000 horse. Jokermish was at the head of 2,000, not doubting that he would lay hands on Jāwulī. After the battle lines had been drawn, Jāwulī charged from the centre against Jokermish's centre. The latter's men fled and he was left alone, incapable of flight because of the hemiplegia he suffered from. Unable to ride, he was carried in a litter. After the flight of his men a black groom defended him stoutly but was slain. One of the sons of Prince Qāvurt Beg ibn Dā'ūd, named Aḥmad, fought alongside him to protect him. He received a spear wound and fled to die later in Mosul. Jāwulī's men were unable to get to Jokermish until the black groom was killed. Then they took him prisoner and brought him before Jāwulī, who ordered him to be watched and guarded.

Jokermish's troops, whom he had summoned, arrived at Mosul two days after he had left. They set out in flying columns to be in time for the battle but they were met by their defeated comrades – 'in order that God might complete a plan which was for Him already achieved!'[4]

[424] Account of Jāwulī Saqāo's siege of Mosul and the death of Jokermish

After his troops were defeated and Jokermish taken prisoner, the news reached Mosul and they put Zankī ibn Jokermish, a boy of eleven years of age, in the seat of authority and made the khutbah in his name. They summoned the notables of the city and asked for their help, which they agreed to give.

---

[4] Koran, viii, 42, 44.

The governor of the citadel was a mamluke of Jokermish, called Qizoghlu, who exercised his office in exemplary fashion. He distributed to the troops the money that Jokermish had amassed and the horses and other items. He wrote to Sayf al-Dawla Ṣadaqa, Qilij Arslān and al-Bursuqī, the prefect of Baghdad, to urge them to make haste and defend them against Jāwulī. They promised each one that they would hand the city over to him. Ṣadaqa made no response and decided to stay loyal to the sultan. As for al-Bursuqī and Qilij Arslān, we shall relate what they did later.

Jāwulī then put Mosul under siege, accompanied by Karbāwī[5] ibn Khurāsān the Turkoman and other emirs. His force was large. He gave orders that Jokermish should be brought every day on a mule and that he should call upon his men in Mosul to surrender the city and so free their lord from his present state. He so ordered them but they were not listening to him. He was being held in a pit and men were assigned to guard him to avoid his being snatched away. One day he was brought out dead. His age was about sixty. His career had risen high and his status had been very great. He had built up and strengthened the walls of Mosul, and had constructed a barbican and dug a moat, fortifying the city as much as he possibly could.

With Jokermish was a man, one of the notables of Mosul, called Abū Ṭālib ibn **[425]** Kasīrāt. The Banū Kasīrāt are until this present day amongst the notables of the inhabitants of Mosul. Abū Ṭālib had achieved great advancement in the eyes of Jokermish, his standing was very high and he had taken control of his affairs. He was present with him at the battle and, when Jokermish was taken prisoner, Abū Ṭālib fled to Irbil. The sons of Abū'l-Hayjā', the lord of Irbil, were also present at the battle with Jokermish and Jāwulī took them prisoner. Jāwulī sent to Abū'l-Hayjā', demanding [Abū Ṭālib] ibn Kasīrāt, who was released and sent to him. Whereupon Jāwulī released Abū'l-Hayjā''s son. When Ibn Kasīrāt came before Jāwulī, he guaranteed him the conquest of Mosul and Jokermish's lands and the acquisition of money. Jāwulī imprisoned him but not harshly.

The cadi of Mosul, Abū'l-Qāsim ibn Wad'ān was an enemy of Abū Ṭalib's. He sent to Jāwulī, saying, 'If you kill Abū Ṭālib, I shall surrender Mosul to you,' so he killed him and sent his head to Abū'l-Qāsim, who showed great delight at his fall and appropriated much of his wealth and deposits. The Turks rose against him, angry at the fate of Abū Ṭālib and the appropriation of all Abū Ṭālib's wealth that was taken, and slew him. One month separated their deaths. We have often seen and heard innumerable times how, for two enemies, the death of one is soon followed by the death of the other.

---

[5] Here and in *Kāmil*, x, 443, the text has: Karmāwī. However, Karbāwī is the reading at x, 539, 540 and 608, and also in al-Nuwayrī, xxvii, 11 (based on the *Kāmil*).

The battle between the emperor of Constantinople and the Franks

During this year there arose a deep antagonism between the emperor of the Byzantines, the ruler of Constantinople, and Bohemond the Frank.[6] Bohemond invaded and plundered the territory of the emperor and aimed to bring him to battle. The emperor sent to Prince Qilij Arslān ibn Sulaymān, the ruler of Konya, Aqṣarāy and other lands, asking for his aid. He provided a detachment of his army. This strengthened the emperor, who marched against Bohemond. They met, formed their battle lines and fought. The Franks held firm, relying on their bravery, while the Byzantines and their allies held firm through their numbers. The battle lasted long and in the event it resulted in the defeat **[426]** of the Franks. The majority were killed and many were captured. Those who survived returned to their lands in Syria. Qilij Arslān's troops also set out for home, intending to join their ruler in the Jazīra. However, news reached them that he had died, as we shall relate, God willing, so they abandoned their move and stayed on.

Account of Qilij Arslān's capture of Mosul

We have previously told that Jokermish's men wrote to Emir Ṣadaqa, Qasīm al-Dawla al-Bursuqī and Prince Qilij Arslān ibn Sulaymān ibn Qutlumish al-Saljūqī, the ruler of Anatolia, summoning each one with the promise to surrender the city to him. Ṣadaqa refused and decided to stay loyal to the sultan. Qilij Arslān, however, marched with his troops and when Jāwulī Saqāo heard that he had arrived at Nisibis, he withdrew from Mosul. As for al-Bursuqī, who was prefect of Baghdad, he went from there to Mosul, arriving after the departure of Jāwulī. He camped on the east bank but nobody paid any attention to him nor sent him a single word. He therefore went back to Baghdad during the remainder of that same day.

After he had come to Nisibis, Qilij Arslān waited there until his force was large. Hearing that he was near, Jāwulī left Mosul for Sinjār and deposited his baggage there. He was joined by Emir Īlghāzī ibn Artuq and a detachment of Jokermish's troops, so that he came to have 4,000 cavalry. Then a letter from Prince Riḍwān arrived, inviting him to Syria and telling him that the Franks in Syria were too weak to resist them. Jāwulī then set out for al-Raḥba.

The people of Mosul and Jokermish's men sent to Qilij Arslān, when he was at Nisibis, **[427]** and asked him to take certain oaths, which he did. He then made them swear to be obedient and loyal and set out with them for Mosul, which he took over on 25 Rajab [22 March 1107] and resided in al-Mu'riqa. Jokermish's son and his men came out to meet him and were given robes of honour. Qilij Arslān

[6] In 1105 Behemond returned to Europe and during 1107-8 led an attack on Byzantine territory, particularly Durazzo (Asbridge, *Principality of Antioch*, 64, Stevenson, *Crusaders*, 79-80.

took his seat on the throne and dropped Sultan Muḥammad's name from the khutbah and added his own after the caliph's. He was generous to the troops but took the citadel from Qizoghlu, Jokermish's mamluke, and placed a castellan of his own there. He abolished the duties that had been wickedly introduced and acted with justice and conciliation towards the populace. He proclaimed, 'Whoever informs on anyone I shall put to death,' so there were no false accusations made against anyone. He confirmed Abū Muḥammad 'Abd Allāh ibn al-Qāsim ibn al-Shahrazūrī in the office of cadi for Mosul and appointed as headman Abū'l-Barakāt Muḥammad ibn Muḥammad ibn Khamīs, who was the father of our teacher, Abū'l-Rabī' Sulaymān. In Qilij Arslān's retinue were Emir Ibrāhīm ibn Yināl al-Turkomānī, lord of Āmid, and Muḥammad ibn Jabaq al-Turkomānī, lord of Castle Ziyād,[7] that is to say, Khartbirt. The reason why Ibrāhīm ibn Yināl held the city of Āmid was that Tāj al-Dawla Tutush gave it to him, when he ruled Diyār Bakr, and it remained in his hands. As for Muḥammad ibn Jabaq, how it came about that he held Castle Ziyād was that this castle had been in the hands of Philateros, the dragoman of the Byzantine emperor, whose lands also comprised Edessa and Antioch. When Sulaymān ibn Qutlumish, the father of this present Qilij Arslān, took Antioch and also when Fakhr al-Dawla ibn Jahīr took Diyār Bakr, Philateros became too weak to supply the necessary provisions and support for Castle Ziyād, so Jabaq took it. Philateros became a Muslim at the hands of Sultan Malikshāh and was made emir of Edessa, where he continued until his death, after which Emir Buzān took it. [**428**] Near Castle Ziyād was another fort in the hands of a Greek whose name was Ifranjī. He preyed on travellers and killed many Muslims. Jabaq sent him a gift and solicited his friendship, suggesting that each should help the other. He agreed to this. Jabaq would help Ifranjī in his brigandage and other matters and likewise Ifranjī would help Jabaq. When their mutual trust was established, Jabaq sent to him, saying, 'I plan to attack certain places,' and asked him to send him his men. This he did, but when they had journeyed on the road with him, he ordered them to be bound and carried them to Ifranjī's castle. He said to their families, 'By God, if you do not surrender Ifranjī to me, I shall cut their heads off and take the castle by force and I shall kill you all for one life.' They therefore opened the castle and gave up Ifranjī. Jabaq flayed him alive and seized his money and his armoury, which was considerable. After Jabaq died, his son Muḥammad succeeded him.

How Qilij Arslān was killed and Jāwulī took Mosul

We have related that when Qilij Arslān came to Nisibis, Jāwulī left Mosul for Sinjār and then for al-Raḥba, where he arrived in Rajab [March 1107]. He besieged it until 24 Ramaḍān [19 May 1107]. The ruler there at that time was

[7] An alternative name for Khartbirt, see Krawulsky, 400.

known as Muḥammad ibn al-Sabbāq, one of the Banū Shaybān, whom Prince Duqāq had installed there when he conquered it. Duqāq took his son as a hostage and carried him to Damascus. When Duqāq died, this Shaybānī tribesman sent some people who snatched his son and brought him back. As soon as he had arrived he threw off his allegiance to Damascus and at a certain time made the khutbah in the name of Qilij Arslān. When Jāwulī came to al-Raḥba and put it under siege, he sent to Prince Riḍwān informing him that he was an ally of his and ready to help him against any who made war on him, and undertaking, if [**429**] he took over the town, that he would march with him to sweep the Franks out of his lands. When terms had been agreed between them, Ridwān came to him and the siege of the inhabitants was intensified and their situation became very difficult for them.

A group who were in one of the towers agreed to send to Jāwulī and asked him to swear to protect them and keep them safe. They told him to attack the tower they were in when the night was half over. This he did and those in the tower lifted up his men by ropes. They blew their trumpets and beat their drums, at which the garrison of the town gave up. Jāwulī's men made their entry on 24 Ramaḍān [19 May 1107] and sacked the town until midday. Then Jāwulī ordered the pillage to stop. Muḥammad al-Shaybānī, the lord of the town, submitted to his rule and joined with him.

When Qilij Arslān had secured Mosul, he departed to make war on Jāwulī Saqāo. He left his son Malikshāh, who was eleven years of age, in the government house with an emir to guide his affairs and a detachment of the army, consisting of 4,000 cavalry with full equipment and excellent mounts.

When his army heard of the strength of Jāwulī, dissension appeared. The first to disobey was Ibrāhīm ibn Yināl, the lord of Āmid. He abandoned his tents and baggage and returned from al-Khābūr to his own territory. Others did the same. When he heard of Jāwulī's strength and the great number of his forces, Qilij Arslān played a waiting game and sent to his own lands calling for his troops because they were with the Byzantine emperor aiding him to fight the Franks, as we have related.[8] When he arrived at al-Khābūr, his force amounted to 5,000. With Jāwulī were 4,000, including Prince Riḍwān and some of his troops, although his picked men were in the majority. Jāwulī took advantage of the fact that Qilij Arslān's army was not large and brought him to battle before [the rest of] his troops reached him. They met on 20 Dhū'l-Qa'da [13 July 1107]. Qilij Arslān charged [**430**] in person and became closely engaged. He severed the standard-bearer's hand and himself reached Jāwulī, to whom he gave a sword-blow which cut his brigandine but without penetrating to his body. Then Jāwulī's men charged and put their enemies to flight, pillaging the baggage and slaughtering the camp-followers. When Qilij Arslān saw that his army was defeated, he understood that, if he were taken, he would be treated as an implacable enemy, especially as he had challenged

[8] See above pp. [**425–6**].

the sultan in his lands and for the title of sultan. He therefore urged his mount into the River Khābūr and shot some arrows to defend himself from Jāwulī's men. His horse carried him downstream to deep water where he drowned. After a few days his body appeared and was buried in al-Shamsāniyya,[9] a village of al-Khābūr.

Jāwulī proceeded to Mosul and on his arrival the populace opened the gates to him. Qilij Arslān's men who were there were unable to prevent them. Jāwulī camped outside the city and took every one of Jokermish's men who had been present at the battle with Qilij Arslān to a secure place.[10] After taking Mosul he restored the khutbah to Sultan Muḥammad and extorted money from several of Jokermish's followers who were there. He then went to Jazīrat Ibn 'Umar, where was Ḥabashī ibn Jokermish with one of his father's mamlukes called Qizoghlu. After a period of siege they made peace with him and contributed 6,000 dinars in addition to mounts and clothing. Jāwulī then left for Mosul and sent Malikshāh, Qilij Arslān's son, to Sultan Muḥammad.

The position of the Baṭinīs at Isfahan and the killing of Ibn 'Aṭṭāsh

This year Sultan Muḥammad conquered the castle which the Bāṭinīs had taken close to Isfahan, called Shāh Diz, and killed its ruler Aḥmad ibn 'Abd al-Malik ibn 'Aṭṭāsh **[431]** and his son. This castle had been built by Malikshāh, after whose death Aḥmad ibn 'Abd al-Malik ibn 'Aṭṭāsh had taken control of it.

The reason for this is that he had associated with a castellan there and when he died Aḥmad took it over. The Bāṭinīs in Isfahan had already given him a crown and collected money for him. They did this only because his father 'Abd al-Malik had been a leader of their sect. He was a learned and eloquent man, possessing a good calligraphic hand, capable of swift extempore composition, and virtuous, but he was unfortunate to become devoted to this sect. However, his son Aḥmad was an ignoramus who knew nothing. Ibn al-Ṣabbāḥ, the lord of the fortress of Alamūt, was asked, 'Why do you revere Ibn 'Aṭṭash when he is so ignorant?' He replied, 'For his father's sake, because he was my mentor.'

Ibn 'Aṭṭāsh acquired numerous support and great strength. His position in the castle flourished. He used to send his men to raid the highway, steal goods and kill whomever they could. They killed a vast number beyond counting and, acting on his behalf, imposed on the sultan's villages and people's property taxes which they collected in return for not harming them. On account of this the sultan was incapable of benefiting from his villages or the people from their properties. The Bāṭinī position prospered through the dispute existing between the two sultans, Barkyāruq and Muḥammad.

---

[9] Krawulsky, 453.

[10] The meaning is doubtful here. The text reads *ilā jiha* and records a variant *wa-akhīhi ya'man fīhā*, neither of which makes sense by itself. The two have been speculatively combined: *ilā jiha ya'man fīhā*.

Once Muḥammad's sultanate was uncontested and no rival remained, there was no project more important to him than to attack and wage war on the Bātinīs and to seek to revenge the Muslims for their tyrannical violence. He decided to begin with the castle at Isfahan which was in their hands, because the harm it caused was the greatest, as it exerted pressure on his capital. He marched out in person and besieged them on 6 Sha'bān [2 April 1107]. He had intended to set out on 1 Rajab [26 February 1107] but their sympathizers in his army were upset by this. They spread the rumour that Qilij Arslān ibn Sulaymān had arrived at Baghdad and taken it. They fabricated correspondence to that effect. Then they pretended that trouble had broken out in Khurasan, so the sultan hesitated [**432**] to implement his plan. When this proved to be false, he showed a proper resolution and intention to fight them. He climbed a hill opposite the castle to the west and set up a throne on the summit. From Isfahan and its hinterland large hosts gathered to fight them because of the revenge they wished to extract from them. They surrounded the castle hill, which was four leagues in circumference. The sultan organized the emirs for the battle, with a [different] emir fighting each day. The situation [of the defenders] became difficult as the siege intensified and they were unable to get provisions.

When their situation had become serious, they wrote a fatwa, which contained, 'What say the learned lawyers, imams of the Faith, concerning a people who believe in God, His scriptures, His prophets and the Last Day, and that what Muḥammad (may God bless him and give him peace) brought is the genuine truth, and only differ about the Imam? Is it permissible for the sultan to make peace and be reconciled with them, accept their allegiance and guard them from all harm?' Most of the lawyers answered that it was permissible but some refrained. They were brought together to dispute the matter. With them was Abū'l-Ḥasan 'Alī ibn 'Abd al-Raḥmān al-Simanjānī, one of the shaykhs of the Shāfi'īs, who said in the presence of the company, 'It is encumbent to fight them. To leave them established in their place is not permissible. That they pronounce the two articles of faith does not help them. Let them be asked, "Tell us about your Imam. If he allows you what the Holy Law has forbidden or forbids you what the Law has allowed, do you accept his command?" They will say "Yes". In that case their blood is forfeit by consensus of the community.' The disputation about this lasted a long time.

Then the Bāṭinīs asked the sultan to send them some people to dispute with them and they specified certain persons amongst the ulema, such as the Cadi Abū'l-'Alā' Ṣā'id ibn Yaḥyā, the shaykh of the Ḥanafīs in Isfahan and their cadi, among others. They went up [into the castle], disputed with them and returned as they had gone up. [**433**] The only aim of the Bāṭinīs was distraction and procrastination. The sultan thereupon pressed the siege and when they realised his really serious purpose, they conceded the surrender of the castle on condition that they would be given in place of it the castle of Khālinjān about seven leagues distant from Isfahan. They said, 'We fear for our lives and our property from the common people. We must have a place where we may defend ourselves against them.' The sultan was advised to agree to their request. They then asked for a delay until Nawrūz[11] to withdraw to Khālinjān and give up their castle. They stipulated that he should not listen to what any adviser had to say about them. If anyone said anything about them he should hand him over to them. Anything he had acquired of theirs should be returned. The sultan granted this. They also requested that they should be supplied with sufficient provisions on a daily basis. All this was granted them. Their aim was to play for time in expectation that some split or mishap might occur.

The sultan's vizier Sa'd al-Mulk made arrangements for the food and fruit and all that they needed to be carried to them daily. They themselves began to send to buy foodstuffs that they stocked to resist further in their castle. Later they deputed one of their adherents to kill an emir who had been very active in fighting them. They surprised and wounded him but he escaped them. At that the sultan ordered the demolition of the castle of Khālinjān and renewed the siege. They asked that, if some of them descended, the sultan would send men with them to protect them until they arrived at Ṭabas, and that the remainder would stay in a high peak of the castle until someone came to tell them that their comrades had arrived and then they themselves would leave and the sultan send people with them to convey them to Ibn al-Ṣabbāḥ in the castle of Alamūt. This was agreed, so some of them left to go to al-Nāẓir and Ṭabas. The sultan took over [**434**] the castle and razed it.

Later there came from those who had gone to the castle of al-Nāẓir and Ṭabas men who informed Ibn 'Aṭṭāsh that they had arrived. However, he did not surrender the peak which remained in his hands. The sultan considered this treachery and a retreat from what had been agreed, so he ordered an assault. A general assault was launched on 2 Dhu'l-Qa'da [25 June 1107]. The numbers of those who could resist and fight were few but they showed great steadfastness and extreme courage. One of their leaders had sought terms from the sultan and said, 'I shall point out to you a weak point of theirs.' He took them to one side of that peak, very difficult of access. He said, 'Climb up here.' It was objected that they have secured that place and stationed men there. He said, 'The weapons and brigandines that you see they have put there to look as though there are men because they have so few.' All that remained were eighty men. The troops attacked by climbing up at that point and took the place. Most of the Bāṭinīs were slain. Some mingled with those who gained entrance and then left with them. However, Ibn 'Aṭṭāsh was taken prisoner. He was left for a week and then orders were given for him to be paraded through the whole town. He was flayed and after surviving [a while] he died. His skin was stuffed with straw. His son was also killed and their heads were taken to Baghdad. His wife threw herself from the top of the castle and perished. She had with her precious jewels which were without parallel. They too were destroyed and lost. The tribulations caused by Ibn 'Aṭṭāsh lasted for a period of twelve years.

---

[11] The Persian New Year's day at the vernal equinox.

[435] Account of the disagreement between Sayf al-Dawla Ṣadaqa and Muhadhdhab al-Dawla, lord of the Marsh

This year there was a disagreement between Sayf al-Dawla Ṣadaqa ibn Mazyad and Muhadhdhab al-Dawla al-Sa'īd ibn Abī'l-Jabr, lord of the Marsh. Ḥammād ibn Abī'l-Jabr became an ally of Ṣadaqa and displayed hostility towards his cousin Muhadhdhab al-Dawla but then they came to an agreement.[12]

The background to all this was as follows. When Sultan Muḥammad gave Ṣadaqa the town of Wāsiṭ as a fief, Muhadhdhab al-Dawla took it over as a tax-farm and handed the administration of it to his sons and his subordinates. They flagrantly laid their hands on the money and squandered it. At the end of the year Ṣadaqa claimed money from him and put him in prison. Badrān ibn Ṣadaqa, Muhadhdhab al-Dawla's son-in-law, intervened to secure his release, got him out of prison and sent him back to his lands in the Marsh.

Ḥammād ibn Abī'l-Jabr took on the tax-farm of Wāsiṭ and Muhadhdhab al-Dawla found much of his position undermined. In the end the matter led to a dispute after they had been in agreement.

Now al-Muṣṭani' Ismā'īl, Ḥammād's grandfather, and al-Mukhṭaṣṣ Muḥammad, Muhadhdhab al-Dawla's father, who were brothers, both of them sons of Abū'l-Jabr, had both held the headship of their family and their following. Al-Muṣṭani' died and his son Abū'l-Sayyid al-Muẓaffar, who was Ḥammād's father, took his place. Al-Mukhṭaṣṣ Muḥammad died and his son Muhadhdhab al-Dawla took his place. The two began to act as rivals of Ibn al-Haytham, lord of the Marsh, and they fought with him until Muhadhdhab al-Dawla seized him in the days of Goharā'īn and handed him over to the latter, who bore him away toward Isfahan, although he perished on the road. The position of Muhadhdhab al-Dawla grew mighty and Goharā'īn created him lord of the Marsh. His cousin [al-Muẓaffar] and many others became subject to his authority.

[436] Ḥammād was a youth, whom Muhadhdhab al-Dawla respected and married to one of his daughters, He added to his fief, so that his wealth became great but he began to envy Muhadhdhab al-Dawla and harbour a hatred for him. At times it was plain to see but Muhadhdhab al-Dawla did his best to humour him. After the death of Goharā'īn, Ḥammād broke with Muhadhdhab al-Dawla and revealed his inner feelings. Muhadhdhab al-Dawla strove to bring him back to what had been but he refused and would not talk. Al-Nafīs ibn Muhadhdhab al-Dawla gathered a force and attacked Ḥammād, so the latter sent to Ṣadaqa to inform him of this. Ṣadaqa sent him a large part of his army. Muhadhdhab al-Dawla determined to wage war in order not to be thought weak. His family advised him not to leave the position he was in because it was a strong one but he did not comply and

[12] As is often the case, the mention of 'ibn Abī'l-Jabr' does not mean directly 'son of...' but 'descended from' (cf. 'Jesus Christ, son of David' in Matthew, i, 1). As is clear from what follows, Muhadhdhab al-Dawla was a grandson of Abū'l-Jabr and Ḥammād a great-grandson. They were therefore first cousins once removed.

despatched his ships and his men by the waterways. Ḥammād and his brother, having prepared an ambush for him, retired before his advance. Muhadhdhab al-Dawla's men were eager and pursued them. Then the ambush was sprung and the only survivors were those whose alloted end had not yet come. A large number were killed or taken prisoner. Ḥammād's ambition grew and he applied to Ṣadaqa for more reinforcements, who sent the commander of his army, Sa'īd ibn Ḥamīd al-'Umarī, and other officers. They assembled their ships to attack Muhadhdhab al-Dawla but they found a solid defence and were not able to break in. Now while Ḥammād was miserly, Muhadhdhab al-Dawla was generous. He sent abundant supplies and many gifts to Sa'īd ibn Hamīd and was successful in winning him over. They met and an agreement was reached that Muhadhdhab al-Dawla would send his son al-Nafīs to Ṣadaqa, who showed him his favour and made peace between them and their cousin, Ḥammād. They returned to a happy state of harmony. Peace was made in Dhū'l-Ḥijja of the year 500 [24 July-21 August 1107].

[437] **How the sultan's vizier was killed and Aḥmad ibn Niẓām al-Mulk appointed to that office**

In Shawwāl of this year [26 May-23 June 1107] Sultan Muḥammad arrested his vizier, Sa'd al-Mulk Abū'l-Maḥāsin, seized his wealth and crucified him at the gate of Isfahan. He also crucified four of his leading associates who were clients of his. The vizier was accused of treachery to the sultan, whereas the other four were said to be of the Bāṭinī persuasion. He had been vizier for two years and nine months. At the beginning of his career he had been an associate of Tāj al-Mulk Abū'l-Ghanā'im, after whom he had been unemployed. Then Mu'ayyad al-Mulk ibn Niẓām al-Mulk appointed him as head of the Bureau of Financial Control and he gave excellent service to Sultan Muḥammad when his brother Sultan Barkyāruq besieged him in Isfahan. When Muḥammad left Isfahan he held it successfully and fulfilled his role admirably. Muḥammad appointed him vizier and rewarded him with extensive fiefs and gave him full authority in the state, but then cast him down - and this is the end result of service for princes! How excellent is the saying of 'Abd al-Malik ibn Marwān: 'The man most blessed in life is he who has enough to live on and a wife who pleases him and who knows not these wicked courts of ours and the harm they can do.'

After arresting the vizier the sultan consulted about the appointment of a successor. Several names were mentioned and the sultan said, 'My ancestors showered blessings on Niẓām al-Mulk and he owed them a great deal. His sons are nurtured by our bounty. They are indispensable.' He then commanded this Abū Naṣr Aḥmad to be made vizier and he was given the titles of his father, Qiwām al-Dīn Niẓām al-Mulk Ṣadr al-Islām.[13]

---

[13] i.e. the Support of Religion, Order of Kingship, Leader of Islam.

The reason why he came to the sultan's court was that, when he saw the collapse of his family's power, [**438**] he remained close in his house at Hamadhan. It happened that the headman of Hamadhan, namely the Sharīf Abū Hāshim, did him an injury, so he went to the sultan to complain and seek redress. The sultan had arrested his vizier while Aḥmad was on the way to him. On his arrival he remembered him and invested him with the robe of the vizierate, giving him full authority. His position became powerful. This is a case of 'Deliverance after Adversity', for he came complaining with a petition and ended in power with a commission.

Miscellaneous events

This year in Ṣafar [October 1106] the Vizier Abū'l-Qāsim 'Alī ibn Jahīr, the caliph's vizier, was dismissed. He made his way to the residence of Sayf al-Dawla Ṣadaqa in Baghdad to seek refuge there, for it was a refuge for every person wronged. Ṣadaqa sent someone to take him to Ḥilla. His vizierate had lasted three years, five months and some days. The caliph ordered his residence in the Commoners' Gate district to be demolished. There is a lesson here, because his father Abū Naṣr ibn Jahīr built it with material from people's demolished properties and used most of what had gone into them for it. It [too] was soon destroyed. After his dismissal the Cadi Abū'l-Ḥasan ibn al-Dāmghānī acted as deputy, and then in Muḥarram of the year 501 [22 August–20 September 1107] the vizierate was assigned to Abū'l-Ma'ālī Hibat Allāh ibn Muḥammad ibn al-Muṭṭalib and he was given a robe of investiture.

The following died in this year:

In Shawwāl [26 May–23 June 1107] Emir Abū'l-Fawāris Surkhāb ibn Badr ibn Muhalhil, known as Ibn Abī'l-Shawk the Kurd. He possessed vast sums of money and horses beyond counting. He was succeeded as emir by Abū Manṣūr ibn Badr. The emirate had remained in his family for 130 years. Of his history we have already given a sufficient account.[14]

[**439**] Abū'l-Fatḥ Aḥmad ibn Muḥammad ibn Aḥmad ibn Sa'īd al-Ḥaddād al-Isfahānī, the cousin of 'Abd al-Raḥmān ibn Abī 'Abd Allāh ibn Manda, who was born in 408 [1017–18]. He was very active in the field of Ḥadīth and was a renowed transmitter.[15]

Abū Muḥammad Ja'far ibn Aḥmad ibn al-Ḥusayn al-Sarrāj al-Baghdādī in Ṣafar [October 1106]. He was active in transmission of Ḥadīth and is the author of excellent books and charming poetry, one of the outstanding men of the age.[16]

---

[14] There are previous references to Surkhāb but no general account. He was a member of the dynasty of the Banū 'Annāz in northern Iraq (see *EI(2)*, i, 512–13, s.v. 'Annāzids).

[15] He died in Rajab/March 1107 (*Muntaẓam*, ix, 151).

[16] Born 416/1025–6, died eve of Sunday 20 Ṣafar/21 October 1106 (*Muntaẓam*, ix, 151–2).

'Abd al-Wahhāb ibn Muḥammad ibn 'Abd al-Wahhāb Abū Muḥammad al-Shīrāzī, the lawyer. He was appointed professor at the Niẓāmiyya in Baghdad in the year 483 [1090-91] and was also a transmitter of Ḥadīth.[17]

Abū'l-Ḥusayn al-Mubārak ibn 'Abd al-Jabbār ibn Aḥmad al-Ṣayrafī, known as Ibn al-Ṭuyūrī al-Baghdādī. Born in the year 411 [1020-21] he was active in Ḥadīth studies, reliable, upright and pious.[18]

Abū'l-Karam al-Mubārak ibn al-Fākhir ibn Muḥammad ibn Ya'qūb, the grammarian. He heard Ḥadīth from Abū'l-Ṭayyib al-Ṭabarī and al-Jawharī and others and was a leading scholar in grammar and lexicography.[19]

---

[17] He died in Ramāḍan/April-May 1107 (*Muntaẓam*, ix, 152-3).

[18] He died in the middle of Dhū'l-Qa'da/8 July 1107 (*Muntaẓam*, ix, 154).

[19] Died in Dhū'l-Qa'da/June-July 1107 (*Muntaẓam*, ix, 153).

[**440**]

The Year 501 [1107-1108]

The death of Ṣadaqa ibn Mazyad

In Rajab of this year [15 February-15 March 1108] Emir Sayf al-Dīn Ṣadaqa ibn Manṣūr ibn Dubays ibn Mazyad al-Asadi, the Emir of the Arabs, was killed. He is the one who built al-Ḥilla, called [after him] al-Sayfiyya, in Iraq. His career was very significant and his standing high. His prestige spread far and wide and people great and small sought and received his protection.

He paid much attention to the affairs of Sultan Muḥammad and gave him support and backing against his brother Barkyāruq, to the extent that he was openly hostile to the latter and never ceased to be a sincere ally of Sultan Muḥammad. Muḥammad increased the size of his fief, which included the town of Wāsiṭ, and allowed him to take Basra. In due course the 'Amīd Abū Ja'far Muḥammad ibn al-Ḥusayn al-Balkhī undermined their relationship. One of the things he said about him was, 'Ṣadaqa's power and position have grown great and his high-handedness has increased. He spreads throughout the state his protection for all who flee to him from the sultan. This is something that princes cannot tolerate from their children. If you were to send one of your men he could seize his lands and his wealth.'

Later he went further than that and impugned his orthodoxy and claimed that he and his populace belonged to the Bāṭinī sect. He lied, for Ṣadaqa was of the Shiite persuasion, nothing more. Arghūn al-Sa'dī backed up Abū Ja'far the 'Amīd and Ṣadaqa heard of this. Arghūn's wife and family were in Ḥilla [**441**] but Ṣadaqa did not pursue them for any of the arrears of taxes that he was owed there. He ordered that they should be completely cancelled and given over to his wife.

It came about that Ṣadaqa was killed in the following way. As we have related, he used to give protection to all who were fearful of caliph, sultan or any other. Sultan Muḥammad was enraged at Abū Dulaf Surkhāb ibn Kaykhusro, the lord of Sāveh and Āveh, who fled from him and made for Ṣadaqa to seek asylum with him, which he granted. The sultan sent asking Ṣadaqa to surrender him to his deputies but he refused and answered, 'I cannot do it. Indeed, I shall defend him and I say what Abū Ṭālib said to Quraysh when they demanded he give up the Prophet of God (God bless him and give him peace),

"We shall protect him until we are laid low around him,
Unmindful of our children and our wives." '

Other matters arose which displeased the sultan, so he set out for Iraq to settle this business. When Ṣadaqa heard, he consulted his followers about what to do. His son Dubays advised that he should be sent to the sultan with money, horses and gifts to win back the sultan's favour. Sa'īd ibn Ḥamīd, Ṣadaqa's army commander, advised armed resistance, mobilisation of the army and distribution of money to them. He spoke at length on the matter and Ṣadaqa inclined to his view. He therefore summoned his troops, and 20,000 horsemen and 30,000 infantry answered the summons. Al-Mustaẓhir bi-Allāh sent to him warning of the consequences of this course of action and forbidding him to rebel against the sultan and offering to mediate. Ṣadaqa answered, 'I am a loyal subject of the sultan but I do not feel secure about meeting him.' The caliph's envoy on that occasion was the Chief Syndic 'Alī ibn Ṭirād al-Zaynabī.

[**442**] The sultan sent the Chief Cadi Abū Sa'd[1] al-Harawī to Ṣadaqa to conciliate him and remove his fear, also to bid him to be easy in his mind as was his custom. He was also to tell him of his intention to attack the Franks and to order him to prepare for a joint expedition. Ṣadaqa replied, 'The sultan's men have poisoned his mind against me and changed my relationship with him. The favour I deserved from him has disappeared.' He rehearsed his past service and loyal assistance. Sa'īd ibn Ḥamīd, the commander of his army, said, 'We have no hope left of making peace with the sultan. We shall surely see our cavalry disbanding.'[2] Ṣadaqa refused to meet with the sultan.

On 20 Rabī' II [8 December 1107] the sultan arrived at Baghdad, accompanied by his vizier, Niẓām al-Mulk Aḥmad ibn Niẓām al-Mulk. He despatched al-Bursuqī, the prefect of Baghdad, with several emirs to Ṣarṣar,[3] which they put under siege. The sultan had arrived with a light force. His troops did not amount to 2,000 cavalry. When it was known for certain in Baghdad that Ṣadaqa had declared hostilities, the sultan sent to the emirs ordering them to come to him, to hurry and make all haste. They came to him from every direction.

In Jumādā I [18 December 1107–16 January 1108] a letter from Ṣadaqa reached the caliph, telling that he would stand by whatever arrangement was made and whatever position he might be assigned with the sultan. Whatever he was ordered he would carry it out. The caliph forwarded the letter to the sultan, who said, 'I will obey the orders of the caliph. I have no wish to differ.' So the caliph sent to Ṣadaqa to tell him that the sultan agreed to what was asked of him and bidding him despatch his trusted representative to settle terms and to secure the sultan's oath to whatever was agreed. However, Ṣadaqa backed away from that idea and said, 'If the sultan withdraws from Baghdad I shall support him with money, men and whatever is needed for the Jihad, but now, while he is in Baghdad and his troops

---

1 Correct the text's 'Sa'īd', cf. p. [**446**] below and *Muntaẓam*, ix, 165, 223, 234: Zayn al-Islām Abū Sa'd al-Harawī. In Alptekin, *Reign of Zangi*, 23, note 2, he is named Abu Sa'īd Muḥammad ibn Naṣr.

2 This is based on the reading of the Mss. given in the edition's footnotes, which I interpret as *la-narayanna khuyūlanā yaḥullūna*.

3 The name of two places in Baghdad province: i) a village on the south bank of Sīb Canal; ii) a small town on north bank of the Sīb Canal on the pilgrim road from Baghdad (see Krawulsky, 505).

at King's Canal, [**443**] then I have no money or anything else. Jāwulī Saqāo and Īlghāzī ibn Artuq have written to me that they obey me and are in agreement with me to fight the sultan and any other. Whenever I wish for them they will come to me with their troops.'

The following joined the sultan, Qirwāsh ibn Sharaf al-Dawla, Karbāwī ibn Khurasān the Turkoman and Abū 'Imrān Faḍl ibn Rabī'a ibn Ḥāzim ibn al-Jarrāḥ al-Ṭā'ī. The latter's ancestors had been lords of al-Balqā' and Jerusalem, among them Ḥassān ibn al-Mufarrij whom al-Tihāmī praised in verse.[4] Faḍl was at one time with the Franks and at another with the Egyptians. When Ṭughtakīn the Atabeg saw him behaving like that, he drove him out of Syria. After he had been driven out he sought refuge with Ṣadaqa and made a compact with him. Ṣadaqa honoured him and gave him many gifts, including 7,000 dinars in cash.

At the time of this crisis between Ṣadaqa and the sultan, Faḍl marched in the vanguard but then he fled to the sultan. On his arrival he and his followers were rewarded and he lodged in Ṣadaqa's residence at Baghdad. When the sultan set out to fight Ṣadaqa, Faḍl asked permission to take the desert route to prevent Ṣadaqa's flight if he had that in mind. Permission given, he crossed the river at al-Anbār and that was the last that was heard of him.

During Jumādā I [18 December 1107–16 January 1108] the sultan sent Emir Muḥammad ibn Būqā the Turkoman to Wāsiṭ, who expelled Ṣadaqa's governor and gave guarantees of security for all the population, apart from Ṣadaqa's men. They scattered and no one was despoiled. Ibn Būqā sent his cavalry to Qūsān,[5] which was part of Ṣadaqa's territory, pillaged it most dreadfully and remained for some days. Ṣadaqa sent against him Thābit ibn Sulṭān, his cousin, with an army. Once they had arrived there, the Turks left. Thābit occupied it with the Tigris separating them.

Ibn Būqā sent across the river a picked detachment of his soldiers, whose bravery he knew, and they occupied a raised position above Nahr Sālim, about fifty cubits high. [**444**] Thābit and his troops attacked them but were unable to close with the Turks because of their archery, while reinforcements were joining them from Ibn Būqā. Thābit was wounded in the face and many of his men were wounded. He and those with him fled and were pursued by the Turks, who killed some of them and captured others. A group of the Turks plundered the town of Wāsiṭ and Thābit's infantry mingled with them and plundered alongside them. Hearing of this, Ibn Būqā rode there and stopped them, when they had already sacked part of the town, and proclaimed that the populace were to be protected. Towards the end of Jumādā I the sultan assigned Wāsiṭ as a fief to Qasīm al-Dawla al-Bursuqī and ordered Ibn Būqā to attack and sack Ṣadaqa's town, where plunder beyond measure was taken.

---

[4] Ḥassān ibn al-Mufarrij was a member of the minor Arab dynasty of the Jarrāḥids in Palestine. Abū'l-Ḥasan 'Alī ibn Muḥammad al-Tihāmī died at Cairo in 416/1025 (see *EI(2)*, x, 482; Sezgin, ii, 478–9).

[5] A district in 'Irāq al-'Arab on both sides of the Shaṭṭ al-Nīl (Krawulsky, 503).

The sultan left Baghdad to go to al-Za'farāniyya on 2 Jumādā II [18 January 1108]. The caliph sent him his vizier, Majd al-Dīn ibn al-Muṭṭalib, ordering him to halt and not be so hasty, fearing murder and plunder for the populace. The cadi of Isfahan advised the same and that the caliph's order be followed. The sultan complied. Then the caliph sent the Chief Syndic 'Alī ibn Ṭirād and Jamāl al-Dawla Mukhtaṣṣ the Eunuch to Ṣadaqa. They came to him and conveyed the caliph's message, ordering him to obey the sultan and forbidding opposition. Ṣadaqa made his excuses and said, 'I have not cast off my allegiance, nor have I interrupted the khutbah in my lands.' He made arrangements for his son Dubays to go with the two of them to the sultan.

While the envoys and Ṣadaqa were in these talks, news arrived that a detachment of the sultan's army had crossed at Maṭīrābādh and that fighting between them and Ṣadaqa's men was in progress. On account of the envoys Ṣadaqa acted with restraint, although he was eager to ride to his men because he feared for them. The envoys, when they heard this news, condemned it because they had commanded the army, when they passed through them, that no one should start any hostilities until they returned, for a peace settlement was imminent. Ṣadaqa said to the envoy, 'How can I trust sending my son [**445**] now? How can I feel that he will be safe, now that what you see has happened? If you personally guarantee his return to me, I shall send him.' They did not dare to give this guarantee, so he wrote to the caliph apologising for not sending his son because of what had happened.

This situation came about because when the sultan's army saw the envoys they believed that peace was going to come and so some of them said, 'Our best plan is to seize some plunder before the peace.' Some agreed and others refused. Those that agreed crossed the river and then those that had not agreed did not stay behind to avoid being called weak and cowardly and to prevent any mishap befalling those that crossed, which would be a source of shame and trouble. So these also crossed over after the others. They were met by Ṣadaqa's men and a battle followed. The Turks suffered a defeat and a large number of them were killed and several of their leaders and many others were taken. Some of them drowned, including Emir Muḥammad ibn Yaghī Siyān, whose father had been the lord of Antioch. He was twenty odd years old. He loved the ulema and the men of religion and had built in his fief in Azerbayjan a number of madrasahs. The Turks did not dare to inform the sultan of the money and mounts that had been taken from them because they were afraid of him, seeing that they acted without his order.

The Arabs were buoyed up by this defeat [of the Turks] and manifested their pride, arrogance and ambition. They announced that they sold each prisoner for a dinar and that three men sold a prisoner for five *qīrāṭ*s and ate bread and *harīsa*[6] with the proceeds. They began to chant, 'Who will lunch on a prisoner and sup on another?' The Turks were clearly greatly perturbed,

---

6 A dish of meat and rice.

The caliph renewed his correspondence with Ṣadaqa about drawing up terms of peace. Ṣadaqa replied that he would not disobey [**446**] any order given, and he also wrote to the sultan arguing against the reports made about him and with excuses for the battle that had occurred between his men and the Turks, saying that the sultan's soldiers had crossed over to attack his men, who defended themselves, while he knew nothing about it and was not present at the battle, and that he had not cast off his allegiance nor had he terminated the sultan's khutbah in his territory. Ṣadaqa had not written to him before this letter.

The caliph sent the Chief Syndic and Abū Sa'd al-Harawī, who first went to the sultan and secured his promise to guarantee the safety of any of Ṣadaqa's relatives who came to him. When they then repaired to Ṣadaqa, they said to him, speaking for the caliph, 'Any move to placate the sultan's heart depends on releasing prisoners and giving back all that was taken from the defeated army.' Initially Ṣadaqa responded with humility and obedience but then he said, 'Were I able to give way before the sultan, I would do so, but behind me are three hundred women, my dependants and those of my father and grandfather. No place will sustain them. If I knew, if I come to the sultan in submission, that he would receive me and take me into his service, I would do so, but I fear that he will not pardon my stumblings and not forgive my error. As for what has been plundered, the people [involved] are numerous and I have men I do not know. They have taken their booty and gone into the countryside. I have no control over them. However, if the sultan will not challenge me in what I hold nor over those I protect, if he confirms Surkhāb ibn Kaykhusro in his fief at Sāveh and orders that Ibn Būqā restore what he has plundered from my lands and that the caliph's vizier should go and get him to swear oaths that I can trust to maintain the position between me and himself, then shall I serve him with my wealth and later do obeisance to him.'[7]

They returned with this message, accompanied by Abū Manṣūr ibn Ma'rūf, Ṣadaqa's envoy. The caliph sent them back and with them the sultan sent the Cadi of Isfahan Abū Ismā'īl. However, the latter [**447**] did not reach Ṣadaqa but turned back on the way. Ṣadaqa persisted with his first statement. Thereupon the sultan set out from al-Za'farāniyya on 8 Rajab [22 February 1108]. Ṣadaqa with his forces proceeded to the village of Maṭar and ordered his soldiers to don their armour. Thābit ibn Sulṭān ibn Dubays ibn 'Alī ibn Mazyad, the cousin of Ṣadaqa, sought the protection of Sultan Muḥammad. He was envious of Ṣadaqa and is the one we have said was in Wāsiṭ, and that the sultan treated him with honour and kindness and promised him the fief.

The sultan's armies came to join him, including the sons of Bursuq and 'Alā' al-Dawla Abū Kālījār Garshasp ibn 'Alī ibn Farāmurz Abī Ja'far ibn Kākūya, whose ancestors were lords of Isfahan (Farāmurz is the one who surrendered it to Ṭughril Beg) and whose father was slain with Tutush. The sultan's army crossed the Tigris but not he himself. They were thus now on the same side as Ṣadaqa with a canal between them.

[7] Literally 'tread his carpet.'

They met in battle on 19 Rajab [4 March 1108]. The wind had been in the faces of the sultan's troops but when battle was joined it became behind their backs and was now in the faces of Ṣadaqa's men. The Turks loosed their arrows and with each volley 10,000 arrows were discharged. There was not an arrow that did not fall on a horse or a horseman. Whenever Ṣadaqa's men charged, the water and arrows prevented them from reaching the Turks. Any of them that did cross did not return. The 'Ubāda and Khafāja stood idly by and Ṣadaqa began to cry out, 'On, on, the Khuzayma! On, on, the Nāshira! On, on, the 'Awf!' He promised the Kurds every favour for any courage they would show. He was mounted on a horse with its tail fully docked and no one else had one like it. This horse was wounded three times and was taken by Emir Aḥmadīl after Ṣadaqa was killed. He sent it by boat to Baghdad but it died on the way.

Ṣadaqa had another horse which his chamberlain Abū Naṣr ibn Tuffāḥa had ridden. When he saw [**448**] that the enemy had surrounded Ṣadaqa, he rode away on it. Ṣadaqa called out to him but he did not respond. Ṣadaqa charged the Turks, and a mamluke amongst them struck him a disfiguring blow on the face. He then said, 'I am the king of the Arabs. I am Ṣadaqa.' An arrow then hit him in the back and a mamluke called Buzghush came up to him, now unable to move, grappled him, being unaware of who he was, and dragged him from his horse. He and the mamluke fell to the ground. Ṣadaqa recognized him and said, ' Buzghush, mercy!' but he struck him with his sword and killed him. He took his head and carried it to al-Bursuqī, who bore it to the sultan. Seeing the head, the sultan embraced him and ordered a gift to be given to Buzghush.

Ṣadaqa remained where he fell until the sultan left and then a man from al-Madā'in buried him. He was fifty-nine years of age and his rule had lasted twenty-one years. His head was taken to Baghdad. More than 3,000 of his mounted followers were killed, amongst them several members of his house. Ninety-five men of the Banū Shaybān were killed and his son, Dubays ibn Ṣadaqa, was taken prisoner, as was Surkhāb ibn Kaykhusro the Daylamī, who was the cause of this conflict. He was brought before the sultan and begged for his life. The sultan said, 'I have sworn to God that I will not slay any prisoner, but if it is established that you are a Bāṭinī, I shall kill you.' Sa'īd ibn Ḥamīd al-'Umarī, the commander of Ṣadaqa's army, was captured but Badrān ibn Ṣadaqa fled to al-Ḥilla, took what money and other things he could and sent his mother and womenfolk to the Marsh to Muhadhdhab al-Dawla Abū'l-'Abbās Aḥmad ibn Abī'l-Jabr. Badrān was Muhadhdhab al-Dawla's son-in-law, married to his daughter.

The quantity of goods plundered was beyond estimation. Ṣadaqa possessed a great many manuscripts, thousands of volumes, written by reputable hands. He himself [**449**] read well but could not write. He was generous, mild, honest, very charitable and kind. He was ever a refuge for every unfortunate, meeting all who sought him out with kindness and courtesy. He welcomed and visited those who made their way to him. He was just. With him his subjects were safe and secure. His sexuality was restrained. He took only his one wife and had no concubines. So what would you expect about anything else? He extorted money from none of his deputies nor held them to account for an old offence. His men used to deposit their wealth in his treasury and had a free and easy way with him like sons with a father. No subjects have ever been known to love their emir as his subjects loved him. He was modest, long-suffering, knew a stock of poetry by heart and was eager for an interesting anecdote. God have mercy on him! He was indeed one of the ornaments of this world.

The sultan returned to Baghdad and did not go to al-Ḥilla. He sent a guarantee of safety for Ṣadaqa's wife to the Marsh and ordered her to appear. She therefore went up to Baghdad. The sultan freed her son Dubays and sent several emirs with him to meet her. When her son met her, they both wept bitterly. On her arrival at Baghdad the sultan summoned her and apologised for the killing of her husband. He said, 'I wanted him to be brought to me, so that I could treat him with the favour and kindness that people would admire. However, I was defeated by fate.' He made her son Dubays swear that he would not engage in any wickedness.

Account of the death of Tamīm ibn al-Mu'izz, the ruler of Ifrīqiya, and the succession of his son Yaḥyā

In Rajab of this year [February 1108] the ruler of Ifrīqiya Tamīm ibn al-Mu'izz ibn Bādīs died.[8] He was energetic, brave and clever with a good learning. He was also mild-mannered and very forgiving of [**450**] major offences. He was the author of some good poetry. For instance, there was a conflict between two groups of Arabs, namely the 'Adī and the Riyāḥ. One of the latter was killed but peace was made and they left his blood unavenged. Peace between them was something that was harmful to Tamīm and his lands, so he composed some verses to urge the demand for blood revenge. They are:

When your blood remains unavenged,
Is there no one among you capable of seeking revenge?
Is there any profit, moreover any peace, if you are cowards?
Your ancestors were not so base.
You slumber rather than seek blood revenge until
It seems that honour among you has dwindled away.
For that cause you have broken no lance tips,
No swords have been notched, not even drawn.

The brothers of the victim then took the step of killing an emir of the 'Adī. Fighting between them intensified and many were killed until the Banū 'Adī were expelled from Ifrīqiya.

---

8 He died the eve of Saturday 15 Rajab/29 February 1108 (Idris, *La Berbérie*, 302).

It has been reported that Tamīm bought a slave girl for a great price. He then heard that her master who had sold her was out of his mind with sorrow at having parted with her. Tamīm summoned him to his presence and sent the slave girl to his house along with a large amount of clothes, silver vessels and other things such as perfumes. He ordered her master to go home, unaware of all of this. Having arrived at his house and seeing her in her former state, he collapsed in a swoon for excess of joy. He recovered and on the following day he took the price paid and all that had come with her and carried it to Tamīm's residence. Tamīm rebuked him and commanded him to take all of it back to his house.

In his lands he had intelligence agents to whom he paid magnificent pensions that they might inform him of his subordinates' behaviour to stop them wronging the populace. In Qayrawān there was a rich and prosperous merchant. One day the merchants talked about Tamīm and blessed his name. This merchant was present but he blessed his father al-Mu'izz and made no reference to Tamīm. This was reported to Tamīm who summoned him to his palace and asked, 'Have I wronged you?' 'No,' he replied. 'Has one of my subordinates wronged you?' 'No.' Then he said, 'Why did you licence your tongue to find fault with me yesterday?' The merchant was silent. Tamīm continued, 'Were it not that people might say, "He coveted [**451**] his wealth," I would kill you!' He gave orders for him to be beaten a little in his presence and then allowed him to leave. His friends who were waiting asked what had happened. He said, 'The secrets of princes are not to be divulged.' This became proverbial in Ifrīqiya.

Tamīm died when he was seventy-nine years of age. His rule had lasted forty-six years, ten months and twenty days. Of male children he left more than one hundred and of daughters sixty. When he died, his son Yaḥyā ibn Tamīm came to power, who had been born in al-Mahdiyya when four days remained of Dhū'l-Ḥijja in the year 457 [28 November 1065]. When he succeeded he was aged forty-three years, six months and twenty days. After his accession he distributed vast sums of money and ruled his subjects well.

Account of Yaḥyā's conquest of the castle of Kelibia

After Yaḥyā ibn Tamīm had succeeded his father, he despatched a sizeable army to the castle of Kelibia, one of the most fortified of Ifrīqiya's castles, and, camping around it, placed it under an intense siege. He did not move until he had taken it,[9] and then he strengthened its fortifications. His father Tamīm had wished to take it but had been unable to do so. Yaḥya continued to be triumphant and victorious. Not a single army of his was defeated.

---

9 Kelibia (in the text Qulaybiyya) on the coast south of Cape Bon was taken in 502/1108–9 (Idris, *La Berbérie*, 308).

[452] How Ibn 'Ammār came to Baghdad appealing for aid

During this year in the month of Ramaḍān [14 April–13 May 1108] the Cadi Fakhr al-Mulk Abū 'Alī ibn 'Ammār, the lord of Tripoli in Syria, came to Baghdad, seeking the court of the Sultan Muḥammad, to ask for aid against the Franks and requesting the sending of troops to drive them away.[10] What prompted him to do that was that, after the Frankish siege of Tripoli had lasted a long time, as we have recounted, provisions became difficult to obtain and in short supply. The situation became serious for him and the populace. In the year 500 [1106–7] God kindly supplied them with some provisions by sea from Cyprus, Antaliya and the islands of the Adriatic.[11] Their hearts were invigorated and they found the strength to hold on to the city after they had been about to surrender.

When Fakhr al-Mulk had heard that Sultan Muḥammad was well established and that every rival had disappeared, he decided for his own and the Muslims' sake to go to him and ask for his support. He left as his deputy in Tripoli his cousin Dhū'l-Manāqib, ordered him to hold on there and made arrangements for his forces both by land and by sea, giving them six months' salary in advance and assigning every position to someone who was to be responsible for its defence, so that his cousin had no need to do anything of that sort. He then left for Damascus but his cousin disobeyed him and rebelled against him by proclaiming allegiance to the Egyptians. Learning of this, Fakhr al-Mulk wrote to his men ordering them to arrest him and take him to the fortress of al-Khawābī.[12] They carried out his order.

Ibn 'Ammār had taken with him gifts such as no comparable prince ever had in his possession, precious objects, rare items and thoroughbred horses. When he arrived at Damascus, he was met by the local forces and Ṭughtakīn the Atabeg, and he camped outside the city. Ṭughtakīn asked him to enter, which he did one day for a feast, and he was also invited to use his bath-house. He then left Damascus with Ṭughtakīn's son escorting him on his way.

[453] When he reached Baghdad, the sultan ordered all the emirs to meet him with respect. He sent him his barge (*shabbāra*) on which was his throne where he would sit when travelling in her. When Ibn 'Ammār embarked he sat in front of the sultan's place. One of the sultan's courtiers on board said to him, 'We have been instructed that you should sit on the sultan's throne.' When he came into the sultan's presence, he asked him to be seated, showed him honour and paid attention to what he had to say.

The caliph sent his courtiers and several of his officials to receive Ibn 'Ammār. He also gave him lodgings and bestowed on him a large allowance. The sultan treated him likewise. Indeed, he was treated in a way that no similar prince at their

---

[10] For Ibn 'Ammār's mission to Baghdad, see Richard, *Comté de Tripoli*, 16.

[11] In the text 'the islands of the Venetians.' Note that the text and *Kāmil* (Thornberg), x, 316, read Antioch. In Arabic script Antaliya is a simple (and necessary) emendation.

[12] About 15 miles south of Antartus.

court had been. All this was the fruit of his Jihad in this world, although the reward of the next world is greater.

When he came to his meeting with the sultan, he presented his gift and the sultan questioned him about his situation and what he had to bear in his struggle with the infidels and his hardships from the dangers he met in fighting them. Ibn ‘Ammār told him of the situation, the strength of the enemy and the length of the siege, and of his request for military support. He guaranteed that, if troops were sent with him, he would provide them with everything they might ask for. The sultan promised him that that would be done.

He then came to the Caliphal Palace and related more or less what he had told to the sultan. He brought a valuable and handsome gift. He remained until the sultan departed from Baghdad in Shawwāl [14 May–11 June 1108]. The sultan summoned him to himself at al-Nahrawān, having commanded that Emir Ḥusayn ibn Atabeg Qutlughtakīn should send with him the troops that he had despatched to Mosul with Emir Mawdūd to fight Jāwulī Saqāo and that they were to march with him to Syria. The sultan, having rewarded him with a costly robe of honour and given him much, bade him farewell. He set out, accompanied by Emir Ḥusayn, but did not find this of any use. The sequel we shall tell of later, God willing.

[**454**] Fakhr al-Mulk ibn ‘Ammār returned to Damascus in the middle of Muḥarram in the year 502 [26 August 1108], remained there a few days and then set out with a force from Damascus to Jabala, which he entered and received the allegiance of the populace. As for the people of Tripoli, they had made contact with al-Afḍal Emir al-Juyūsh in Egypt, requesting from him a governor to be with them and bring provisions by sea. He sent them Sharaf al-Dawla ibn Abī'l-Ṭayyib to act as governor, with corn and other things that the city needed during the siege. Having arrived there he arrested several of Ibn ‘Ammār's family and followers and took his treasures, equipment and other items that he found. All of this he shipped to Egypt.

Miscellaneous events

In Sha‘bān of this year [16 March–13 April 1108] Sultan Muḥammad waived customs and non-canonical taxes, sales tax, transit dues[13] and other similar ones in Iraq. Tablets were inscribed to this effect and put up in the markets.

In the month of Ramaḍān [14 April–13 May 1108] the Cadi Abū'l-‘Abbās ibn al-Raṭbī took on the office of market inspector at Baghdad.

In the same month the caliph dismissed his vizier, Majd al-Dīn ibn al-Muṭṭalib, according to a written instruction from the sultan. Later, with the permission of the sultan he was restored to the vizierate. Certain stipulations were imposed on him,

[13] A possible meaning of *ijtiyāzāt*, from the basic sense of the root, ‘to pass.’ Duties were perhaps demanded from river-borne commerce (cf. Mez, *Renaissance*, 490–91).

including justice and fair dealing and that he should not employ any of the Dhimmī community.

[**455**] This year the General Ṣabāwa returned from Damascus. He had fled after the killing of Ayāz. When he arrived, the sultan honoured him and assigned him as a fief the Square (Raḥba) of Mālik ibn Ṭawq.

On 7 Shawwāl [20 May 1108] the sultan left Baghdad, intending to return to Isfahan. On this occasion his sojourn there had been five months and seventeen days.

During Dhū'l-Ḥijja [12 July–9 August 1108] Ibn Jarada's Ruins caught fire and many people perished there.[14] As for goods, property and furniture, the loss was beyond measure. A crowd of people escaped through a hole that they bored in the district's wall into the Abraz Gate cemetery. A number of Jews were there. They brought nothing out because they held to their Sabbath. Some of the inhabitants had crossed to the West Bank for recreation according to their custom on the Saturday next to the Festival. They returned and found their houses in ruins, their families burnt and their wealth destroyed.

Fires in several places followed, for example, in the Street of the Pitch-maker[15] and Ibn Razīn' Garden.[16] The people were worried at this and interrupted their livelihoods, spending day and night guarding their houses in the alley-ways and on the roofs. They kept water by them ready to extinguish any fire. It emerged that the cause of the [original] fire was that a servant-girl, who had fallen in love with a man, arranged for him to spend the night secretly with her in her master's house. She prepared something that he could steal when he left, and take her with him too. After he had taken her,[17] they set fire to the house, but God revealed their guilt and brought swift shame upon them. They were seized and imprisoned.

In this year Baldwin, the king of the Franks, assembled an army and marched to the city of Tyre to besiege it. He ordered a fort to be built near it on the Hill of the Beloved (Tall al-Ma'shūqa) and spent a month besieging the city. He was bought off [**456**] by the governor for 7,000 dinars. He took the money and departed and moved against Sidon, which he put under siege by land and by sea, erecting a wooden tower to attack it. The Egyptian fleet arrived to defend the town and protect the inhabitants. The Frankish fleet engaged them and the Muslims proved victorious. News then reached the Franks that the army of Damascus had set out to aid the people of Sidon, so they left without gaining anything.

This year a large comet with a tail appeared, remained for many nights and then disappeared.

---

14 See Makdisi, 'Topography', 293, note 11 (for this fire, 294–5). *Kharāba* ('Ruins') denotes an urban area where at some time people lived amid decayed and abandoned buildings.

15 *Darb al-Qayyār*, in East Baghdad (see Makdisi, 'Topography', 288, note 12).

16 *Qarāḥ Ibn Razīn*, in the centre of East Baghdad (see Makdisi, 'Topography'. 295, note 1).

17 This pronoun in Ibn al-Athīr's reworking of his source, *Muntaẓam*, ix, 157, can only refer to 'the girl', but in the original it refers to the stolen object, namely a *zanfalīja*, i.e. 'a basket,' presumably filled with valuable items.

There died during this year:

In Sha‘bān [16 March–13 April 1108] Ibrāhīm ibn Mayyās ibn Mahdī, Abū Isḥāq al-Qushayrī al-Dimashqī, who studied much Ḥadīth with al-Khaṭīb al-Baghdādī and others.

In Dhū'l-Qa‘da [12 June–11 July 1108] Abū Sa‘īd[18] Ismā‘īl ibn ‘Amr ibn Muḥammad al-Nīsābūrī, the Traditionist. He used to teach Ḥadīth to foreigners and he read the *Ṣaḥīḥ* of Muslim with ‘Abd al-Ghāfir al-Fārisī twenty times.

---

18 *Muntaẓam*, x, 158, and a variant in the text have Abū Sa‘d.

[457] The Year 502 [1108-1109]

How Mawdūd and the sultan's army conquered Mosul and Mawdūd became governor

In Ṣafar of this year [10 September-8 October 1108] Mawdūd and the army that the sultan had sent with him conquered the city of Mosul. They took it from Jāwulī Saqāo's men. We have already mentioned under the year 500 [1106-7] Jāwulī's conquest of it and what happened between him and Jokermish and Prince Qilij Arslān and the destruction of both of them at his hands. After that he acquired a large army, complete equipment and much money. Sultan Muḥammad had appointed him governor of every town he could conquer and he gained control of a lot of territory and wealth.

How the territory was taken from him was as follows. After he had gained control of it and its vast wealth, he brought none of it to the sultan. When the sultan came to Baghdad to attack the lands of Sayf al-Dawla Ṣadaqa, he sent to Jāwulī summoning him to bring his troops. He despatched further envoys but Jāwulī did not appear. He gave specious arguments against travelling down to him and put it out that he feared to meet with him. Not content with that he even wrote to Ṣadaqa and announced that he was with him and ready to help to fight the sultan, encouraging him to disobey and rebel.

When the sultan had dealt with Ṣadaqa and killed him, as has been related, he commanded the emirs, the sons of Bursuq, Sukmān al-Quṭbī, Mawdūd ibn Altūntakīn, Āqsunqur al-Bursuqī, Naṣr [**458**] ibn Muhalhil ibn Abī'l-Shawk al-Kurdī and Abū'l-Hayjā', the lord of Irbil, to march to Mosul and Jāwulī's territory and take it from him. They set out for Mosul and found Jāwulī in rebellion, already having built up the walls of Mosul and strengthened what Jokermish had constructed. He had also prepared supplies, foodstuffs and military equipment. He laid hands on the notables in Mosul and put them in prison. He also expelled more that 20,000 of the city militia and publicly proclaimed, 'If any two citizens gather to talk about this situation, I shall execute them.'

He moved out of the city and plundered the hinterland, having left his wife, Bursuq's daughter, in the city, whom he installed in the citadel along with 1,500 Turkish cavalrymen, apart from others and apart from the infantry. The [emirs'] army came to besiege the city in the month of Ramaḍān of the year 501 [April 1109]. Jāwulī's wife extorted money from those left in the city and oppressed the womenfolk of those who had left. She took extreme measures to guard herself against the people, which alienated them and led them to turn from her. Meanwhile, the inhabitants were under continous attack. The siege from without and the oppression within lasted until the end of Muḥarram [29 August 1109]. The troops inside prevented any common citizen from approaching the city wall.

After the populace had suffered this for a long time, a band of plasterers, whose leader was a plasterer called Sa'dī, plotted to surrender the city, swearing to support one another. At the time of Friday prayers, when people were in the mosque, they met and went up into a tower. They locked the doors and killed the troops who were there. They had been sleeping and were slain before they knew what was happening. They took their weapons and threw the bodies down to the ground. Then they seized another tower but a shout was raised and 200 cavalry attacked them, shooting arrows. They fought back, calling out the sultan's slogan. The troops of the sultan advanced and, gaining entrance at that sector, took the city. Emir Mawdūd entered and a proclamation was made, calling for calm and promising security and that people should return to their homes and possessions. Jāwulī's wife remained in the citadel for eight [**459**] days, then made contact with Emir Mawdūd, asking that he allow her to depart and that he swear to guard and protect her. This he did, so she left to go to her brother, Bursuq ibn Bursuq, taking her property and what she had acquired. Mawdūd assumed the governorship of Mosul and its attached lands.

Jāwulī's situation during the period of the siege

When the sultan's army came to Mosul and put it under siege, Jāwulī left and took with him the Count, the lord of Edessa, whom Suqmān had taken prisoner and whom Jokermish had taken from him, but we have mentioned this already. Jāwulī went to Nisibis, which at the time belonged to Emir Īlghāzī ibn Artuq. He wrote to him, asked for a meeting and invited him to support him, both of them acting as one. He told him that their fear of the sultan ought to unite them in securing protection from him. Īlghāzī did not respond but departed from Nisibis, having installed his son there and ordered him to hold it against Jāwulī, to fight him if he attacked, and he himself went to Mardīn.

Hearing this, Jāwulī vered away from Nisibis and made for Dārā. He sent a second time to Īlghāzī on these matters and himself followed his envoy. While his envoy was with Īlghāzī in Mardīn, before the latter realised it, Jāwulī was alongside him in the citadel, alone, with every intention of gaining his support and sympathy. When he saw him, Īlghāzī rose and did obeisance. Seeing Jāwulī so confident of a good reception and not wary of him, he found it impossible to deny him. He left the citadel with him and they came to camp together outside Nisibis. From there they went to Sinjār, which they besieged for a while but the person in charge there did not agree to terms. So they left and moved towards al-Raḥba. Īlghāzī was making a show of cooperating with Jāwulī but was harbouring opposition and looking for an opportunity [**460**] to leave him. After they arrived at 'Arābān,[1] in the Khābūr valley, Īlghāzī fled at night and made for Nisibis.

---

1 According to Krawulsky, 427–8, the modern name is Tell al-'Ajjāja.

How Jāwulī released the Frankish Count

After Īlghāzī's flight Jāwulī set out for al-Raḥba. Having arrived at Māksīn,[2] he released the Frankish Count who had been his prisoner at Mosul and whom he had taken with him. His name was Baldwin and he was lord of Edessa, Sarūj and other places. Up to this moment he had remained in captivity. He had offered large sums of money but he was not set free. However, at this time, Jāwulī released him and gave him a robe of honour. His stay in prison was almost five years. It was stipulated that he should pay a ransom, free the Muslim captives he held in prison and that he should give aid in person and with his troops and money, when that was wanted.

When this was agreed, Jāwulī sent the Count to Qal'at Ja'bar and handed him over to the ruler there, Sālim ibn Mālik, until Joscelin, his cousin and one of the Franks' brave knights, ruler of Tell Bāshir and elsewhere, came to him. Joscelin had been taken prisoner with the Count in the same battle but had ransomed himself for 20,000 dinars. After he came to Qal'at Ja'bar, he remained there in the Count's place as a hostage. The Count was released and travelled to Antioch. Jāwulī took Joscelin from Qal'at Ja'bar and set him free, taking in his place his wife's brother and the Count's brother-in-law, and sent him to the Count to strengthen him and to urge him to free the prisoners and send the money and what he had guaranteed. When Joscelin reached Manbij he raided and sacked it, while he had with him a detachment of Jāwulī's men. They objected and called it treacherous behaviour. He replied, 'This city is not yours.'

[461] Account of what occurred between this Count and the lord of Antioch

After the release of the Count and his journey to Antioch, Tancred, its ruler, gave him 30,000 dinars, horses, weapons, apparel and other things. Tancred had taken Edessa from the Count's men when he was captured. The latter now proposed that it should be restored to him but this was not done, so he left Tancred to go to Tell Bāshir, where Joscelin joined him, having been released by Jāwulī, much to the delight and joy of the Count.

Tancred, ruler of Antioch, now marched against them with his troops to bring them to battle before they became powerful and assembled an army and before Jāwulī could join forces with them to bring them support. They fought together but when the fighting was over, they met, feasted and conversed with one another. The Count freed one hundred and sixty Muslim prisoners, all of them from the hinterland of Aleppo, clothed them and sent them on their way.

Tancred retired to Antioch without having settled any matter as regards Edessa.[3]

---

[2] A town on the Khābūr River, modern name Markada (see Krawulsky, 443–4).

[3] For the dispute over control of Edessa after the release of Joscelin of Courtenay in 1107 and Baldwin of Bourg in 1108, see Asbridge, *Principality of Antioch*, 112ff.

The Count and Joscelin then went on a raid of Tancred's forts and took refuge in the area controlled by Kogh Basil,[4] an Armenian, who had with him a large body of apostates and others and who was the lord of Ra'bān, Kaysūm[5] and other fortresses north of Aleppo. He supplied the Count with 1,000 cavalry from amongst the apostates, and 2,000 infantry. Tancred moved to meet them and they argued about who was to control Edessa. Their Patriarch,[6] who is for them like the Imam for the Muslims, whose authority is not to be opposed, acted as intermediary. Several metropolitans and priests bore witness that Bohemond, Tancred's uncle, had said to him, when he planned to sail the sea and return home, [**462**] that Edessa should be restored to the Count when he was set free from captivity. Tancred duly restored it on 9 Ṣafar [18 September 1108]. The Count crossed the Euphrates to hand the ransom money and prisoners to Jāwulī's subordinates. On his way he released a large number of captives from Ḥarrān and elsewhere.

In Sarūj there were three hundred indigent Muslims. Jāwulī's men repaired their mosques. The headman of Sarūj was a Muslim who had apostatised. Jāwulī's men heard him speaking disparagingly of Islam, so they beat him and because of him there arose a dispute between them and the Franks. This was reported to the Count, who said, 'This is no good either for us or for the Muslims,' and he put him to death.

What happened to Jāwulī after the release of the Count

After Jāwulī had released the Count at Māksīn, he proceeded to al-Raḥba, where Abū'l-Najm Badrān and Abū Kāmil Manṣūr, the sons of Sayf al-Dawla Ṣadaqa, came to him. After the killing of their father they had been at Qal'at Ja'bar with Sālim ibn Mālik. They reached an agreement to help and support one another and Sālim promised them both that he would go with them to al-Ḥilla. Their intention was to make Baktāsh ibn Tutush ibn Alp Arslan their commander. While they had this plan the General Ṣabāwa came to them. He had sought out the sultan who had assigned him al-Raḥba as a fief, as we have mentioned. He met with Jāwulī and advised him to go to Syria, for the land there was empty of troops since the Franks had conquered much of it. He told him that, if ever he aimed at Iraq while the sultan was there or nearby, he could not be sure that some evil would not come upon him. He accepted what he said and left al-Raḥba. Envoys of Sālim ibn Mālik, lord of Qal'at Ja'bar, came to him, [**463**] seeking his aid against the Banū Numayr.

---

4 In the text Kawāsīl. He died in the year 506/1112, see below p. [**493**].

5 Ra'bān: town and castle between Sumaysāṭ and Aleppo, near the Euphrates. Kaysūm: fort above the village of the same name in the district of Sumaysāṭ (Le Strange, *Palestine*, 475, 517).

6 i.e. Bernard, Patriarch of Antioch (Runciman, ii, 113).

Raqqa had been in the possession of his son, ʻAlī ibn Sālim, but Jawshan al-Numayrī along with a group of the Banū Numayr surprised and killed ʻAlī and seized Raqqa.

Riḍwān heard of this and he set out for Ṣiffīn from Aleppo. He encountered ninety Franks who had with them some part of the ransom of the Count, lord of Edessa, which he had sent off to Jāwulī. Riḍwān seized it and took a number of them prisoner. He came to Raqqa and made peace with the Banū Numayr in return for some payment and then left them to return to Aleppo. Sālim ibn Mālik asked Jāwulī for military aid and requested him to go to Raqqa and take it, promising him what he might need. So Jāwulī marched to Raqqa and besieged it for seventy days. The Banū Numayr guaranteed to give him money and horses. He sent to Sālim, saying, 'I am engaged in a project more important than this. I am face to face with an enemy, with whom I must concern myself rather than anyone else. I am planning to go down to Iraq. If my cause succeeds, then Raqqa and other places will be yours. I will not be distracted from this important matter by besieging five individuals of the Banū Numayr.'

Then there came to Jāwulī Emir Ḥusayn, the son of the Atabeg Qutlughtakīn. His father was been the atabeg of Sultan Muḥammad but the latter put him to death. However, his son prospered at the court of the sultan and became an intimate of his. The sultan sent him with Fakhr al-Dīn ibn ʻAmmār to repair his relations with Jāwulī and to command the troops to march with Ibn ʻAmmār to wage Jihad against the infidels. He came to Jāwulī, ordered him to surrender his lands and put his heart at rest regarding the sultan, guaranteeing him fair treatment, if he yielded his lands and declared his obedience and subordination. Jāwulī answered, ' I am the sultan's humble servant and will obey him,' and he had money and apparel of great value handed over to him and said, 'Go to Mosul and withdraw the army from the city. I will send with you someone who will deliver my son to you as a hostage, and let the sultan despatch someone to take charge of the city [**464**] and collect its taxes.' Ḥusayn did this and set out with Jāwulī's man. When they arrived at the army which was besieging Mosul, not yet having captured it, Ḥusayn ordered them to withdraw. All agreed except for Emir Mawdūd, who said, 'I will only withdraw on the orders of the sultan,' and he arrested Jāwulī's man and remained before Mosul until he took it, as we have related.

Ḥusayn ibn Qutlughtakīn returned to the sultan and put before him a good case on behalf of Jawulī. Jāwulī went to the city of Bālis, arriving on 13 Ṣafar [22 September 1108], but the populace resisted him. Those men of Prince Riḍwān, the lord of Aleppo, who were there, fled. Jāwulī besieged it for five days and took it after mining one of the towers, which fell on the sappers, killing several of them. He took the city and crucified a group of notables where the mine had been. He summoned the Cadi Muḥammad ibn ʻAbd al-ʻAzīz ibn Ilyās, who was a pious lawyer, and put him to death. Then he sacked the city and took a great amount of money.

Account of the battle between Jāwulī and the Franks

In Ṣafar this year [10 September-8 October 1108] a battle took place between Jāwulī Saqāo and Tancred the Frank, the ruler of Antioch. The reason was that Prince Riḍwān corresponded with Tancred informing him of Jāwulī's treacherous, sly and deceitful behaviour, warning against him and telling that he was intending to attack Aleppo and that, if he conquered it, the Franks would no longer maintain their presence in Syria. He asked Tancred for aid and for an alliance to resist him. Tancred responded to this and marched out of Antioch. Riḍwān sent him 600 cavalry. Having heard news of this, Jāwulī sent to the Count, **[465]** lord of Edessa, inviting him to provide aid, and he waived the outstanding ransom money. Upon that, the Count proceeded to join forces with Jāwulī, who was at Manbij. In this state of affairs Jāwulī received intelligence that the sultan's army had conquered Mosul and seized his treasury and property. This distressed him greatly and many of his followers abandoned him, including Atabeg Zankī ibn Āqsunqur and Baktāsh al-Nihawandī. He was left with a thousand horsemen but a large crowd of volunteers joined him and he camped before Tell Bāshir.

Tancred drew near, leading 1,500 Frankish cavalry and 600 of Prince Riḍwān's followers, not counting the foot-soldiers. On his right wing Jāwulī placed Emir Aqsiyān, Emir Altūntāsh al-Abarī and others, and on the left wing Emir Badrān ibn Ṣadaqa, General Ṣabāwa and Sunqur Darāz and in the centre Count Baldwin and Joscelin, the two Franks. The battle commenced and the men of Antioch charged the Count. The fighting was fierce and Tancred drove the centre from its position. Then Jāwulī's left charged the infantry of the lord of Antioch and slew a great many of them. The defeat of the lord of Antioch seemed imminent but at that moment Jāwulī's men turned to the Count's spare horses and those of Joscelin and other Franks. They mounted them and fled the field. Jāwulī went after them to call them back but they did not return. His authority over them had been lost after Mosul had been taken from him. When he saw that they would not return with him, he took thought for himself, feared to stay and fled. The rest of his army then fled.

The General Ṣabāwa went towards Damascus, Badrān ibn Ṣadaqa to Qal'at Ja'bar and the son of Jokermish set out for Jazīrat Ibn 'Umar. As for Jāwulī, **[466]** he made for al-Raḥba. A host of Muslims were killed and the lord of Antioch plundered their belongings and their baggage train. They suffered much from the Franks. The Count and Joscelin fled to Tell Bāshir and a great number of Muslims sought refuge with them. They treated them well. They nursed the wounded, clothed the naked and sent them to their own lands.

How Jāwulī returned to the sultan

After Jāwulī Saqāo's defeat he made for al-Raḥba. When he had drawn near, he spent the night just short of it with a number of horsemen. It so happened that a detachment of Emir Mawdūd's army that had taken Mosul from Jāwulī raided some Arab tribesmen who lived near al-Raḥba and they came close to Jāwulī quite unawares. Had they known they would have captured him.

When he saw how things were, Jāwulī realised that he was able to remain neither in the Jazīra nor in Syria. He had no means of preserving himself, nothing to resort to and no way to treat his ills apart from repairing to the sultan's court willingly and of his own free will. He had trust in the Emir Ḥusayn ibn Qutlughtakīn, so, although fearful and cautious, having concealed his person and kept his whereabouts a secret, he set out and went to where the sultan's army was, in the vicinity of Isfahan. He arrived within seventeen days of leaving because he made forced marches. He came into the sultan's presence with his shroud under his arm and was given a guarantee of life and limb. The emirs came to him with their congratulations. The sultan meanwhile asked him for Prince Baktāsh ibn Tutush, who, after he had been handed over, was imprisoned in Isfahan.

[467] The battle between Ṭughtakīn and the Franks and the subsequent treaty

There was a fierce battle this year between Ṭughtakīn the Atabeg and the Franks which came about because Ṭughtakīn went to Tiberias after the nephew[7] of Baldwin the Frank, king of Jerusalem, had arrived there. They came to open hostilities. Ṭughtakīn had 2,000 cavalry and a large number of infantry, while the king of Jerusalem's nephew led 400 knights and 2,000 infantry.

After some intense fighting, the Muslims retreated. Ṭughtakīn dismounted and addressed the Muslims with words of encouragement. They returned to the fray and broke the Franks, capturing the king's nephew who was taken to Ṭughtakīn. Ṭughtakīn proposed his conversion to Islam but he refused and offered 30,000 dinars and the liberation of 500 captives to ransom himself. Ṭughtakīn was not satisfied with anything but his conversion and, when he would not agree, killed him with his own hand. He sent the prisoners he made to the caliph and the sultan. Later Ṭughtakīn and Baldwin, the king of the Franks, agreed to a cessation of hostilities for four years. This was for the Muslims a blessing from God Almighty. Had it not been for this treaty the Franks would have attained a great success over the Muslims after the defeat which is about to be mentioned.

How Ṭughtakīn fled from the Franks

In this year, during the month of Sha'bān [March 1109], the Atabeg Ṭughtakīn was

---

[7] 'The son of the king's sister.' Gervase of Tiberias is intended.

defeated by the Franks. This happened as follows. The fortress of ʻArqa, in the district of Tripoli, was in the hands of a mamluke of the Cadi Fakhr al-Mulk Abū ʻAlī ibn ʻAmmār, the lord of Tripoli, and was very strong. [**468**] He rebelled against his master but ran short of food and his supplies were interrupted because the Franks had remained so long in the area. He therefore sent to Atabeg Ṭughtakīn, lord of Damascus, and said to him, 'Send someone to whom I can surrender this fortress. I am incapable of holding it and that Muslims should take it is better for me in this world and the next than that the Franks should.' Ṭughtakīn sent him one of his subordinates, called Isrā'īl, with 300 men and he took over the fortress. After Ibn ʻAmmār's mamluke had descended from the fortress Isrā'īl shot him with an arrow in the 'humours'[8] and killed him. His purpose in doing so was to stop him informing the Atabeg Ṭughtakīn of the money he had left in the citadel.

Tughtakīn planned to go to the fortress to inspect it and put a strong garrison in it with provisions and war materials. However, for two months there was rain and snow night and day which prevented him. When that had passed he set out with 4,000 cavalry. He conquered several forts of the Franks, including the fort of al-Akma. When the Frankish Count of Cerdagne,[9] while besieging Tripoli, heard of Ṭughtakīn's coming, he set out with 300 knights. This company came in sight of Ṭughtakīn's troops and the latter fled, leaving their baggage train, their personal effects and their horses for the Franks, who took the booty, became much strengthened by it and much better equipped.

The Muslims arrived at Homs in an extremely bad state of disarray, although no one had been killed because there had been no battle. The Count of Cerdagne came to ʻArqa and after he had invested it, the garrison asked for terms. He guaranteed them their lives and took over the fort. When the garrison left he arrested Isrā'īl and said, ' I will only free him in return for the freeing of so-and-so,' meaning a certain Frank, prisoner in Damascus for the last seven years. This exchange was accepted and both were freed together.

[**469**] When Ṭughtakīn arrived at Damascus after this defeat, the king of Jerusalem sent to him, saying, 'Do not imagine that I will break our treaty because of the defeat that you have undergone, for princes suffer worse than what you have suffered and then their affairs return to order and a sound state.' Ṭughtakīn had feared that after this set-back the king would attack him and acquire any of his lands that he chose.

Account of the Sunnis' and Shiites' settlement at Baghdad

This year in Shaʻbān [March 1109] the common people of Baghdad, Sunni and

---

[8] How one can be shot in *al-akhlāṭ*, the four 'humours' of the body? Perhaps the text is corrupt.

[9] In Arabic al-Sirdānī al-Faranjī, i.e. William Jordan, Count of Cerdagne, who initially succeeded Raymond I.

Shiite, reached a settlement. They had been the cause of trouble over a long period. Caliphs, sultans and prefects had struggled to improve the situation but it had proved impossible for them until God Almighty gave his leave and it came about without any intermediary.

The reason was that after Sultan Muḥammad had killed the King of the Arabs Ṣadaqa, as we have recounted, the Shia in Baghdad, the inhabitants of Karkh and elsewhere, were fearful because Ṣadaqa and his family were Shiites and the Sunnis exposed them to rude taunts on account of the dismay and anxiety that came upon them because of his death. So the Shiites were fearful and put up with what they were hearing. Their fears continued until Sha'bān. At the commencement of this month the Sunnis made their preparations for the pilgrimage to the tomb of Muṣ'ab ibn al-Zubayr,[10] which they had not performed for many years, having been prevented from doing so to put a stop to the disturbances which resulted from it.

When they made their preparations for their progress, they agreed to take their route through Karkh. They announced this and the general opinion of the inhabitants of Karkh was that they should not object nor resist them. The Sunnis began to send off the inhabitants of each quarter one after the other, accompanied by much decorative display and weaponry. The population of the Gate of Degrees came with an elephant made of wood with armed men upon it. All of them made for Karkh to cross through it, and the inhabitants met them with incense, **[470]** perfume, chilled water and display of weapons. With every sign of joy they conducted them through and out of their quarter.

On the eve of the middle of the month the Shia went out to the shrine of Mūsā ibn Ja'far[11] and to others and not a single Sunni impeded them. People were astonished at this. When [the Sunnis] returned from their visit to the tomb of Muṣ'ab, the inhabitants of Karkh met them with joy and delight. It chanced that the elephant of the Gate of Degrees group fell apart at the Ḥarb Gate bridge. Some persons appositely recited, 'Did you not see how your Lord dealt with the followers of the elephant ...,' down to the end of the chapter.[12]

Miscellaneous events

This year Manṣūr ibn Ṣadaqa ibn Mazyad returned to the sultan's court and was generously received. After the death of his father he had been a fugitive until this moment. His brother, Badrān ibn Ṣadaqa had attached himself to Emir Mawdūd to whom the sultan had given Mosul as a fief. He made him an honoured and

[10] The brother of the 'anti-caliph' 'Abd Allāh ibn al-Zubayr, for whom he served as governor of Iraq. He died in battle with the Umayyad 'Abd al-Malik in 72/619 (*EI(2)*, vii, 649-50).

[11] Mūsā al-Kāẓim, the seventh of the twelve Imāms, died at Baghdad in 183/799.

[12] See Koran, cv, 1-5. The reference is to the Abyssinian army under Abraha which unsuccessfully attacked Mecca *c*.570 A.D. Either this passage was quoted jocularly or, as one suspects, sectarian animosities had not entirely ceased.

welcome member of his company.

In Nīsān of this year [April 1109] the Tigris rose greatly and the roads were made impassable. The winter and summer crops were inundated and a great famine ensued in Iraq. A *kāra* of roughly ground wheat reached ten Imāmī dinars and bread was quite impossible to find. The people ate dates and green beans. As for the inhabitants of the hinterland, they had nothing to eat the whole of Ramaḍān and for half of Shawwāl [4 April-18 May 1109] except for grass and mulberries.

In Rajab [4 February-5 March 1109] the caliph's vizier, Abū'l-Ma'ālī Hibat Allāh ibn al-Muṭṭalib was dismissed and the office was taken by [**471**] Abū'l-Qāsim 'Alī ibn Abī Naṣr ibn Jahīr.

In Sha'bān [March 1109] the Caliph al-Mustaẓhir bi-Allāh married the daughter of Sultan Malikshāh, the sister of Sultan Muḥammad. The person who proposed the match was the Cadi Abū'l-'Alā' Ṣā'id ibn Muḥammad al-Nīsābūrī al-Ḥanafī, and the person who acted to accept the contract as agent for the caliph was Niẓām al-Mulk Aḥmad ibn Niẓām al-Mulk, the sultan's vizier. The dowry was 100,000 dinars, and jewels and dinars were scattered when the contract was made at Isfahan.

This year Mujāhid al-Dīn Bahrūz was appointed prefect of Baghdad. This was because Sultan Muḥammad had arrested Abū'l-Qāsim al-Ḥusayn ibn 'Abd al-Wāḥid, the head of the Storehouse, and Abū'l-Faraj, son of Ra'īs al-Ru'asā',[13] and imprisoned them both. At this time he released them and imposed on them a fine to pay. He sent Mujāhid al-Dīn Bahrūz to collect the money and also ordered him to repair the Sultan's Residence. He complied, repaired the Residence and ruled the populace well. When the sultan came to Baghdad, he appointed him as prefect of the whole of Iraq and also gave a robe of honour to Sa'īd ibn Ḥamīd al-'Umarī, Ṣadaqa's army chief, and put him in charge of al-Ḥilla al-Sayfiyya. Sa'īd was stern, resolute but a man of good sense and patience.

In Shawwāl [May 1109] Emir Sukmān al-Quṭbī, the lord of Khilāṭ, took the city of Mayyāfāriqīn on terms after a siege and blockading the inhabitants for several months. Foodstuffs were unobtainable there and the populace's hunger became extreme, so they surrendered the city.

In Ṣafar of this year [10 September–8 October 1108] the cadi of Isfahan, 'Ubayd Allāh ibn 'Alī al-Khaṭībī, was killed in Hamadhan. He had devoted his full attention to the Bātinī problem and taken to wearing a mail shirt as a precaution and observing other security measures. One Friday a man from Persia sought him out, [**472**] got between him and his guards and killed him. Ṣā'id ibn Muḥammad ibn 'Abd al-Raḥmān, Abū'l-'Alā', the qādī of Nishapur, was killed the day of the Feast[14] [4 May 1109], assassinated by a Bāṭinī, who was himself slain. Born in the year 448 [1056-7], he was a scholar of Ḥadīth and a member of the Ḥanafī school of law.

---

[13] 'Alī ibn al-Muslima, the vizier of the Caliph al-Qā'im, who was killed by Emir al-Basāsīrī during his year's control of Baghdad in 450/1058-9 (see Richards, *Annals*, 119-23).

[14] The *'īd al-fiṭr*, to mark the end of Ramaḍān, celebrated 1 Shawwāl.

This year a large caravan left Damascus for Egypt, intelligence of which came to the King of the Franks. He therefore set out and opposed its passage, capturing all who were part of it. Only a few of them escaped but those who did escape the Bedouin seized.

Also this year at the Christians' Easter a group of Bāṭinīs, a hundred strong, rose up in the fortress of Shayzar, taking the inhabitants by surprise, seized it and drove them out. They closed the gate and went up into the citadel which they took over. The rulers there, the Banū Munqidh, had descended to attend the Christians' festival. They had treated those who now caused this mischief very well. The people of the town hastened to the barbican and their women pulled them up through the windows by ropes to join them. The Banū Munqidh emirs, the rulers of the fortress, also came on the scene and climbed up to join them and overcame the Bāṭinīs in battle. They were foiled and fell before the sword on every side. Not one of them escaped and those in the town of like persuasion were also put to death.

Three strangers came to al-Mahdiyya this year. They wrote to the local emir, Yaḥyā ibn Tamīm, to say that they practised alchemy. He summoned them and ordered them to perform something of their art that he could witness. They replied, 'We shall make an ingot.' He provided the equipment and other things that they asked for. He then took his seat amongst them, he and the Sharīf Abū'l-Ḥasan and the commander of his army, called Ibrāhīm, both of whom were intimate with him. When the alchemists saw that the place was empty of company, [**473**] they attacked them. One of them struck Yaḥyā ibn Tamīm on his head, but the dagger hit his turban and had no effect. Yaḥyā kicked him and threw him down on his back, then went through a door and locked himself in. The second man struck and killed the Sharīf. The commander Ibrāhīm drew his sword and fought with the alchemists. A commotion ensued, whereupon Emir Yaḥyā's men entered and slew the alchemists. Their dress was that of men from Andalusia, so several men in the town dressed in a similar way were put to death. Emir Yaḥyā was told that some people had seen these men with al-Muqaddam ibn Khalīfa. It also happened that Emir Abū'l-Futūḥ ibn Tamīm, Yaḥyā's brother, came to the palace at that time with his followers, fully armed. He was prevented from entering and Emir Yaḥyā became convinced that this had been instigated by the two of them. He summoned al-Muqaddam ibn Khalīfa and the latter's nephews, on Yaḥyā's orders, killed al-Muqaddam in retaliation for having killed their father. He expelled Emir Abū'l-Futūḥ and his wife, Ballāra, daughter of al-Qāsim ibn Tamīm and his cousin, and put them under guard in Ziyād's palace between al-Mahdiyya and Sfax, where they remained until the death of Yaḥyā. His son 'Alī succeeded in the year 509 [1115–16] and he sent Abū'l-Futūḥ and his wife Ballāra to Egypt by sea. They arrived at Alexandria, as we shall narrate, God willing.[15]

---

[15] This whole passage is discussed in Idris, *La Berbérie*, 310–14, where other versions are examined. For the succession, see below pp. [**512–13**]. However, Ibn al-Athīr does not mention what he promised.

In Muḥarram [August 1109] ‘Abd al-Wāḥid ibn Ismā‘īl ibn Aḥmad ibn Muḥammad Abū’l-Maḥāsin al-Rūyānī al-Ṭabarī, the Shāfi‘ī lawyer, born in the year 415 [1024-5], was killed. He was well versed in his law school. He used to say, ‘Were all the writings of al-Shāfi‘ī to be burnt, I could dictate them all by heart.’

The following died this year:

In Jumādā II [January 1109] the preacher, Abū Zakarīyā’ Yaḥyā ibn ‘Alī al-Tabrīzī al-Shaybānī, a scholar of [the Arabic] language, the author of well-known works and a poet of no merit.

In Rajab [4 February–5 March 1109] al-Sayyid Abū Hāshim Zayd al-Ḥasanī al-‘Alawī, the headman [**474**] of Hamadhan. He was a strong and effective administrator, whose headship lasted for forty-seven years. His maternal grandfather was al-Ṣāḥib Abū’l-Qāsim ibn ‘Abbād.[16] He was an extremely rich man and, as an indication of that, Sultan Muḥammad on one occasion took from him 700,000 dinars, to raise which he neither sold a single property nor borrowed a single dinar. After that for several months he supplied Sultan Muḥammad with money for whatever he wanted. He did little in the way of good works.

In Dhū’l-Ḥijja [July 1109] Abū’l-Fawāris al-Ḥasan ibn ‘Alī al-Khāzin, a famous secretary who wrote an excellent hand. He produced some poetry, for example:

This world is a trouble to those that seek it. The wise ascetic takes his ease.
He has learnt what the world is and has seen that temptations are all that it brings.
For every prince who gains its baubles the only lasting share is a shroud.
Either he acquires wealth or he leaves it; in both cases he is deceived.
My hope is to be sure that I shall be guaranteed to meet God.
I hate the world and how should one not? What it offers is a dream.
It has never endured for anyone before me, so why this anxiety and care?

It is reported that he died in the year 499 [1105-6] and he has been mentioned there.[17]

---

[16] Ismā‘īl ibn ‘Abbād (326–85/938–95), Būyid vizier and man of letters (see *Encyclopedia of Arabic Literature*, ii, 675–6).

[17] An earlier obituary notice under the year 499/1105–6 is given on p. [**415**], where he is called al-Ḥusayn ibn ‘Alī ibn al-Ḥusayn ibn al-Khāzin.

The Year 503 [1109-1110]

How the Franks captured Tripoli and Beirut in Syria

On 11 Dhū'l-Ḥijja this year[1] the Franks captured Tripoli. This came about as follows. Tripoli had been controlled by the ruler of Egypt through his deputy there. The city had received supplies from him. We have mentioned this under the year 501 [1107-8]. In Sha'bān of this present year[2] a great fleet came by sea from the Frankish lands, commanded by a great count, whose name was Raymond, son of [Raymond of] St. Gilles.[3] The ships were loaded with men, weapons and provisions. He besieged Tripoli, which had previously been besieged by the Count of Cerdagne,[4] the nephew of [Raymond of] St. Gilles, who is not the nephew of this Raymond. On the contrary, he is another count.[5] There was dissession between them which ended in trouble and fighting. Tancred, ruler of Antioch, came to Tripoli to aid the Count of Cerdagne. Then King Baldwin, king of Jerusalem, came with his army and made peace between them. All the Franks together descended on Tripoli and began to attack it and press hard on its population from the beginning of Sha'bān.[6] They brought their towers into close contact with the city wall. When the garrison and the populace saw this, they despaired and their spirits sank. The late arrival of the Egyptian fleet with supplies and reinforcements increased their vulnerable state.

The fleet was late because, when it was ready and everything needed had been supplied,[7] they argued about it for more **[476]** than a year. It then set sail but the wind drove it back, and they were unable to get to Tripoli, 'in order that God might fulfil his foreordained plan.'

---

1 This is an error, also found in *Muntaẓam*, ix, 163. The year should be 502 (see Ibn Qal., 163), which, with the 'Monday' given below, makes the date 12 July 1109.

2 Correct this also to Sha'bān 502/ 6 March-3 April 1109.

3 In fact it was Bertrand, son (probably illegitimate) of Raymond I. For an overview of the St. Gilles dynasty, see Richard, *Comté de Tripoli*, 4-8.

4 The count, William Jordan, was Raymond I's cousin, not his nephew.

5 Ibn al-Athīr is confused here and the text possibly corrupt. Even in its own terms the text is not easily explained. The translation (of a slightly different text) in *Recueil*, i, 273 - 'Au contraire Raymond n'était pas fils de soeur; il était comte lui-même ...' - does not convince.

6 See note 2 above.

7 The second half of this clause in the text and in *Kāmil* (Thornberg), x, 334 (*wa'l-ḥathth 'alayhi*) is syntactically awkward and gives no good meaning. Thornberg's footnote gives a variant *irtajjat* [?]. However, in Ms. Pococke 346, fol. 4a. the verb has no diacritical points and the whole phrase should surely be read as *uzīḥat 'illatu-hu*. For this expression (meaning literally 'its excuse was removed') see Dozy, *Supplément*, ii, s.v. *'illatun*.

The Franks intensified[8] their fighting from the siege-towers and their assaults. Finally they assailed the city and took it by force of arms on Monday 11 Dhū'l-Ḥijja [502=12 July 1109]. They sacked the town, taking the men prisoner, enslaving the women and children and seizing property. The amount of money, goods and endowed books from institutions of learning that they plundered from the inhabitants was beyond computation or estimation. The local population was one of the richest and most commercially developed. The governor who was there and some of the garrison, who had asked for terms before it fell, got away safely and came to Damascus. The Franks submitted the populace to all sorts of torture and their hidden treasures and stores were seized from the places where they had hidden them.[9]

The Franks' conquest of Jubayl and Banyās

When the Franks had finished with Tripoli, Tancred, the lord of Antioch, went to Bānyās and, after a siege, took the place and guaranteed the lives of its inhabitants.[10] He then invested the town of Jubayl, where was Fakhr al-Mulk ibn 'Ammār, the former lord of Tripoli. Provisions there were very short. Tancred fought the town until he took possession of it on terms on 22 Dhū'l-Ḥijja of this year.[11] Fakhr al-Mulk ibn 'Ammār left in safety.

A little after the conquest of Tripoli the Egyptian fleet arrived with men, money, food-stuffs and other things, sufficient for a year. The fleet came to Tyre eight days after the fall of Tripoli [**477**] on account of the fate that had been decreed to befall Tripoli's populace. The provisions and stores it brought were distributed in the areas put in need of[12] them, Tyre, Sidon and Beirut.

Fakhr al-Mulk ibn 'Ammār made his way to Shayzar, where he was honourably and respectfully received by its ruler, the Emir Sulṭān ibn 'Alī ibn Munqidh al-Kinānī, who asked him to stay with him. He declined and went to Damascus, where Ṭughtakīn welcomed him and made abundant provision for him and gave generous gifts. He assigned him the district of al-Zabadānī as a fief, a large district,

---

8 Reading *shadda* as in Ms. Pococke 346, fol. 4a. *Kāmil* (Thornberg), x, 334, has *sadda*, a misprint. Cf. Ibn Qal., 163, line 18.

9 Beyond the mention in the rubric nothing is said about Beirut. According to Ibn Qal., 167–8, it fell on Friday 21 Shawwāl 503/13 May 1110.

10 This too was in the year 502. Ibn Qal., 163–4, dates the fall of Bānyās to Shawwāl 502/May 1109.

11 Correct the year to 502. Ibn Qal., 164, gives Friday 22 Dhū'l-Ḥijja [502]/=23 July 1109.

12 This reading is from Ms. Pococke 346, fol. 4b (*al-mufqara* with dotless *fā'*). The editions' *al-munfadha ilayhā* ('the ones sent to') is possible, as Ibn Qal., 164, makes it clear that the supplies were intended for other Fatimid-held towns on the coast, as well as Tripoli, but strict grammar would demand *al-munfadh ilayhā*.

one of the dependent areas of Damascus. This was in Muḥarram of the year 502.[13]

The conflict between Muḥammad Khān and Sāghir Beg

This year Sāghir Beg returned and gathered large forces of Turks and others and attacked the areas controlled by Muḥammad Khān at Samarqand and elsewhere. Muḥammad Khān sent to ask for assistance from Sanjar, who despatched troops to him. Many other forces also gathered around him and he marched against Sāghir Beg. They met in battle in the region of al-Khashab. Sāghir Beg and his troops fled and [their enemies'] swords wreaked their will upon them. Many of them were taken prisoner and much booty seized. When hostilities were over and Muḥammad Khān felt secure from the evil of Sāghir Beg, Sanjar's army returned to Khurasan and crossed the river to Balkh.

Miscellaneous events

In Muḥarram of this year [August 1109] the sultan sent his vizier, Niẓām al-Mulk[14] Aḥmad ibn Niẓām al-Mulk, to the fortress of Alamūt to fight al-Ḥasan ibn al-Ṣabbāḥ and the Ismā'īlīs who were with him. [**478**] They began a siege but winter descended on them, so they withdrew without having achieved any purpose.

During Rabī' II [28 October–25 November 1109] the sultan came to Baghdad and left in Shawwāl, also of this year [23 April–21 May 1110].

In Sha'bān this year [23 February–23 March 1110] the Vizier Niẓām al-Mulk went to the Friday Mosque and was leapt on by some Bāṭinīs, who struck him with daggers, wounding him in the neck. For a while he remained ill but later recovered. The Bāṭinī who wounded him was seized, plied with wine until he was drunk and then questioned about his accomplices. He named several persons in the Ma'mūniyya Mosque.[15] They were taken and put to death.

The caliph's vizier, that is Abū'l-Ma'ālī ibn al-Muṭṭalib, was dismissed this year and replaced by al-Za'īm Abū'l-Qāsim ibn Jahīr. Ibn al-Muṭṭalib, he and his sons, left the Caliphal Palace in disguise and sought protection in the sultan's palace.[16]

---

[13] Ibn al-Athīr's chronology is impossibly muddled here, bearing in mind his dating previous events to later in the year 503. Read Muḥarram 503/31 July–29 August 1109, as in Ibn Qal., 165.

[14] The parallel passage in *Muntaẓam*, ix, 163, calls him Niẓām al-Dīn, as does the text under the year 517, but see s.a. 500, p. [**437**]. This son of the great vizier was also styled Ḍiyā' al-Mulk (see Bundārī, 96, 101 and Klausner, 126, note 45).

[15] That is, the mosque in the Ma'mūniyya quarter (the south-east corner of East Baghdad).

[16] This dismissal and the appointment have been mentioned under the previous year, see above p. [**470–71**]. *Muntaẓam*, ix, 159, dates the dismissal 11 Rajab 502/14 February 1109 and under this year (503) mentions only the flight in disguise (ix, 163).

During this year Yaḥyā ibn Tamīm, the lord of Ifrīqiya, equipped fifteen galleys and sent them towards the Byzantine lands. The Byzantine fleet, which was large, met them and there was a battle. Six of the Muslims' galleys were taken but after this no other force of Yaḥyā met a defeat at sea or on land. He sent his son, Abū'l-Futūḥ, to the city of Sfax to be governor there. The populace rebelled against him and sacked his palace. They intended to kill him but Yaḥyā continued to employ various stratagems until he spread dissension amongst them and broke their united front. He seized their persons and imprisoned them but pardoned their bloodshed and their crimes.[17]

This year Emir Ibrāhīm [ibn] Yināl, lord of Āmid, died. He was a wicked ruler, notorious for injustice. Many of the inhabitants emigrated because of his tyranny. After him his son took power and he was a better man in his ways.[18]

On 8 Dhū'l-Qa'da [29 May 1110] a comet appeared in the sky from the east with a tail stretching to the south. It remained in view until the end of Dhū'l-Ḥijja [19 July 1110] and then disappeared.

---

17 The appointment of Abū'l-Futūḥ is dated to 504/1110–11, but no date given for the plot, see Idris, *La Berbérie*, 309 and sources there cited.

18 Fakhr al-Dawla Ibrāhīm's father, the Turkoman chief Yināl, began his rule in Āmid in about 490/1096–7. Ibrāhīm was succeeded by Sa'd al-Dawla Īkaldi (Ĭl-aldï), who died in Jumādā I 536/December 1141. Āmid remained in the family's hands until 572/1176 (Ibn Qal., 275 and note 3; 131, note 1; Hillenbrand, *Muslim Principality,* 102, note 95).

[479] The Year 504 [1110–1111]

Account of the Franks' capture of Sidon

In Rabīʿ II of this year [October 1110] the Franks gained possession of the city of Sidon on the coast of Syria. This came about because there arrived by sea to Syria sixty ships of the Franks, loaded with men and supplies, accompanied by one of their princes, intent on making a pilgrimage to Jerusalem and on waging war, as he asserted, against the Muslims.[1] Baldwin, the king of Jerusalem, met with them and an agreement was made between them that they would attack Islamic territory. They set out from Jerusalem and besieged the city of Sidon on 3 Rabīʿ II [19 October 1110] and pressed it hard by land and sea.

The Egyptian fleet was anchored at Tyre but was unable to aid Sidon. The Franks constructed a wooden tower very solidly. They put on it a protective covering against fire and stones and moved it forward for an assault. When the inhabitants of Sidon saw it, their hearts sank and they feared that the same would befall them as had befallen the people of Beirut, so they sent the cadi and a number of the city's shaykhs to the Franks. They requested terms from the king, who gave a guarantee of their lives and property to them [**480**] and to the troops amongst them. To whomsoever wished to remain there with them they granted terms but whoever wanted to depart was not stopped. An oath to that effect was given them. The governor left and also a large number of the notables of the city on 20 Jumādā I [=5 December 1110] to go to Damascus. A great number remained in the city under the guarantee. The siege had lasted forty-seven days.

Baldwin left for Jerusalem but then returned to Sidon after a little while and imposed on the Muslims who had remained there payment of 20,000 dinars. He impoverished them and swallowed up their wealth.

How the Egyptians took control of Ascalon

Ascalon had belonged to the Alid [caliphs] of Egypt but then the Caliph al-Āmir bi-Aḥkām Allāh appointed as governor there a man called Shams al-Khilāfa. He made contact with Baldwin, king of the Franks in Syria, arranged a truce with him and gave him gifts of money and goods. With Baldwin's support he avoided Egyptian control, except where he was willing to accept it, without proclaiming that openly.

---

[1] This prince was King Sigurd I of Norway, who had sailed from Bergen in 1107 (Runciman, ii, 92).

Knowledge of this reached al-Āmir bi-Aḥkām Allāh, ruler of Egypt, and his vizier, al-Afḍal Emir al-Juyūsh. Both were outraged and equipped a force which they sent to Ascalon with a great general of theirs. They announced that his purpose was to make war [on the Franks] but they secretly informed the general that he should arrest Shams al-Khilāfa when he presented himself before them and that he himself should remain in his place at Ascalon as emir. The army set out but Shams al-Khilāfa understood how things were and refused to appear amongst [**481**] the Egyptian army. He proclaimed his rebellion openly and expelled the Egyptian troops he had with him for fear of them.

When al-Afḍal learnt of that, he feared that he might surrender Ascalon to the Franks, so he sent to him, reconciled him and calmed his fears. He confirmed him in his office and restored to him his fief in Egypt. Next Shams al-Khilāfa became fearful of the people of Ascalon and so summoned a group of Armenians whom he enlisted as troops. Things remained like this until the end of the year 504 [June–July 1111]. The townsfolk were unhappy with the situation. Some of the notables pounced on him while he was out riding and wounded him. He fled from them back to his residence but they followed and killed him. They plundered his house and all the contents and also plundered some houses belonging to others, men of wealth, on this pretext. They sent to Egypt with a full report of the matter to al-Āmir and al-Afḍal, who were delighted and were generous to those who brought this good news. They despatched a governor to reside there and to exercise goodwill and fair government towards the populace. This was done and the fears they had were removed.

Account of the Franks' taking of the fortress of al-Athārib and others

This year the lord of Antioch gathered his forces amongst the Franks and mobilised cavalry and infantry. He marched towards the fortress of al-Athārib which is near the city of Aleppo, about three leagues distant. He besieged it and cut off its supplies. The situation for the Muslims there became serious. They dug a mine from the citadel, planning to emerge from it and attack the lord of Antioch's tent and kill him. When they did this and drew close to his tent, an Armenian youth sought sanctuary with him and told of the plan. The lord took precautions and guarded against them. He pressed the attacks strongly until the fortress was taken by force of arms. Two thousand men of the populace were killed and the rest were enslaved and made captive.[2]

[**482**] He then proceeded to the fortess of Zardanā, which he besieged and took. He treated the populace as at al-Athārib. When the inhabitants of Manbij heard of this, they abandoned the town for fear of the Franks, and the people of Bālis did

---

2 For Tancred's taking of al-Athārib in October 1110 and other gains, see Asbridge, *Principality of Antioch*, 65-6.

likewise. The Franks went to the two towns but when they saw them devoid of any living soul they withdrew from them.

A force of Franks went to Sidon and the people there asked them for terms, which were granted, and they took over the city. The Muslims' fear of them was great and their hearts were in their throats, convinced that the Franks would gain control of all Syria because there was no one to protect and defend it. The rulers of the Syrian territories in Muslim hands began to negotiate truces with them but the Franks refused to grant them except for a short period on payment of tribute. Prince Riḍwān, the lord of Aleppo, made peace with them on payment of 32,000 dinars and other items, including horses and clothing. The lord of Tyre made a truce on payment of 7,000 dinars, as did Ibn Munqidh, lord of Shayzar, for 4,000 dinars. The lord of Ḥāma, 'Alī the Kurd, made peace with them for 2,000 dinars. The period of truce was until the ripening and harvesting of the crops.

Some ships set sail from Egypt bearing merchants and their large amount of merchandise. They were intercepted by Frankish ships and seized. All that the merchants had became booty and they themselves were made prisoner.

A number of the inhabitants of Aleppo travelled to Baghdad to seek aid against the Franks. Having arrived at Baghdad[3] they were joined by a host of canon lawyers and others. They marched to the Sultan's Mosque and pleaded for help. They prevented prayer and smashed the pulpit. The sultan promised to send troops for the Jihad and he sent a pulpit to the Sultan's Mosque from the Caliphal Palace. On the following Friday they marched to the Palace Mosque in the caliphal residence, accompanied by the people of Baghdad. The palace chamberlain denied them access but they overwhelmed him and entered the mosque, where they broke the grille of the *maqṣūra*.[4] **[483]** They also attacked and demolished the pulpit. The Friday prayer was again cancelled. The caliph sent to the sultan on this matter, ordering him to concern himself with this shortcoming and to remedy it. Thereupon the sultan commanded the emirs with him to return to their lands and to prepare for the Jihad. He sent his son, Prince Mas'ūd, with Emir Mawdūd, lord of Mosul. They went first to Mosul with the intention that the emirs would join them and proceed to fight the Franks. Thus the year came to an end and they set out during the year 505 [1111]. There followed what we shall relate, God Almighty willing.

Miscellaneous events

This year Niẓām al-Mulk Aḥmad was dismissed from office as vizier of the sultan

---

3 These protestors ('a Hashemite *sharīf* from Aleppo and several sufis, merchants and canon lawyers') arrived 'the first Friday in Sha'bān'/17 February 1111 (Ibn Qal., 173).

4 The secure, separate area reserved for the ruler when attending prayers, normally near the *miḥrāb* (see *EI(2)*, vi, 661–2).

and Khaṭīr al-Mulk Muḥammad ibn al-Ḥusayn al-Maybudī became vizier to follow him.

An envoy from the Byzantine emperor came to the sultan, seeking his support against the Franks and urging him to fight them and drive them from the lands. His arrival[5] preceded the arrival of the people from Aleppo, who said to the sultan, 'Are you not ashamed before God Almighty that the Byzantine emperor shows greater zeal for Islam than you, so that he has sent to you concerning Jihad against them?'

In Ramaḍān [March 1111] the daughter of Sultan Malikshāh was led in bridal procession to the caliph. Baghdad was decorated [**484**] and closed off.[6] Great celebrations were held, the like of which people had never witnessed.

This year a black wind blew in Egypt which darkened the world and took away people's breath. No one was able to open his eyes. Anyone who did could not see his hand before him. Sand descended on people and they despaired of life, convinced they would perish. Then it brightened a little and clear skies returned. That lasted from the beginning of the afternoon until after sunset.

In Muḥarram[7] [July 1111] al-Kiyā al-Harrās al-Ṭabarī died. His name was Abū'l-Ḥasan 'Alī ibn Muḥammad ibn 'Alī and he was one of the outstanding Shāfi'ī lawyers who learnt his canon law from the Imam of the Two Sanctuaries al-Juwaynī and taught after him in the Niẓāmiyya at Baghdad, where he died. He was buried in the tomb of the Shaykh Abū Isḥāq. His successor as professor at the Niẓāmiyya was the Imam Abū Bakr al-Shāshī.

In this year also there died Abū'l-Ḥusayn Idrīs ibn Ḥamza ibn 'Alī al-Ramlī, the Shāfi'ī lawyer, a citizen of Ramla in Palestine, who studied law with Abū'l-Fatḥ Naṣr ibn Ibrāhīm al-Muqaddasī and the Shaykh Abū Isḥāq al-Shirāzī. He went away to Khurasan and held a professorship at Samarqand, where he died.

---

5 In Jumādā II/15 December 1110–12 January 1111 (Ibn Qal., 173).

6 *Muntaẓam*, ix, 166, has 'the market-places were closed and domes were erected' and dates the procession to 'the eve of 10 Ramaḍān'/22 March.

7 On Thursday 1 Muḥarram/20 July (*Muntaẓam*, ix, 167).

[485] The Year 505 [1111-1112]

How the armies went to fight the Franks

This year the armies, which the sultan ordered to go to fight the Franks, gathered. There were Emir Mawdūd, the lord of Mosul, Emir Sukmān al-Quṭbī, lord of Tabrīz and part of Diyār Bakr, the two emirs, Īlbakī and Zankī, the sons of Bursuq, who held Hamadhan and its neighbourhood, and Emir Aḥmadīl, who had Marāgha. Emir Abū'l-Hayjā', lord of Irbil, Emir Īlghāzī, lord of Mardīn, and the Bakjiyya emirs were written to, ordering them to join Prince Mas'ūd and Mawdūd. This they did, except for Īlghāzī, for he sent his son Ayāz and himself stayed at home. When they had gathered they set out for Sinjār. They took several castles held by the Franks and killed those who were in them. For a while they besieged the city of Edessa and then withdrew without having taken it.

The reason for their withdrawal was that all the Franks united, their horse and their foot, and marched to the Euphrates to cross over and defend Edessa from the Muslims. When they reached the Euphrates they heard how numerous the Muslims were, so they did not advance beyond it but camped at the Euphrates. Seeing this, **[486]** the Muslims moved away from Edessa towards Ḥarran to tempt the Franks to cross the Euphrates and bring them to battle. After their move the Franks came to Edessa, bringing with them provisions and stores. They put in the city all that they could require, after it had been short of provisions and on the brink of being taken. They took anyone who was incapacitated, weak or poor and returned to the Euphrates, crossing to the Syrian side. They raided the district of Aleppo, destroying and plundering what was there and killing and capturing. A vast number were enslaved.

The reason for this was that, when the Franks crossed into Mesopotamia, Prince Riḍwān, the lord of Aleppo, entered the districts that the Franks had taken and recovered some of them after ravaging and killing. When the Franks crossed back over the Euphrates, they in their turn did likewise in his districts.

As for the sultan's army, when they heard of the Franks' withdrawal and crossing of the Euphrates, they marched to Edessa and besieged it. They faced a formidable task. The spirits of the city's inhabitants had been strengthened by the stores that had been left with them and by the great number of those fighting for them. The army could find there nothing to encourage them and so they retired. They crossed the Euphrates, besieged the citadel of Tell Bāshir for forty-five days and then departed without having achieved any purpose.

They came to Aleppo, where Prince Riḍwān closed the city gates and would not meet with them. Later Emir Sukmān al-Quṭbī fell ill there and, having set out for home still sick, died at Bālis. His men placed him in a coffin and carried him back to his lands. Īlghāzī attacked to seize them and make booty of their belongings. They put his coffin in their centre and fought in its presence. After Īlghāzī had been put to flight, they seized *his* property as booty and proceeded to their lands.

[**487**] After Prince Ridwān had closed the gates of Aleppo and refused to join with the sultan's forces, they left for Ma'arrat al-Nu'mān and were met by Ṭughtakīn, lord of Damascus. He lodged with Emir Mawdūd but, becoming aware that the emirs had evil intentions towards him and fearing that Damascus might be taken from him, he secretly embarked on peace talks with the Franks, who had refrained from meeting this Muslim force in battle. However, this came to nothing and the armies broke up.

The reason why they broke up was that Emir Bursuq ibn Bursuq, one of the greatest emirs, suffered from gout and was transported in a litter; Sukmān al-Quṭbī died, as we have mentioned; Emir Aḥmadīl, lord of Marāgha, wished to return to request the sultan to grant him the lands that Sukmān had had, and Atabeg Ṭughtakīn, lord of Damascus, feared for himself from the emirs and was not well-disposed towards them, except that amity and friendship developed between himself and Mawdūd, lord of Mosul. For these reasons they broke up. Mawdūd and Ṭughtakīn remained in Ma'arrat al-Nu'mān but then left and camped on the River Orontes.

When the Franks heard that the armies of Islam had broken up, they became ambitious, having all united after disord and dissension, and marched to Apamea. Sulṭān ibn Munqidh, lord of Shayzar, heard of them, went to Mawdūd and Ṭughtakīn, portrayed the Franks as an easy target and urged them to wage the Jihad. They proceeded to Shayzar and camped there. The Franks camped near them. The Muslim army made their provisioning difficult and kept up constant attacks on them, while the Franks guarded themselves and did not give battle. When they had seen how strong the Muslims were, they returned to [**488**] Apamea. The Muslims followed them and snatched any of their rearguard they caught up with. In Rabī' I [7 September-6 October 1111] they returned to Shayzar.

Account of the Franks' siege of Tyre

After the armies had broken up, the Franks agreed to attack and besiege the city of Tyre. They marched there with King Baldwin, ruler of Jerusalem, having mobilised and concentrated their forces. They descended on the city and put it under siege on 25 Jumādā I [29 November 1111]. They constructed three wooden towers, the height of each being seventy cubits and each containing a thousand men, on which they erected trebuchets. They brought one of the towers up close to the city wall and cleared it of defenders.

Tyre was in the possession of al-Āmir bi-Aḥkām Allāh the Alid and his deputy there, 'Izz al-Mulk al-A'azz. The latter summoned the populace and consulted them concerning some device to save them from the evil of the towers. An old man, a citizen of Tripoli, stood up and guaranteed that he could set them on fire. He took with him a thousand men, fully armed, each one having a bundle of firewood. They engaged the Franks until they reached the tower that was close up against the city, threw down the firewood on all sides of it and set fire to it. Fearing that the Franks in the tower might busy themselves with putting out the flames and so escape, he pelted them with bags, which he had prepared, full of excrement. When these fell on them, they concentrated on them and the evil smell and contamination that they brought. The fire gained hold of the tower and all within perished, except for [**489**] a few. The Muslims dragged away what they could with grappling-irons. Then he took large grape baskets and left in them firewood which he had soaked with naphtha, tar, flax and sulphur and hurled seventy baskets at them, setting fire to the other two towers.

The populace of Tyre dug tunnels beneath the earth, so that the Franks would fall into them if they made an assault and so that any siege-tower would be swallowed up if they made one and moved it forward. A few Muslims sought refuge with the Franks and informed them of what had been done, so they took precautions against that.

The citizens sent to Atabeg Ṭughtakīn, lord of Damascus, asking for his aid and requesting him to come so that they could hand the city over to him. He moved with his troops to the region of Bānyās and sent them two hundred cavalry as reinforcements. They entered the city and added to its defence. The Franks fought ever more fiercely, fearing that reinforcements would continue to come. The [tipped] arrows of the Turks were all used up, so they fought on shooting the wood[en shafts].[1] The naphtha was exhausted too but they commandeered an underground cellar containing naphtha. No one knew who had stored it there.

Later 'Izz al-Mulk, governor of Tyre, sent money to Ṭughtakīn to persuade him to raise more troops and come to take over the city. Ṭughtakīn sent a pigeon with a message to tell him that the money had arrived and ordering him to prepare a ship in a place which he named so that the men could come to it. The pigeon alighted on a Frankish ship and two men, a Muslim and a Frank, caught it. The Frank said, 'Shall we let it go? Perhaps it brings deliverance to them.' The Muslim would not allow this and took it to King Baldwin, who, having read it, sent a ship to the place that Ṭughtakīn mentioned. In it were a number of Muslims who had left Tyre to seek protection with the king. The troops duly arrived and, as they were addressed in Arabic, they found nothing suspicious and embarked. They were then all made prisoners and carried to the Franks, who slew them [**490**] and became confident of success against Tyre.

Ṭughtakīn was raiding Frankish territory from all directions. He made for the castle of al-Ḥabīs in al-Sawād, part of the Damascus district, which belonged to the Franks. He besieged it and took it by the sword and killed the garrison. He then

---

[1] The additions in square brackets are an attempt to explain the bare text, which ends with 'they fought with wood' (*qātalū bi'l-khashab*).

returned to the Franks who were at Tyre and cut off their provisions by land but they brought them in by sea. They built a ditch around themselves and did not emerge to attack him. Ṭughtakīn went to Sidon and raided its suburbs. He killed several sailors and burnt about twenty ships on the shore. All the while he was in constant contact by letter with the people of Tyre, ordering them to hold firm although the Franks were keeping up their assaults. The inhabitants of Tyre fought like those who despaired of life. The fighting lasted until the time the crops ripened. The Franks feared that Ṭughtakīn would seize the crops of their lands, so they withdrew from the city to Acre on 10 Shawwāl [10 April 1112]. Ṭughtakīn's troops returned to him and the people of Tyre gave them money and other things. They repaired the city wall and moat that had been damaged. The Franks had filled the latter in.

The defeat of the Franks in Andalusia

During this year Alphonse the Frank, ruler of Toledo in Andalusia, marched into the lands of Islam there, seeking to conquer them and take control. He assembled and recruited a very large army. His ambition had grown because of the death of the Emir of the Muslims Yūsuf ibn Tāshfīn. The Emir of the Muslims 'Alī ibn Yūsuf ibn Tāshfīn heard this news and marched to meet him with his armies and his levies. They met and fought a very fierce fight. Victory went to the Muslims and the Franks were routed. [**491**] They were slain devastatingly and many men were taken prisoner. Some were enslaved and booty was taken from them in amounts beyond measure. After this the Franks feared him and declined to attack his territory. Alphonse was humbled at this time and learnt that the lands had a protector and defender.

In Jumādā II of this year [December 1111] the Imam Abū Ḥāmid Muḥammad ibn Muḥammad ibn Muḥammad al-Ghazālī, the celebrated Imam, died.[2]

---

[2] Born 450/1058 and died Monday 14 Jumādā II/18 December 1111 (*Muntaẓām*, x, 168-70). See *Encyclopedia of Arabic Literature*, i, 252–3; W.M. Watt, *Muslim Intellectual*, Edinburgh, 1963. Al-Ghazālī's 'autobiography', the *Deliverer from Error*, was edited and translated into French by F. Jabre, Beirut, 1959.

[492] The Year 506 [1112-1113]

In Muḥarram of this year [July 1112] the lord of Mosul, Mawdūd, went to Edessa, descended upon it and his troops grazed their mounts on its crops. He then moved to Sarūj where he did likewise. He ignored the Franks and took no precautions against them. Before he was aware of it Joscelin, lord of Tell Bāshir, fell upon them. His army's mounts were scattered over where they were pasturing, so the Franks seized many of them and killed many of the troops. When the Muslims arrayed themselves for battle, Joscelin retired to Sarūj.

This year Sultan Muḥammad departed from Baghdad. This time his stay there had been five months. After arriving at Isfahan he arrested Zayn al-Mulk Abū Sa'd al-Qumī and delivered him to Emir Kāmyār because of the enmity that was between them. After he reached Rayy, Kāmyār mounted him on a horse with a gold saddle and announced that the sultan had rewarded him with office in return for a sum of money that he demanded from him. In this way Kāmyār acquired a large amount from al-Qumī's people and then crucified him. The reason for his arrest was that he made many defamatory remarks about the caliph and the sultan.

There was a man from North Africa in Baghdad this year who, as he claimed, practised alchemy. His name was Abū 'Alī. He was taken to the Caliphal Palace and that was the last that was heard of him.

There came to Baghdad Yūsuf ibn Ayyūb al-Hamadhānī, the preacher. He was one of the ascetics, [**493**] the men of piety. He preached to the populace there and a man, a student of the Law called Ibn al-Saqqā', rose up and attacked him on a certain question, persistently. Yūsuf said to him, 'Sit down. I detect a whiff of unbelief in what you say. It may well be that you will die a non-Muslim.' It came about a little while later that Ibn al-Saqqā' went away into Byzantine lands and became a Christian.

In Dhū'l-Qa'da [19 April-18 May 1113] the sound of a great crash was heard in Baghdad at a time when there were no clouds in the sky to make one think that it was the sound of thunder. No one knew what sound it was.

During this year the following died:

Basil the Armenian,[1] lord of the Passes in the lands of Ibn Leon. Tancred, lord of Antioch, went to his lands at the beginning of Jumādā II [23 November 1112], eager to conquer them. However, he fell ill on the way and returned to Antioch where he died on 8 Jumādā II [30 November 1112].[2] His nephew Roger[3] took these

---

1 For the death of Kogh Vasil, see Matthew of Edessa, *Chronicle*, 211-12.

2 There is some doubt about the date. 30 November was a Saturday but according to Ibn Qal., 183, Tancred died on *Wednesday* 8 Jumādā II. Gibb (*Damascus Chronicle*, 132) emended the date to 18 Jumādā II, which gives 10 December 1112, a Tuesday.

3 Roger of Salerno, son of Richard, regent of Edessa. His mother was a sister of Tancred.

lands after his death and his position became well established after a dispute had arisen between the Franks because of him. Their priests and monks settled the matter between them.

Qarāja, ruler of Homs, who was a wicked man. His son Khīr Khān[4] took his place and was like him in his evil ways.

Al-Mu'ammar ibn 'Alī, Abū Sa'd ibn Abī 'Imāma, the preacher from Baghdad. He was born in the year 429 [1037–8], a man of sharp mind and excellent wit. His preaching consisted mostly of the tales of the pious.[5]

Aḥmad ibn al-Faraj ibn 'Umar al-Dīnawarī, the father of Shuhda. He transmitted [Ḥadīth] [**494**] from Abū Ya'lā ibn al-Farrā', Ibn al-Ma'mūn, Ibn al-Muhtadī, Ibn al-Naqūr and others. He was a man of a good life and an ascetic.[6]

Abū'l-'Alā' Ṣā'id ibn Manṣūr ibn Ismā'īl ibn Ṣā'id, the preacher from Nishapur. He was one of the leading canon lawyers, held the cadiship of Khwārazm and was a transmitter of Ḥadīth.[7]

The *Kāmil* text has S.r.*khāla*, with a variant S.r.*khāl*. Ibn Qal., 183, reads, with the small change of a diacritical point, S.r.*jāl*, although the Ms. had *Sīr R.jāl*. Below p. [**511**] the edition's reading is *Rūjīl*.

4 He is called Khīr Khān in Ibn Qal., 182. The name in *Kāmil* is given as Q.r.jān.

5 A long homily which he delivered before Niẓām al-Mulk is quoted in *Muntaẓam*, ix, 173–4. He died in Rabī' I/26 August–24 September 1112.

6 He died in Jumādā I/24 October–22 November 1112. His daughter Shuhda is described by Ibn al-Jawzī as 'our teacher (*shaykha*)', see *Muntaẓam*, ix, 172.

7 According to *Muntaẓam*, ix, p. 172, he died in Ramaḍān/19 February–20 March 1113.

The Year 507 [1113-1114]

How the Franks were fought and defeated and how Mawdūd was killed

In Muḥarram of this year [18 June-17 July 1113] the Muslims assembled, including Emir Mawdūd ibn Altūntakīn, lord of Mosul, Tamīrak, lord of Sinjār, Emir Ayāz ibn Īlghāzī and Ṭughtakīn, lord of Damascus. The reason why they did so was that Baldwin, the king of the Franks, made a series of raids on Damascus lands towards the end of the year 506 [early summer 1113], plundering and destroying. Supplies to Damascus were cut off, prices rose there and food-stuffs were scarce. Ṭughtakīn, the ruler there, sent to Emir Mawdūd, explaining the situation to him, seeking his aid and urging him to come quickly. The latter collected his army together, set out, and crossed the Euphrates at the end of Dhū'l-Qa'da of the year 506 [18 May 1113]. The Franks were fearful of him.

Ṭughtakīn heard his news and went to meet him, which he did at Salamiyya. They agreed to [**496**] attack Baldwin, king of Jerusalem, and marched to the Jordan. The Muslims camped at al-Uqḥuwāna and the Franks camped with their king Baldwin and Joscelin, the commander of their army, and other leaders and renowned knights. The Muslims with Mawdūd entered Frankish territory and the Franks were assembled. They met in a fierce battle on 13 Muḥarram [30 June 1113]. Both sides held firm but then the Franks turned in flight and many of them were either killed or taken prisoner. One of those taken was Baldwin, their king, but he was not recognized. His armour and weapons were seized but he was set free and so reached safety. Many of them drowned in Lake Tiberias and the River Jordan and the Muslims took their goods and equipment. The Franks reached a pass below Tiberias where they were met by the troops of Tripoli and Antioch. Their spirits were strengthened thereby and they resumed the battle. The Muslims surrounded them on all sides and the Franks climbed a hill west of Tiberias, where they remained for twenty-six days, while the Muslims faced them, shooting arrows at them and hitting those who were close to them. They cut off their provisions in the hope that they would come out to fight but nobody did. The Muslims moved to Baysān and ravaged and ruined Frankish territory between Acre and Jerusalem. They killed any Christians who fell into their hands but they ran short of provisions because they were far from their own lands, so they returned and camped at Marj al-Ṣuffar.

Emir Mawdūd allowed his troops to return and rest, with the intention of assembling in the spring to renew the campaign. He remained with his special retinue and entered Damascus on 21 Rabī' I [5 September 1113] to stay with Ṭughtakīn until the spring. On [the last][1] Friday in Rabī' I [12 September 1113] he

[1] 'The last' is missing in the *Kāmil* text. Logic might well demand it but it is in any case

entered the mosque to attend prayers with Ṭughtakīn. When they had completed their prayers and he had gone out into the courtyard [**497**] of the mosque hand in hand with Ṭughtakīn, a Bāṭinī leapt on him and struck him, wounding him four times. The Bāṭinī was killed and his head removed. No one knew who he was, and his corpse was burnt.

Mawdūd was in the middle of a fast. He was carried to Ṭughtakīn's house and efforts were made to get him to break his fast but he would not. He said, 'I am determined to be fasting when I meet God.' He died that day (may God have mercy on him!). It has been said that the Bāṭinīs in Syria killed him because they feared him, or that Ṭughtakīn feared him and so arranged for someone to assassinate him.

He was a good man, just and very charitable. My father told me, 'The king of the Franks wrote a letter to Ṭughtakīn after the killing of Mawdūd, a section of which contained, "A people that has killed its main prop on its holy day in its house of worship truly deserves that God should destroy it."'

After his murder Tamīrak, lord of Sinjār, took over the treasures and armaments that he had and carried them to the sultan. Mawdūd was buried in Damascus in the tomb of Duqāq, its [former] ruler, and later on was transported to Baghdad and buried in the vicinity of Abū Ḥanīfa, but then moved to Isfahan.

Account of the difference between Sultan Sanjar and Muḥammad Khān and the settlement that was made

During this year it was often reported to Sanjar that Muḥammad Khān ibn Sulaymān ibn Dā'ūd had laid his hands on the property of his subjects and greatly oppressed them and that by his oppression and evil-doing he had ruined the lands and that he had begun to make light of Sanjar's orders and not pay attention to any of them. Sanjar made his preparations, assembled his armies and marched away, planning to seek him out in Transoxania. Fearful, [**498**] Muḥammad Khān sent to Emir Qimāj, the greatest emir with Sanjar, asking him to repair the situation between him and Sanjar. He also sent to the Khwārazmshāh with the same message and asked them both to procure him the sultan's goodwill. He acknowledged that he had been mistaken. Sanjar agreed to be reconciled on condition that he attend in person and do obeisance before him. Muḥammad Khān sent, saying that, because of his own wicked conduct, he was afraid but that he would attend to bow before the sultan, with the River Oxus between them, and then later present himself again and enter into his very presence. They urged Sanjar to accept this and to turn his attention to other matters. First he refused but then he agreed.

So Sanjar stood on the bank of the Oxus on the western side and Muḥammad Khān came to the eastern side. He dismounted and kissed the ground, while Sanjar remained mounted. Each one returned to his tents and then went home. Discord between them was stilled.

---

present in Ibn Qal., 187.

Miscellaneous events

This year a great caravan went from Damascus to Egypt. News reached Baldwin, king of Jerusalem, who moved to meet and intercept it in open country. He seized everyone in it. Only a few escaped and those that did escape the Bedouin caught,

This year the following died:

The Vizier Abū'l-Qāsim 'Alī ibn Muḥammad ibn Jahīr, the vizier of the Caliph al-Mustaẓhir bi-Allāh. The office of vizier was taken after him by al-Rabīb Abū Manṣūr, son of the Vizier Abū Shujā' Muḥammad ibn al-Ḥusayn, the sultan's vizier.

[**499**] Prince Riḍwān ibn Tāj al-Dawla Tutush ibn Alp Arslān, lord of Aleppo.[2] His son, Alp Arslān the Mute, succeeded him in Aleppo at the age of sixteen years. Riḍwān's deeds were not worthy of praise. He killed his brothers, Abū Ṭālib and Bahrām, and in many of his affairs, because of his lack of religion, he used to call on the help of the Bāṭinīs. After [Alp Arslān] the Mute became ruler, affairs were dominated by Lu'lu' the Eunuch and the Mute had only the semblance of authority as sultan, while Lu'lu' had the reality. In fact, Alp Arslān was not mute. There was simply an impediment in his speech and a stammer. His mother was the daughter of Yaghī Siyān, who had been ruler of Antioch. The Mute killed two brothers of his, one of them called Malikshāh, who shared the same mother and father, and the other named Mubārakshāh, on the father's side only. His father had done just the same and then after his death his two sons were killed in retribution for what he had done to his two brothers.

During Riḍwān's reign the Bāṭinīs became numerous in Aleppo, so that Ibn Badī', the headman, and the notables amongst the population feared them. After his death Ibn Badī' suggested to Alp Arslān that he put them to death and persecute them. He gave orders for this and their leader, Abū Ṭāhir the Goldsmith (*al-Ṣā'igh*), and all his followers were arrested. Abū Ṭāhir and several of their notables were put to death. The property of the rest was seized but they were released. Some of them went to join the Franks or were dispersed about the land.

Abū Bakr Aḥmad ibn 'Alī ibn Badrān al-Ḥulwānī, the ascetic. He died in Baghdad in the middle of Jumādā I [28 October 1113]. He transmitted Ḥadīth from the Cadi Abū'l-Ṭayyib al-Ṭabarī, Abū Muḥammad al-Jawharī, Abū Ṭālib al-'Ushārī and others. A vast number heard and transmitted from him. One of the latest was Abū'l-Faḍl 'Abd Allāh ibn al-Ṭūsī, the preacher of Mosul.

Isma'īl ibn Aḥmad ibn al-Ḥusayn ibn 'Alī, Abū 'Alī ibn Abī Bakr al-Bayhaqī, the Imam, son of the Imam, who was born in the year 428 [1036-7] and died in the city of Bayhaq. His father[3] is the author of many famous works.

---

2 He died in Jumādā II/December 1113. For a study of his reign, see Eddé, 'Riḍwān'.

3 Al-Bayhaqī, Abū Bakr Aḥmad (384–458/994–1066), author of major Shāfi'ī texts (see *Encyclopedia of Arabic Literature*, i, 145).

[**500**] Shujā‘ ibn Abī Shujā‘ Fāris ibn al-Ḥusayn ibn Fāris, Abū Ghālib al-Dhuhlī, the *Ḥāfiẓ*. He was born in the year 430 [1038-9] and was a transmitter from his father, Abū'l-Qāsim, Ibn al-Muhtadī, al-Jawharī and others.

The man of letters, Abū'l-Muẓaffar Muḥammad ibn Aḥmad ibn Muḥammad al-Abīwardī,[4] the well-known poet, the author of an excellent collection. An example of his verse is:

My fate has scorned me and knew not that I am precious,
While the events of this age are of little worth.
It ever shows me difficulties, how hostile they are;
And I am left to show it how endurance should be.[5]

He also wrote:

I mounted my noble steed and it shed its tears in sorrow
At my parting from them, harbouring despair.
It said: 'How long will you distress me? If good fortune
attends your affairs, then ride me [back] to your folk!'[6]

His death occurred in Isfahan and he was a descendant of ‘Anbasa ibn Abī Sufyān ibn Ḥarb the Umayyad.

Abū Bakr Muḥammad ibn Aḥmad ibn al-Ḥusayn ibn ‘Umar al-Shāshī,[7] the Imam and Shāfi‘ī lawyer, in Shawwāl [11 March–8 April 1114]. He was born in the year 427 [1035-6] and heard Ḥadīth from Abū Bakr al-Khaṭīb, Abū Ya‘lā ibn al-Farrā' and others. He studied law with Abū ‘Abd Allāh Muḥammad ibn al-Kāzarūnī in Diyār Bakr and with Abū Isḥāq al-Shīrāzī in Baghdad and with Abū Naṣr ibn al-Ṣabbāgh.

Abū Naṣr al-Mu'tamin ibn Aḥmad ibn al-Ḥasan al-Sājī, the *Ḥāfiẓ* from Jerusalem, who was born in the year 445 [1053-4]. He had a copious knowledge of Ḥadīth and studied law with Abū Isḥāq. He was a reliable authority.

---

4 See *Encyclopedia of Arabic Literature*, i, 22.

5 See al-Abīwardī, *Dīwān*, ii, 55.

6 See al-Abīwardī, *Dīwān*, ii, 153.

7 For a survey of his life and works, see Makdisi, *Ibn ‘Aqīl*, 208-9.

[501]
The Year 508 [1114-1115]

Account of Āqsunqur al-Bursuqī's expedition to Syria to fight the Franks

This year Sultan Muḥammad sent Emir Āqsunqur al-Bursuqī to Mosul and its districts to act as governor there, after he had heard of the death of Mawdūd, and he sent his son, Prince Mas'ūd, with him at the head of a vast army, and ordered him to fight the Franks. All the emirs were instructed by letter that they should obey him. He came to Mosul and its troops joined him, amongst them being 'Imād al-Dīn Zankī ibn Āqsunqur, who subsequently came to rule Mosul, both he and his descendants. He was valiant in the extreme. The lord of Sinjār, Tamīrak, and others also mustered.

Al-Bursuqī marched to Jazīrat Ibn 'Umar. Mawdūd's deputy surrendered it to him and continued in his company to Mārdīn. After a siege by al-Bursuqī, its ruler Īlghāzī submitted and sent with him a force under his son Ayāz. From there al-Bursuqī proceeded to Edessa, leading 15,000 cavalry, and began a siege during Dhū'l-Ḥijja [28 April-26 May 1115]. The Franks stoutly resisted his assaults and exploited some carelessness on the part of the Muslims. They seized nine men and crucified them on the city wall. The fighting then intensified and the Muslims attacked with burning zeal, killing fifty of the Franks' leading knights. The siege continued for two months and several days.

However, supplies ran short for the Muslims, so they withdrew from Edessa to Sumaysāṭ after laying waste the territory of Edessa, Sarūj and Sumaysāṭ. The lord of Mar'ash offered al-Bursuqī his allegiance, as **[502]** we shall relate. The latter then returned to Shabakhtān[1] and arrested Ayāz ibn Īlghāzī, seeing that his father had not presented himself, and ravaged the agricultural lands of Mārdīn.

How the lord of Mar'ash and others submitted to al-Bursuqī

One of the counts of the Franks died this year, known as Kogh Basil,[2] the lord of Mar'ash, Kaysūm, Ra'bān and elsewhere. His wife seized power, fortified herself

---

[1] The reading in the *Kāmil* text, Sh.ḥ.nān, is doubtful. The reading adopted here comes from *Zubdat al-ḥalab*, ii, 158 (Ms.: S.kh.tān) and Yāqūt (i, 864, 869). Note that Ibn Qal., 174, has S.n.j.tān (in Arabic script the same basic consonantal outline, if diacritical points are disregarded).

[2] Mention of the Franks here points to a confused situation. The Armenian Kogh Basil died probably in late 1112 A.D. (Asbridge, *Principality of Antioch*, 67) and for a while the Franks interferred in his territories.

against the Franks and gave generously to the troops. She made contact with Āqsunqur al-Bursuqī, when he was at Edessa, and asked him for one of his subordinates to whom she could give her obedience. He sent her Emir Sunqur Dizdār, lord of al-Khābūr. When he came to her, she received him with honour and brought him a large sum of money.

While he was with her, a detachment of Franks arrived and gave battle to his men, being about a hundred horse. After a fierce battle the Muslims overcame the Franks and killed most of them. Sunqur Dizdār returned, taking with him presents from her for Prince Mas'ūd and al-Bursuqī and her acceptance of their authority. Learning of this, many of the Franks who were in her service returned to Antioch.

Account of hostilities between al-Bursuqī and Īlghāzī and the capture of the latter

After al-Bursuqī had arrested Ayāz, son of Īlghāzī, the latter went to Ḥiṣn Kayfā and asked its lord, Emir Rukn al-Dawla Dā'ūd, the son of his brother Suqmān, for aid. He joined him with his army and brought [**503**] a mighty host of Turkomans. They both marched against al-Bursuqī and late in the year they met in a fierce battle in which all held firm but in the end al-Bursuqī and his army were defeated. Ayāz ibn Īlghāzī was freed from captivity. The sultan sent threats to Īlghāzī, so, fearful of this, he went to his father-in-law, the lord of Damascus Ṭughtakīn, in Syria and stayed several days with him.

Ṭughtakīn had also fallen out of favour with the sultan because the sultan attributed the murder of Mawdūd to him. Ṭughtakīn and Īlghāzī agreed to defend themselves and to have recourse to the Franks and seek support from them. They made overtures to the lord of Antioch and allied themselves with him. He met with them at Lake Qadas near Homs, where they renewed their oaths. He returned to Antioch and Ṭughtakīn to Damascus, while Īlghāzī left for al-Rastan[3] with the intention of making for Diyār Bakr and enlisting Turkomans before coming back again. He stopped at al-Rastan to rest but was attacked by Khīr Khān[4] ibn Qarāja, lord of Homs, after Īlghāzī's men had scattered. Khīr Khān overwhelmed him and took him prisoner, along with several of his retinue. He sent to the sultan to inform him of this and to ask him speedily to despatch troops to prevent Ṭughtakīn forcibly recovering Īlghāzī.

Hearing this news Ṭughtakīn returned to Homs and sent to ask for his release but Khīr Khān refused and swore that, if Ṭughtakīn did not withdraw, he would kill Īlghāzī. The latter sent to Ṭughtakīn, saying, 'Persistance is harmful to me and

---

[3] On the Orontes, about 13 miles north of Homs.

[4] Khīr Khān succeeded his father at Homs in 505/1111-12 (Ibn Qal., 182). His name is often given as Q.r.jān or variants of that. I have followed throughout the form found in Ibn Qal. and *Zubdat al-ḥalab*, ii, see indices.

will lead to my bloodshed. The best course is for you to return to Damascus,' so he did.

Khīr Khān waited for the arrival of the sultan's troops but they were delayed and he feared that his men would be deluded by Ṭughtakīn into surrendering Homs to him. He therefore changed his mind and proposed a settlement with Īlghāzī, that he would free him, take his son Ayāz as a hostage, make a marriage alliance with him and that Īlghāzī would defend him from Ṭughtakīn and others. This was accepted, so he set him free and they swore oaths to each other. Īlghāzī handed over his son Ayāz and then left Homs [**504**] for Aleppo, where he assembled Turkomans and then returned to Homs and demanded his son Ayāz. He besieged Khīr Khān until the troops of the sultan arrived, at which Īlghāzī withdrew, as we shall relate.

The death of 'Alā' al-Dawla ibn Sabuktakīn, the accession of his son and what happened to him and Sultan Sanjar

During Shawwāl this year [March 1115] the Prince 'Alā' al-Dawla Abū Sa'd Mas'ūd ibn Abī'l-Muẓaffar Ibrāhīm ibn Abī Sa'd Mas'ūd ibn Maḥmūd ibn Sabuktakīn, the lord of Ghazna, died there and was succeeded by his son, Arslanshāh, whose mother was a Saljūq princess, the daughter of Sultan Alp Arslān ibn Dā'ūd. He arrested his brothers and put them in prison. One of his brothers, called Bahrām, fled to Khurasan and came to Sultan Sanjar ibn Malikshāh, who contacted Arslānshāh on his behalf. However, he did not listen to him nor pay any attention to what he said, so Sanjar made his preparations to march to Ghazna and establish Bahrāmshāh in power.

Arslānshāh sent to Sultan Muḥammad to complain about his brother Sanjar, The sultan sent to his brother Sanjar ordering him to make peace with Arslānshāh and to stop interfering with him. He said to his envoy, 'If you see that my brother has already set out on his march towards them or is on the point of setting out, do not stop him and do not deliver the message, for that will sap his strength and weaken him and he will not return. That my brother should win temporal success is what I want most.' The envoy came to Sanjar when he had already despatched his troops to Ghazna and had put Emir Unur, the commander of his army, along with Prince Bahrāmshāh in his vanguard. They made their way until they reached Bust, where they were joined by Abū'l-Faḍl Naṣr ibn Khalaf, lord of Sijistān.

[**505**] Arslānshāh heard this news and sent out a vast army, which was defeated and plundered. The survivors returned to Ghazna in the worst state possible. At that, Arslānshāh became submissive and sent to Emir Unur guaranteeing him large sums of money if he withdrew and recommended withdrawal to Sultan Sanjar. This he refused to do.

After Unur Sultan Sanjar prepared to march in person. Arslānshāh sent him the wife of his uncle Naṣr to ask for pardon and the abandonment of his plan. She was the stepsister of Sanjar[5] 'Alā' al-Dawla Abū Sa'd had killed her husband, prevented her from leaving Ghazna and married her. Arslānshāh now sent her [on this mission]. When she reached her brother she delivered the money and gifts she had. Among other things she had 200,000 dinars. Sanjar was requested to hand over Arslānshāh's brother, Bahrām, to him.

She harboured hatred for Arslānshāh, so she belittled him to Sanjar, fed the latter's desire to take his lands and urged that it would be an easy task. She told him how he had treated his brothers. Some he killed and others he blinded although they had not rebelled. The sultan therefore marched out and, having reached Bust, he sent a eunuch of his personal retinue to Arslānshāh with a letter. He was arrested in one of the fortresses, so thereupon Sanjar made all speed. Hearing of his near approach, Arslānshāh released the envoy. Sanjar arrived at Ghazna and a battle followed between them one league from Ghazna in the open country around Shahrābādh. Arslānshāh led 30,000 cavalry and a great host of infantry. He also had 120 elephants with four persons on each elephant. The elephants charged the centre, where Sanjar was, and his men gave way. Sanjar told his Turkish mamlukes to shoot arrows at the elephants. Three thousand mamlukes advanced and released one complete volley at the elephants, killing a number of them. The [remaining] elephants veered away from the centre to the left wing, where was Abū'l-Faḍl, lord of Sijistān, and ran them down. The left wing was weakened but Abū'l-Faḍl encouraged them **[506]** and told them how fearful defeat would be so far from their homelands. He himself dismounted from his horse and charged the biggest and leading elephant. He went beneath it and split open its belly. He also killed two other elephants.

Emir Unur on the right wing saw the fighting the left wing were engaged in and was fearful for them. He charged behind the army of Ghazna and made for the left wing, mingled with them and brought them support. Defeat came upon the Ghaznavid troops. Those mounted on the elephants had tied themselves on with chains. When they felt the bite of battle and the sword went to work amongst them, they threw themselves down and were left hanging from them.

On 20 Shawwāl in the year 510 [25 February 1117] Sanjar entered Ghazna, accompanied by Bahrāmshāh. The great castle which contained the treasury, situated nine leagues from the city, was vast and there was no hope of taking it, no point of access to it. Arslānshāh had imprisoned there his brother Ṭāhir the Treasurer, a friend of Bahrāmshāh, and had also incarcerated the wife of Bahrāmshāh there. When Arslānshāh had been defeated, his brother Ṭāhir won over the governor and offered him and the troops pay increases. They surrendered the castle to Sultan Sanjar. As for the citadel in the city, that is where Arslānshāh had imprisoned Sanjar's envoy. After his release, Arslānshāh's mamlukes remained there but they too surrendered the citadel without any resistance.

[5] This is understood to be the meaning of *hiya ukht al-Malik Sanjar min al-Sulṭān Barkyāruq*, 'she [was] the sister of Prince Sanjar through Sultan Barkyāruq', i.e. that Barkyāruq's half-sister was daughter of a wife of Malikshāh who was stepmother to Sanjar.

Bahrāmshāh and Sanjar had already agreed between them that Bahrām alone should sit on the throne of his ancestor, Maḥmūd ibn Sabuktakīn, and that the khutbah in Ghazna should be in the names of the caliph, Sultan Muḥammad, Prince Sanjar and then of Bahrāmshāh. When they made their entry into Ghazna, Sanjar was mounted and Bahrāmshāh went before him on foot, until he came to the throne. Bahrāmshāh ascended and took his seat [**507**] upon it and Sanjar withdrew. In the khutbah Sanjar was entitled Prince while Bahrāmshāh was addressed as Sultan in the fashion of his ancestors. This was one of the strangest things ever heard of.

Sanjar's followers acquired untold amounts of money from the sultan and the populace. Among the palaces of their princes were several with silver panels on the walls and there were water-wheels supplying the gardens which were also of silver. Most of this was prised off and seized as plunder. When Sanjar heard what was being done, he prevented it energetically and crucified several until his men desisted.

Among that which Sanjar acquired were five crowns, each one of which was worth more than 2,000,000 dinars, and 1,300 items of jewel-encrusted gold and silver metal work and seventeen gold and silver thrones. He remained in Ghazna for forty days until Bahrāmshāh was well established and then he set out back to Khurasan. No Saljūq ruler had ever been named in the khutbah at Ghazna before this time. Even Sultan Malikshāh, despite his power and the size of his realm did not aspire to this. Whenever he expressed the wish for it, Niẓām al-Mulk held him back.

Arslānshāh, after his defeat, set out for Hindūstān, where his men flocked to him and his offensive power grew, After Sanjar had returned to Khurasan, he made his way to Ghazna. Becoming aware of his hostile moves, Bahrāmshāh set out for Bāmiyān and sent to Sanjar to tell him of the situation. Sanjar sent him some troops.

Arslānshāh stayed in Ghazna for one month and then went in search of his brother Bahrāmshāh. The news of the arrival of Sanjar's troops reached him, so he retreated without a fight because of the fear that acted on the hearts of his soldiers. He sought refuge in the mountains of Ūghnān.[6] His brother Bahrāmshāh and Sanjar's troops pursued him and laid waste to the country he was in. They sent out threats to the populace, who, after they had been hard pressed, handed him over. He was held by the commander of Sanjar's army, who wished to take him to his ruler. Bahrāmshāh was anxious [**508**] about that and offered the commander money, who then handed him over. Bahrāmshāh strangled him and buried him in his father's tomb at Ghazna. He was twenty-seven years old and was the most handsome of his brothers. His death fell in Jumādā II of the year 512 [19 September–17 October 1119]. We have mentioned this here simply for the sake of narrative continuity.

---

[6] Unidentified. Perhaps the modern district of Urgun in Afghanistan, see Bosworth, *Later Ghaznavids*, 98.

Miscellaneous events

In Jumādā II [November 1114] there was a violent earthquake in the Jazīra, Syria and elsewhere. It destroyed much of Edessa, Ḥarrān, Sumaysāṭ, Bālis and other places. A great number of people perished under the rubble.

This year Tāj al-Dawla Alp Arslān ibn Riḍwān, the lord of Aleppo, was killed. His mamlukes killed him in the citadel of Aleppo. After him they set up his brother, Sulṭān Shāh ibn Riḍwān, although he was under the control of Lu'lu' the Eunuch.

This year there died the Sharīf Nasīb [al-Dawla] Abū'l-Qāsim 'Alī ibn Ibrāhīm ibn al-'Abbās al-Ḥusaynī at Damascus in Rabī' II [September 1114].[7]

---

7 He was a teacher of the scholar and historian, Ibn 'Asākir. He died the eve of Sunday 24 Rabī' II/27 September. See Ibn Qal., 191 and note 1.

[**509**] The Year 509 [1115-1116]

Account of the defeat of the sultan's army by the Franks

We have mentioned already the rebellion that Īlghāzī and Ṭughtakīn made against the sultan and how the Franks grew powerful. When this came to the attention of Sultan Muḥammad, he prepared a large force and put Emir Bursuq ibn Bursuq, lord of Hamadhan, in command. With him were Emir Juyūsh Beg and Emir Kuntughdī and the troops of Mosul and the Jazīra. The sultan ordered them first of all to engage Īlghāzī and Ṭughtakīn and, when they had dealt with them, to march into Frankish territory, wage war on them and harass their lands.

They set out in Ramaḍān of the year 508 [February 1115] with a very numerous army. At the end of the year [spring 1115] they crossed the Euphrates at al-Raqqa and, when they drew near to Aleppo, they made contact with the ruling authority there, Lu'lu' the Eunuch, and the commander of the local forces, who was known as Shams al-Khawāṣṣ, ordering them to surrender Aleppo. They presented them with the sultan's letters that ordered the same. The two of them gave a deceitful answer[1] and sent for Īlghāzī and Ṭughtakīn to bring them assistance. These two set out with 2,000 cavalry and entered Aleppo. The defenders then defied the sultan's troops and openly declared their rebellion. Emir [**510**] Bursuq ibn Bursuq went to the city of Hama, which was subject to Ṭughtakīn and where his baggage train was, and put it under siege. He then took it by storm and sacked it for three days, before handing it to Emir Khīr Khān, lord of Homs. The sultan had commanded that every town they took should be given to him. Seeing this the emirs became dispirited and their purpose faltered, insomuch as their lands might be taken and handed to Khīr Khān. After Ḥamā was given to Khīr Khān, he handed over Ayāz ibn Īlghāzī. Īlghāzī himself, Ṭughtakīn and Shams al-Khawāṣṣ had previously gone to Antioch and sought the protection of its ruler, Roger, and asked him to help them to defend the city of Ḥamā, as they had not heard that it had fallen.

Baldwin, lord of Jerusalem, and the lord of Tripoli and other Frankish devils came to them at Antioch and they agreed not to risk battle because the Muslims were so numerous. They said, 'At the onset of winter they will disperse.' They gathered at the fortress of Apamea, where they remained about two months. When September (*Aylūl*) was half over and they saw that the Muslims were planning to stay, they [themselves] disbanded. Īlghāzī returned to Mārdīn, Ṭughtakīn to Damascus and the Franks to their lands.

Apamea and Kafarṭāb were held by the Franks. The Muslims went to Kafarṭāb

1 In the light of the following narrative this reading (*ghālaṭā fī'l-jawāb*) seems preferable to the plausible variant 'gave a rude answer' (*ghālaẓā ...*).

and besieged it. When the blockade intensified and the Franks saw destruction facing them, they slew their women and children and burnt their possessions. The Muslims made a forced entry into the town, captured its ruler and killed all the Franks that remained there. They then marched to the fortress of Apamea but they saw that it was strongly defended, so they withdrew to al-Ma'arra, which was also held by the Franks. The Emir Juyūsh Beg parted from them and went to the valley of Buzā'a, which he took possession of. From al-Ma'arra the troops proceeded to Aleppo, while their baggage and their mounts went before them [**511**] as is the normal practice, and the troops followed close on their tracks. They felt secure, not imagining that anyone would dare to approach them.

Roger,[2] lord of Antioch, when he heard that Kafarṭāb was besieged, set out at the head of 500 knights and 2,000 infantry to prevent it. He came to the place where the tents of the Muslims had been pitched, without knowing they were there. He saw that they were devoid of fighting men, because they had not yet arrived. He plundered everything there and killed many of the camp-followers and the army's pages. The troops arrived in disorder and the Franks were killing them all as they arrived.

The Emir Bursuq arrived with about one hundred horse. He saw the situation and climbed a hill there, along with his brother, Zankī. Some of the camp-followers and the pages surrounded them and sought protection with them, preventing Emir Bursuq from descending. His brother and those with him advised him to go down and save himself, but he said, 'I shall not do so. I shall be slain on the path of God and be a sacrifice for the Muslims.' They convinced him to give up this plan, so he and those with him made their escape. The Franks pursued them for about a league but then returned and completed the plundering and slaughter. They burnt many of our people. The army was scattered, each man taking what route he could.

When those guarding the prisoners taken at Kafarṭāb heard this news, they put them to death and the person guarding Ayāz ibn Īlghazī acted similarly and killed him too. The population of Aleppo and other Muslims towns in Syria were fearful. They had been hoping for a victory from this army but what they had not counted upon befell them. The troops retired to their own lands.

Bursuq and his brother Zankī both died in the year 510 [1116–17]. Bursuq was a good, religious man. He was full of remorse for this defeat and was preparing to make a repeat expedition when his appointed time came.

[512] How the Franks conquered Rafaniyya and how it was taken back from them

In Jumādā II this year [22 October–19 November 1115] the Franks conquered

---

2 In the text Rūjīl.

Rafaniyya in Syria, which was held by Ṭughtakīn, lord of Damascus. They strengthened it with men and supplies and did their utmost to fortify it. Ṭughtakīn was concerned at this and increased his determination to attack Frankish lands, bringing plunder and destruction. Intelligence came to him that Rafaniyya was devoid of any force capable of defending it. Only the Franks stationed as a garrison were there. Taking no baggage train, Ṭughtakīn set out and before the men there realised it he had assaulted the town and entered by force of arms. The Franks there were taken prisoner. Some he killed and others he spared. The Muslims filled their hands with plunder from their crops, their livestock and their stores, and returned safely to their own territory.

The death of Yaḥyā ibn Tamīm and the succession of his son, 'Alī

Yaḥyā ibn Tamīm ibn al-Mu'izz ibn Bādīs, the ruler of Ifrīqiya, died suddenly this year on the Festival of Sacrifice [25 April 1116]. An astrologer had said to him in Monastir, his birth-place, that this day he was under an inauspicious star and he should not ride, so he did not. His sons and his men of state went to the Oratory and when the prayer was completed they came to greet and congratulate him. The Koran readers recited, the poets declaimed and then they went to eat. Yaḥyā rose to pass through another door to join them at the meal. He had not walked three paces before he collapsed dead. His son 'Alī was [**513**] in Sfax. He was summoned and installed as successor. Yaḥyā was buried within the palace and then transferred to his tomb in Monastir. He was fifty-two years and fifteen days old and his reign had lasted eight years, five months and twenty-five days. He left thirty sons.

'Abd al-Jabbār ibn Muḥammad ibn Ḥamdīs al-Ṣiqillī[3] mourned him and congratulated his son 'Alī on his accession as follows:

No sword is sheathed without another blade being drawn,
No moon is hidden but another appears.
By the death of Yaḥyā all people were consigned to die,
Until, when 'Alī came, they were raised again.
If they are resurrected in joy at his coming to power,
Yet in grief at Yaḥyā's fate are they buried.
'Alī has fulfilled his destiny, and sovereignty's face[4] is smiling,
While its eye sheds tears for his father.
The raiments of noble deeds have been torn in sorrow,
On every horizon the bright stars have wept for him.

---

[3] Ibn Ḥamdīs (447-527/1056-1133), born in Syracuse, had a career as court poet in Spain and North Africa. For a brief life and further references, see *Encyclopedia of Arabic Literature*, 330. For the complete poem, see Ibn Hamdīs, *Dīwān*, 221ff.

[4] Literally 'tooth'.

The son of Tamīm is little saddened at his lot;
He is scornful of every great grief.
Now that Yaḥyā is lifeless the proof stands,
That death spares and overlooks none.

Yaḥyā was just to his people, firmly in control of affairs of state and a manager of all his circumstances. He was merciful to the weak and the poor, giving much in alms to them. He used to favour the men of religion and learning and himself was knowledgeable in history, ancient lore and medicine. He was handsome, blue-eyed and rather tall.[5]

After ʿAlī had become established in power, he despatched a fleet to the island of Jerba. The reason was that [**514**] the inhabitants had been interrupting commerce and seizing merchants. He blockaded the island and made things very hard for the people, so they entered under his sway and undertook to give up their trouble-making and guaranteed to improve traffic. He thereupon ceased his hostilities against them, the maritime situation improved and travellers became secure.[6]

Miscellaneous events

In Rajab of this year [20 November–19 December 1115] Sultan Muḥammad came to Baghdad. Atabeg Ṭughtakīn, lord of Damascus, visited him in Dhū'l-Qaʿda [17 March–15 April 1116]. He sought his goodwill, which the sultan gave and rewarded him with a robe of honour and sent him back to Damascus.

This year the Imam al-Mustaẓhir bi-Allāh ordered the sale of al-Badriyya, which was named after Badr, the mamluke of al-Muʿtaḍid bi-Allāh. It was one of the most beautiful of the caliphal palaces. It used to be the residence of al-Rāḍī bi-Allāh but it fell into ruin and became a mound. Al-Qādir bi-Allāh ordered a wall to be built around it because it was [contiguous] with the Imām's Palace. This was done. At this present time the sale that was ordered was carried out and people developed the site.[7]

Rioting among the common people occurred in Shaʿbān [20 December 1115–17 January 1116]. The cause of it was that, when they returned from the

---

[5] In Arabic *ilā'l-ṭūl mā huwa*. For this form of expression, see Wright, ii, 276.

[6] For more details on Yaḥyā's death, ʿAlī's succession and the submission of Jerba, see Idris, *La Berbérie*, 315–18.

[7] Badr (died 289/902) and the Caliph al-Muʿtaḍid are linked with two Badriyyas. The first was an extension of some sort to the palace/mosque complex of al-Manṣūr on the West Bank (see Lassner, *Topography*, 96, 189). Probably what is intended here was the palace built by Badr outside the palace area on the East Bank, opposite the Badr Gate. See Salmon, *Introduction*, 147, and Le Strange, *Baghdad*, 270. *Al-Dār al-Imāmiyya* is taken to be the whole walled complex on the East Bank.

pilgrimage to the tomb of Muṣ'ab, they argued about who should enter first. They came to blows and several of them were killed. There was a renewal of the disturbances between the inhabitants of the quarters as in the past, but then they quietened down.

This year Sultan Muḥammad gave Mosul and what had been held by Āqsunqur al-Bursuqī to Emir Juyūsh Beg as a fief and sent his son, Prince Mas'ūd [to him]. Al-Bursuqī remained in al-Raḥba, which was his fief, [**515**] until the death of Sultan Muḥammad. What happened then we shall relate, God willing.

Ismā'īl ibn Muḥammad ibn Aḥmad ibn Milla al-Iṣbahānī, Abū 'Uthmān ibn Abī Sa'īd, the preacher, died this year. He heard and transmitted much Ḥadīth in Baghdad and elsewhere.[8]

There also died 'Abd Allāh ibn al-Mubārak ibn Mūsā al-Saqaṭī, Abū'l-Barakāt. He wrote a book on his scholarly travels and other works too, as he was a man of letters.[9]

---

[8] He died in Isfahan. Ibn al-Athīr omits Ibn al-Jawzī's critical comments on his scholarship (see *Muntaẓam*, ix, 183).

[9] Ibn al-Jawzī calls him Hibat Allāh ibn al-Mubārak and reports doubts about his Ḥadīth transmission. He died in Rabī' I/July–August 1115 (see *Muntaẓam*, ix, 183).

[516] The Year 510 [1116-1117]

Account of the killing of Aḥmadīl ibn Wahsūdān

At the beginning of Muḥarram [16 May 1116] Atabeg Ṭughtakīn, lord of Damascus, attended at the palace of Sultan Muḥammad in Baghdad. Several emirs were present, including Aḥmadīl ibn Ibrāhīm ibn Wahsūdān al-Rawādī al-Kurdī, the ruler of Marāgha and other places in Azerbayjan. He was sitting alongside Ṭughtakīn. A man who claimed to have a grievance approached him, weeping and holding a petition in his hand, to ask him to convey it to the sultan. Aḥmadīl took it from his hand and then the man struck him with a dagger. Aḥmadīl dragged him down and pinioned him beneath him. An accomplice of the Bātinī then leapt up and struck Aḥmadīl another blow with a dagger. Swords cut them both down but a [third] accomplice came forward and stabbed Aḥmadīl yet again. People were amazed at his audacity after the killing of his two companions. Ṭughtakīn and those present thought that Ṭughtakīn was the intended target of the assassination and that it was on the orders of the sultan. When it was gathered that they were Bāṭinīs this suspicion was removed.

The death of Jāwulī Saqāo and what he had previously done in Fars

Jāwulī Saqāo died this year.

The sultan in Baghdad had intended to remain there but was obliged to go to Isfahan to be close to Fars to prevent its rising against him. [**517**] We have told of Jāwulī's position in Mosul before it was eventually conquered and taken from him by the sultan. After he had visited the sultan and gained his goodwill, he was given Fars as a fief, to which he went, taking with him the sultan's son Chaghrī, who was a child aged two years. The sultan ordered him to repair the situation there and suppress those disturbing the peace. The first thing he was careful to do after his arrival was not to meddle with the lands of Emir Baldajī, one of the great mamlukes of Sultan Malikshāh. Part of his territory was Kalīl and Sarmāh,[1] on which lands he had a powerful hold.

Jāwulī wrote to him to come and pay his respects to Chaghrī, the sultan's son. He taught Chaghrī to say 'Arrest him' in Persian. When Baldajī made his entry, Chaghrī said, as he often did, 'Arrest him.' He was seized, killed and his possessions plundered.

---

[1] Kalīl: Yāqūt, iv, 303, simply has 'a place'! Sarmāh (with Ms. variations) has not been identified. It is perhaps a corruption of Sarmsā, a town in Fars on the route Qūmisa-Iṣṭakhr (see *Die Kernländer*, 159).

One of Baldajī's fortresses was the castle of Iṣṭakhr, one of the strongest and most fortified. His family and his treasure were there. His deputy who held it for him was an official of his, known as al-Jahrumī. He rebelled and sent away Baldajī's family and part of his treasure. Iṣṭakhr remained in al-Jahrumī's hands until Jāwulī came to Fars and took it from him and put his own treasure there.

In Fars there were several emirs of the Shabānkāra, a people too numerous to be counted. Their chief was al-Ḥasan ibn al-Mubāriz, known as Khusro, who held Fasā and other places. Jāwulī wrote to him to come and pay his respects to Chaghrī, but he replied, 'I am the servant of the sultan and loyal to him. However, there is no way that I shall attend, because I have learnt of your practice with Baldajī and others, but I will provide the sultan with what he chooses.' Having heard this answer, Jāwulī realised that there was no future **[518]** for him in Fars with this man there. He let it be known that he was returning to the sultan, loaded his baggage on his pack-animals and set off, as though on his way to the sultan. Khusro's messenger went back to him and told him the news. Misled by this, he began a drinking session and felt secure.

Jāwulī, however, retraced his route towards Khusro, leaving his baggage and leading a small detachment. He arrived and surprised him when he was in a drunken sleep. He brother Faḍlūh tried to rouse him but he would not wake up. He then poured cold water over him and he came to, mounted up immediately and fled. His men scattered and Jāwulī plundered his baggage and his money and did much slaughter among his men. Khusro escaped to his fortress,which was between two hills, one of which was called Unju.

Then Jāwulī went to Fasā and received its surrender. He ravaged much of the land of Fars, including Jahrum, and made his way to Khusro, whom he besieged for a while very closely. However, he saw that his castle was so strong and powerful and so well provisioned that he realised that the time [needed for a siege] would long detain him, so he came to terms with him, to be free to deal with the rest of Fars. He left for Shīrāz, where he stayed a while before proceeding to Kāzarūn, which he seized. He blockaded Abū Sa'd Muḥammad ibn Mammā in the citadel, which he invested for two years, summer and winter. Jāwulī made him overtures of peace but his envoy was killed. He then sent him a group of Sufis but Abū Sa'd fed them stew and honey-cakes and then ordered that their anuses be sewn up and that they be thrown out in the sun. They all perished. Later Abū Sa'd's supplies were exhausted, so he asked for terms which were granted, and the citadel was surrendered.

Jāwulī subsequently treated him badly, so he fled. His sons were arrested and men were sent to pursue him. One of these saw a black slave who was carrying something. He said, 'What do you have there?' He replied, 'My provisions.' He searched him and saw [that he had] a chicken and sugar confectionery. 'This is not your food,' he said and beat him. Then the slave confessed that he was taking it to Abū Sa'd. They made their way to where he was, in a mountain ravine. The soldier seized him and took him to Jāwulī, who put him to death.

[**519**] Jāwulī went to Dārābjird, whose ruler, named Ibrāhīm, fearing him, fled to Kirman, for there was a relationship by marriage between him and the ruler of Kirman, who was Arslānshāh ibn Kirmānshāh ibn Arslān Beg ibn Qāwurt. He said to him, 'If we support one another, Jāwulī will not prevail against us,' and he asked for assistance,

After Ibrāhīm's flight Jāwulī came to besiege Ratīl Ranana (meaning the Pass of Ranana),[2] which was a place that had never been taken by force because it was a valley about two leagues [long] in the heart of which was an impregnable castle on a high mountain. Whenever they were fearful, the inhabitants of Dārābjird took refuge there securely and remained there, guarding the high pass.

When Jāwulī saw its strength he left, making for the open country towards Kirman but concealing his real purpose. He turned back from the road to Kirman towards Dārābjird, making it appear that he was part of the Lord of Kirman Arslānshāh's army. The people in the castle did not doubt that they were reinforcements for them with their lord. They showed their delight and allowed Jāwulī to enter the pass. After entering he put the people there to the sword and only a few escaped. He plundered the property of the inhabitants of Dārābjird and then returned home. He wrote to Khusro to tell him that he was planning to go to Kirman and inviting him to join him. Khusro found no way not to agree, obediently came to him and travelled in his company to Kirman. Jāwulī sent the Cadi Abū Ṭāhir 'Abd Allāh ibn Ṭāhir, cadi of Shiraz, to its ruler ordering him to send back the Shabānkāra, because they were subjects of the sultan, saying that, if he sent them back, he would give up his plan to attack his lands, but otherwise he would descend upon them. The ruler of Kirman gave an answer, interceding for the Shabānkāra, seeing that they had sought refuge with him.

When his envoy came to Jāwulī, he treated him well and rewarded him handsomely but suborned him from [**520**] his master and got him to spy for him. He arranged with him that the army of Kirman should be made to retire, so that he could enter the country while they were deceived. When the envoy returned and reached al-Sīrajān[3] where the troops of Kirman's ruler were and his vizier, the commander of his army, he informed the vizier how Jāwulī was prepared for an accommodation and that he was abandoning what they objected to, and he added many things of this sort. He said, 'Jāwulī is reluctant to gather his troops at al-Sīrajān, for his enemies are eager to use this army of yours against him. Your best plan is for your troops to return home.'

The vizier and the army retired and al-Sīrajān was left empty. Jāwulī followed on the track of the envoy and descended on Furj,[4] on the border between Fars and Kirman, which he put under siege. When the ruler of Kirman heard that, he

---

[2] This follows the text of the edition, but the Mss. readings are doubtful. Could it be that Rūnīz is intended? Rūnīz is 'a small town' one day's march south-west of Dārābjird (see Le Strange, *Caliphate*, 291, and Krawulsky, 154–5).

[3] One of the main cities of Kirmān (see Yāqūt, iii, 213).

[4] *Die Kernländer*, 55, and Krawulsky, 153, s.v. Porg.

summoned the envoy and blamed him for the withdrawal of the army but he made his excuses. With the envoy was a servant of Jāwulī's, ready to take information back to him. The vizier had his suspicions about him and tortured him until he gave evidence against the envoy, who was crucified and his possessions seized. The servant was also crucified.

The troops were ordered to march against Jāwulī and they set out, numbering 6,000 cavalry. The area which was the borderland between Fars and Kirman was in the hands of a man called Mūsā, who was politic and cunning. He joined this force and advised them to leave the highway, saying, 'Jāwulī is watching it.' He led them on an unfrequented route amongst mountains and narrow passes.

Jāwulī was besieging Furj and had pressed hard on the garrison, while himself drinking excessively. He despatched an emir with a detachment of his army to meet the troops sent from Kirman. The emir travelled some distance but saw nobody, so he thought that they had gone back. He returned to Jāwulī and said, 'The army [**521**] was small and has withdrawn for fear of us.' At that Jāwulī felt confident and continued his excessive wine-drinking.

The army of Kirman arrived at night when he was drunk and asleep. One of his men woke him up with the news but he refused to listen. Another man came, aroused him and informed him of the situation. Now wide awake, Jāwulī mounted a horse and fled. His troops were scattered in rout and many were killed or captured. Khusro and the son of Abū Sa'd, whose father Jāwulī had killed, caught up with him and rode with him, attended by their own men. Jāwulī looked around and could not see one of his Turkish followers, so that he feared for his life. They said to him, 'We will do no treachery towards you. You will see nothing but good treatment and protection from us.' They travelled on until the city of Fasā was reached, where his defeated followers joined him. Meanwhile, the lord of Kirman released his prisoners and sent them on their way. This battle took place during Shawwāl in the year 508 [March 1115].

While Jāwulī was arranging his affairs to return to Kirman and take his revenge, Prince Chaghrī, son of Sultan Muḥammad, died, aged five years. His death occurred in Dhū'l-Ḥijja of the year 509 [16 April–14 May 1116]. This weakened Jāwulī's position. The ruler of Kirman sent an envoy to the sultan, who was at Baghdad, asking him to stop Jāwulī's attacks on him. The sultan replied that it was necessary for him to placate Jāwulī and surrender Furj to him. The envoy returned in Rabī' I in the year 510 [14 July–12 August 1116]. Then Jāwulī died and so their fears no longer troubled them. Hearing of this, the sultan left Baghdad and went to Isfahan, fearing a threat to Fars from the ruler of Kirman.

Account of the conquest of Mount Wasilāt and Tunis

During this year the army of the ruler of Ifrīqiya, 'Alī ibn Yaḥyā, besieged the city of Tunis, in which was Aḥmad ibn Khurāsān, and pressed hard on the inhabitants.

Its ruler came to terms with 'Alī according to the wishes of the latter.

[**522**] Also in this year he conquered Mount Wasilāt[5] in Ifrīqiya and established control there. It is an inaccessible mountain, whose inhabitants had continued for ages to attack people and practise brigandage. When there was no end to this, 'Alī sent a force against them. The mountain folk used to descend towards the army and engage them very fiercely. The commander of the force carried out a clever move by climbing the mountain up a ravine which nobody had thought he would be able to climb. When he got to the top, leading a detachment of his men, the mountain folk rushed to attack him but he held firm and fought them very hard with the men he had. More of his force climbed up to him one after another and the men of the mountain were beaten. Many of them were killed and some threw themselves down the mountain and were broken to pieces. Yet others escaped and a large group sought refuge in a fort on the mountain. When the troops surrounded them, they asked to be sent someone to negotiate terms. The commander sent them several Arabs and soldiers but they turned on these with their weapons and killed some of them. The survivors climbed onto the roof of the fort and called on their comrades in the army. They came to their help and fighting continued, partly from on top of the fort and partly from below. The men of the mountain within gave themselves up and were all put to death.[6]

Account of rioting in Ṭūs

At the time of 'Āshūrā' [25 May 1116] there was a serious riot in Ṭūs, in the shrine of 'Alī ibn Mūsā al-Riḍā[7] (peace be upon him!). It was caused because an Alid disputed with one of the canon lawyers of Ṭūs in the shrine on the day of 'Āshūrā'. This led to an exchange of blows, although the disturbance was cut short. However, each of them sought the assistance of his sympathisers. A serious riot broke out which involved all the population of Ṭūs. Some surrounded the shrine and vandalised it, killing [**523**] those they found. On both sides several were killed and a great deal of property was plundered, before they separated.

The people at the shrine ceased to make the khutbah there on Fridays. Later, 'Aḍud al-Dīn Garshasp[8] ibn 'Alī built a strong wall around it to protect people in the shrine from those who wished to do them ill. Its construction was in the year 515 [1121-2].

---

5 Between Tunis and Kairouan.

6 For these events, see Idris, *La Berbérie*, 318-19.

7 The Alid Imam who in 817 A.D. was designated (for a while) heir of the 'Abbāsid al-Ma'mūn.

8 The text has Farāmurz incorrectly. 'Alā' al-Dawla 'Aḍud al-Dīn Garshasp ibn 'Alī ibn Farāmurz was a late member of the Kākūyid dynasty, ruler of Yazd. See Bosworth, 'Dailamīs etc.', 88.

Miscellaneous events

During this year a fire occurred in the yards next to the Niẓāmiyya Madrasah at Baghdad. The timber there was burnt and the flames spread to the Alley of the Chain and sparks flew as far as the Gate of Degrees, where a number of houses were burnt down. The library of the Niẓāmiyya was destroyed by the fire, although the books were saved because the student lawyers became aware of the fire and moved them out.[9]

In this year the following died:

'Abd Allāh ibn Yaḥyā ibn Muḥammad ibn Bahlūl, Abū Muḥammad al-Andalusī al-Saraqusṭī. He was a canon lawyer and a man of learning. He came to Iraq about the year 500 [1106–7] and, having travelled to Khurasan, he took up residence in Marv al-Rūdh, where he died.

He was the author of some good poetry. Here is an example:

How many a slender youth struts in his garments,
[as] the supple branch sports beneath the strong wind.
I beheld his cheek in the mirror of my thoughts,
Imitated the movement of his eyelids with my limbs.
I did not reckon that the action of my imagination
Would have so strong an effect and wound my limb.
No wonder, if [my] imagining wounds his cheek:
Sorcery works on what is distant and remote.

Abū'l-Qāsim 'Alī ibn Muḥammad ibn Aḥmad ibn Bayān al-Razzāz in Sha'bān [December 1116] [**524**]. He was born in Ṣafar of the year 413 [May 1022] and was the last to relate Ḥadīth on the authority of Abū'l-Ḥasan ibn Mukhlid and Abū'l-Qāsim ibn Bishrān.

Abū Bakr Muḥammad ibn Manṣūr ibn Muḥammad ibn 'Abd al-Jabbār al-Sam'ānī, the head of the Shafi'īs in Marv. He was born in the year 446 [1054–5].[10] He heard much Ḥadīth and wrote books on the subject, including some excellent *Dictations*. He gave lectures on Ḥadīth and whatever he wished to do he did well.

Maḥfūẓ ibn Aḥmad ibn al-Ḥasan al-Kalūdhānī, Abū'l-Khaṭṭāb the Ḥanbalī lawyer. His birth date was the year 432 [1041] and he studied canon law under Abū Ya'lā ibn al-Farrā'.

---

9 For this fire and further references, see Makdisi, 'Topography', 295–6.

10 *Muntaẓam*, ix, 188, gives 466/1073–4 as the year of his birth and supports that by adding that he died aged somewhat over 43.

[525]

The Year 511 [1117-1118]

The death of Sultan Muḥammad and the accession of his son Maḥmūd

On 24 Dhū'l-Ḥijja [18 April 1118] the Sultan Muḥammad ibn Malikshāh ibn Alp Arslān died. His illness had begun in Sha'bān [December 1117] and he gave up riding. His illness increased and became chronic and rumours of his death circulated. When the Feast of the Sacrifice came [4 April 1118], the sultan and his son Sultan Maḥmūd both attended the banquet which the people 'demolished'.[1] Permission was then given and they entered into the presence of Sultan Muḥammad, after he had made a great effort to take his seat with a large feast spread before him. The people ate and departed.

When Dhū'l-Ḥijja was halfway through [9 April] the sultan despaired of his life. He summoned his son Maḥmūd, kissed him and both of them wept. Muḥammad ordered him to go out, take his seat on the throne of the sultanate and consider the business of the people. At that time he was somewhat more than fourteen years old. He said to his father, 'It is not an auspicious day', meaning, as concerns the stars. 'You speak truly,' he replied, 'but only for your father. For you, it is auspicious by your accession to the sultanate.' So Maḥmūd went out and took his place on the throne, wearing the crown and the two bracelets.

On Thursday 24 Dhū'l-Ḥijja [18 April] the emirs were summoned and informed of Muḥammad's death. His last testament to his son Maḥmūd was read, in which he ordered him to be just and do good. On Friday 25th of that month [19 April] the khutbah was made in the name of Maḥmūd as sultan.

Sultan Muḥammad, who was born on 18 Sha'bān in the year 474 [21 January 1082], was thirty-seven years, four months and six days of age. He had been first saluted **[526]** as sultan in Baghdad during Dhū'l-Ḥijja of the year 492 [19 October-16 November 1099]. Several times the khutbah in his name was stopped, as we have related. He encountered hardships and dangers beyond counting. However, after his brother Barkyāruq died, his position as sultan was uncontested and he was held in great respect. His armies and his wealth increased. The people were united under him for twelve years and six months.

---

1 Literally 'plundered.' One might look askance at this passage if it were not for *Mufarrij*, v, 14–15: 'He [al-Kāmil] spread a great banquet to be plundered in the fashion of the Turks and made high towers of halvah around it ... The common people and the pages (*ghilmān*) climbed up the towers of halvah to plunder them ... while the sultan [and his son] were laughing etc.'

Some account of his way of life

He was a just man, of good conduct and brave. An example of his justice is that he purchased some mamlukes from certain merchants. He paid them by a draft on the financial official of Khūzistān, who gave them part but deferred the rest. They came before the court and took with them the cadi's servants. When the sultan saw them, he said to his chamberlain, 'Look into the situation of these men.' He duly questioned them and they said, 'We have a case against a person who should attend the court with us.' 'Who is that,' he asked, and they replied, 'The sultan.' They explained their plea, which he then told to the sultan, who was mortified and felt constrained. He ordered the official to be summoned and to deliver their money and pay a heavy fine. He punished him to prevent others doing the same thing. After that he used to say, 'I was very sorry that I did not attend the court with them, as an example to others and so that no one will refuse to attend and fulfil his obligations.'

Another instance of his justice is that he had a treasurer, called Abū Aḥmad al-Qazwīnī, who was killed by the Bāṭinīs. After his murder the sultan ordered a review of the Treasury. A casket was shown to him in which were many precious jewels. He said, 'A few days ago he showed me these jewels. They belong to his friends.' He handed them **[527]** to a servant to keep them safe, investigate who his friends were and return them. After enquiries they were [found to be] foreign merchants, who were convinced they had lost the jewels, despaired of them but held their peace. The sultan summoned them and restored the jewels to them.

A further example is that he waived non-canonical taxes and imposts in all his lands. He was not known for any wicked deed. The emirs knew his conduct and not one of them dared to do an injustice and refrained from all such acts.

One of the excellent things he did was his handling of the Bāṭinīs, as we shall now relate.

The state of the Bāṭinīs in the reign of Sultan Muḥammad

We have already related what steps he took to besiege their fortresses. Here we shall tell what extra trouble he took to deal with them. When he realised (God Almighty have mercy on him) that the interests of his lands and his people depended on eliminating them, destroying their haunts and conquering their fortresses and castles, he made it his constant care to harass them.

During his reign their leader and upholder of their cause was al-Ḥasan ibn al-Ṣabbāḥ al-Rāzī, the lord of the castle of Alamūt. He had been long in power and it was nearly twenty-six years since he had taken Alamūt. His neighbours were in a very bad state on account of his many raids and the killing and capturing of their men and enslaving of their women. The sultan sent troops against them, as we have recounted, but they returned without achieving any purpose. When this sickness defied all [other] treatment, he commissioned Emir Anūshtakīn Shīrkīr, lord of Abeh, Saveh and elsewhere, to fight them. He overcame several of their forts, including the castle of Kulām,[2] which he took in Jumādā I of the year 505 [5 November–4 December 1111]. The commander there was known as 'Alī ibn Mūsā, who was given terms along with his men. They were sent **[528]** to Alamūt. He also conquered the castle of Bīra, which was seven leagues from Qazwīn. He gave its garrison terms and also sent them to Alamūt.

With the troops he had he then marched to Alamūt. The sultan sent him a number of emirs as reinforcements and he began a siege. He was the one, among the emirs, who possessed the talent and insight to fight them, along with good sense and bravery. He built quarters for himself and his men to live in and appointed certain months for each group of emirs to reside there on a rota basis, while he constantly pressed the siege. The sultan transported provisions, supplies and men to him and the situation of the Bāṭinīs became difficult. Foodstuffs and other things grew short. When things became critical, they sent down their women and children to sue for terms. They asked him to clear a route for them and their menfolk to leave under a guarantee of security. This was not granted and he sent them back to the castle, with the intention that they should all die of hunger.

Ibn al-Ṣabbāḥ issued each person daily with a loaf and three walnuts. When their situation had reached a stage which could not become any worse, news of the death of Sultan Muḥammad came to them. Their morale was raised and their hearts gladdened. The news reached the besieging army a day afterwards and they determined to withdraw. However, Shīrkīr said, 'If we withdraw and this becomes widely known, they will come down and take the food and supplies that we have prepared. Our right course is to remain besieging the castle until we conquer it, or, if we do not remain, then we must wait three days to send away our baggage and what we have amassed and burn what we cannot transport so that the enemy cannot take it.'

When they heard what he said, they knew that he spoke the truth and undertook to act in concert and be united. Nevertheless, when **[529]** evening came, they departed without any consultation and only Shīrkīr remained. The Bāṭinīs came down from the castle and Shīrkīr fought and resisted them, protecting the army's traders and camp-followers who were left behind. When he eventually left the castle, the Bātinīs seized as booty what was abandoned.

Account of the siege of Gabès and al-Mahdiyya

This year 'Alī ibn Yaḥyā, ruler of Ifrīqiya, sent a fleet by sea to Gabès and blockaded it. The reason for this was that the ruler there, Rāfi' ibn Makkan al-

2 Le Strange, *Caliphate*, 374, tentatively places this castle (named Kalām) on the Shāh Rūd [river]. In *Order of the Assassins*, 97, note 44 it is called Kīlām, but in Yāqūt, iv, 297, Kulām, 'an ancient fortress in the mountains of Ṭabaristān'.

Dahmānī, constructed a ship on the shore to carry the overseas merchants. This was at the end of the reign of Emir Yaḥyā, who did not disapprove in accordance with his normal easy-going ways. When ʻAlī came to power after his father, he rejected this and said, 'No-one in Ifrīqiya may compete with me in maintaining merchants ships at sea.' When Rāfiʻ was afraid that ʻAlī might stop him, he sought protection from Roger, king of the Franks in Sicily, and relied on his support. Roger promised to give him aid and help him keep his ship at sea. Immediately he sent a fleet to Gabès. They sailed by al-Mahdiyya and that was when ʻAlī became convinced that they had come to an agreement, having dismissed it as false.

After Roger's fleet passed al-Mahdiyya, ʻAlī despatched his fleet in pursuit. All came together at Gabès. When its ruler saw the Frankish and the Muslim fleets, he did not send his ship out. However, the Frankish fleet withdrew and ʻAlī's fleet remained besieging Rāfiʻ at Gabès, blockading him very closely.

[**530**] They returned to al-Mahdiyya and Rāfiʻ continued his opposition to ʻAlī. He gathered the Arab tribes and marched with them to besiege al-Mahdiyya. He tried to trick ʻAlī. He said, 'I have only come to put myself under your allegiance,' and he asked for someone to start peace negotiations, but his actions gave the lie to his words. Not a word was given him in answer. ʻAlī put his forces in the field and they charged Rāfiʻ and his men savagely, forcing them back to their tents. The attackers reached the tents and, seeing this, the womenfolk cried out and wailed. The Arabs' honour was aroused and they took up the struggle again. The fighting was fierce until sunset and then they separated. Many men in Rāfiʻ's army were slain but in ʻAlī's force only one man in the infantry was killed.

ʻAlī's army marched out one more time and a battle was fought, fiercer than the first. Victory went to ʻAlī's army. When Rāfiʻ saw that he could not match them he left al-Mahdiyya by night to go to Qairawan. The inhabitants refused to allow him to enter, so he fought them for a few days and then entered. ʻAlī sent a force from al-Mahdiyya which besieged him there until he left and returned to Gabès. A number of notables of Ifrīqiya, Arabs and others, asked ʻAlī for peace. He refused but later agreed and a treaty was made.[3]

Account of a difference between Roger and Emir ʻAlī

Between Roger, lord of Sicily, and Emir ʻAlī, ruler of Ifrīqiya, there was a strong friendship until the former helped Rāfiʻ, as we have mentioned above. They became estranged from one another. Roger addressed him in terms that were not customary and the estrangement became deeper. Roger sent a letter full of rough language. ʻAlī took precautionary measures and ordered the renewal of his fleet and the preparation of equipment to confront the enemy. He made contact with the

---

[3] For a fuller account of the events in this section, see Idris, *La Berbérie*, 319–23.

Almoravids in Marrakech about cooperating to invade Sicily. Thereupon Roger refrained from the measures he had been taking.[4]

[531] The death of the ruler of Aleppo and Īlghāzī's taking control

During this year Lu'lu' the Eunuch was killed. He had taken control of the citadel of Aleppo and its surrounding districts after the death of Prince Riḍwān. He became atabeg for Riḍwān's son, Alp Arslān, and when the latter died, he set up Sulṭānshāh ibn Riḍwān in power to succeed him and during his reign wielded more authority than he had in his brother's reign. When it was this present year he went from Aleppo to Qal'at Ja'bar to meet with the Emir Sālim ibn Mālik, its ruler. When he was at Qal'at Nādir,[5] he dismounted to pass water. A group of his followers, Turks, charged towards him and shouted, 'A rabbit! A rabbit!' and gave him to understand that they were hunting one, but they shot their arrows at him and he was killed. After his death they ransacked his treasure-chest but the people of Aleppo came out against them and recovered what they had taken.

The atabegate of Sulṭānshāh ibn Riḍwān was then held by Shams al-Khawāṣṣ Yārūqtāsh, who lasted one month but was then dismissed. He was followed by Abū'l-Ma'ālī ibn al-Malaḥī al-Dimashqī but he too was dismissed and mulcted. It is said that the reason for the killing of Lu'lu' was that he planned to kill Sulṭānshāh as he had killed his brother Alp Arslān, but Sulṭānshāh's men learnt his purpose and put him to death. It is said that he was killed in the year 510 [1116–17] and God knows best.

The inhabitants of Aleppo were fearful of the Franks so they handed over the city to Najm al-Dīn Īlghāzī. When he took charge, he found neither money nor stores there, because the Eunuch had distributed everything. Prince Riḍwān had amassed a very great deal, but God supplied it to others, not his children. Seeing the empty state of the city's treasury, Īlghāzī extorted from the eunuch servants money with which he bought off the Franks and made a truce with them for a short period, which would be enough to allow him to journey to Mārdīn, gather his forces and return. **[532]** When the truce was concluded, he set out for Mārdīn with this intention. As his deputy in Aleppo he left his son, Ḥusām al-Dīn Timurtāsh.

Miscellaneous events

This year on 14 Ṣafar [17 June 1117] there was a total eclipse of the moon.

---

4 Cf. Idris, *La Berbérie*, 323–4.

5 Situated between Aleppo and Bālis. See Eddé, *Description*, 11, 13 and references cited.

In this year the Franks attacked the suburbs of Ḥāma in Syria. They killed more than one hundred of the population and then they retired.[6]

On the day of ʻArafāt[7] [3 April 1118] there was an earthquake in Iraq, the Jazīra and much of the area. In Baghdad many houses were destroyed on the West Bank.

This year the following died:

Aḥmad al-ʻArabī in Baghdad.[8] He was one of the pious devotees of God, who worked miracles. His tomb at Baghdad is a site of pilgrimage.

Abū ʻAlī Muḥammad ibn Saʻd ibn Ibrāhīm ibn Nuhbān, the clerk, in Shawwāl of this year [February 1118]. He was one hundred years of age. His transmission of Ḥadīth had very high authority. He transmitted on the authority of Abū ʻAlī ibn Shādhān and others.[9]

Al-Ḥasan ibn Jaʻfar, Abū ʻAbd Allāh al-Shaqqāq, the inheritance specialist and mathematician. He was the leading scholar of his age in the science of the Koranic shares and in mathematics. He also heard Ḥadīth from Abū'l-Ḥasan ibn al-Muhtadī and others.[10]

Alexius,[11] the ruler of Constantinople. His son John,[12] who followed his pattern of rule, succeeded him.

The duke[13] of Antioch died and God saved us from his wickedness.

---

[6] According to Ibn Qal., 199, this raid was on 15 Muḥarram/19 May 1117 (for him, also the date of the eclipse), and 120 were killed.

[7] i.e. 9 Dhū'l-Ḥijja, the day the pilgrims gather at Mt. ʻArafāt.

[8] Also called Aḥmad al-Qazwīnī, he died in Ramaḍān/January 1118 (*Muntaẓam*, ix, 193-4).

[9] Born 411/1020-21, died Sunday 7 Shawwāl/ =3 February 1118 (*Muntaẓam*, ix, 195).

[10] In *Muntaẓam*, ix, 194, named as al-Ḥusayn ibn Aḥmad ibn Jaʻfar (died in Dhū'l-Ḥijja/April 1118).

[11] This is Alexius I Comnenus (1081-1118). The Arabic (with some variant readings) has something like Alikzāyakus.

[12] John II Comnenus (1118-43).

[13] In Arabic *dūqas*. The same note is found in Ibn Qal., 199. Is this perhaps an anticipation of the death of Roger of Salerno in 513/1119. See below p. [**555**].

[533]

The Year 512 [1118-1119]

Account of what the Sultan Maḥmūd did in Iraq and how al-Bursuqī was appointed prefect of Baghdad

After the death of Sultan Muḥammad and the accession of his son Maḥmūd, affairs of state were managed by the Vizier Rabīb al-Dawla Abū Manṣūr. He sent to the Caliph al-Mustaẓhir bi-Allāh, asking for the khutbah to be pronounced in Maḥmūd's name at Baghdad. This was done on Friday 23 Muḥarram[1] [=17 May 1118]. The prefect in Baghdad was Bahrūz.

Emir Dubays ibn Ṣadaqa had been with Sultan Muḥammad since his father was killed, as we have related. The sultan treated him well and assigned him a large fief. After the death of Sultan Muḥammad, Dubays spoke to Sultan Maḥmūd about returning to his town, al-Ḥilla, and did so, after permission for this had been given. A large host of Arabs, Kurds and others flocked to him. Āqsunqur al-Bursuqī was resident in al-Raḥba, which was his fief, although no governmental responsibilities were in his hands. He had left his son, 'Izz al-Dīn Maḥmūd, as his deputy and travelled to Sultan Muḥammad before his death, intending to appeal to him for an increase in his fief. However, before he reached Baghdad, he heard of the death of Sultan Muḥammad.

Mujāhid al-Dīn Bahrūz, apprised of his approach to Baghdad, sent to him, to prevent him from entering the city. However, he set off to see Sultan Maḥmūd and was met, when he was in Ḥulwān, by the sultan's rescript appointing him prefect of Baghdad and dismissing Bahrūz. The emirs around the sultan wanted al-Bursuqī and had banded together in his support, while they disliked [**534**] Mujāhid al-Dīn Bahrūz and envied him because of the closeness to Sultan Muḥammad that he had had. They feared that he might become more prominent and more powerful with Sultan Maḥmūd. When al-Bursuqī took on the prefecture of Baghdad, Bahrūz fled to Takrit, which was held by him.

Later the sultan appointed Emir Mankūbars as prefect of Baghdad, a great emir who had gained authority in the regime of Sultan Maḥmūd. When given this office he sent his step-son, Emir Ḥusayn ibn Uzbak, one of the Turkish emirs and lord of Asadābādh, to deputize for him in Baghdad and Iraq. Ḥusayn left the sultan at the gate of Hamadhan, and several of the Bakjiyya emirs and others joined him.

When al-Bursuqī heard of this, he appealed to the Caliph al-Mustaẓhir bi-Allāh, to order Ḥusayn to stop where he was until the sultan had been written to, when

---

[1] The text has 13 Muḥarram, which gives 6 May, a Monday! *Muntaẓam*, ix, 196, has the 23 Muḥarram date (easily confused with 13 in Arabic script), which by the conversion tables is 16 May, a Thursday!

he would carry out whatever order he might receive. The caliph made contact with Ḥusayn and he replied, 'If the caliph orders a return, I shall go back, but otherwise I must enter Baghdad.' Al-Bursuqī gathered his followers and moved against him. They met and fought. A brother of Ḥusayn was killed and he himself and those with him were defeated and returned to the sultan's camp. This took place in the month of Rabīʿ I [22 June–21 July 1118] some days before the death of al-Mustaẓhir bi-Allāh.

Account of the death of al-Mustaẓhir bi-Allāh

This year on 16 Rabīʿ II [3 August 1118] al-Mustaẓhir bi-Allāh Abū'l-ʿAbbās Aḥmad ibn al-Muqtadī bi-Amr Allāh died. He had been ill with a gastric condition.[2] He was forty-one years, six months and six days old and his caliphate had lasted twenty-four years, three [**535**] months and eleven days. The following served him as vizier, ʿAmīd al-Dawla Abū Manṣūr ibn Jahīr, Sadīd al-Mulk Abū'l-Maʿālī al-Mufaḍḍal ibn ʿAbd al-Razzāq al-Iṣbahānī, Zaʿīm al-Ruʾasāʾ Abū'l-Qāsim ibn Jahīr, Majd al-Dīn Abū'l-Maʿālī Hibat Allāh ibn al-Muṭṭalib and Niẓām al-Dīn Abū Manṣūr al-Ḥusayn ibn Muḥammad. Amīn al-Dawla Abū Saʿd ibn al-Mawṣilāyā and Chief Cadi Abū'l-Ḥasan ʿAlī ibn al-Dāmghānī acted as deputy viziers. Three sultans, whose names were mentioned in the khutbah at his court, died during his reign. They were Tāj al-Dawla Tutush ibn Alp Arslān, and Sultan Barkyāruq and Muḥammad, two sons of Malikshāh.

It is a strange coincidence that al-Qāʾim bi-Amr Allāh died [soon] after the death of Sultan Alp Arslān, that al-Muqtadī bi-Amr Allāh died after Sultan Malikshāh, and that al-Mustaẓhir bi-Allāh died after Sultan Muḥammad.

Some account of his character and his manner of rule

He was (God be pleased with him) gentle and noble in character. He loved to shower benefits on people and do good. He was eager to perform pious acts and good deeds. His efforts were appreciated and he never refused a favour that was asked of him.

He showed great trust in those he appointed to office, not hearkening to any slanderer nor paying attention to what such a one might say. Capriciousness was

[2] The text reads *al-tarāqī*. *Muntaẓam*, ix, 200, which dates the caliph's death to the eve of Thursday 26 Rabīʿ II/=15 August 1118, has *ʿillat al-tarāqī*, meaning 'illness of the shoulder blades' (!) or 'of the upper chest' (cf Koran, lxxv, 26–7). An emendation is suggested by *Wāfī*, vii, 117: *ʿillat al-marāqiyā* (sic). *Marāqq* is the *hupokhondrion*, 'the belly', and Ibn Zuhr, 95ff., refers to a stomach illness called *al-marāqqiyya*. Ibn al-ʿImranī, 208, dates his death to Rabīʿ I/June-July and says that the illness was dropsy (*al-istisqāʾ*).

unknown in him nor did his resolution wilt under the urging of those with special interests.

His days were days of happiness for his subjects, like festive days, so good they were. When he heard of that, he rejoiced and was very happy. Whenever any sultan or deputy of his set out to harm anyone, he did all he could to condemn and prevent it.

[536] He had a good hand and his minuting of documents was excellent. No one came near him in that, which showed his rich culture and wide learning. When he died, his son al-Mustarshid bi-Allāh said the last prayers over him and pronounced *Allāhu akbar* four times. He was buried in a chamber of his which he used to frequent. Here is an example of his poetry:

The heat of passion melted what had frozen in my heart
When I stretched forth my hand for the formal farewell.
How shall I fare along the path of patient endurance,
Seeing my paths over the chasm of love to be cords?
A new moon whom I loved has broken his promise
After my fate had fulfilled what it promised.
If I break the compact of love in my heart
After this, then may I never behold him more.

The Imam al-Mustarshid bi-Allāh's accession to the caliphate

After the death of al-Mustaẓhir bi-Allāh his son, al-Mustarshid bi-Allāh Abū Manṣūr al-Faḍl ibn Abī'l-'Abbās Aḥmad al-Mustaẓhir bi-Allāh, was proclaimed his successor. He was heir apparent in whose name the khutbah had been made for twenty-three years. Allegiance to him was pledged by his two brothers, sons of al-Mustaẓhir bi-Allāh, namely Abū 'Abd Allāh Muḥammad and Abū Ṭālib al-'Abbās, his uncles, the sons of al-Muqtadī bi-Amr Allāh, and others, such as the emirs, cadis, imams and notables.

The person who undertook to take the oaths of allegiance was the Cadi Abū'l-Ḥasan al-Dāmghānī, who was acting as deputy vizier. Al-Mustarshid bi-Allāh confirmed him in the office. No cadi ever administered these oaths other than this man and Aḥmad **[537]** ibn Abī Dā'ūd, who took the oaths for al-Wāthiq bi-Allāh, and the Cadi Abū 'Alī Ismā'īl ibn Isḥāq, who took them for al-Mu'tamiḍ bi-Allāh.

Later al-Mustarshid dismissed the Chief Cadi from the deputy vizierate and appointed as vizier Abū Shujā' Muḥammad, son of Rabīb al-Dawla Abū Manṣūr, Sultan Muḥammad's vizier. His father had made approaches on behalf of his son and he was finally appointed. The head of the Storeroom, Abū Ṭāhir Yūsuf ibn Aḥmad al-Ḥuzzī,[3] was arrested.

---

[3] *Muntaẓam*, ix, 198, has al-Kharazī. The same source mentions the rumour that Abū Ṭāhir

The flight and then the return of Emir Abū'l-Ḥasan, brother of al-Mustarshid

When people were busy with al-Mustarshid bi-Allāh's installation, his brother, Emir Abū'l-Ḥasan ibn al-Mustaẓhir bi-Allāh, took ship with three persons and went down to al-Madā'in. From there he went to Dubays ibn Ṣadaqa at al-Ḥilla, who received him with honour and learnt from him of the death of al-Mustaẓhir bi-Allāh. Dubays provided him with lavish maintenance. When al-Mustarshid bi-Allāh learnt this information it worried him and made him anxious. He sent to Dubays asking that he send him back. The reply was, 'I am the servant of the caliph and wait upon his orders. Nevertheless, he has sought my protection and entered my house. I can never compel him to any action.'

The envoy was the Chief Syndic Sharaf al-Dīn 'Alī ibn Ṭirād al-Zaynabī. He sought out Emir Abū'l-Ḥasan, talked to him about returning and guaranteed on behalf of the caliph all he might wish for. Abū'l-Ḥasan agreed to go back and said, 'I did not leave my brother because of any evil I planned. It was fear that brought me to leave him. If he gives me guarantees, I shall go to him.' Dubays pledged to make things right **[538]** personally and to go with him to Baghdad. The syndic returned and informed the caliph of the situation. The latter consented to what was asked of him.

Then there occurred the affair between al-Bursuqī, Dubays and Mankūbars which we have already mentioned, and the matter was delayed.

Emir Abū'l-Ḥasan remained with Dubays until 12 Ṣafar in the year 513 [25 May 1119]. Then he left al-Ḥilla for Wāsiṭ, where his following became numerous and there were strong rumours of his growing power. He took the city of Wāsiṭ and became a danger. The Caliph al-Mustarshid bi-Allāh ordered that the khutbah be proclaimed for his heir apparent, his son Abū Ja'far al-Manṣūr, who was twelve years of age. His name was added to the khutbah on 2 Rabī' II [13 July 1119] **[513]** at Baghdad. Letters ordering the same went out to the lands and the caliph sent to Dubays ibn Mazyad on the subject of Emir Abū'l-Ḥasan, pointing out that he had now left his protection and laid hands on the caliph's estates and resources. He ordered that he be attacked and dealt with before he grew [too] powerful. Dubays sent his troops against him, so he abandoned Wāsiṭ. He and his men were at a loss what to do, and lost their way. Dubays' troops arrived and surprised them at al-Ṣilḥ[4] and sacked his baggage. The Kurds and Turks amongst his men fled. The rest returned to Dubays.

Emir Abū'l-Ḥasan remained with ten followers, thirsty and five leagues from any water. It was the time of summer heat and he was convinced he would perish. Two

and some others who were also arrested had incited the actions of Emir Abū'l-Ḥasan (see next section). *Op. cit.*, ix, 203, records Abū Ṭāhir's execution in Jumādā I this year/ 20 August–17 September 1118.

4 The name of a canal and a town on east bank of Tigris 'seven leagues above Wāsiṭ' (see Le Strange, *Caliphate*, 38).

Bedouin followed him. He wanted to flee from them but could not. They seized him when his thirst had become severe. They gave him something to drink and took him to Dubays, who sent him to Baghdad and had him carried to the caliph, after he had offered Dubays 20,000 dinars. He was taken to the Palace (*al-dār al-'azīza*). There were eleven months between his leaving Baghdad and his return.

When he came into the presence of al-Mustarshid bi-Allāh, he kissed his foot. Al-Mustarshid kissed him in return and they both wept. The caliph settled him [**539**] in a handsome residence where he himself had lodged before he became caliph, and had robes of honour and many gifts brought to him. He put his mind at rest and guaranteed his safety.

Account of the coming of Prince Mas'ūd and Juyūsh Beg to Iraq and what happened between them and between al-Bursuqī and Dubays

In Jumādā I of this year [20 August–18 September 1118] al-Bursuqī took the field and camped below al-Raqqa[5] with his troops and other followers. He announced that he was intending to attack al-Ḥilla and expel Dubays ibn Ṣadaqa. Dubays gathered together large bodies of Arabs and Kurds and distributed large sums of money and weapons.

Prince Mas'ūd, son of Sultan Muḥammad, was at Mosul with his atabeg, Ay Aba Juyūsh Beg. A number of people in their service advised them both to head for Iraq, for there was no one to defend it. So they set out at the head of large forces. With Prince Mas'ūd was his vizier, Fakhr al-Mulk Abū 'Alī ibn 'Ammār, the [former] lord of Tripoli, and 'Imād al-Dīn[6] Zankī ibn Āqsunqur, the ancestor of our present rulers in Mosul, who was courageous in the extreme. With them also was the lord of Sinjār, the lord of Irbil, Abū'l-Hayjā', and Karbāwī ibn Khurasān al-Turkomānī, the lord of al-Bawāzīj. When al-Bursuqī learnt of their approach, he was fearful of them.

In the past Sultan Muḥammad had made al-Bursuqī atabeg for his son Mas'ūd, as we have mentioned, and it was only Juyūsh Beg he feared. When they drew near Baghdad, he marched to confront them and block their route. Having learnt of this, Mas'ūd and Juyūsh Beg sent him Emir [**540**] Karbāwī to make peace. He informed al-Bursuqī that they had merely come to reinforce him against Dubays, so they came to terms, made an agreement and united.

Mas'ūd came to Baghdad and lodged in the Sultan's Palace. Then news came to them of the arrival of Emir 'Imād al-Dīn Mankūbars, who has been mentioned before, with a large army. Al-Bursuqī left Baghdad to meet him and bring him to battle and keep him away from the city. Hearing this, Mankūbars went to al-Nu'māniyya, crossed the Tigris there and effected a junction with Dubays ibn Ṣadaqa.

5 This is not the town on the Euphrates but either a town west of Baghdad or a village a league below that.

6 The edition has 'Qasīm al-Dawla' which was the title of his father Āqsunqur.

Dubays was fearful of Prince Mas'ūd and al-Bursuqī and his strategy was based on playing for time and seeking conciliation. He now presented Mas'ūd, al-Bursuqī and Juyūsh Beg with a handsome gift. However, when the news of Mankūbars's arrival reached him, he made contact, won him to his side and made him swear an oath. They both agreed to cooperate and aid one another. They united and each one was strengthened by the other. After this Prince Mas'ūd, al-Bursuqī and Juyūsh Beg with their followers marched to al-Madā'in to meet Dubays and Mankūbars. Having arrived there, they received intelligence of the large forces the two had. Al-Bursuqī and Mas'ūd withdrew and crossed the Ṣarṣar Canal and held the crossing places. Both sides plundered the countryside disgracefully, the [districts of] King's Canal, the Ṣarṣar Canal and Īsā Canal, and they violated the womenfolk.

Al-Mustarshid bi-Allāh sent to Prince Mas'ūd and al-Bursuqī, disapproving of this state of affairs and ordering them to stop bloodshed and to cease their wicked ways and ordering them to be conciliatory and make peace. The envoys were Sadīd al-Dawla ibn al-Anbārī and the Imam al-As'ad al-Mayhanī, the professor of the Niẓāmiyya. Al-Bursuqī denied that anything of that sort had been caused by them and he agreed to return to Baghdad. Then a report came that Mankūbars and Dubays had equipped 3,000 cavalry under Manṣūr, the brother of Dubays, and Emir Ḥusayn ibn Uzbak, Mankūbars' step-son, and had despatched them to cross at Darzījān[7] and to block the crossing-point at Diyālā on the road to Baghdad because it was devoid of [**541**] troops to defend and hold it.

Al-Bursuqī returned to Baghdad and crossed the bridge to avoid frightening the population who did not know the news. He left his son, 'Izz al-Dīn Mas'ūd, with the army at Ṣarṣar and took with him 'Imād al-Dīn Zankī ibn Āqsunqur. He came to Diyālā where the troops of Mankūbars prevented him from crossing. Two days he remained there and then he received a letter from his son, 'Izz al-Dīn Mas'ūd, telling him that peace had been arranged between the two sides. His spirit was broken since this had come about without his knowledge, and he retired to Baghdad and crossed to the West Bank. Manṣūr and Ḥusayn crossed and followed behind him with their troops. They came to Baghdad in the middle of the night and camped at the Sultan's Mosque.

Al-Bursuqī travelled to Prince Mas'ūd and collected his equipment and treasure, then returned to Baghdad, where he camped at the Old Bridge.[8] Prince Mas'ūd and Juyūsh Beg came up river and camped at the Hospital. Dubays and Mankūbars did the same and camped below al-Raqqa. 'Izz al-Dīn Mas'ūd, son of al-Bursuqī, remained with Mankūbars, separated from his father.

The reason for this peace was that Juyūsh Beg had sent to Sultan Maḥmūd, demanding more for himself and for Prince Mas'ūd. His envoy's letter came back from the sultan's camp, telling that he had met with great kindness from the sultan

---

[7] Yāqūt, ii, 567: 'a large village below Baghdad on west bank of Tigris.'

[8] i.e. al-Qanṭara al-'Atiqa, across the Sarāt Canal opposite Kufa Gate, south-west of the original Round City (see Le Strange, *Baghdad*, index).

and that he assigned them both Azerbayjan. When the sultan heard of their setting-out for Baghdad he believed that the two had rebelled against him, so he retracted what he had agreed to. The envoy also said that the sultan had dispatched a force to Mosul. The letter fell into the hands of Mankūbars and he sent it to Juyūsh Beg, guaranteeing that he would repair his and Prince Mas'ūd's relations with the sultan. Mankūbars was **[542]** married to Prince Mas'ūd's mother, whose name was Sarjahān, and for that reason preferred to do what was good for him. Peace therefore was settled but both feared that al-Bursuqī would resist it, so they agreed to send their troops to Darzījān, so that al-Bursuqī would use up his resources facing them, his troops leave him and an agreement be the result. What happened when he marched there has been mentioned already.

Because of his good rule among them al-Bursuqī was loved by the people of Baghdad. When peace was made and the emirs came to Baghdad, his men and his levies left al-Bursuqī, and his ambition to take control of Iraq without the order of the sultan came to nothing. He left Iraq to go to Prince Mas'ūd with whom he remained. Mankūbars was established as prefect of Baghdad. Dubays ibn Ṣadaqa took leave of him and returned to al-Ḥilla, after he had made a claim for his father's residence in Fayrūz Lane, which had been incorporated into the Sultan's Mosque at Baghdad. He received a monetary compensation for it.

Mankūbars remained in Baghdad, acting wickedly, ill-treating the population and extorting money. People of wealth hid and several moved into the Harem of the Caliphal Palace for fear of him. People's livelihoods were ruined and his men did many evil things. Indeed, a woman, whom a certain citizen of Baghdad had married, was conducted to him in her bridal procession, and one of Mankūbars' men, hearing of this, came to him, broke down the door, wounded the husband several times and then violated his wife. Loud were the pleas made day and night and the people clamoured for help because of this state of affairs and closed down the markets. The soldier in question was taken to the Caliphal Palace, where he was imprisoned for several days but then released.

The sultan heard what Mankūbars was doing in Baghdad and he sent to summon him and to urge him to attend on him, but he made excuses and temporised. The more the sultan asked for him, the more he devoted himself to collecting money and extortion. However, when the people of Baghdad realised that the sultan had turned against him and had demanded his presence, they were emboldened. At that stage Mankūbars departed, fearing that they would rise against him, and so people were saved from his wickedness and those who had been in hiding appeared again.

[543] The death of the king of the Franks and what happened between the Franks and the Muslims

In Dhū'l-Ḥijja of the year 511 [26 March–23 April 1118] Baldwin, the king of the

Franks, died. He had marched towards Egypt with an assemblage of Franks, aiming to conquer and take control of it. His eagerness to take Egypt was strong. He came opposite Tinnīs and took a swim in the Nile, and a former wound reopened. When he felt close to death, he returned to Jerusalem, and there he died. He willed his lands to the Count, lord of Edessa, the one whom Jokermish had made captive and Jāwulī Saqāo set free. It chanced that this count had gone to Jerusalem on a pilgrimage to the Church of the Sepulchre. When he was designated as king, he accepted and united Jerusalem and Edessa in his hands.

Atabeg Ṭughtakīn had marched from Damascus to fight the Franks and camped between Job's Monastery[9] and Kafar Baṣl on the Yarmūk River. The death of Baldwin remained unknown to him until he heard the news eighteen days later, when about two days' journey separated the two forces. The envoys of the king of the Franks came to him, asking for a truce. Ṭughtakīn demanded that the crop-sharing that existed between them for Jabal 'Awf, al-Ḥannāna, al-Ṣalt and the Jordan Depression be abandoned. The king did not accept this and made a show of force. Ṭughtakīn then proceeded to Tiberias and plundered it and the surrounding country. Then he set out towards Ascalon.

It belonged to the Egyptians and their forces were there, whom they had despatched after the deceased king of Jerusalem had withdrawn from Egypt. They amounted to 7,000 cavalry. Ṭughtakīn joined them and their commander informed him that their caliph had ordered him to follow Ṭughtakīn's plans and to act in accordance with his decisions. They remained at Ascalon for two months but effected nothing against the Franks. Ṭughtakīn returned to Damascus. A plea for help came to him, reporting that 130 Frankish knights had taken [**544**] a fortress in his lands, known as al-Ḥabas and also as the Fortress of Jaldak, which the castellan had surrendered to them. The Franks also raided Adhri'āt[10] and sacked it. When Tāj al-Mulūk Būrī, son of Ṭughtakīn, was sent against them, they retired to a hill where they were surrounded. His father arrived and ordered him to hold back but he refused to do so and was eager to deal with them. The Franks, with no way out, fought like men prepared to embrace death. They left their hill-top and made a full-blooded charge on the Muslims who were put to flight. A great many of them were made prisoner or killed and the remnants returned to Damascus in a most wretched state.

Ṭughtakīn went to Aleppo where Īlghāzī was and asked him for assistance, requesting that they cooperate against the Franks. Īlghāzī promised to march with him. While he was at Aleppo, he received intelligence that the Franks had attacked the Ḥawrān, part of Damascus territory. They plundered, killed and took captives before withdrawing. Both Ṭughtakīn and Īlghāzī were in accord that Ṭughtakīn should return to Damascus and protect his lands and that Īlghāzī should return to Mārdīn and raise troops and that they should meet to fight the Franks. Īlghāzī made

---

9 i.e. Dayr Ayyūb. See Yāqūt, ii, 645: 'a village in Ḥawrān.'

10 The modern Dir'ā, north of Damascus on the road to Homs (Krawulsky, 587).

a truce with the Franks who were his neighbours, as has been mentioned already. He crossed over the river [Euphrates] to Mārdīn to assemble troops. We shall narrate the sequel in the year 513 [1119-20], God willing.

Miscellaneous events

This year rainfall was interrupted and in much of the land there was a shortage of crops. The worst effects were in Iraq. Prices rose and the population of the Sawād emigrated. People fed themselves on what was left after sieving. The situation of the citizens of Baghdad was worsened by the treatment they had from Mankūbars.

This year al-Mustarshid bi-Allāh cancelled every unjust demand in the fief that was specific to him and ordered that nothing should be taken except what was according to ancient custom. He waived the tax-farm on gold thread. [**545**] The manufacturers of siglaton and gold brocade and others who worked with it used to meet with trouble and hardship from those that administered it.

The departure of the pilgrims was delayed this year, because of which there was a rumour that the pilgrimage from Iraq had been cancelled. The caliph appointed Emir Naẓar, the eunuch of Yumn, the commander of the army, and gave him the same authority over the pilgrimage that the commander of the army used to have. He also gave him the money that he would need for the journey and sent him on his way. They accomplished their pilgrimage and Naẓar's competence was manifested.

Two large ships arrived with supplies and reinforcements for the Franks in Syria but they were wrecked and sank. The people had been fearful of the men they brought.

During this year the envoy of Īlghāzī, the lord of Aleppo and Mārdīn, came to Baghdad to raise men to fight the Franks, telling of what they did to the Muslims in the lands of the Jazīra, that they had seized a castle by Edessa and killed its emir, Ibn 'Uṭayr. Letters telling of this were sent to Sultan Maḥmūd.

Also this year [the body of] al-Mustaẓhir was transferred to al-Rusāfa, along with all who were buried in the Caliphal Palace, including the grandmother of al-Mustaẓhir, al-Muqtadī's mother. Her death occurred after al-Mustaẓhir's. She lived to see the fourth generation of her descendants.[11]

The situation of the urban gangs on the West Bank at Baghdad became serious this year. The prefect's deputy crossed to deal with them leading fifty Turkish mamlukes. After a battle he fled from them. Then on the next day he crossed over

---

[11] She was Urjuwān, the Armenian slave-girl of Dhakhīrat al-Mulk, son of the Caliph al-Qā'im, by whom, before his early death, she conceived al-Muqtadī. She died during this year (see *Muntaẓam*, ix, 200). According to Ibn al-'Imrānī, 201, she was of Abyssinian origin. The hospice she founded in Baghdad is mentioned under 516/1122-3.

again with two hundred mamlukes but did not subdue them. The gangs sacked Quṭuftā[12] on that day.

The following died this year:

In Sha'bān [17 November–15 December 1118] Abū'l-Faḍl Bakr ibn Muḥammad ibn 'Alī ibn al-Faḍl al-Anṣārī, a descendant of Jābir ibn 'Abd Allāh. Born in Bukhara, he was one of the outstanding Ḥanafī lawyers, an authority for that school of law.

Abū Ṭālib al-Ḥusayn ibn Muḥammad ibn 'Alī ibn al-Ḥasan al-Zaynabī, the chief syndic at Baghdad, during Ṣafar [June 1118]. He had retired from that office and been succeeded by his brother Ṭirād. He was one of the leading **[546]** Ḥanafīs and transmitted much Ḥadīth.

In Dhū'l-Ḥijja [15 March–12 April 1119] Abū Zakarīyā Yaḥyā ibn 'Abd al-Wahhāb ibn Manda al-Iṣbahānī, the renowned Ḥadīth expert from a family of Ḥadīth scholars. He is the author of some excellent works.

Abū'l-Faḍl Aḥmad ibn al-Khāzin, who was a witty man of letters, the author of good poetry. These are some of his verses, which he extemporised after he had gone to visit a friend of his but failed to see him. The servants ushered him into a garden in the house and a bath-house:

I came to his house and saw no fellow
That did not meet me with a laughing face.
A joyful welcome in a servant's face is the result
Of the previous brightness of the master's face.
I entered his Paradise and visited his Hell
And thanked Riḍwān and Mālik[13] for his compassion.

---

[12] A suburb of West Baghdad, situated between the Dajjāj and 'Īsā Canals and stretching from the Basra road to the Tigris (see Le Strange, *Baghdad*, 97).

[13] Respectively they are the guardian of Paradise (see *EI(2)*, viii, 519) and the angel who watches over Hell (Koran, xliii, 77).

[547] The Year 513 [1119-1120]

Account of the rebellion of Prince Ṭughril against his brother Sultan Maḥmūd

When his father died, Prince Ṭughril, son of Muḥammad, who was born in Muḥarram of the year 503 [August 1109], was in the fortress of Sarjahān.[1] In the year 504 [1110-11] his father had assigned him Sāveh, Āveh and Zanjān and appointed as his atabeg the Great Emir Shīrkīr who has been mentioned before concerning the besieging of the Ismāʿīlī castles. Ṭughril's dominion increased through the castles conquered by Shīrkīr. Sultan Maḥmūd sent Emir Kuntughdī to him to be his atabeg, to administer his affairs and to bring him to the sultan. After his arrival, Ṭughril persuaded him to disobey his brother and not to go back to him. They came to an agreement on this.

Sultan Maḥmūd, having heard this news, sent Sharaf al-Dīn Anūshirwān ibn Khālid with robes of honour, gifts and 30,000 dinars. He promised his brother a large fief in addition to what he had, if he would come to him and meet with him. Agreement to meet was not forthcoming. Kuntughdī answered, 'We are loyal to the sultan. We shall proceed in whatever direction he chooses and we have the troops with which to face whoever he orders to be attacked.'

While embarking on these talks with them, Sultan Maḥmūd rode out from the gate of Hamadhan, during Jumādā I [10 August-8 September 1119], with 10,000 cavalry, without heavy baggage, and concealed his objective. His plan was to surprise his brother and Emir Kuntughdī. One of his retinue saw a Turk, one of Prince Ṭughril's men. He informed the sultan who arrested him. However, a comrade who was with the man, grasped the situation and travelled twenty **[548]** leagues in one night. He arrived to find Emir Kuntughdī drunk. After some difficulty he woke him and informed him of the situation. The emir sought out Prince Ṭughril, gave the news and took him away in disguise, making for the castle of Samīrān. They lost their way and ended up at the fortress of Sarjahān, which they had recently left and where they gathered their forces. Their losing their way actually guided them to safety, for Sultan Maḥmūd took his route via Samīrān, saying [to himself] that it was the castle which held their stores and treasure, and, when they learnt of his coming, they would make for it and possibly he would encounter them on the road. Thus they escaped from him through what they thought was a disaster for them.

However, the sultan came upon their army, surprised and routed it. He seized

[1] Krawulsky, 308-9: Sar-e Ǧahān, 'five leagues east of Sulṭāniyya on a high hill, overlooking Abhar and Zanjān.'

from his brother's treasure chest 300,000[2] dinars, which was the money that he had sent him. Sultan Maḥmūd remained in Zanjān and then from there set out for Rayy. Ṭughril left Sarjahān and he and Kuntughdī made their way to Ganja. His followers sought him there and his offensive capacity grew. The estrangment between him and his brother Maḥmūd deepened.

Account of hostilities between Sanjar and Sultan Maḥmūd

In Jumādā I of this year [10 August–8 September 1119] there were serious hostilities between Sanjar and his nephew, Sultan Maḥmūd. We shall here give the narrative background to this.

We have mentioned under the year 508 [1114–15] how Sanjar went to Ghazna and conquered it and what he did there. Later he returned to Khurasan and when he heard of the death of his brother, Sultan Muḥammad, and the accession of the latter's son, Sultan Maḥmūd, who was the husband of Sanjar's daughter, he was overcome by a great sadness [**549**] at the death of his brother and displayed unheard-of anguish and sadness. He sat among ashes[3] to receive condolences and instructed the preachers to rehearse the good deeds of Sultan Muḥammad, such as his fighting the Bāṭinīs, waiving uncanonical taxes and other matters.

Sanjar used to have the honorific title Nāṣir al-Dīn (Aider of the Religion). After the death of his brother Muḥammad, he adopted the title Mu'izz al-Dīn (Strengthener of the Religion), which was the title of his father Malikshāh. He determined to set out for the Uplands and Iraq and the territory in the possession of Maḥmūd, his nephew. He regretted having put to death his Vizier Abū Ja'far Muḥammad ibn Fakhr al-Mulk Abī'l-Muẓaffar ibn Niẓām al-Mulk. The reason why he killed him was that he alienated the emirs and slighted them. They loathed and hated him and complained of him to the sultan [Sanjar], when he was at Ghazna. Sanjar informed them that he would like to kill him but it was impossible to do that in Ghazna.

Sanjar had had his change of heart towards his vizier for various reasons. One was that he had advised him to make the expedition to Ghazna, but, when Bust had been reached, its ruler Arslānshāh sent to the vizier and guaranteed him 500,000 dinars to deflect Sanjar from his purpose. The vizier therefore advised Sanjar to make peace and retire and he did the same thing in Transoxania. Another reason was that it was reported of him that he took from Ghazna splendid possessions of great value. Yet another was his alienation of the emirs, as has been mentioned, and

[2] This figure clearly contradicts that of 30,000 given above, but there is no telling which is correct.

[3] This appears to be meant literally. In response to the loss of life during the attack on Damascus by the Second Crusade there was, according to *Muntaẓam*, x, 131, 'weeping and wailing in the city and ashes were spread (*furisha*) for several days.'

there were other reasons besides. When he returned to Balkh he was arrested, then put to death and his property seized. He had jewels and wealth unlimited. The cash that he was found to possess was one million dinars. After he was killed, the next vizier to be appointed was Shihāb al-Islām ʿAbd al-Razzāq, the nephew of Niẓām al-Mulk, who was known as Ibn al-Faqīh,[4] although he did not have the high status of [Muḥammad] ibn Fakhr al-Mulk in people's eyes. After hearing of the death of his brother, Sanjar regretted the vizier's killing because through him he achieved such aims and power as he could not attain through large numbers of troops, because of the people's liking and high regard for him.

Sultan Maḥmūd sent to his uncle, Sanjar, Sharaf al-Dīn Anūshirwān [**550**] ibn Khālid and Fakhr al-Dīn Ṭughāyuruk ibn Ilyazan, both bearing gifts and curiosities, and he offered to cede him Māzandarān and provide him with 200,000 dinars annually. They came to him and delivered their message. Sanjar prepared to set out for Rayy but Sharaf al-Dīn Anūshirwān advised him not to fight or make war. Sanjar's reply to that was, 'My brother's boy is a child. His vizier and the Chamberlain ʿAlī have acquired a dominance over him.'

When Sultan Maḥmūd heard that his uncle was marching towards him and that Emir Unur with his vanguard had arrived at Jurjān, he ordered Emir ʿAlī ibn ʿUmar, who had been Sultan Muḥammad's chamberlain and after his death became the chamberlain of Sultan Maḥmūd, to take the field and attached to him a large gathering of troops and emirs. Altogether 10,000 cavalry assembled and they set out until they drew close to Sanjar's vanguard, of which Emir Unur was the commander. Emir ʿAlī ibn ʿUmar made contact with Unur to inform him of Sultan Muḥammad's behest that Sanjar should be respected and his orders and prohibitions deferred to and his good pleasure sought; furthermore that he had expected that Sanjar would preserve the sultanate for his son Maḥmūd and make us swear to do likewise. 'It is not for us to disobey him and now that you have come to our lands, we will not tolerate this and cannot overlook it. I have learnt that 5,000 cavalry are with you. I will send against you less than that so that you may learn that you cannot withstand us nor prevail over us.'

When Emir Unur heard this, he withdrew from Jurjān. Some of Sultan Maḥmūd's army caught up with him and seized a group of his camp followers and made prisoners of a number of his men. Sultan Maḥmūd had arrived at Rayy. Emir ʿAlī ibn ʿUmar returned to him there and received his thanks and praise for his actions, as did the troops with him.

[**551**] Sultan Maḥmūd was advised to hold fast to Rayy and take up residence there. It was said, 'When the troops of Khurasan know that you reside there, they will not pass their own frontiers nor go beyond their own area of authority.' However, he did not accept the advice, became tired of staying there and went to Jurjān.

Sultan Maḥmūd and Emir Mankūbars arrived from Iraq [sic] leading 10,000

---

[4] i.e. Son of the Canon Lawyer.

cavalry and accompanied by Emir Manṣūr ibn Ṣadaqa, Dubays' brother, the Bakjiyya emirs and others. Maḥmūd proceeded to Hamadhan, where his vizier Rabīb [al-Dawla] died.[5] As his successor he appointed Abū Ṭālib al-Sumayramī. He heard of his uncle Sanjar's arrival at Rayy and marched towards him, intending to give battle. They met near Sāveh on 2 Jumādā I of this year [11 August 1119]. Sultan Maḥmūd's army already knew the desertic region which lay before Sanjar's army and took eight days to cross. They got to the source of water first and held it against them.

The Khurasanian army was 20,000 strong and had with it eighteen elephants, the name of whose lead elephant was Bādhhū. Among their senior emirs were the son of Emir Abū'l-Faḍl, the lord of Sijistān, Khwārazmshāh Muḥammad, Emir Unur and Emir Qumāj. The force was joined by 'Alā' al-Dawla Garshāsp ibn Farāmurz ibn Kākūya, lord of Yazd, who was related by marriage to Sultan Muḥammad and Sanjar through their sister. He had been very intimate with Sultan Muḥammad, but when Sultan Maḥmūd came to power, he delayed his attendance on him, so his lands were granted to Qarāja al-Sāqī, who became lord of Fars. Thereupon 'Alā' al-Dawla, one of the princes of the Daylam, went to Sanjar, whom he informed of local conditions, the route to invade these lands, the seizure of property carried out by the emirs and the disparity of views among them. He encouraged him to attack these lands.

Sultan Maḥmūd's army was 30,000 strong and among his senior emirs were Emir 'Alī ibn 'Umar the chamberlain, Emir Mankūbars, Atabeg Ghuzoghlu, the sons of Bursuq, [**552**] [Aq]sunqur al-Bukhārī and Qarāja al-Sāqī. The army had nine hundred loads of armaments.

Maḥmūd's army because of their numbers, their valour and the quantity of their cavalry made light of his uncle's troops. When they met, the spirit of the Khurasanians failed when they saw the power and size of the opposing army. Sanjar's right and left wing broke and his men fell into confusion and great disarray. They fled the field, not stopping for anything. A large amount of their baggage was plundered and the local peasantry killed many of them.

Sanjar stood amongst the elephants with a detachment of his followers, facing Sultan Maḥmūd who had Atabeg Ghuzoghlu with him. Forced by necessity when the crisis really threatened him, Sanjar ordered the elephants to be brought forward to battle. Those men that remained with him advised flight but he said, 'Victory or death, but flight - never!' When the elephants advanced and Maḥmūd's horses saw them, they turned tail with their riders. Sanjar was anxious for Sultan Maḥmūd at this juncture and said to his men, 'Do not frighten the boy with elephant charges', so they restrained them. Maḥmūd and those with him in the centre fled. Atabeg Ghuzoghlu was captured. He had been writing to Sultan [Sanjar], promising to deliver his nephew to him. Blamed for his failure to do so, he pleaded that it was

5 See under 'Miscellaneous events' for this year.

impossible but Sanjar put him to death. He was a wicked man who oppressed the people of Hamadhan beyond measure. God expedited his punishment!

When Sanjar's victorious triumph was complete, he sent after his men who had fled to bring them back. The news came to Baghdad within ten days. Emir Dubays ibn Ṣadaqa sent to al-Mustarshid bi-Allāh suggesting that the khutbah be made for Sultan Sanjar. This was done on 26 Jumādā I [4 September 1119] and the khutbah for Sultan Maḥmūd was dropped.

As for Sultan Maḥmūd, he left the scene of his defeat for Isfahan, accompanied by his vizier Abū Ṭālib al-Sumayramī, Emir 'Alī ibn 'Umar and Qarāja. Sanjar, on the other hand, proceeded to Hamadhan. He saw how small his army was and how troops rallied to his nephew, so he made overtures for peace. His mother was advising him to do that, **[553]** saying, 'You have already gained control of Ghazna and its districts and Transoxania. You have gained boundless territory and you have confirmed it all in the hands of its rulers. Treat your brother's son like one of them.'

Sanjar's mother was Sultan Maḥmūd's grandmother. He accepted what she said. Later the troops with Sanjar grew in number. Among them was al-Bursuqī, who had been with Prince Mas'ūd in Azerbayjan from the time when he left Baghdad up to this present moment. Sanjar grew powerful because of them. His envoy returned and, speaking for the emirs who were with Sultan Maḥmūd, informed him that they would not make peace with him until he returned to Khurasan. This he did not accept. He moved from Hamadhan to Karaj and sent another embassy to Maḥmūd to discuss peace, promising that he would make him his heir apparent. Maḥmūd agreed to this and the matter was settled between them with the making of mutual oaths.

During Sha'bān [7 November–5 December 1119] Sultan Maḥmūd went to his uncle Sanjar and lodged with his grandmother, Sanjar's mother. His uncle went to great lengths to receive him with honour and Maḥmūd brought him a magnificent present, which he accepted publicly but gave back in private. All that he accepted was five Arab horses. Sultan Sanjar wrote to all the lands in his possession, such as Khurasan, Ghazna, Transoxania and other dominions, that Sultan Maḥmūd should be mentioned in the khutbah after his own name. He wrote in similar fashion to Baghdad. He restored to Maḥmūd all the lands he had taken, apart from Rayy. By keeping it he intended to have a base in these areas so that Sultan Maḥmūd would not be tempted to rebel.

Account of Īlghāzī's raid on Frankish territory

This year the Franks marched from their lands into the districts of Aleppo. They took Buzā'a and elsewhere and they laid waste to the area around Aleppo and besieged the city. Aleppo did not have sufficient supplies for a single month and the inhabitants were greatly afraid of the Franks. Had they been allowed to fight, not one man would have remained in the city, [**554**] but they were prevented from taking that action. The Franks came to terms with the Aleppans on the basis of sharing the produce of their estates at the gates of Aleppo. The citizens sent to Baghdad appealing for assistance and pleading for aid but none was forthcoming.

Emir Īlghāzī, the lord of Aleppo, was in Mārdīn gathering troops and volunteers for the Holy War. About 20,000 men came to join him. With him were Usāma ibn al-Mubārak ibn Shibl al-Kilābī and Emir Ṭughān Arslān[6] ibn Ilmakar, lord of Bitlis and Arzan. He set out with them to Syria, purposing to fight the Franks.

The Franks, who were 3,000 horse and 9,000 infantry, when they realised the strength of his purpose to confront them, went and camped near al-Athārib, at a place called Tell 'Ifrīn amongst mountains to which there was access by only three routes. This is the place where Sharaf al-Dawla Muslim ibn Quraysh was killed.[7]

The Franks believed that no one would move against them because of the difficult access and they settled down to play a waiting game, as was their practice, when they saw that the Muslims were strong. They contacted Īlghāzī, saying, 'Do not fatigue yourself by marching towards us. We will come to you.' He informed his followers of what they had said and consulted them about what he should do. They advised mounting up immediately and attacking them. This is what he did. He set out towards them and his men entered by the three routes. The Franks were convinced that no one could get to them because the access was so difficult. However, before they were aware of it, the Muslim advance guard was upon them. The Franks gave a redoutable charge and the Muslims turned their backs in flight. They met the rest of the army coming on in waves, so rallied with them. An intense battle ensued. The Franks were surrounded on all sides and the sword fell upon them from all directions. Only a small group escaped. [**555**] All [the others] were slain or captured.

Among the prisoners taken were ninety and more of their leading knights. They were taken to Aleppo and they offered for their persons 300,000 dinars but this was not accepted. The Muslims also seized vast amounts of booty from them.

As for Roger, lord of Antioch, he was killed and his head taken. This battle took place in the middle of Rabī' I [=28 June 1119].[8] Among the verses concerning this battle and in praise of Īlghāzī are the lines of al-'Aẓīmī:

Say what you will. Your words are the welcome ones.
After the Creator our reliance is upon you.
The Koran rejoiced when you brought it victory.

---

6 A vassal of the Artuqids whose death is recorded under the year 532/1137-8. He is called Shams al-Dawla al-Aḥdab (Crook-back) by al-Fāriqī (Hillenbrand, *Muslim Principality*, 39, quoted in Ibn al-Qal., 205, note 1) and 'son of Ḥusām al-Dīn' in Ibn al-Qal., 209.

7 In 478/1085 (see Richards, *Annals*, 218-20).

8 This battle, in which Roger of Salerno was killed, is known as *Ager Sanguinis* (the Field of Blood). For events around this battle, see Asbridge, *Principality of Antioch*, 74-81.

The Gospel wept for the loss of its followers.

Later the survivors of the battle joined with others and they too were met by Īlghāzī and defeated. He took from them the fortress of al-Athārib and Zardanā, then returned to Aleppo, put its affairs on a sound and proper footing and crossed over the Euphrates to go to Mārdīn.

Account of another battle with the Franks

This year Joscelin, the lord of Tell Bāshir, set out from Tiberias with a band of Franks, about 200 knights, and surprised a group of the Ṭayy, known as the Banū Khālid. [**556**] He seized them and their possessions and questioned them about the rest of their people, the Banū Rabī'a. They told him that they were beyond the stony desert, in the Wadi al-Salāla between Damascus and Tiberias. Joscelin sent off 150 knights and himself rode with 50 by a different route. He gave the others a morning rendezvous to ambush the Banū Rabī'a. News of this reached them, however, and they wished to break camp but their emir of the Banū Rabī'a prevented them. They were 150 horsemen strong. The 150 Frankish knights came to them, in the belief that Joscelin had already arrived before them or that he would soon be catching them up, but he had lost his way. The numbers were therefore equal. Battle was joined. The Bedouin speared the Franks' horses and reduced most of them to fighting on foot. Their emir showed courage, good tactics and excellent sense. Seventy of the Franks were killed and twelve of their commanders were taken prisoner, each one of whom offered considerable sums of money and a number of captives to ransom himself.

As for Joscelin, who had lost his way, he heard the news of the battle and travelled to Tripoli, where he gathered a force and made a night march to Ascalon. He raided the surrounding country but the Muslims there drove him off and he withdrew, in a beaten state.

The killing of Mankūbars

This year Emir Mankūbars, who was prefect of Baghdad, was killed. His circumstance have already been mentioned. The reason for his death was that, when he, along with Sultan Maḥmūd, suffered defeat and returned towards Baghdad, he plundered several places on the Khurasan road and wished to enter Baghdad. Dubays ibn Ṣadaqa sent men who prevented this. He went back, after peace had been established between the two sultans, Sanjar and Maḥmūd, [**557**] and sought out Sanjar. He entered into his presence, bearing a sword and a winding sheet. Sanjar said to him, 'I am not blaming anyone,' and handed him over to Sultan Maḥmūd, saying, 'This is your mamluke. Do with him what you will.' Maḥmūd arrested him.

He harboured a serious grudge against Mankūbars for various reasons, including that, when Sultan Muḥammad died, he took his concubine, the mother of Prince Mas'ūd, by force before the expiration of her waiting period.[9] Another reason was his high-handed behaviour and the way he dominated affairs to the exclusion of Maḥmūd and his going to take up the prefecture of Baghdad, despite the disapproval of the sultan, although he could do nothing to stop him. There were also his tyrannical actions in Iraq and other matters. Therefore he killed him in cold blood and so relieved the people and the land of his wickedness.

Account of the killing of Emir 'Alī ibn 'Umar

During this year Emir 'Alī ibn 'Umar, Sultan Muḥammad's chamberlain, was killed. He had become the senior emir of Sultan Maḥmūd and the troops were obedient to him. The other emirs were envious of him and poisoned his relationship with Sultan Maḥmūd, encouraging the latter to put him to death. Learning of this, 'Alī fled to the fortress of Barjīn, which is between Barūjird and Karaj, where he had his family and his wealth. From there he set out with 200 horse to Khūzistān, which was in the hands of Āqbūrī ibn Bursuq and his two nephews, Urughlī ibn Ilbakī and Hindū ibn Zankī. He sent to them and received from them guarantees for his security and protection.

However, when he set out, they sent an army which prevented his coming to them. They met him at six leagues from Tustar and fought a battle. He and his men were defeated. His horse refused to move, so he transferred to another but its tail was entangled in his original saddle. He freed it but it became attached again, which delayed him. His enemies caught him and made him prisoner. They wrote to Sultan Maḥmūd for instructions and he ordered them to put him to death. This was done and his head taken to the sultan.

[558] Account of the discord between the Almoravids and the population of Cordoba

During this year, although the year 514 [1120–21] is also mentioned, there was discord between the troops of the Emir of the Muslims 'Alī ibn Yūsuf and the population of Cordoba. This came about because the Emir of the Muslims appointed as governor there Abū Bakr Yaḥyā ibn Rawwād. When it was the Day of the Sacrifices [13 March 1120] and the people came out to view the festivities, one of the slaves of Abū Bakr laid his hands on a woman and seized her. She called on her fellow Muslims for help and they came to her aid. Serious disturbances

[9] In Arabic the *'idda*, the waiting period which must elapse before a woman, whether widowed or divorced, whether free or not, can marry again.

occurred between the slaves and the townsfolk which lasted all that day with open warfare breaking out between them. Night intervened and they dispersed. News of this came to Emir Abū Bakr. The lawyers and notables gathered in his presence and said, 'The politic course is for you to kill one of the slaves who instigated this discord,' but he refused that and was angry. On the morrow he brought out weapons and equipment intending to fight the townsfolk. The lawyers, notables and the young men of the population mounted up, gave battle and put him to flight. He barricaded himself in the palace but they besieged it and scaled the walls. After some hardship and exhaustion he fled from them. They plundered the palace, burnt all the residences of the Almoravids and plundered their wealth. They expelled them from the town in a very wretched state.

The news reached the Emir of the Muslims who expressed his disapproval and outrage. He gathered his troops from the Ṣanhāja, Zenāta and the Berbers among others. A large host answered his call. He crossed the straits in the year 515 [1121–22] and put the town of Cordoba under siege. The population fought him like men who desire to protect their blood, womenfolk and property. When the Emir of the Muslims saw how fiercely they fought, envoys got to work between them and tried to make peace. The Emir agreed to this on condition that the population of Cordoba should pay a fine to compensate the Almoravids for their plundered property. An agreement was reached on this basis and he withdrew from the assault.

[559] **Account of 'Alī ibn Sukmān's taking of Basra**

'Alī ibn Sukmān took control of Basra during this year. This came about because Sultan Muḥammad had assigned Basra as a fief to Emir Āqsunqur al-Bukhārī, who appointed a deputy there called Sunqur al-Bayātī. His rule was so good that, when water at Basra became salinated, he organised boats and a large barge for the poor and for travellers to bring them sweet water. When Sultan Muḥammad died, this Emir Sunqur decided to arrest an emir whose name was Ghuzoghlu, the leader of the Ismā'īlī Turks, who was well-known and had led people on pilgrimage via Basra for several years, and also another emir named Sunqur Alp, the leader of the Buldaqī Turks. They both united against him, arrested and chained him. They took the citadel and his possessions that they found there.

Sunqur Alp wished to put him to death but Ghuzoghlu told him not to. However, he did not accept this and after he had killed him, Ghuzoghlu attacked Sunqur Alp and slew him. He then made a proclamation to the people calling for calm and all settled down.

The Emir of the Pilgrimage from Basra this year was an emir named 'Alī ibn Sukmān, one of the Buldaqī Turks. In Ghuzoghlu's heart there was ill-will towards him since he led the pilgrimage and because he feared that he would seek revenge for Sunqur Alp, as he had been leader of the Buldaqī Turks. Ghuzoghlu sent to the

Bedouin in the desert ordering them to attack and rob the pilgrims. Encouraged by this, they attacked and fought the pilgrims. Ibn Sukmān defended them with gallant action. He began to fight them while on the way to Basra until he was still two days' journey distant. Ghuzoghlu sent men against him to stop him from reaching Basra, so he made for al-'Awnī[10] below the Euphrates, this while the Bedouin were attacking him. After he had reached al-'Awnī, he made an all-out charge against the Bedouin and put them to flight.

Ghuzoghlu marched towards 'Alī ibn Sukmān with a numerous force, while 'Alī had few men. [**560**] Hostilities began and both sides entered the fray. An arrow hit Ghuzoghlī's horse. He fell and was killed. 'Alī came to Basra and, having entered, seized the citadel and confirmed the officials and deputies of Āqsunqur al-Bukharī, to whom he wrote offering his allegiance. Āqsunqur was with the sultan and he asked him whether he could be his deputy in Basra. When Āqsunqur did not agree to this, he drove out Āqsunqur's representatives and took control of the town and acted like a ruler, taking everything into his hands. His position became established and he ruled well until the year 514 [1120-21], when Sultan Maḥmūd sent an army to Basra with Emir Āqsunqur al-Bukhārī, who took it from 'Alī ibn Sukmān.

Miscellaneous events

This year Sultan Sanjar ordered the restoration of Mujāhid al-Dīn Bahrūz as prefect of Iraq. The deputy of Dubays ibn Ṣadaqa held the office and he was dismissed.

In Rabī' I [12 June–11 July 1119] Vizier Rabīb al-Dawla, the vizier of Sultan Maḥmūd, died and was succeeded by Kamāl al-Dīn al-Sumayramī. Rabīb al-Dawla's son, who was the vizier of al-Mustarshid, was dismissed. After him 'Amīd al-Dawla Abū 'Alī ibn Ṣadaqa, who had the title Jalāl al-Dīn, was appointed. This vizier is the uncle of the Vizier Jalāl al-Dīn Abū'l-Riḍā Ṣadaqa, who acted as vizier for al-Rāshid and the Atabeg Zankī, as we shall relate.

This year the tomb of Abraham, the Friend of God (*al-Khalīl*), was found and also the tombs of his sons, Isaac and Jacob, near Jerusalem.[11] Many people saw them with their bodies uncorrupted and lamps of gold and silver around them in the cave. This is what Ḥamza ibn Asad al-Tamīmī related in his history.[12] God knows best!

[**561**] In Muḥarram of this year [14 April–13 May 1119] the Chief Qāḍī Abū'l-Ḥasan 'Alī ibn Muḥammad al-Dāmghānī died. He was born in Rajab of the year

---

[10] Unidentified.

[11] i.e in the shrine at Hebron (al-Khalīl). For various accounts of this 'invention', see Riant, 'L'invention de la sépulture etc.'

[12] i.e. the history of Ibn al-Qalānisī (see Ibn Qal., 202).

449 [September 1057]. He was appointed as cadi at the Ṭāq Gate with jurisdiction from Baghdad to Mosul when he was twenty-six years old. This is something unique to him. After his death the post of Chief Cadi was taken by Akmal al-Dīn Abū'l-Qāsim 'Alī ibn Abī Ṭālib al-Ḥusayn ibn Muḥammad al-Zaynabī, who was installed on 3 Ṣafar [16 May 1119].

This year the caliph's Tāj Palace on the Tigris was demolished because of fears that it would collapse. This Tāj was built by the Commander of the Faithful al-Muktafī after the year 290 [903].

This year the pilgrimage was delayed. The people cried for help and threatened to smash the pulpit in the Palace Mosque. The caliph sent to Dubays ibn Ṣadaqa, asking him to aid the Emir Naẓar in conveying the pilgrims. He agreed to do this and they left Baghdad on 12 Dhū'l-Qa'da [14 February 1120]. They met with continuous rains as far as Kufa.

Dubays ibn Ṣadaqa sent Cadi Abū Ja'far 'Abd al-Wāḥid ibn Aḥmad al-Thaqafī, the cadi of Kufa, to Īlghāzī ibn Artuq at Mārdīn this year, to seek the hand of his daughter. Īlghāzī gave her to him in marriage and al-Thaqafī brought her back with him to al-Ḥilla, passing by Mosul.

In Jumādā I [August 1119] there died Abū'l-Wafā 'Alī ibn 'Aqīl ibn Muḥammad ibn 'Aqīl, the leading Ḥanbalī of his age at Baghdad. He was an excellent debater and a man of quick wit. In his youth he studied the school of thought of the Mu'tazila with Abū'l-Walīd. The Ḥanbalīs wished to kill him and for a number of years he sought sanctuary at the Gate of Degrees. He then announced his repentance and thus was able to appear in public. He is the author of various works, including *The Book of Disciplines*.[13]

---

[13] For the life and works of Ibn 'Aqīl, see G. Makdisi's study, *Ibn 'Aqīl*, 385-532. For *Kitāb al-Funūn*, his most important work, see *op. cit.*, 510-12.

The Year 514 [1120-1121]

Account of Prince Mas'ūd's rebellion against his brother Sultan Maḥmūd and the battle between them

In Rabī' I of this year [June 1120] there was a battle between Sultan Maḥmūd and his brother Prince Mas'ūd, the latter at that time holding Mosul and Azerbayjan. The reason for this was that Dubays ibn Ṣadaqa was corresponding with Juyūsh Beg, Mas'ūd's atabeg, urging him to seek the sultanate for Prince Mas'ūd and promising him help. His aim was that there should be dissension so that he would acquire the prestige and high status that his father had acquired through the dissension of the two sultans, Barkyāruq and Muḥammad, sons of Malikshāh, as we have related.

Qasīm al-Dawla al-Bursuqī, atabeg of Prince Mas'ūd, had given up the prefecture of Baghdad, and Mas'ūd had assigned him Marāgha, in addition to al-Raḥba. There was an entrenched enmity between him and Dubays. The latter wrote to Juyūsh Beg, advising him to arrest al-Bursuqī and accusing him of favouring Sultan Maḥmūd. He offered him a lot of money to effect his arrest. Al-Bursuqī learnt of this and abandoned them to go to Sultan Maḥmūd, who received him with honour, gave him a high position and increased his leading role.

Master Abū Ismā'īl al-Ḥusayn ibn 'Alī al-Iṣbahānī al-Ṭughrā'ī joined [the service of] Prince Mas'ūd. [**563**] His son, Abū'l-Mu'ayyad Muḥammad ibn Abī Ismā'īl, used to write the *ṭughrā'*[1] with the prince, but when his father arrived Mas'ūd appointed him as his vizier, after he had dismissed Abū 'Alī ibn 'Ammār, the [former] lord of Tripoli, in the year 513 [1119-20] at the gates of Khoy. Abū Isma'īl approved of the tenor of Dubays' correspondence, namely opposition to Sultan Maḥmūd and abandonment of allegiance to him.

Their position in this respect became public and news of it reached Sultan Maḥmūd, who wrote threatening them if they broke with him and promising them generous treatment if they remained loyal and in accord. They did not listen to his words but manifested the plans they were concealing. They proclaimed Prince Mas'ūd sultan in the khutbah and played the five daily musical salutes for him. This was at a time when the troops of Sultan Mahmūd were dispersed, which further encouraged them. They made forced marches to confront him when his forces were not a full strength. He assembled 15,000 men and also moved against them. They met near the Pass of Asadābādh in the middle of Rabī' I [14 June 1120] and they fought from early morning to the end of daylight.

---

[1] The *ṭughrā* was originally a tribal mark and later the elaborately written names and titles of a ruler, which served as authentication of official documents.

Al-Bursuqī was in Sultan Maḥmūd's vanguard and did heroic deeds that day. Prince Mas'ūd's army was defeated at the end of the day and a large number of their notables and commanders were taken prisoner. Mas'ūd's vizier, Master Abū Ismā'īl, was made captive and the sultan ordered him to be killed, saying, 'I am quite convinced of the wickedness of his religion and creed.' His period as vizier had lasted a year and a month, and he was more than sixty years old. He was excellent in the art of secretaryship and poetry, with an inclination to the craft of alchemy, concerning which he was the author of works which caused the waste of untold amounts of people's money.

As for Prince Mas'ūd, when his men were defeated and scattered, he made for a hill twelve leagues from the battle and hid there with some young mamlukes. He sent his equerry 'Uthmān to his brother to seek a safe-conduct. He duly went to Sultan Maḥmūd and informed him of the state of his brother Mas'ūd. [**564**] He had pity on him and bestowed a safe-conduct, ordering Āqsunqur al-Bursuqī to go to him, calm his fears, tell him he was forgiven and bring him back. After he had sent his request for safe-conduct, Mas'ūd had been joined by a certain emir who persuaded him that it was a good idea to make for Mosul, which was held by him along with Azerbayjan, and advised him to write to Dubays ibn Ṣadaqa with the aim of joining him, increasing his following and renewing the quest for the sultanate. He left his current position accompanied by this emir.

When al-Bursuqī arrived, he did not find Mas'ūd. Told of his departure, he set off on his tracks, determined to pursue him, even to Mosul. He pressed on and overtook him thirty leagues from where he started. Having told him that his brother had forgiven him and having guaranteed whatever he wished for, he sent him back to the army. Sultan Maḥmūd ordered the troops to welcome him with respect, which they did, and he ordered him to be lodged with his mother. He held a council and summoned his brother. They embraced and wept. Maḥmūd was sympathetic towards him and fulfilled all he had offered him. He associated him with himself in all his doings. This was reckoned to be generous behaviour on the part of Maḥmūd. The khutbah had been made for Mas'ūd as sultan in Azerbayjan, Mosul and the Jazira for twenty-eight days.

As for Atabeg Juyūsh Beg, he went to the Pass of Asadābādh and waited for Prince Mas'ūd. When he did not appear, he waited for him in another place but again he did not come. Despairing of him, he went to Mosul and camped outside. He gathered crops from the hinterland into the city and his troops joined him. When he heard how the sultan had treated his brother and that the latter was with the sultan, he realised that in these circumstances his position was untenable. He left as though his aim was to go hunting. He came to the Zāb and said to the men with him, 'I have decided to go to Sultan Maḥmūd and to put my life at risk.' He set out and came to him at Hamadhan. When he came into his presence, the sultan calmed his fears, gave him guarantees and treated him with liberality.

As for Dubays, who was in Iraq, when he heard of the defeat of Prince Mas'ūd,

[**565**] he plundered and laid waste to the land and perpetrated wicked deeds there, until the envoy of Sultan Maḥmūd came to him and [tried to] win him over but he paid no attention.

Account of Dubays' situation and his subsequent course of action

When he had carried out in Baghdad and its hinterland unparalleled deeds of plundering, killing and wickedness, the Caliph al-Mustarshid bi-Allāh sent a mission to him, deploring his actions and ordering him to desist, but he did not. The sultan sent to him, offering conciliation, and ordered him to stop the wicked actions of his men but he refused. He went in person to Baghdad and pitched his pavilions opposite the Caliphal Palace. He revealed the hatred that was hidden in his heart for the way his father's head had been paraded in public. He threatened the caliph, saying, 'You have sent to summon the sultan. Unless you make him turn back, I shall deal harshly with you.' A response to this was delivered, namely, 'It is impossible for the sultan to turn back, as he has set out from Hamadhan, but we shall repair your relations with him.' The envoy was the Chief Shaykh Ismā'īl. Dubays ceased [his threats] on the understanding that emissaries should be despatched to make an agreement between himself and the sultan. He withdrew from Baghdad in Rajab [26 September–25 October 1120].

In Rajab the sultan arrived at Baghdad and Dubays sent him his wife, the daughter of 'Amīd al-Dawla ibn Jahīr, with a large sum of money and a precious gift. He asked for pardon, which was granted him, but on terms that he could not accept. He remained recalcitrant and plundered some horses and cattle belonging to the sultan. The sultan left Baghdad in Shawwāl [24 December 1120–21 January 1121] to attack Dubays in al-Ḥilla, taking with him 1,000 boats to cross the river. Learning that the sultan had set out, Dubays sent to request a guarantee of security which was granted. His aim was to deceive the sultan so that he could make his own preparations. He sent his womenfolk to the Marshlands and, taking his treasury, he left al-Ḥilla, after plundering the place, to seek refuge with Īlghāzī. The sultan came to al-Ḥilla and found nobody there. He spent one night there and then returned.

[**566**] Dubays remained with Īlghāzī and accompanied him on his travels. Later he sent his brother Manṣūr with an army from Qal'at Ja'bar to Iraq. Manṣūr inspected al-Ḥilla and Kufa and went down to Basra. He sent to Yarunqush al-Zakawī, asking him to repair his relations with the sultan, but this was without success. He made contact with his brother Dubays to inform him of this and to call him to Iraq. In the year 515 [1121–22] Dubays left Qal'at Ja'bar to go to al-Ḥilla, which he entered and took control of. He then sent to the caliph and the sultan with excuses for his actions and promising his personal allegiance, but there was no response to this.

Troops were then sent against him and when they had drawn near, he abandoned al-Ḥilla and entered al-Azbar, which is the canal of Sindād.[2] The troops came to al-Ḥilla, which was deserted as the inhabitants had been expelled. There were no means of support there. Provisions were brought in from Baghdad. The commander of the force was Sa'd al-Dawla Yarunqush al-Zakawī, who left 500 cavalry in al-Ḥilla and another detachment in Kufa to hold the roads against Dubays. He instructed the troops of Wāsiṭ that they should watch the route to the Marsh. This they did and the sultan's army crossed the river to move against Dubays. Between the two sides there remained a canal which was fordable in places. Yarunqush and Dubays opened talks and they agreed that Dubays should send his brother Manṣūr as a hostage and pursue a course of obedience. This he did and the army retired to Baghdad in the year 516 [1122-23].

[567] The Georgian incursion into the lands of Islam and the conquest of Tiflis

During this year the Georgians, otherwise the Jurz,[3] invaded the lands of Islam. They used to carry out raids in the past but they stopped them in the reign of Sultan Malikshāh and until the end of the reign of Sultan Muḥammad. However, when this year came, they invaded, accompanied by the Qipjaqs[4] and other neighbouring peoples. The emirs, who were neighbours of the Georgian lands, gathered together after an exchange of correspondence, namely, Emir Īlghāzī, Dubays ibn Ṣadaqa, who was with the former at the time, Prince Ṭughril ibn Muḥammad and his atabeg, Kuntughdī. Ṭughril held the area of Arrān and Nakhchevan as far as the Araxes. They gathered together and marched against the Georgians. When they approached Tiflis - and the Muslims were in a large force that reached 30,000 - they met and both sides drew up their lines for battle. Two hundred men of the Qipjaqs came forward. The Muslims thought that they were seeking terms and took no precautions against them. They mingled with the Muslims, shot their arrows and caused confusion in the Muslim line. Those at some distance thought that it was a defeat and fled. Our men followed one another in a rout and because of the tight press of men trampled on one another. A great many of them were killed.

---

2 The reading 'al-Azbar' is dubious. The Mss. do not give a clear consonantal outline. Sindād is 'a canal between al-Ḥīra and Ubulla' (Yāqūt, iii, 164).

3 'Khazars', the reading of *Kāmil*, is clearly an error; they were Turkish and converts to Judaism. The suggested variant, al-Jurz, is an alternative for the normal al-Kurj (Georgians).

4 The Qipjaqs were a confederation of Turkish tribes who spread westwards along the steppes to the north of Islamic lands. They were known to the Russians as the Polovsty and to Europeans as the Cumans. In the thirteenth and early fourteenth centuries they provided much of the manpower of the Mamluk state. See *EI(2)*, v, 125-6 and 373, s.v. Ḳipčak and Ḳumān.

The infidels pursued them for ten leagues, killing and taking prisoners. Most were killed but 4,000 men were made captive. Prince Ṭughril, Īlghāzī and Dubays escaped. The Georgians returned, plundered the lands of Islam and put Tiflis under siege. They engaged the garrison strongly. The situation was serious and the inhabitants faced a crisis. The siege continued until the year 515 [1121–22], when the Georgians took the city by assault.

When they were face to face with disaster, the inhabitants sent the local cadi and preacher to the Georgians to **[568]** ask for surrender terms. The Georgians did not listen to them but treated them harshly. They made a forced entry into the city, which they gave over to rapine and plunder. In the year 516 [1122–23] refugees came to Baghdad, crying for help and seeking assistance. They heard that Sultan Maḥmūd was in Hamadhan, so they made their way to him and pleaded with him for aid. He went to Azerbayjan, where he remained in the city of Tabriz for the month of Ramaḍān [November 1122]. He sent an army against the Georgians and the account of what it did will be given, if God Almighty wills.

Account of the expeditions of Īlghāzī this year

This year al-Mustarshid bi-Allāh sent Sadīd al-Dawla ibn al-Anbārī with robes of honour for Najm al-Dīn Īlghāzī, thanked him for the attacks on the Franks that he was carrying out and ordered him to banish Dubays from his side. Abū ʻAlī ibn ʻAmmār, who had been lord of Tripoli, journeyed with Ibn al-Anbārī to Īlghāzī to remain with him, living his days on what Īlghāzī bestowed on him. Īlghāzī apologised for not dismissing Dubays but promised to do so. Then he marched against the Franks, having assembled a large force to confront them. They met at a place called Dānīth[5] in the region of Aleppo. Battle was joined and the fighting was intense. Victory went to Īlghāzī.[6]

Then Īlghāzī and Atabeg Ṭughtakīn, lord of Damascus, joined forces and besieged the Franks in Ma'arrat al-Nu'mān for a day and a night. Atabeg Ṭughtakīn suggested the siege be lifted so that their fear would not incite them to death-defying resistance in a sortie against the Muslims, when perhaps they might be victorious. **[569]** His fear arose mostly on account of the shortcoming of the Turkoman cavalry and the excellence of the Frankish cavalry. Īlghāzī therefore raised the siege, so the Franks moved from their position and escaped. Īlghāzī could not remain long in Frankish territory because it was through their desire for booty that he had brought the Turkomans together. Each one of them would arrive with a bag of wheat and a sheep and would count the hours until he could take

---

[5] The edition's reading, Dhāt al-Baql (the place of vegetables), should be replaced by the reading of the Bodleian Ms., Dānīth al-Baql. Cf. Ibn Qal., 200–201: 'a place called Sharmadā [Sarmadā] or Dānīth al-Baql.'

[6] This is a duplicate reference to *Ager Sanguinis* (see under the previous year, 513/1119).

some quick booty and then go home. If their stay was extended, they would disperse. Īlghāzī did not have money that he could distribute to them.

Account of the beginning of the career of Muḥammad ibn Tūmart and 'Abd al-Mu'min and their coming to power

In this year the career of the Mahdi Abū 'Abd Allah Muḥammad ibn 'Abd Allāh ibn Tūmart al-'Alawī al-Ḥasanī began. His tribe, part of the Maṣmūda, was known as the Hargha in the Sūs Mountains of the Maghrib. They settled there when the Muslims with Mūsā ibn Nuṣayr conquered it. Under this year we shall give an account of the Mahdi and of 'Abd al-Mu'min up to the completion of the conquest of the Maghrib to give a continuous narrative.[7]

In his youth Ibn Tūmart travelled to the lands of the East in search of learning. He was a lawyer, a man of culture, well versed in the Sharia and a student of Ḥadīth. He was knowledgeable in the fundamentals of religion and canon law and had a solid learning in the Arabic language. He was pious and an ascetic. On his journeys he came to Iraq and met with al-Ghazālī and al-Kiyā. In Alexandria he associated with Abū Bakr al-Ṭarṭūshī. It is reported that he had a conversation with al-Ghazālī concerning the power that he had achieved in the Maghrib. Al-Ghazālī said to him, 'This is not feasible in these lands. It is impossible for that to happen for the likes of us.' A certain historian of the Maghrib gave this account, but the truth is that he never met him.

He went on pilgrimage from there [**570**] and returned to the Maghrib. When he took ship from Alexandria to go west, he changed the wicked conduct on board and obliged the crew to observe the prayer times and to recite the Koran, until eventually he arrived in the year 505 [1111-12] at Mahdiyya, where the ruler at that time was Yaḥyā ibn Tamīm. He settled in a mosque to the south of the Saturday Mosque. He possessed nothing but a coffee pot and a staff. The townsfolk heard reports of him and sought him out to study various branches of learning under him. Whenever he was aware of something reprehensible, he reformed or abolished it. After many examples of this the Emir Yaḥyā summoned him along with a group of ulema and, when he saw his character and heard his words, he paid him honour and respect and asked him for his prayers.

He left the city and resided at Monastir with a group of pious men for a while. He then went to Bougie, where he acted as before. He was expelled from there to a village nearby, called Mallāla. There he met 'Abd al-Mu'min ibn 'Alī. In him he saw such nobility and enterprise as he interpreted to indicate leadership and an ability to succeed. He asked him his name and his tribe and was told that he was from Qays 'Aylān, and then from the Banū Sulaym. Ibn Tūmart said to him, 'This

---

7 Cf. the 'excursus into Maghribī History' in Hillenbrand, *Muslim Principality*, 89ff., and Ibn Qal., 291-3.

is what the Prophet (God bless him and give him peace) foretold, when he said, "God will give victory to this religion at the end of time through a man from Qays." He was asked, "From which branch of Qays?" and he replied, "From the Banū Sulaym." He was delighted with 'Abd al-Mu'min and rejoiced at meeting him. 'Abd al-Mu'min was born in the city of Tājara[8] in the district of Tlemcen. He was from the 'Ā'idh, a branch of Kūmara, who settled in this region in the year 180 [796–7].

The Mahdi continued zealously to order what is good and forbid what is evil on his travels until he arrived at Marrakech, the capital of the Emir of the Muslims, Yūsuf ibn 'Alī ibn Tāshfīn. There he witnessed more reprehensible behaviour than he had observed on his travels. He increased his ordering of the good and forbidding of evil, so his following became extensive and the people held a high opinion of him. One day on his travels he saw the sister of the Emir of the Muslims in her ceremonial procession, accompanied by her maid-servants, [**571**] beautiful, numerous and unveiled. This was the custom of the Veiled Ones,[9] whose women uncovered their faces while the men veiled theirs. When he saw the women like this he expressed his disapproval, ordered them to cover their faces, and he and his followers struck out at their mounts. The sister of the Emir of the Muslims fell from her horse, which incident was reported to the Emir of the Muslims, 'Alī ibn Yūsuf who summoned him and summoned the lawyers to debate with him. The Mahdi began to preach and put the fear of God into the Emir who was reduced to tears. He ordered the lawyers to dispute with him but there was amongst them no one who could stand against him because of the power of his arguments in support of what he had done.

In the service of the Emir of the Muslims was a certain vizier called Mālik ibn Wuhayb. He said, 'O Emir of the Muslims, this man, by God, does not wish to order what is good and forbid what is evil. His only aim is to foment discord and to seize control of some region. Execute him and place the responsibility for his blood on me.' When the Emir refused, he said, 'If you will not kill him, then imprison him and shut him away, for otherwise he will provoke trouble which cannot be mended.' He then ordered his imprisonment but one of the leaders of the Veiled Ones, called Bayān ibn 'Uthmān, prevented this, so the Emir ordered his expulsion from Marrakech. He went to Aghmāt and stayed in the mountain,[10] where he travelled until he came in the year 514 [1120–21] to Sūs, where the Hargha tribe was and other members of the Maṣmūda, who came to him and flocked to join him.

---

8 Yāqūt, i, 810: 'a small town in the Maghrib in the district of Hunayn ... in the coastal regions of Tlemcen province.'

9 In Arabic *al-Mulaththamūn*. A designation of the Almoravids (see *EI(2)*, vii, 583–91, s.v. *Murābiṭūn*). The tribesmen of the West and Central Saharan regions wore a face-muffler (*lithām*).

10 i.e. the High Atlas range.

The inhabitants of these regions exchanged reports about him and came to pay him visits. Their notables attended on him and he began to preach to them, reminding them of 'the days of God', and expound to them the ordinances of Islam, what had been corrupted and what new tyranny and wickedness had been introduced and also that obedience to any of these regimes was not binding because they followed what was false but rather it was obligatory to fight them and stop them doing what they were doing. He continued thus for about a year and the Hargha, his tribe, followed him. He called his followers the Almohads[11] and taught them that the Prophet (God bless him and give him peace) had promised a Mahdi who would fill the earth with justice and that the place where he would appear was the Furthest Maghrib. Ten men arose to support him, one of whom was 'Abd al-Mu'min. They said, 'All this applies only to you. You are the Mahdi,' and they swore allegiance to him on this basis.

[572] Reports about him reached the Emir of the Muslims, who prepared a force of his followers and sent them against the Mahdi. When they drew near the mountain where he was, the Mahdi said to his men, 'These people seek me but I fear what they may do to you. The best course is for me to leave these lands so that you may remain secure.' Ibn Tūfiyān, one of the shaykhs of the Hargha, said to him, 'Are you fearful of anything from the heavens?' 'No,' was the reply, 'rather from the heavens will your victory come.' So Ibn Tūfiyān said, 'Then let the whole world come against us.' All the tribe agreed with him, so the Mahdi said, 'Rest assured that with this little band will come victory and triumph. After a little while you will extirpate their regime and inherit their land.' They therefore descended from the mountain. So strong was their belief that the Mahdi spoke the truth that they were victorious as he had told them.

Tribes came to him in droves from the settlements around, both to east and west, and pledged him their loyalty. The tribe of Hintāta, one of the strongest of the tribes, offered him their allegiance. He welcomed them and placed much reliance on them. Envoys of the people of Tīnmāl[12] came to him to tell of their submission and to request him to come to them. He set out for the mountain of Tīnmāl and settled there. He composed a book on the oneness of God for them and also a treatise on the creed. He laid down for them how they should behave one to another, that they should limit themselves to short, inexpensive clothing, and urged them to fight their enemies and to expel any evil men from their midst.

He dwelt in Tīnmāl and built himself a mosque outside the city. There he would perform the daily prayers, he and a group of those around him. After the last prayer of the day he would enter the city. When he saw how numerous were the inhabitants of the mountain and how strong the city, he feared they would turn against him, so he ordered them to present themselves without weapons. They did

[11] In Arabic *al-Muwaḥḥidūn*, meaning 'the Unitarians'.

[12] The edition reads Tīn Mallal. Tīnmāl is in the valley of Nafis in the High Atlas (see Hopkins, *Medieval Muslim Government*, 88–9, and Abun-Nasr, *Maghrib*, 105).

this for several days, then he ordered his followers to kill them. They attacked [**573**] them, taking them by surprise, and killed them in that mosque. He then entered the city, where he carried out a massacre, enslaved the women and plundered property. The number of the slain was 15,000. He divided their houses and land amongst his followers and built a wall around the city and a citadel on the summit of a high hill.

In the Tīnmāl mountain there are running rivers, trees and fields of crops. Access is difficult. There is no mountain more impregnable. It is said that, when he feared the inhabitants of Tīnmāl, he looked about him and saw that many of their offspring were fair-haired and blue-eyed, while brown colouring was dominant for their fathers. The Emir of the Muslims had a large number of Frankish and [other] Christian[13] mamlukes, whose colouring was predominantly fair. Once every year they used to go up into the mountain to take the money assigned them by the sultan. They would reside in the houses of the inhabitants, expelling their owners from them. When the Mahdi saw their offspring, he questioned them, 'Why is it that I see you brown in colouring, and I see your children to be fair and blue-eyed?' They told him their story in connection with the mamlukes of the Emir of the Muslims. He censured their toleration of that and expressed his scorn for them and his horror at their situation. They replied, 'What is to be done to get rid of them? We do not have the power to deal with them.' He said, 'When they come to you at the customary time and disperse to their lodgings, let each one of you rise up against his lodger and kill him. Then guard your mountain, for it is very defensible and not easily taken.' They waited patiently until those mamlukes arrived, then they killed them as the Mahdi had prescribed. Having done this, they feared what the Emir might do to them, so they fortified themselves in the mountain and closed off any passable route. This strengthened the Mahdi's spirit.

Later the Emir of the Muslims sent a powerful force against them, which besieged them in the mountain, imposing a tight blockade and preventing the passage of provisions. Food became scarce for the Mahdi's followers, [**574**] until bread was unobtainable. Each day just enough broth was cooked. To feed themselves, each person dipped his hand in the broth and then withdrew it. For that day he had to make do with whatever stuck to it. The notables of the Tīnmāl population met together and desired to repair their relations with the Emir of the Muslims. News of this came to the Mahdi Ibn Tūmart. There was with him a man called Abū 'Abd Allāh al-Wansharīshī, who appeared to be simple-minded and lacking in any knowledge of the Koran and religious studies. Spittle would drop on to his chest and it was as though he was out of his wits. Nevertheless the Mahdi showed him favour and honour and used to say, 'God has a mysterious purpose for this man which will be revealed.'

In fact al-Wansharīshī was assiduous in studying the Koran and religious

---

[13] In Arabic *al-Rūm*, an ambiguous term.

learning in secret so that nobody should know about it. When it was the year 519 [1125-6] and the Mahdi was fearful of the inhabitants of the mountain, he went out one day to pray the morning prayer and alongside the *miḥrāb*[14] he saw a man, handsomely dressed and nicely perfumed. He pretended not to know him and said, 'Who is this?' 'I am Abū 'Abd Allāh al-Wansharīshī,' was the reply. The Mahdi said to him, 'How amazing this is!' He began his prayers and when he had finished, he called the people to gather together and said, 'This man claims that he is al-Wansharīshī. Examine him and establish his identity.' When daylight had fully broken, they knew him. The Mahdi asked him, 'What has happened to you?' He replied, 'Last night an angel came to me from the heavens and washed my heart. God taught me the Koran and *al-Muwaṭṭa'*[15] and other religious knowledge and ḥadīths.' In the presence of the people the Mahdi wept and said, 'We shall test you.' 'Do so,' was the answer.

He began to recite the Koran most excellently, starting from whatever point was requested, and likewise with *al-Muwaṭṭa'* and other books of law and jurisprudence. This astonished the people and they were awestruck. He said to them, 'God Almighty has given me a light by which I may tell the people of Paradise from the people of **[575]** Hellfire. I command you to kill the people of Hellfire and not to touch the people of Paradise. God has sent down angels to the well which is in such-and-such a place who will bear witness to my truthfulness.'

The Mahdi along with the people, all in tears, went to that well. At its mouth the Mahdi prayed and said, 'O angels of God, Abū 'Abd Allāh al-Wansharīshī has asserted such-and-such.' The reply from within was 'He has spoken the truth.' The Mahdi had placed some men there to give that testimony. When that reply came from the well, the Mahdi said, 'This is a purified and hallowed place into which the angels have descended. The right course is to fill it in lest any pollution or something unacceptable fall into it.' They threw in stones and earth sufficient to fill it. Then the Mahdi summoned the people of the mountain to gather at that spot and they assembled for 'the discrimination.'[16] Al-Wansharīshī would pick out a man whose attitude was threatening and say, 'This man is one of the people of Hellfire,' and he would be cast down dead from the mountain. He would also pick out an inexperienced youth or someone not to be feared and say, 'This man is one of the people of Paradise,' and so he would be left on the right hand. The number of those slain was 70,000. When this was completed, the Mahdi felt secure for himself and his followers and his cause prospered.

This is what I have heard several learned men of the Maghrib say about 'the discrimination.' I have heard others say, 'When Ibn Tūmart saw the many wicked and corrupt people among the inhabitants of the mountain, he summoned the

---

[14] The niche marking the *qibla*, the direction of prayer.

[15] Literally *The Beaten Path*, a law book written by Mālik ibn Anas, the eponymous founder of the Mālikī school of law.

[16] In Arabic *al-tamyīz*, in effect, a purge.

shaykhs of the tribes and said to them, "You have no true religion and it will only become strong by ordering what is good and forbidding what is evil and by expelling the corrupt from your midst. Seek out all those wicked and corrupt people among you. Tell them to desist and if they do not, write down their names and report them to me that I may look into their case." They did so and wrote down for him their names in every tribe. He ordered them to do this a second and a third time. Then he gathered all the lists and took from them the names that were repeated and made a record of them. He gathered all the people together, produced the names that he had written down and handed them to al-Wansharīshī, known as the Bringer of Good News (*al-Bashīr*). He commanded him to review the tribes and put the evil-doers on the left side and the rest on the right. [**576**] He carried this out and it was ordered that those on al-Wansharīshī's left should have their hands tied, which was done. He then said, "These are wretched people who must be put to death." He ordered each tribe to kill those wretches in their ranks. They were killed to the last man. This was the day of discrimination.'

After Ibn Tūmart had completed 'the discrimination', he saw his surviving followers to be truly well-disposed with hearts united in obedience. He equipped an army of them and sent them to the mountains of Aghmāt, where was a force of the Almoravids. There was a battle and the followers of Ibn Tūmart, whose commander was Abū 'Abd Allāh al-Wansharīshī, were defeated. Many of them were killed and 'Umar al-Hintātī, one of his greatest men, was wounded. His senses were gone and his pulse had ceased. 'He is dead,' they said, but al-Wansharīshī said, 'Truly he is not dead. He will not die until he conquers the land.' After a while he opened his eyes and his strength returned to him. The people were deceived and led astray by this. They returned defeated to Ibn Tūmart who preached to them and thanked them for their steadfastness.

After this he continued to send out squadrons into the far reaches of Muslim lands. If they saw an army, they clung close to their mountain and so were safe. The Mahdi had organised his followers in grades. The first was called *Ayt 'Ashara*, meaning 'the People of Ten'. Of these the first was 'Abd al-Mu'min, followed by Abū Ḥafṣ ['Umar] al-Hintātī and then the others. These are the noblest of his followers and his close confidants, the first to follow him. The second grade was *Ayt Khamsīn*, meaning 'the People of Fifty', lower in rank but consisting of a number of the leaders of the tribes. The third was *Ayt Sab'īn*, meaning 'the People of Seventy', lower than the preceding ranks. The generality of his followers and those who entered into his allegiance were called 'Almohads' (*Muwaḥḥidūn*). If the Almohads are mentioned in their histories, the Mahdi's followers and those of 'Abd al-Mu'min after him are intended.[17]

Ibn Tūmart's position continued to grow until the year 524 [1130]. He fitted out [**577**] a mighty army, amounting to 40,000, most of whom were infantry, and put al-Wansharīshī in charge. He sent 'Abd al-Mu'min with them. They marched down

[17] For a discussion of this hierarchy, see Hopkins, *Medieval Muslim Government*, 87–91.

to Marrakech and put it under siege, pressing hard on it. The Emir of the Muslims 'Alī ibn Yūsuf was there. The siege continued for twenty days. The Emir of the Muslims sent to the governor of Sijilmāsa ordering him to come with his troops. The latter assembled a large force and set out. When he drew near the Mahdi's army, the people of Marrakech made a sortie from the opposite direction. Battle was joined and became fierce. Many of the Mahdi's followers were killed, including their commander al-Wansharīshī. They rallied around 'Abd al-Mu'min and appointed him commander.

The fighting continued most of the day. 'Abd al-Mu'min performed the prayer as in time of danger at both the noon and afternoon prayer times while the battle was in progress. It had not been performed previously in the Maghrib. When the Maṣmūda tribes saw how numerous the Almoravids were and how strong, they placed their backs up against a large orchard there. The orchard was called by them 'the Lake' (*al-Buḥayra*) and thus one speaks of 'the battle of the Lake' and 'the year of the Lake.' They were now fighting on one front until they were overtaken by nightfall. Most of the Maṣmūda had been killed. When al-Wansharīshī was killed, 'Abd al-Mu'min buried him. The Maṣmūda looked for his body but could not find it amongst the slain. They said, 'The angels have lifted him up.' When night fell, 'Abd al-Mu'min and the survivors set out for the mountain.

The death of the Mahdi and the succession of 'Abd al-Mu'min

After he had sent the army to Marrakech, the Mahdi fell seriously ill. When he heard the news of the defeat, his illness worsened. He asked about 'Abd al-Mu'min and was told that he was safe. He said, 'No one has died; **[578]** the cause still stands and he is the one who will conquer the country.' He enjoined his followers to follow 'Abd al-Mu'min, to make him their leader, to hand over authority to him and obey him. He dubbed him 'Commander of the Faithful.'

The Mahdi then died. He was fifty-one years old, although some say fifty-five. He had held power for twenty years. 'Abd al-Mu'min returned to Tīnmāl and took up residence there, conciliating hearts and behaving generously to people. He was magnanimous, bold in war and firm in times of commotion. The year 528 [1133-4] began and he made his preparations and set out with a large army. He marched along the Mountain until he came to Tādala,[18] whose inhabitants put up an armed resistance but he overcame them. He conquered that town and all the adjacent country, then marched through the mountains, conquering any place that resisted him. The Ṣanhāja of the Mountain gave him their allegiance.

The Emir of the Muslims had appointed his son as his heir apparent but he died, so the Emir summoned his [other] son Tāshfīn from Andalusia, where he was ruler. After his arrival, he made him his heir apparent in the year 530 [1135-6]. He

[18] Near Tlemcen according to Yāqūt, i, 810.

assigned an army to Tāshfīn, who began to manoeuvre in the plain, keeping opposite ‘Abd al-Mu’min in the mountains.

In the year 532 [1137–8] ‘Abd al-Mu’min was in al-Nawāẓir, which is a high mountain with a commanding view, while Tāshfīn was in the lowlands. From both sides men went forth to exchange shots and to clash with one another, but there was no [major] engagement between them. It was called ‘the year of al-Nawāẓir’.

In the year 533 [1138–9] ‘Abd al-Mu’min set out, following the mountain chain in the scrub, until he came to Mt. Karnāṭa. He camped on firm ground among trees and Tāshfīn camped opposite him in the plain in an area where there was no vegetation. It was the winter season and there was continuous rain for many days without interruption. The terrain where Tāshfīn and his men were became very [**579**] muddy and their horses sank into it up to their chests. It was impossible for a man to walk there. Their supply routes were cut off. They used their spears and the pommels of their saddles as fuel but they perished from hunger, cold and the dreadful conditions.

‘Abd al-Mu’min and his men were on hard, firm ground in the mountain, not troubled by anything as they received constant supplies. At that time ‘Abd al-Mu’min sent a force to Wajra in the district of Tlemcen, commanded by Abū ‘Abd Allāh Muḥammad ibn Raqū, one of ‘the People of Fifty’. Information about them reached Muḥammad ibn Yaḥyā ibn Fānnū, the governor of Tlemcen. He marched out with an army of ‘Veiled Ones’. They met at a place called the Ditch of Wine. ‘Abd al-Mu’min’s force defeated them, killing Muḥammad ibn Yaḥyā and many of his men. They seized their baggage as booty and returned. Then ‘Abd al-Mu’min and all his troops proceeded to Ghumāra. Tribe after tribe submitted to him and he remained amongst them for a while.

‘Abd al-Mu’min continued to campaign in the mountains, while Tāshfīn shadowed him in the lowlands. He continued in this manner until the year 535 [1140–41] when the Emir of the Muslims ‘Alī ibn Yūsuf died at Marrakech and his son Tāshfīn succeeded him. ‘Abd al-Mu’min’s territorial ambition increased, yet he still did not descend into the lowlands.

In the year 538 [1143–4] ‘Abd al-Mu’min marched to Tlemcen and besieged it, setting up his tents on the mountain overlooking it. Tāshfīn camped on the further side of the city. There was some skirmishing between them which lasted until the year 539 [1144–5]. Then ‘Abd al-Mu’min withdrew to Mt. Tājara and sent an army with ‘Umar al-Hintātī to the city of Wahrān, on which the latter made a surprise attack, and he and his troops gained an entry. [Tāshfīn][19] heard the news and made his way there. ‘Umar left the city and Tāshfīn camped outside Wahrān by the sea in the month of Ramaḍān of the year 539 [began 25 February 1145] [**580**]. The eve of the 27th of the month [23 March] came, a night that the people of the Maghrib revere. Outside Wahrān is a hill overlooking the sea and at the top is a pass where worshippers gather, a place revered by them. Tāshfīn with a small group of his men

[19] The edition supplies ‘Abd al-Mu’min as the subject of the verb, but this is surely an error.

went there secretly. Only the few persons he was with knew about it. His intention was to gain spiritual benefit from attending at that spot with that group of pious men. However, 'Umar ibn Yaḥyā al-Hintātī heard of this and immediately set out with all his troops to that place of worship, which he surrounded, taking control of the hill. When Tāshfīn feared that he might be taken, he mounted his horse and spurred it towards the sea, but he fell from a high cliff on to rocks and perished. His corpse was hoisted on a gibbet and all who were with him were killed.

It is said that Tāshfīn went to a fort there on a hill, where he had a large orchard with all kinds of fruit. It happened that 'Umar al-Hintātī, the commander of 'Abd al-Mu'min's army, sent a squadron to that fort, telling them of the weakness of the garrison. They did not know that Tāshfīn was there. They set fire to and burnt down the gate. Tāshfīn wished to flee, mounted his horse, which leapt from within the fort beyond the wall. It fell into the fire. Tāshfīn was taken and revealed his identity. They wanted to take him to 'Abd al-Mu'min but he died at that moment because his neck was broken. His corpse was exhibited and all who were with him were killed. His army dispersed and never again mustered. He was succeeded by his brother, Isḥāq ibn 'Alī ibn Yūsuf.

After the death of Tāshfīn, 'Umar sent the news to 'Abd al-Mu'min, who came from Tājara that very day with all his forces. The army of the Emir of the Muslims scattered and some of them took refuge in the city of Wahrān. After 'Abd al-Mu'min's arrival he entered by force of arms. The persons killed there were more than could be counted. He then went to Tlemcen, which is two cities, a horse's gallop apart, one being Tahert, [**581**] where the Muslim army was, and the other Agadir, built in olden times. Agadir resisted and closed its gates, and the inhabitants prepared for a fight.

Tahert is where Yaḥyā ibn al-Ṣaḥrāwiyya was. He fled with his troops to the city of Fez, but 'Abd al-Mu'min came there and entered it after the troops had again fled. The inhabitants met him with humble submission and yet he did not accept that but slew most of them. His army made their entry and he reorganised the city, then departed. He left an army to besiege Agadir and marched to Fez in the year 540 [1145–6]. He made camp on a mountain overlooking the city and besieged it for nine months. Yaḥyā ibn al-Ṣaḥrāwiyya was there with his troops that had fled from Tlemcen. When his stay became lengthy, 'Abd al-Mu'min turned to a river that entered the city and dammed it with timbers, earth and other things and stopped it entering the city. It became a lake on which boats could sail but then he demolished the dam and the water came in a rush and destroyed the city wall and all the city that was in the neighbourhood of the river. 'Abd al-Mu'min wished to enter the city but the inhabitants fought him outside the wall, so the entry he had counted on was impossible.

In Fez, acting as governor of the city and all its districts, was 'Abd Allāh ibn Khiyār al-Jayyānī. He and several notables of the city came to an agreement and wrote to 'Abd al-Mu'min to seek surrender terms for the population. They were granted and so they opened one of the city gates. The Almohad army entered and

Yaḥyā ibn al-Ṣaḥrāwiyya fled. Fez fell at the end of the year 540 [ended in June 1146] and Yaḥyā made his way to [**582**] Tangier. 'Abd al-Mu'min organised affairs in the city of Fez and gave orders for a proclamation: 'Anyone who retains weapons or military equipment may be killed with impunity.' Everyone in the city who possessed weapons brought them in and they were seized. He then returned to Meknes and made the same arrangements with the population, but the cavalrymen and other soldiers there he killed.

The troops who were besieging Tlemcen fought with the inhabitants. They erected mangonels and wooden towers and attacked with their siege engines. The commander in the city was 'Uthmān the Lawyer. The siege lasted about a year. When the situation of the inhabitants became parlous, a number of them gathered together and made contact with the Almohads, the followers of 'Abd al-Mu'min, without the knowledge of 'Uthmān the Lawyer. They let them into the city and before the defenders were aware of what was happening they were falling to the sword. Most were slain. The children and the womenfolk were taken as captives. Untold amounts of property were plundered and jewels of immeasurable value. Those who were not slain were sold at minimal prices. The numbers of the slain reached 100,000.

It is said that 'Abd al-Mu'min was the one who besieged Tlemcen and that he went from there to Fez. God knows best! 'Abd al-Mu'min despatched a squadron of cavalry to Meknes. They besieged it for a while, and then the inhabitants surrendered the town on terms, which were honoured.

From Fez 'Abd al-Mu'min proceeded to Salé and conquered it. A group of the notables of Ceuta came before him and entered into his allegiance. He agreed to give them guarantees. This was in the year 541 [1146–7].

[583] **How 'Abd al-Mu'min conquered the city of Marrakech**

After 'Abd al-Mu'min had finished with Fez and those regions, he went to Marrakech, the seat of the Veiled Ones' kingdom, one of the largest and greatest of cities. At that time its ruler was Isḥāq ibn 'Alī ibn Yūsuf ibn Tāshfīn, who was still a boy. 'Abd al-Mu'min besieged the city in the year 541 [1146–7] and pitched his tents to the west on a small hill, where he constructed a settlement for himself and his army. He built a mosque there and a high building for himself from which he could look down on the city and see the condition of the inhabitants and of those of his followers who were engaged in the fighting. The city was hard-pressed and was besieged for eleven months. The Almoravids within used to come out to fight outside the city. The hunger of the inhabitants became severe and they were unable to acquire supplies.

One day he ordered an assault and positioned an ambush, saying to them, 'When you hear the sound of the drum, come forth.' He took his seat at the top of the watch-tower he had built to observe the fighting. His troops advanced, fought and held firm. Then they gave way before the men of Marrakech to make them follow them to the prepared ambush. The Veiled Ones pursued them as far as 'Abd al-Mu'min's settlement and demolished most of its wall. The Maṣmūda called out to 'Abd al-Mu'min to order the drum to be beaten for the ambush to be sprung but he said to them, 'Wait until every would-be warrior in the city has come out.' When most had done so, he ordered the drum to be beaten and the ambushers emerged. The Maṣmūda tribesmen who were retreating turned on the Almoravids and killed them at will. It was now the turn of the Almoravids to flee. There died in the crush at the gates a multitude that only God (praised be He!) could number.

[**584**] The shaykhs of the Almoravids used to administer Isḥāq ibn 'Alī ibn Yūsuf's state. It came about that one of their number, called 'Abd Allāh ibn Abī Bakr, went to surrender to 'Abd al-Mu'min and informed him of their weak spots and defects. His eagerness to overcome them grew stronger and their tribulations intensified. Mangonels and towers were erected to attack them and their foodstuffs ran out, so they ate their horses. More than 100,000 of the common people died of starvation, and the city stank from the smell of the dead.

In Marrakech there was a force of Franks whom the Almoravids had enlisted and who had come to fight for them. After the situation had dragged on, they made contact with 'Abd al-Mu'min to seek guarantees for themselves, which were granted. They opened one of the city gates, called the Aghmāt Gate, and 'Abd al-Mu'min's troops entered, sword in hand, and took the city by force of arms, killing those they found. They came to the residence of the Emir of the Muslims and brought out the Emir Isḥāq and all the Almoravid emirs who were with him. The latter were put to death and Isḥāq, in his desire to survive, began to tremble and to bless 'Abd al-Mu'min and weep. The Emir Sīr ibn al-Ḥājj, who was alongside him with his hands tied, rose and spat in his face, saying, 'Are you crying for your father and mother? Be steadfast like a man. This fellow is a man who neither fears God nor has any religion.' The Almohads set about him with wooden clubs and beat him to death. He was a brave man, renowned for his bravery. Isḥāq was brought forward, despite his tender years, and his head cut off. This was in the year 542 [1147–8]. He was the last of the Almoravid rulers and with him their dynasty came to an end. Their period of rule lasted seventy years. Four of them held power, Yūsuf, 'Alī, Tāshfīn and Isḥāq.

After 'Abd al-Mu'min had taken Marrakech, he made it his place of residence and his regime became well established. When 'Abd al-Mu'min carried out many executions among the inhabitants of Marrakech, many of them went into hiding. Seven days later a proclamation of guaranteed security for the remaining population was ordered. People emerged from hiding. The Maṣmūda wished to kill them but 'Abd al-Mu'min prevented this and said, 'These are craftsmen and market people [**585**] who can be useful for us,' and so they were left alone. He ordered the dead to be taken out of the city, which was done, and he built a great mosque in the palace and decorated it with very excellent work. He ordered the demolition of the mosque which the Emir of the Muslims Yūsuf ibn Tāshfīn had built.

Yūsuf ibn Tāshfīn did a wicked act in the way he treated al-Mu'tamid ibn 'Abbād and committed an evil crime in imprisoning him in the state that has been mentioned.[20] It is no wonder then that, to punish him, God gave him into the power of those who went further in their ill-treatment of him. Blessed be the Living God, the Everlasting King, whose kingdom has no end! Such is the way of this world (woe upon it!). We pray God to make our deeds end with a good reward and to make the best of our days the day we meet Him through Muḥammad and his family.

Account of 'Abd al-Mu'min's seizure of Dukkāla

In the year 543 [1148–9] one of the Almoravids went to Dukkāla, where the local tribes gathered around him. They began to raid the districts of Marrakech, although 'Abd al-Mu'min paid them no attention. When their raids increased, he moved against them during the year 544 [1149–50]. Hearing of this, all the Dukkala tribes congregated on the coast in a force of 200,000 infantry and 20,000 cavalry. They were renowned for their courage. 'Abd al-Mu'min had countless troops. The position the Dukkāla were in was very stony and rugged. They laid ambushes to surprise 'Abd al-Mu'min if he came that way. It was a fortunate circumstance for him that he came upon them not from the direction where the ambushes were. The plan they had laid was undone and they abandoned their position. They fell prey to the sword and ran to [**586**] the sea, where most of them were slain. Their camels, flocks and other goods became booty and their women and children were made captive. Handsome girls were sold for a few dirhams. 'Abd al-Mu'min returned to Marrakech in victorious triumph. His rule was now established and people in the whole of the Maghrib feared him and yielded to him in submission.

Account of the siege of the city of Kutunda

In this year, that is, the year 514 [1120–21] one of the Frankish kings in Andalusia, called Ibn Rudmīr,[21] took the field and came to Kutunda,[22] which is near Murcia in the east of Andalusia. He besieged it and pressed hard on the inhabitants. At that time the Emir of the Muslims 'Alī ibn Tāshfīn was in Cordoba with a large army

[20] After Seville was taken from al-Mu'tamid in 484/1091, he and his family were kept in harsh confinement at Aghmāt in the Maghrib (*Kāmil*, x, 190). He died in prison in 488/1095 (*Kāmil*, x, 248).

[21] i.e. Alfonso I of Aragon (1105–34), who was a son of Sancho I Ramīrez, son of Ramiro I.

[22] In Yāqūt, iv, 37, spelt Qutunda. It is situated at Doroca in the district of Saragossa (see *Nafḥ al-ṭīb*, ii, 92, note 4).

of Muslims and volunteer troops, whom he sent against Ibn Rudmīr. They met in a fierce battle, in which Ibn Rudmīr inflicted a shocking defeat on the Muslims and killed many of them. Amongst those slain was Abū 'Abd Allāh ibn al-Farrā', the cadi of Almeria, who was one of the learned ulema, careless of the things of this world and just in the exercise of his office.

Miscellaneous events

This year Balak [ibn Bahrām] ibn Artuq defeated Gavras[23] the Byzantine and killed 5,000 of the Byzantines at the castle of Sarmān in the area of Andukān.[24] Gavras and many of his army were taken prisoner.

[**587**] Also this year Joscelin the Frank, lord of Edessa, raided the forces of the Arabs and the Turkomans, who were camped at Ṣiffīn, west of the Euphrates. He seized much of their money, horses and herds as booty. On his return he destroyed Buzā'a.

Atabeg Ṭughtakīn, lord of Damascus, took over control of Tadmor and al-Shaqīf.[25]

Sultan Maḥmūd ordered Emir Juyūsh Beg to go to fight his brother Ṭughril. He set out and when Ṭughril and his atabeg, Kuntughdī, heard of this, they withdrew before the army to Ganja and no battle took place.

The following died this year:

In Muḥarram [April 1120] Khāliṣat al-Dawla Abū'l-Barakāt Aḥmad ibn 'Abd al-Wahhāb ibn al-Sībī, the head of the Storehouse at Baghdad.[26] His place was taken by Kamāl al-Dīn Abū'l-Futūḥ Ḥamza ibn Ṭalḥa, known as Ibn al-Baqshalāmī,[27] the father of 'Alam al-Dīn, the celebrated secretary.

In Jumādā I [August 1120] Abū Sa'd 'Abd al-Raḥīm ibn 'Abd al-Karīm ibn Hawāzin al-Qushayrī, the Imam and son of the Imam. He received his religious learning from his relatives and likewise his [Sufi] path. He also studied with the Imam of the Two Sanctuaries Abū'l-Ma'ālī al-Juwaynī and heard Ḥadīth from

---

[23] Text has 'Afrās. This is Gavras, the Byzantine governor of Trebizond.

[24] This toponym is not fully pointed in the text. Ibn Qal., 202 has An.d.kān. There was an Andukān (or Andījān) in Ferghāna (Transoxania) and Andukān was also a village at Sarakhs in Khurasan (see Le Strange, *Caliphate*, 478, and Yāqūt, i, 375). Neither seems likely in this context.

[25] Shaqīf Arnūn is probably intended, i.e. Belfort overlooking the bend of the Litani river.

[26] See *Muntaẓam*, viii, 91–2. His grandfather, Hibat Allāh ibn 'Abd Allāh, served as cadi for the Mazyadids. Sīb is said to be a village near Qaṣr Hubayra which is midway between Kufa and Baghdad on the Euphrates (*Ansāb*, vii, 334–5).

[27] Given without the final 'ī' in the text, but cf. *Kāmil*, xi, 42. This name is fancifully explained as resulting from an ancestor's lengthy complaints about his experience with bedbugs (*buqq*) in Shalām, a village near Baghdad (see *Ansāb*, ii, 283–4).

several persons and transmitted it. He was an excellent preacher and a man of quick intellect. When he died, people in distant lands held sessions of condolence, even at Baghdad in the Hospice of the Chief Shaykh.

[588] The Year 515 [1121-1122]

Al-Bursuqī is granted Mosul as a fief

In Ṣafar of this year [21 April-19 May 1121] Sultan Maḥmūd assigned the city of Mosul and its districts and dependent territories, such as Jazīrat [Ibn 'Umar], Sinjār and elsewhere, to Emir Āqsunqur al-Bursuqī. The reason for this was that in Sultan Maḥmūd's service he had been a loyal adviser and a constant ally in all his wars. He had played an excellent role in the aforementioned war between Sultan Maḥmūd and his brother Prince Mas'ūd. He it was who brought Mas'ūd to his brother Maḥmūd, which greatly impressed the latter. After Juyūsh Beg had joined the sultan's entourage and Mosul was left without a governor, he put al-Bursuqī in charge there and commanded all the emirs to obey him. He ordered him to wage jihad against the Franks and to take their lands. Al-Bursuqī proceeded to Mosul with a large force and took control there. He took up residence, administering its affairs and improving its conditions.

The death of Emir 'Alī and the succession of his son al-Ḥasan in Ifrīqiya

The Emir 'Alī ibn Yaḥyā ibn Tamīm, the lord of Ifrīqiya, died this year in the last ten days of Rabī' II [5-14 September 1121]. He was born in Mahdiyya and sufficient has been mentioned previously concerning his wars [**589**] and deeds to indicate his lofty aspirations. After his death his son al-Ḥasan succeeded him according to his father's testament. The business of governing was undertaken by Ṣandal the Eunuch, because at that time al-Ḥasan was only twelve years old and unable to rule independently. Ṣandal undertook the task of guarding and preserving but his days did not last long before he died. Dissension followed among al-Ḥasan's courtiers and commanders, each one of them saying, 'I am the chief of all and in my hands is the power to loose and bind.' So they continued until al-Ḥasan entrusted matters of state to a general, one of his father's men, called Abū 'Azīz Muwaffaq, and affairs improved.

Account of the killing of Emir al-Juyūsh

On 23 Ramaḍān this year [5 December 1121] Emir al-Juyūsh al-Afḍal ibn Badr al-Jamālī, who was the holder of influence and power in Egypt, was killed. He had ridden to the Armoury to distribute weapons to the soldiers according to the custom on festival days. A large host of infantry and cavalry went with him and he became inconvenienced by the dust. He ordered people to keep their distance and proceeded separately, accompanied by two persons. In the Metal-polishers Market two men accosted him and wounded him with blows from their daggers. A third approached from behind and stabbed him in the side and then he fell from his horse. His companions turned back and killed the three men. They carried him to his house and the caliph came to see him and commiserated with him. He asked him about his money and he replied, 'As for what is easily accessible, the secretary Abū'l-Ḥasan ibn Usāma knows about that.' He was a man from Aleppo, whose father had held the post of cadi of Cairo. 'As for what is hidden away, Ibn al-Baṭā'iḥī knows about that.' They both said, 'That is true.'

After al-Afḍal's death quantities of his property were taken away that none but God Almighty could take the measure of. The caliph remained in his house for about forty days, with his secretaries in attendance, while pack-animals were loading and transporting night [**590**] and day. He was found to have such precious objects and strange rare things as were never found in the possession of anyone else. His children were imprisoned. He was fifty-seven years old and had exercised power after his father for twenty-eight years, including the end of al-Mustanṣir's reign, all of al-Musta'lī's and up to this year in the reign of al-Āmir.

The Ismā'īlīs hated him for several reasons, for example, for his tight rein on their Imam, his failure to treat them as they thought he ought to, his failure to oppose the Sunnīs over their creed, indeed his forbidding opposition to them and his allowing people to proclaim their beliefs and to argue for them. Foreigners became numerous in Egypt.

He was a good and just ruler. It is related that, after his death and the oppression that was manifest subsequently, several people gathered and pleaded with the caliph for succour. As part of what they said they cursed al-Afḍal. The caliph asked why they cursed him and they replied, 'He was just and an excellent ruler. We abandoned our lands and homes and came to his land because of his justice. Now, since his death, we have been hit by the present oppression, so he is the cause of our hardship.' The caliph gave generously to them and ordered generous treatment for the people [at large].

Another reason [for their hatred] was that his master, al-Āmir bi-Aḥkām Allāh, the ruler of Egypt, disparaged him, and the reason for that is what we have related previously. Relations between them became bad and al-Āmir planned to arrange for someone to assassinate him when he came to the palace for a levée or during festival days. His cousin, Abū'l-Maymūn 'Abd al-Majīd, who was his eventual successor in Egypt, prevented him from doing that. He said to him, 'To do such a thing means abomination and infamy, because he and his father have served the dynasty for fifty years and people have known [**591**] from them nothing but loyal counsel for us and love of our dynasty. This has travelled throughout all regions of the land and it is impossible that such an shameful reward should come from us. In addition, we have to appoint someone else in his place and rely on him in his office, powerful in the same way or similarly. He will fear that we will treat him as we have this man and he will take care not to come into our presence, out of fear for his life. If he does come before us, he will be fearful and ready to resist. Such behaviour would diminish our standing. The best course is for you to write to Abū 'Abd Allāh ibn al-Baṭā'iḥī, for he is influential with al-Afḍal and privy to his secrets, and promise him that you will appoint him to al-Afḍal's position and ask him to arrange for his assassination by someone who will attack him when he rides out. When we seize whoever kills him, we shall put that person to death and make a show of seeking revenge for his blood and sorrowing for him. Thus we will achieve our aim and escape any evil report.' This is what they did and he was killed as we have mentioned.

After his murder he was succeeded by Abū 'Abd Allāh ibn al-Baṭā'iḥī, who was given the title al-Ma'mūn. He became powerful in the state and remained so, ruling the land, until the year 519 [1125–6], when he was crucified, as we shall relate, God willing.

Account of the rebellion of Sulaymān ibn Īlghāzī against his father

This year Sulaymān ibn Īlghāzī ibn Artuq, who had just past twenty years of age, rebelled against his father in Aleppo. Several of his entourage incited him to that action. His father heard the news and immediately set out on a forced march. Sulaymān had no inkling of this until he made his surprise appearance. He went to his father to apologise and the latter refrained from punishing him but arrested those who had given him this counsel, including an emir whom Artuq, Īlghāzī's father, had adopted and brought up, named Nāṣir. He gouged out his eyes and cut out his tongue. Another emir was **[592]** a man from Hama, a well-established family, whom Īlghāzī had promoted over the people of Aleppo and made the headman. This was how they requited Īlghāzī, so he cut off his hands and feet and blinded him. He later died.

He summoned his son, who was drunk, and had a mind to put him to death, but the tender-heartedness of a father held him back, so he spared him. The son then fled to Damascus and Ṭughtakīn sent to intercede for him, which was not accepted. Īlghāzī appointed as his deputy in Aleppo the son of his brother 'Abd al-Jabbār ibn Artuq and gave him the title Badr al-Dawla. He then returned to Mardin.

Account of the grant of Mayyafariqin to Īlghāzī

This year Sultan Maḥmūd assigned the city of Mayyafariqin to Emir Īlghāzī as a fief. This came about because Īlghāzī sent his son Ḥusām al-Dīn Timurtāsh, aged seventeen, to the sultan to intercede for Dubays ibn Ṣadaqa and to offer obedience on his behalf and the payment of money, horses and such like and that he would guarantee a daily revenue from al-Ḥilla of 1,000 dinars and a horse. The negotiator on his behalf was Cadi Bahā' al-Dīn Abū'l-Ḥasan 'Alī ibn al-Qāsim ibn al-Shahrazūrī. Discussions continued to and fro but nothing was settled. When he decided to return, the sultan gave his father Mayyafaraqin as a fief, which had been held by Emir Sukmān, lord of Khilat. Īlghāzī took it over and it remained in his hands and the hands of his descendants until Ṣalāḥ al-Dīn[1] Yūsuf ibn Ayyūb conquered it in the year 580 [1184–5]. We shall relate this later, God willing.

[593] How Balak ibn Bahrām besieged Edessa and captured its lord

This year Balak ibn Bahrām, Īlghāzī's nephew, marched to Edessa, held by the Franks, and put it under siege, which continued for a while but without any success, so he withdrew. A Turkoman came to him and informed him that Joscelin, lord of Edessa and Sarūj, had gathered together the Franks under him, intending to take him in ambush. Balak's men had dispersed and he remained with 400 cavalry. He took up a position, prepared to give battle.

The Franks advanced and by God's grace to the Muslims the Franks arrived at ground which had soaked up water and become mud, into which their cavalry sank, unable to manoeuvre quickly or gallop because of the weight of their armour and horses. Balak's men loosed their arrows at them and not one of them escaped. Joscelin was taken and sewn into a camel's skin. The surrender of Edessa was demanded but he refused and offered large sums of money and many prisoners as his ransom. This was not accepted and he was carried to the castle of Khartbirt and incarcerated there. His cousin, called William, one of the Infidels' devils, was captured with him. Balak also captured several of their celebrated knights and imprisoned them with him.

Miscellaneous events

During this year there died the paternal grandmother of Sultan Maḥmūd, who was the mother of Sultan Sanjar. She was Turkish and called the Lady Safariyya.[2] She died in Marv. [**594**] Maḥmūd held a session of condolence in Baghdad, which was a occasion the like of which had never been witnessed.

In Fars this year Khaṭīr al-Mulk Muḥammad ibn al-Ḥusayn al-Maybudhī died, while he was vizier for Prince Saljūq, son of Sultan Muḥammad. Formerly he had served as vizier for the two sultans, Barkyāruq and Muḥammad. He was generous and forbearing. He heard that al-Abīwardī had satirized him. When he heard the satire, he suffered but bit his thumb and forgave him, giving him a robe and some remuneration.

---

1 i.e. Saladin.

2 She had been a concubine of Malikshāh. In her days of power she sent for her mother and sisters after forty years of separation (*Muntaẓam*, ix, 228–9).

Also this year Shihāb al-Dīn Abū'l-Maḥāsin 'Abd al-Razzāq ibn 'Abd Allāh died, the vizier of Sultan Sanjar and a cousin of Niẓām al-Mulk. Formerly he studied law under the Imam of the Two Sanctuaries al-Juwaynī. He used to give fatwas and record administrative decisions. After him Abū Ṭāhir Sa'd ibn 'Alī ibn 'Īsā al-Qumī became vizier but he died within a few months. The next vizier was 'Uthmān al-Qumī.

In Jumādā I [18 July–16 August 1121] Atabeg Ṭughtakīn fell upon a detachment of Franks, whom he killed or captured. He sent some of the prisoners and booty to the sultan and the caliph.

This year the south corner of the Sacred House (may God add to its glory!) was weakened by an earthquake. Part of it collapsed and some of the Prophet's sanctuary was damaged (may God bless him and give him peace). Other lands suffered too and much damage occurred in Mosul.

The sultan's palace, built by Mujāhid al-Dīn Bahrūz for Sultan Muḥammad and completed a little before his death, caught fire this year and at the present time was destroyed by fire. The cause of the fire was that a servant girl was adorning herself at night and leant a candle against the canvas screen, which caught fire and the flames spread around the palace. Sultan Maḥmūd's wife, the daughter of Sultan Sanjar, lost in the fire untold quantities of jewels, ornaments, furnishings and clothes. The cleaners were put to work to recover the gold and whatever else could be recovered. All the gems had been destroyed except for the red rubies.[3]

[**595**] The sultan left the palace without any repair. He considered it ill-omened because his father had never enjoyed it and then all this great amount of property had been burnt there. A week previously the mosque at Isfahan had burnt down, one of the largest and most handsome of mosques. A group of Ismā'īlīs set fire to it at night. The sultan had intended to impose a sales tax and renew other non-canonical taxes in Iraq on the advice of the Vizier al-Sumayramī. The occurrence of these two fires was enough to disturb him. He drew a lesson from them and gave up his plan.

In Rabī' I [20 May–18 June 1121] a meteor [lit. blinding star] fell to earth and had a great light. When it fell to earth it caused the collapse of structures and at the same time a great rumbling sound was heard, like an earthquake.[4]

There appeared this year in Mecca an Alid who 'ordered the good'. His following became numerous and he challenged the Emir of Mecca, Ibn Abī Hāshim. His cause prospered and he determined to have the khutbah said in his name. Ibn Abī Hāshim returned, seized him and expelled him from the Hijaz to Bahrain. This Alid was one of the lawyers of the Niẓāmiyya in Baghdad.

---

3 *Muntaẓam*, ix, 223–4: the fire occurred on Sunday 4 Jumādā II/= 21 August 1121 and note: 'the cleaners (*ghassālūn*) washed the rubble and recovered lumps of gold and jewelry.'

4 Where this occurred is not mentioned and there is no parallel passage in *Muntaẓam*. 'Meteor' must in the context be the meaning of *kawkab 'ishā'* but the second word is puzzling. I am grateful to Dr Emilie Savage-Smith for her suggestions.

This year the sultan obliged the Dhimmīs in Baghdad to wear the distinguishing badge.[5] There followed discussions about this which ended in the imposition of a payment of 20,000 dinars by them to the sultan and 4,000 to the caliph.

This year Sultan Maḥmūd and his brother Prince Mas'ūd attended on the caliph who gave them robes of honour, as he did also to several of the sultan's entourage, such as his vizier, Abū Ṭālib al-Sumayramī, Shams al-Mulk 'Uthmān ibn Niẓām al-Mulk, the Vizier Abū Naṣr Aḥmad ibn Muḥammad ibn Ḥāmid the Comptroller and others among the emirs.

In Dhū'l-Qa'da, that is, 21 Kānūn II [21 January 1122] there was a great fall of snow over the whole of Iraq, from Basra to Takrit, which lay on the ground for fifteen days to the thickness of a cubit. The orange, the citron and the lemon trees perished. [**596**] A certain poet said about this:

O leaders of the age, this is not excessive,
what we have seen in the lands of Iraq.
It is just that your iniquity has spread to all creation,
So the heads of the far horizons have turned white.

This year a black wind blew for three days in Egypt. It caused the death of many people and of animals too.

This year Abū Muḥammad al-Qāsim ibn 'Alī ibn Muḥammad ibn 'Uthmān al-Ḥarīrī, the author of the famous *Maqāmas*,[6] died, as did Hazārasb ibn 'Iwaḍ al-Harawī, who had heard much Ḥadīth.

---

[5] In Arabic *al-ghiyār*. Various distinctive forms of apparel (often a yellow patch) were at different times obligatory for the Dhimmīs or *Ahl al-Dhimma* (people of the Covenant), protected non-Muslims living under Muslim jurisdiction.

[6] For al-Ḥarīrī, see *Encyclopedia of Arabic Literature*, i, 272–3, where the year of his death is given as 516/1122; and for the *maqāma* (short narrative in rhymed prose with some verse passages), see *op. cit.*, ii, 507-8.

[597]

The Year 516 [1122-1123]

Account of Prince Ṭughril's submission to his brother Sultan Maḥmūd

In Muḥarram of this year [12 March-10 April 1122] Prince Ṭughril submitted to his brother Sultan Maḥmūd, having earlier cast off his allegiance, as we have related. In the previous year he went to Azerbayjan to seize control of it. His atabeg Kuntughdī encouraged him in that and strengthened his purpose, but it happened that Kuntughdī fell ill and died in Shawwāl of the year 515 [13 December 1121-10 January 1122]

Emir Āqsunqur al-Aḥmadīlī, lord of Marāgha, was with the sultan at Baghdad. He sought leave to go to his fief, which was granted. After he had left the sultan, he thought that he might take Kuntughdī's place with Prince Ṭughril, so he went to join him, and suggested that he break openly with his brother, Sultan Maḥmūd. He said to him, 'When you arrive at Marāgha, 10,000 horse and foot will attach themselves to you.' So he went with him, but when they reached Ardabil, the gates were closed in their faces. They therefore went on to near Tabriz. News came to them that Sultan Maḥmūd had sent Emir Juyūsh Beg to Azerbayjan and given him the area as a fief and that he had stopped at Marāgha with a mighty army provided by the sultan.

When they had verified this, they turned aside to Khūnaj[1] and their project collapsed. They made overtures to Emir Shīrkīr, who had been Ṭughril's atabeg during the reign of his father, inviting him to give them assistance. Kuntughdī had arrested him after the death of Sultan Muḥammad, as we have related, and then he had been released [**598**] by Sultan Sanjar. He returned to his fief, Abhar and Zanjan. They [now] wrote to him and he responded by joining them and went with them to Abhar. However, what they planned came to nothing, so they made contact with the sultan, offering allegiance, which was accepted. The terms were agreed and settled at the beginning of this year.

Account of Dubays ibn Ṣadaqa's situation and his subsequent course of action

Under the year 514 [1120-21] we have mentioned Dubays ibn Ṣadaqa's situation, his making peace through the agency of Yarunqush al-Zakawī, his residence at al-Ḥilla and Yarunqush's return to the sultan, accompanied by Manṣūr ibn Ṣadaqa,

[1] Two days north of Zanjan within the large bend of the Safīd Rūd (Yāqūt, ii, 500; Le Strange, *Caliphate*, 224-5).

Dubays' brother, and his son[2] as a hostage. When the caliph heard of this, he was not content. He wrote to Sultan Maḥmūd to have Dubays removed from Iraq to some other region.

There was an exchange of correspondence about this. When the sultan decided to go to Hamadhan, the caliph repeated his complaint about Dubays and mentioned that he was hounding people because of his grudges, for example, because of the killing of his father. He suggested that the sultan should summon Āqsunqur al-Bursuqī from Mosul and appoint him prefect of Baghdad and Iraq and let him confront Dubays. The sultan took this course and summoned al-Bursuqī. On his arrival he married him to the mother of Prince Mas'ūd and made him prefect of Baghdad, ordering him to fight Dubays if the latter interfered in that region.

The sultan left Baghdad during Ṣafar of this year [11 April–9 May 1122].[3] His stay in Baghdad had been one year, seven months and fifteen days. After his departure from Baghdad and Iraq, Dubays openly pursued a course that disturbed al-Mustarshid bi-Allāh, so he ordered al-Bursuqī to march against him and oust him from al-Ḥilla. Al-Bursuqī sent to Mosul and summoned his troops, then set out for al-Ḥilla. [**599**] Dubays advanced towards him and they met at the Canal of Bashīr, east of the Euphrates. A battle ensued and al-Bursuqī's force was defeated.

The reason for the defeat was that al-Bursuqī saw some disorder on his left flank, where the Bakjiyya emirs were, so he ordered his tent to be struck and erected on the left wing to strengthen the hearts of those stationed there. When they saw that the tent had fallen, they thought that it was because of some reverse, so they fled and the army and al-Bursuqī followed them.

There is a different version. He was handed a note which said that a number of the emirs, including Ismā'īl al-Bakjī, were planning to assassinate him, so he took to flight and the army followed him. He entered Baghdad on 2 Rabī' II [10 June 1122].

In the army was Naṣr ibn al-Nafīs ibn Muhadhdhab al-Dawla Aḥmad ibn Abī'l-Jabr, who was the inspector of the Marsh for Rayḥān Maḥkawayh, a eunuch of the sultan, because it was part of his fief. Al-Muẓaffar ibn Ḥammād ibn Abī'l-Jabr was also present. There was great enmity between the two of them. At the time of the defeat they confronted one another at the Arcade of 'Īsā Canal. Al-Muẓaffar killed Naṣr ibn al-Nafīs, then went to Wāsiṭ and from there to the Marsh, of which he took control. He wrote to Dubays and accepted his authority.

Dubays caused no trouble at King's Canal or anywhere else. He sent to the caliph, claiming to be loyal and that, had that not been so, he would have captured al-Bursuqī and everyone with him. He requested that the inspector should go out to the villages, which belonged to the caliph's personal estate, to collect their revenues

The battle was in Ḥazīrān [June]. Dubays protected the area and the caliph praised his actions. There followed an exchange of messengers and the settlement

[2] Under the year 514 there is no mention of any son as a hostage.

[3] Cf. *Muntaẓam*, ix, 232: Wednesday 1 Rabī' I/10 May 1122.

agreed on was that al-Mustarshid bi-Allāh should arrest his vizier, Jalāl al-Dīn Abū 'Alī ibn Ṣadaqa, to allow Dubays to return to obedience. The vizier was duly arrested and his house plundered as were the houses of his followers and dependents. Jalāl al-Din's nephew, Abū'l-Riḍā, fled to Mosul. When the sultan heard the news of the battle, he arrested Manṣūr ibn Ṣadaqa, Dubays' brother, and also his son, and took them up into the castle of Barjīn,[4] which is near Karaj.[5]

[600] Later Dubays ordered several of his men to proceed to their fiefs in Wāsiṭ. They did so, but the Turks in Wāsiṭ resisted them, so Dubays sent an army against them, commanded by Muhalhil ibn Abī'l-'Askar, and he sent to al-Muẓaffar ibn Abī'l-Jabr in the Marsh to urge him to cooperate with Muhalhil and aid him in the fight with the Wāsiṭī Turks. The two agreed that they should act together on 9 Rajab [13 September 1122]. The Wāsiṭīs wrote to al-Bursuqī seeking support and he supplied them with some of his troops. Muhalhil, commanding Dubays' troops, anticipated and did not wait for al-Muẓaffar in the belief that he could gain the desired end on his own and win a victory by himself. He and the Wāsiṭīs clashed on 8 Rajab [12 September]. Muhalhil and his troops were routed and the Wāsiṭīs were victorious. Muhalhil and several of the notables of his force were taken prisoner and more than a thousand were killed. Only a single Wāsiṭī was killed.

As for al-Muẓaffar ibn Abī'l-Jabr, he came up from the Marsh, plundering and causing disturbance. His men behaved abominably. When he drew near Wāsiṭ, he heard of the defeat and went back down country.

One of the things that the Wāsiṭī army took from Muhalhil was a memorandum in Dubays' hand, in which he ordered him to seize al-Muẓaffar ibn Abī'l-Jabr and to demand from him large sums of money that he had taken from the Marsh. They sent this document to al-Muẓaffar, saying, 'This is in the hand of the person you favour and for whose sake you have angered God and all men.' He therefore went over to their side. When Dubays' men suffered as we have related at the hands of the Wāsiṭīs, he abandoned all restraint in his wickedness. He heard that the sultan had blinded his brother, so he cropped his hair, donned black and ravaged the lands, taking everything that belonged to the caliph at King's Canal and driving the people away to Baghdad.

The army of Wāsiṭ marched to al-Nu'māniyya and expelled Dubays' troops and took control **[601]**. There was an engagement in which victory went to the Wāsiṭīs. The caliph commanded al-Bursuqī to take the field to wage war on Dubays. He did so in Ramaḍān [November 1122] and there took place what we shall later recount, God willing.

---

4 Correct the text's Barḥīn. For Barjīn (or Farjīn), see Krawulsky, 269-70.

5 Dubays had behaved with moderation, contrary to all expectation. An understanding was reached with the caliph but Dubays' demands were not met: for example, the Vizier Ibn Ṣadaqa was not executed, al-Bursuqī was not removed from Baghdad, and his own brother Manṣūr was not freed. Hostilities began again. See details in *Muntaẓam*, ix, 233, 235.

Account of the killing of al-Sumayramī

This year Vizier Abū Ṭālib al-Sumayramī, Sultan Maḥmūd's vizier, was killed the last day of Ṣafar [9 May 1122].[6] He had prepared to leave with the sultan to go to Hamadhan. He visited the baths and left, preceded by his foot-soldiers and cavalry, in great state. He traversed the Madrasah Market, which Khumārtakīn al-Tutushī had built, and passed through a narrow passage where there were thorn barriers. Because the place was narrow his men went in front. A Bāṭinī leapt at him and struck at him with a dagger, but [the blow] fell on his mule. The man fled towards the Tigris, followed by the vizier's attendants, which left the place empty. A second man appeared and struck the vizier in his side with a dagger, dragged him from the mule to the ground and struck him several more blows. The vizier's men returned but, when attacked by two Bāṭinīs, they ran away. They came back again but the vizier's throat had been cut like a sheep's. His corpse was carried away with thirty or more wounds in it. His assassins were all killed [later].

When he was in the bath, the astrologers were casting his horoscope for his departure. They declared, 'This is an excellent moment. If you delay, the auspicious star will be missed.' So he saddled his horse and rode out. He wished to eat some food but they prevented him because of the ascendant star. Then he was murdered, so what they said did him no good.

His vizierate lasted for three years and ten months. His wealth was plundered and the sultan took his library. [**602**] To succeed him, Shams al-Mulk ibn Niẓām al-Mulk became vizier. Al-Sumayramī's wife had already departed this same day with a large retinue, accompanied by about one hundred slave girls and a number of eunuchs, all with gold accoutrements. After they heard of his assassination they returned, bare-footed and with heads uncovered, having exchanged pomp for abasement and joy for grief. Praise be to Him whose kingdom has no end!

Al-Sumayramī was tyrannical. He frequently extorted money from people and he followed wicked ways. After his murder the sultan cancelled the taxes that the vizier had introduced and his impositions on the merchants and shop-keepers.

The capture of Ibn Ṣadaqa, the caliph's vizier, and 'Alī ibn Ṭirād's appointment as deputy

In Jumādā I [July 1122][7] the caliph arrested his vizier, Jalāl al-Dīn ibn Ṣadaqa. Mention of this has been made before. The Chief Syndic Sharaf al-Dīn 'Alī ibn Ṭirād al-Zaynabī was installed as deputy vizier. The sultan sent to al-Mustarshid bi-Allāh on the matter of appointing Niẓām al-Mulk Abū Naṣr Aḥmad ibn Niẓām

6 Ibn al-Jawzī has a confirmatory 'Tuesday' in the date and more details of the assassination (*Muntaẓam*, ix, 239–41).

7 *Muntaẓam*, ix, 233: Thursday 20 Jumādā I/27 July. 'Alī was made deputy the next day.

al-Mulk as vizier. He was the brother of Shams al-Mulk 'Uthmān ibn Niẓām al-Mulk, Sultan Maḥmūd's vizier. The suggestion was accepted and he was appointed vizier in Sha'bān [October 1122].

He had previously served as vizier for Sultan Muḥammad in the year 500 [1106–7]. On his dismissal he kept to a house he built in Baghdad until this present year. When now given his robe of office and having taken his seat in the Dīwān, he requested that Ibn Ṣadaqa should leave Baghdad. Hearing this, Ibn Ṣadaqa asked the caliph to send him to Ḥadīthat 'Āna to be with Emir Sulaymān ibn Muhārish. This request was granted.

He set out for Ḥadītha and on the road he was waylaid by a Turkoman brigand called [**603**] Yūnus the Robber, who took him prisoner and plundered his companions. The vizier feared that Dubays might find out and send to Yūnus with an offer of money to lay hands on him because of the enmity between them. He therefore agreed with Yūnus to pay 1,000 dinars, with 300 as a down payment and the rest delayed until he send it from Ḥadītha.

The financial agent of al-Furāt wrote a letter about freeing him and sending someone to guarantee the outstanding amount he owed. The agent employed a trick. He fetched a peasant and dressed him in fine robes and a *ṭaylasān*,[8] put him on a horse and sent him off with some retainers. He ordered him to go to Yūnus, claim that he was the cadi of al-Furāt and guarantee the money owed. The peasant duly went to Yūnus. When he came to the vizier and Yūnus, they both received him with respect. The peasant stood surety for the person of the vizier, saying to Yūnus, 'I will stay with you until the money arrives with one of the men you send with the vizier.' Yūnus accepted that all this was genuine and released the vizier, sending with him several of his own men. On arriving at Ḥadītha, the vizier seized those that had come with him. Yūnus later freed the peasant and returned the money he had received, in return for the vizier's release of his men, now that he understood the trick that he had fallen for. When the vizier left Yūnus, he met a man of whom he became suspicious. He seized him and found on him a letter from Dubays to Yūnus, offering 6,000 dinars for his person. His escape was really an amazing matter!

Account of the killing of Juyūsh Beg

Emir Juyūsh Beg, who had been ruler of Mosul, was killed this year. We have already mentioned his rebellion against Sultan Maḥmūd and his return to his service. After the sultan was reconciled with him, he assigned him Azerbayjan as a fief [**604**] and made him commander of his army. Rivalry and disputes followed between him and a number of the emirs, who incited the sultan against him. Eventually he put him to death at the gates of Tabriz in Ramaḍān [November 1122].

[8] A pointed hood or cowl, distinctive item of dress for the ulema and cadis.

Juyūsh Beg was a Turk, one of the mamlukes of Sultan Muḥammad, a just man of upright life. When he became governor of Mosul and the Jazīra, the Kurds in those regions were widely scattered, caused much disruption and had numerous fortresses. The population were in difficult straits with them and the roads were dangerous. He targeted them and besieged their fortresses, many of which he conquered in the lands of the Hakkārīs, in Zawzān and the lands of the Bashnawīs. The Kurds feared him for he led the attack on them in person. They fled from him into the mountains, woods and passes, leaving the main roads safe. The population spread around and felt secure. The Kurds were left not daring to carry arms because they were in awe of him.

The death of Īlghāzī and the subsequent state of Aleppo

In the month of Ramadān this year [November 1122] Īlghāzī ibn Artuq died at Mayyafariqin. His son Ḥusām al-Dīn Timurtāsh seized the citadel of Mardin and his other son Sulaymān seized Mayyafaraqin. His nephew Badr al-Dīn Sulaymān ibn ʻAbd al-Jabbār ibn Artuq was in Aleppo and continued there until his cousin took it.

Miscellaneous events

This year Sultan Maḥmūd assigned to Emir Āqsunqur al-Bursuqī the city of Wāsiṭ and its districts, in addition to the governorship of Mosul and other places that he held already, and also the office of prefect of Iraq. After having been assigned them, al-Bursuqī sent ʻImād al-Din Zankī, son of Āqsunqur who had been [**605**] ruler of Aleppo, and ordered him to administer them for him. Zankī set out in Shaʻbān [October 1122] and took charge there. We have related Zankī's history in our book *al-Bāhir*[9] on the history of his rule and that of his descendants who are our rulers at the present. Reference may be made to that book.

This year a copper mine was found in Diyār Bakr, near the Castle of the Two-Horned One.[10]

This year the Euphrates rose greatly to a previously unheard-of extent. Water entered the suburb of Qalʻat Jaʻbar. At that time the Euphrates flowed close to it. Most of its palaces and houses were inundated and a horse was carried away from the suburb and borne over the wall into the Euphrates.

---

[9] This monograph on the Zankid dynasty, entitled *al-Taʼrīkh al-Bāhir fīʼl-Dawla al-Atābakiyya*, was edited by A. A. Tolaymat, Cairo, 1962.

[10] Qalʻat Dhīʼl-Qarnayn, i.e. of Alexander the Great, given this epithet in Koran, xviii, 83, 86, 94. It is in the mountains north of Āmid (Diyarbakır), near the tributaries of the Tigris, one of which is called Zulkar. See Krawulsky, 433.

A madrasah for the followers of al-Shāfiʿī was built in Aleppo this year.

The daughter of Sultan Sanjar, the wife of Sultan Maḥmūd, died this year.

In Shaʿbān [October 1122] Burhān al-Dīn Abū'l-Ḥasan ʿAlī ibn al-Ḥusayn al-Ghaznawī came to Baghdad and held sermon sessions in all parts. After him there arrived Abū'l-Qāsim ʿAlī ibn Yaʿlā al-ʿAlawī, who lodged in the Hospice of the Chief Shaykh and preached in the Palace Mosque, in the Tājiyya and the Hospice of Saʿāda. He was very well received by the Ḥanbalīs. He gained a great sum of money because he proclaimed his agreement with them.

After him came Abū'l-Futūḥ al-Isfarā'īnī, who also lodged in the Hospice of the Chief Shaykh and preached in the same places and in the Niẓāmiyya. He proclaimed the teaching of al-Ashʿarī and had a great reception from the Shāfiʿīs. The Caliph al-Mustarshid bi-Allāh attended his circle and entrusted to him the Hospice of al-Urjuwaniyya,[11] the mother of al-Muqtadī bi-Allāh, in the Alley of Zākhī.

The following died this year:

ʿAbd Allāh ibn Aḥmad ibn ʿUmar, Abū Muḥammad al-Samarqandī, the brother of Abū'l-Qāsim ibn al-Samarqandī.[12] He was born in Damascus in the year 444 [1052–3] and grew up in Baghdad. He studied with al-Ṣarīfīnī, Ibn al-Naqūr and others, and travelled much. He knew Ḥadīth by heart [**606**] and was learned in that subject.

In Dhū'l-Ḥijja [February 1123][13] ʿAbd al-Qādir ibn Muḥammad ibn ʿAbd al-Qādir ibn Muḥammad ibn Yūsuf, Abū Ṭālib, born in the year 436 [1044–5]. He studied with al-Barmakī, al-Jawharī and al-ʿUshārī, and was a reliable source and a learned scholar of Ḥadīth.

---

[11] Also called Urjuwān, see above under year 512/1118–19, p. [**545**] and note 1.

[12] He died Monday 12 Rabīʿ II/=19 June 1122 (*Muntaẓam*, ix, 239).

[13] *Muntaẓam*, ix, 23: Saturday 18 Dhū'l-Ḥijja/17 February 1123.

[**607**] The Year 517 [1123-1124]

Account of al-Mustarshid bi-Allāh's campaign to make war on Dubays

In this year there was warfare between the Caliph al-Mustarshid bi-Allāh and Dubays ibn Ṣadaqa. This came about because Dubays freed 'Afīf, the caliph's eunuch, whom he held captive, and made him the bearer of a missive in which he threatened the caliph for sending al-Bursuqī to fight him and supporting him with money and also because the sultan had blinded his brother. He made extreme threats, donned black, cut his hair and swore that he would sack and destroy Baghdad. The caliph was outraged at this communication and in his anger commanded al-Bursuqī to take the field to wage war on Dubays, which he did in Ramaḍān of the year 516 [November 1122].

The caliph made his preparations and left Baghdad. He summoned his troops. Sulaymān ibn Muhārish, the lord of Ḥadītha, came to him with the tribe of 'Uqayl. Qirwāsh ibn Musallim also came and others too. Dubays sent men to King's Canal and sacked it. His men perpetrated every dreadful wickness and its inhabitants came to Baghdad. The caliph ordered a proclamation in Baghdad that none of the troops should fail to muster and also that those common people who wished to serve as soldiers should present themselves. A huge number came forward and he distributed money and weapons among them.

[**608**] When Dubays learnt the state of affairs, he wrote to the caliph to seek reconciliation and ask for his good will. There was no response to this, and the caliph's tents were brought out on 20 Dhū'l-Ḥijja 516 [19 February 1123]. He appealed to the people of Baghdad, 'To arms, to arms! To war, to war!' Great was the commotion among the people and a vast crowd of them, more than could be counted, left the city. The caliph left on 14 Dhū'l-Ḥijja [13 February 1123] and crossed the Tigris, wearing his black gown, black turban and shawl, with the Cloak[1] over his shoulders, the sceptre in his hand and a bronze[2] belt about his waist. He took up quarters in the tents, along with his vizier, Niẓām al-Mulk[3] Aḥmad ibn Niẓām al-Mulk, the syndic of the Alids, the Chief Syndic 'Alī ibn Ṭirād and the Chief Shaykh Ṣadr al-Dīn Ismā'īl and other notables.

Al-Bursuqī had camped at the village of Chahār Ṭāq with his troops. When they heard that the caliph had left Baghdad, they returned to wait upon him. When they

---

[1] The *Burda*, the Prophet's cloak preserved by the caliphs as a holy relic until the Mongol capture of Baghdad, although it is also claimed to survive in Istanbul (see *EI(2)*, i, 1314).

[2] The text has *ḥadīd ṣīnī*, literally 'Chinese iron.' It seems that high tin bronze is intended (see the detailed discussion in Allan, *Persian Metal etc.*, 45-55).

[3] The text has Niẓām al-Dīn.

caught sight of his parasol, they all dismounted and kissed the ground at some distance from him.

This present year began and the caliph camped on 1 Muḥarram [1 March 1123] at Ḥadītha, at King's Canal. He summoned al-Bursuqī and the emirs and made them swear to be loyal in the conflict. They then proceeded to al-Nīl and camped at al-Mubāraka. Al-Bursuqī drew up his men for battle and the caliph positioned himself in the rear of all with his special guard. Dubays formed his men in a line, a left and right wing and a centre, placing his infantry before the cavalry as a protective screen.[4] He had promised his men the sack of Baghdad and the capture of women. When the two forces caught sight of each other, Dubays' followers made the first move, preceded by slave girls beating their tambourines and androgynes with their musical instruments. In the caliph's army only men reciting the Koran, counting rosaries and praying were to be seen. A fierce battle began.

Emir Karbāwī ibn Khurasān was with the caliph's banners, while in the rear-guard was Sulaymān ibn Muhārish. On the right wing of Bursuqī's force was Emir Abū Bakr ibn Ilyās with the Bakjiyya emirs. 'Antar ibn Abī'l-'Askar with a detachment of Dubays' army charged the right wing [**609**] of al-Bursuqī, which gave ground. A nephew of Emir Abū Bakr al-Bakjī was killed. 'Antar withdrew and then made a second charge on the right wing. The way it retreated was just like the first occasion. When the troops of Wāsiṭ, whose commander was the Martyr[5] 'Imād al-Dīn Zankī ibn Āqsunqur, saw this, they along with him attacked 'Antar and his men. They came upon them from behind and 'Antar was caught in the middle, with 'Imād al-Dīn and the troops of Wāsiṭ behind them and the Bakjiyya emirs before them. 'Antar was taken, as were Barīk ibn Zā'ida and all with them. Not one escaped.

Al-Bursuqī was standing on a rise in the ground. Emir Āqbūrī was in an ambush with 500 horse. When the combatants were fully engaged, the ambush fell upon Dubays' force. They all fled and threw themselves into the water. Many of them drowned and many were killed.

When the caliph saw the battle's intensity, he drew his sword, shouted 'God is great', and advanced towards the action. After the flight of Dubays' army, when the prisoners were brought before him, the caliph ordered that all should be summarily decapitated. Dubays' army had consisted of 10,000 cavalry and 12,000 infantry, while that of al-Bursuqī was 8,000 cavalry and 5,000 infantry. Only twenty of the caliph's followers were killed. Dubays' wives and his concubines became captives, except for the daughter of Īlghāzī and the daughter of 'Amīd al-Dawla ibn Jahīr, for Dubays had left them at the Shrine.[6]

The caliph returned to Baghdad which he entered on the day of 'Ashūrā' of this year [10 March 1123]. When the caliph returned, the mob rioted in Baghdad and

---

4 The text has 'with [their] weapons.' *Muntaẓam*, ix, 242, has 'with [their] large shields.'

5 Zankī is routinely called 'Martyr' (*al-Shahīd*), anticipating his death while campaigning.

6 Probably at the shrine of Imam 'Alī ibn Ḥusayn at Karbalā', about 60 miles south of Baghdad, or possibly at Najaf further south, the burial place of 'Alī himself.

plundered the shrine at the Straw Gate. They wrenched off the doors. The caliph condemned this and ordered Naẓar, the Emir of the Pilgrimage, to ride to the shrine and discipline the perpetrators and recover what had been plundered. He obeyed and recovered some but the rest remained hidden.

As for Dubays ibn Ṣadaqa, at the time of the defeat, he escaped with his horse and his weapons. The cavalry caught up with him [**610**] but he eluded them and crossed the Euphrates. An old woman saw him after he had crossed and said, 'You have come in poor shape.' He replied, 'Those who have not come are [the ones] in poor shape!'[7] Afterwards all news of him was lost and it was rumoured that he had been killed. Then it became apparent that he had made his way to the Ghuzayya, some Bedouin of Nejd. He asked them to be his allies but they refused, saying, 'We shall only annoy the caliph and the sultan.' He therefore left and went to the Muntafiq, with whom he agreed to attack and seize Basra. They made their way there and, having entered the town, plundered the inhabitants.[8] Emir Sakht Kumān, the commander of the local force, was killed and the population expelled.

The caliph wrote to al-Bursuqī, reprimanding him for his failure to deal with Dubays, with the result that the latter had managed to ruin Basra. Al-Bursuqī made preparations to go down south, so Dubays, hearing of that, abandoned Basra and travelled overland to Qal'at Ja'bar, where he joined the Franks. He was present with them at the siege of Aleppo and encouraged them to attempt to take it, but they did not succeed and withdrew. He then parted from them and joined with Prince Ṭughril, son of Sultan Muḥammad. He remained with him and incited him to attack Iraq. We shall tell of this under the year 529 [1134–5], if God Almighty wills.

Account of the Franks' taking control of the fortress of al-Athārib

In Ṣafar this year [April 1123] the Franks took the fortress of al-Athārib in the district of Aleppo. This came about because they had made many attacks on Aleppo and its district with raids of destruction and burning. At that time Aleppo was held by Badr al-Dawla Sulaymān ibn 'Abd al-Jabbār ibn Artuq, but he was not strong enough to deal with the Franks, whom he feared. He therefore made a truce with them on the basis that he would surrender al-Athārib and they would refrain from attacking his lands. They agreed to this and took over the fortress. The truce between them was concluded, which improved the situation of the populace in the districts of Aleppo, because foodstuffs and other things were now imported. Al-Athārib remained in the hands of the Franks until it was taken by Atabeg Zankī ibn Āqsunqur, as we shall relate, God willing.

---

7 The same passage is in *Muntaẓam*, ix, 243. Although the root *d.b.r.* has meanings that may support the translation 'in poor shape', there is no dictionary entry for *dubayr* itself, which is interpreted solely according to the context.

8 In Rabī' I/ May 1123 (*Muntaẓam*, ix, 245).

[611] How Balak took Ḥarrān and Aleppo

In Rabī‘ I [May 1123] Balak ibn Bahrām took the city of Ḥarrān after a siege and, when he had taken it, he went from there to Aleppo. The reason why he went there was that he had heard that its ruler, Badr al-Dawla, had surrendered the citadel of al-Athārib to the Franks. This dismayed him but he also realised that Badr al-Dawla was incapable of defending his lands. His eagerness to take Aleppo grew. He set out and descended on it in Rabī‘ I [May]. He closely encircled the city, prevented any supplies and burnt the crops. His cousin surrendered the city and the citadel to him on terms on 1 Jumādā I [27 June 1123]. He married the daughter of Prince Riḍwān and remained the ruler of the place until he was killed, as we shall relate.

Account of the warfare between the Franks and the Muslims in Ifrīqiya

We have already mentioned that Emir ‘Alī ibn Yaḥyā, the lord of Ifrīqiya, after his estrangement from Roger, ruler of Sicily, renewed the fleet he had and enlarged its complement and its equipment. He wrote to the Emir of the Muslims, ‘Alī ibn Yūsuf ibn Tāshfīn, in Marrakech proposing an alliance to attack the island of Sicily. When Roger heard of this, he desisted from some of what he had been doing.

It happened that ‘Alī [ibn Yaḥya] died in the year 515 [1121] and was succeeded by his son al-Ḥasan, whom we have mentioned before. After the beginning of the year 516 [1122] the Emir of the Muslims despatched a fleet which overcame Nicotera on the coast of Calabria. Roger had no doubt that ‘Alī **[612]** was behind that, so he made great efforts to construct galleys and other ships and to enlist men, as many as possible. He put an embargo on travel to Ifrīqiya and other parts of the Maghrib. As a result of this he assembled more than had ever been known; some say three hundred vessels.

After the interruption of communications with Ifrīqiya Emir al-Ḥasan ibn ‘Alī expected that the enemy would descend upon Mahdiyya, so he ordered war materials to be prepared, the walls to be repaired and soldiers to be mustered. A great number of locals and Arabs came to him.

In Jumādā I[9] of the year 517 [June–July 1123] the Frankish fleet set sail with 300 ships carrying a thousand and one horses.[10] However, after they had left Marsā ‘Alī,[11] the wind scattered them and many ships sank. The survivors made landfall on the island of Qawṣara[12] which they conquered, killing the people there, taking captives and plunder. From there they arrived at Ifrīqiya and descended on the

9 Correct Jumādā II in the text.

10 Not as a precise figure but meaning a large quantity.

11 i.e. ‘Alī's Harbour, otherwise Marsala.

12 i.e. present-day Pantelleria (see *EI(2)*, iv, 805).

fortress known as al-Dīmās towards the end of Jumādā I [late July 1123]. A body of Arabs who were there gave battle. Al-Dīmās is an impregnable fortress, overlooking the sea, with a second fort in its centre.

Al-Ḥasan sent the troops that he had against the Franks, while he remained in Mahdiyya with a detachment to guard it. The Franks took al-Dīmās, while encircled by the Muslim forces. A few nights later the fighting for the inner fort intensified. At night-time the Muslims gave a great shout which made the earth shake and cried out 'God is great.' Terror struck the hearts of the Franks, who did not doubt that they were under attack by the Muslims. They rushed to their galleys and with their own hands killed many of their horses. However, the Muslims took four hundred horses as booty. Only one horse got away with the Franks. The Muslims acquired all that the Franks left behind and killed all who were unable to climb aboard their ships.

After the Franks had embarked on their ships, they stayed for eight days, unable to disembark [**613**] and land. When they despaired of freeing their comrades who were in al-Dīmās, they set sail, while the Muslims taunted them with shouts of 'God is great' and insults. The forces of the Muslims remained besieging the fortress of al-Dīmās with multitudes too numerous to count, but they could not take it because it was so impregnable and strong. When there was no more water for the Frankish defenders and they became tired of constant fighting night and day, they opened the fortress gate and came out. They were slain to the last man. That was on Wednesday 15 Jumādā II this year [8 August 1123]. Their occupation of the fortress had lasted sixteen days.

When the Franks returned defeated, Emir al-Ḥasan sent out victory announcements to all the lands.[13] Poets made many verses about this episode but we have not mentioned any for fear of being tedious.

How the Franks took Khartbirt and then lost it again

In Rabīʿ I [May 1123] the Franks conquered Khartbirt in Diyār Bakr. This came about as follows. Balak ibn Bahrām ibn Artuq, who was lord of Khartbirt, besieged the castle of Karkar,[14] which is near to Khartbirt. The Franks in Syria heard this news and Baldwin, king of the Franks, marched there with his troops to raise the siege, fearing that Balak would grow powerful if he captured it. When Balak heard of his approach, he moved to meet him. They clashed in battle during Ṣafar [April 1123] and the Franks were defeated. Their king was taken prisoner along with a number of their leading knights. Balak imprisoned them in the citadel of Khartbirt, where were also Joscelin, lord of Edessa, and other Frankish leaders whom he had made captive in the year 515 [1121–2]. In Rabīʿ I [May 1123] Balak left Khartbirt

[13] For these events and a victory letter, by ʿAbd al-ʿAzīz ibn Shaddād, see Tijānī, *Riḥla*, 335–9.

[14] The modern Gerger in Turkey, a fortress south-east of Malatya (see Krawulsky, 606).

and went to Ḥarrān, which he captured. Meanwhile the Franks employed a trick to win over some of the garrison, emerged from prison and seized the citadel.

[**614**] King Baldwin rode off under cover of darkness[15] and made his way to his own lands. The news reached Balak, lord of Khartbirt, who returned there with his troops and put it under siege. He pressed hard on the defenders in the citadel and so recovered it from the Franks. He stationed troops there to guard it and again left.

The killing of the sultan's vizier and the return of Ibn Ṣadaqa to the caliph's vizierate

During this year Sultan Maḥmūd arrested his vizier, Shams al-Mulk 'Uthmān ibn Niẓam al-Mulk, and put him to death. The reason for this was that, when he advised the sultan to withdraw from the war with the Georgians and the sultan went against him (which was his best course), the sultan had a change of heart towards him. His enemies spread evil reports about him, called attention to his irresponsibility and his lack of learning and understanding of good government. The sultan's opinion of him became very bad.

Later Shihāb al-Dīn Abū'l-Maḥāsin, Sultan Sanjar's vizier, died. He was a nephew of Niẓām al-Mulk. Abū Ṭāhir al-Qumī, an enemy of the house of Niẓām al-Mulk, followed him as vizier. He worked on Sultan Sanjar until the latter sent to Sultan Maḥmūd ordering him to arrest his vizier, Shams al-Mulk. The arrival of the messenger coincided with his change of attitude towards him, so he arrested him and handed him over to Ṭughāyuruk, who sent him to his town, Khalkhāl, and imprisoned him there.

Abū Naṣr the Comptroller, dubbed al-'Azīz, said to Sultan Maḥmūd, 'We cannot be sure that Sultan Sanjar will not send to ask for the vizier. If he joins him, we cannot be sure that he will not be the cause of some trouble.' There was enmity between the two. The sultan therefore ordered his execution. When the executioner[16] entered his cell to kill him, [**615**] Shams al-Mulk said, 'Allow me a moment to pray two *rak'a*s.' When he performed his prayer, he began to tremble. He said to the executioner, 'My sword is better than yours. Kill me with mine and do not make me suffer.' He was killed on 2 Jumādā II [28 July 1123]. When the Caliph al-Mustarshid bi-Allāh heard of that, he dismissed his brother, Niẓām al-Mulk Aḥmad from his vizierate and restored Jalāl al-Dīn Abū 'Alī ibn Ṣadaqa to that office. Niẓām al-Mulk took up residence in the Octagon[17] which is in the

---

[15] The literal translation of the text is 'took the night as a camel.' A literary reference?

[16] In *Muntaẓam*, ix, 247, named as 'Antar the Eunuch. Note the continuation: 'He took the executioner's sword, inspected it and said, "My sword if sharper (*amḍā*) than this..."'

[17] In Arabic *al-Muthammana*. Presumably the same structure is intended in *Muntaẓam*, ix, 249: 'In Jumāda I [518] the construction of the Octagon was completed' (June–July 1124). The Octagon is also mentioned below under the year 530. See p. [**43**]. It is where al-Muqtafī was enthroned (*ujlisa*) and received oaths of allegiance.

Niẓāmiyya Madrasah at Baghdad. Al-ʿAzīz the Comptroller's days in office did not last long before he was killed, as we shall relate, recompense for bringing about the death of the vizier [Shams al-Mulk].

Account of Sultan Maḥmūd's success against the Georgians

This year the damage caused by the Georgians in Islamic lands became serious and the situation was very hard for the people, especially the inhabitants of Darband Shirwān.[18] A large body of their notables travelled to the sultan and complained to him about what they had to suffer and informed him of their weakness and inability to defend their land. The sultan came to them after the Georgians had reached Shamākhī[19] and camped in an orchard there. The Georgians advanced towards him and his army were in great fear of them.

The Vizier Shams al-Mulk ʿUthmān ibn Niẓām al-Mulk advised the sultan to retire. When the inhabitants of Shirwān heard of that, they sought out the sultan and said to him, 'We shall fight as long as you remain with us. If you withdraw and leave us, Muslim spirits will weaken and they will be destroyed.' He accepted what they said and remained where he was.

The army spent the night in great trepidation, anxious about the intended battle. However, God brought them a deliverance [**616**] of His making. He cast dissension and enmity between the Georgians and the Qipjāq, who came to blows that night and departed like men defeated. God spared the Muslims the need to fight. The sultan remained in Shirwān for a while and then returned to Hamadhan, where he arrived in Jumāda II [27 July–24 August 1123].

Conflict between the Maghribis and the army of Egypt

A large gathering of Lawāta tribesmen from the Maghrib arrived in Egypt this year, where they caused serious disturbances and depredations. They did some terrible things. Al-Ma'mūn ibn al-Baṭa'iḥī, who had become the vizier in Egypt after al-Afḍal, gathered the Egyptian army and, having marched against them, fought and defeated them. He captured or killed a vast number of them, and imposed on them a fixed annual tribute. They returned to their own lands and al-Ma'mūn returned to Egypt in triumph and victorious.

Miscellaneous events

In Ṣafar [April 1123] al-Mustarshid bi-Allāh ordered the Baghdad wall to be built

[18] Modern Derbent on the coastal strip between the Caucasus and the Caspian Sea.
[19] Modern Shemakha, west of Baku at the eastern end of the Caucasus.

and that the necessary expenditure should be raised from the city. This was a hardship for the inhabitants but a great amount was collected. When the caliph learnt of the inhabitants' dislike of this, he ordered the repayment of what had been taken from them, which made them happy and brought down many blessings on his head. It is said that Vizier Aḥmad ibn Niẓām al-Mulk offered 15,000 dinars of his own money and said, 'We shall raise what is outstanding in instalments from the leading men of the state.' [**617**] The people of Baghdad themselves worked on this project, doing the work in shifts. The inhabitants of each quarter worked separately to the sound of drums and pipes. They decorated the city and built [festive] domes there.[20]

This year the syndic of the Alids was dismissed and the house of 'Alī ibn Aflaḥ was demolished. The caliph used to honour the latter but it transpired that both men were spies for Dubays, keeping him informed of affairs. The caliph added the function of syndic of the Alids to that of syndic of the Abbasids, held by 'Alī ibn Ṭirād.

Emir Balak gathered his troops together this year and went to invade Syria. The Franks confronted him and a battle was fought, in which the Franks were defeated and a large number of their commanders and their infantry were killed.

In most lands this year there was a severe famine, worst of all in Iraq. The price of a *kāra* of coarsely ground wheat reached six dinars and ten *qīrāṭ*s. High mortality resulted and chronic diseases from which many people died.

This year 'Abd Allāh[21] ibn al-Ḥasan ibn Aḥmad ibn al-Ḥasan, Abū Nu'aym ibn Abī 'Alī al-Ḥaddād al-Iṣbahānī died. He was born in the year 463 [1070–71] and was one of the leading Ḥadīth scholars who travelled much in search of Ḥadīth.

This year Ṭughtakīn, lord of Damascus, went to Homs and attacked the city. He plundered and burnt much of it and put it under siege. The local lord Khīr Khān[22] was in the citadel. He sent for aid to Ṭughān Arslān,[23] who set out with a large force, so Ṭughtakīn retired to Damascus.

This year the Egyptian fleet met the fleet of the Venetians in battle. Victory went to the latter and a number of ships of the Egyptian fleet were captured. The rest returned safely.

[**618**] Emir Maḥmūd ibn Qarāja, lord of Hama, this year went to the fortress of Apamea and made a surprise attack on the suburb. An arrow from the citadel hit him in the arm and gave him great pain. He returned to Hama and extracted the arrow-head from his arm but it turned gangrenous and he died as a result. The people he governed gained release from his wickedness and tyranny. When

---

[20] This section is much abbreviated from its source, *Muntaẓam*, ix, 245, which makes it clear that the decorating of the city etc. was to celebrate the circumcision of the caliph's sons and nephews.

[21] Called 'Ubayd Allāh in *Muntaẓam*, ix, 247.

[22] Following the variant reading of the name, as previously.

[23] See above p. [**554**].

Ṭughtakīn heard the news, he sent an army to Hama, seized it and added it to his lands. He appointed a governor and installed a force there to protect it,

[619] The Year 518 [1124–1125]

Account of the death of Balak ibn Bahrām ibn Artuq and Timurtāsh's acquisition of Aleppo

In Ṣafar of this year [20 March–17 April 1124] Balak ibn Bahrām ibn Artuq, lord of Aleppo, arrested Emir Ḥassān al-Ba'labakkī, lord of Manbij, and then marched to Manbij and put it under siege. The city fell and then he besieged the citadel but it held out. The Franks set out to make him raise the siege, to prevent his becoming stronger by its acquisition. When they drew near, he left men to engage the citadel and with the rest of his troops marched towards the Franks. He met, fought and broke them, killing a great many. He then returned to his siege of Manbij, but, while he was fighting the defenders, he was hit and killed by an arrow, shot by an unknown person. The army fell into confusion and dispersed, and Ḥassān escaped from confinement.

Ḥusām al-Dīn Timurtāsh ibn Īlghāzī ibn Artuq was with his cousin Balak. He carried his dead body back to the outskirts of Aleppo and then took over the town on 20 Rabī' I [7 May 1124]. The siege of the citadel of Manbij was discontinued and its lord Ḥassān returned. Meanwhile Timurtāsh became established in Aleppo and took control there. He then appointed a deputy whom he trusted and assigned him the troops and other personnel that he needed, before returning to Mardin, because he saw that Syria was a frequent battle-ground with the Franks and he was a man who loved calm and the easy life. After his return to Mardin, he lost Aleppo, as we shall relate, God willing.

[620] Account of the Franks' conquest of Tyre in Syria

The city of Tyre belonged to the Alid caliphs in Egypt and continued to do so until the year 506 [1112–13]. There was a governor there, acting for al-Afḍal Emir al-Juyūsh, the vizier of al-Āmir bi-Ahkām Allāh the Alid, and he was entitled 'Izz al-Mulk. The Franks had besieged the city and pressed hard on it. They ravaged its land more than once. When the year 506 came, the king of the Franks made his preparation and gathered his forces to march to Tyre. The inhabitants were fearful and sent to Atabeg Ṭughtakīn, lord of Damascus, beseeching him to send them an emir of his to take charge of them and protect them. The city would be his. They said to him, 'Unless you send us a governor and troops, we will surrender the place to the Franks.' He therefore sent a force and appointed a governor for them, called Mas'ūd, who was determined, brave and knowledgeable in war and its stratagems. He reinforced him with troops and sent them supplies and money, which he distributed among them.

The morale of the inhabitants improved but the khutbah for al-Āmir, the ruler of Egypt, was not changed, nor was the coinage. A letter was sent to al-Afḍal in Egypt informing him of the situation and saying, 'When someone arrives from Egypt to take control and defend the place, I shall surrender it to him,' and asking that the fleet would continue to provide men and materials. Al-Afḍal expressed his thanks for this, praised Ṭughtakīn and approved of his decision to act as he had done. He equipped a fleet and sent it to Tyre, so that the situation of the inhabitants improved and remained so until the year 516 [1122–3] after the death of al-Afḍal. A fleet was then despatched as normal and the commander of the fleet was ordered to trick Emir Mas'ūd, the governor of Tyre appointed by Ṭughtakīn, arrest him and take over the city.

The reason for this was that the people of Tyre had made many complaints about him to al-Āmir bi-Aḥkām [**621**] Allāh, the ruler of Egpt, because of his actions in opposition to them and the harm he did them. They followed the plan. The fleet set sail and anchored at Tyre. Mas'ūd came to greet the commander and, when he went aboard the commander's ship, he was locked up. The commander went ashore and seized the city. The fleet returned to Egypt with Emir Mas'ūd, who was well received, recompensed and then sent back to Damascus.

The governor sent by the Egyptians put the population's minds at rest and contacted Ṭughtakīn with humble prayers and offers of support and explained that the reason for what he had done was the complaints against Mas'ūd from the people of Tyre. Ṭughtakīn gave him a friendly reply and himself offered assistance.

When the Franks heard that Mas'ūd had left Tyre, their desire for the city grew stronger and they convinced themselves that they would conquer it. They began to muster and equip themselves to undertake a siege. The governor for the Egyptians heard the news and realised that he lacked the strength and the forces to repel the Franks, because he was short of troops and supplies. He communicated that to al-Āmir, who saw that he should restore Ṭughtakīn to the governorship of Tyre. He sent to tell him that, so Ṭughtakīn took power in Tyre and stationed troops and other personnel there that he thought sufficient.

The Franks came and put it under siege in Rabī' I of this year [18 April–17 May 1124]. They tightened their grip with constant attacks. Food ran short and the defenders became tired of fighting and their morale weakened. Ṭughtakīn came to Bānyās to be near them and to protect his territory, with the hope that, if the Franks saw that he was close, they might withdraw, but they made no move. They persevered with the siege. Ṭughtakīn sent to Egypt for help but no help was sent. The days passed by and the population faced destruction. Ṭughtakīn then opened talks and it was agreed that he would surrender the city to the Franks, who would allow the troops and the populace there to leave [**622**] with whatever of their money, goods and other things that they could manage. These were the terms agreed upon. The gates of the city were opened and the Franks took control. The population departed and was scattered throughout the lands, having carried away what they could manage and abandoned what they could not. The Franks did not interfere with anybody and only the weak, who were incapable of moving, remained behind.

The Franks took over the city on 23 Jumādā I [8 July 1124]. Its conquest greatly weakened the Muslims, for it was one of the strongest and most impregnable of cities. May God restore it to Islam and assuage the hearts of the Muslims with its recovery, through Muḥammad and his family.

The dismissal of al-Bursuqī as prefect of Iraq and the appointment of Yarunqush al-Zakawī

This year al-Bursuqī was removed from the office of prefect of Iraq and Sa'd al-Dawla Yarunqush al-Zakawī was appointed to it. This came about because al-Bursuqī was shunned by al-Mustarshid bi-Allāh, who sent to Sultan Maḥmūd requesting him to dismiss al-Bursuqī from Iraq and send him back to Mosul. The sultan agreed with this and accordingly sent to al-Bursuqī commanding him to return to Mosul and occupy himself with Jihad against the Franks. When he learnt of this, al-Bursuqī embarked on a collection of taxes. Yarunqush's deputy arrived and al-Bursuqī handed over authority to him. The sultan sent a young son of his with his mother to be with al-Bursuqī. When the youngster came to Iraq, the troops and other officials went out to greet him and all necessaries were provided for him. The day he made his entrance was a memorable day. Al-Bursuqī took charge of him and set out for Mosul with the young child and his mother.

When al-Bursuqī went to Mosul, 'Imād al-Dīn Zankī ibn Āqsunqur was in Basra, where al-Bursuqī had sent him to run its affairs. His management had clearly been such as to win the admiration of people. He constantly [**623**] pursued the Arabs and fought them in their settlements until he drove them away into the desert. Then al-Bursuqī sent ordering him to join him but Zankī said to his followers, 'We are tired of our present situation. Every day Mosul has a new emir, who wants[1] us to serve him. I have thought that I might go to the sultan and join him.' They recommended this course, so he set out and came to the sultan at Isfahan. He was received with honour, assigned Basra and sent back there.

How al-Bursuqī took control of Aleppo

In Dhū'l-Ḥijja of this year [9 January–6 February 1125] Āqsunqur al-Bursuqī took the city of Aleppo and its citadel. This came about because, after the Franks had taken the city of Tyre, as we have related, their ambitions grew and their morale

---

[1] Reading *yurīd* instead of *nurīd* of the edition.

was high. Convinced that they could take the whole of Syria, they collected large numbers of troops. Dubays ibn Ṣadaqa, lord of al-Ḥilla, came to them and fed their ambitions further, especially for Aleppo. He said, 'Its inhabitants are Shiites. They lean towards me for sectarian reasons. When they see me, they will surrender the city to me.' He offered them many promises in return for help, and said, 'I shall be here as an obedient deputy for you.' They therefore marched against and besieged Aleppo, keeping up fierce attacks. They reconciled themselves to a long stay and agreed that they would not leave until they had taken it. They built houses against the heat and the cold.

Seeing this, the defenders' spirits weakened and they feared they were doomed. Their lord Timurtāsh's weakness and incompetence were plain to see and they were short of food. When they saw to what end they were being driven on this account, they put their minds to finding a way of escape and they realised that there was none but al-Bursuqī, lord of Mosul. So they sent to him for assistance, asking [**624**] him to come so that they could surrender the city to him. Al-Bursuqī gathered his troops and set out, sending, while on the way, to those in the city to say, 'I cannot come to you, while the Franks are engaging you in battle, unless you surrender the citadel to my deputies and my men take control of it. I do not know what God Almighty may have in store when I meet the Franks. If we are defeated when Aleppo is not in the hands of my men to serve as a refuge for me and my army, not one of us will survive, and then Aleppo and other places will fall.'

They accepted this and handed over the citadel to his deputies. Once they were established there and in control, he proceeded with his troops. When he came in sight of Aleppo, the Franks withdrew, while he watched them. Those in his advance guard wished to charge them but he personally stopped them, saying, 'We have been spared their evil purposes and we have saved the city. The best plan is to leave them until Aleppo is settled and we put its affairs to right and build up its monetary resources. Then we shall attack them and bring them to battle.' After the withdrawal of the Franks, the inhabitants emerged and welcomed him joyfully. He resided there until he had organised and settled its affairs.

Miscellaneous events

The rains did not come this year in Iraq, Mosul, the Jazīra, Syria, Diyār Bakr and many lands. Foodstuffs were in short supply and prices rose high in all lands. This lasted until the year 519 [1125].

This year Manṣūr ibn Ṣadaqa, the brother of Dubays, came to Baghdad in custody. He fell ill there and the caliph summoned doctors and ordered them to treat him. He was brought to the palace, placed in a chamber and his own men given access to him.

[**625**] Dubays left Syria this year after his departure from Aleppo and sought out Prince Ṭughril, whom he incited against the caliph and urged to attack Iraq. The

result was what we shall relate under the year 519 [1125-6], God willing.

This year the leader of the Ismāʿīlīs and lord of Alamūt, al-Ḥasan ibn al-Ṣabbāḥ, died. We have already mentioned such of his history as allows one to understand where he stood for bravery, wisdom and experience.

This year the people of Āmid rose up against the Ismāʿīlīs who were there and had become very numerous. They killed about seven hundred of them and their position there weakened after this event.

David, the King of the Abkhāz, died this year, as did the following:

Shams al-Dawla [Sulaymān] ibn Najm al-Dīn Īlghāzī.[2]

In Ṣafar [April 1124] Muḥammad ibn Marzūq ibn ʿAbd al-Razzāq al-Zaʿfarānī,[3] one of the pupils of al-Khaṭīb al-Baghdādī.

Aḥmad ibn ʿAlī ibn Burhān, Abū'l-Fatḥ, the lawyer, known as Ibn al-Ḥammāmī, because his father was a bath-house (*ḥammām*) keeper. He was a Ḥanbalī and studied law with Ibn ʿAqīl. He later became a Shāfiʿī and studied with al-Ghazālī and al-Shāshī.

---

2 The Artuqid prince of Mayyafariqin, see Ṣibṭ ibn al-Jawzī, 117; Hillenbrand, *Muslim Principality*, 44-8.

3 According to *Muntaẓam*, ix, 249, he died the previous year, on 29 Ṣafar/28 April 1123.

The Year 519 [1125-1126]

How Prince Ṭughril and Dubays ibn Ṣadaqa came to Iraq and then withdrew

We have already mentioned that Dubays ibn Ṣadaqa came to Prince Ṭughril from Syria. When he came, Ṭughril met him with honour and kindness and made him one of his leading intimates and emirs. Dubays encouraged him to attack Iraq, presented it as an easy operation and guaranteed that he would conquer it. Ṭughril therefore set out with him and they arrived at Daqūqā with a large force. Mujāhid al-Dīn Bahrūz wrote from Takrit to give the caliph intelligence of their movements. The caliph made preparations to march to intercept them, and ordered Yarunqush al-Zakawī, the prefect of Iraq, to be ready for war and to mobilise the troops, the Bakjiyya emirs and others. The number of troops amounted to 12,000, apart from the infantry and the people of Baghdad. Weapons were distributed.

The caliph moved out on 5 Ṣafar [13 March 1125], preceded by his men of state on foot, and left by the Gate of Victory, which he had ordered to be opened[1] during those days and to which he had given that name. He camped in the open country at al-Shammāsiyya, while Yarunqush camped at al-Sabtī.[2] Later he moved and camped at al-Khāliṣ on 9 Ṣafar [17 March 1125].

When Ṭughril heard that the caliph had left Baghdad, he turned aside to the Khurasan road and his followers scattered to plunder and pillage. He himself lodged at the Hospice of Jalūlā'. The Vizier Jalāl al-Dīn Ibn Ṣadaqa marched towards him with a large force and halted at al-Daskara. Ṭughril and Dubays moved to al-Hārūniyya, while the caliph came and camped at al-Daskara, he together with his vizier. It was settled between [**627**] Dubays and Ṭughril that they should march to cross Diyālā and Tāmarrā, cut the bridge at al-Nahrawān, and that Dubays should remain to guard the crossings while Ṭughril went on before to Baghdad to take and sack it. They set out with this plan and both crossed Tāmarrā. Ṭughril halted between it and Diyālā.

Dubays moved to join up with Ṭughril but God Almighty decreed that Prince Ṭughril was stricken by a severe fever. Rain, the like of which had never been seen, fell on them. The waters rose and flash floods followed, while the caliph was at al-Daskara. Dubays took 200 horse and made for Ma'arrat al-Nahrawān,[3] ill and suffering from lack of sleep. He and his men suffered from the rain and wet they encountered. They also had nothing to eat, under the impression that Ṭughril and

---

[1] A new gate in the palace wall opposite the polo ground (*al-ḥalba*).

[2] Of doubtful spelling, it is a village in the Baghdad region (cf. *Muntaẓam*, x, 246, s.a. 569).

[3] This should probably be *mashra'at* of al-Nahrawān, see the following note.

his men would join them, but these were delayed due to what we have mentioned. Dubays' men halted, starving and overcome by the cold. Suddenly thirty camels came into view, carrying clothing, turbans, tunics, bonnets and other items, and also carrying various sorts of prepared meals, all brought out of Baghdad for the caliph. Dubays seized everything. They put on the new clothes, having discarded their wet garments, ate the food and went to sleep in the sun after what they had suffered the previous night.

When the people of Baghdad heard the news, they donned their weapons and remained on guard night and day. The report came to the caliph and his troops that Dubays had taken Baghdad, so the caliph left al-Daskara, and his troops came in a rout as far as al-Nahrawān. They abandoned their baggage, thrown down on the road and disregarded by all. Had it not been that God was kind to them through Prince Ṭughril's fever and delay, the army would have perished and the caliph too. They would have been caught, as the irrigation courses were filled with mud and water from the flash floods. They were in tatters and if a hundred horsemen had caught up with them, they would have been destroyed.

The caliph's banners arrived while Dubays and his men were sleeping. The caliph advanced [**628**] and came in sight of Diyālā. Dubays was camped west of al-Nahrawān [Canal] and the [pontoon] bridge was attached the east side of it. When Dubays caught sight of the caliph's parasol, he kissed the ground in obeisance to the caliph and said, 'I am his cast-off slave. May the Commander of the Faithful forgive his slave.' The caliph showed him mercy and intended to make peace with him until the Vizier Ibn Ṣadaqa arrived and persuaded him to change his mind. Dubays mounted his horse and took a position opposite the army of Yarunqush al-Zakawī, conversing with them and joking. Then, on the orders of the vizier, at the end of the day the infantry crossed to fasten the bridge. Thereupon Dubays left to return to Prince Ṭughril and the caliph sent a force with the vizier to pursue him, and himself entered Baghdad again, from which he had been absent twenty-five days.[4]

---

[4] Although clearly a source for Ibn al-Athīr, *Muntaẓam*, ix, 252–3, has differences:

Ṭughril and Dubays camped at Rādhān and when they learnt that the caliph had left [Baghdad], they turned off [sic] the Khurasan Road and camped at the Hospice of Jalūlā'. Vizier Abū 'Alī ibn Ṣadaqa went with a large force to al-Daskara. Prince Ṭughril went to al-Hārūniyya, while the caliph moved to camp at Daskara. Ṭughril and Dubays planned to cross the Diyāla and Tāmarrā to make a surprise attack on Baghdad and cut the bridge at Nahrawān. Dubays would guard the crossings and Ṭughril would occupy himself with the plundering of Baghdad. They both crossed Tāmarrā and, while Ṭughril camped between Diyāla and Tāmarrā, Dubays crossed Diyāla with the understanding that the prince would follow him. However, that night the prince fell ill, continous rain followed and the water rose in the Diyāla. The caliph was in camp at Daskara, unaware of Dubays' plan. Dubays came to the wharf (*mashra'a*) of Nahrawān with 200 horse and no baggage. He camped there, exhausted. They had rain all night and were without tents, supplies and fodder. [The capture of the caliph's supply caravan and panic in Baghdad] The caliph made a swift march to Nahrawān and before Dubays knew what was happening the caliph's banners came into

Subsequently Prince Ṭughril and Dubays withdrew and went to Sultan Sanjar. They passed by Hamadhan and imposed the payment of a large sum on its inhabitants, which they took and then concealed themselves in those regions. Information about them reached Sultan Maḥmūd who marched speedily towards them but they retreated before him, pursued by his armies. They entered Khurasan, the land of Sultan Sanjar, and complained to him of the caliph and Yarunqush al-Zakawī.

Account of al-Bursuqī's capture of Kafarṭāb and his defeat by the Franks

This year al-Bursuqī assembled his armies and went to Syria, where he attacked Kafarṭāb, besieged it and took it from the Franks. He then went to the castle of 'Azāz, in the district of Aleppo to the north, whose lord was Joscelin, and put it under siege. The Franks gathered, their knights and foot-soldiers, and set out to raise the siege. Al-Bursuqī met them in a pitched battle in which all fought fiercely and stubbornly. In the end the Muslims were defeated and men killed or captured. The number of the Muslim dead was more than one thousand. Al-Bursuqī returned defeated to Aleppo, [**629**] left his son Mas'ūd in charge there and crossed the Euphrates to Mosul to assemble troops and return to the battle. There followed what we shall relate, if God Almighty wills.

The killing of Ma'mūn al-Baṭā'iḥī

In Ramaḍān [October 1125] al-Āmir bi-Aḥkām Allāh the Alid, the ruler of Egypt, arrested his vizier, Abū 'Abd Allāh ibn al-Baṭā'iḥī, who bore the title al-Ma'mūn. He crucified him and his brothers.

His career began as follows. His father was one of al-Afḍal's spies in Iraq, who died without leaving anything. His mother married again and left him poor. He attached himself to a man to learn the building trade in Egypt. Later he started to carry goods in the Great Market. Time after time he entered al-Afḍal Emir al-Juyūsh's house with the porters. Al-Afḍal noticed that he was nimble and lithe, well-coordinated and pleasant of speech. Impressed by him, he asked about him and was told that he was the son of so-and-so. He took him into service as one of his household attendants. He made progress in his service, gained a great position and rose ever higher until he became vizier.

He was generous, magnanimous, a warrior, given to shedding blood but extremely cautious. He used to enquire a great deal into the affairs of people, both

---

view. When he saw them he kissed the earth where he was (*fī makānihi*) ... The caliph sent Naẓar the Eunuch to Baghdad to calm the people. A proclamation was made in Baghdad that the army should leave quickly to pursue Dubays with Vizier Ibn Ṣadaqa. The caliph returned to his palace after an absence of 25 days.

commoners and the elite throughout the lands, Egypt, Syria and Iraq. During his period of office denunciations became very prevalent.

As for the reason for his killing, he had sent Emir Ja'far, al-Āmir's brother, to kill al-Āmir and become caliph. This was what had been agreed between the two of them. Abū'l-Ḥasan ibn Abī Usāma, who was a favourite of al-Āmir and close to him, heard of this. He had suffered harm and rejection from the vizier, [**630**] so he came before al-Āmir and told him of the plan. The caliph arrested and crucified al-Ma'mūn. This is the reward of those who repay kindness with wickedness.

Miscellaneous events

During this year the following died:

Shams al-Dawla Sālim[5] ibn Mālik, lord of Qal'at Ja'bar, formerly known as Qal'at Dūs.

Cadi Abū Sa'd Muḥammad ibn Naṣr ibn Manṣūr al-Harawī in Hamadhan, assassinated by the Bāṭinīs. He had gone to Khurasan with a message from the caliph for Sultan Sanjar. He was killed on his return. He was a man possessed of abundant virtue and a very high position in the Saljūq state.

Hilāl ibn 'Abd al-Raḥmān ibn Shurayḥ ibn 'Umar ibn Aḥmad, a descendant of Bilāl ibn Ribāḥ, the muezzin of God's Prophet (may God bless him and give him peace). His *kunya* was Abū Sa'd.[6] He travelled extensively, studied Hadīth and recited the Koran. He died in Samarqand.

---

5 An Uqaylid prince, cousin of Sharaf al-Dawla Muslim (see Eddé, *Description*, 8, note 4 and references cited; Hillenbrand, *Muslim Principality*, 65, note 96).

6 According to *Muntaẓam*, ix, 154, his grandfather's name was Surayj and his *kunya* Abū Sa'īd.

The Year 520 [1126-1127]

Hostilities between the Franks and the Muslims in Andalusia

This year the power of Ibn Rudmīr the Frank became great in Andalusia and he lorded it over the Muslims. He took the field with a great gathering of Franks and reconnoitred deep into Muslim territory. He even arrived close to Cordoba and indulged in much plundering, enslaving and killing. The Muslims assembled in a large force, exceedingly numerous, and marched against him. He was not strong enough to meet them, so took secure refuge in a powerful fortress called Arnisol.[1] They besieged him there but he surprised them with a night attack. The Muslims fled and many were killed. He then returned to his lands.

Account of the attack on Ismā'īlī lands in Khurasan

This year the Vizier [Mu'īn al-Mulk] Mukhtaṣṣ al-Mulk[2] Abū Naṣr Aḥmad ibn al-Faḍl, Sultan Sanjar's vizier, ordered an attack on the Bāṭinīs, that they should be killed wherever they were and wherever they were seized, their property looted and their women enslaved. He sent one army to Ṭuraythīth,[3] a place of theirs, and another to Bayhaq in the district of Nishapur. In this district there was a settlement which was special to them, called Ṭazar.[4] Their leader there was a man called al-Ḥasan ibn Samīn.

[632] The vizier sent a detachment of the army to every part of their districts and urged them to kill each and everyone they might meet. Each detachment set out in the direction it had been sent to. As for the settlement in the area of Bayhaq, the main force made for that and killed all there. Likewise the force despatched to Ṭuraythīth massacred its inhabitants, seized their property as booty and then returned.

How the Ismā'īlīs took the castle of Bānyās

This year the fortunes of the Ismā'īlīs in Syria prospered and their offensive power grew great. In Dhū'l-Qa'da [18 November-17 December 1126] they took Bānyās. This came about because Bahrām, the nephew of al-Asadābādhī, when his uncle

---

1 Arabic: Arnīsūl, near Lucena, about 40 miles south-east of Cordoba.

2 This vizier bore two titles.

3 A small town, between Kāshmar and Torbat-e Haydariyya (cf. Krawulsky, 132-3).

4 The edition has Ṭarz. For Ṭazar, see Yāqūt, iii, 537, and Krawulsky, 119.

was killed in Baghdad, as we have mentioned, fled to Syria and became the leader of the Ismā'īlīs there. He travelled all over the country, calling the riff-raff and the lowly to his creed. Those with no wits responded to him and his following became numerous, except that he was concealing his person, so as not to be recognised. He dwelt in Aleppo for a while and grew close to[5] its ruler, Īlghāzī.

Īlghāzī wanted to gain his backing because the people feared his and his men's wickedness, for they would kill all who opposed them and attacked their allies. Īlghāzī advised Ṭughtakīn, lord of Damascus, to instal him in his service for this reason. He accepted this idea and took him in. At this juncture Bahrām made his identity public and proclaimed his mission. His following grew among all who desired evil-doing and trouble-making. The Vizier Abū 'Alī Ṭāhir ibn Sa'd al-Mazdaqānī[6] helped him, wishing to use him for his own ends. Bahrām's wickedness increased and his position became immensely powerful. His following became many times larger than it had been. Were it not for the fact [**633**] that the common people of Damascus were predominantly of the Sunnī persuasion and that they were strongly opposed to his creed, he would have seized the city.

Bahrām saw that the Damascenes were fiercely hostile to him and feared their enmity. He asked Ṭughtakīn for a fortress in which he and his followers could take refuge. The vizier suggested that he be given the castle of Bānyās. This was done and after he had gone there, his supporters flocked to him from all directions. He now became a serious danger and his public preaching a huge challenge. The situation became very difficult for the lawyers, the ulema and the men of religion, especially the Sunnīs and the respectable and peaceable men, and yet they were unable to utter a single word, firstly for fear of their authorities and secondly for fear of the wickedness of the Ismā'īlīs. Nobody dared condemn the state of affairs and they waited on the turn of events.

The death of al-Bursuqī and the succession of his son, 'Izz al-Dīn Mas'ūd

On 8 Dhū'l-Qa'da [25 November 1126] the lord of Mosul, Qasīm al-Dawla Āqsunqur al-Bursuqī, was killed in Mosul. The Bāṭinīs assassinated him on Friday in the congregational mosque, when he was at the Friday prayers with the people. The previous night he had seen in his dream that several dogs attacked him. He killed some but the rest did him some harm. He related this dream to his companions and they advised him not to leave the house for several days. He said, 'I shall not miss Friday prayers for anything.' They overcame his determination, however, and prevented him from going out to the service. He had a mind to go,

---

5 *Nafara ilā*, the opposite of *nafara 'an*, 'to shun.' The variant reading, *nafaqa 'alā*, would mean 'to find a welcome with.'

6 The text has Abū Ṭāhir ... al-Marghīnānī. For correct name, see Ibn Qal., 215, and below p. [**652**].

nevertheless, and took a Koran copy to consult it. The first thing he saw was 'God's purpose was a fore-ordained decree.'[7] He therefore rode to the mosque in his normal way. He was praying in the first rank when he was leapt on by [**634**] ten or more persons, the same number as the dogs he had dreamed of. They wounded him with their daggers and he with his own hand wounded three of them but he was slain (God have mercy on him).

He was a Turkish mamluke, benevolent and a lover of men of religion and the righteous. He saw what was just and did it. He was one of the best governors, observing prayers at their proper times and keeping vigil for prayers during the night.

My father (God bless him) told me the following from someone who used to serve him, who said: 'I was a household servant with him. Every night he used to pray a lot. He would personally perform his ritual ablutions and not use anyone's services. I saw him one winter's night at Mosul, when he had risen from his bed, dressed in a short woollen gown. He had a pitcher in his hand and he walked towards the Tigris to fetch some water. The cold stopped me from rising, but then I was frightened of him and so rose to face him and take the pitcher from him. He stopped me and said, "You poor thing! Go back to bed. It is cold." I endeavoured to take the pitcher but he refused to give it me and sent me back to bed. He then performed his ablutions and began his prayers.'

When he was killed, his son 'Izz al-Dīn Mas'ūd was in Aleppo, guarding it against the Franks. His father's men sent him the news and he set out for Mosul, which he entered the beginning of Dhū'l-Ḥijja [18 December 1126]. He was good to his father's men there and confirmed his vizier, al-Mu'ayyad Abū Ghālib ibn 'Abd al-Khāliq ibn 'Abd al-Razzāq, in his office. The emirs and the troops gave him their allegiance. He travelled down to wait upon Sultan Maḥmūd, who received him kindly and sent him back. Nobody in his father's lands disputed his position.

An enquiry about those Bāṭinīs and a full investigation into their background took place. It was said that they had been apprenticed to a cobbler in the Īliyā Lane.[8] He was summoned and promised generous treatment if he confessed, but he did not. He was threatened with death, and then said, 'They came to kill him several years ago, but they had no opportunity until [**635**] this present time.' His hands, his feet and his penis were cut off and he was stoned to death.

It is remarkable that the lord of Antioch sent to 'Izz al-Dīn ibn al-Bursuqī to tell him of the killing of his father before the news reached him [from elsewhere]. The Franks had heard it before him because of their intense interest in learning about Muslim affairs.

---

7 Koran, xxxiii, v. 38.

8 Darb Īliyā, presumably in Mosul but unidentified. Perhaps a sort of apprenticeship is intended by the phrase *jalasa ilā* (lit. 'sit towards'). Cf. Dozy, *Supplément*, i, 207: a student 'sits towards' a study group (*ḥalqa*).

After ‘Izz al-Dīn was established in control, he arrested Emir Bābakr ibn Mīkhā'īl, one of the senior emirs. He demanded that his nephew surrender the castle of Irbil to Emir Faḍl and Abū ‘Alī, the sons of Abū'l-Hayjā'. His nephew had taken it from him in the year 517 [1123–4]. He wrote to his nephew and he duly surrendered Irbil to the two persons mentioned.

Account of the disagreement that arose between al-Mustarshid bi-Allāh and Sultan Maḥmūd

An antipathy had arisen between Yarunqush al-Zakawī, the prefect of Baghdad, and the agents of the Caliph al-Mustarshid bi-Allāh, which led to the caliph's threatening him. He feared for his life, so left Baghdad to go to Sultan Maḥmūd in Rajab of this year [23 July–21 August 1126]. He complained to him, warned him of the caliph, telling him that he had led armies, experienced battles and grown in stature. If the sultan did not deal speedily with him by attacking Iraq and entering Baghdad, the caliph would grow in strength and manpower and would defy him. Then to recover what the sultan now had would be impossible.

The sultan set out for Iraq and the caliph sent to him, telling him of the poverty and weakness that the land and its people were experiencing because of Dubays and the evil-doings of his troops there, and that the people were suffering a serious famine because of the lack of crops and other foodstuffs, as the peasants had fled their lands. He asked [**636**] the sultan on this occasion to delay until the state of the country improved and then to return. None would resist him. A large sum of money was offered him to do this.

When the sultan heard this communication, he was the more convinced of what al-Zakawī had stated and he refused to delay but persisted in his plan and marched on with all haste. On receipt of this news the caliph, his family and womenfolk and the descendants of caliphs with him crossed to the West Bank in Dhū'l-Qa‘da [18 November–17 December 1126], manifesting anger and a determination to abandon Baghdad, if the sultan moved against it. When he left his palace everybody wept copiously. The like had never been seen before. Learning of this, the sultan was extremely upset and affected. He sent to conciliate the caliph and ask him to return to his palace. The caliph replied that it was essential for the sultan to withdraw at this time. The people were dying because of the great famine and the ruin of the land and the sultan could not think it in his religion to add to their suffering, as he witnessed their state. If the sultan did not withdraw, he himself would depart from Iraq to avoid witnessing what the people would meet with through the coming of his soldiers.

These words angered the sultan, who continued towards Baghdad. The caliph remained on the West Bank, and when the Feast of Sacrifice [27 December 1126] came, he preached to the people and led them in the prayers. They wept to hear his address. He despatched ‘Afīf the Eunuch, one of his closest courtiers, with an army to Wāsiṭ to deny it to the lieutenants of the sultan. The sultan sent against him 'Imād al-Dīn Zankī ibn Āqsunqur, who at that time held Basra. He had broken with al-Bursuqī and joined the sultan, who had given him Basra as his fief.

When 'Afīf reached Wāsiṭ, 'Imād al-Dīn moved towards him and camped on the east bank, while 'Afīf was on the west bank. 'Imād al-Dīn sent threatening him with battle and ordering him to retire, but he refused to do so. 'Imād al-Dīn crossed the river and battle was joined. [**637**] 'Afīf's troops were routed and a great number were slaughtered. A similar great number were captured. 'Afīf was ignored and escaped because of the friendship that existed between the two of them.

The caliph gathered together all the boats and blocked up the gates of the Caliphal Palace, except for the Nubian Gate. He ordered the palace chamberlain, Ibn al-Ṣāḥib, to remain there to protect the palace. Apart from him not one of the caliph's household remained on the East Bank.

On 20 Dhū'l-Ḥijja [6 January 1127] the sultan arrived at Baghdad and camped at the Shammāsiyya Gate. Some of the troops entered Baghdad and lodged in the houses of the populace, who complained of that to the sultan. The latter ordered their ejection but those who owned a house remained in the city. The sultan continued to write to the caliph about coming back and the search for an accommodation but this was refused. There were skirmishes between the two forces and the common folk were abusing the sultan from the West Bank most abominably. In due course a detachment of the sultan's troops entered the Caliphal Palace and sacked the Tāj and the caliph's apartments on 1 Muḥarram in the year 521 [17 January 1127]. At that, the people of Baghdad raised a clamour, gathered together and called for military action, coming forward from every direction. When the caliph saw them, he left his pavilion with the parasol over his head and the vizier before him, ordered the drums and trumpets to sound, and cried at the top of his voice. 'Onward, scions of Hāshim!' He ordered the boats to be brought out and the pontoon bridge to be assembled. The people crossed in one rush. In the palace the caliph had a thousand men hidden in the cellars. They emerged, while the sultan's troops were occupied in their plundering. Several of their emirs were seized. The mob sacked the house of the sultan's vizier, the houses of several of the emirs and those of 'Azīz al-Dīn the Comptroller and Master Awḥad al-Zamān, the doctor. A great crowd of soldiers were killed in the alleys.

Next the caliph crossed to the East Bank, accompanied by 30,000 fighting men from the people of Baghdad and the countryside. He ordered ditches to be dug, which was done at night, and so they protected Baghdad from the sultan's army. A scarcity of provisions fell upon the army and their situation became serious. There was fighting every [**638**] day at the city gates and along the bank of the Tigris. The caliph's forces planned to make a surprise attack on the sultan's army but Emir Abū'l-Hayjā' the Kurd, lord of Irbil, betrayed them. He went out as though he was intending to fight but he and his troops joined the sultan.

The sultan had sent to 'Imād al-Dīn in Wāsiṭ, commanding him to come in person, with his troops in boats and also overland on horseback. He collected every boat in Basra, loaded them with fighting men, and amassed much military equipment. He set out upstream and, when he was near Baghdad, he ordered all in the boats and on land to don their gear and to make a show of their firmness and zeal. The boats sailed on and the land troops on the Tigris bank spread far and wide. Together they filled the scene on land and water. The people beheld an amazing sight, which dazzled and astounded them. The sultan and his troops rode to meet them and saw a sight the like of which they had never seen before. 'Imād al-Dīn became a great figure in their eyes. At that moment the sultan decided to storm Baghdad and make every effort by land and on water. When the Imam al-Mustarshid bi-Allāh saw affairs in this shape and that Emir Abū'l-Hayjā' had left him, he agreed to make peace. Envoys went to and fro and terms were settled. The sultan apologised for what had occurred. He was forebearing, hearing vituperation directed at him but not punishing it. He pardoned the whole people of Baghdad.

The enemies of the caliph advised the sultan to burn Baghdad but he did not do so. He said, 'Not for the whole world is it worth doing such a thing.' He remained in Baghdad until 4 Rabī' II 521 [19 April 1127]. The caliph paid him cash according to the terms of agreement and presented him with weapons, horses and other thing. The sultan then fell ill at Baghdad and his doctors advised him to leave. He set out for Hamadhan and recovered after his arrival there.

[639] The battle between Ṭughtakīn the Atabeg and the Franks in Syria

This year the Franks, their princes and counts, united and marched to the district of Damascus. They camped in Marj al-Ṣuffar at a village called Shaqḥab[9] close to Damascus. The position was serious for the Muslims and their fear intense. Atabeg Ṭughtakīn, the lord, wrote to the emirs of the Turkomans in Diyār Bakr and elsewhere and mobilised them. He himself had set out from Damascus to meet the Franks and left his son Tāj al-Mulūk Būrī in charge there. As often as[10] a group came to him there, he welcomed them most hospitably and sent them on to his father. When they were assembled, Ṭughtakīn rode with them against the Franks. They met towards the end of Dhū'l-Ḥijja [ended 15 January 1127][11] and fought a fierce battle. Ṭughtakīn fell from his horse and his men thought that he had been killed, so they fled. Ṭughtakīn remounted and caught them up, as they were pursued by the Franks. The Turkomans were left unable to catch up with the Muslims in their rout. They were left behind. When they saw that the Frankish knights had pursued those that fled and that the camp and their infantry had no guard and protector, they charged the foot-soldiers and killed them. Only the odd

[9] Correct the text's Saqḥabā. The Mamlukes defeated the Mongols in 702/1303 at Shaqḥab, about 18 miles from Damascus, north-west of Ghabaghib.

[10] Both the edition and *Kāmil* (Thornberg), x, 451, have *kamā*. Ms. Pococke 346, fol. 53b, has *kullamā*, which is the reading followed.

[11] Ibn Qal., 212–14, places these events towards the end of 519/early 1126.

fugitive survived. The Turkomans plundered the Franks' camp, their tents and their money and all that they had with them, including an altar with gold and gems beyond value. They plundered all this and returned to Damascus safe and sound, not having lost anyone. When the Franks came back from the trail of those that had fled and saw their infantry slain and their baggage ransacked, they departed in a full-scale rout with every man for himself. This was a strange occurrence, for two sides to be routed each one by the other.

[640] Miscellaneous events

This year the Franks besieged Rafaniyya in Syria, which was in Muslim hands. They pressed very hard on the place and took it.

There died this year Abū'l-Fatḥ Aḥmad ibn Muḥammad ibn Muḥammad al-Ghazālī, the preacher. He was the brother of the Imam Abū Ḥāmid Muḥammad [al-Ghazālī]. Abū'l-Faraj ibn al-Jawzī found fault with him[12] in many things, for example, that in his sermons he cited ḥadīths that he did not consider to be genuine. It is amazing that he attacked him in this manner, since his own writings and sermons are stuffed full of the like. We pray God to save us from ever slandering people. Would to God I understood! Did not al-Ghazālī possess a single virtue worth mentioning alongside the bad things that he mentioned and attributed to him, to avoid being himself accused of partiality and bias?

---

[12] Ibn al-Jawzī's strictures are in *Muntaẓam*, ix, 260–62.

[641] The Year 521 [1127-1128]

The Martyr, Atabeg Zankī, is appointed prefect of Iraq

In Rabīʿ II this year [16 April-14 May 1127] Sultan Maḥmūd entrusted the office of prefect of Iraq to ʿImād al-Dīn Zankī ibn Āqsunqur. The reason for this was that, when ʿImād al-Dīn came up from Wāsiṭ with his superbly equipped body of men, as we have mentioned, and performed in the protection of Wāsiṭ and Basra and those regions in a manner that was beyond anyone else, he gained a place in the sultan's heart and in the hearts of his emirs. When the sultan decided to leave Baghdad, he considered who was suitable to exercise the prefecture of Iraq and who would look after his interests with the caliph. He reviewed his emirs and the leading men of the state and saw amongst them nobody who could undertake this office as ʿImād al-Dīn would. He consulted on this and everyone suggested him. They said, 'We cannot patch up this break nor restore the prestige of this office. No one is strong enough in spirit to tackle this perilous task but ʿImād al-Dīn.' This agreed with his views, so he made the appointment and entrusted him with the office in addition to the fief that he held. He then left Baghdad with a heart at ease as regards Iraq. Matters were as he anticipated.

[642] The sultan's return from Baghdad and the vizierate of Anūshirwān ibn Khālid

This year on 10 Rabīʿ II [25 April 1127] Sultan Maḥmūd left Baghdad after settling its affairs. When he decided to depart, the caliph sent him robes of honour and many mounts. The sultan accepted everything and left.

When he was far away from Baghdad, he arrested his vizier, Abū'l-Qāsim ʿAlī ibn al-Qāsim al-Anasābādhī in Rajab [13 July-11 August 1127] as he suspected him of siding with al-Mustarshid bi-Allāh because he undertook the caliph's cause and concluded peace in a way that gave clear evidence of that. His enemies undermined his position. After his arrest the sultan sent to Baghdad and summoned Sharaf al-Dīn Anūshirwān ibn Khālid, who was resident there. When this became known, presents arrived for him from all and sundry, even the caliph. He left Baghdad on 5 Shaʿbān [16 August 1127] and came to the sultan when he was at Isfahan. The vizieral robe was bestowed upon him and he kept it for about ten months. Then he resigned and gave up the position, and returned to Baghdad in Shaʿbān of the year 522 [August 1128].

As for the Vizier Abū'l-Qāsim, he remained under arrest until Sultan Sanjar came to Rayy in the year 522 [1128], released him from confinement in Dhū'l-

Ḥijja [26 November–24 December 1128] and restored him to Sultan Maḥmūd's vizierate, this being his second period in office.

[643] The death of 'Izz al-Dīn ibn al-Bursuqī and the appointment of 'Imād al-Dīn Zankī as governor of Mosul and its districts

This year 'Izz al-Dīn Mas'ūd ibn al-Bursuqī, lord of Mosul, died. His death occurred in al-Raḥba. The course of events that led to his going there was as follows. After his affairs became well settled in his area and he had written to Sultan Maḥmūd and petitioned him to be appointed to his father's governorship in Mosul and elsewhere, the sultan acceded to his request. 'Izz al-Dīn organised and arranged matters and his troops became numerous. He himself was brave and energetic. He was ambitious to seize control of Syria, so gathered his forces and set out, intending to attack Damascus. He began with al-Raḥba, which, when he arrived, he put under siege. An acute illness took hold of him, while he was besieging it. He accepted the submission of the citadel but shortly afterwards died. The defenders regretted their surrender of the citadel.

After his death he was left lying on a carpet, unburied. His troops disbanded and plundered one another, too occupied to deal with him, but then later he was buried. A young brother of his succeeded him but his lands fell under a mamluke of al-Bursuqī's, called al-Jāwulī. He administered the youngster's affairs and sent to the sultan requesting that the lands should be settled on al-Bursuqī's son, and he offered large sums of money to achieve that.

The envoys on this business were the Cadi Bahā' al-Dīn Abū'l-Ḥasan 'Alī ibn al-Qāsim al-Shahrazūrī and Ṣalāḥ al-Dīn Muḥammad, the emir-chamberlain of al-Bursuqī. They came to the court of the sultan to speak to him on this matter. They were afraid of al-Jāwulī and not happy about his loyalty nor the freedom with which he ruled. Ṣalāḥ al-Dīn and Naṣīr al-Dīn Jaqar, who became Atabeg 'Imād al-Dīn's deputy in Mosul, had a meeting. They were connected by marriage. Ṣalāḥ al-Dīn mentioned to him the matter **[644]** concerning which he had come and revealed his hidden thoughts. Naṣīr al-Dīn warned him against Jāwulī and condemned his loyalty to him. He convinced him that Jāwulī only spared him and people like him because he needed them. If and when his request was granted, he would spare none of them.

Naṣīr al-Dīn discussed with him the possibility of petitioning for 'Imād al-Dīn to be appointed and promised him offices and many fiefs, and the same for the Cadi Bahā' al-Dīn al-Shahrazūrī. Ṣalāḥ al-Dīn agreed and together they went to Bahā' al-Dīn and broached this matter with him. They promised him whatever he wanted. He agreed with what the two of them asked. He and Ṣalāḥ al-Dīn rode to the vizier's residence (at that time the vizier was Sharaf al-Dīn Anūshirwān ibn Khālid) and said to him, 'You know, as the sultan does too, that the lands of the Jazīra and Syria are in the hands of the Franks. Their power is great and they have seized most of them. Their dominion is now from the borders of Mardīn to 'Arīsh in Egypt, apart from the towns surviving in Muslim hands. With his valour, experience and the loyalty of his troops al-Bursuqī restrained part of their hostility and evil. Since his death their ambition has increased. Here we have his son, a young infant. The lands must have an energetic, brave man, endowed with good sense and experience, to defend and protect them and guard their integrity. We have reported the state of affairs to avoid shortcomings or any source of weakness for Islam and the Muslims. Blame would attach itself to us particularly and people would say, "Why did you not inform us clearly of the situation?'"

The vizier reported what they said to the sultan, who approved it and thanked them for it. He summoned them and consulted them about who was fit for the position. They mentioned several, including 'Imād al-Dīn Zankī, **[645]** and presented on his behalf, as an offering for the sultan's treasury, a considerable sum. The sultan consented to appoint him because he knew of his competence for the job. He summoned Zankī and appointed him to all Mosul's lands and wrote his letters patent for the post.

Zankī set out and started with al-Bawāzīj, to take it and make it a source of strength and support, because he feared that Jāwulī might perhaps block his access to his lands. After entering al-Bawāzīj he proceeded to Mosul. When Jāwulī heard of his approach, he marched out to meet him with all his army. When he saw him, Jāwulī dismounted, kissed the ground before him and returned to Mosul in attendance on him. Zankī entered the city in Ramaḍān [10 September–9 October 1127] and sent Jāwulī to al-Raḥba, which he assigned him as a fief. He himself remained in Mosul, reforming its affairs and settling its organisation. He appointed Naṣīr al-Dīn as governor of the citadel at Mosul and made him governor of all the other castles. He made Ṣalāḥ al-Dīn Muḥammad his emir-chamberlain and Bahā' al-Dīn chief cadi in all his territories, giving the latter increased properties, fiefs and respect. Zankī initiated nothing without consulting him.

Having finished matters at Mosul, he left to go to Jazīrat Ibn 'Umar, held by mamlukes of al-Bursuqī. They resisted him, so he besieged them and then negotiated, offering large sums if they gave up. They did not respond, so he intensified his attacks. The Tigris was between him and the city. He ordered his men to take to the water and cross to the city. They did so. Some swam across, some crossed in boats and yet others on inflated skins. They overwhelmed the citizens who had emerged from the city on to the land between the city and the Tigris, known as al-Zallāqa, to prevent any attempted crossing of the Tigris. When the troops crossed, they engaged them and tried to stop their landing, but 'Imād al-Dīn's soldiers were too many for them, so the defenders fled back into the city and shut themselves behind its walls. 'Imād al-Dīn thus gained al-Zallāqa. Seeing this, those within lost heart and weakened, realising for sure that the city would be taken [one way or another], either by surrender or by force of arms. They therefore sent asking for terms, which Zankī agreed to. **[646]** He was with his troops at al-Zallāqa. The city was yielded to him and he and his army made their entrance.

That very night the Tigris rose so much that it lapped the city walls and al-Zallāqa was covered with water. Had he remained there that day he and his army would have been drowned without a single survivor. Having witnessed this people were convinced that fortune favoured him and that a career which began like this was destined to be great.

He then left Jazīrat Ibn 'Umar for Nisibis, which was held by Ḥusām al-Dīn Timurtāsh, lord of Mardin. When Zankī began a siege, Ḥusām al-Dīn went to his cousin, Rukn al-Dawla Da'ūd ibn Suqmān ibn Artuq, lord of Ḥiṣn Kayfā and other places, and asked for assistance against Atabeg Zankī. Dā'ūd promised to help him in person and mobilised his troops. Timurtāsh returned to Mardin and sent messages by pigeon post to Nisibis to tell the troops there that he and his cousin were coming with a large army to raise 'Imād al-Dīn's siege, and ordering them to hold out for five days.

While the Atabeg was in his tent a pigeon landed on a tent facing him. He ordered it to be caught and saw it had a message. He read its contents and ordered a different message to be written, as follows: 'I have sought out my cousin Rukn al-Dawla, who has promised to aid me and gather his troops. His arrival will not be delayed more than twenty days.' It also ordered them to hold the city for this period until they came. He attached it to the pigeon and released it. It entered Nisibis and when the defenders read the message, they were dismayed and knew that they were unable to hold the city for this time. Therefore they sent to the Martyr and reached a peaceful settlement. They yielded him the city and the plans of Timurtāsh and Dā'ūd were frustrated. This is indeed a strange tale.

Having taken Nisibis, Zankī marched to Sinjār, where the inhabitants resisted but then came to terms with him [**647**] and handed him the town. From there he sent prefects to al-Khābūr, all of which he took. Then he went to Ḥarrān, which was in Muslim hands. Edessa, Sarūj, al-Bīra and all those regions belonged to the Franks, on account of whom the people of Ḥarrān were suffering greatly and very hard-pressed, as those lands were devoid of a champion to protect them or any authority to defend them. When Zankī approached Ḥarrān, the citizens came out to offer him allegiance and hand the town over to him. Having taken it, he sent to Joscelin, lord of Edessa and those regions, with a proposal, and made a truce for a short period. His aim was to be free to repair the lands and to raise troops. The most important project for him was to cross the Euphrates into Syria and gain the city of Aleppo and others in Syrian lands. Peace was now arranged and the people gained security. We shall be telling how Aleppo was taken, if God Almighty wills.

Miscellaneous events

In this year Mu'īn al-Mulk Abū Naṣr Aḥmad ibn al-Faḍl, Sultan Sanjar's vizier, was killed. The Bāṭinīs assassinated him, for he had an excellent record for fighting them and a goodly intention [to pursue that end]. God bestowed martyrdom upon him.

This year the sultan appointed as prefect of Baghdad Mujāhid al-Dīn Bahrūz when Atabeg Zankī left for Mosul.

Al-Ḥasan ibn Salmān[1] was appointed professor at the Niẓāmiyya in Baghdad.

This year Sultan Sanjar dealt a blow to the Bāṭinīs at Alamūt. He killed a great number of them. It was said that the dead exceeded 10,000 souls.

[648] There died this year:

'Alī ibn al-Mubārak, Abū'l-Ḥasan al-Muqrī, known as Ibn al-Fā'ūs, a Ḥanbalī of Baghdad, in Shawwāl [October 1127]. He was a pious man.

Also in Shawwāl, Muḥammad ibn 'Abd al-Malik ibn Ibrāhīm ibn Aḥmad, Abū'l-Ḥasan ibn Abī'l-Faḍl al-Hamadhānī al-Farḍī, the historian.[2]

---

1 Correct the text's 'Sulaymān', cf. *Muntaẓam*, x, 5. For the death of Ibn Salmān, see below p. [**670-71**].

2 *Muntaẓam*, x, 8: he died the eve of Saturday 6 Shawwāl/15 October 1127. See the brief discussion about him in Cahen, 'Historiography', 61-2.

[649] # The Year 522 [1128]

Account of Atabeg 'Imād al-Dīn Zankī's taking the city of Aleppo

At the beginning of Muḥarram this year [6 January 1128] 'Imād al-Dīn Zankī ibn Āqsunqur took the city of Aleppo and its citadel. We shall relate how this came about. We have mentioned that al-Bursuqī took Aleppo and its citadel in the year 518 [1124–5] and left his son Mas'ūd there as his deputy. When al-Bursuqī was killed, Mas'ūd went away to Mosul and took control there, having left as his lieutenant in Aleppo an emir called Qūmān. Later he appointed an emir named Qutlugh-Aba, whom he sent to Qūmān with a written order for the hand-over of the city. Qūmān said, 'Between 'Izz al-Dīn [Mas'ūd] and me there is a secret sign which I have not seen here. I shall not hand over without it.' Their agreed sign was a picture of a gazelle. Mas'ūd ibn al-Bursuqī could draw very well. Qutlugh-Aba returned to Mas'ūd, who had been besieging al-Raḥba, but found that he had died, so he hurried back to Aleppo again.

The people learnt of his death and the headman, Faḍā'il ibn Badī', gave the city up. The leading men offered Qutlugh-Aba their obedience and brought Qūmān down from the citadel after he had verified that his master Mas'ūd was dead. They gave him one thousand dinars. Qutlugh-Aba took over the citadel on 24 Jumādā II in the year 521 [7 July 1127]. After some days the extent of his tyranny and wickedness became evident. He laid his hands on people's property, especially inheritances which he appropriated. Evil men became his associates, while most people felt a deep aversion.

Present in the city was Badr al-Dawla Sulaymān ibn 'Abd al-Jabbār ibn Artuq, who had formerly been **[650]** the ruler there. The populace followed him and rose up on the eve of Tuesday 2 Shawwāl [= 9 October 1127]. They arrested all the followers of Qutlugh-Aba who were in the city, most of whom were drinking on the morning of the Feast. They moved against the citadel, where Qutlugh-Aba and those with him took refuge, and put it under siege. Ḥassān, the lord of Manbij, and Ḥasan, the lord of Buzā'a, arrived at Aleppo to repair the situation but had no success.

The Franks heard of this and Joscelin with his troops advanced towards the city but was bought off and retired. After him came the ruler of Antioch with a body of Franks. The Aleppans dug a ditch around the citadel and prevented any entry from outside the city or any departure. The people were facing great danger up to the middle of Dhū'l-Ḥijja [22 December 1127].

'Imād al-Dīn had taken possession of Mosul and the Jazīra and had sent to Aleppo Emir Sunqur Darāz and Emir Ḥasan Qarāqūsh, senior emirs of al-Bursuqī, who had joined 'Imād al-Din with a powerful force. The latter had a document from the sultan appointing him to Mosul, the Jazīra and Syria. It was settled that Badr al-Dawla ibn ʻAbd al-Jabbār and Qutlugh-Aba should go to ʻImād al-Dīn in Mosul. This they did, and Ḥasan Qarāqūsh remained in Aleppo acting as a temporary governor. When Badr al-Dawla and Qutlugh-Aba arrived, ʻImād al-Dīn settled their differences but did not send either one of them back to Aleppo. He sent his chamberlain, Ṣalāḥ al-Dīn Muḥammad al-Yāghīsiyānī, with an army, who went up into the citadel, organised its affairs and put a governor in charge.

ʻImād al-Dīn Zankī set out for Syria with his levies and his standing troops and on the way he took Manbij and Buzāʻa. The people of Aleppo came out to welcome him and were delighted at his coming. He entered the town, took control of it and organised its affairs. He assigned its dependent lands as fiefs to his troops and emirs. After he had completed what he wanted, he seized Qutlugh-Aba's person and handed him over to Ibn Badīʻ, who blinded him in his house at Aleppo. Qutlugh-Aba died subsequently.[1] Ibn Badīʻ became apprehensive and fled to Qalʻat Jaʻbar, to whose ruler he appealed for protection, which was granted.

[651] As headman of Aleppo ʻImād al-Dīn appointed Abū'l-Ḥasan ʻAlī ibn ʻAbd al-Razzāq. Were it not for the fact that God Almighty was gracious to the Muslims by giving power to the Atabeg in Syrian lands, the Franks would have taken them. This was because they had been engaged in the siege of a certain Syrian town and, when Ẓahīr al-Dīn Ṭughtakīn learnt of that, he had gathered his forces and attacked, harassed and raided their lands, forcing the Franks to raise the siege to defend their lands against him. However, God decreed that he died this year and Syria lay open to them on all sides, lacking a man to undertake to fight for His people. God graciously gave to the Muslims ʻImād al-Dīn as ruler, whose deeds against the Franks we shall tell of, God willing.

Account of Sultan Sanjar's coming to Rayy

This year Sultan Sanjar left Khurasan to come to Rayy with a large army. The reason was that, when Dubays ibn Ṣadaqa came to Sanjar along with Prince Ṭughril, as we have already related, he continued to encourage Sanjar's ambitions concerning Iraq and to declare how easy it would be to attack it. He also kept suggesting to him that al-Mustarshid bi-Allāh and Sultan Maḥmūd were acting together to stop him. He persisted in this until Sanjar agreed to an expedition to Iraq. After setting out, he came to Rayy, when the Sultan Maḥmūd was at Hamadhan. Sultan Sanjar sent to summon him to see whether he was still obedient or whether he had changed as Dubays asserted. When the envoy came, Maḥmūd hastened to go to his uncle, who ordered all his army to welcome him on his arrival, gave him a seat with him on the royal dais and went to great lengths to honour him. He remained with him until the middle of Dhū'l-Ḥijja [10 December

[1] Note that *Zubdat al-ḥalab*, ii, 607, says that Zankī put him to death.

1128] and then Sultan Sanjar returned to Khurasan. He entrusted Dubays to Sultan Maḥmūd and enjoined him to honour him and restore him to his lands. Maḥmūd returned to Hamadhan, accompanied by Dubays, and then they both went to Iraq. When [**652**] they drew near to Baghdad, the vizier came out to meet the sultan. He arrived on 9 Muḥarram of the year 523 [2 January 1129].

The Vizier Abū'l-Qāsim al-Anasābādhī had been arrested by Sultan Maḥmūd but at his meeting with Sultan Sanjar he had been ordered to release him and this he had done. Sanjar established Abū'l-Qāsim as vizier for his daughter whom he married to Sultan Maḥmūd. When he came with him to Baghdad, Maḥmūd restored him to his vizierate on 24 Muḥarram [17 January 1129]. This was his second time in office.

Miscellaneous events

This year on 8 Ṣafar [12 February 1128] Atabeg Ṭughtakīn, lord of Damascus, died. He was a mamluke of Prince Tutush, son of Alp Arslān, and was wise and generous. He raided and waged Jihad against the Franks frequently, and ruled his subjects well, eager to be just to them. His honorific name was Ẓahīr al-Dīn (Upholder of the Religion). After his death his son Tāj al-Mulūk Būrī, the oldest of his sons, succeeded him according to the testament of his father, which named him as successor. He confirmed his father's vizier, Abū 'Alī Ṭāhir ibn Sa'd al-Mazdaqānī, in post.

On the first day of Rajab [1 July 1128] the Vizier Jalāl al-Dīn Abū 'Alī ibn Ṣadaqa, the caliph's vizier, died. His manner of life was good and his religious life excellent. He was modest and loved the men of religion, showing them much respect. He wrote some good poetry, and here is an example in praise of al-Mustarshid bi-Allāh:

> I have found men like water in taste and fineness:
> The Commander of the Faithful is its ice-cold drink.
> I have imagined the idea of wisdom as a figure drawn;
> The Commander of the Faithful is its model.
> Were it not for the path of religion, law and piety,
> I would say in reverence, 'Exalted is his glory!'

[**653**] After his death Sharaf al-Dīn 'Alī ibn Ṭirād al-Zaynabī was set up as a deputy, but later made full vizier. He was installed at the end of Rabī' II in the year 523 [21 April 1129]. He is the only Hāshimite[2] who served as vizier for the Abbasid caliphs.

[2] i.e. a descendant of the Banū Hāshim to which both the Prophet Muḥammad and al-'Abbās, the eponym of the Abbasid dynasty, belonged.

This year a strong wind blew which blackened the horizons. It brought red dirt resembling sand. Columns, as though they were flames, appeared in the sky. The people were terrified and turned to prayer and contrition, but their fears were lifted from them.

[654] The Year 523 [1128-1129]

Account of Sultan Maḥmūd's coming to Baghdad

In Muḥarram this year [25 December 1128-23 January 1129] Sultan Maḥmūd came to Baghdad after his return from meeting with his uncle, Sultan Sanjar. He was accompanied by Dubays ibn Ṣadaqa to repair his relations with the Caliph al-Mustarshid bi-Allāh. Dubays delayed behind the sultan but then entered Baghdad and lodged in the Sultanian Palace. He sought to be reconciled with the caliph but the caliph refused to agree to invest Dubays with any lands, although he offered 100,000 dinars for that.

Atabeg Zankī learnt that the sultan wanted to appoint Dubays to Mosul, so he produced 100,000 dinars and came in person to wait upon the sultan. Before the sultan had any inkling of his coming Zankī was waiting before the curtain,[1] having brought with him splendid gifts. He remained with the sultan for three days, who invested him with a robe of honour and sent him back to Mosul.

The sultan went out hunting and the shaykh of al-Mazrafa[2] prepared a great banquet for him at which all the sultan's army was fed. He showed him into a bath in his residence and prepared rose water instead of normal water. The sultan remained until 4 Jumādā II [25 May 1129] and then left for Hamadhan. He appointed Bahrūz as prefect of Baghdad, and al-Ḥilla was given to him as well.

[655] Account of Dubays' deeds in Iraq and the sultan's return to Baghdad

After the departure of the sultan to Hamadhan his wife died. She was the daughter of Sultan Sanjar and she it was who interested herself in the cause of Dubays and protected him. When she died, Dubays' position fell apart.

Then the sultan fell seriously ill. Dubays took a young son of his and set out for Iraq. When al-Mustarshid bi-Allāḥ heard of this, he set about raising troops. Bahrūz, who was in al-Ḥilla, fled from there and Dubays entered in the month of Ramaḍān [18 August-16 September 1129]. Having heard the news about Dubays, the sultan summoned the two emirs, Qizil and al-Aḥmadīlī. He said, 'You gave me an undertaking to produce [the person of] Dubays. I want you both to deliver him.' Al-Aḥmadīlī set out for Iraq to prevent Dubays from doing evil in those lands and bring him to the sultan. Dubays heard this news and sent to win the support of the

---

[1] This is probably to be understood as being the equivalent of 'in the ante-room' before being ushered into the immediate presence.

[2] Yāqūt, iv, 520: 'a large village on the Tigris above Baghdad (about 3 leagues distant).'

caliph, saying, 'If you show me goodwill, I shall give back much more than I have taken and be your humble slave.' Messengers went backwards and forwards, while Dubays was collecting money and men. Ten thousand horse assembled with him, who had arrived with 300. In Shawwāl [17 September-15 October 1129] al-Aḥmadīlī arrived at Baghdad and set out to follow Dubays' tracks.

Later the sultan came to Iraq, and hearing of this, Dubays sent him gifts of great value and presented 300 horses, shoed with gold, and 200,000 dinars to win the goodwill of the sultan and the caliph, but this was not forthcoming. The sultan arrived at Baghdad in Dhū'l-Qa'da [16 October-14 November 1129] and was met by the Vizier al-Zaynabī and other officials. When he verified that the sultan had arrived, Dubays departed into the desert. He made his way to Basra and took large sums of money and whatever revenue of the caliph and the sultan was there. The sultan sent 10,000 cavalry on his track but Dubays abandoned Basra and entered the desert.

[656] Account of the massacre of the Ismā'īlīs at Damascus

In what has preceded we have mentioned the killing of Ibrāhīm al-Asadābādhī at Baghdad, the flight of his nephew Bahrām to Syria and his gaining the citadel of Bānyās, to which he made his way. When he left Damascus he set up a deputy there to summon people to his beliefs. They multiplied and spread. He himself gained several fortresses, including, for example, al-Qadmūs. In Wādī al-Taym in the district of Baalbek there were the adherents of various sects, such as the Nuṣayrīs, the Druze and the Magians and others too. Their emir was called al-Ḍaḥḥāk. Bahrām marched against them in the year 522 [1128], laid siege to, and fought with, them.[3] Al-Ḍaḥḥāk came out to meet him with 1,000 men and, surprising Bahrām's troops, put them to the sword, killing a great number of them. Bahrām was slain. The survivors fled and entered Bānyās in a wretched state.

In Bānyās Bahrām had left as his lieutenant one of his leading followers whose name was Ismā'īl. He took his place and regrouped those that returned to him. He spread missionaries throughout the land and was also supported by al-Mazdaqānī. He took heart despite the rage he felt at this set-back and his anxieties.

In Damascus al-Mazdaqānī installed in place of Bahrām a man called Abū'l-Wafā', whose power and importance increased greatly. His following became numerous. He rose in Damascus and came to dominate the Muslims there. His sway was greater than that of the ruler Tāj al-Mulūk. In due course al-Mazdaqānī contacted the Franks to surrender to them the city of Damascus and for them to hand over the city of Tyre to him. This was agreed between them and they settled on a date, a Friday which they named. Al-Mazdaqānī agreed with the Ismā'īlīs that

---

[3] Enmity already existed because Bahrām had killed al-Ḍaḥḥāk ibn Jandal's brother, called Barq and described as a *muqaddam* (leader, chief) of Wādī al-Taym (Ibn Qal., 221-2).

[657] on that day they should seal off the gates of the mosque and not allow anyone to leave, in order that the Franks might come and seize the city. Knowledge of this reached Tāj al-Mulūk, lord of Damascus, who summoned al-Mazdaqānī. He came and when they were alone, Tāj al-Mulūk killed him and suspended his head from the citadel gate. He proclaimed about the city, 'Kill the Bāṭinīs', and 6,000 of them were put to death. That was in the middle of Ramaḍān [early September 1129].[4] Thus God saved the Muslims from their wickedness and turned their plotting back upon the infidels.

When this disaster had finished the Ismā'īlīs in Damascus, Ismā'īl, the ruler of Bānyās, feared that its populace might rise against him and his followers, which could lead to their destruction. He made contact with the Franks and offered to surrender Bānyās to them and move to their lands. On their agreement, the castle was given over to them and he, along with his followers, shifted into Frankish territory, where they experienced hardship, humiliation and shame. Ismā'īl died early in the year 524 [began 15 December 1129] and God saved the Believers from their wickedness.

Account of the Franks' siege of Damascus and their defeat

When the Franks heard of the killing of al-Mazdaqānī and the Ismā'īlīs at Damascus, they were very dismayed and regretted that they had not been able to achieve the take-over of Damascus. The disaster fell upon all of them. They all gathered, the king of Jerusalem, lord of Antioch, lord of Tripoli and other Frankish [rulers] and their counts and also those who had come by sea for trade or for pilgrimage. They gathered in a great host of about 2,000 knights and of infantry beyond counting. They marched to put Damascus under siege.

Hearing of this Tāj al-Mulūk gathered the Arab bedouin and the Turkomans. Eight thousand horsemen assembled with them. The Franks arrived during Dhū'l-Ḥijja [15 November–13 December 1129] and camped about the city. They sent to the dependent districts **[658]** of Damascus to forage and to raid. Tāj al-Mulūk heard that a large detachment had gone to Ḥawrān to plunder and fetch provisions, so he sent one of his emirs, known as Shams al-Khawāṣṣ, with a body of Muslims to meet them. They left on a wintry night of heavy rain and came upon the Franks the next day. They engaged them in battle and both sides held firm. Eventually the Muslims overcame and slew them. Only their commander and forty men with him escaped. What they had with them was seized, 10,000 loaded pack-animals, and 300 men were taken prisoner. The Muslims returned to Damascus without a scratch. When the Franks besieging Damascus learnt this, God cast terror into their

---

4 According to Ibn Qal., 223, Tāj al-Mulūk gave a signal to a trusted retainer who struck the fatal blows. The vizier was killed on Wednesday 17 Ramaḍān/4 September. The news spread immediately and the massacre began.

hearts and they departed as in a rout, having burnt the munitions and provisions that they were unable to carry. The Muslims pursued them in pouring rain and intense cold, killing all the stragglers. A great many of them were slain. Their investment of the city and their withdrawal happened during Dhū'l-Ḥijja.

Account of 'Imād al-Dīn Zankī's taking of the city of Hama

During this year[5] 'Imād al-Dīn Zankī ibn Āqsunqur, lord of Mosul, took Hama. This came about because he crossed over the Euphrates into Syria and announced that he was planning to wage Jihad against the Franks. He sent to the lord of Damascus, Tāj al-Mulūk Būrī, son of Ṭughtakīn, asking for his aid and requesting help in this Jihad. Būrī responded to his wish and sent men to secure undertakings and guarantees. When a written pact arrived, he despatched a force from Damascus with several emirs. He also sent to [**659**] his son Savinj, who was in Hama, ordering him to join up with this force and proceed with it to Zankī. He obeyed and all went to meet Zankī, who gave them a generous and kindly welcome. He did nothing for several days but then, in an act of treachery against them, arrested Savinj, Tāj al-Mulūk's son, and the emirs, officers in his army, seizing their tents and all the horses and mules they had, and imprisoned them in Aleppo. The rest ran away and that same day Zankī went to Hama, which, when he arrived there, was empty of fighting men to defend it, so he took complete control of it.

He then moved on to Homs. Its lord, Khīr Khān[6] ibn Qarāja, was with him in his army and he was the person who had suggested his treacherous dealing with Tāj al-Mulūk's son. Zankī now arrested him and besieged Homs, demanding from its lord, Khīr Khān, that he order his lieutenants and his son who were within to surrender it. He sent this order to them but they did not accept it and paid no attention to his words. Zankī continued his siege and his assaults on the defenders for a long time but was unable to take it. He therefore withdrew back to Mosul and took with him Savinj, son of Tāj al-Mulūk, and the Damascene emirs who were with him. To discuss their release messengers travelled to and fro between Zankī and Tāj al-Mulūk. A ransom of 50,000 dinars was stipulated, which was agreed by Tāj al-Mulūk, but nothing was actually concluded.

Miscellaneous events

This year Bohemond, the lord of Antioch,[7] took the castle of al-Qadmūs from the Muslims.

---

[5] This whole section is based on Ibn Qal., 227–8, but is there given under 524/1129–30.

[6] In the edition Q.r.jān. For support of this variant reading, see Ibn Qal., 228.

[7] i.e. Bohemond II (ruled 1126–30). Bohemond I had died in the West in 1111.

Also in this year the Ismāʿīlīs attacked ʿAbd al-Laṭīf ibn al-Khujandī, the leader [**660**] of the Shāfiʿīs in Isfahan, and killed him. He was a man of great qualities of leadership and much authority.

This year there died:

The Imam Abū'l-Fatḥ Asʿad ibn Abī Naṣr al-Mīhanī, the Shāfiʿī lawyer and professor at the Baghdad Niẓāmiyya. He was famous for his practice of disputation between the legal schools. He had studied with Abū'l-Muẓaffar al-Samʿānī. The caliph, the sultan and everybody held him in the greatest esteem.[8]

Ḥamza ibn Hibat Allāh ibn Muḥammad al-Sharīf al-ʿAlawī al-Ḥasanī al-Nīsābūrī. He heard and transmitted a great deal of Ḥadīth. He was born in the year 429 [1037–8]. He united nobility of lineage with nobility of soul and piety. In his own beliefs he was a Zaydī.[9]

---

8 See *Muntaẓam*, x, 13.

9 He died in Muḥarram/January 1129 (*Muntaẓam*, x, 13–14), an adherent of a moderate branch of Shiism that recognised the imamate of Zayd ibn ʿAlī ibn al-Ḥusayn ibn ʿAlī and thereafter admitted no automatic inheritance of religious leadership. See s.v. al-Zaydiyya in *EI(2)*, xi, 477–81.

[**661**]

The Year 524 [1129-1130]

How Sultan Sanjar took the city of Samarqand from Muḥammad Khān and how Maḥmūd, the son of the same Muḥammad Khān, succeeded

In Rabīʿ I [12 February-13 March 1130] Sultan Sanjar took the city of Samarqand. This came about because, when he first took it, he established there Arslān Khān Muḥammad ibn Sulaymān ibn Bughrā Khān Dā'ūd. The latter became semi-paralysed and made his son his deputy, known as Naṣr Khān, who was energetic and brave. There was in Samarqand an Alid, a lawyer and a madrasah teacher, who had the power of 'loosing and binding' and authority in the city. He and the city headman conspired to kill Naṣr Khān, which they did at night. His father Muḥammad Khān, who was absent, was outraged and dismayed. He had another son who was absent in the land of Turkistan, so he sent a messenger and summoned him. When he approached Samarqand, the Alid and the headman went out to welcome him, but he killed the Alid immediately and arrested the headman.

His father Arslān Khān [Muḥammad] had despatched a messenger to Sultan Sanjar to bid him come, thinking that his son would not successfully establish his position with the Alid and the headman. Sanjar made his preparations and set out for Samarqand. After Arslān Khān's son had overcome those two, he regretted that Sanjar had been summoned, so he sent to tell him that he had dealt with the Alid and the headman and that he and his son remained loyal but asked him to return to Khurasan. This infuriated Sanjar. He halted for a few days and while he was hunting he caught sight of twelve men, fully armed. He arrested and tortured them, and they confessed that Muḥammad Khān had sent them to assassinate him. He put them to death and marched to Samarqand, which he took [**662**] by assault, sacked part but protected the rest. Muḥammad Khān took refuge from him in one of the fortresses there, from which after a while Sanjar persuaded him to come down on offer of terms. When he did so, Sanjar honoured him and sent him to his daughter, who was Sultan Sanjar's wife, and he remained with her until he died.

For a while Sanjar stayed in Samarqand until he had taken its money, munitions and stores. He then entrusted the city to Emir Ḥasan Takīn and returned to Khurasan. It was not long before Ḥasan Takīn died. Sanjar installed as his successor Maḥmūd ibn Muḥammad Khān ibn Sulaymān ibn Dā'ūd aforementioned. It has been claimed that the circumstances were not as we have related. An account of the different version will be given under the year 536 [1141-2] because it is necessary to mention it there.

‘Imād al-Dīn Zankī’s conquest of the fortress of al-Athārib and the defeat of the Franks

When ‘Imād al-Dīn Zankī had finished his business with the Syrian towns, Aleppo and its dependencies, having taken and reorganised them, he returned to Mosul and the Jazīra to rest his army. Then he ordered them to prepare for a military expedition, which they did fully and completely. He returned to Syria and made for Aleppo. He strengthened his determination to attack and besiege the fortress of al-Athārib because it caused serious damage to the Muslims.

This fortress is distant about three leagues from Aleppo and lies between it and Antioch. The Franks there took a proportion of Aleppo’s revenues from all its western districts, even from a mill outside the Gardens’ Gate belonging to the Aleppans and only the width of the highroad from the city. The populace suffered extreme hardship and oppression from the Franks, who every day raided them and plundered their property. When the Martyr [Zankī] saw this state of affairs, he determined to besiege this fortress. He duly set out and descended upon it.

[663] Learning of this, the Franks gathered their cavalry and infantry. They realised that this was a battle which would determine the future. They mobilised all and left none of their potential strength unexploited. When they were ready, they marched towards Zankī. He consulted his companions about what he should do and each one advised withdrawal from the fortress, for to meet the Franks in their own territory was a dangerous risk, the outcome of which nobody could know. He said to them, ‘If the Franks see that we have given way before them, they will be emboldened, will follow us and destroy our lands. Come what may we must confront them.’

He left the fortress and advanced towards them. They met and drew up their battle lines. Each side stood firm before its enemy and the fighting became furious. Then God Almighty sent down His aid for the Muslims and they were victorious. The Franks were routed very badly and many of their knights fell into captivity and large numbers were slain. ‘Imād al-Dīn ordered his troops to be ruthless. He said to them, ‘This is the first battle we have had with them. Let us make them so taste of our might that the fear of it remains in their hearts.’ They did as he commanded them. I passed over this terrain at night in the year 584 [1188–9] and I was told, ‘Until the present time many bones still remain here.’

When the Muslims had completed their victory, they returned to the fortress and took it by assault. They killed or took prisoner all within. ‘Imād al-Dīn demolished it and and razed it to the ground.[1] Until now it has remained a ruin. From there he went to the citadel of Ḥārim, also a Frankish possession, in the vicinity of Antioch,

---

[1] The chronology is dubious and Ibn al-Athīr is inconsistent. According to *Zubdat al-ḥalab*, ii, 259, Athārib did not fall to Zankī until 1 Rajab 529/17 April 1135. It was occupied by the Muslims until they abandoned it to the Byzantines in 532/1138, as Ibn al-Athīr himself records (see below p. [**57**]).

and besieged it. The inhabitants offered him half the revenue of the town of Ḥārim and proposed a truce. He agreed to this and left them, after the Muslims had ridden all over those regions. The morale of the Infidels was weakened and they realised that something they had not reckoned on had come to their lands. The most they hoped for now was to preserve what they held, after they had aspired to a total conquest.

[664] How 'Imād al-Dīn Zankī also took Sarjā and Dārā

Having finished his business with al-Athārib and those regions, he returned to the Jazīra. Stinging attacks by Ḥusām al-Dīn Timurtāsh ibn Īlghāzī, lord of Mardin, and his cousin Rukn al-Dawla Dā'ūd ibn Suqmān, lord of Ḥiṣn Kayfā, had already come to his ears. He returned to deal with them and besieged Sarjā,[2] which is between Mardin and Nisibis. Ḥusām al-Dīn, Rukn al-Dawla, the lord of Āmid and others too came together and gathered a large host of Turkomans, that reached 20,000 in number. They marched against 'Imād al-Dīn and prepared for battle in those regions, but he defeated them and took Sarjā.

My father told me the following: 'When Rukn al-Dawla Dā'ūd was defeated, he made for Jazīrat Ibn 'Umar and sacked it. 'Imād al-Dīn heard of this, he set out for the Jazīra and wished to enter Dā'ūd's land but withdrew because of the narrowness of the routes and the ruggedness of the mountains on the way there. He went to Dārā,[3] one of the castles in those parts, and took possession of it.'

Account of the death of al-Āmir and the caliphate of al-Ḥāfiẓ the Alid

On 2 Dhū'l-Qa'da of this year [7 October 1130] al-Āmir bi-Aḥkām Allāh Abū 'Alī ibn al-Musta'lī the Alid, lord of Egypt, was killed. He visited a pleasure ground of his and on his return the Bāṭinīs leapt on him and slew him, because he was a bad ruler of his subjects. His reign had lasted twenty-nine years **[665]** and five months. He was thirty-four years of age and the tenth of the descendants of the Mahdi 'Ubayd Allāh, who began his career in Sijilmasa and built al-Mahdiyya in Ifrīqiya. He was also the tenth Alid caliph of al-Mahdi's progeny.

When he was killed, he had no son to succeed him, so his cousin, [al-Ḥāfiẓ] al-Maymūn 'Abd al-Majīd, son of Emir Abū'l-Qāsim ibn al-Mustanṣir bi-Allāh, came to the throne. He was not proclaimed as caliph but only proclaimed as a supervisor of affairs, as a deputy until it might be discovered whether al-Āmir had fathered an as yet unborn son, who would be caliph while 'Abd al-Majīd deputized for him.

---

2 A fortress, originally Byzantine, near to Nisibis, Dunaysir and Dārā (Yāqūt, iii, 70).

3 Yāqūt, ii, 516–17: 'A town at the foot of a mountain between Nisibis and Mardin.' See also Krawulsky, 432–3.

Al-Ḥāfiẓ was born in Ascalon, because his father went there from Egypt in the Great Crisis[4] and took up residence. Thus his son ʻAbd al-Majīd was born there. When he came to power, he appointed as vizier Abū ʻAlī Aḥmad ibn al-Afḍal ibn Badr al-Jamālī, who monopolised power and dominated and confined al-Ḥāfiẓ, keeping him in a closet, visited only by those whom Abū ʻAlī wished. A nominal position was left to al-Ḥāfiẓ with no substance to it. Abū ʻAlī transferred all the money and other things that were in the palace to his own residence. This remained the situation until Abū ʻAlī was killed in the year 526 [1131–2]. Al-Ḥāfiẓ's affairs then improved, he became the authority in the state and he gained a secure hold on his position and his lands.

Miscellaneous events

During this year the Lady, daughter of Sultan Sanjar, died. She was the wife of Sultan Maḥmūd.

[666] This year Bohemond the Frank, lord of Antioch, was killed.[5]

In Shaʻbān [10 July–7 August 1130] Naṣīr al-Dīn Maḥmūd ibn Mu'ayyad al-Mulk ibn Niẓām al-Mulk died at Baghdad. After his death a fire broke out in his house and in the stores of firewood and the Market of Tutush.[6] Much property was lost by the people.

This year the headman, Abū'l-Dhu'ād al-Mufarrij ibn al-Ḥasan ibn al-Ṣūfī became the vizier of the ruler of Damascus, Tāj al-Mulūk.

This year the astronomical observations took place in the Sultanian Palace in the east of Baghdad. It was undertaken by al-Badīʻ al-Aṣṭurlābī but was not completed.[7]

At Baghdad flying scorpions with two stings appeared. The populace were very fearful of them and suffered much.

In Dhū'l-Ḥijja [5 November–3 December 1130] Prince Masʻūd ibn Muḥammad left Khurasan, where he had been with his uncle Sultan Sanjar, and came to Sāveh. The rumour arose that his strong intention was to oppose his brother Sultan Maḥmūd and that his uncle Sultan Sanjar had ordered this. Maḥmūd was

---

[4] Early in the second half of the eleventh century there began a period of political and economic chaos in Fatimid Egypt, which ended in 1074 with the vizierate of the military man, Badr al-Jamālī.

[5] Bohemond II died in battle in Cilicia early in 1130 (Asbridge, *Principality of Antioch*, 90).

[6] This market in East Baghdad ran from the Niẓāmiyya Madrasa to the Azaj Gate. It was originally built by a mamluke of Tutush (see Le Strange, *Baghdad*, 298).

[7] This well-known scholar, Abū'l-Qāsim Hibat Allāh ibn al-Ḥusayn, died at Baghdad in 534/1139-40 (*Wāfī*, xxvii, 269–70). According to *EI(2)*, i, 858, 'It is probable that the tables of Maḥmūd composed by him and dedicated to the Sultan [Maḥmūd ibn Muḥammad] are the results of these observations.'

apprehensive and left Baghdad for Hamadhan. When he arrived at Kirmānshāhān his brother Prince Mas'ūd came to him and did obeisance. The rumours turned out to be without substance. The sultan assigned him as fief the city of Ganja with its dependencies and sent him off there.

In Iraq, the Uplands, Mosul and the Jazīra there was a great earthquake in Rabī' I [12 February-13 March 1130] which caused much destruction.[8]

This year Sultan Maḥmūd took the citadel of Alamūt.

During this year the following died:

Ibrāhīm ibn 'Uthmān ibn Muḥammad, Abū Isḥāq al-Ghazzī, a man from Gaza, a city in Palestine (part of Syria). He was born in the year 441 [1049-50] and was a skilled poet.[9] These are some verses of his from an ode describing the Turks:

> **[667]** Among the youths of the Turkish troops their charges
> Have robbed the thunder of noise and éclat.
> If welcomed, they are as beautiful as angels,
> But, if fought, they are very devils.

And again on asceticism:

> This life is merely a [passing] pleasure;
> A deluded simpleton is he who chooses it.
> The past is gone and what is hoped for a mystery still;
> You have but the moment in which you exist.

Al-Ḥusayn ibn Muḥammad ibn 'Abd al-Wahhāb ibn Aḥmad ibn Muḥammad al-Dabbās, Abū 'Abd Allāh al-Naḥawī, the poet, known as 'the Skilled One.' On his mother's side he was half-brother of Abū'l-Karam ibn Fākhir al-Naḥawī. He was born in the year 443 [1051-2]. He wrote some charming poetry, for example:

> Give me back my rest and avoid my house.
> I am satisfied with your simulacrum in my sleep.
> Do not imagine that I am likely to seek sleep
> Otherwise than in hope that your image will be kind to me.
> You have left me alone with my passion to overcome it.
> Your night's sleep saved you from a torment that robs me of rest.

This is a long poem.[10]

---

8 It occurred the eve of Friday 16 Rabī' I/= 28 February 1130. Ibn al-Jawzī experienced the effects in a Baghdad mosque (*Muntaẓam*, x, 14).

9 See *Muntaẓam*, x, 15-16.

10 More of this poem and of another is given in *Muntaẓam*, x, 16-19.

Hibat Allāh ibn al-Qāsim ibn Muḥammad ibn ʿAṭā ibn Muḥammad, Abū Saʿd[11] al-Mihrawānī al-Nīsābūrī, born in the year 431 [1039–40]. He was a scholar of Ḥadīth and of the Koran and a man of piety.

[11] *Muntaẓam*, x, 19, has ʿibn Saʿdʾ. He died in Jumādā I/ April–May 1130.

The Year 525 [1130-1131]

The capture of Dubays ibn Ṣadaqa and his being handed over to 'Imād al-Dīn Zankī

In Sha'bān this year [July 1131] Tāj al-Mulūk Būrī ibn Ṭughtakīn, lord of Damascus, captured Emir Dubays ibn Ṣadaqa, lord of al-Ḥilla, and handed him over to Atabeg Zankī ibn Āqsunqur, the Martyr. This came about because, when he left Basra, as we have described, a messenger came to him from Syria, from Ṣarkhad, summoning him, because its lord was a eunuch who had died this year[1] and left a concubine who took control of the citadel and its contents. She realised that she would achieve nothing without allying herself with a man of power and military might. Dubays ibn Ṣadaqa and his numerous tribal following were described to her, as were his circumstances and present situation in Iraq. She sent to invite him to Ṣarkhad so that she could marry him and hand to him the citadel and the money and other things it contained.

Dubays took guides with him and set out from Iraq to Syria. In the vicinity of Damascus his guides led him astray and he came upon some tribesmen of Kalb who were to the east of the Ghūṭa. They seized him and took him to Tāj al-Mulūk, lord of Damascus, who imprisoned him.[2] This came to the ears of Atabeg 'Imād al-Dīn Zankī, whom Dubays used to criticise and attack. He therefore sent to Tāj al-Mulūk requesting him to give Dubays into his hands. In return he would release his son and **[669]** the emirs whom he held prisoner. If he refused to hand him over, he would march against Damascus and besiege it, and destroy, and lay waste to, its lands. Tāj al-Mulūk accepted this, so the Atabeg sent his son Savinj and the emirs who were with him, while Tāj al-Mulūk sent Dubays[3] who was certain that his end had come, but Zankī treated him quite differently from what he expected. He was generous to him, provided him with provisions, weapons and mounts and other goods from his stores. He gave him precedence even over himself and treated him like a great prince.

When al-Mustarshid bi-Allāh heard of his arrest at Damascus, he sent Sadīd al-Dawla ibn al-Anbārī and Abū Bakr ibn Bishr al-Jazarī (from Jazīrat ibn 'Umar) to Tāj al-Mulūk to ask him to surrender Dubays to himself, because of the caliph's well-known enmity towards him. While he was on the way there, Sadīd al-Dawla heard that Dubays had been handed over to 'Imād al-Dīn. He continued to

---

1 He was Fakhr al-Dīn Kumushtakīn al-Tājī who died in Jumādā II/May 1130, according to Ibn Qal., 231, who has no mention of the concubine's invitation to Dubays. The motive for Dubays' departure from Iraq is 'fear of the caliph' (Ibn Qal., 230).

2 On the eve of Monday 6 Sha'bān/6 July 1131 (Ibn Qal., 231).

3 Dubays was exchanged on Thursday 8 Dhū'l-Qa'da/2 October 1131 (Ibn Qal., 231).

Damascus without turning back and, when there, made some disparaging and critical remarks about Atabeg Zankī. News of this came to ‘Imād al-Dīn, so he sent people to intercept him when he returned. They arrested both him and Ibn Bishr on their return from Damascus and took them to ‘Imād al-Dīn. Ibn Bishr he humiliated and treated unpleasantly but Ibn al-Anbārī he put in prison. Al-Mustarshid bi-Allāh interceded for him, so he was set free. Dubays remained with Zankī until he travelled down to Iraq with him, as we shall relate, God Almighty willing.

The death of Sultan Maḥmūd and the succession of his son Dā’ūd

In Shawwāl of this year [27 August–24 September 1131] Sultan Maḥmūd, the son of Sultan Muḥammad, died at Hamadhan. Before he fell ill, his vizier Abū’l-Qāsim al-Anasābādhī had become fearful of a number of emirs and notables of the state, including ‘Azīz al-Dīn Abū Naṣr ibn Ḥāmid the Comptroller, Emir Anūshtakīn, known as Shīrkīr, and his son ‘Umar, who was the sultan’s emir-chamberlain [**670**] among others. He sent ‘Azīz al-Dīn under arrest to Mujāhid al-Dīn Bahrūz at Takrit, where he was later put to death. Shīrkīr and his son were executed in Jumādā II [May 1131].

After this the sultan became ill and died in Shawwāl. His son Prince Dā’ūd was enthroned as sultan with the agreement of Vizier Abū’l-Qāsim and his Atabeg, Āqsunqur al-Aḥmadīlī. The khutbah was made in his name throughout all the Uplands and Azerbayjan. Some disturbances occurred in Hamadhan and the rest of the Uplands but they calmed down. After the people had become quiet and calm, the vizier travelled with his treasure to Rayy, where he felt secure because it was held by Sultan Sanjar.

When he died, Sultan Maḥmūd was about twenty-seven years of age. He had held the sultanate for twelve years, nine months and twenty days. He was mild of temper, generous and intelligent. He would listen to what he found disagreeable without meting out punishment although he had the power to do so. He was seldom greedy for the wealth of his subjects but kept his hands off it and he prevented his men from getting at any of it.

Miscellaneous events

During this year the Bāṭinīs attacked Tāj al-Dīn Būrī ibn Ṭughtakīn, lord of Damascus, and wounded him twice.[4] One wound healed but the other became septic and remained painful. However, he held public sessions and rode out in public despite his weakness.

---

4 In Jumādā II/May 1131 (Ibn Qal., 230).

This year the following died:

Emir Abū'l-Ḥasan ['Alī] ibn al-Mustaẓhir bi-Allāh, the brother of al-Mustarshid bi-Allāh, in Rajab [June 1131].[5]

Al-Ḥasan ibn Salmān ibn 'Abd Allāh, Abū 'Alī, the Shāfi'ī lawyer, [**671**] preacher and professor of the Niẓāmiyya at Baghdad, in Shawwāl [27 August-24 September 1131].[6] He was originally from al-Zawzān.

The Preacher Abū Naṣr Aḥmad ibn 'Abd al-Qādir, known as Ibn al-Ṭūsī, the preacher of Mosul, in Rabī' I [February 1131].[7]

Ḥammād ibn Musallim, the Treacle Seller from al-Raḥba. He was a celebrated ascetic and miracle worker, a student of Ḥadīth and had many followers and pupils. I have seen that Shaykh Abū'l-Faraj ibn al-Jawzī criticised and found fault with him. However, for this shaykh other pious men provide a pattern, for Ibn al-Jawzī composed a book which he entitled *Talbīs Iblīs*,[8] in which he spared not a single righteous Muslim master.[9]

Hibat Allāh ibn Muḥammad ibn 'Abd al-Wāḥid ibn al-Ḥaṣīn al-Shaybānī, the secretary. He was born in the year 432 [1040-41]. He heard Ḥadīth from Abū 'Alī ibn al-Muhadhdhib and Abū Ṭālib ibn Ghaylān and others. He was an authority for the *Musnad* of Aḥmad ibn Ḥanbal, the *Ghaylāniyyāt* and other collections.[10]

Muḥammad ibn al-Ḥasan ibn 'Alī ibn al-Ḥasan, Abū Ghālib al-Māwardī. He was born in the year 450 [1058] at Basra. He heard much Ḥadīth and transmitted the *Sunan* of Abū Dā'ūd al-Sijistānī. He was a righteous man.[11]

---

[5] *Muntaẓam*, x, 20, also records the death by smallpox of an unnamed twenty-one year old son of al-Mustarshid.

[6] See *Muntaẓam*, x, 22.

[7] Ibn al-Jawzī, who calls him Aḥmad ibn Muḥammad ibn 'Abd al-Qādir, heard Hadīth and some of his poetry from him. He moved to Mosul where he died on Saturday 21 Rabī' I/=19 February 1131 (*Muntaẓam*, x, 21).

[8] Translated by D.S. Margoliouth as 'The Devil's Delusion,' *Islamic Culture*, ix-xii (1935-8). See also *The Devil's Deception*, trans. Abu Ameenah Philips, Birmingham, 1996.

[9] Ibn al-Jawzī (*Muntaẓam*, x, 22-3) says that Ḥammād, who died in Ramaḍān/28 July-26 August 1131, was devoid of Sharī'a learning and used to delude the ignorant. Ibn 'Aqīl also warned people against him.

[10] He died 14 Shawwāl/9 September 1131 (*Muntaẓam*, x, 24). Ibn al-Jawzī himself 'heard' from him the *Musnad* (Ḥadīth collection arranged by principal transmitters) of Ibn Ḥanbal (d. 241/855) etc. A Ḥadīth collection called *al-Ghaylāniyyāt* by a Muḥammad ibn 'Abd Allāh al-Shāfi'ī (d. 354/965) was published at Riyāḍ in 1996.

[11] He died in Ramaḍān 28 July-26 August 1131 (*Muntaẓam*, x, 23).

The Year 526 [1131-1132]

The killing of Abū 'Alī, the vizier of al-Ḥāfiẓ, and how Yānis became vizier and then died

During Muḥarram of this year [December 1131] al-Afḍal Abū 'Alī ibn al-Afḍal ibn Badr al-Jamālī, the vizier of al-Ḥāfiẓ li-Dīn Allāh al-'Alawī, ruler of Egypt, was killed. The cause of his murder was that he had confined al-Ḥāfiẓ and prevented him from exercising authority in any affairs, great or small. All that was in the palace he moved to his own residence and dropped from the prayers any mention of Ismā'īl, son of Ja'far ibn Muḥammad al-Ṣādiq, their ancestor after whom the Ismā'īlīs take their name. He also dropped the formula 'Come to the best of work' from the call to prayer and made no khutbah in al-Ḥāfiẓ's name. He ordered the preachers to mention his own name in the khutbah with the titles that he wrote out for them, namely:

> The Lord al-Afḍal the most excellent, lord of the mamlukes of princes, the protector of Islam's heartland, spreader of justice's wing over Muslims near and far, aider of the Imam of Truth when 'hidden' and present, the guarantor of his victory with the sharp blade of his sword and his correct judgement and administration, God's steward of His servants and guide of the cadis to follow and support the path of Truth, and director of the believers' missionaries with his clear exposition and direction, lord of benefactions, remover of injustice from the nations, master of the sword and the pen, Abū 'Alī Aḥmad, son of the most excellent lord al-Afḍal Shāhinshāh Emir al-Juyūsh.

He was an Imāmī[1] by persuasion and used often to criticise and disparage al-Āmir. The Shia turned against him **[673]**, the Alids and their mamlukes. Indeed, they hated him and plotted his death. On 20 Muḥarram [12 December 1131] he went out to the Hippodrome to play polo with his followers. A group, including a Frankish mamluke who belonged to al-Ḥāfiẓ, prepared an ambush. They emerged, the Frank charged and with a thrust slew him, and then they cut off his head. Al-Ḥāfiẓ came out of the closet where he had been, and the people ransacked Abū 'Alī's house, taking untold quantities of plunder. The elite then rode to his house with al-Ḥāfiẓ, who seized what was left and transported it to the palace.

That day al-Ḥāfiẓ was saluted as caliph. He had previously been proclaimed heir apparent and regent for any offspring of al-Āmir's that might be born. When he

[1] The Imāmiyya or Twelver Shiites recognised a line of Imāms after Ja'far al-Ṣādiq, the sixth, which did not include his son Ismā'īl.

was proclaimed he appointed as his vizier Abū'l-Fatḥ Yānis al-Ḥāfiẓī on that very same day. He was given the title Emir al-Juyūsh and was held in great respect, being a man of great depths, but very wicked. While al-Ḥāfiẓ feared for his life, Yānis was apprehensive about al-Ḥāfiẓ and took precautions. He neither ate nor drank anything with him, but al-Ḥāfiẓ contrived to arrange that his body-servant provided polluted water in the ablutions chamber, which Yānis used for washing. The worm descended towards his anus. He was told, 'If you move and stand up, you will die.' He was treated by having fresh meat put in that place, which the worm would attach itself to and so be drawn out. Then a replacement piece would be put there. He came close to being cured. Al-Ḥāfiẓ was told, 'He is much better, but if he moves he will die.' Therefore al-Ḥāfiẓ rode to pay him a sick visit and Yānis stood up and walked forward to meet him. Al-Ḥāfiẓ sat with him and then left. That very night Yānis died. His death was on 26 Dhū'l-Ḥijja of this year [7 November 1132].

When Yānis died, al-Ḥāfiẓ appointed his son Ḥasan as vizier and mentioned him as heir apparent in the khutbah. An account of his murder will be given under the year 529 [1134-5].

We mentioned Abū 'Alī's titles merely out of amazement at them and the folly of the man. If even such a one as the vizier of Egypt's ruler acts thus, then it would be fitting for the vizier of the Saljuq sultans, **[674]** such as Niẓām al-Mulk and others, to lay claim to divinity! However, the soil of Egypt gives rise to that sort of thing. Consider, if you will, how Pharaoh says, 'I am your highest Lord,'[2] and other [similar] things which I will not waste time by mentioning.

The situation of Sultan Mas'ūd and the two princes, Saljūqshāh and Dā'ūd, and the firm establishment of Mas'ūd's sultanate in Iraq

After the death of Sultan Maḥmūd, son of Sultan Muḥammad, and the making of the khutbah for his son, Prince Dā'ūd, in the Uplands and Azerbayjan, as we have related, Dā'ūd left Hamadhan in Dhū'l-Qa'da 525 [25 September-24 October 1131] to go to Zanjan. News came to him that his uncle, Sultan Mas'ūd, had left Jurjan and come to Tabriz, where he took control. Dā'ūd marched there and besieged him. There was fighting between them until the end of Muḥarram 526 [22 December 1131] when they made peace.

Prince Dā'ūd withdrew the distance of a day's journey and Sultan Mas'ūd came out of Tabriz. Troops gathered around him and he moved to Hamadhan, He wrote asking for the khutbah at Baghdad. The envoys of Prince Dā'ūd had gone in advance to ask for the khutbah and al-Mustarshid bi-Allāh had replied that the decision about the khutbah depended on Sultan Sanjar. Whoever he wanted would be given the khutbah. The caliph also wrote to Sultan Sanjar suggesting that

---

2 Koran, lxxix, 24.

neither should be allowed the khutbah, for the khutbah was fittingly his alone. This was well received by Sanjar.

[675] Later Sultan Mas'ūd made contact with 'Imād al-Dīn Zankī, lord of Mosul and elsewhere, asking for his aid and support. Zankī promised him his backing and that made Mas'ūd feel much stronger to seek the sultanate.

Qarāja al-Sāqī,[3] the master of Fars and Khuzistan and the atabeg of Prince Saljūqshāh, son of Sultan Muḥammad, marched with a large army to Baghdad. He arrived there before Sultan Mas'ūd's arrival and lodged in the Sultanian Palace. The caliph gave him an honourable reception and secured an oath of support from him. Then there arrived the envoy of Sultan Mas'ūd, seeking the khutbah and making threats if it was withheld. The request was not granted, so Mas'ūd moved to make camp at 'Abbāsiyyat al-Khāliṣ.[4] The caliph's army and the army of Saljūqshāh and Qarāja al-Sāqī took the field and moved towards Mas'ūd to bring the conflict with Atabeg 'Imād al-Dīn Zankī to a conclusion. A day and a night they marched to al-Ma'shūq[5] and fell upon Zankī and put him to flight. Many of his men were taken prisoner. Zankī himself fled to Takrit and crossed the Tigris there. At that time the castellan was Najm al-Dīn Ayyūb, who provided ferry boats for him. Once across the river he was safe from pursuit. He went on to his own lands to repair his situation and that of his men. This action on Najm al-Dīn Ayyūb's part was the basis for his connection with Zankī and his joining his service, with the ultimate outcome for the family that they became rulers of Egypt, Syria and elsewhere, as we shall relate.[6]

Sultan Mas'ūd moved from al-'Abbāsiyya to al-Malikiyya.[7] The advance guards made contact with one another and skirmishing between Mas'ūd and his brother Saljūqshāh continued for two days. Saljūqshāh sent to Qarāja urging him to come quickly, so he returned in haste and crossed **[676]** over the Tigris to the east bank. When Sultan Mas'ūd learnt of 'Imād al-Dīn Zankī's reverse, he withdrew and sent to the caliph to inform him of Sultan Sanjar's arrival at Rayy and that he was intending to come against the caliph and others, [adding,] 'If you think that we should unite to fight him and drive him out of Iraq, which should then be in the hands of the caliph's representative, then I am in full agreement with that.' The caliph sent him a holding reply.

---

3 i.e. Qarāja the Cupbearer.

4 Al-Khāliṣ is the canal which starts at Bājisrā on the Nahrawān Canal and flows west to the Tigris at Baradān above Baghdad. It is also a district. It is assumed that the 'Abbāsiyya mentioned here was a village in that area. It cannot be identified as the island of 'Abbāsiyya between the Little and the Upper Ṣarāt Canals in West Baghdad.

5 Site of a palace (*Qaṣr al-Ma'shūq*, 'the Beloved's Palace') built by Caliph al-Mu'tamid on the west bank of the Tigris opposite Samarra (Yāqūt, iv, 576).

6 Ayyūb, brother of Asad al-Dīn Shīrkūh, was the father of Saladin.

7 Al-Malikiyya (also al-Mālikiyya) was a village and a cemetery outside the Baradān Gate of East Baghdad (Yāqūt, iv, 397; Le Strange, *Baghdad*, 294, 327).

There was an exchange of emissaries to discuss peace, and eventually they reached an agreement that Iraq should be held by the caliph's representative and Mas'ūd should be sultan with Saljūqshāh as his heir apparent. They exchanged oaths on that. Sultan Mas'ūd then returned to Baghdad and took up residence in the Sultanian Palace while Saljūqshāh lodged in the prefect's residence. Their uniting took place in Jumādā I [20 March–18 April 1132].

Account of the hostilities between Sultan Mas'ūd and his uncle Sultan Sanjar

After the death of Sultan Maḥmūd, Sultan Sanjar came to the Uplands accompanied by Prince Ṭughril, Sultan Muḥammad's son, who was closely attached to him at his court. Sanjar came to Rayy, then proceeded from there to Hamadhan. News of his arrival at Hamadhan reached the Caliph al-Mustarshid bi-Allāh and Sultan Mas'ūd. They had mutually agreed to resist him and that the caliph should be with the troops. The latter made his preparations. While Qarāja al-Sāqī, Sultan Mas'ūd and Saljūqshāh went on ahead towards Sultan Sanjar, al-Mustarshid bi-Allāh delayed marching with them. Qarāja sent to him and put pressure on him, saying, 'What you dread from Sanjar in the future I shall do now!' Thereupon he moved out but proceeded hesitantly and with stops and starts until he arrived at Khānaqīn, where he halted.

The khutbah for Sanjar was discontinued in the whole of Iraq. News came that 'Imād al-Dīn Zankī and Dubays ibn Ṣadaqa had arrived near Baghdad. It has been mentioned that Sultan Sanjar had assigned al-Ḥilla to Dubays as a fief and had sent to al-Mustarshid bi-Allāh submissively, asking for [**677**] his goodwill towards Dubays. The caliph refused to respond to this. As for 'Imād al-Dīn Zankī, it has been related that Sultan Sanjar had given him the office of prefect at Baghdad. Al-Mustarshid bi-Allāh returned to Baghdad, ordered the population to prepare its defence and raised troops to put alongside them.

Sultan Mas'ūd came to Dāy Marj[8] and the vanguard of Sultan Sanjar met them in large numbers. Mas'ūd withdrew to Kirmānshāhān,[9] while Sultan Sanjar camped at Asadābādh with 100,000 cavalry. Mas'ūd and his brother Saljūqshāh went to the two mountains called the Ox and the Fish[10] and camped between them. Sanjar moved camp to Kinkiwar and, when he heard of their turning away, he hastened to pursue them and they retraced their steps the distance of four days' journey in a day and a night. Both armies met at 'Ūlān near Dīnawar.[11] Mas'ūd was

---

[8] Unidentified. Correct the text's 'Dādmarj' (see above p. [**293**], s.a. 493, and below p. [**26**], s.a. 529).

[9] Sometimes called Qarmāsīn, it is the modern Kermanshah (Krawulsky, 371).

[10] In Persian *Gāv* and *Māhī*.

[11] A toponym beginning with *'ayn* is unexpected in the Uplands area al-Jibāl. There is a Qūlān (a plausible correction) in Krawulsky, 546, but nowhere near Dīnawar.

putting off the conflict, awaiting the coming of al-Mustarshid. However, when Sultan Sanjar came upon him, he found it unavoidable to give battle. On his left wing Sanjar put Ṭughril, the son of his brother Muhammad, Qumāj and Amīr-e Amīrān, and on his left wing the Khwārazmshāh Atsiz ibn Muḥammad with a number of emirs. Mas'ūd placed Qarāja al-Sāqī and Emir Qizil on his right wing and Yarunqush Bāzdār[12] and Yūsuf the Herald[13] and others on his left. Qizil had already conspired with Sanjar to flee.

Hostilities began and the fighting grew fierce. It was a memorable day. Qarāja al-Sāqī charged the centre where Sultan Sanjar was with 10,000 cavalry, the elite of his force, and elephants ranged before them. When Qarāja charged the centre, Prince Ṭughril and the Khwārazmshāh came behind his rear and Qarāja found himself surrounded. He fought until he had received several wounds and many of his men were killed, and then he was taken prisoner, suffering from many wounds. Seeing this, Sultan Mas'ūd fled the field of battle to safety. **[678]** Yūsuf the Herald and Ḥusayn Uzbek, both among the senior emirs, were killed. The battle took place on 8 Rajab of this year [25 May 1132].

When the defeat of Mas'ūd was complete, Sanjar made camp and summoned Qarāja whom he cursed when he appeared, saying, 'Trouble-maker! What were you hoping for by fighting me?' He replied, 'I was hoping to kill you and set up a sultan whom I could control.' Sanjar slew him summarily and then sent to summon Sultan Mas'ūd. He presented himself before Sanjar when he had arrived at Khūnaj, and when Sanjar saw him, he kissed him and received him with honour but reprimanded him for his rebellion and disobedience. He sent him back to Ganja and set up Prince Ṭughril, his nephew, as sultan and made the khutbah for him throughout the lands. As his vizier he appointed Abū'l-Qāsim al-Anasābādhī, Sultan Maḥmūd's vizier, and then returned to Khurasan. He arrived at Nishapur on 20 Ramaḍān of the year 526 [4 August 1132]. As for al-Mustarshid bi-Allah, we shall tell later what happened to him.

'Imād al-Dīn Zankī's expedition to Baghdad and his defeat

When al-Mustarshid bi-Allāh, having left Baghdad, heard of Sultan Mas'ūd's defeat, he determined to return to Baghdad. News came to him of 'Imād al-Dīn Zankī's arrival at Baghdad, accompanied by Dubays ibn Ṣadaqa. Sultan Sanjar had written to both of them and ordered them to invade Iraq and take control. Having learnt of this, the caliph made a hasty return to the city, crossed to the West Bank and travelled to al-'Abbāsiyya where he made camp. 'Imād al-Dīn camped at al-Manāriyya in Dujayl. They met at the Castle of the Barmakids[14] on 27 Rajab [13

[12] A Persian court official, literally the falcon holder.

[13] i.e. *Jāwūsh*.

[14] *Mufarrij*, i, 50, in a parallel passage names 'Aqarqūf, a village 30 km west of Baghdad (see *EI(2)*, i, 315; Krawulsky, 463).

June 1132]. Zankī began the battle by charging the caliph's right wing, where Jamāl al-Dawla Iqbāl was, and he put them to flight. Naẓar the Eunuch on the caliph's left wing charged [**679**] the right wing of 'Imād al-Dīn and Dubays. The caliph in person took part in the charge and the fighting became intense. Dubays fled but 'Imād al-Dīn wished to stand firm. However, he saw that his men had scattered and left him, so he too took flight. Several were killed and several made captive. The caliph spent the night there and then the next day returned to Baghdad.

What happened to Dubays after his flight

After the defeat which we have mentioned, Dubays returned to take refuge in the area of al-Ḥilla, where he gathered some followers together. Authority there was held by Iqbāl al-Mustarshidī, who was reinforced with a detachment from Baghdad. He and Dubays came into conflict and Dubays was defeated and hid in a reed-bed there. He remained for three days without any food. He was unable to get away until a dedicated adherent carried him out on his back.

He gathered some support and attacked Wāsiṭ. The local troops joined him, as did Bakhtiyār Washshāq and Ibn Abī'l-Jabr. He continued there until the year 527 [1132-3], when Yarunqush Bāzdār and Iqbāl al-Mustarshidī the Eunuch were despatched against them with an army. The men of Wāsiṭ and Dubays were defeated and Bakhtiyār Washshāq and other emirs were taken prisoner.

Account of the death of Tāj al-Mulūk, lord of Damascus

This year in Rajab [June 1132] Tāj al-Mulūk Būrī ibn Ṭughtakīn, lord of Damascus, died. [**680**] He died because the wound which he had received from the Bāṭiniyya became more serious at this time, weakened him and reduced his strength. He died on 21 Rajab [7 June 1132], having willed that his successor as ruler should be his son Shams al-Mulūk Ismā'īl. He left the city of Baalbek and its dependencies to his [other] son Shams al-Dawla Muḥammad.

Būrī was energetic in the Jihad, brave and daring. He filled the gap left by his father and surpassed him. He was a fit subject for praise. Many are the panegyrical odes written by the poets, especially Ibn al-Khayyāṭ. His son Shams al-Mulūk succeeded him and the administration of his affairs was undertaken by the Chamberlain Yūsuf ibn Fayrūz, the prefect of Damascus, who had been his father's trusted chamberlain. His reign commenced with compassion and kindness towards his subjects and many were the blessings called down upon him and many those who sought out his court.

How Shams al-Mulūk took the castle of al-Labwa and that of Rās and how he besieged Baalbek

Shams al-Mulūk Ismā'īl, lord of Damascus, took the castle of al-Labwa and the castle of Rās[15] during this year. This came about as follows. They had belonged to his father Tāj al-Mulūk and in each one there was a castellan to defend it. After Shams al-Mulūk came to power it came to his knowledge that his brother Shams al-Dawla Muḥammad, lord of Baalbek, had made contact with the two castellans and suborned them. They surrendered both castles to him and he stationed enough troops there to hold them both There was no [immediate] effect from this, but Ismā'īl communicated mildly with his brother, expressing his disapproval of the situation and asking him to hand them both back. He refused to do so. Ismā'īl let this pass but began to make his preparations without informing anyone.

[681] At the end of Dhū'l-Qa'da [12 October 1132] he and his troops set out, making for the north, but then turned to the west, and before the garrison of al-Labwa Castle were aware of it, he had descended upon them and made an immediate assault. The defenders were unable to erect any trebuchet or other engine, and they sued for terms which were offered. The castle was taken over that very day. At the end of the day he moved to Rās Castle and took the garrison by surprise. The situation followed the same pattern as before. He received its surrender and placed men in both to hold them.

He then proceeded to Baalbek and put it under siege. His brother Shams al-Dawla Muḥammad, who was there, had made his preparations and gathered in the citadel the men and stores that he needed. While continuing the siege, Shams al-Mulūk made assaults with cavalry and infantry. The defenders resisted from on the wall but after several attacks the town fell as a result of heavy fighting with many killed. The citadel, with his brother within, held out against attacks. Trebuchets were erected and the action was unremitting. When his brother Shams al-Dawla saw the seriousness of the situation, he sent offering obedience and asking to be confirmed in what he held and what his father had put in his name. Shams al-Mulūk agreed to his request and confirmed him in control of Baalbek and its dependencies. They swore mutual oaths and Shams al-Mulūk returned to Damascus, having satisfactorily established his position.

Account of the conflict between Sultan Ṭughril and Prince Dā'ūd

In Ramaḍān this year [July–August 1132] there was a battle between Prince Ṭughril and his nephew, Prince Dā'ūd ibn Maḥmūd. The reason for this was that

---

[15] The castles of al-Labwa and Rās were both converted antique temples about 10 km apart, near the sources of the Orontes, and controlled the Beirut-Homs route through the Biqā' (see Elisséeff, 242).

Sultan Sanjar had enthroned Ṭughril as sultan, as we have related, and returned to Khurasan because he heard that the lord **[682]** of Transoxania, Aḥmad Khān, had rebelled against him. He hastened to return to repair the torn fabric [of his rule] but, after he had left for Khurasan, Prince Dā'ūd rebelled against his uncle Ṭughril and refused obedience. He gathered troops in Azerbayjan and the area of Ganja and then set out for Hamadhan, where he made camp on the first day of Ramaḍān [16 July 1132] at a nearby village called Wahnān.[16]

Ṭughril marched out to confront him. Each of them drew up his men in battle order. On Sultan Ṭughril's right wing was Ibn Bursuq and on his left Qizil. Qarāsunqur was with the advance guard. On Dā'ūd's right wing was Yarunqush al-Zakawī, who took no part in the action. When the Turkomans saw this, they plundered his tents and all his impedimenta. Dā'ūd's army fell into disarray. Seeing this his atabeg, Āqsunqur al-Aḥmadīlī, turned his back in flight. His men followed him in a rout. Ṭughril captured Yarunqush al-Zakawī and a number of emirs.

After this defeat Prince Dā'ūd was left at a loss until the early days of Dhū'l-Qa'da [began 13 September 1132]. He came to Baghdad, accompanied by his atabeg, Āqsunqur al-Aḥmadīlī. The caliph received him with honour and lodged him in the Sultanian Palace. Prince Mas'ūd was in Ganja, and when he heard of Dā'ūd's defeat he set out for Baghdad, as we shall relate, God willing.

Miscellaneous events

During this year al-Mustarshid bi-Allāh arrested his vizier, Sharaf al-Dīn 'Alī ibn Ṭirād al-Zaynabī. He replaced him with Anūshirwān ibn Khālid after he had initially refused and asked to be excused.

[683] Aḥmad ibn Ḥāmid ibn Muḥammad, Abū Naṣr the Comptroller of Sultan Maḥmūd, entitled 'Azīz [al-Dīn], was killed in the citadel of Takrit. The reason for this has already been given under the year 525 [1130-31].

In Muḥarram [December 1131] Muḥammad ibn Muḥammad ibn al-Ḥusayn, Abū'l-Ḥusayn ibn Abī Ya'lā ibn al-Farrā' al-Ḥanbalī, was killed. He was born in Sha'bān of the year 451 [12 September-10 October 1059]. He studied Ḥadīth with al-Khaṭīb Abū Bakr, Ibn al-Ḥusayn ibn al-Muhtadī[17] and others, and also studied canon law. His servants murdered him and took his money.[18]

---

[16] The text has Wahān. This is probably an error for Wahnān, which still exists a few kilometres west of Hamadhan (Krawulsky, 237).

[17] *Muntaẓam*, x, 29, calls him Abū'l-Ḥusayn, which sounds more likely. However, his father can hardly be the Caliph al-Muhtadī, who died in 256/870, even if one assumes precocious learning and extreme longevity.

[18] 'Servants' translates *aṣḥāb*, an ambiguous word. *Muntaẓam*, x, 29, having noted that Muḥammad lived alone, continues: 'Some people who served him and came often to the house learnt that he had money. They entered one night, stole the money and killed him.'

Aḥmad ibn ʻUbayd Allāh, [known as] Ibn Kādish, Abū'l-ʻIzz al-ʻUkbarī, died this year in Jumādā I [20 March–18 April 1132]. He was a prolific transmitter of Ḥadīth.[19] The following also died:

Abū'l-Faḍl ʻAbd Allāh ibn al-Muẓaffar ibn Ra'īs al-Ru'asā'. He was a man of letters with some good poetry to his credit. An example is what he wrote to Jalāl al-Dīn ibn Ṣadaqa the Vizier:

My lord Jalāl al-Dīn, you whom I shall remind of my past service,
Did you not purpose to be my patron? What has hindered this purpose?

---

[19] His authorities included the celebrated al-Māwardī, but he also admitted forging an *ḥadīth* (see *Muntaẓam*, x, 28).

[684]

The Year 527 [1132-1133]

How Shams al-Mulūk took Bānyās

In Ṣafar of this year [December 1132] the lord of Damascus, Shams al-Mulūk, took the fortress of Bānyās from the Franks. This came about because the Franks considered him to be weak and were eager to attack him. They decided to break the truce between them, so their eyes fell upon the property of a group of Damascene merchants in Beirut and they seized it. The merchants complained to Shams al-Mulūk, who wrote demanding the restitution of what had been taken. He made repeated representations but they returned nothing. His indignation and anger at this state of affairs led him to mobilise his troops and prepare for war, although nobody knew what his objective was.

He marched out towards the end of Muḥarram [ended 11 December], outstripped any news of his move and descended on Bānyās at the beginning of Ṣafar [12 December]. He began operations immediately and carried out a succession of assaults. The Franks were unprepared without sufficient soldiers to resist. He approached the city wall, dismounted, and both cavalry and infantry followed him. They reached the wall, mined it and made an entry by force of arms. [**685**] Such Frankish troops as were there sought refuge in the citadel and fortified themselves within. Many Franks in the town were killed, many made captive and property was seized. He assailed the citadel fiercely day and night and took it on terms of surrender during 4 Ṣafar [15 December]. He then returned to Damascus and arrived on 6th of the month [17 December].

Account of hostilities between the Muslims and the Franks

In Ṣafar [December 1132] the king of the Franks, lord of Jerusalem, marched with his horse and foot to the outlying districts of Aleppo. Emir Sawār, the deputy in Aleppo,[1] went to meet him with the troops that he had. Many Turkomans joined him as auxiliaries. They fought near Qinnisrīn and a large number were killed on both sides. The Muslims retreated to Aleppo and the king of the Franks ranged freely through Aleppan territory. Sawār returned to oppose him with what troops he had. He chanced upon a Frankish detachment and fell upon them, killing and

---

1 Sayf al-Dīn Sawār ibn Aytakīn left Būrī's service and joined Zankī in 524/1130 at Aleppo and was made governor (Ibn al-'Adīm, ii, 245). The text calls him Aswār throughout, but Sawār is generally found, e.g. in Ibn Qal., see index.

capturing many. The survivors returned routed to their lands. Thus the first setback was mended by the later victory. Sawār entered Aleppo with his captives and the heads of the slain. It was a memorable day.

Later a body of Franks from Edessa came to raid the districts of Aleppo. Sawār heard of them and he and Emir Ḥassān al-Ba'labakkī went out to oppose them. They fell upon them and slew them [almost] to the last man in the northern territories. Those who were not killed they took prisoner and then returned safely to Aleppo.

[686] Sultan Mas'ūd's return to the sultanate and the defeat of Prince Ṭughril

It has already been mentioned how Sultan Mas'ūd was defeated at the hands of his uncle Sultan Sanjar, how he returned to Ganja, how Prince Ṭughril became sultan and how he and Prince Dā'ūd, his brother Maḥmūd's son, fought together, leading to Dā'ūd's defeat and entry into Baghdad. When Sultan Mas'ūd heard that Dā'ūd had been defeated and made his way to Baghdad, he too went to Baghdad. On his approach Dā'ūd met him, dismounted before him and did obeisance. They then entered Baghdad together.

Mas'ūd took up residence in the Sultanian Palace in Ṣafar [December 1132] and made a request for the khutbah in his name. This was granted and his name was mentioned with Dā'ūd's coming next. Both were given robes of honour and had an audience with the caliph who received them graciously. It was agreed that Mas'ūd and Dā'ūd should proceed to Azerbayjan and that the caliph should send an army with them. They set out and when they came to Marāgha, Āqsunqur al-Aḥmadīlī provided a large sum of money and abundant provisions. Mas'ūd took control of all Azerbayjan. The emirs who were there, such as Qarāsunqur, retreated before him. Many of them fortified themselves in the city of Ardabil. Mas'ūd followed them and besieged them there. A great many of them met their deaths and the survivors fled.

Afterwards Mas'ūd went to Hamadhan to wage war on his brother, Prince Ṭughril. When Ṭughril heard of his approach, he went forth to meet him. They fought until midday but then Ṭughril fled and made for Rayy. Sultan Mas'ūd took control of Hamadhan in Sha'bān [7 June–5 July 1133]. After Mas'ūd had become established in Hamadhan, Āqsunqur al-Aḥmadīlī was killed. It was the Bāṭinīs who killed him, although it is said that Sultan Mas'ūd arranged to have him put to death.

[687] After reaching Qum, Ṭughril retired further to Isfahan and planned to make it his stronghold. His brother Mas'ūd came to put him under siege there, and Ṭughril realised that the populace of Isfahan would not obey him to undergo a siege, so he left to go to Fars. Mas'ūd seized Isfahan and the populace welcomed him with joy. From Isfahan he set out for Fars, dogging the footsteps of his brother

Ṭughril. He came to a place in the vicinity of White [Castle].[2] One of his brother's emirs along with 400 mounted men offered to submit to him. He gave them guarantees of protection. Ṭughril then feared that his troops would defect to his brother, so he fled at his approach and made for Rayy in Ramaḍān [6 July–4 August 1133]. On the way during Shawwāl [5 August–2 September 1133] his vizier, Abū'l-Qāsim al-Anasābādhī, was killed. He was murdered by the mamlukes of Emir Shīrkīr, who had plotted to have him killed, as has already been mentioned.[3]

Sultan Mas'ūd went in pursuit and caught up with Ṭughril at a place called Dhakrāwar, where a pitched battle ensued. When close engagement had begun, Prince Ṭughril fled. His army became bogged down in ground which was muddy where water had soaked in. Several of his emirs were taken prisoner, including the Chamberlain Tankiz and Ibn Bughrā. Mas'ūd set them free. In this battle only a few persons were killed. Sultan Mas'ūd returned to Hamadhan.

[Vol. xi] [5] Account of al-Mustarshid bi-Allāh's siege of Mosul

In this year al-Mustarshid bi-Allāh besieged the city of Mosul on 20 Ramaḍān [25 July 1133]. This was because of the previous attack on Baghdad by Zankī the Martyr, as we have related above.

At the present time a group of Saljuq emirs made their way to al-Mustarshid's court and joined with him, thus adding to his power. Meanwhile the Saljuq sultans were preoccupied with the differences between them. The caliph sent the Shaykh Bahā'l-Dīn Abū'l-Futūḥ al-Isfarā'inī, the preacher, to 'Imād al-Dīn Zankī with a message full of harsh words, to which Abu'l-Futūḥ added more, trusting in the power of the caliph and the prestige of the caliphate. Zankī arrested him humiliatingly and gave him some unwelcome treatment. Whereupon Mustarshid sent to the Sultan Mas'ūd to tell him of the situation that had come about with Zankī and to inform him that he intended to march to Mosul and besiege it. Days passed by until Sha'bān came, and then in the middle of the month [20 July 1133] he left Baghdad with a force of thirty thousand.

When he drew near to Mosul, Atabeg Zankī with part of his army moved out of the city, leaving the remainder behind **[6]** with his deputy, Naṣīr al-Dīn Jaqar, the commander of the citadel and the chief man in his state, with orders to hold on to it. The caliph invested the city and attacked, pressing the defenders hard. 'Imād al-Dīn went to Sinjār and rode every night to intercept the [caliphal] army's supplies. Every person he captured he took away and dealt with severely.

---

2 Here simply al-Bayḍā' but otherwise al-Qal'a al-Bayḍā' (White Castle) as below p. [**70**]. It was about 15 miles north of Shirāz, west of Kor River (Le Strange, *Caliphate*, 280; Krawulsky, 161, s.v. Beizā).

3 Presumably a reference to the report on p. [**669–70**] above.

Matters were also difficult for his own forces. Several plasterers in Mosul conspired to surrender the city, but they were informed on, arrested and gibbeted. The siege of Mosul lasted for three months, but no part of it was taken, nor did the caliph hear of any weakness on the part of the garrison or of any shortage of supplies and food. He abandoned the siege and returned to Baghdad. It is said that Naẓar the Eunuch came to him from the sultan's camp with a message from Sultan Mas'ūd that necessitated his departure and return to Baghdad. It is also said that he heard that Sultan Mas'ūd was planning to invade Iraq, so he returned without delay and travelled down the Tigris in a pinnace (*shabbāra*)[4] and arrived at Baghdad on 'Arafat day[5] [11 October 1133].

Account of Shams al-Mulūk's conquest of the city of Hama

In this year also, in Shawwal [August 1133], Shams al-Mulūk Ismā'īl ibn Tāj al-Mulūk, the lord of Damascus, took the city of Hama with its citadel, which was a possession of Zankī ibn Āqsunqur who had taken it from Taj al-Mulūk, as we have related.

When Tāj al-Mulūk had taken the citadel of Bālis he remained in Damascus until the month of Ramaḍān this year, and then went to Hama in the last third of that month [24 July–3 August]. The reason for his ambitious venture was that he had heard that al-Mustarshid was planning to besiege Mosul, and that encouraged him. The governor in Hama had also received the news and strengthened his defences, increasing his garrison and his stores. There was not [7] one of Shams al-Mulūk's men who did not advise him against attacking it, because of the power of its lord, but he did not listen to them. He marched to put the city under siege and engaged the defenders on the Feast Day [4 August], immediately carrying out an assault. The garrison stoutly resisted and for that day he withdrew.

On the next day early he made an assault on the town from all sides and entered by force. The inhabitants asked for terms, which he granted. He then besieged the citadel, which was not as impregnable and as lofty as it is today. Taqī al-Dīn 'Umar, the nephew of Saladin, excavated the hill it is on and over several years made it what it is now. When it was besieged, the governor was unable to hold it and surrendered. Shams al-Mulūk took it and all the stores and armaments etc. which it contained. He then left for the citadel of Shayzar, whose lord was one of the Banū Munqidh. He besieged it and sacked the town. Its lord sent envoys and negotiated his withdrawal to Damascus in return for a sum of money which he paid over. He arrived back in Damascus during Dhū'l-Qa'da of this year [September 1133].

---

4 See Makdisi, 'Topography', 192, note 5 and references cited. 'Pinnace' is used not in any technical sense but solely to suggest 'a small light vessel.'

5 The day when the pilgrims congregate at Mt. 'Arafāt to the east of Mecca for *al-Wuqūf* (the Standing), i.e. 9 Dhū'l-Ḥijja.

Account of the defeat of the Frankish lord of Tripoli

This year a large band of Turkomans crossed into Syria from the Jazīra and raided the territory of Tripoli, taking booty and killing many. The Count, lord of Tripoli, took the field with his troops. When the Turkomans pulled back, he followed them but they turned to fight him and put him to flight, killing many of his army. He and the survivors with him went to the castle of Ba'rīn, where he sought a safe refuge and held out against the Turkomans. They besieged him and, when the siege had lasted some time, the lord of Tripoli, accompanied by twenty knights, some of his leading companions, secretly left the castle. They escaped and went to Tripoli, leaving the remainder in Ba'rīn to hold it. When he arrived [**8**] at Tripoli, he wrote to all the Franks, and after a great host had answered his call he marched with them towards the Turkomans to force them to raise the siege of Ba'rīn. Hearing of this, the Turkomans went to meet them and they clashed. On both sides many were killed and the Franks were close to a defeat. However, they steaded themselves and made a safe tactical withdrawal to Rafaniyya. It was difficult for the Turkomans to pursue them into the middle of their lands, so they retired.

Miscellaneous events

In this year the Ismā'īlīs in Syria purchased the fortress of al-Qadmūs from its lord, Ibn 'Amrūn. They went up into it and waged war on their neighbours, both Muslims and Franks, all of whom were unhappy to have them in the vicinity.

A dispute occurred among the Franks in Syria this year, and they fought one another. Before this year they had not been wont to act like this. A number of them were killed.[6]

In Jumādā II [9 April-7 May 1133] the Emir Sawār, commander of Zankī's troops in Aleppo, raided Tell Bāshir territory and took much booty. The Franks in a large body came out to meet him and gave battle. He was victorious and killed many of them. The number of their dead was about one thousand. He returned safely.

On 9 Rabī' II [17 February 1133] Shams al-Mulūk, the lord of Damascus, was attacked by one of the mamlukes of his grandfather Ṭughtakīn. He struck him with his sword but the blow was ineffectual. Shams al-Mulūk's mamlukes overpowered and seized him. He was interrogated about what had induced him to do it. He said,

---

[6] *Kāmil*'s source is Ibn Qal., 236 (Gibb, *Damascus Chronicle*, 215). This refers to the revolt of Hugh du Puiset, count of Jaffa, and Roman du Puy, lord of Transjordan, against King Fulk, one-time count of Anjou. Mayer argues that it was not an affair of marital jealousy (cf. Runciman, ii, 190-93) but that the two factors were their disputing Fulk's attempt to rule without the participation of his wife, Queen Melisende (in opposition to the will of her father, King Baldwin II) and their opposition to Fulk's favouring Angevin newcomers (Mayer, 'Angevins *versus* Normans', 2-3).

'I wanted to deliver the Muslims from your evil and tyranny.' He was beaten unremittingly until he named several persons as instigators **[9]** of his action. Without further confirmation Shams al-Mulūk had them executed. Along with them he put his brother Savinj to death. This outraged people and turned them against him.

The following persons died this year:

The Shaykh Abū'l-Wafā' al-Fārisī. He had a memorable funeral which was attended by the notables of Baghdad.

The Cadi Abū'l-'Abbās Aḥmad ibn Salāma ibn 'Abd Allāh ibn Makhlad, known as Ibn al-Raṭbī, the Shāfi'ī lawyer and cadi of al-Karkh, in Rajab [8 May–6 June 1133]. He studied law with Abū Isḥāq and Abū Naṣr ibn al-Ṣabbāgh. He heard and transmitted Ḥadīth, and was close to the caliph, acting as tutor to his children.

Abū'l-Ḥusayn 'Alī ibn 'Abd Allāh ibn Naṣr, known as Ibn al-Zāghūnī, the Ḥanbalī lawyer and preacher. He was a master of many disciplines. He died in Muḥarram [12 November–11 December 1132].

'Alī ibn Ya'lā ibn 'Awaḍ ibn al-Qāsim al-Harawī al-'Alawī. He was a preacher with a great following in Khurasan, and he was a prolific scholar of Ḥadīth.

Muḥammad ibn Aḥmad ibn 'Alī, Abū 'Abd Allāh al-'Uthmānī al-Dībājī, who was a descendant of Muḥammad ibn 'Abd Allāh ibn 'Amr ibn 'Uthmān ibn 'Affān. Muḥammad was called al-Dībājī because of his good looks. His family was originally from Mecca, but he was from Nablus. He was an extreme supporter of the Ash'arī school [of theology] and used to preach. He died in Ṣafar [12 December 1132–9 January 1133].[7]

Abū Fulayta, Emir of Mecca, who was succeeded by his son, al-Qāsim.

Al-'Azīz ibn Hibat Allāh ibn 'Alī, al-Sharīf al-'Alawī. He died suddenly in Nishapur. His grandfather was chief syndic in Khurasan, and this al-'Azīz was offered the post of syndic **[10]** of the Alids in Nishapur, but he declined it. He was also offered the post of vizier to the sultan, but he refused. He clung to his secluded life and his concern for the affairs of the life to come.

The Chief Cadi of Khurasan, Abū Sa'īd Muḥammad ibn Aḥmad ibn Sā'id, a good and pious man.

---

[7] Note the claim for his descent from the third caliph, 'Uthmān. *Dībāj* means 'silk brocade.'

[11] The Year 528 [1133–1134]

How Shams al-Mulūk took Shaqīf Tīrūn and ravaged Frankish territory

In Muḥarram this year [November 1133] Shams al-Mulūk Ismā'īl marched from Damascus to Shaqīf Tīrūn,[1] which is on a hill overlooking Beirut and Sidon. It was held by al-Ḍaḥḥāk ibn Jandal, the headman of Wādī al-Taym. He had seized it and made it his strong fortress. Both the Muslims and the Franks were wary of him, while he claimed the protection of each side against the other. During this year Shams al-Mulūk moved against him and took the castle from him. Its capture upset the Franks because al-Ḍaḥḥāk had not interfered with any of the lands that were in his neighbourhood but they feared Shams al-Mulūk. They embarked on a mobilisation and when it was complete, they marched into the Ḥawrān, destroyed the major settlements and plundered all they could on a large scale.

When he saw that they were mobilising, Shams al-Mulūk also gathered and raised troops. A large force of Turkomans and others joined him. He camped opposite the Franks and for a number of days there was skirmishing between them. Then Shams al-Mulūk made a move with part of his army, left the rest facing the Franks, who were unaware of what was happening, and raided their territory, Tiberias, Nazareth, Acre and the neighbouring **[12]** areas, plundering, destroying and burning. He ruined most of the land and took women and children captive. The hands of those who were with him were filled with booty. The news reached the Franks. They were alarmed and immediately withdrew in precipitous haste and sought their own territory.

Shams al-Mulūk meanwhile returned to his army by a route different from that taken by the Franks and arrived safely. When the Franks reached their lands, they saw it in ruins. Greatly reduced in strength, they disbanded and sent envoys to discuss a renewal of the truce. This was settled in Dhū'l-Qa'da [23 August–21 September 1134].

Account of Prince Ṭughril's return to the Uplands and the flight of Sultan Mas'ūd

This year Prince Ṭughril ibn Muḥammad ibn Malikshāh conquered all the Uplands province and expelled his brother, Sultan Mas'ūd. It came about like this. When Mas'ūd returned from war with his brother, he received the news that Dā'ūd, his brother Muḥammad's son, had rebelled in Azerbayjan. He moved against him and

[1] i.e. Tyron.

besieged him in the castle of Rū'īn Diz,[2] where Dā'ūd had fortified himself. While he was busy with this siege, Prince Ṭughril gathered his troops together and won the support of some emirs of Sultan Mas'ūd's. Ṭughril continued to make gains of territory and, his army having grown numerous, he attacked Mas'ūd. When he drew near to Qazwin, Mas'ūd moved out to meet him. After the two armies had come within view of one another, Mas'ūd was abandoned by those emirs whom Ṭughril had won to his side and was left in a very small force. He turned and fled at the end of Ramaḍān [2 July 1134].

He sent to ask al-Mustarshid bi-Allāh's permission to come to Baghdad, which was given. His lieutenant in Isfahan was Alpqush al-Silāḥī who had the Prince Saljūqshāh with him. When he had heard of Mas'ūd's flight, he also came to Baghdad. Saljūqshāh stayed at the Sultan's Palace, and was nobly received [**13**] by the caliph, who sent him 10,000 dinars. In due course Mas'ūd came to Baghdad, with most of his retinue riding camels for lack of other mounts. He met with hardships on the road, but the caliph sent mounts, tents and equipment, in addition to money and clothing. He entered the Caliphal Palace in the middle of Shawwāl [8 August 1134]. Ṭughril remained at Hamadhan.

Account of Atabeg Zankī's siege of Āmid, the conflict between him and Dā'ūd, and Zankī's capture of the castle of al-Ṣūr

During this year the Atabeg Zankī, lord of Mosul, and Timurtāsh, the lord of Mardin, together attacked the city of Āmid and put it under seige. Its lord sent to Dā'ūd ibn Suqmān ibn Artuq, the lord of Ḥiṣn Kayfā, to ask his aid. The latter gathered what forces he could and marched to Āmid to raise the siege. The confrontation took place at the gate of Āmid and the battle lines were drawn up in Jumādā II [29 March–26 April 1134]. Dā'ūd was defeated and retired in rout. Several in his army were killed. Zankī and Timurtāsh continued their siege of Āmid, cut down the trees and pillaged the countryside, but then retired without achieving their aim. Zankī marched to the castle of Ṣūr in Diyār Bakr and put that under a close seige. He took it in Rajab of this year [27 April–26 May 1134]. Ḍiyā' al-Dīn Abū Sa'īd ibn al-Kafartūthī joined Zankī's service and was appointed vizier by him. He was a right-thinking man, an outstanding administrator and government official, and a friend of virtue and the virtuous.

[14] Account of Zankī's capture of the Ḥumaydī Kurds' castles

In this year 'Imād al-Dīn Zankī took control of all the castles of the Ḥumaydī

[2] See Le Strange, *Caliphate*, 164: Ruwīn Diz, 'three leagues distant from Marāgha.'

Kurds, such as the castles of al-'Aqr[3] and Shūsh.[4] When he had become master of Mosul, he confirmed the ruler, Emir 'Īsā al-Ḥumaydī, in his control of them and their dependent territories and interfered in no part of what he possessed. However, when al-Mustarshid besieged Mosul, this same 'Īsā joined him and raised a large force of Kurds for him. After al-Mustarshid had retired from Mosul, Zankī ordered their castles to be besieged. The sieges lasted a long time and there was some fierce fighting until they were taken in this year. Then there was some security for the people in the countryside of Mosul, those living in the neighbourhood of these tribesmen, for they had suffered a lot from their plundering of their flocks and ravaging of the land.

Account of the taking of the castles of the Hakkārīs and of Kawāshī

It has been related on the authority of a certain learned man of the Kurds, knowledgable in their affairs, that when Atabeg Zankī gained the castles of the Ḥumaydīs and expelled them, Abū'l-Hayjā' ibn 'Abd Allāh, the lord of Āshib[5] castle, al-Jazīra and Nūshī, became fearful and sent Atabeg Zankī someone to ask him to swear on oath [i.e. that his intentions were peaceful] and to take him money. Abū'l-Hayjā' came to Zankī in Mosul and stayed for a while, but then died and was buried at Tell Tawba.[6] When he left Āshib for Mosul, he had removed his son Aḥmad ibn Abi'l-Hayjā' **[15]** from there, fearing that it might be taken by force. He gave him the castle of Nūshī. This Aḥmad is the father of the 'Alī ibn Aḥmad, known as al-Mashṭūb, one of the greatest of Saladin's emirs in Syria.

When his father removed him from Āshib, he appointed as his lieutenant there a Kurd, called Bāv al-Arajī. On his father's death, Aḥmad set out from[7] Nūshī to Āshib to seize it, but Bāv resisted him, intending to hold it for a young son of Abu'l-Hayjā', whose name was 'Alī. Then Zankī marched with his army, descended on Āshib and took it.

Its capture came about like this. The inhabitants all came down to fight him and Zankī let them all approach and drew them on until they were at some distance from the castle. Then he rounded on them and put them to flight. A massacre ensued and many were killed or taken captive. Zankī took over the castle immediately and brought before him a number of Kurdish leaders, including Bāv, whom he put to death. He then returned to Mosul. When he later left the city again,

---

3 A village on the Tigris between Takrit and al-Qayyāra. Ruins still survive (Tulūl 'Aqīr), see Krawulsky, 427.

4 18 km south-west of Dezful (see Krawulsky, 355).

5 Yāqūt, i, 63: 'It was one of the most famous of the castles of the Hakkārīs in the area of Mosul. Zankī demolished it and in place of it built al-'Imādiyya close by.' It was at the head waters of the Upper Zāb river (Le Strange, *Caliphate*, 92–3).

6 'Hill of Repentance', site of Nineveh opposite Mosul (Le Strange, *Caliphate*, 89).

7 Correcting the edition's *bn* to *min*.

in his absence Naṣīr al-Dīn Jaqar, his lieutenant, sent and destroyed Āshib and evicted all from Kuhayja, Nūshī and the castle of Jullāb,[8] otherwise known as the 'Imādiyya castle. He also sent to besiege al-Sha'bānī castle, Faraḥ, Kūshar, al-Za'farān, Alqī[9] and Nayrūh, which are Mihrānī castles, and took them all. The situation in the Uplands and al-Zawzān was now well settled and the peasantry were secure from the Kurds.

As for the remainder of the Hakkārī castles, Jallaṣawrā,[10] Harūr,[11] al-Malāsī, Mābaramā, Bābūkhā, Bākazā and Nisbās,[12] they were conquered by Qarāja, the lord of 'Imadiyya, a long time after the murder of Zankī . This Qarāja was an emir to whom Zayn al-Dīn 'Alī assigned the Hakkārī lands as a fief after the death of Zankī. I have not learnt the date of the conquest of these castles and that is why I have mentioned it here.

Another learned Kurd has told a different and opposed version, as follows. When Zankī had conquered and demolished Āshib, there was only the lord of Jallaṣawrā and the lord of Harūr left amongst the Hakkārīs, and they had no power to be a threat to anyone. Zankī returned to Mosul, **[16]** feared by the lords of the Uplands castles. It so happened that 'Abd Allah ibn 'Īsā ibn Ibrāhīm, the lord of al-Rabiyya, Alqī, Faraḥ and other places, died and was succeeded by his son, 'Alī. His mother, Khadīja, the daughter of al-Ḥasan, was the sister of Ibrāhīm and 'Īsā, two emirs who were with Zankī in Mosul. Her son, 'Alī, sent her to her two brothers, who asked Zankī to guarantee his position and security. They asked him to swear, which he did. Thereupon 'Alī came to do obeisance and Zankī, having confirmed him in control of his castles, busied himself with the conquest of the Hakkārīs' castles. Al-Sha'bānī was in the hands of a Mihrānī emir, whose name was al-Ḥasan ibn 'Umar. Zankī took it from him, but showed him favour because of his great age and his quietism.

Naṣīr al-Dīn Jaqar hated 'Alī, the lord of al-Rabiyya and other castles. He urged Zankī that it would be a good plan to seize him. He gave his approval for that, so he was taken, but then Zankī regretted his arrest and sent to Naṣīr al-Dīn to release him, but found him already dead. It is reported that Naṣīr al-Dīn had killed him. Then he sent his army to the castle of al-Rabiyya, on which they made a surprise attack and which they took in an hour. All the offspring of 'Alī and his brothers and his sisters who were there were all taken prisoner. His mother, Khadīja, was absent and was not found later. Zankī was delighted when he heard the news of the taking of al-Rabiyya. He ordered the troops to go to the rest of 'Alī's castles. This was done and they were put under siege, but they found them strong. Zankī made

8 On a river of the same name (modern Colab) north of Harrān (see Yāqūt, ii, 96).

9 Yāqūt, i, 352: 'a strong castle in the district of Zawzan'. Yaqūt, iv, 859, makes the same comment for Nayrūh.

10 Spelt thus in Yāqūt, ii, 103: 'a castle in the Hakkārī Mts. in the territory of Mosul.'

11 Yāqūt, iv, 970: 'a strong castle in the Mosul region, 30 leagues to the north of it.'

12 These five toponyms have not been identified. Perhaps Mābaramā (?) should be corrected to Bārimmā on the Lesser Zab in the province of Mosul (Krawulsky, 469).

contact with the defenders and promised them generous treatment. They agreed to surrender on condition that all their people in prison should be freed. Zankī would not agree to this, unless they would also surrender the castle of Kawāshī.[13] Khadīja, 'Alī's mother, went to the lord of Kawāshī, whose name was Khūl Wahrūn, a Mihrānī, and asked him to give up Kawāshī. He agreed to that, so Zankī took over the castles and freed the captives. Such a thing had never been heard of. Zankī said, 'He gives up a place like Kawāshī when a women asks! Either he is the most noble and generous man ever, who never turns anyone away from his door, or he is the most stupid man ever.' Zankī's control of the Uplands was now well established.

[17] Miscellaneous events

In this year the Danishmand, lord of Malatya, defeated the Franks in Syria, and killed and captured many of them, and also the caliph and Atabeg Zankī made peace.

In Rabī' I [30 December 1133–28 January 1134] Sharaf al-Dīn Anūshirwān ibn Khālid was dismissed from the post of caliph's vizier.

The mother of al-Mustarshid bi-Allāh died, and al-Mustarshid sent an army to Takrit to besiege Mujāhid al-Dīn Bahrūz, who negotiated their withdrawal in return for a payment of money.

This year a part of Sanjar's army assembled with Emir Arghush and besieged the castle of Girdkūh in Khurasan, which belonged to the Ismā'īlīs. They pressed hard on the defenders during a long siege. Food ran out and the inhabitants suffered agues and spasms. Many were unable to stand, let alone fight. When signs that the city would fall were plain, Emir Arghush withdrew. It was reported that they brought him a lot of money and precious items, and that was why he left.

This year the following persons died:

Emir Sulaymān ibn Muhārish al-'Uqaylī, Emir of the Banū 'Uqayl. The position was held after him by his sons despite their young age. They were paraded in Baghdad to mark what was owed to their grandfather Muhārish, for he was the one who entertained the Caliph al-Qā'im bi-Amr Allāh in al-Ḥadītha when al-Basāsīrī did what we have already related.[14]

Abū 'Alī al-Ḥasan ibn Ibrāhīm ibn Farhūn al-Shāfi'ī al-Fāriqī, in Muḥarram [November 1133]. He was born in Mayyafariqin in the year 433 [1041-2] and

[13] In a later context (the year 552/1158) *Bāhir*, 112–13, mentions Kawāshī, along with Faraḥ and al-Za'farān, as 'castles in the sphere of Jazīrat ibn 'Umar.' Under the year 615/1218-9 Kawāshī is described as 'the strongest, highest and most defensible of Mosul's castles' (*Kāmil*, xii, 341).

[14] The occupation of Baghdad by the Turkish emir al-Basāsīrī and the recognition of the Fatimid caliph there in the year 450-51/1058-59 (Richards, *Annals*, 118–28).

studied law there under Abū 'Abd Allāh al-Kāzarūnī. When the latter died, he came down to Baghdad and studied with Abū Isḥāq al-Shīrāzī and Abū Naṣr al-Ṣabbāgh. He became cadi at Wāsiṭ and was a good and learned man, neither penalising nor favouring anyone in his judgments.

[18] 'Abd Allāh ibn Muḥammad ibn Aḥmad ibn al-Ḥasan, Abū Muḥammad ibn Abī Bakr, the Shafi'ī lawyer. He studied with his father and gave fatwas and engaged in disputation. He gave sermons and his discourse was full of word-play, for example:

> Where are the tall (*al-'āliya*) frames and the rosy (*al-wardiyya*) cheeks; by God, al-'Āliya and al-Wardiyya are full of them.

These are [the names of] two cemeteries at Nahr al-Mu'allā. Here is an example of his poetry:

> Tears flow like blood from my eyelids.
> If I live with such weeping, how dreadful will I be!
> My prison is my grief and my cares have distressed me.
> My reproacher has named me with blame.
> Telling them of me increases my woes;
> Their laments along with the doves have grieved me.
> My dwelling places cannot contain the reach of my desire;
> Separation has given me the extension of my sorrows.[15]

Ibn Abī al-Ṣalt, the poet.[16] An example of his verse, finding fault with a ponderous dullard, is:

> I have an acquaintance and I wonder how it is possible
> For this earth and these hills to support him.
> I pay him due respect but in my heart
> The slightest thought of him makes the hills sink.
> He is like the gray hairs whose appearance I dislike,
> Yet I protect and respect them.

He also wrote:

> Insignificant people have power in this age of ours.
> May it not endure and may it not exist.

---

[15] The translation of these verses is speculative and follows some variant readings in the text.

[16] Umayya ibn 'Abd al-'Azīz ibn Abī'l-Ṣalt al-Andalusī, born 460/1068, died, according to Yāqūt, *Irshād*, ii, 361–5, in Muḥarram 529/October 1134.

As in a chess game, whenever it is about to end,
The pawn is turned into a queen.

Muḥammad ibn ʻAlī ibn ʻAbd al-Wahhāb, Abū Rashīd, the Shāfiʻī lawyer from Ṭabaristan. He also heard and transmitted Ḥadīth. He was a pious ascetic who lived in isolation on an island for several years, worshipping God Almighty. He returned to Āmul, where he died. His tomb is visited by pilgrims.

[19] The Year 529 [1134–1135]

Account of Prince Ṭughril's death and Mas'ūd's taking power in the Uplands

We have mentioned that Sultan Mas'ūd came to Baghdad fleeing from his brother, Prince Ṭughril ibn Muḥammad. On his arrival at Baghdad the caliph received him with honour and provided him with all that a person of his rank needed. He commanded him to go to Hamadhan, to gather troops and to challenge his brother Ṭughril for the sultanate and the country. Mas'ūd was making promises and procrastinating. The caliph was urging him on and promised him that he would accompany him in person, and ordered his tents to be brought out to the caliph's gate.

Emir Alpqush and other emirs had joined the caliph and asked to serve him. He took them into his service and reached an understanding with them. Now it happened that a certain person was seized on whom were found some private messages from Ṭughril to these emirs and his promise under seal to give them fiefs. Seeing this, the caliph arrested one of their number, called Oghulbeg, and sequestered his property. The other emirs who were with the caliph took fright and fled to the army of Sultan Mas'ūd. The caliph sent to Mas'ūd asking for them to be handed back, which he failed to do, providing various excuses. This outraged the caliph and resulted in a coolness between them which caused the delay of his expedition. The [sultan] sent to him, firmly demanding that he set out with him.

In this situation there came the news of his brother Ṭughril's death, which happened in Muḥarram of this year [22 October–20 November 1134]. He had been born in Muḥarram of the year 503 [August 1109]. He was good, intelligent and just, close to his subjects and kind toward them. Before his death he had left his palace, intending to move against his brother, Sultan Mas'ūd. The people prayed for him and he said, [**20**] 'Pray for our success for the sake of the Muslims.'

When he died and the news reached Mas'ūd, he set out immediately for Hamadhan and all the troops joined him. He appointed as his vizier Sharaf al-Dīn Anūshirwān ibn Khālid, who together with his family had accompanied him. Arriving at Hamadhan, Mas'ūd took control and all the territories and the populace submitted to him.

The murder of Shams al-Mulūk and the succession of his brother

On 14 Rabīʿ II [= 30 January 1135][1] Shams al-Mulūk Ismāʿīl ibn Tāj al-Mulūk Būrī ibn Ṭughtakīn, the ruler of Damascus, was killed. The reason for this was that he followed a dreadful course of tyranny and extortion of his officials and others in the city's financial administration. He used extreme tortures to extract money and manifested excessive greed and meanness of spirit, so that he did not scorn to use violence to take derisory amounts. In addition there were other blameworthy traits, so his family, his followers and his subjects loathed him.

It became known that he wrote to ʿImād al-Dīn Zankī to surrender Damascus to him, urging him to come quickly. He emptied the city of stores and money and transferred it all to Ṣarkhad. He sent a succession of envoys to Zankī, urging him to come and saying, 'If you neglect to come, I shall hand it to the Franks.' Zankī set out therefore, but news of this became public in Damascus. The retainers of Shams al-Mulūk's father and grandfather became very worried and anxious at this and informed his mother of the state of affairs. She was vexed and alarmed but promised relief from this situation.

She kept on eye open for an opportunity of finding him alone without his mamlukes. When she saw such a chance she ordered her mamlukes to kill him, which they did. She gave orders for him to be thrown down in a place in the palace so that he could be seen by his mamlukes [**21**] and his followers. When they saw him they rejoiced at his downfall and their release from his wickedness.

He was born on the eve of Thursday 7 Jumādā II in the year 506 [= 28 November 1112]. It is said that the cause of his death was that his father had a chamberlain called Yūsuf ibn Fayrūz, who dominated him and exercised authority in his state and continued like that in the reign of Shams al-Mulūk. There were rumours about him and Shams al-Mulūk's mother, news of which reached him. He intended to kill Yūsuf but he fled to Tadmor and sought safe refuge there, proclaiming his loyalty to Shams al-Mulūk. The latter planned to kill his mother, but she, hearing of this, killed him first as she was afraid of him. God knows best!

His brother Shihāb al-Dīn Maḥmūd ibn Tāj al-Mulūk Būrī succeeded and sat on his throne. Everyone swore allegiance to him and his rule became firmly established. God knows best!

How Atabeg Zankī besieged Damascus

During this year Atabeg Zankī besieged Damascus. He descended upon it at the beginning of Jumādā I [17 February 1135]. The cause was what we have mentioned, Shams al-Mulūk's sending to him and summoning him to take over.

---

[1] By the tables 14 Rabīʿ II is 1 February but that was a Friday. Ibn Qal., 246, specifies Wednesday.

When the letters and the envoys arrived with this offer he set out for Damascus. However, before he could arrive, Shams al-Mulūk was murdered. When Zankī crossed the Euphrates he sent him messengers to arrange the terms of the hand-over but they saw that the opportunity was lost. However, they were received with respect and kindness and sent back with a handsome letter. Zankī learnt of Shams al-Mulūk's murder and that their choice had settled on Shihāb al-Dīn and they had united in allegiance to him. Zankī paid no attention to this letter [**22**] but set off for Damascus and put it under siege. The peasants of the local countryside took refuge in Damascus and gathered there to resist him.

Initially he camped to the north but later moved to the Pebble Hippodrome.[2] He carried out assaults but witnessed in the opposition to him manifest strength, great valour and an absolute unity of purpose. Mu'īn al-Dīn Unur, a mamluke of Shihāb al-Dīn's grandfather Ṭughtakīn, played a notable role in this crisis at Damascus. His knowledge of siege operations and warfare and his capability proved to be unparalleled and were the cause of his advancement and his taking over all affairs of state, as we shall relate, God willing.

While the siege of the city was in progress, the envoy of the Caliph al-Mustarshid bi-Allāh, namely Abū Bakr ibn Bishr al-Jazarī (from Jazīrat Ibn 'Umar), arrived with robes of honour for Atabeg Zankī and a command that he make peace with the ruler of Damascus [and leave. He made peace with them and made the khutbah in Damascus][3] for Prince Alp Arslān Maḥmūd who was with Atabeg Zankī. Zankī departed from Damascus two days from the end of Jumādā I of this year [16 March 1135].

Account of the killing of Ḥasan ibn al-Ḥāfiẓ

We have mentioned already under the year 526 [1131–2] that al-Ḥāfiẓ li-Dīn Allāh, ruler of Egypt, appointed his son Ḥasan as vizier and proclaimed him as heir apparent in the khutbah. He lived until this present year and then died, poisoned. This was because his father al-Ḥāfiẓ made him vizier although he was rashly eager to shed blood and because al-Ḥāfiẓ harboured rancorous feelings against the emirs who had aided Abū 'Alī ibn al-Afḍal. Wishing to avenge himself on them without any direct action of his own, he ordered his son Ḥasan to do it. He took over the whole matter and acted quite independently, leaving no decision to his father. He put to death some Egyptian emirs and also some local notables. He even killed forty emirs in a single night.

2 The text has *Maydān al-Ḥiṣār*, otherwide unknown and almost certainly an error for *Maydān al-Ḥaṣā*. Ibn Shaddād, *Damas*, 184, places the latter 'south of Damascus'.

3 What is added between brackets is from Ms. Pococke 346, fol. 73a: *wa'l-raḥl 'anhā fa-ṣālaḥa-hum wa-khaṭaba bi-dimashq* (*lil-malik*). It is missing from the published text and also from *Kāmil* (Thornberg), xi, 12–13.

[**23**] When his father saw how he dominated him, he sent out one of the senior eunuchs of the palace, who assembled a following and raised a large crowd of infantry and then advanced towards the city. Ḥasan sent against them several of his retinue and his men. There was a battle and the eunuch was defeated and a large number of the infantry with him were killed. The survivors crossed to the Giza bank.[4] Al-Ḥāfiẓ was humiliated but endured the restrictions which were placed on him. Later the surviving Egyptian emirs met and agreed to kill Ḥasan. They sent to his father al-Ḥāfiẓ and said, 'Either you hand your son over to us to kill him or we shall kill you both.' He summoned his son and placed a guard over him. He sent to the emirs to tell them that but they said, 'We will not be satisfied unless he is killed.' He saw that, if he handed him over, they would be emboldened against himself, but there was no way he could save him. He called for two doctors he had, one a Muslim and the other a Jew. He said to the Jew, 'We want some fatal poison we can give to this boy to escape from this dilemma.' He replied, ' I only know infusions and barley water and those sorts of potions.' Al-Ḥāfiẓ said, 'I want something to save me from this awful situation.' 'I know nothing,' the Jew said. He summoned the Muslim doctor, who, when he was asked about that, concocted something. It was given to the boy to drink and he died immediately. The emirs said, 'We want to see him.' Some of them were brought in, they looked at him and thought that some trick had been done, so they made cuts on his lower legs. When no blood flowed, they knew that he was dead and left.

After Ḥasan was buried, al-Ḥāfiẓ summoned the Muslim doctor and said to him, 'It would be best for you to leave the palace and our service. All the perquisites and the salary that you have you may keep.' He summoned the Jew and increased his salary, and said, 'I know that you understand what I asked of you. However, you are intelligent, so you may stay in the palace with us.'

Ḥasan was wicked, tyrannical and reckless in the shedding of blood and seizing of property. Poets satirised him and an example of that is what al-Mu'tamid ibn al-Anṣārī,[5] the author of celebrated letters, said:

O Ḥasan, you did not perform among mankind any good deed (*ḥasan*),
And you did not see the truth in any matter, temporal or religious.
[**24**] Killing people for no crime and no cause,
And oppression in seizing the property of the poor!
With no learning and no culture you have united
The arrogance of princes and the behaviour of the insane.

---

[4] The text has *ilā barr al-jazīra*, but both Ms. Pococke 346, fol. 73b, and *Kāmil* (Thornberg), xi, 13, have *ilā al-jīza*.

[5] Is this perhaps Mu'tamid al-Dawla 'Alī ibn Ja'far ibn Ghassān, known as Ibn al-'Asāf, who in 527/1132–3 headed the Fatimid bureacracy as *nāẓir al-dīwān* and was arrested and killed by Ḥasan in 528/1133–4 (see *Itti'āẓ*, iii, 148–9; Ibn Muyassar, 76).

It is said that al-Ḥāfiẓ, when he saw that his son had dominated government, arranged for someone to give him poison, from which he died.

After the death of Ḥasan, al-Ḥāfiẓ appointed as vizier Emir Tāj al-Mulk Bahrām, who was a Christian. He took full control of affairs and put Armenians in authority over the people. They humiliated the Muslims. An account of this will be given under the year 531 [1136–7], God willing.

Account of al-Mustarshid's expedition against Sultan Mas'ūd and his defeat

In this year in the month of Ramaḍān [15 June–14 July 1135] there took place the war between the Caliph al-Mustarshid and Sultan Mas'ūd. The cause was that when Sultan Mas'ūd went from Baghdad to Hamadhan after the death of his brother Ṭughril and took that city, a number of his leading emirs deserted him, such as Yarunqush Bāzdār, Qizil Ākhur, Sunqur al-Khumārtakīn, the governor of Hamadhan, and 'Abd al-Raḥmān ibn Tughāyaruk and others, in fear of him and feeling estranged. With them was a large contingent and they were joined by Dubays ibn Ṣadaqa. They sent to the caliph asking for his safe-conduct to allow them to present themselves at his service. He was told that this was a ruse, because Dubays was with them. They then went to Khuzistan and came to an agreement with Bursuq ibn Bursuq. The caliph sent them Sadīd al-Dawla ibn al-Anbārī with rescripts addressed to the emirs mentioned above, bidding them put their minds at rest and commanding them to present themselves before him.

[**25**] These emirs had already decided to arrest Dubays and to win favour with the caliph by bringing him to him. However, Dubays heard of this and fled to Sultan Mas'ūd. In Rajab [began 17 April 1135] the emirs went to Baghdad and were well received by the caliph who provided them with all necessaries and robes of honour. All prayers for Sultan Mas'ūd were dropped in Baghdad, and on 20 Rajab [8 May 1135] the caliph left his palace with the intention of going to fight Mas'ūd. He stopped at al-Shufay'ī. The lord of Basra, Beg-Aba rebelled against the caliph and fled to his city. The caliph wrote to him, offering to guarantee his security, but he did not return.

The caliph delayed his march, while these emirs were urging him to set out and making light of the whole undertaking, assuring him how weak Sultan Mas'ūd was. He despatched his vanguard to Hulwan, which they plundered in a riotous manner which no one rebuked them for at all. On 8 Sha'bān [24 May 1135] the caliph set out and was joined on the way by Emir Bursuq ibn Bursuq, whose complement of men reached 7,000 horse. Three thousand remained behind in Iraq with Iqbāl, al-Mustarshid's eunuch.

Sultan Mas'ūd was in Hamadhan with about 1,500 horse. Most of the regional rulers were in correspondance with the caliph, offering him allegiance, but while the caliph delayed his march, Sultan Mas'ūd came to terms with most of them, so that his numbers grew to about 15,000 horse. A large part of the caliph's army deserted, so that he was left with 5,000. The Atabeg Zankī sent reinforcements, but they failed to join him.

Prince Dā'ūd, son of Sultan Maḥmūd, who was in Azerbayjan, sent to the caliph, advising him to turn aside to Dinawar to allow Dā'ūd with his army to join him. Al-Mustarshid did not do this, but pressed on to Dāy Marj, where he drew up his troops for battle. On the right wing he placed Yarunqush Bāzdār, Nūr al-Dawla Sunqur, Qizil Ākhur and Bursuq ibn Bursuq, and on the left he placed Jawlī [**26**], Bursuq the Butler[6] and Oghulbeg, whom the caliph had arrested and then released from prison.

On hearing news of them Sultan Mas'ūd moved quickly towards them and gave battle at Dāy Marj on 10 Ramadan [24 June 1135]. The caliph's left wing withdrew from the field, as treacherously agreed with Sultan Mas'ūd, and joined him. The caliph's right wing and the sultan's left fought a desultory battle. The sultan's army encircled the caliph, who held firm, not moving from his position. His forces fled and he himself was taken captive, along with a large number of his men, such as Vizier Sharaf al-Dīn 'Alī ibn Ṭirād al-Zaynabī, the chief cadi, the head of the Treasury, Ibn Ṭalḥa, Ibn al-Anbārī, the preachers, lawyers and notaries and others. The caliph was put in a tent and the contents of his camp, which were considerable, were ransacked. The vizier, the chief cadi, Ibn al-Anbārī and the head of the Treasury and other notables were taken to the castle of Sarjahān. All the rest were sold for trifling sums. Not one person was killed in this battle, which is one of the most surprising things to relate.

The sultan returned to Hamadhan and ordered the following proclamation: 'Any men of Baghdad who follow us to Hamadan we will execute.' All made their way back in the worst possible state, not knowing the route and having no mounts. The sultan sent Emir Beg-Aba al-Muḥammadī to Baghdad as prefect. He arrived at the end of Ramaḍān [14 July 1135] with some slaves. They seized all the estates of the caliph and took their stores of grain.

Many of the Baghdad common people rioted, broke the minbar and the grille,[7] and prevented the making of the khutbah. They went out into the markets, heaping dust on their heads, weeping and crying aloud. Women went out into the markets bare-headed, beating their breasts. The prefect's men and the Baghdad populace came to blows, and more than 150 people were killed. The governor and the palace chamberlain fled.

[**27**] The sultan meanwhile left Hamadhan for Marāgha to fight Prince Dā'ūd, the son of his brother Maḥmūd, who had rebelled against him. He camped two leagues from Marāgha, with al-Mustarshid in train. Envoys went back and forth between the caliph and the sultan on the subject of an accord. A basis was settled on, as we shall relate, God willing, and God is the giver of all success.

---

6 i.e. *Sharāb Salār*.

7 Probably one of the caliph's private 'pew', the *maqṣūra*.

Account of the killing of al-Mustarshid and the succession of al-Rāshid as caliph

When al-Mustarshid bi-Allāh Abū Manṣūr ibn al-Faḍl ibn al-Mustaẓhir bi-Allāh Abī'l-'Abbās Aḥmad was taken, as we have related, Sultan Mas'ūd put him in a tent, arranged for him to be kept under guard and provided for all the service he needed. They exchanged messengers to discuss terms and to come to an agreement, namely that the caliph would pay some money, not assemble an army again nor leave his palace. The sultan accepted this, provided a mount for the caliph to ride in state with the Saddle Covering[8] borne before him, and all that remained was for the caliph to return to Baghdad. Then news came that Emir Qirān Khuwān had arrived as an envoy from Sanjar, so the caliph's departure was put off. Everyone went out with Sultan Mas'ūd to meet the envoy. Some of those entrusted with watching the caliph left him. His tent was isolated from the main army. Twenty-four members of the Bātinīs made their way to him, entered his tent and killed him. They inflicted more than twenty wounds on him, mutilated him by cutting off his nose and ears, and left him naked. Some of his attendants, for example Abū 'Abd Allāh ibn Sukayna, were killed with him. His assassination took place on Thursday 17 Dhū'l-Qā'da [29 August 1135] at the gates of Marāgha. He was left to be buried by the inhabitants of the town. Ten of the Bāṭinīs were killed or, according to another account, all were killed. God knows best!

[**28**] He was forty-three years and three months old when he was killed, and his caliphate had lasted seven years, six months and twenty days. His mother had been a slave. He was strong and courageous, very bold and with far-reaching aspirations. The events of his reign are evidence of this. He had an excellent command of Arabic, was eloquent and wrote a fine hand. I have seen the excellent quality of his penmanship and I have also seen his responses to petitions which are very well written and superlatively well expressed.

After the murder of al-Mustarshid his son, Abū Ja'far al-Manṣūr was proclaimed and given the title al-Rāshid bi-Allāh.[9] Al-Mustarshid had had him proclaimed as heir apparent during his lifetime. After the assassination oaths of allegiance to him were renewed on Monday 27 Dhū'l-Qa'da [Monday[10] = 9 September 1135]. Sultan Mas'ūd wrote to Beg-Aba, the prefect of Baghdad, who also swore his allegiance. Everyone of importance came to the swearing of allegiance, as did twenty-one members of the caliphal family. The Shaykh Abū'l-Najīb performed the ceremony and gave a sermon, which was full of uplifting matter. Jamāl al-Dawla Iqbāl, who was in Baghdad with a detachment of the army, crossed over to the West Bank

---

8 *al-Ghāshiya*. From the Saljuqs onwards this remained one of the emblems of sovereignty. See, for the Mamluke period, Vermeulen, 'Une note sur les insignes,' 359, and references there cited.

9 i.e. the One Rightly-guided by God.

10 If the 17th of Dhūl-Qa'da was a Thursday (see above), then this Monday ought to be the 28th. The 27th would be a Sunday.

when these events occurred and travelled up to Takrit. He made contact with Mujāhid al-Dīn Bahrūz, got him to swear an oath and then joined him in the castle.

Account of Sultan Sanjar's expedition to Ghazna and his return

This year during Dhū'l-Qa'da [August-September 1135], Sultan Sanjar marched from Khurasan to Ghazna. The reason for this was that he had received reports about the ruler there, Bahrām Shāh, that his loyalty had become doubtful, and that his grasping hand was wronging his subjects and despoiling their wealth.

[**29**] It was Sultan Sanjar who had conquered Ghazna, as we have related under the year 509 [1115-16]. When he heard these disturbing reports, he set out for Ghazna to take it or to make peace with Bahrām Shāh. Far along his march, he was overtaken by a winter of severe cold and much snow. Provisions and fodder were impossible to come by. The army complained of this to the sultan and told him of the hardship they suffered and their lack of all necessities. However, they found him quite determined to march on. On their approach to Ghazna, Bahrām Shāh sent Sanjar envoys to express his submission and to ask for pardon for his misdeeds and forgiveness for his faults. In reply to his communication, Sanjar sent back his greatest emir, the Favourite[11] Jawhar, the eunuch, part of whose fief was the city of Rayy, to grant him forgiveness, if he came before his presence and returned to his obedience. When he came to Bahrām, the latter agreed to the demand that he should return to obedience, pay money and attend in person before the sultan, and he made a great show of allegiance and submission to the sultan's orders.

The Favourite Jawhar returned to Sanjar with Bahrām Shah. Jawhar went first to Sultan Sanjar and informed him of Bahrām Shāh's arrival and that he would early on the next day attend on him. Jawhar went back to Bahrām Shāh to be ready to present him, and on the morrow Sanjar rode out in state for the meeting. Bahrām Shāh, accompanied by Jawhar, advanced towards Sanjar. When he caught sight of Sanjar's retinue and the parasol over his head, he turned to withdraw, but the Chamberlain took hold of his bridle, censured what he was doing and warned him of the dreadful consequences. Nevertheless, Bahrām Shāh would not go on, but turned and fled, not believing himself secure and thinking that Sanjar would seize him and take his lands. Several of his men and his courtiers followed him. He went on past Ghazna, which Sanjar then entered and took possession of, laying hands on all it contained and collecting its taxes. He wrote a letter to Bahrām Shāh, blaming him for his action and swearing that he had no evil intention towards him. Regarding his city he had no ambitions and he was not one of those who vexed his

---

[11] This epithet, *al-muqarrab*, meaning 'treated as an intimate', is used like a title. *Muntaẓam*, x, 87, which refers to him as 'the Abyssinian eunuch' (*al-khādim al-ḥabashī*), shows this to be so: 'known as the Favourite' (*al-ma'rūf bi'l-muqarrab*).

servants or requited their faithful service with evil. His only plan was to repair their relations. Bahrām Shāh sent back a reply full of excuses and self-vindication, saying that his fear [**30**] had prevented his attendance and that no blame attached to one who feared someone like the sultan. He begged him to return to his former goodwill. Sanjar agreed to restore him to his city, and so left Ghazna for home. He arrived at Balkh during Shawwāl of the year 530 [July 1136]. Thus Bahrām Shāh's rule of Ghazna was confirmed and he returned there as ruler in complete charge.

Account of the death of Dubays ibn Ṣadaqa at this time

The Sultan Mas'ūd had Dubays ibn Ṣadaqa killed this year at the door of his pavilion outside Khūnaj. He ordered an Armenian mamluke to kill him. He stood just behind him, as he was scratching the ground with his finger, and struck off his head without his knowing anything about it. His son Ṣadaqa was in al-Ḥilla and his father's troops and mamlukes rallied to him. His following became numerous and Emir Qutlugh Takīn sought protection with him. Sultan Mas'ūd ordered Beg-Aba to take al-Ḥilla, and part of the army went to al-Madā'in, where they remained for some while, waiting for Beg-Aba to join them, but he failed to come because of cowardice and an inability to attack al-Ḥilla because of the large number of troops there with Ṣadaqa. The latter remained in al-Ḥilla until Sultan Mas'ūd came to Baghdad in the year 531 [1136–7]. He then sought him out, repaired their relations and became his constant servant.

This sort of thing happens quite often, namely the near simultaneous death of two enemies, for Dubays was an enemy of al-Mustarshid and hated his being caliph. He did not realise that he was only preserved by the sultans because they used him as an instrument to oppose al-Mustarshid. When the motive was no more, the result was lost too, but God knows best about that.

[31] How Yaḥyā's army besieged al-Mahdiyya

This year Yaḥyā[12] ibn al-'Azīz ibn Ḥammād, lord of Bougie, sent a force to besiege Mahdiyya, where al-Ḥasan[13] ibn 'Alī ibn Tamīm ibn al-Mu'izz ibn Bādīs was the ruler. The reason was that al-Ḥasan was attached to Maymūn ibn Ziyād, the emir of a large group of Arabs, and favoured him over the rest of the Arabs, who were envious. The Arab emirs sent their sons to Yaḥyā ibn al-'Azīz and put them in his hands as hostages, when they asked him to send a force with them to conquer

---

[12] The last of the Hammādid dynasty, succeeded circa 515/1122 and died in 557/1161–2 (see Idris, *La Berbérie*, 325, 364–70).

[13] Prince of the Zīrid dynasty, born 502/1109, ruled 515–43/1121–48 (see *EI(2)*, xi, 513–15; Idris, *La Berbérie*, i, 333ff., and for this attack on Mahdiyya, 342–5).

Mahdiyya for him. He agreed to that, although with no urgency. It happened that letters came to him from some of the shaykhs of Mahdiyya suggesting the same thing. He trusted in what he had received and despatched a powerful force over whom he placed a great commander, one of his learned companions, called Muṭṭarif ibn Ḥamdūn.

This Yaḥyā and his ancestors were jealous of al-Mu'izz ibn Bādīs and his descendants.[14] The troops, horse and foot, accompanied by a large gathering of Arabs, marched until they descended upon Mahdiyya and besieged it by land and by sea. Muṭṭarif displayed austere piety and an unwillingness to shed blood. He said, 'I have only come at this time to take over the city without a fight.' His expectation was disappointed and he waited for several days without any engagement, but then they commenced direct hostilities. The people of Mahdiyya got the upper-hand and had some affect on them. The fighting continued uninterruptedly and in all of it success went to the city's inhabitants. A sizeable number of the rebels were slain.

When he despaired of a surrender, Muṭṭarif gathered his troops and made a land and sea assault with very fierce fighting. His galleys dominated the shore and his men drew close to the wall. A crisis point arrived and al-Ḥasan ordered the opening of the gate on the shoreward side and was one of the first to sally forth. He and the men with him charged, as he cried, 'I am al-Ḥasan.' When those opposing him heard his call, they saluted him [**32**] and gave way before him out of reverence. Al-Ḥasan at that moment sent his galleys out the harbour. Four of the enemy ships were taken and the rest were put to flight. Reinforcements from Roger the Frank, ruler of Sicily, then arrived by sea in twenty vessels. The galleys of the ruler of Bougie were surrounded but al-Ḥasan ordered that they be set free, which was done. Then Maymūn ibn Ziyād arrived with a large body of Arabs to aid al-Ḥasan. Seeing this and also that reinforcements were coming to al-Ḥasan by land and by sea, Muṭṭarif realised that he was powerless to match them, so he withdrew from Mahdiyya, disappointed. Roger the Frank continued to pretend to al-Ḥasan that he was at peace with him and an ally, while nevertheless building galleys and increasing their numbers.

How the Franks took the island of Jerba

The island of Jerba, off the coast of Ifrīqiya, had fully developed its abundant agriculture and natural advantages. However, its population were unruly and would not accept being subject to any authority. They were known as trouble-makers and pirates. A force of Franks from Sicily invaded it with a large fleet and

[14] The text's reading has 'the descendants of al-Manṣūr Abū'l-Ḥasan.' This cannot be an oblique way of referring to al-Mu'izz, who was Abū Tamīm Sharaf al-Dawla (see *EI(2)*, vii, 481–4). *Kāmil* (Thornberg), xi, 19, has a bizarre version, but at least refers to al-Mu'izz directly. The translation here follows Ms. Pococke, 346, fol. 76a.

sizeable numbers, which included several of the famous knights of the Franks. They disembarked and encircled it with their ships on all sides.

The inhabitants gathered together and resisted strongly. A fierce battle took place between the two sides. The people of Jerba held firm and many men were killed. Then they were defeated and the Franks took the island. They seized property and enslaved the women and children. Most of the men perished but those that survived secured guarantees for themselves from Roger, ruler of Sicily, and they redeemed their prisoners, captives and womenfolk. God knows best about that!

[33] Account of the Franks' acquisition of the castle of Rūṭa in Andalusia

This year al-Mustanṣir bi-Allāh ibn Hūd[15] and the Frankish princeling,[16] lord of Toledo in Andulusia, made peace for a period of ten years. The princeling had vigorously raided and waged war on the lands of al-Mustanṣir, to the extent that al-Mustanṣir became too weak to resist him because he had few troops and the Franks were so many. He decided to make peace for a period during which he and his troops could recuperate and prepare for [further] hostilities. There was an exchange of envoys and a treaty was arranged on condition that al-Mustanṣir would surrender to the princeling the castle of Rūṭa[17] in Andalusia, one of the strongest and largest castles. Agreement was reached, peace concluded and the Franks took over the castle. Al-Mustanṣir had done something that nobody before him had ever done.

Account of Ibn Rudmīr's siege of the city of Fraga, his defeat and his death

During this year Ibn Rudmīr the Frank besieged the city of Fraga[18] in the east of Andalusia. Emir Yūsuf ibn Tāshfīn ibn 'Alī ibn Yūsuf was in Cordoba and he sent al-Zubayr ibn 'Amr al-Lamtūnī, governor of Cordoba, with 2,000 horse. He also sent with him to Fraga a great amount of provisions.

The celebrated emir, Yaḥyā ibn Ghāniya, was emir of Murcia and Valencia in the east of Andalusia and governed them for the Emir of the Muslims 'Alī ibn Yūsuf. He took the field with 500 horse. 'Abd Allāh ibn 'Iyāḍ, who was ruler of Lérida, set out at the head of 200 horse. They met and marched, carrying supplies with them, until they came in sight of Fraga. Al-Zubayr positioned the supplies in front

---

[15] Al-Mustanṣir Abū Ja'far Aḥmad III was a member of the Ḥūdids, centred on Saragossa (see *EI(2)*, iii, 542–3), who were from the eleventh century important among the 'Party Kings' (*Reyes des Taifas*).

[16] In Arabic *al-sulayṭīn al-faranjī*. Alfonso VII is intended.

[17] i.e. Rueda de Jalon, about 20 miles west of Saragossa.

[18] In Arabic Ifrāgha, situated on the River Cinca, about 15 miles south-west of Lérida.

of himself, Ibn Ghāniya before the supplies and Ibn ʻIyāḍ in front of Ibn Ghāniya. He was a brave warrior, as were all those with him.

[**34**] Ibn Rudmīr led 12,000 cavalry. He despised all the Muslims that were arriving and said to his men, 'Go out and take this gift which the Muslims have sent you.' Carried away by arrogance, he sent forward a large contingent from his army. When they approached the Muslims, Ibn ʻIyāḍ charged and broke them, forcing them back on one another and dealing death. When the battle was fully engaged, Ibn Rudmīr arrived in person with all his troops, overconfident in their numbers and their courage. Ibn Ghāniya and Ibn ʻIyāḍ made a frontal attack. As the battle became hot and the fighting intensified, many of the Franks were slain. At that moment the people of Fraga, men and women, young and old, came out to the Frankish tents. The men occupied themselves with killing those they found in the camp and the women with plundering. Everything in the camp, food, equipment, engines, weapons and such like, was borne back to the city.

While the Muslims and the Franks were fighting, al-Zubayr arrived with his troops. Ibn Rudmīr was beaten and turned his back in flight. His whole army was overwhelmed with destruction. Only a few escaped. Ibn Rudmīr reached Saragossa. Having seen how many of his men were slain, within twenty days of the defeat he died of grief. He was the bravest of the Frankish kings, the most dedicated to making war on the Muslims and the most determined. He used to sleep on his shield without any mattress. It was said to him, 'Why do you not take a concubine from the daughters of the Muslim nobles whom you have taken captive?' He replied, 'It is proper for a fighting man to associate with men not women.' God did away with him and saved the Muslims from his wickedness.

Miscellaneous events

In Shawwāl of this year [17 July–12 August 1135] there was an earthquake in Iraq, Mosul, the Uplands and elsewhere. It was very severe and many people perished. God knows best.

[35]

The Year 530 [1135-1136]

Account of the battle between the armies of al-Rāshid and Sultan Mas'ūd

In Muḥarram of this year [11 October–9 November 1135] Yarunqush al-Zakawī arrived from Sultan Mas'ūd requesting from the caliph the money that al-Mustarshid had agreed to pay, that is 400,000 dīnars. He replied that he had nothing and that all the treasury had been with al-Mustarshid and was plundered in the defeat mentioned above. Al-Rāshid bi-Allāh was then informed that Yarunqush intended to raid the caliphal palace and search it to take the money, so he gathered his troops to defend the palace, put Kuj-Aba in command and repaired the fabric of the walls.

When Yarunqush became aware of this, he and Beg-Aba, the prefect of Baghdad, who was one of the sultan's emirs, agreed to attack the caliphal palace on Friday. Hearing of this, al-Rāshid made preparations to resist them. Yarunqush accompanied by the sultanian forces, the Bakjiyya emirs and Muḥammad ibn 'Akar, at the head of about 5,000 horse, took the field, and were met by the caliph's army, led by Kuj-Aba, and a fierce battle was fought. The populace aided the caliph's forces in their fight against the sultan's troops, and eventually forced them out towards the sultan's palace. When night fell, they took the road to Khurasan. Beg-Aba went down river to Wāsiṭ, Yarunqush left for Bandanījayn, and the Baghdad citizens sacked the sultan's palace.

[36] Account of the uniting of the provincial rulers to make war on Mas'ūd in Baghdad and their rebellion against him

This year many of the emirs and the rulers of the provinces agreed to abandon their allegiance to Sultan Mas'ūd. Prince Dā'ūd, son of Sultan Muḥammad, marched with the army of Azerbayjan to Baghdad, arriving on 4 Ṣafar [13 November 1135]. He stayed in the sultanian palace. The Atabeg 'Imād al-Dīn Zankī arrived from Mosul, and there also came Yarunqush Bāzdār, the ruler of Qazvin and other places, Alpqush the Elder, lord of Isfahan, Ṣadaqa ibn Dubays, the lord of Ḥilla, accompanied by 'Antar ibn Abī'l-'Askar al-Jāwānī to manage his affairs and supplement the shortcomings of his youth, Ibn Bursuq and Ibn al-Aḥmadīlī. From the army of Baghdad Kuj-Aba, al-Ṭurunṭay and others came out to join them, and Prince Dā'ūd appointed Yarunqush Bāzdār to be prefect of Baghdad. The caliph arrested Nāṣiḥ al-Dawla Abū 'Abd Allāh al-Ḥasan ibn Jahīr, the palace major-domo, who had been behind his accession, and also Jamāl al-Dawla Iqbāl al-Mustarshidī, who had joined his service from Takrit, and other notables of his state. The attitude of his men towards him changed and they became frightened of him.

Jamāl al-Dawla was interceded for by Atabeg Zankī with the sort of intercession behind which lay [the threat] of compulsion. He was released and joined [Zankī's] staff.

The caliph's retinue along with his vizier, Jalāl al-Dīn Abū'l-Riḍā ibn Ṣadaqa went to 'Imād al-Dīn to greet him on his arrival. Thereupon the vizier stayed with him and asked him to protect him against the caliph, which Zankī agreed to do. The caliph's cortege therefore returned without a vizier. Zankī sent men to guard the residence [**37**] of the vizier from being plundered, and later he put things right between [the vizier] and the caliph and restored him to his office. In the same way Chief Cadi al-Zaynabī crossed to join [Zankī] and travelled with him to Mosul.

The caliph pressed on assiduously with the repair of the walls, but Prince Dā'ūd sent men to dismantle the gates and to demolish a part of the walls. People in Baghdad became very alarmed and transferred their property into the caliphal palace. The khutbah for Sultan Mas'ūd was dropped and was said in the name of Prince Dā'ūd. Oaths were taken between the caliph, Prince Dā'ūd and 'Imād al-Dīn Zankī and the caliph sent Atabeg Zankī 30,000 dīnars for his expenses.

Prince Saljuqshāh came to Wāsiṭ, which he entered, and arrested Emir Beg-Aba and seized his wealth. Atabeg Zankī travelled down the river to drive him out, but they came to a peaceful agreement and Zankī returned to Baghdad, then crossed to the Khurasan road, urging all the forces to give battle to Sultan Mas'ūd. Prince Dā'ūd also took the Khurasan road and his troops plundered the region and committed misdemeanours. News came that Sultan Mas'ūd had set out for Baghdad to confront the prince. Prince Dā'ūd and Atabeg Zankī withdrew. The latter returned to Baghdad, parted from Prince Dā'ūd and let him know that he would proceed to Marāgha if Sultan Mas'ūd left Hamadan. Al-Rāshid moved to the outskirts of Baghdad on 1 Ramaḍān [3 June 1136], then he entered the city again on the 5th [7 June]. He sent to Dā'ūd and the rest of the emirs ordering them to return to Baghdad, which they did. They camped in their tents and decided to fight Sultan Mas'ūd from within the walls of Baghdad.

The envoys of Sultan Mas'ūd arrived offering to the caliph his personal allegiance and cooperation, and threatening those who had gathered around him. The caliph showed the letter to them and all advised war. The caliph replied, 'I am also with you in that.'

[38] Account of Shihāb al-Dīn's taking of Homs

This year on 22 Rabī' I [30 December 1135] Shihāb al-Dīn Maḥmūd, ruler of Damascus, took over the city of Homs and its citadel. This came about because the rulers, the sons of Emir Khīr Khān ibn Qarājā, and the man who governed there on their behalf became tired of the amount of trouble caused to the city and its surrounding districts by 'Imād al-Dīn's troops and their making life difficult for the soldiers and the ordinary citizens. They made contact with Shihāb al-Dīn about the possibility of their surrendering the city to him in return for his giving them Tadmor. He responded positively and went to take it over on the date mentioned, and handed over Tadmor. He assigned Homs as a fief to a mamluke of his grandfather's, Mu'īn al-Dīn Unur, and placed there a deputy for him, one of his leading comrades whom he could trust. He then returned to Damascus.

When Zankī's troops who were in Aleppo and Hama, saw that Homs had gone out of their hands, they carried out a series of plundering raids on its territory and took control of much of it. Several battles took place but, after Shihāb al-Dīn had written to Zankī on the matter, peace was arranged between them and each side refrained from attacking the other.

Account of discord at Damascus

In Damascus this year there was discord between the ruler and the troops. This occurred because the Chamberlain Yūsuf ibn Fayrūz, who had been the greatest chamberlain in his father's and his grandfather's service, came to fear the ruler's brother, Shams al-Mulūk, and fled from him to Tadmor. When this present year came, he asked **[39]** to come to Damascus, although he was fearful of a group of mamlukes because he had wronged them and treated them most abominably. Consequently they all felt resentment towards him, especially over the incident for which Tāj al-Mulūk had left. This has already been dealt with. He had advised that several innocent persons should be put to death and that Sivanj, the son of Tāj al-Mulūk, should be executed. They all became enemies full of hate.

When he now requested to be allowed to come to Damascus, this was granted. However, several emirs and mamlukes disapproved of his presence and feared that he might treat them as he had earlier treated others. He continued to seek good relations with them until eventually he swore oaths to them and secured oaths from them. He undertook not to take any role in affairs of state.

Later, however, he began to interfere in many affairs, so his enemies conspired to kill him. While he was riding with Shams al-Mulūk in the Hippodrome, conversing with an emir named Bazwāj[1] alongside him, the latter struck him a blow with his sword and killed him. He was borne away and buried in the tomb of his father at al-'Uqayba.

Fearful of Shams al-Mulūk, Bazwāj and the other emirs did not enter the city but camped outside. They sent seeking bases for agreement but they made high-handed demands. He agreed to some but they could not accept this and left for Baalbek, which was ruled by Shams al-Dawla Muḥammad ibn Tāj al-Mulūk, and

[1] This name is variously given as Bazwāj or Bazwāsh (cf. Ibn Qal., see index). William of Tyre has Bezeuge (cf. Stevenson, *Crusaders*, 137, note 1).

joined his service. Many Turkomans and others attached themselves to them and embarked on a course of disturbance and wickedness. The situation required that they should be written to, handled indulgently and allowed their demands. The position was resolved in this manner. They all swore mutual oaths and returned to the outskirts of Damascus but did not enter. Shihāb al-Dīn, ruler of Damascus, went out and met with them. Sworn undertakings were renewed and Bazwāj became commander of the army with full powers. This was in Sha'bān [May 1136]. All discord ceased and they entered the city. God knows best!

[40] How the forces of the Atabeg raided Frankish lands

In Sha'bān of this year [May 1136] the forces of Atabeg Zankī, lord of Aleppo and Hama, gathered with his deputy in Aleppo, Emir Sawār, and marched into Frankish territory, taking them by surprise. They suddenly attacked the districts of Lattakia, whose population was unable to move away and take precautionary measures. The troops took more plunder than it is possible to describe. They killed and captured, doing in the land of the Franks what no others had ever managed against them.

The captives amounted to 7,000 men, women and children. They seized 100,000 animals, that is, horses, mules, donkeys, cattle and sheep. As for other things, such as clothing, coins or jewellery, they were beyond counting. They destroyed Lattakia and the neighbouring areas. Only very little escaped. They then safely left for Shayzar with their booty in the middle of Ramaḍān [17 June 1136]. Syria was full of captives and riding animals and the Muslims rejoiced greatly at this. The Franks were incapable of doing anything to respond to this disaster because they were weak and impotent.

Account of Sultan Mas'ūd's arrival in Iraq, the dispersal of the local rulers, al-Rāshid's move to Mosul and his deposition

When Sultan Mas'ūd heard of the assembling of the princes and emirs in Baghdad in opposition to him [**41**] and that the khutbah had been delivered for Prince Dā'ūd, the son of his brother Sultan Maḥmūd, he gathered his forces and marched towards Baghdad, camping at al-Malakiyya. Some of his opponents, among whom was one of Atabeg Zankī's emirs, Zayn al-Dīn 'Alī, came to within shooting distance of his forces, but they drove them off and they withdrew. The sultan then arrived and camped before Baghdad, putting it and all the troops within under siege.

The urban gangs in Baghdad and all its suburbs arose in disorderly riot and plunder. They caused loss of life too, and even when one of Atabeg Zankī's men came with letters, they attacked him, took the documents and killed him. A number of the inhabitants of the quarters came to Atabeg Zankī and suggested that he should plunder the western districts, for there was nothing but urban gangs and trouble-makers there. This he refused to do, but later he sent people to sack the Ṭāhirī Harem,[2] from which large amounts of goods were seized. The reason for this was that the urban gangs were numerous there and they had taken others' property. The troops also ransacked other districts besides the Harem.

The sultan besieged them for fifty days or so without any success. He withdrew to Nahrawan, with the intention of returning to Hamadhan. Ṭuruntay, the lord of Wāsiṭ, then arrived with many boats, so the sultan came back and crossed in them to the west bank of the Tigris. The Baghdad army tried to prevent him, but he managed to cross before they could do so. Then unity broke down and Prince Dā'ūd returned to his lands during Dhū'l-Qa'da [August 1136], and the emirs dispersed.

'Imād al-Dīn Zankī was on the west bank. The Caliph al-Rāshid crossed over to him and together they went to Mosul with a small band of Zankī's men. When Sultan Mas'ūd heard that the caliph and Zankī had left Baghdad he entered the city and took up residence there, preventing his followers from harming [the populace] and looting. He made his entry in the middle of Dhū'l-Qa'da [15 August]. The inhabitants became calm and felt secure after having been extremely fearful. The sultan ordered a gathering of the cadis, notaries and lawyers, and the oath which al-Rāshid had sworn to Mas'ūd was presented to them. **[42]** It contained, written in his own hand, 'If ever I raise an army and go forth to meet any of the sultan's men with the sword, I thereby dismiss myself from my office.' They gave it as their opinion that he had abandoned the caliphate. There is a different version of these events and we shall record it under the caliphate of al-Muqtafī.

Vizier Sharaf al-Dīn 'Alī ibn Ṭirād, the head of the Treasury Kamāl al-Dīn Ibn al-Baqshalāmī, and Ibn al-Anbārī had come with the sultan, because they had been with him since they were taken prisoner along with al-Mustarshid. They now impugned al-Rāshid, and all the office holders of Baghdad agreed with them in that, except for very few, because they feared him, as he had arrested some and extorted money from others. There was general agreement in finding him at fault, so the sultan ordered his deposition and the elevation of someone suitable for the caliphate. He was therefore deposed and his name dropped from the khutbah in Baghdad during Dhū'l-Qa'da [August 1136] and in the rest of the lands. He had been caliph for eleven months and eleven days and he was assassinated by the Bāṭinīs, as we shall relate, God willing.

Account of the accession of the Caliph al-Muqtafī li-Amr Allāh

After the dropping of al-Rāshid from the khutbah, the sultan consulted a number of Baghdad notables, including among others Vizier 'Alī ibn Ṭirād and the head of

---

[2] This was built as a palace for the Ṭāhirid family (*floruit* ninth century) in West Baghdad, north of al-Manṣūr's Round City (see Le Strange, *Baghdad*, 119–21).

the Treasury, concerning a suitable person to hold the office of caliph. The vizier said, 'One of al-Rāshid's uncles - he is a suitable person.' 'Who is that?' asked [the sultan]. He replied, 'One whose name I cannot say openly lest he should be killed.' The sultan ordered them to write a report on the deposition of al-Rāshid, which they did, mentioning his faults such as extortion and other things which nullified his status as Imam. They then wrote their legal opinion (*fatwa*): 'What say the ulema concerning a person of this description? Is he fit to be Imam or not?' They stated their opinion that a man of this description was not fit to be Imam. When they had completed [**43**] this, they brought in Cadi Abū Ṭāhir ibn al-Karkhī and gave testimony to that effect before him. He duly ruled that [al-Rāshid] was 'immoral' (*fāsiq*) and [hence] deposed. Others also gave their rulings after him. The chief cadi was not present to give a ruling, because he was with Atabeg Zankī in Mosul.

Then Vizier Sharaf al-Dīn told the sultan of Abū 'Abd Allāh al-Ḥusayn (or some say, Muḥammad), the son of al-Mustarshid, his deep religion, his intelligence, his probity and tractability. The sultan came to the caliphal palace, accompanied by Vizier Sharaf al-Dīn al-Zaynabī, and the head of the Treasury Ibn al-Baqshalāmī and others, and ordered Prince Abū 'Abd Allāh, son of al-Mustarshid, to be summoned from the place where he was residing. This was done and he was enthroned in the Octagon (*al-Muthammana*),[3] where the sultan, along with Vizier Sharaf al-Dīn, came to see him. They swore mutual oaths and the vizier arranged the terms of their mutual compact. Then the sultan left and the emirs and all the officials, the cadis and the lawyers came and swore allegiance to him on 18 Dhū'l-Ḥijja [7 September 1136]. He was given the title of al-Muqtafī li-Amr Allāh.[4]

The reason for this title, it is said, was that he saw the Prophet (God bless him and give him peace) [in a dream] six days before his accession, who said to him, 'This charge is going to fall on you. Follow my example (*iqtafi bī*),' so he made use of that for his title. When he became caliph, legal certifications of his accession were despatched to all the main centres. He maintained Sharaf al-Dīn 'Alī ibn Ṭirād al-Zaynabī as his vizier and he sent to Mosul to summon Chief Cadi Abū'l-Qāsim 'Alī ibn al-Ḥusayn al-Zaynabī, the vizier's uncle, whom he restored to his post. He confirmed Kamāl al-Dīn Ḥamza ibn Ṭalḥa in his office as head of the Treasury, and affairs proceeded in excellent order.

I have heard that Sultan Mas'ūd sent to the Caliph al-Muqtafī about arranging for a fief to serve as his privy purse. The answer was, 'In the palace there are eighty mules that transport water from the Tigris. Would the sultan consider what is required for those who drink that [amount of] water and make due provision.' The settlement proposed was [**44**] that his allowance should be what al-Mustarshid had had, and this was accepted. When the sultan heard what his response had been, he

---

3 See above p. [**615**].

4 i.e. Follower of God's command.

said, 'We have put an impressive man in the caliphate. We pray God to keep us safe from him.'[5]

Al-Muqtafī was the uncle of al-Rāshid. He and al-Mustarshid, sons of al-Mustaẓhir, both held the caliphate. Likewise al-Saffāḥ and al-Manṣūr were brothers, so were al-Mahdī and al-Rashīd, and al-Wāthiq and al-Mutawakkil. Three brothers, all of whom became caliph, were al-Amīn, al-Ma'mūn and al-Mu'taṣim, sons of al-Rashīd, and also al-Muktafī, al-Muqtadir and al-Qāhir, sons of al-Mu'taḍid, and al-Rāḍī, al-Muttaqī and al-Mutī', sons of al-Muqtadir. For four brothers who were caliphs, one has al-Walīd, Sulaymān, Yazīd and Hishām, sons of 'Abd al-Malik ibn Marwān. No other case is known.

When al-Muqtafī was installed in the caliphate, al-Rāshid sent an envoy to him from Mosul with the envoy of Atabeg Zankī. Al-Rāshid's envoy was not given audience, but Atabeg Zankī's envoy, who was Kamāl al-Dīn Muḥammad ibn 'Abd Allāh al-Shahrazūrī, was brought before the Dīwān and the message he brought was listened to.

My father told me the following on the authority of [Kamāl al-Dīn]:

> When I went before the Dīwān, I was asked, 'Do you recognise the Commander of the Faithful?' I replied, 'The Commander of the Faithful is with us in Mosul. He has the prior claim to allegiance on the necks of the people.' There was a long discussion and then I returned to my residence. That night an old woman came to me secretly. We talked together and she delivered a message from al-Muqtafī, which censured me for what I had said and requested that I retract it. I said, 'Tomorrow I shall do him a service to some obvious effect.' Next day I was again summoned to the Dīwān and asked about the meaning of the oath of allegiance (*al-bay'a*). I answered, 'I am a lawyer and a cadi. I may not take such an oath until after I have established in legal form that the previous holder is deposed.' Notaries were brought in and they gave evidence before me in the Dīwān that confirmed the fact of his deposition. I said, 'This is established and there can be no dispute about it, but we must gain some advantage from this affair, because the Commander [**45**] of the Faithful has acquired God's caliphate throughout the lands, the sultan has disembarrassed himself of an enemy, but we - what shall we take back?' The matter was referred to the caliph, who commanded that Atabeg Zankī should be given Ṣarifayn, Darb Harūn and Ḥarbā[6] as his own property (they were part of the caliph's personal estate) and that he should be given further titles. He said, 'This is an arrangement that no provincial ruler has ever been granted, to receive a portion of the caliph's personal estate.' I then gave the oath of allegiance and returned with all my aims achieved and having acquired a goodly amount of money and gifts.

---

[5] *Kāmil* (Thornberg), xi, 28, omits this sentence. The text, through an error, has only the first word, *nas'al*. Ms. Pococke 346, fol. 83b supplies *nas'al Allāh an yakfiyanā amra-hu.*

[6] Described as the chief town of Dujayl district, between Baghdad and Takrit (see Le Strange, *Baghdad*, 51; Krawulsky, 485).

The oath of allegiance and the khutbah for al-Muqtafī followed at Mosul in Rajab of the year 531 [25 March–23 April 1137]. When Kamāl al-Dīn Ibn al-Shahrazūrī returned, he was sent back with the certification, which had been drawn up concerning the deposition of al-Rāshid, in his hands. Chief Cadi al-Zaynabī in Mosul, who was there with Atabeg Zankī, ruled it to be valid.

Miscellaneous events

In this year Sultan Mas'ūd dismissed his vizier, Sharaf al-Dīn Anūshirwān ibn Khālid. He returned to Baghdad and remained in his house without employment. Kamāl al-Dīn Abū'l-Barakāt ibn Salama al-Darkazīnī, who was from Khurasan, became vizier after him.

The urban gangs rioted in Baghdad when the army assembled there. They openly committed murder and violent theft of property and the evil they did was great. The prefect raided Slave Market Street to seek out the gangs, but the populace of the western quarters rose against him and met him with force. He set fire to the street and a large number of people were burnt to death. People transferred their property to the Ṭāhirī Harem, but the prefect entered it and seized much property.

[**46**] Then there arose discord between the inhabitants of the Azaj Gate [district] and those of Ma'mūniyya. Several people on both sides were killed, but they later made a peaceful settlement.

This year Qarāsunqur marched with a large army to attack Prince Dā'ūd, the son of Sultan Maḥmūd. Sultan Mas'ūd remained in Baghdad. Qarāsunqur kept up his pursuit of Dā'ūd until he caught up with him at Marāgha. They met in a pitched battle and both armies fought fiercely, but Dā'ūd was defeated. Qarāsunqur remained in Azerbayjan. Dā'ūd, however, made for Khuzistan and large forces of Turkomans and others gathered around him there. Their numbers reached 10,000 horsemen. He then marched to Tustar and put it under siege. His uncle, Prince Saljuqshāh, son of Sultan Muḥammad, was in Wāsiṭ, and he sent to his brother, Sultan Mas'ūd, to ask for his assistance. The latter supplied some troops, so [Saljuqshāh] moved against Dā'ūd, while he was besieging Tustar. A battle was fought, and Saljuqshāh was defeated.

This year the following died:

Muḥammad ibn Ḥamawayh, Abū 'Abd Allāh al-Juwaynī. He is one of the celebrated shaykhs of the Sufis, known for many miracles and the transmission of Ḥadīth.

Muḥammad ibn 'Abd Allāh ibn Aḥmad ibn Ḥabīb al-'Āmirī al-Ṣūfī, the author of the commentary on *al-Shihāb*.[7] When death was upon him, he recited:

---

[7] Both *Muntaẓam*, x, 64 and *Wāfī*, iii, 349 (calling him al-'Ārī), by adding *kitāb*, show that a book title is intended. But which? Possibly by al-Murtaḍā (d. 436/1044), see *GAL*, ii, 405.

Here I stretch out my hand to You. Return it to me
With grace and not with the curses of my enemies.[8]

Abū 'Abd Allāh Muḥammad ibn al-Faḍl ibn Aḥmad al-Furāwī al-Ṣā'idī, the transmitter of the *Ṣaḥīḥ* of Muslim on the authority of al-Ghāfir al-Fārisī. His line of transmission is today the highest authority. Scholars travelled to him from east and west. He was a lawyer, a debater and a witty man who used to wait on his visitors in person. He used to say, 'The man from Furāwa (*al-Furāwī*) is a thousand relators (*alfu rāwī*).' May God have mercy on him and show him His good pleasure.

8 According to *Muntaẓam*, x, 65, the verse is by the Sufi Abū Naṣr al-Qushayrī.

[47] The Year 531 [1136–1137]

Account of the break-up of Sultan Mas'ūd's army

In Muḥarram of this year [October 1136] Sultan Mas'ūd allowed his troops who were with him in Baghdad to return to their lands, when he heard that al-Rāshid had left Atabeg Zankī and moved from Mosul. He had kept his forces together with him for fear that Zankī might descend on Iraq with al-Rāshid and take it from him. When he decided to give Emir Ṣadaqa ibn Dubays permission [to depart], he gave his daughter to him in marriage to maintain a hold on him.

A number of emirs who had fought against him with Prince Dā'ūd, among them Alpqush al-Silāḥī, Bursuq ibn Bursuq, lord of Tustar, and Sunqur al-Khumārtakīn, prefect of Hamadhan, came to Sultan Mas'ūd, who received them into his good pleasure and gave them guarantees. Alpqush became prefect of Baghdad and treated the populace with harshness and injustice.

After the dispersal of his army, Sultan Mas'ūd remained with a thousand horsemen. The caliph married the sultan's daughter, the Lady Fāṭima, in Rajab [25 March–23 April 1137] with a bride-price of 100,000 dinars. The agent in the acceptance of the marriage contract was the caliph's vizier, 'Alī ibn Ṭirād al-Zaynabī, while the sultan's agent was *his* vizier, Kamāl al-Dīn al-Darkazīnī. The sultan now felt secure, seeing that both the caliph and Ṣadaqa ibn Dubays ibn Ṣadaqa had become his sons-in-law and that al-Rāshid had left Zankī the Atabeg, but God knows best!

[48] The dismissal of Bahrām as al-Ḥāfiẓ's vizier and the appointment of Riḍwān

In Jumādā I of this year [25 January–23 February 1137] Tāj al-Dawla Bahrām, the vizier of al-Ḥāfiẓ li-Dīn Allāh the Alid, ruler of Egypt, fled. He had been appointed by al-Ḥāfiẓ after the killing of his son Ḥasan in the year 529 [1134–5]. He was an Armenian Christian, who became powerful in the land, gave positions to Armenians and dismissed Muslims. He treated the latter badly, and he and the Armenians whom he put in office humiliated and exploited them. The only Egyptian who scorned to bear this was Riḍwān ibn al-Walakhshī.[1] When it upset and disturbed him, he gathered a considerable force and marched on Cairo. Bahrām heard of this and fled to Upper Egypt without any resistance or any battle.

[1] The text has al-Rayḥīnī but the correct name is indicated by two variant readings. See Imad, *Vizierate*, 169, 193.

He made for the city of Aswan but the governor prevented him from entering and fought him. The black troops killed many of the Armenians. Unable to enter Aswan, Bahrām wrote to al-Ḥāfiẓ asking for a guarantee of safe conduct. This was granted and he returned to Cairo. He was imprisoned in the palace where he remained for a while but later left prison after becoming a monk.[2]

Riḍwān became vizier for al-Ḥāfiẓ and took the title al-Malik al-Afḍal. He was the first vizier of the Egyptians who took a title using 'al-malik'. Later relations between him and al-Ḥāfiẓ became bad and al-Ḥāfiẓ worked to remove him. When there was a rising against him in the middle of Shawwāl in the year 533 [June 1139], he fled from his residence and abandoned everything in it. The people took from it more plunder than could ever be detailed or counted. Al-Ḥāfiẓ rode out and calmed the people, before transferring what was left in Riḍwān's house to his own palace. As for Riḍwān, he set out for Syria, to seek aid and support from the Turks. Al-Ḥafiẓ sent Emir Ibn Maṣāl to him, to get him to return with a safe conduct and an undertaking that he would do him no harm. He therefore returned to Cairo, where al-Ḥāfiẓ imprisoned him near him in the palace.

A variant account says that he went to Syria (and that is [**49**] true) but that he went to Ṣarkhad, where he arrived in Dhū'l-Ḥijja [August 1139] and stopped with its ruler, Amīn al-Dawla Kumushtakīn. He was received with honour and respect and remained with him. Then in the year 534 [1139–40] he returned to Egypt with an army, fought the Egyptians at the Gate of Victory[3] and defeated them, killing a good many. He remained for three days but many of the men with him dispersed, so he decided to return to Syria. Al-Ḥāfiẓ sent Emir Ibn Maṣāl to him, who brought him back and imprisoned him in the caliph's palace, united with his family.

He stayed in the palace until the year 543 [1148–9], when he broke through the prison walls and escaped. Horses had been prepared for him to flee on. He crossed the Nile to Giza and raised support, gathering Maghribis and others, before going back to Cairo, where he fought the Egyptians near the Mosque of Ibn Ṭūlūn and put them to flight. He entered Cairo, stopped at the Mosque of al-Aqmar and sent to al-Ḥafiẓ demanding money to distribute, as was their custom. Whenever the caliphs appointed a vizier, they sent him 20,000 dinars to distribute. On this occasion al-Ḥāfiẓ sent 20,000 dinars which were divided up but the influential people importuned Riḍwān and demanded more. The caliph sent another 20,000 dinars. These were distributed but then his men scattered and slipped away from him. There was an outbreak of shouting and noise and a large company of black troops came against him. Al-Ḥāfiẓ had encouraged them in this. They charged Riḍwān's mamlukes and a battle ensued. Riḍwān prepared to ride out and one of his men brought forward a horse for him to mount. When he went to do so, the man struck him on the head with his sword and killed him. His head was carried to al-Ḥāfiẓ who sent it to his wife. It was placed in her lap but she threw it down

---

2 For a sketch of Bahrām's life, see Imad, *Vizierate*, 109–19.

3 The Bāb al-Naṣr, one of the two gates on the north side of Fatimid Cairo.

and said, 'This is what men come to.' Al-Ḥāfiẓ did not appoint anyone as vizier after him but took personal charge of affairs until he died.

[50] How the Muslims captured the fortress of Wādī Ibn al-Aḥmar from the Franks

In Rajab of this year [25 March–23 April 1137] the troops of Damascus with their commander Emir Bazwāj went to Tripoli in Syria. A large host of volunteer warriors for the Faith and Turkomans assembled with him. When the Count, its ruler, heard that they were near his lands he marched to meet them with his troops and levies. The Franks were defeated in the battle that followed and they returned to Tripoli in bad shape, many of their knights and brave men having been killed. The Muslims took much booty from their lands and besieged the fortress of Wādī Ibn al-Aḥmar, which they took by force of arms and seized everything within. The fighting men they killed and the women and children they enslaved. The men whom they took ransomed themselves for considerable sums of money. The troops returned to Damascus in safety. God knows best![4]

Zankī's siege of Homs

In Sha'bān [24 April–22 May 1137] Atabeg Zankī moved against Homs. He sent on before him his senior emir, Ṣalāḥ al-Dīn Muḥammad al-Yāghīsiyānī, a cunning and wily man. He sent him to intrigue with the garrison to engineer their surrender of the town to him. He arrived and the governor and man in authority there was Mu'īn al-Dīn Unur, who was also the senior emir in Damascus. Homs was his fief, as has been mentioned before. The plotting had no success with him. Then Zankī arrived, besieged the city and made several contacts with Unur about a surrender, sometimes with promises and sometimes with threats. Unur argued that it was the possession of his lord, Shihāb al-Dīn, and that he himself held it in trust and would only give it up **[51]** if forced to. Zankī continued his siege until 20 Shawwāl [11 July 1137] without having achieved any success, then departed and went to Ba'rīn which he besieged. What happened between him and the Franks we shall relate, God Almighty willing.

---

4 Count Pons was killed at this time (according to William of Tyre, ii, 82, near Mount Pilgrim) and was succeeded by his son, Raymond II. This is the only reference to a Wādī Ibn al-Aḥmar in *Kāmil*. According to Ibn Qal., 262, the battle was at a place called al-Kūra and the castle there (unnamed) was plundered and the defenders killed. A tentative identification of the Wādī Ibn al-Aḥmar castle with Chastel-Rouge is made in Richard, *Comté de Tripoli*, 20–21.

How Zankī took the fortress of Ba'rīn and defeated the Franks

In Shawwāl [July 1137] Atabeg Zankī left Mosul for Syria and besieged the fortress of Ba'rīn, which was close to Hama and was one of the Franks' strongest and most impregnable castles. Having descended upon it, he made some assaults. The Franks gathered their horse and foot and marched with all their forces, their princes, counts and barons, to make Atabeg Zankī raise the siege of Ba'rīn. However, he did not retire but waited for them to come to him. He then met them in a battle, the fiercest that people had ever seen. Both sides held firm but the outcome became clear, a defeat for the Franks. From all quarters Muslim swords fell upon them. Their princes and knights took refuge in the fortress of Ba'rīn because it was close. Zankī besieged them there and prevented them from receiving anything, even news. Those Franks that were there could gather no information about what was happening in their lands because the roads were watched so closely and Zankī's troops were in such awe of him

The priests and monks went into Byzantine territory and the Frankish lands, seeking assistance against the Muslims. They told people that, if Zankī took the castle of Ba'rīn and the Franks who were there, he would conquer all their territory very quickly and that the Muslims had only one aim and that is to attack Jerusalem. Thereupon the Christians came together and set out despite **[52]** difficulties and setbacks. They marched towards Syria and we shall relate what happened to them.

Zankī meanwhile exerted himself in his fight with the Franks, but they held out, although their supplies ran short, for they were unprepared and had not believed that anyone would challenge them. On the contrary they were expecting to conquer the rest of Syria. When their supplies were low, they ate their riding animals and announced that they would surrender if Zankī would grant them safe conduct and allow them to return to their lands. He did not agree to this but [later] when he heard of the mobilisation of the remaining Franks and the arrival of their near neighbours, he gave the defenders of the fortress terms. He demanded a payment of 50,000 dinars from them. After they had accepted this, he allowed them to depart and they handed over the castle. Once they had abandoned it they heard of the gathering of those who had mobilised on their account and they regretted their surrender when all regrets were useless. No news at all had been getting through to them and that is why they gave up the castle.

During the period of his siege Zankī took Ma'arrat [al-Nu'mān] and Kafarṭāb from the Franks. The population of these two and of all the areas between Aleppo and Hama, along with the people of Ba'rīn, were in a parlous state because of the constant warfare between them and the plundering and killing that never stopped. When Zankī conquered it, people gained some security, the land was cultivated and revenue increased considerably. It was a conspicious victory and anyone who witnessed it knows the truth of what I say.

One of the best and fairest things that Zankī did for the people of Ma'arrat [al-

Nu'mān] was as follows. When the Franks took the city, they seized their wealth and properties. After Zankī had recovered it at this time, the surviving inhabitants and also the descendants of those who had perished came before him and asked for their properties back. He asked them for their title deeds, to which they replied, 'The Franks took all we had [**53**] and the deeds for the properties there.' Zankī said, 'Seek out the registers for Aleppo and anyone who paid land tax for a property let it be given to him.' They did this and so he restored people's property to them. This is a very good and just thing to have done.[5]

Account of the Byzantine emperor's expedition to Syria

It has already been mentioned that the Franks sent to the emperor of Constantinople[6] seeking his aid, informing him what Zankī had done among them and urging him to come to their lands before they were conquered and his arrival be of no benefit. He made his preparations and set out, making all haste. He first took ship and came to Antalya,[7] a possession of his on the coast. He anchored there and stayed to await the arrival of the ships bringing his baggage and military equipment. When this had arrived, he left for the city of Nicaea, which he put under siege. He came to terms with the population for a payment of money. Alternatively it is said that he took it by force. He then went to Adana and Maṣīṣa, both in the possession of Leo[8] the Armenian, lord of the castles of the Passes. He besieged and took both places. He then moved to 'Ayn Zarba, which he took by assault, and also seized Tell Ḥamdūn. He transferred the population to the island of Cyprus. He restored[9] the port of Iskanderun, then emerged into Syria and besieged Antioch in Dhū'l-Qa'da [August 1137]. He pressed hard on the population, whose ruler was Raymond the Frank. Envoys went to and fro between them and they came to an agreement. The emperor moved on to Baghrāṣ and from there he entered the territory of Leo the Armenian. Leo offered him large sums of money and agreed to be his subject. God know best!

---

5 According to Ḥanafī law (and Zankī was a Ḥanafī), the public treasury should own property recovered by reconquest.

6 i.e. John II Comnenus (ruled 1118-43).

7 Ibn Qal., 258, has, oddly, *ilā jazīrat Anṭākiya* ('to the island of Antioch'). Ms. Pococke 346, fol. 80a also has Anṭākiya but a marginal correction gives Anṭāliya (easily confused).

8 Leo I, Roupenian prince of Cilicia (see Matthew of Edessa, *Chronicle*, 239).

9 The text and *Kāmil* (Thornberg), xi, 35 read *'abara* ('passed by') but the reading of Ms. Pococke 346, fol. 80a. (*'ammara*) is preferable. That is also the reading of Ibn Qal., 258.

[54] Miscellaneous events

On 24 Ayyār of this year [24 May 1137][10] black clouds appeared over Syria which made the world dark. The sky was as black as at night. Afterwards red clouds rose up, as though it was a fire that lit up the world. A violent wind blew which threw down many trees. This was at its worst in Ḥawrān and Damascus. It was followed by heavy rain and large hailstones.

This year Mu'ayyad al-Dīn Abū'l-Fawāris al-Musayyib ibn 'Alī ibn al-Ḥusayn, known as Ibn al-Ṣūfī, returned to Damascus from Ṣarkhad. He and his family had been expelled from Damascus and had remained in Ṣarkhad until this moment. After their return Abū'l-Fawāris assumed the position of headman in Damascus. He was beloved by the population and gained a powerful hold. He was a man of strong leadership and manifest valour.

There was much illness this year in Baghdad. Unexpected deaths became common in Isfahan and Hamadhan.

This year Atabeg Zankī went to Daqūqā and conquered it, after a siege and a hard fight to overcome the citadel.

There died during this year:

Abū Sa'īd Aḥmad ibn Muḥammad ibn Thābit al-Khujandī, the leader of the Shāfi'īs in Isfahan.[11] He studied law with his father and lectured at the Niẓāmiyya in Isfahan.

Abū'l-Qāsim Hibat Allāh ibn Aḥmad ibn 'Umar al-Ḥarīrī. Born on the day of 'Āshūrā' in the year 435 [=18 August 1043], he was the last to transmit Ḥadīth from Abū'l-Ḥasan, the husband of al-Ḥurra. Al-Khaṭīb Abū Bakr ibn Thābit[12] also transmitted from this source and al-Khaṭīb's death occurred in the year 463 [1071].[13]

---

[10] These phenomena are noted by Ibn Qal., 256, under the year 530 and Wednesday is specified. However, 24 May 1136 was a Sunday. That date in 1137 fell on a Monday.

[11] Born 443/1051-2, died 1 Sha'bān/24 April 1137; he is called Abū Sa'd in *Muntaẓam*, x, 70.

[12] This is al-Khatīb al-Baghdādī Abū Bakr Aḥmad ibn 'Alī ibn Thābit, author of the famous biographical dictionary of Baghdad scholars (see *Encyclopedia of Arabic Literature*, ii, 438-9).

[13] Abū'l-Qāsim was born on a Thursday and died Thursday 2 Jumādā I/= 28 January 1137, aged 96 (*Muntaẓam*, x, 71).

[55] The Year 532 [1137-1138]

How Atabeg Zankī took Homs and other dependencies of Damascus

In Muḥarram of this year [19 September-18 October 1137] Atabeg Zankī came to Hama and from there went to the Baalbek Valley. He took the fortress of al-Majdal which belonged to the ruler of Damascus. The castellan of Bānyās, also a possession of the ruler of Damascus, made contact with Zankī and submitted to him. Zankī marched to Homs and put it under siege, keeping up a prolonged attack on it. After the Byzantine emperor descended on Aleppo, Zankī withdrew to Salamiyya, but when the Byzantine danger was over, as we have mentioned,[1] he resumed the siege of Homs. He sent to Shihāb al-Dīn, the ruler of Damascus, to seek the hand of his mother in marriage. Her name was the Lady Zumurrud, the daughter of Jāwulī, and she it was who killed her son, Shams al-Mulūk, and built the madrasah[2] outside Damascus, which overlooks the Wadi of Shaqrā[3] and the River Baradā.

Zankī duly married her and received the surrender of Homs along with its citadel. The Lady was escorted to him in Ramaḍān [13 May-11 June 1138]. He was only motivated to marry her because he saw that she had a dominant influence in Damascus and he thought that by uniting himself to her he would take control of that city. However, his hopes were disappointed after his marriage. He gained nothing and later neglected her.

[56] The arrival of the Byzantine emperor in Syria, his conquest of Buzāʻa and treatment of the Muslims

Under the year 531 [1137] we have already related how the emperor marched from his lands and was busy with the Franks and Leo. When this year began, he came to Syria and people were in great dread of him. He attacked and besieged Buzāʻa, a small town six leagues from Aleppo. Several of the notables of Aleppo made their way to Zankī when he was besieging Homs and begged him for help and support. He dispatched with them many men of his army who entered Aleppo ready to defend it against the Byzantines if they began a siege.

---

1 Thus in the text, but 'as we shall mention' fits better.

2 This Ḥanafī madrasah on the 'southern eminence' (*al-sharaf al-qiblī*) was endowed by Ṣafwat al-Mulūk Zumurrud in 526/1131-2 (see Ibn Shaddād, *Damas*, 218-19).

3 A pleasure ground or park overlooking the Green Meadow (Ibn Shaddād, *Damas*, 321 and note 3).

Then the emperor began direct operations against Buzā'a. He erected trebuchets to bombard it and tightened his grip on the defenders. On 25 Rajab[4] [= 9 April 1138] the place fell after terms had been given. However, he treacherously killed some of the inhabitants and captured and enslaved others. The number of the inhabitants who were wounded was 5,800. The local cadi and several of the notables, about 400 persons, accepted Christianity.

After taking it the Byzantines remained for ten days, hunting those who had gone into hiding. They were told that a large number of the inhabitants of this region had gone down into the caves. Fires were lit to smoke them out and they perished in the caves.

The Byzantines then moved away towards Aleppo and camped on the Quwayq with the Franks from the Syrian littoral. The next day with their horse and foot they assaulted Aleppo. The Aleppan militia came out to meet them and fought a fierce battle with them. A host of Byzantines were killed or wounded. One killed was a general[5] **[57]** of noble standing among them. They withdrew in disarray, waited three days but, not seeing any chance of success, then moved to al-Athārib, where the Muslim population was in great fear. On 9 Sha'bān[6] [= 21 April 1138] they fled, so the Byzantines seized it and left their prisoners and captives from Buzā'a there along with a detachment of Byzantines to guard them and hold the citadel. The main force left and when Emir Sawār in Aleppo heard this he set out with the troops he had to al-Athārib and fell upon the Greeks there. He killed them, freed the prisoners and captives and returned to Aleppo.

As for 'Imād al-Dīn Zankī, he left Homs and went to Salamiyya, where he invested the town. He sent his baggage across the river to Raqqa and remained with minimal baggage to follow the Byzantines and cut off their supplies. The Byzantines meanwhile attacked the castle of Shayzar, one of the strongest fortresses. They only attacked it because it was not held by Zankī and he would not have a great interest in protecting it. It belonged to Emir Abū'l-'Asākir Sulṭān ibn 'Alī ibn Muqallid ibn Naṣr ibn Munqidh al-Kinānī. They came down on it and began a siege, setting up eighteen trebuchets. The ruler sent to Zankī asking for his aid. The latter set out and camped on the River Orontes near the castle, between it and Hama. Every day he and his troops rode to Shayzar and halted in view of the Greeks. Zankī would send out squadrons which seized any of them they intercepted

Later Zankī sent to the emperor, saying, 'You have sought safety from me in these hills. Come down to the open country where we may meet. If I defeat you, then I shall have saved the Muslims from you, but if you are victorious, you may relax and take Shayzar and other places.' In fact he did not have the strength to meet them. He only tried to frighten them with these and similar words. The

4 Ibn Qal., 265, specifies Saturday.

5 In Arabic *biṭrīq* (patrician).

6 According to Ibn Qal., 265, this was a Thursday.

Franks of Syria advised the emperor to give battle and declared that it would be easy to defeat him. However, he took no action but said, 'Do you imagine that he has no troops other than those you see? His one wish is that you engage him and then he will be joined by Muslim reinforcements beyond number.'

[**58**] Zankī was also sending to the emperor to make him believe that the Franks of Syria were fearful of him and that, if he left his position, they would abandon him. He also was sending messages to the Syrian Franks warning them of the emperor and saying, 'If he conquers a single fortress in Syria, he will then take all your lands.' Each side was apprehensive of the other. In Ramaḍān [13 May–11 June 1138] the emperor moved away from Shayzar, where he had remained for twenty-four days, and left his trebuchets and siege engines where they were. Atabeg Zankī pursued the rear-guard and seized many stragglers. He also appropriated all that they had left behind.

When the Franks were at Buzā'a, Zankī sent Cadi Kamāl al-Dīn Abū'l-Muẓaffar Muḥammad ibn 'Abd Allāh ibn al-Qāsim al-Shahrazūrī to Sultan Mas'ūd to ask him for aid and to request troops. He went to Baghdad and reported the situation to the sultan, informing him of what would result from failure to act and that he would be sure to find that the Byzantines would conquer Aleppo and descend the Euphrates to Baghdad. Kamāl al-Dīn found him unwilling to move, so arranged for one of his men to go to the Palace Mosque on Friday, accompanied by a number of non-Arab ruffians. He instructed him to start them rioting when the preacher mounted the pulpit and to shout with them, 'Woe for Islam, woe for the religion of Muhammad' and to tear his clothes and cast his turban from his head, and to go to the sultan's palace with the people calling for support in this same way. He also set up another man to do the same in the sultan's mosque.

When the preacher went up into the pulpit, this man stood up, beat his head, threw off his turban and tore his garments, along with these others, who shouted [their slogans]. The congregation wept and abandoned their prayer. They cursed the sultan and left the mosque, following the shaykh to the sultan's palace. They found the congregation in the sultan's mosque had acted likewise. The people surrounded the sultan's residence, calling for his support and weeping. The sultan was fearful and said, 'Summon Ibn al-Shahrazūrī to me,' which was done. Kamāl al-Dīn said, 'I feared his reaction to what I had seen. When I entered his presence, he said to me, "What a riot you have stirred up!" I replied, "I have not done anything. I was in my house. It is the people who are simply roused on behalf of the faith and Islam. They fear [**59**] the outcome of this prevarication." He said, "Go out to the people and disperse them from our doors. Come tomorrow and choose what troops you wish." I sent the people away and told them of his order for the mobilization of troops. The next day I came to the Dīwān, and they equipped a large contingent of troops for me. I sent to Naṣīr al-Dīn in Mosul to inform him of this, but warning him that the troops, if they descended on the region, would take it. He sent back a reply, "No doubt the land will be lost, but that Muslims should take it is better than that the infidels should." We started loading for our departure, when there came a letter from Atabeg Zankī in Syria with the news that the Byzantine emperor had withdrawn and ordering me not to bring a single soldier with me. I told the sultan of that and he said, "The troops are all prepared. The expedition to Syria must take place." However, after much trouble and the bestowal of a large consideration on him and his advisers, he recalled his troops.'

After the Byzantine emperor had withdrawn from Shayzar, poets praised Atabeg Zankī extravagantly. An example is what al-Muslim ibn Khiḍr ibn Qusaym al-Ḥamawī[7] wrote in an ode that begins:

> By your resolution, O mighty prince, difficulties bow before you and are set to rights.

It also contains the following:

> Did you not see that the Byzantine cur, when it appeared that he was the 'merciful prince',[8]
> Came covering the open plains with cavalry, a host like black night.
> Fate waited upon his good pleasure and the great enterprise submitted to his plan.
> But when you hurled yourself against him in your serried ranks, he knew for sure that this could not last.
> He saw you in your coat of mail a whole army and stopped short,[9] neither going nor staying.
> You were like a gleam of light in the dust of battle, burning bright, while he was an accursed devil.[10]
> He wished to save his life, so turned in flight, yet he had no friend but death.

[60] It is a long ode. A strange story that is told is that, when the emperor decided to besiege Shayzar, the people there heard of this and Emir Murshid ibn 'Alī, the brother of the ruler, said, as he was opening a copy of the Koran, 'O God, by the truth of him to whom You revealed this, if You have decreed that the Byzantine emperor is to come, then take me to You.' He died a few days afterwards.

---

7 Abū'l-Majd al-Muslim died in 540s/1145–54. See *Rawḍatayn*, i, 91, note 6, and a longer extract of this poem, 124–5.

8 A surprising epithet, even used ironically. Perhaps it is an echo of Kaloịoannes (John the Good), which appears as Kiyālyānī (?) in Ibn Qal., 258. See Runciman, ii, 212, note 1.

9 The text has *fa-aḥraba*, 'waged war'. Correct to *fa-aḥrana* from *Rawḍatayn*, i, 124.

10 A reference to Koran, xv, 17–18.

Account of the battle between Sultan Mas'ūd and Prince Dā'ūd and those emirs with him

When al-Rāshid bi-Allāh parted from the Atabeg Zankī in Mosul, he went towards Azerbayjan and came to Marāgha. Emir Mankūbars, lord of Fars, his deputy in Khuzistan, Emir Būz-Aba, Emir 'Abd al-Raḥmān [ibn] Ṭughāyuruk, lord of Khalkhāl, and Prince Dā'ūd, son of Sultan Maḥmūd, were apprehensive about Sultan Mas'ūd and in fear of him. They met and persuaded al-Rāshid to join them to act as one and to restore him to the caliphate. He agreed, but he did not actually join them.

When Sultan Mas'ūd was at Baghdad the news that they had united came to him. He left the city in Sha'bān [14 April–12 May 1138] to march towards them. They met at Banjan Kusht and fought a battle. Sultan Mas'ūd defeated them, took Emir Mankūbars prisoner and had him summarily executed in his presence. Mas'ūd's army scattered to plunder and pursue the fugitives.

Būz-Aba and 'Abd al-Raḥman [ibn] Ṭughāyuruk were on an eminence. They saw that Sultan [**61**] Mas'ūd's troops had dispersed and left him, so they charged him, while he was attended by only a few. He did not stand his ground but fled. Būz-Aba seized a number of emirs, including Ṣadaqa ibn Dubays, lord of Ḥilla, the son of Atabeg Qarāsunqur, lord of Azerbayjan, 'Antar ibn Abī'l-'Askar and others. He kept them with him, but when he heard that his lord, Mankūbars, had been killed, he killed all of them. Both armies left in disarray. It was a most remarkable occurrence.

Sultan Mas'ūd made for Azerbayjan, while Prince Dā'ūd made for Hamadhan. Al-Rāshid arrived there after the battle. All their ideas were at variance. Some advised going to Iraq and taking it over by force, while others advised pursuing Sultan Mas'ūd to finish him off. Once he was removed things would be easy for them. Būz-Aba, the senior one of the group, did not hold that view. His aim was to proceed to Fars and take it over, now that its lord, Mankūbars, was dead, before anyone there could resist him. He vetoed the others' plans, marched to Fars and took it, so that it became his along with Khuzistan.

Saljuqshāh, the son of Sultan Muḥammad, marched to Baghdad to take it, but Alpqush, the prefect there, and Naẓar the Eunuch, emir of the Pilgrimage, came out to confront him, fought him and drove him off. He was incompetent and weak. After the death of Ṣadaqa ibn Dubays, Sultan Mas'ūd assigned Ḥilla to the former's brother, Muḥammad ibn Dubays, and appointed Muhalhil ibn Abī'l-'Askar, the brother of the slain 'Antar, to direct his affairs.

When Alpqush, the prefect of Baghdad, was fighting with Saljuqshāh, the urban gangs in Baghdad rioted, plundering property and murdering people. The situation became so serious that they were quite openly attacking wealthy persons and taking whatever they wanted, carrying away goods on the backs of porters. On his return, the prefect executed some of them and displayed their bodies. Prices rose and the prefect's injustice increased. He seized respectable citizens, claiming they belonged to the gangs. People emigrated to Mosul and other places, leaving Baghdad.

[62] Account of the killing of al-Rāshid bi-Allāh

When al-Rāshid bi-Allāh came to Hamadhan, where Prince Dā'ūd, Būz-Aba and their remaining emirs and troops were after the defeat of Sultan Mas'ūd and the dispersal of the armies, as has been mentioned, he and Prince Dā'ūd set out for Khuzistan, accompanied by Khwārazm Shāh. They drew near al-Ḥawīza and Sultan Mas'ūd proceeded to Baghdad to deny them access to Iraq. Prince Dā'ūd returned to Fars and Khwārazm Shāh also returned to his lands, leaving al-Rāshid alone. When he despaired of troops from Persian lands he went to Isfahan.

On 25 Ramaḍān [6 June 1138] a small band of Khurasanians who were in his service attacked and killed him, as he was about to take a siesta. He was at the tail-end of an illness, from which he had recently recovered. He was buried outside Isfahan at Shahristān. His followers made a foray and killed members of the Bāṭinī sect.[11]

When the news came to Baghdad, they held a one-day session of condolence in the Audience Chamber.[12] Al-Rāshid was pale-skinned and fair-haired. His complexion was good and his face handsome. As a person he inspired respect and was very powerful and forceful.

Abū Bakr al-Ṣūlī said, 'People claim that every sixth person to rule since the beginning of Islam is inevitably deposed and often killed. I thought about this and saw that it was correct. The first person to rule this community was Muḥammad, the Prophet of God (God bless him and give him peace). Then came Abū Bakr, 'Umar, 'Uthmān, 'Alī and al-Ḥasan (God be pleased with them). The last named was deposed. Then came Mu'āwiya, Yazīd, his son, Mu'āwiya ibn Yazīd, Marwān, 'Abd al-Malik ibn Marwān, and 'Abd Allāh ibn al-Zubayr, who was deposed and killed. Next came al-Walīd ibn 'Abd al-Malik, his brother Sulaymān, 'Umar ibn 'Abd al-'Azīz, Yazīd and Hishām, the sons of 'Abd al-Malik, and al-Walīd ibn Yazīd ibn 'Abd al-Malik, who was deposed and killed. After that the cause of the Umayyads fell into disorder. Then there ruled al-Saffāḥ, **[63]** al-Manṣūr, al-Mahdī, al-Hādī, al-Rashīd and al-Amīn, the last of whom was deposed and killed. Next came al-Ma'mūn, al-Mu'taṣim, al-Wāthiq, al-Mutawakkil, al-Muntaṣir, and al-Musta'īn, who was deposed and killed; then al-Mu'tazz, al-Muhtadī, al-Mu'tamid, al-Mu'taḍid, al-Muktafī and al-Muqtadir, who was deposed, then restored but killed later; then al-Qāhir, al-Rāḍī, al-Muttaqī, al-Mustakfī, al-Muṭī', al-Ṭā'i', who was deposed; then al-Qādir, al-Qā'im, al-Muqtadī, al-Mustaẓhir, al-Mustarshid and

---

[11] *Muntaẓam*, x, 72, expressly attributes the murder to the Assassins, the Bāṭinīs.

[12] In Arabic *bayt al-nawba*, seemingly not referring to the caliphal musical band. Receptions, investitures, public readings of documents and sessions of the vizier were held in the palace's *bayt al-nawba* according to the term's uses in *Mir'āt al-Zamān*, see index.

al-Rāshid, who was deposed and killed.' My personal comment is that this is open to argument, because Ibn al-Zubayr was proclaimed caliph before the proclamation of 'Abd al-Malik ibn Marwān and there is no justification for his having put him before Ibn al-Zubayr. Al-Ṣūlī only mentioned reigns up to that of al-Muqtadir. Those that followed him were mentioned by a different person.[13]

The circumstances of Ibn Bakrān, the brigand

In Dhū'l-Ḥijja [10 August-7 September 1138] the position of the brigand Ibn Bakrān in Iraq became powerful and his following increased greatly. He took to riding openly with a band of malefactors. Sharīf Abū'l-Karam, the chief of the Watch in Baghdad, feared him, and he ordered Abū'l-Qāsim, his nephew and the person responsible for security in Azaj Gate district, to take a strong line with him to protect people from his evil doings.

Ibn Bakrān resided frequently in the Sawād, with a comrade of his called Ibn al-Bazzāz. They finally went so far as to intend to strike coins in their own names at al-Anbār. The prefect and Vizier Sharaf al-Dīn al-Zaynabī sent to the chief of the Watch, Abū'l-Karam, saying, 'Either you kill Ibn Bakrān or we shall kill you.' He summoned his nephew and told him what had happened. He said to him, 'Either you choose me and yourself or you choose Ibn Bakrān,' to which he replied, 'I shall kill him.' Ibn Bakrān was in the habit of coming some evenings to Abū'l-Karam's nephew and staying in his house to drink with him. When he came as usual and began to drink, Abū'l-Qāsim took his weapons, leapt [**64**] on him and killed him, thus saving the people from his wickedness. A little while later he captured his comrade Ibn al-Bazzāz, who was crucified. Several of the brigands were killed with him and the population gained peace and security and the disturbances subsided.

The death of Vizier al-Darkazīnī and al-Khāzin's period of office

This year Sultan Mas'ūd arrested his vizier, Kamāl al-Dīn Abū'l-Barakāt ibn Salama al-Darkazīnī, and appointed to follow him Kamāl al-Dīn Muḥammad ibn al-Ḥusayn al-Khāzin (the Treasurer). Kamāl al-Dīn was vigorous, brave and just, an effective administrator and a man of goodly life. He cancelled non-canonical taxes and removed grievances. He provided the sultan's supplies and met his regular outgoings and also gathered vast stores of treasure. He uncovered many things that were concealed, where there had been corruption and theft. He bore

---

[13] That person was Ibn al-Jawzī (see *Muntaẓam*, x, 76). Abū Bakr Muḥammad al-Ṣūlī was a courtier and man of letters at Baghdad. He died *c.*335/946 (see *Encyclopedia of Arabic Literature*, ii, 744).

down hard on the clerks and tax officials, so they caused trouble between him and the emirs, especially Qarāsunqur, lord of Azerbayjan. The latter parted from the sultan and sent to say, 'Either you send the vizier's head or we shall serve another sultan.' The emirs present at court advised that the vizier should be killed and warned the sultan of discord that would be impossible to repair, so he put him to death, although unwillingly. He sent his head to Qarāsunqur, who was satisfied. He had been vizier for seven months and his execution took place in the year 533 [1138–9].

Abū'l-'Izz Ṭāhir ibn Muḥammad al-Barūjirdī, Qarāsunqur's vizier, became vizier after him and was given the title 'Izz al-Mulk. Sultan Mas'ūd lost freedom of action and the emirs took lands as fiefs without reference to his wishes. None of the land was left to him at all but only the empty title of sultan.

[65] Miscellaneous events

During this year Ḥusām al-Dīn Timurtāsh [ibn] Īlghāzī, lord of Mardin, conquered the fortress of al-Hattākh[14] in the province of Diyār Bakr. He took it from one of the Marwanids who had been rulers of the whole of Diyār Bakr. This was the last of that line to rule anywhere. Glory be to the Living, Everlasting God whose kingdom has no end and who is untouched by change and decay!

This year the covering[15] for the Kaabah failed to arrive because of the disputes that we have mentioned. Rāmisht the Persian merchant provided its covering. He draped it with all the rich textiles that he could manage. The cost amounted to 18,000 Egyptian dinars. He was a rich merchant, one of those who travelled to India.

The Lady Zubayda, daughter of Sultan Barkyāruq and wife of Sultan Mas'ūd, died this year. After her he married Sufrā, daughter of Dubays ibn Ṣadaqa, in Jumāda I [15 January–13 February 1138]. He also married the daughter of Qāwurt, a member of the Saljuq house, although he drank wine without stop day and night and thus his name and reputation suffered.

This year Sultan Mas'ūd put to death Alpqush al-Silāḥī,[16] the prefect of Baghdad. He had wronged and oppressed people and indeed had done wrongs that nobody else had ever done. He was arrested and sent to Takrit, where he was incarcerated in the house of Mujāhid al-Dīn Bahrūz. Later his execution was ordered. When they were purposing to carry this out, he threw himself into the Tigris and drowned. His head was taken and brought to the sultan. Mujāhid al-Dīn Bahrūz was made prefect of Iraq by the sultan and he did some good works; for example

---

[14] For possible locations, see Hillenbrand, *Muslim Principality*, 85, note 86.

[15] In Arabic *kiswa*, the black embroidered covering, renewed annually and in the past provided either by Baghdad or Cairo.

[16] The text has 'the son of Alpqush' etc., corrected on the basis of *Muntaẓam*, x, 72 and 74, and Sibṭ ibn al-Jawzī, 163.

he constructed the jetty at al-Nahrawān and others like it. He governed very well and did many kindnesses.

[**66**] This year Shaykh Abū Manṣūr ibn al-Razzāz lectured at the Niẓāmiyya in Baghdad.

Atabeg Zankī was instructed by letter to free Chief Cadi al-Zaynabī. This was done and he travelled down to Baghdad, where the caliph gave him a robe of honour and re-established him in his post.

In Khurasan there was a protracted and severe famine. It became so serious that people ate dogs and cats and other animals. Most of the population fled abroad because of hunger.

Ṭughān Arslān, lord of Bitlis and Arzan in Diyār Bakr, died this year. He was succeeded by his son, Qurtī,[17] who became well established.

In Ṣafar [19 October–16 November 1137] there was a large earthquake in Syria, the Jazīra, Diyār Bakr, Mosul, Iraq and elsewhere. It destroyed most of these areas and great numbers of people perished in the collapsed buildings.

The following also died this year:

Aḥmad ibn Muḥammad ibn [Aḥmad, Abū] Bakr ibn Abī'l-Fatḥ al-Dīnawarī,[18] the Ḥanbalī lawyer, in Baghdad. He used often to recite the following verses:

You hoped to become a lawyer and a leading exponent
Without effort. Madness takes many forms!
The acquisition of money is not without trouble.
You have accepted that. How then should it be with learning!

Muḥammad ibn 'Abd al-Malik ibn 'Umar, Abū'l-Ḥasan al-Karkhī. He was born in the year 458 [1066]. He was a lawyer and a scholar of Ḥadith, who heard it in Karkh, Isfahan, Hamadhan and elsewhere.

Cadi Abū'l-'Alā' Ṣā'id ibn al-Ḥusayn ibn Ismā'īl ibn Ṣā'id, in Sha'bān [14 April–12 May 1138]. He was a cousin of Cadi Abū Sa'īd and himself became cadi at Nishapur after Abū Sa'īd.

---

[17] The text has F.r.niyy. 'Qurtī' (with the same basic consonantal outline) is supplied by Ibn Qal., 267.

[18] He was a teacher of Ibn al-Jawzī, from whom (*Muntaẓam*, x, 73) the bracketed text has been taken.

[67] The Year 533 [1138-1139]

Account of the war between Sultan Sanjar and Khwārazm Shāh

In Muḥarram [8 September-7 October 1138] Sultan Sanjar ibn Malikshāh marched to Khwārazm to make war on Khwārazm Shāh Atsiz ibn Muḥammad. The reason was that Sanjar had heard that Atsiz was tempted to defy him and cast off his allegiance to him. This had already become clear to many of his officials and emirs and it made it necessary to attack him and take Khwārazm from him. He therefore gathered his armies and set off towards him. When he came close to Khwārazm, Khwārazm Shāh came out against him with his forces and came face to face with him. Each one drew up his troops and his followers, and battle was joined. The Khwārazmians were not strong enough for the sultan and they did not hold firm but turned and fled. Many of them were killed and among those killed was a son of Khwārazm Shāh. His father grieved greatly for him and felt the loss severely.

Sanjar seized Khwārazm and assigned it as a fief to Ghiyāth al-Dīn Sulaymān Shāh, the son of his brother Muḥammad. He appointed a vizier, an atabeg and a chamberlain to serve him and established the bases of his government. During Jumādā II [February 1139] he returned to Marv. However, after he had left Khwārazm on his way home, Khwārazm Shāh seized his opportunity and returned. The local people hated Sanjar's army and preferred the return of Khwārazm Shāh. When that happened, they helped him to take the country. Sulaymān Shāh and those with him abandoned it and he went back to his uncle, Sultan Sanjar. Relations between Sanjar and Khwārazm Shāh became bad. They were totally opposed after having reached an agreement. In the year 536 [1141-2] Khwārazm Shāh did in Khurasan what we shall later recount, God willing.

[68] Account of the death of the ruler of Damascus and the succession of his brother Muḥammad

The ruler of Damascus, Shihāb al-Dīn Maḥmūd ibn Tāj al-Mulūk [Būrī] ibn Ṭughtakīn, was murdered in his bed during Shawwāl [June 1139]. Three of his mamlukes, his intimates and the closest people to him in private or in public, were his killers. They used to sleep by him at night. After they had killed him, they left the citadel and fled. One escaped but the other two were taken and crucified.

A letter was sent from Damascus to his brother, Jamāl al-Dīn Muḥammad ibn Būrī, the ruler of Baalbek, with an account of what had happened. They summoned him to take control after his brother. He came as quickly as he could and when he entered the city he held a session of condolence for his brother and received the oaths of the troops and his notable subjects. The people remained calm and he entrusted the affairs of state to Mu'īn al-Dīn Unur, his grandfather's mamluke, whose high position he further increased, so that he became the ultimate authority in every matter.[1] Unur was a good and wise man, of excellent conduct. Under him affairs proceeded in the very best order.

How Zankī gained Baalbek

In Dhū'l-Qa'da [July 1139] 'Imād al-Dīn Atabeg Zankī ibn Āqsunqur went to Baalbek, besieged and then took it. This came about because, when the ruler of Damascus, Maḥmūd, was murdered, his mother, the Lady Zumurrud, was in Atabeg Zankī's household at Aleppo, as he had married her. She was greatly upset at the death of her son and grieved for him. She sent to Zankī, when he was in [**69**] the Jazīra, to tell him of this sad event and ask him to set out for Damascus to avenge her son. After he had read this letter, immediately with no hesitation or delay he hastened to go there with all speed to make this a means of taking the city. He crossed the Euphrates with the intention of making for Damascus. Those there took precautions; they made preparations and collected lots of stores. They neglected nothing they might need but made every effort to acquire it, and remained in expectation of his arrival. He therefore left them alone and went to Baalbek.

It has been said that the conquest of Baalbek came about differently. Baalbek was held by Mu'īn al-Dīn Unur, as we have mentioned, and he was in love with a slave girl of his. When he married Jamāl al-Dīn's mother, he sent the girl to Baalbek. When Zankī set out for Syria, intending to go to Damascus, he sent to Unur offering him huge rewards if he would surrender Damascus to him, but he would not. Zankī went to Baalbek instead, arriving on 20 Dhū'l-Ḥijja [18 August 1139]. He besieged it with his troops and blockaded it tightly. He made great efforts to assault the city and set up fourteen trebuchets that maintained a bombardment day and night. The people there were faced with imminent destruction so they asked for terms and gave the city up. Only the citadel held out, defended by brave Turks. Zankī continued to attack them and when they despaired of any help or support, they too asked for terms and, when they were granted, surrendered the citadel. After they had come down and the citadel was taken, he treacherously ordered their crucifixion. This was done and only a few of them escaped. The local people disapproved of what he had done and were outraged. People elsewhere were fearful and became very wary of him, especially the people of Damascus, for they said, 'Had he conquered us, he would have treated us just like these.' Their aversion to him increased, as did their determination to resist him.

[1] Literally 'he became the sum and the detail.'

After Zankī had gained Baalbek, he took Mu'īn al-Dīn Unur's slave girl, who was there, and married her in Aleppo, where she remained until his death. His son, Nūr al-Dīn Maḥmūd, then sent her back to [**70**] Mu'īn al-Dīn Unur, and this was the most important reason for the friendship between Nūr al-Dīn and Unur. God knows best!

Account of Qarāsunqur's seizing of Fars and his withdrawal

This year Atabeg Qarāsunqur, lord of Azerbayjan, gathered and enlisted many troops and marched to seek revenge for his son[2] whom Būz-Aba had killed in the battle which has been mentioned previously. When he was near Sultan Mas'ud, he sent to him, requesting him to execute his vizier Kamāl al-Dīn. He put him to death as we have already mentioned.[3] After his execution, Qarāsunqur went to Fars and on his approach Būz-Aba fortified himself within White Castle. Qarāsunqur ravaged the country with complete freedom, as there was no defence or resistance. However, he was unable to remain there. He took the towns in Fars and handed the country to Prince Saljuqshāh, son of Sultan Muḥammad,[4] saying, 'These lands are yours. Conquer what is left.' He then returned to Azerbayjan. At that, Būz-Aba came down from the [White] Castle (in the year 534 [1139–40]), defeated Saljuqshāh and recovered the lands. He took Saljuqshāh prisoner and incarcerated him in a castle in Fars.

Miscellaneous events

In Ṣafar [8 October–5 November 1138][5] Vizier Sharaf al-Dīn Anūshirwān ibn Khālid died in Baghdad when out of office. The caliph's vizier and other lesser officials attended his funeral. He was buried in his residence but was later transferred to Kufa and buried in the shrine of the Commander of the Faithful, 'Alī ibn Abī Ṭālib [**71**] (peace be upon him), as he had Shiite leanings. He was the instigator of the composition of al-Ḥarīrī's *Maqāmas*.[6] An intelligent and energetic man, and a good and religious one, he served as vizier for the Caliph al-Mustarshid and for Sultan Maḥmūd and Sultan Mas'ūd. He asked permission to resign the

---

2 The text and *Kāmil* (Thornberg), xi, 46, read 'his father' (*abīh*) here. Above, p. [**61**], we read of the capture and death of his son (*walad*). I prefer to read *ibnihi* here (Ms. Pococke 346, fol. 90a, has the ambiguous consonantal outline with no dots), rather than emend the earlier *walad*, the reading of the Ms., fol. 87a, to *wālid* ('father') .

3 See above p. [**64**].

4 *Kāmil* in error reads 'Maḥmūd'. He was Saljuqshāh's brother.

5 According to *Muntaẓam*, x, 77–8, Anūshirwān died in Ramaḍān 532/May–June 1138.

6 See above (s.a. 515) p. [**596**], note 1.

vizierate, which was granted, but then he was sought again for the post, which he accepted unwillingly.

In Rabīʿ I [6 November–5 December 1138] Sultan Masʿūd came to Baghdad. It was the winter season and he was now in the habit of wintering in Iraq and spending the summer in the Uplands. When he came he abolished the non-canonical taxes and set up inscriptions recording this act. The tablets were put on the doors of the mosques and in the markets. He commanded that no soldier should take a billet in the house of any ordinary citizen of Baghdad except with permission. Many blessings and much praise were given him. The person behind that was Kamāl al-Dīn al-Khāzin, the sultan's vizier.

In Ṣafar [October 1138] there were many frightening earth tremors in Syria, the Jazīra and many lands. The worst were in Syria. There was a series of them over several nights, with a number of tremors every night. Much of the country was ruined, especially Aleppo. The people there, when the tremors became too much for them, left their homes and went out into open country. In a single night they counted eighty tremors. In Syria they experienced earthquakes from 4 Ṣafar until the 19th [11–26 October], accompanied by a roaring and terrible shocks.

This year the Franks raided the district of Bānyās. The troops of Damascus pursued them but failed to catch them, so returned.

The following died this year:

Abū'l-Qāsim Zāhir ibn Ṭahir al-Shaḥḥāmī al-Nīsābūrī at Nishapur. He was born in the year 446 [1054–5] and was a leading scholar of Ḥadīth, a prolific transmitter of high authority.

ʿAbd Allāh ibn Aḥmad ibn ʿAbd al-Qādir ibn Muḥammad ibn Yūsuf, Abū'l-Qāsim ibn Abī'l-Ḥusayn al-Baghdādī in Baghdad. He was born in the year 452 [1060-61].

ʿAbd al-ʿAzīz [**72**] ibn ʿUthmān ibn Ibrāhīm, Abū Muḥammad al-Asadī al-Bukhārī, who was cadi of Bukhārā. He was a lawyer, a scion of a scholarly family and a man of a goodly life.

Muḥammad ibn Shujāʿ ibn Abī Bakr ibn ʿAlī ibn Ibrāhīm al-Laftuwānī[7] al-Iṣfahānī. He died in Isfahan in Jumādā II [February 1139] and was born in the year 497 [1103–4]. He studied Ḥadīth intensively in Isfahan, Baghdad and elsewhere.

---

7 According to *Muntaẓam*, x, 84, Laftuwān was one of Isfahan's villages.

[73] The Year 534 [1139–1140]

How Atabeg Zankī besieged Damascus

This year Atabeg Zankī besieged Damascus twice. The first time was in Rabī‘ I [November 1139] when he came to besiege it from Baalbek after he had successfully dealt with that place, settled its administration and corrected what was disordered there. He stopped in the Biqā‘ and sent to the ruler of Damascus, Jamāl al-Dīn, offering him any town he might suggest, if he would surrender Damascus to him, but he did not accept this proposal. So Zankī moved to attack Damascus. On 13 Rabī‘ I [7 November 1139] he halted at Dārayyā and the advance guards clashed in battle. Victory went to Zankī's troops and the Damascenes retired defeated. Many of them were killed.

Next Zankī advanced to Damascus, where he camped. A large gathering of the regular troops of Damascus, the local militia and foot-soldiers from the Ghūṭa met him in battle and suffered a defeat. They fell to the sword in great numbers and likewise many were taken prisoner. The survivors returned wounded. That day the city was on the point of being taken, but Zankī withdrew from the battle and held back for several days. He sent a succession of envoys to the ruler of Damascus and offered him Baalbek, Homs and other places that he might choose. He inclined towards surrender but others of his entourage turned it down and pointed out the likely dangerous consequences, adding that Zankī might deal treacherously with him, as he had with the men of Baalbek. After his refusal to surrender Zankī resumed the fighting and the assaults.

Later Jamāl al-Dīn, ruler of Damascus, fell ill and died on 8 Sha‘bān [29 March 1140]. Eager [**74**] then for the city, Zankī carried out a fierce assault, in the expectation that differences might arise among the leading men and the emirs and that thus he would gain his aim. What he hoped for was far from coming about. After the death of Jamāl al-Dīn, his son Mujīr al-Dīn Abaq succeeded while Mu‘īn al-Dīn Unur took on the office of regent. There was no obvious effect from the death of his father, even though their enemy was at the gates of the city. When Unur saw that Zankī did not depart nor stop the siege, he contacted the Franks and summoned them to his aid, asking them to agree to defend Damascus from Zankī. He offered them inducements, including that he would besiege Bānyās, capture it and give to over to them. He painted them a frightening picture, if Zankī should take Damascus. They knew that what he said was true, namely that, if Zankī gained it, there would be no remaining in Syria for them with him there. The Franks met and decided to march to Damascus to join with its ruler and troops in fighting Zankī. When Zankī learnt of this he went to the Ḥawrān on 5 Ramaḍān [24 April 1140], planning to engage the Franks before they linked up with the

Damascenes. The Franks heard this news and stayed in their own territory. Seeing that this was so, Zankī returned to the siege of Damascus and camped to the north of the city at Adhrā on 6 Shawwāl [25 May 1140]. He burnt several villages in the Meadow (al-Marj)[1] and in the Ghūṭa, but then departed back to his own lands.

The Franks came to Damascus and joined its ruler after Zankī had withdrawn. They then went back but Mu'īn al-Dīn Unur with the troops of Damascus marched to Bānyās, which was obedient to Zankī, as we have mentioned, to besiege it and deliver it to the Franks. The governor there had previously gone to Tyre with a force he had assembled to raid the local country. He encountered the ruler of Antioch who was making his way to Damascus to bring reinforcements to its ruler against Zankī. A battle followed in which the Muslims were defeated and the governor of Bānyās taken and killed. The survivors escaped to Bānyās and gathered many men from the Biqā' and elsewhere to hold the citadel. Mu'īn al-Dīn camped before it, engaged the defenders and pressed them hard. He had a detachment of Franks with him. After he had taken the place he handed it to the Franks.

[75] As for the second siege of Damascus, when the Atabeg heard the news of the siege of Bānyās, he returned to Baalbek in order to defend Bānyās against those besieging it. He remained at Baalbek awhile, but when the army of Damacus returned after they had taken Bānyās and given it to the Franks, Atabeg Zankī divided his troops to raid the Ḥawrān and the districts around Damascus. He himself, with his close staff but without his main baggage train, descended upon Damascus at dawn without any of the population having any inkling of this. When the people woke up and saw his troops, they were fearful and the city was in an uproar. The troops and the common people gathered on the city wall. The gates were opened and the regulars and the infantry sallied forth to fight. Zankī did not allow his troops to take any military initiative because the main part of his army had scattered around the country to plunder and cause havoc. He had only moved against Damascus to prevent any troops moving out against his own when they were widely scattered. During the fighting that day there were several losses on both sides and then Zankī disengaged, retired to his tents and moved to Marj Rāhiṭ, where he remained awaiting the return of his troops. When they did so, their hands were full of booty, because they had fallen on the country when the inhabitants were unprepared. After they had mustered again he led them back to his lands.

Account of Zankī's conquest of Shahrazūr and its districts

This year Atabeg Zankī conquered Shahrazūr, its districts and the neighbouring fortresses. They were in the possession of Qipjāq ibn Arslān Tāsh the Turkoman. His writ was effective over Turkomans both distant and near at hand. His word was

[1] Probably Marj Rāhiṭ, a plain north of Damascus near Adhrā (see just below).

never gainsaid. They considered obedience to him a duty and rulers avoided any move against him. They did not interfere in his domain because of this and also because it was inaccessible with many narrow passes. His power grew and his following increased. The Turkomans came to him from every remote nook.

When this year came, Atabeg Zankī sent an army against him. Qipjāq gathered his men and met Zankī's troops in a pitched battle. Qipjāq was defeated and his army given over to slaughter. The forces of [**76**] the Atabeg pursued them and besieged their fortresses and castles, all of which they took. They offered safe conduct to Qipjāq who joined them and was assimilated into the ranks of the army. He and his sons continued to serve the Atabeg house in impeccable fashion until a little after the year 600 [1203–4] when they left its service.

Miscellaneous events

This year there was a dispute between the Commander of the Faithful al-Muqtafī li-Amr Allāh and Vizier Sharaf al-Dīn 'Alī ibn Ṭirād al-Zaynabī. The cause was that the vizier opposed every order of the caliph, who objected to this. The vizier was angry, but later became fearful and made his way by barge to the residence of the sultan at midday. He entered and demanded protection. The caliph sent proposing that he return to his office but he refused. Official documents were still being issued under his name and the Chief Cadi al-Zaynabī, the cousin of the vizier, acted as deputy. The caliph sent messengers on the matter of the vizier to the sultan, who gave permission for his dismissal. At that, his name was dropped from documents. He stayed in the sultan's residence, and al-Zaynabī was dismissed from the deputy's post, which was taken by Sadīd al-Dawla ibn al-Anbārī.

During this year the Favourite Jawhar, one of Sultan Sanjar's eunuchs, was killed. He had gained great authority throughout the whole of Sanjar's state. Part of his fief was Rayy and one of his mamlukes was 'Abbās, the man in charge [**77**] of Rayy. All of Sanjar's army used to attend on him and stand at his gate. He was killed at the hands of the Bāṭinīs. A group of them waited on him, dressed as women, and pleaded for his help. He stopped to listen to what they had to say and they slew him. After his assassination his man 'Abbās gathered troops and attacked the Bāṭinīs, killing very many of them. He did more against them than any other had done. He continued to campaign against them, killing them and ravaging their territory, until his death.

This year Ganja and other parts of Azerbayjan and Arran suffered an earthquake. It was most severe in Ganja and destroyed much of it and killed so many people that they could not be counted. It was said that the dead reached 230,000. Among those that perished were two sons of Qarāsunqur, the ruler of the land. A castle there that belonged to Mujāhid al-Dīn Bahrūz collapsed and he lost a great amount of stores and money.

During the year Mujāhid al-Dīn Bahrūz embarked on the development of al-Nahrawānāt.[2] He built a great dam to make the water return to its original course. He dredged the old water course and opened up a channel to take water from Diyālā. Later there was a breach and the water flow avoided the dam, which was left isolated,[3] of no use to anyone. Nobody made any attempt to restore the water to its course at the dam until this present age of ours.[4]

This year the rains at Baghdad and in Iraq failed. Rain fell only once in Ādhar [March 1140], then it stopped again. A famine followed and provisions were lacking in Iraq.

In Jumādā II [23 January-20 February 1140] the caliph took to wife the Lady Fāṭima, daughter of Sultan Muḥammad.[5] The day she was conveyed to the Caliphal Palace was a memorable one. Baghdad was bedecked[6] for several days and put *en fête*. The marriage of Sultan Mas'ūd to the daughter of the Caliph al-Muqtafī li-Amr Allāh was arranged. The marriage contract was drawn up but it was agreed that her wedding procession should be delayed for five years because of her young years.

In Rabī' I [25 October-23 November 1140] Cadi Abū'l-Faḍl Yaḥyā, the son of the cadi of Damascus, known as al-Zakī, died.

---

2 By this plural form I understand the numerous branches either side of the main Nahrawan canal and the areas they irrigated.

3 Adopting the reading in *Kāmil* (Thornberg), xi, 51: *fī'l-barr* (lit. 'in open country'). The text has *fīl-bi'r* ('in the well'), which does not give good sense.

4 *Muntaẓam*, xi, 95, records (s.a. 536/1141-2) the completion of Bahrūz's development, the building of a village, named al-Mujāhidiyya, and a mausoleum for himself. There was talk of waste of money (the cost was 70,000 dinars). Bahrūz was temporarily dismissed (see below p. [**89**]). For a study of irrigation in lower Iraq since the advent of Islam, see Adams, *Land behind Baghdad*, 84-111.

5 The text in error has Mas'ūd, who was Fāṭima's brother. Correct from *Muntaẓam*, x, 85, and Lambton, *Continuity and Change*, table II, p. 390. *Muntaẓam* gives the preceding month, Jumādā I.

6 The text and *Kāmil* (Thornberg), xi, 51, read *ughliqat* ('closed'). Very little change (chiefly the dropping of the diacritical point on the first radical) allows one to adopt a preferable reading indicated by *Muntaẓam*, x, 84-5, *'ulliqat*. Note also *al-ta'ālīq* ('the decorative hangings').

The Year 535 [1140-1141]

The expedition of Chahārdānikī to Iraq and what he did

This year Sultan Mas'ūd ordered Emir Ismā'īl, known as Chahārdānikī,[1] and Alpqush Kūn-Khar[2] to proceed to Khuzistan and Fars and take them both from Būz-Aba. He issued them with expenses drawn on Baghdad. They set out with their followers to Baghdad, but Mujāhid al-Dīn Bahrūz would not allow them to enter the city. They would not accept this, but he sent to the ferries and had them holed and sunk. He also made great efforts to repair the city wall, blocked up the Ẓafariyya Gate and the Kalwādhā Gate and closed the rest of the gates, on which he hung protective material.[3] He also pitched tents for the soldiers.

When the two emirs learnt this, they crossed the Ṣarṣar and made for al-Ḥilla. They were denied access, so they went to Wāsiṭ. Emir Ṭurunṭāy came out to meet them in battle but was defeated. They entered Wāsiṭ and sacked it. They also sacked Qūsān[4] and al-Nu'māniyya. Ṭurunṭāy allied himself with Ḥammād ibn Abī'l-Jabr,[5] the lord of the Marsh, and the troops of Basra also agreed to cooperate. Some of their troops abandoned Ismā'īl and Alpqush and joined with Ṭurunṭāy. Weakened by that, the two went to Tustar. Ismā'īl approached the sultan through intercessors and was pardoned.

[79] Miscellaneous events

This year the envoy of Sultan Sanjar came,[6] bringing with him the Prophet's Cloak (may God bless him and give him peace) and his Staff. They had been taken from al-Mustarshid but at this present time Sanjar restored them to al-Muqtafī.

Atabeg Qarāsunqur, lord of Azerbayjan and Arran, died this year in the city of Ardabīl, having suffered chronically from consumption. He was one of the

---

1 The main course of Dujayl passed west of Tustar and was known as Chahār Dānika, "four sixths" (see Le Strange, *Caliphate*, 236; Krawulsky, 356).

2 This rather colourful nickname, 'Ass's backside', is also the reading of *Kāmil* (Thornberg), xi, 51, and Rāwandī, *Rāḥat*, see index. Bosworth, 'The Iranian world', 130, has Khūn-Kar, meaning 'Blood-shedder' (?).

3 This is a speculative translation of 'he suspended *silāḥ* on them', lit. 'arms, armour', understood as referring to padded hangings to aborb the shock of missiles or materials treated with substances to prevent combustion.

4 The text reads Fursān but for Qūsān, given as a variant and supported by Ms. Pococke 346, fol. 92b, see Krawulsky, 503: a province in Iraq al-'Ajam, including al-Nu'māniyya.

5 Following the reading in the text's footnote.

6 In Dhū'l-Qa'da/June-July 1141, according to *Muntaẓam*, xi, 90.

mamlukes of Prince Ṭughril. Azerbayjan and Arran were given to Emir Jāwulī al-Ṭughrilī. Qarāsunqur's high position had overshadowed the sultan, who was afraid of him.

This year there was a fierce battle between Atabeg Zankī and Dā'ūd [ibn] Suqmān ibn Artuq, lord of Ḥisn Kayfā. The latter was defeated and Zankī took the castle of Bahmard, one of his possessions. However, winter overtook Zankī and he returned to Mosul.

This year the Ismā'īlīs gained control of the castle of Masyāf in Syria. The castellan there was a mamluke of the Banū Munqidh, the lords of Shayzar. By tricking and outwitting him, they went up into the castle to meet him, killed him and seized the castle. It remains in their hands until today.

This year Sadīd al-Dawla ibn al-Anbārī died. After him the caliph appointed as vizier Niẓām al-Dīn Abū Naṣr al-Muẓaffar[7] ibn Muḥammad ibn Jahīr. Previously he had been major-domo.

Yarunqush Bāzdār, lord of Qazwīn, also died this year.

In Rajab [10 February–11 March 1141] the son of the Dānishmand, lord of Malaṭyā and other places in that region, overcame a force of Byzantines, killed them and took what they had as booty.

[80] In Ramaḍān [10 April–9 May 1141] a detachment of Franks in Syria went to Ascalon to raid the surrounding country, which belonged to the ruler of Egypt. The troops based in Ascalon came out to meet them in battle and won a victory, killing many of the Franks, who withdrew in flight.

This year the Kamāliyya Madrasah was built in Baghdad.[8] It was built by Kamāl al-Dīn Abū'l-Futūḥ ibn Ṭalḥa, the head of the Storehouse. On its completion Shaykh Abū'l-Ḥasan ibn al-Khall gave an [inaugural] lecture, which was attended by officials and all the lawyers.

This year in Rajab [10 February–11 March 1141] Cadi Abū Bakr Muḥammad ibn 'Abd al-Bāqī al-Anṣārī, the cadi of the Hospital, died, aged a little over ninety years.[9] As a transmitter of Ḥadīth he had very high authority and he was knowledgeable in logic, arithmetic, geometry and other disciplines of the Ancients. He was the last man in the world to relate Ḥadīth on the authority of Abū Isḥāq al-Barmakī, Cadi Abū'l-Ṭayyib al-Ṭabarī, Abū Ṭālib al-'Ushārī and Abū Muḥammad al-Jawharī and others.

The following also died this year:

---

7 Although the text and Ms. Pococke 346, fol. 93a, read Muḥammad, the reading of *Muntaẓam*, xi, 88, has been adopted. See also *EI(2)*, ii, 385a. Bundārī, 194, gives no personal name.

8 Opened in Shawwāl/May–June 1141 at the Commoners' Gate district (*Muntaẓam*, xi, 89).

9 He died on Wednesday 2 Rajab/=12 February 1141. An 'ibn' following 'Abū Bakr' has been dropped, following *Muntaẓam*, xi, 92-3, where Ibn al-Jawzī gives a rather personal account. Abū Bakr spent a year and a half in Byzantine captivity. He learnt 'Byzantine writing' (*al-khaṭṭ al-rūmī*). He retained all his senses into old age and could read small script from a distance.

The Imam and Koran scholar Abū'l-Qāsim Ismā'īl ibn Muḥammad ibn al-Faḍl al-Iṣfahānī on 10 Dhū'l-Ḥijja [8 July–5 August 1141]. He was born in the year 459 [1066-7] and is the author of celebrated works.

Yūsuf ibn Ayyūb ibn Yūsuf ibn al-Ḥasan, Abū Ya'qūb al-Hamadhānī, a citizen of Burūjird who resided in Marv. He studied law under Abū Isḥāq al-Shīrāzī and transmitted Ḥadīth. He also occupied himself with religious and spiritual exercises. He delivered a sermon at Baghdad and a student of law, called Ibn al-Saqqā', rose and questioned him in a hostile manner. Yūsuf said, 'Silence! I catch a whiff of unbelief from you.' The man travelled later to Byzantine lands and became a Christian.[10]

Abū'l-Qāsim 'Alī ibn Aflaḥ, the famous poet.[11]

---

[10] Ibn al-Athīr perhaps forgot that he had mentioned this incident s.a. 506/1112–13 when Yūsuf ibn Ayyūb's coming to Baghdad is recorded (see above p. [**492–3**]). The incident is also mentioned by *Muntaẓam*, xi, 95, with a reference back to the full version s.a. 506 (*Muntaẓam*, x, 171).

[11] He was in high favour with al-Mustarshid, who gave him four houses in Darb al-Shākiriyya. He bought others nearby and then demolished them all to build one large house (with hot and cold running water), for which the caliph gave him 500 dinars, 100 tree trunks and 200,000 bricks. His fall and the destruction of the house followed the disclosure that he was acting as a spy for Dubays. His death notice (*tarjama*) is in *Muntaẓam*, x, 80–84, s.a. 533/1138–9.

[81] The Year 536 [1141-1142]

Account of Sultan Sanjar's defeat by the Qarakhitay Turks and their conquest of Transoxania

Concerning this event historians have recorded various reports, all of which we shall mention to take responsibility for none of them.

In Muḥarram of this year [August 1141] Sultan Sanjar suffered a defeat at the hands of the infidel Turks. The reason for this was that Sanjar had killed a son of Khwārazm Shāh Atsiz ibn Muḥammad, as we have previously mentioned. Khwārazm Shāh sent to the Qarakhitay,[1] when they were in Transoxania, encouraging them to attack the lands [of Sanjar] and promoting their interest in them. He also made a marriage alliance with them and urged them to invade Sultan Sanjar's realm. They eventually set out with 300,000 horsemen. Sanjar marched against them with his armies and they met in a fierce battle in Transoxania. Sanjar with all his armies was defeated and 100,000 of them were killed, including 11,000 who were all men of the turban, and 4,000 women. Sultan Sanjar's wife was made captive, but Sanjar managed to flee to Tirmidh and from there proceeded to Balkh.

After Sanjar's defeat Khwārazm Shāh made for the city of Marv, which he entered to humiliate Sultan Sanjar. He carried out some executions and seized Abū'l-Faḍl al-Kirmānī, the Ḥanafī lawyer, and several other lawyers and other notables of the city.

Up to this moment Sultan Sanjar had always been blessed by fortune; his banner had never been defeated. After suffering **[82]** this reverse, he sent to Sultan Mas'ūd, granting him permission to act independently in Rayy and its associated territories on the same basis as his father Sultan Muḥammad, and he ordered him to reside there with his armies, so that, if there was a necessity, he could call on him, all because of this defeat. 'Abbās, the governor of Rayy, came to Baghdad with his troops and paid his respects to Sultan Mas'ūd with lavish gifts. The sultan set out for Rayy in obedience to the command of his uncle Sanjar.

The following account has also been given. The land of Turkistan, namely Kāshghar, Balāsāghūn, Khotan, Ṭirāz and other parts of Transoxania that are in the vicinity of these places, were held by rulers of the Qarakhānid Turks, who were Muslims from the lineage of Afrāsiyāb the Turk. However, they did not agree

[1] The Khitan nomads, possibly Mongol in origin, became Chinese in culture and language. In the mid-tenth century in northern China they established a dynasty known as the Liao. They were overthrown by fresh invaders, the Jurchens, *c.*1120. Led by Yelu Dashi, they migrated westward and formed the Qarakhitay or the Western Liao. See Bosworth, 'The Iranian world', 147–9. For an account of their origins and history, see Juvaini, *History*, i, 354–61, and the major study, Biran, *Empire of the Qara Khitai*.

amongst themselves. The reason for the conversion of their early ancestor to Islam, whose name was Satuq[2] Qarākhāqān, was that he dreamt that a man descended from the heavens and said in Turkish what amounted to, 'Accept Islam and you will be at peace (*taslam*) in this world and the next,' and in his dream he converted. Waking in the morning, he duly professed Islam. After his death his place was taken by his son, Mūsā ibn Satuq, and his descendants continued to rule in those regions until Arslān Khān Muḥammad ibn Sulaymān ibn Dā'ūd Bughrā Khān ibn Ibrāhīm (entitled Ṭamghāch Khān) ibn Īlik (known as Naṣr Arslān) ibn 'Alī ibn Mūsā ibn Satuq. Qadir Khān rebelled against him and wrested power from him. However, Sanjar killed Qadir Khān, as we have related, under the year 495 [1101-2][3] and restored the rule of Arslān Khān, whose hold on power became well established. Then rebels appeared, so he sought the aid of Sultan Sanjar, who again helped him and restored him to power.

His army consisted of two groups of Turks, called the Qarluq and the Oghuz Turks. The latter plundered Khurasan, as we shall relate, God willing. They formed two groups, one called Üch-Oq, whose leader was Ṭūṭī ibn Dād Beg, and the other called Bozuq, whose leader was Qurghūt ibn 'Abd al-Ḥamīd.[4] The Sharīf al-Ashraf ibn Muḥammad ibn Abī Shujā' al-'Alawī al-Samarqandī persuaded the son of Arslān Khān, known as Naṣr Khān, to seek to take the kingship from his father [**83**] and fed his ambition. Muḥammad [Arslān] Khān became aware of this and killed both his son and the Sharīf al-Ashraf.

A lack of understanding grew up between Arslān Khān and the Qarluqs in his army, which led them to rebel against him and deprive him of his position as king. He renewed his plea for assistance from Sultan Sanjar, who crossed the Oxus with his troops in the year 524 [1129-30]. The two were related by marriage. Sanjar came to Samarqand and the Qarluqs fled before him.

It chanced that Sultan Sanjar went hunting and caught sight of a band of cavalry. He seized them and they confessed that Arslān Khān had engaged them to kill him. Thereupon he returned to Samarqand and besieged Arslān Khān in the citadel. He took it, made him prisoner and sent him to Balkh where he died. It has been claimed that Sanjar dealt treacherously with him, having invited him to be his guest, that he seized the city from him and then spread this report about him.

After he had taken Samarqand, he appointed as governor Qilij Ṭamghāch Abū'l-Ma'ālī al-Ḥasan ibn 'Alī ibn 'Abd al-Mu'min, known as Ḥasan Takīn, who was one of the nobles of the Qarakhānid house, although Arslān Khān had cast him off. His rule in Samarqand did not last long. He soon died and Sanjar put in his place Prince Maḥmūd ibn Arslān Khān Muḥammad ibn Sulaymān ibn Dā'ūd Bughrā

---

[2] The text has S.b.q and *Kāmil* (Thornberg), xi, 54, reads Sh.b.q. The first convert is traditionally said to be Satuq Bughra Khan (see Bosworth, 'The Iranian world', 5).

[3] Correct the '494' in the text. See above p. [**348**].

[4] For Sanjar's conflict with the incoming nomadic Turks, see Bosworth, 'The Iranian world', 152ff. The spelling of the two groups has been adopted from the same source. Our text has ['.j.q.] and [b.r.q.]. Bundārī, 281, calls the two leaders Ṭūṭī Beg and Q.r.ghūd.

Khān, the son of the person from whom Sanjar had taken Samarqand. This Maḥmūd was Sanjar's nephew.[5]

Before this, in the year 522 [1128], al-A'war al-Ṣīnī (the One-eyed Chinaman) had come to the borders of Kāshghar leading vast numbers that God alone could comprehend. The ruler of Kāshghar, [Arslān] Khān Aḥmad ibn al-Ḥasan, prepared for him, gathered his troops and marched to meet him. They fought a battle and al-A'war al-Ṣīnī was defeated and many of his men killed. He died after this and was succeeded by Gūr Khān[6] al-Ṣīnī. In the language of China 'gūr' is a title for the greatest of their princes and 'khān' is a title of the Turks, also meaning 'the greatest of princes.'[7] He used to wear the dress of their rulers, that is, the *miqna'a* and the *khimār*.[8] He was a Manichean **[84]** in belief.[9] When he emerged from China into Turkistan, the Khiṭay Turks joined him. They had previously come out of China and were in the service of the Qarakhānids, lords of Turkistan.

Arslān Khān Muḥammad ibn Sulaymān used to dispatch 10,000 tents every year and settle them on the routes between him and China, to prevent any prince from attacking his lands. For that they received allowances and allotments. It came about that one year he was angry with them and kept them from their womenfolk to prevent them breeding. This upset them but they did not know any means of getting at him. They were at a loss. It chanced that a large caravan passed by with much money and precious goods. They seized it, brought the merchants before them and said, 'If you hope for your property, tell us of a broad land with plentiful pasturage, big enough for us and our flocks.' The merchants agreed on the land of Balāsāghūn, which they described to them. They then restored the merchants' property, seized and bound the men who were watching over them to keep them from their women, collected their women and proceeded to Balāsāghūn. Arslān Khān used to raid them and wage war on them often, so they feared him greatly.

When some time had passed and Gūr Khān al-Ṣīnī appeared, they allied themselves with him. They grew in importance and their following multiplied, so that they came to control the land of Turkistan. Whenever they took a city, they did not change anything for the inhabitants. From every household in the towns, and also in the villages, they took a dinar. The crops and other things remained for the

---

5 According to Bosworth, 'The Iranian world', 140, Ibrāhīm, a brother of Arslān Khān, was installed as ruler for a while before Maḥmūd.

6 The text in error has 'Kūkhān' and 'Kū'.

7 *Gür* in Mongolian means 'world/universal'. Thus Gūr Khān means 'world ruler'. See Pelliot, *Notes on Marco Polo*, i, 225–6; see also Wittfogel et al., *Chinese Society*, 431; Biran, *Empire of the Qara Khitai*, 38–9.

8 The first term normally denotes a sort of linen coif and the second a veil or headdress, particularly for women. What precisely the terms meant in the Qarakhitay context is unknown. Certainly Qarakhitay dress differed from that of their Muslim subjects: see Juvainī, *History*, i, 65, 352 (I owe these references to Dr Michal Biran).

9 The Qarakhitay practised religious tolerance. Buddhism was also represented among them.

inhabitants. To the waist of every prince that submitted to them they attached a sort of silver tablet, which was the mark of those obedient to them.

They then marched into Transoxania, where Khāqān Maḥmūd ibn Muḥammad met them at the limits of Khujanda[10] in Ramaḍān of the year 531 [23 May–21 June 1137]. A battle took place and Khāqān Maḥmūd ibn Muḥammad was defeated and withdrew to Samarqand. A great disaster threatened its inhabitants, [**85**] fear and anxiety grew and day and night they were expecting their testing time to come. It was the same with the inhabitants of Bukhara and other towns in Transoxania. Khāqān Maḥmūd sent to Sultan Sanjar asking for aid, telling him what had befallen the Muslims and urging him to help them. Sanjar gathered his forces and was joined by the princes of Khurasan, the lord of Sijistan and the Ghūr, the ruler of Ghazna, the ruler of Mazandaran and others. More than 100,000 horseman assembled and the review lasted six months.

Sanjar marched to confront the Turks and crossed the Oxus in Dhū'l-Ḥijja of the year 535 [8 July–5 August 1141]. Maḥmūd ibn Muḥammad Khān complained to him about the Qarluq Turks, so Sanjar made a move against them but they sought refuge with Gūr Khān al-Ṣīnī and his infidel followers. Sanjar remained at Samarqand. Gūr Khān wrote him a letter which contained intercession on behalf of the Qarluq Turks and a request for him to forgive them, but his plea for them was not accepted. Sanjar replied, inviting him to become a Muslim, with menaces if he failed to comply, and threatening him with the size and description of his army. He exaggerated their prowess in fighting with all sorts of weapons. He even said, 'They split hairs with their arrows.' His vizier, Ṭāhir ibn Fakhr al-Mulk ibn Niẓām al-Mulk did not approve of this letter but Sanjar paid no attention to him and sent it off. When the letter was read out to Gūr Khān, he ordered the beard of the envoy to be plucked, gave him a needle and the task of splitting a hair from his beard. When he was unable to do it, Gūr Khān said, 'How can someone else split a hair with an arrow when you are incapable of splitting it with a needle!'

Gūr Khān prepared for war, having with him troops from the Turks, the Chinese, the Khiṭay and others. He moved against Sultan Sanjar and the two armies clashed, like two mighty seas, at a place called Qaṭwān.[11] Gūr Khān circled around his opponents and eventually forced them into a wadi called Dargham.[12] On Sanjar's right wing was Emir Qumāj and on his left wing the ruler of Sijistan with the baggage train [**86**] behind them. The battle was fought on 5 Ṣafar 536 [9 September 1141].[13]

---

[10] Otherwise Khojend, a town south of the Jaxartes, between Samarqand and Khokand.

[11] A steppe area in Ushrūsana, east of Samarqand (see Bosworth, 'The Iranian world', 149). Knowledge of this major battle (for which see Biran, *Empire of the Qara Khitai*, 41–5) gave a boost to the legend of Prester John; see Beckingham, 'The achievements of Prester John,' 3; and for a general account of the legend, Nowell, 'The historical Prester John.'

[12] Dargham is mentioned as a district of Samarqand, south of the River Zarafshān in Barthold, *Turkestan*, 92.

[13] According to *Muntaẓam*, xi, 97, the battle was in Muḥarram/6 August–4 September 1141.

The Qarluq Turks who had fled from Sanjar were some of the fiercest fighters. On that day in the army of Sanjar there was no better fighter than the lord of Sijistan but the battle resulted in the defeat of the Muslims, whose dead were almost too many to count. The valley of Dargham contained 10,000 dead and wounded. Sultan Sanjar fled the field and the lord of Sijistan, Emir Qumāj and Sultan Sanjar's wife, the daughter of Arslān Khān, were captured, although the infidels freed them later. Among those killed was Ḥusām al-Dīn 'Umar ibn 'Abd al-'Azīz ibn Māza al-Bukhārī, the celebrated Ḥanafī lawyer. In the history of Islam there was no battle greater than this, nor any in Khurasan in which more were slain than in this.

The state of the Khiṭay and the infidel Turks became well established in Transoxania. Gūr Khān lived until Rajab of the year 537 [20 January–18 February 1143] and then he died. He was a handsome and good-looking man who wore only Chinese silk. His men held him in great awe. He gave no emir authority over any fief but paid them from his own resources. He used to say, 'Whenever they take a fief they become oppressive.' No emir was given command of more than one hundred horseman, so that he was unable to rebel against him. He prohibited injustice by his men and banned drunkenness which was a punishable offence. However, he did not prohibit nor abhor adultery or fornication.

A daughter of his succeeded him but she died after a short reign. Her mother, Gūr Khān's wife and cousin, ruled after her. Transoxania remained in the hands of the Khiṭay until 'Alā' al-Dīn Muḥammad Khwārazm Shāh took it from them in the year 612 [1215–16], as we shall relate, if God wills.

[87] Account of what Khwārazm Shāh did in Khurasan

We have previously mentioned Sultan Sanjar's expedition to Khwārazm, his taking it from Khwārazm Shāh Atsiz, the latter's return there, the killing of his son and the fact that he was the person who made contact with the Khiṭay and encouraged them to attack the lands of Islam. After Sultan Sanjar had met them and returned defeated, Khwārazm Shāh went to Khurasan and attacked Sarakhs in Rabī' I of this year [October 1141].

When he arrived there he was met by the Imam Abū Muḥammad al-Ziyādī, a man who united asceticism and learning. Khwārazm Shāh received him with much honour and departed to Marv al-Shāhijān. The Imam Aḥmad al-Bākharzī sought him out and interceded on behalf of the population of Marv. He asked that no soldier should interfere with them and this was granted. Khwārazm Shāh camped outside the city and summoned Abū'l-Faḍl al-Kirmānī, the lawyer, and the city notables. However, the common people of Marv rose up and killed one of Khwārazm Shāh's men, expelled his followers from the city and shut the gates, preparing to resist. Khwārazm Shāh fought with them, entered the city on 17 Rabī' I [20 October 1141] and killed many of the inhabitants.

Among those killed were Ibrāhīm al-Marwazī, the Shāfi'ī lawyer, and 'Alī ibn Muḥammad ibn Arslān, a master of many learned disciplines. The Sharīf 'Alī ibn Isḥāq al-Mūsawī, who was a leader of discord and propagator of evil, was also killed. Khwārazm Shāh killed many notables of the city and then returned to Khwārazm, taking with him many of the local ulema, among them Abū'l-Faḍl al-Kirmānī, Abū **[88]** Manṣūr al-'Ibādī, Cadi al-Ḥusayn ibn Muḥammad al-Arsābandī, Abū Muḥammad al-Khiraqī, the philosopher, and others.

In Shawwāl [May 1142] he went to Nishapur. Several local lawyers, ulema and ascetics came out to him and requested him not to treat the people of Nishapur as he had treated those of Marv. He granted their request but carried out a thorough search for the wealth of the sultan's followers, which he seized. Sultan Sanjar's name was dropped from the khutbah at the beginning of Dhū'l-Qa'da [28 May] and his own name added. When the preacher omitted Sultan Sanjar's name and mentioned Khwārazm Shāh's, the people raised a clamour and rioted. There was nearly an outbreak of rebellion and a return of troubles, but wise and intelligent men stopped the people going that far, in view of what the outcome could be. The change in the khutbah lasted until 1 Muḥarram 537 [27 July 1142] and then it was restored in the name of Sultan Sanjar.

Khwārazm Shāh sent an army to the districts of Bayhaq, where they remained fighting the inhabitants for five days. The army then marched away from there, plundering the land, and perpetrated dreadful deeds in Khurasan. Sultan Sanjar was prevented from doing battle with Atsiz Khwārazm Shāh because of his fear of the power of the Khiṭay in Transoxania and their proximity to Khwārazm and other places in the lands of Khurasan.

Miscellaneous events

This year Atabeg Zankī ibn Āqsunqur took the town of al-Ḥadītha. He moved those members of the house of Muhārish[14] who were there to Mosul and placed his own men in the town.

Zankī's name was added to the khutbah in the town of Āmid and its ruler submitted to him. Previously he had been an ally of Dā'ūd in his fight with Zankī, but when he saw Zankī's power he joined with him.

[89] This year Mujāhid al-Dīn Bahrūz was dismissed as prefect of Baghdad, which office was taken by Qizil, Marshal of Horse, one of Sultan Maḥmūd's mamlukes, who held Barūjird and Basra. The office of prefect was given to him in addition. Later Sultan Mas'ūd came to Baghdad, saw the licence and trouble-making of the urban gangs, something that displeased him greatly, so reinstated Bahrūz as prefect. Many of the gangs repented but that did not benefit the population, because the vizier's son and the sultan's brother-in-law were in partnership with the gang members and Bahrūz was unable to prevent their

[14] Correct the text's [M.h.rā.sh].

activities.[15]

This year 'Abd al-Raḥmān [ibn] Ṭughāyuruk became the sultan's chamberlain and took control of affairs of state. Emir Tatar al-Ṭughrilī was removed from the post and ended up walking in the retinue of 'Abd al-Raḥmān.

Ibrāhīm al-Sihāwī,[16] the leader of the Ismā'īlīs, died this year. The son of 'Abbās, governor of Rayy, cremated his body in his coffin.

Kamāl al-Dīn ibn Ṭalḥa, the head of the Storeroom, went on pilgrimage this year. When he returned, he had donned the garb of the Sufis and retired from all his activities. He remained at home, untroubled and secure in his faith.

The sultan came to Baghdad this year. The Vizier al-Zaynabī was in the Sultanian Palace, as we have said, and he asked the sultan to intercede for him so that the caliph might allow him back in his house. The sultan sent his own vizier to the Caliphal Palace, along with Vizier Sharaf al-Dīn al-Zaynabī, and made representations about his returning to his house. Permission for this was granted and his brother was reinstated as chief syndic. The vizier stayed close at home and only came out to go to the mosque.

[**90**] From Aleppo the troops of Atabeg Zankī raided Frankish territory. They plundered and burned and overwhelmed a detachment of Franks, of whom they killed many. Those killed numbered seven hundred.

This year the Banū Khafāja caused much trouble in Iraq. Sultan Mas'ūd sent a detachment of his troops against them, who ravaged their settlement, killing those they seized there. They returned safely.

The lord of Sicily, Roger the Frank, sent a fleet this year to the coast of Ifrīqiya. They captured some ships that had been sent from Egypt to al-Ḥasan, the ruler of Ifrīqiya. Al-Ḥasan was betrayed by Roger but later made contact with him and renewed the truce for the sake of transporting grain from Sicily to Ifrīqiya, because there was a serious famine there and high mortality.

The following died this year:

Abū'l-Qāsim 'Abd al-Wahhāb ibn 'Abd al-Wāhid al-Ḥanbalī al-Dimashqī, who was a pious scholar.

Ḍiyā' al-Dīn Abū Sa'īd ibn al-Kafartūthī, Atabeg Zankī's vizier.[17] His conduct was excellent during his vizierate and he was a generous and outstanding man.

Abū Muḥammad ibn Ṭā'ūs, the imam of the [Umayyad] Mosque in Damascus, during Muḥarram [6 August-4 September 1141]. He was a pious and learned man.

Abū'l-Qāsim Ismā'īl ibn Aḥmad ibn 'Umar ibn Abī'l-Ash'ath, known as Ibn al-Samarqandī. He was born in Damascus in the year 454 [1062] and was a prolific scholar of Ḥadīth.[18]

---

[15] For further developments, see below p. [**95**].

[16] He is named Ibrāhīm al-Sahūlī in *Muntaẓam*, x, 95.

[17] He was appointed vizier by Zankī in the year 528/1133-4 (*Bāhir*, 48).

[18] He died in Baghdad on the eve of Tuesday 26 Dhū'l-Qa'da/= 23 June 1141. A dream he recounted in which he saw the Prophet ill, was interpreted as presaging some weakening of Islam and was shortly followed by news of the Frankish capture of Jerusalem.

[**91**] The Year 537 [1142–1143]

How Atabeg Zankī took the castle of Āshib and others from the Hakkārīs

In this year Atabeg Zankī sent an army to the castle of Āshib, which was the greatest of the castles of the Hakkārī Kurds and the strongest, where they kept their wealth and their families. He besieged it and pressed hard on the defenders, until he took it[1] and then ordered its destruction and the construction of the castle known as al-'Imādiyya to replace it. Among their fortresses this al-'Imādiyya had been a great one, but they destroyed it on account of its size, because it was very large indeed and they were incapable of holding it. At this present time Āshib was demolished and al-'Imādiyya was rebuilt. It was called al-'Imādiyya with reference to Zankī's title. Naṣīr al-Dīn Jaqar, his deputy in Mosul, had already conquered most of the castles in the Uplands.

Account of the Frankish siege of western Tripoli

During this year the Franks' ships sailed from Sicily to western Tripoli and put it under siege. The reason was that its inhabitants in the reign of Emir al-Ḥasan, ruler of Ifrīqiya, did not submit willingly to his authority but continued to be at odds with him and rebellious. They had put over themselves shaykhs of the Banū Maṭrūḥ to govern them. When the ruler of Sicily saw this state of affairs, he sent a sea-borne army against them, which arrived on 9 Dhū'l-Ḥijja [25 June 1143] and camped around the city and attacked it. [**92**] They attached grappling hooks to the wall and also mined it.

The next day a party of Arabs arrived to help the inhabitants who were much heartened by them. They sallied out against the men of the fleet and made a crushing charge. The Franks fled in a terrible rout. A large number of them were killed. The survivors gained their ships but abandoned their weapons, baggage and animals, all of which the Arabs and the men of the city plundered. The Franks returned to Sicily, re-equipped themselves with weapons and came back to the Maghrib, arriving at Jījal.[2] When the population saw them, they fled into the countryside and the hills. The Franks entered the town, enslaved those they caught there and demolished it. They burnt the palace that Yaḥyā ibn al-'Azīz ibn

---

1 On 23 Ramaḍān/11 April 1143 (*Zubdat al-ḥalab*, ii, 276–7).

2 Yāqūt, ii, 170, spells out the name without giving a location. It is on the coast of modern Algeria. See *EI(2)*, ii, 537–8, s. v. Djidjelli, captured this year by George of Antioch, Roger II's admiral.

Ḥammād had built for his pleasure, then they withdrew.[3]

Miscellaneous events[4]

This year Ḥasan, emir of the Arabs, rebelled against Sultan Sanjar in Khurasan.

Muḥammad ibn Dānishmand, the ruler of Malaṭya and the Marches, died this year. His lands were conquered by Prince Mas'ūd ibn Qilij Arslān, the ruler of Konya and one of the Saljuqs [of Rūm].

This year a large army came into Syria from Byzantine lands. They besieged the Franks in Antioch. Its ruler went out to meet with the Byzantine emperor. He restored his good relationship with him and then returned to Antioch. [The emperor] died in Ramaḍān of this year [April 1143]. After the emperor had reached an understanding with the ruler of Antioch, he [had] moved to Tripoli, which he besieged but then departed.[5]

During this year Sultan Mas'ūd arrested Emir Turshak, who was one of the intimates of the caliph and one of those who had been brought up with him and in his palace. This displeased the caliph. The sultan later freed him to placate the caliph.[6]

In Egypt this year there was a great plague, which caused the death of most of the population.

---

3 For this section, see Idris, *La Berbérie*, i, 349.

4 Various events that the text mentions under the year 536 (Sanjar's grant of authority to Mas'ūd in Rayy and its region, Ibn Ṭalḥa's retirement after his pilgrimage and Zankī's taking of al-Ḥadītha and displacing the Muhārish family) are given in *Muntaẓam*, x, 102, under this present year.

5 Here Ibn al-Athir has confused his sources. In the Arabic the only possible subject of the verb 'died' is the prince of Antioch, Raymond of Poitiers, who in fact died in battle in June 1149. The emperor, John II, died in April 1143, as Ibn Qal., 277, reports, after a hunting accident. See Runciman, ii, 224 and 326.

6 According to *Muntaẓam*, i, 105, Turshak was arrested in the following year 538.

[93] The Year 538 [1143–1144]

Account of the peace made between the Martyr [Zankī] and Sultan Mas'ūd

This year Sultan Mas'ūd came to Baghdad[1] as was his annual custom, gathered troops and prepared to march against Atabek Zankī, towards whom he nourished an intense resentment. The reason for this was that the provincial rulers at variance with Sultan Mas'ūd were rebelling against him, as we have already related, and he blamed that on Atabeg Zankī, claiming that he was the one who engineered and advised it, as the sultan knew that they all acted on his suggestion. Without any doubt Atabeg Zankī was doing this to prevent the sultan's being free to overpower him or anybody else. However, when during this year the sultan was free, he assembled his troops to march to Zankī's lands. The latter sent to placate him and win him over. The sultan dispatched Abū 'Abd Allāh ibn al-Anbārī to draw up terms of an agreement. It was settled that Zankī should pay 100,000 dinars to secure the sultan's withdrawal. He paid up 20,000 dinars, most of that in kind.[2] Later the sultan's circumstances changed and he needed to cultivate the Atabeg's goodwill, so he waived the outstanding sum to win his support and his sympathy. The main reason for the sultan's holding back was his knowledge of how defensible Zankī's lands were and how plentiful his troops and money.

What the Martyr did during this difficult time shows the excellence of his policy. His eldest son [**94**] Sayf al-Dīn Ghāzī, on the orders of his father, continued to attend the sultan, whether at home or on his travels. At the present juncture he sent ordering him to flee from the sultan to Mosul and at the same time sent to his deputy there, Naṣīr al-Dīn Jaqar, telling him not to allow him to enter or make contact. Ghāzī duly fled and the news came to his father, who sent orders for him to return to the sultan and would not meet him. With him he sent an envoy to the sultan to say, 'My son fled for fear of the sultan, because he saw how his attitude towards me had changed. I have sent him back to your service and would not meet with him. He is your servant and our lands are yours.' This was very well received by the sultan.

Account of the Atabeg's conquest of parts of Diyār Bakr

This year Atabeg Zankī went to Diyār Bakr and conquered a number of towns and

---

1 In Rabī' II/13 October–10 November 1143 (*Muntaẓam*, x, 105).

2 *Muntaẓam*, x, 105, specifies 'to be paid in textiles (*thawb*)' and that the sum Zankī actually paid was 30,000 dinars.

fortresses there, for example, the towns of Ṭanza,[3] Is'ird,[4] and Khīzān,[5] and the castles of al-Rūq, Qaṭalbas, Bātāsā,[6] Dhū'l-Qarnayn and others that have not gained the fame of these places. He also took from the territory of Mardin that was in the hands of the Franks, Jamalīn,[7] al-Muwazzar, Tell Mawzan and other castles of Joscelin. He organised the affairs of all and garrisoned them with troops to hold them. He also made his way to Āmid and Ḥānī[8] and besieged them. He remained in those regions, putting in order what he had taken and besieging what he had not.

[95] The situation of the urban gangs in Baghdad

During this year the urban gangs became more of a problem and increased in numbers because they were safe from prosecution owing to the vizier's son and a son of Qāwurt, a brother-in-law of the sultan,[9] since they were receiving a share of whatever the gangs took.

The deputy prefect of Baghdad at this time was a mamluke called Īldakīn, who was stern, bold and wicked. His forwardness brought him to present himself before the sultan, who said to him, 'Public order is failing and the people are ruined.' He replied, 'O sultan of the world, when the controllers of the gangs are your vizier's son and your wife's brother, what power do I have to deal with the malefactors?' He explained the situation to him and the sultan said, ' You are to move immediately, fall upon them wherever they are and crucify them. If you do not, I shall crucify you.' He took the sultan's ring, set out and raided the vizier's son without finding him at home, but he seized those who were there. He also raided Qāwurt's son, seized and crucified him. In the morning the vizier's son fled. The news of what had happened spread and Qāwurt's son could be seen on the gibbet. Most of the gang members fled. Those who stayed were arrested and the population was delivered from their evil-doing.

---

3 Ṭanza was near Hattākh, north of Mayyafariqin, whereas Ṭanzī was south of Is'ird (Hillenbrand, *Muslim Principality*, 84, note 75). Given the other places named in this context one should probably emend the text here to Ṭanzī.

4 The modern Turkish Siirt. See Le Strange, *Caliphate*, 114; Krawulsky, 452.

5 Khīzān (correcting the text's Ḥīzān) was a fortress south of Lake Van, between it and Is'ird (see Hillenbrand, *Muslim Principality*, 104 and references there cited).

6 These three places in the region of Is'ird cannot be firmly located. In *Bāhir*, 66, they appear as al-Z.w.q, F.ṭ.līs and Batāsā. Correct the present text's Qaṭlīs and Nātāsā (see Hillenbrand, *Muslim Principality*, 60).

7 The text has Ḥ.m.l.y.n. This fortress and al-Muwazzar are west of Tell Mawzan, present Viranshehir (see Elisséeff, 139–40).

8 Situated about 40 miles N.N.E. of Āmid (see Le Strange, *Caliphate*, 110).

9 Mas'ūd was married to Mustaẓhiriyya, a daughter of Qāwurt. *Muntaẓam*, x, 106, has 'the sultan's cousin.'

How Sanjar blockaded Khwārazm and made peace with Khwārazm Shāh

Under the year 532 [1137–8] we mentioned Sanjar's expedition to Khwārazm, his conquests there, Atsiz Khwārazm Shāh's return and his recovery of the area and what he subsequently did in Khurasan. In this present year Sanjar again went to Khwārazm and Khwārazm Shāh **[96]** gathered his forces, fortified himself in the main town but did not venture out to fight because he knew he was not strong enough for Sanjar.

Fighting between the two sides took place across the city wall. One day it came about that one of Sanjar's emirs called Sunqur made an assault from the eastern side and gained an entry. Another emir, named Mithqāl al-Tājī, entered from the western side. There was nothing to prevent the imminent capture of the city by force of arms. However, Mithqāl withdrew because he was jealous of Sunqur. Khwārazm Shāh Atsiz then overwhelmed him and expelled him from the city. That left Sunqur alone, who strove hard to hold the city. When the sultan saw how strong the city was and its resistance, he resolved to retire to Marv but he was unable to do so without a settlement agreed between them. It chanced that Khwārazm Shāh sent envoys offering money, allegiance and service and a return to his former obedience. This was accepted and they made peace. Sanjar returned to Marv and Khwārazm Shāh remained in Khwārazm.

Miscellaneous events

This year Atabeg Zankī sent an army to the town of 'Āna in the Euphrates district and took control of it.

The following died this year:

Abū'l-Barakāt 'Abd al-Wahhāb ibn al-Mubārak ibn Aḥmad al-Anmāṭī,[10] the Koran scholar, in Muḥarram [July 1143] at Baghdad. He was born in the year 462 [1070].[11]

Abū'l-Futūḥ Muḥammad ibn al-Faḍl ibn Muḥammad al-Isfarā'īnī, the preacher from Isfarā'īn in Khurasan. He remained for a while in Baghdad, preaching, and then went back to Khurasan, where he died at Bisṭām. He was an outstanding scholar and divine. Between him and 'Alī al-Ghaznawī there was a rivalry.[12] **[97]** When he died, al-Ghaznawī came to offer condolences at Baghdad and wept copiously. One of Abū'l-Futūḥ's followers gave a discourse in which he spoke harshly of al-Ghaznawī. When the latter rose to leave, one of Abū'l-Futūḥ's pupils

---

[10] The text has al-Anbāṭī, but Ms. Pococke 346, fol. 98a and *Muntaẓam*, x, 108, have the attested al-Anmāṭī (lit. the Rug-seller).

[11] Born Rajab 462/April–May 1170; died Thursday 11 Muḥarram/26 July 1143 = Monday! (*Muntaẓam*, x, 108–9).

[12] The rivalry was based on theological differences. Abū'l-Futūḥ was a strong Asharite. He was born in 474/1081–2 and died in Dhū'l-Ḥijja/June–July 1144 (*Muntaẓam*, x, 110–12).

criticised him for attending the session of condolence and for weeping a lot, saying, 'You were hostile to this man. Now that he is dead, you come to give condolence, weep plentifully and make a show of sorrow!' His reply was, 'I was weeping for myself. People used to speak of him and me [in one breath]. When one's twin is lost, it's surely nearly time to go!' He recited these verses:

Al-Mubarrad departed and his days ended,
And after al-Mubarrad Tha'lab will surely pass away.[13]
A house of letters of which half has become a ruin,
While a half survives yet, will surely be ruined utterly.
Learn from Tha'lab, for from that which al-Mubarrad drank
Will Tha'lab shortly be drinking too.
I enjoin you to record your breaths,
If breaths are something that can be recorded.

The Vizier Sharaf al-Dīn 'Alī ibn Ṭirād al-Zaynabī in Ramaḍan [March 1144], while out of office.[14] He was buried in his residence at Azaj Gate but later was transferred to al-Ḥarbiyya.

Abū'l-Qāsim Maḥmūd ibn 'Umar al-Zamakhsharī,[15] the grammarian and Koranic exegete. Zamakhshar is one of the villages of Khwārazm.

---

[13] Mubarrad, who died *c.*286/900, and Tha'lab, who died 291/904, were notorious rivals. Both were famous grammarians and philologists (see *EI(2)*, vii, 279–82 and x, 433).

[14] He was born in 462/1069–70 and died Wednesday 1 Ramaḍān/=10 March 1144. His residence was at Bāb al-Marātib (the Gate of Degrees) according to *Muntaẓam*, x, 109. Ḥarbiyya was on the west bank at Baghdad.

[15] Amongst his varied literary output his Koran commentary, *al-Kashshāf*, despite Mu'tazilī ideas, was influential (see *Encyclopedia of Arabic Literature*, ii, 820–21). Born 467/1075 in Khwārazm, he died on the eve of 'Arafāt Day/13 June 1144 (*Muntaẓam*, x, 112).

The Year 539 [1144–1145]

The conquest of Edessa and other places in the Jazīra that had been in the hands of the Franks

On 6 Jumādā II [4 December 1144][1] Atabeg 'Imād al-Dīn Zankī ibn Āqsunqur conquered the city of Edessa from the Franks and also other fortresses of theirs in the Jazīra. The harm they caused had been general throughout the lands of al-Jazīra and their wickedness had spread far and wide. Their raids reached all quarters and corners of it. They extended to Āmid, Nisibis, Ra's 'Ayn and Raqqa.

Their domain in those regions stretched from near Mardin to the Euphrates, including such as Edessa, Sarūj, al-Bīra, Sinn Ibn 'Uṭayr, Jamalīn, al-Muwazzar, al-Qurādī and others. These areas, along with others that were to the west of the Euphrates, belonged to Joscelin. He was the chief policy-maker of the Franks and the commander of their armies because of his courage and cunning.

The Atabeg knew that, if he attempted to besiege Edessa, the Franks would gather forces there to defend it and he would be unable to take it because of its strength. He therefore busied himself with Diyār Bakr to make the Franks imagine that he was not free to attack their territory. When they thought that he was not able to leave the Artuqid rulers and other princes of Diyār Bakr, seeing that he was at war with them, they felt confident and Joscelin departed from Edessa and crossed the Euphrates to his western possessions. The Atabeg's spies came to him with this information. **[99]** He announced that his troops should mobilise and that none should fail to assemble before Edessa later than the following day. He gathered his emirs together and said, 'Bring out the food,' and added, 'Let none eat with me at this my table except those who will wield their sword with me tomorrow at the gates of Edessa.' Only one emir and an unknown page came forward to join him, because his boldness and bravery were well known, as also was the fact that no one could rival him in battle. That emir said to the page, 'What have you to do with this?' The Atabeg said, 'Let him be! By God, I see a brave heart[2] that will not let me down.'

He marched with his troops and came to Edessa. He was the first to charge the Franks and that page was with him. A knight of the Frankish cavalry charged the

---

[1] This date also given in *Kāmil* (Thornberg), xi, 64. Various others found; Ms. Pococke 346, fol. 98b and *Zubdat al-ḥalab*, ii, 279, have 16 Jumādā II. *Muntaẓam*, x, 112, has Saturday 15 Jumadā II. For a discussion of the date, see Stevenson, *Crusaders*, 151 and note 1. The accepted date (Saturday 23 December 1144) is supported by Ibn Qal., 279, and Bundārī, 205: Saturday 26 Jumādā II.

[2] Literally 'a face.'

Atabeg from the side but that emir intercepted him and fatally pierced him, saving the Martyr's life. He invested the city and for twenty-eight days attacked it, carrying out several assaults. He sent the sappers forward, who mined the city wall. He maintained a constant attack for fear that the Franks would gather, march against him and rescue the city. The curtain wall, which the sappers had mined, fell and the city was taken by force of arms. He besieged the citadel and took it too. Our people plundered property, enslaved the women and killed the men.

When he had seen the city, he was impressed with it and thought that no sensible policy would permit the demolition of such a place. He therefore ordered a proclamation to be made among his troops that they should return the men, women and children they had seized to their houses and restore the furnishings and goods they had taken as booty. Every last person was brought back. No one was lost except for the very rare case when someone had been taken and his captor had already left the camp. The city returned to its former state and Zankī stationed a garrison there. He also took over Sarūj and all the other places that the Franks had held east of the Euphrates, apart from al-Bīra, for it was strong and well fortified and on the banks of the Euphrates. He went there and besieged it but they had prepared plenty of provisions and a large garrison. [**100**] He continued to blockade it but later withdrew, as we shall narrate, God willing.

It has been told that a certain scholar, a genealogist and historian, said:

> The ruler of Sicily had sent a squadron by sea to Tripoli in the west and nearby regions, where they plundered and killed. There was in Sicily a Muslim scholar, a man of piety, whom the ruler of Sicily honoured and respected. He paid attention to what he said and gave him precedence over the priests and monks at his court. The people of his realm used therefore to claim that this meant that he was a Muslim. One day he was sitting in a belvedere of his that overlooked the sea, when a small ship appeared. Those on board told him that his troops had entered Islamic territory and ravaged, killed and conquered. The Muslim scholar was at his side, dozing. The king said to him, 'Do you not hear what they say?' 'No,' he replied. Repeating their news, the king went on, 'Where was Muḥammad, abandoning those lands and their folk?' The Muslim said, 'He has been victorious on their behalf. He was at the conquest of Edessa, for the Muslims have now taken it.' The Franks present laughed and the king said, 'Laugh not, for by God he only ever says what is true.' After a few days news of its capture came from the Franks in Syria.

Several religious and pious men have told me that a pious man saw the Martyr in a dream. He asked him, 'How has God treated you?' to which he replied, 'He has forgiven me because of the conquest of Edessa.'

The killing of Naṣīr al-Dīn Jaqar and Zayn al-Dīn ʻAlī Kuchuk's taking control of the citadel of Mosul

In Dhū'l-Qaʻda of this year [25 April–24 May 1145] Naṣīr al-Dīn Jaqar, Atabeg Zankī's deputy in Mosul and all its dependencies east of the Euphrates, was killed.

[**101**] This came about as follows. Prince Alp Arslān, known as al-Khafājī, a son of Sultan Maḥmūd, was with the Atabeg. The latter pretended to the caliph, Sultan Masʻūd and the provincial rulers that his lands were the possessions of this prince and that he himself was his deputy in them. He was [in fact] waiting for the death of Sultan Masʻūd to proclaim Alp Arslān sultan in the khutbah and to conquer the lands in his name. This year the prince was at Mosul and every day Naṣīr al-Dīn would visit him to perform any service that might arise. A certain wicked trouble-maker encouraged the prince to seek power. He said to him, 'If you kill Naṣīr al-Dīn, you can take Mosul and other towns. Not a single cavalryman will remain with Atabeg Zankī.' This was well received by the prince who thought it was true. When Naṣīr al-Dīn entered his presence, the Atabeg's troops and mamlukes who were with the prince attacked Naṣīr al-Dīn and put him to death. They threw his head to his followers, thinking that they would scatter and that the prince could emerge and take the country.

What happened was the opposite of what they expected. Naṣīr al-Dīn's men and those of the Atabeg who served him, when they saw his head, fought the prince's men in the palace. A large number flocked to their side. The Atabeg's realm was full of steadfast men of good sense and experience.

Cadi Tāj al-Dīn Yaḥyā ibn al-Shahrazūrī[3] went to the prince and pressed false advice on him. When he saw that he was upset, one of the things he said to him was, 'My lord, why are you bothered by this dog? He and his master are your mamlukes. Praise be to God who has saved us from him and his master at your hands. Why do you stay inactive here in the palace? Rise and go up into the citadel. Take the money and weapons. Take the town and assemble troops. Once Mosul is yours, there is nothing to prevent your taking all the lands.'

Up he rose with Tāj al-Dīn and rode to the citadel. When he drew near, the officer and troops within were minded to resist. Tāj al-Dīn went forward and said to them, 'Open the gate, take him and do with him what you will.' So they opened the gate and the prince and the cadi entered the citadel, along with those who helped to kill Naṣīr al-Dīn. They were then thrown into prison while the cadi departed.

[**102**] Atabeg Zankī heard the news, when he was besieging the citadel of al-Bīra and on the point of taking it. He feared that the eastern lands might fall into disarray after the murder of Naṣīr al-Dīn, so he left al-Bīra and sent Zayn al-Dīn ʻAlī ibn Baktakīn to the citadel of Mosul to govern there on the same basis as Naṣīr al-Dīn.[4]

---

3 Born 495/1101-2, died 556/1161. He was the brother of Kamāl al-Dīn Muḥammad.

4 According to *Rawḍatayn*, i, 151, Ibn al-Athīr is at error in this section. Zankī was Atabeg

Miscellaneous events

This year Sultan Mas'ūd arrested his vizier, al-Burūjirdī. After him the office was taken by al-Marzubān Ibn 'Ubayd Allāh ibn Naṣr al-Iṣfahānī. Al-Burūjirdī was given into his charge and he was made to disgorge his wealth before he died while in custody.

During this year Atabeg 'Imād al-Dīn Zankī, after taking Edessa, was besieging al-Bīra, one of the strongest fortresses, which was in Frankish hands, lying east of the Euphrates. He pressed it hard and was close to taking it, when news of the killing of Naṣīr al-Dīn, his deputy in Mosul, reached him. He withdrew from al-Bīra and sent a deputy to Mosul. He halted, waiting for news. The Franks in al-Bīra feared that he might come back; they were very fearful of him indeed, so they sent to Najm al-Dīn, the lord of Mardin, and surrendered the place to him, so that it became a Muslim possession.

This year the Frankish fleet sailed from Sicily to the coast of Ifrīqiya and the West. They conquered the city of Brashk[5] and killed its inhabitants. They enslaved the womenfolk and sold them to Muslims in Sicily.

The lord of the West, Tāshfīn ibn 'Alī ibn Yūsuf, died this year. His reign lasted somewhat longer than four years[6] and he was succeeded by his brother [Isḥāq]. The power of the Veiled Ones waned and 'Abd al-Mu'min grew stronger. We have mentioned this under the year 514 [1120-21].

[**103**] In Shawwāl [April 1145] a large star with a tail appeared from the direction of the East. It lasted until the middle of Dhū'l-Qa'da [May 1145], then disappeared. Later it rose again in the West. It was said that it was the same one but others claimed that it was different.

This year there was a serious disturbance between Emir Hāshim ibn Fulayta al-'Alawī al-Ḥusaynī, Emir of Mecca, and Emir Naẓar the Eunuch, the emir of the Pilgrimage. Hāshim's men plundered the pilgrims, while they were in the mosque performing the circumambulation of the Kaabah and praying. They observed towards them 'no obligation either of kin or faith.'[7]

The following died during this year:

In Dhū'l-Ḥijja [25 May-2 June 1145] 'Abd Allāh ibn Aḥmad ibn Muḥammad ibn 'Abd Allāh ibn Ḥamdawayh, Abū'l-Ma'ālī al-Marwazī, at Marv. He travelled

---

to two sons of Sultan Maḥmūd, Alp Arslān, imprisoned at Sinjār, and Farrukhshāh at Mosul (this latter was the one called al-Khafājī). For this and the attempted coup of Farrukhshāh and his probable death, see Bundārī, 205-7. According to *Zubdat al-ḥalab*, ii, 280-81, Zankī went to Mosul where he arrested and killed the Sultan's son, Farrukhānshāh (sic). After these events Alp Arslān was taken up by Zankī (Bundārī, 207). Later after Zankī's death he made an unsuccessful bid for power (see *Bāhir*, 84-6).

5 A small town and harbour west of Algiers, now called Sidi Brahim (see Forstner, *Das Wegenetz*, 252-3).

6 In fact he ruled from the death of his father in 1143 till his own death in March 1145.

7 Cf. Koran, ix, 8 and 10.

much and heard much Ḥadīth. In Marv he built a hospice and left many books there in a permanent trust (*waqf*). He was a man of great charity and devotion.

Muḥammad ibn ʻAbd al-Malik ibn Ḥasan ibn Ibrāhīm ibn Khayrūn, Abū Manṣūr al-Muqrī. He was born in Rajab of the year 454 [11 July–9 August 1062] and was the last person to relate from al-Jawharī by licence. He died in Rajab [January 1145].[8]

Abū Manṣūr Saʻīd ibn Muḥammad ibn ʻUmar, known as Ibn al-Razzāz, professor of the Niẓāmiyya at Baghdad. He was born in the year 462 [1069–70], studied law under al-Ghazālī and al-Shāmī and was buried in the tomb of the Shaykh Abū Isḥāq.[9]

[8] *Muntaẓam*, x, 115, puts his death on the eve of Monday 16 Rajab, but this would give 12 January 1145, which was a Friday. Perhaps 16 is an error for 26. If the change is made, 26 Rajab corresponds to Monday 22 January 1145.

[9] He died on Wednesday 11 Dhū'l-Qaʻda/= 6 June 1145 (*Muntaẓam*, x, 113).

The Year 540 [1145-1146]

[104]

How Būz-Aba and 'Abbās conspired to oppose the sultan

During this year Būz-Aba, lord of Fars and Khuzistan, went with his troops to Qāshān, accompanied by Prince Muḥammad, son of Sultan Maḥmūd. They were joined by Prince Sulaymān Shāh, son of Sultan Muḥammad. Būz-Aba and Emir 'Abbās, lord of Rayy, met and agreed to abandon their allegiance to Sultan Mas'ūd. They proceeded to take control of much of his lands.

News of this came to Mas'ūd when he was at Baghdad, in the company of Emir 'Abd al-Raḥmān [ibn] Ṭughāyuruk, his emir-chamberlain and the dominant man in the state, whose sympathies, however, lay with the two emirs. In Ramaḍān [15 February–16 March 1146] the sultan left Baghdad. Emir Muhalhil, Naẓar and a group of Bahrūz's mamlukes remained there. The sultan set out with 'Abd al-Raḥmān and the two armies drew close to one another. Nothing was wanting but for the pitched battle to begin. However, Sulaymān Shāh joined his brother Mas'ūd and 'Abd al-Raḥmān embarked on making a peaceful settlement on terms that the emirs wanted. In addition to what he already held 'Abd al-Raḥmān was given the governorship of Azerbayjan and Arrāniyya. Abū'l-Fatḥ ibn Dārust, who was Būz-Aba's vizier, became the vizier of Sultan Mas'ūd. Thus the sultan came to be under their strict control. They removed Beg Arslān ibn Balankirī, known as Khaṣṣ Beg, who was the sultan's close adviser and mentor. He transferred to the service of 'Abd al-Raḥmān to save his life. All became in outward appearances servants of the sultan but there was no substance behind this. God knows best!

[105] Account of 'Alī ibn Dubays ibn Ṣadaqa's taking control of al-Ḥilla

This year 'Alī ibn Dubays fled to al-Ḥilla and took control there. This came about because, when the sultan wished to leave Baghdad, he was advised by Muhalhil to imprison 'Alī ibn Dubays in the citadel of Takrit. The latter learnt of this and fled with a small band, about five persons, and went to al-Azīz. He gathered the Banū Asad and others and marched to al-Ḥilla, where his brother, Muḥammad ibn Dubays, was. In the fight that followed Muḥammad was defeated and 'Alī took al-Ḥilla.

At first the sultan thought him of little consequence but his power grew and he attached to himself a body of his own mamlukes and those of his father, his relatives and their troops. His following became numerous. Muhalhil, with the troops he had in Baghdad, moved against him and a pitched battle was fought. 'Alī broke those troops and they returned in rout to Baghdad.

The population of Baghdad were firm supporters of 'Alī ibn Dubays and whenever Muhalhil and some of his men rode in public, they would shout, 'O 'Alī, eat him!' This happened so often that Muhalhil refused to go riding.

'Alī laid hands on the emirs' fiefs at al-Ḥilla and treated them as his own property. The prefect of Baghdad and others there became fearful of him. The caliph assembled a body of men and stationed them on the city wall to guard it. He also wrote to 'Alī, who sent in reply, 'I am your obedient servant. Whatever I am ordered I shall perform.' The people were then reassured. Later news arrived that Sultan Mas'ūd's opponents had scattered before him, which made the people even more reassured and calm.

[106] Miscellaneous events

This year the pilgrimage was led by Qāymāz al-Arjuwānī, one of the men of the Emir of the Pilgrimage, Naẓar. Naẓar argued that his equipment had been plundered in the defeat at al-Ḥilla and that there had been such hostilities between himself and the Emir of Mecca as made it impossible for him to perform the pilgrimage while he was there.

This year the caliph heard things about his brother Abū Ṭālib that he disapproved of, so he kept a tight rein on him and also kept an eye on other relatives of his.

This year the Franks (God curse them) took the city of Santarem, Beja, Merida, Lisbon and all the fortresses in their neighbourhood in Andalusia. They had belonged to the Muslims but they became disunited, so the enemy became ambitious and took these cities, gained strength thereby and became confident of capturing all the lands of Islam in Andalusia. However, God frustrated their expectations. We shall relate what the sequel was.

This year the Frankish fleet sailed from Sicily and conquered the island of Kerkenna, part of Ifrīqiya. They killed the men and made captives of the women. Al-Ḥasan, the ruler of Ifrīqiya, sent to Roger, king of Sicily, reminding him of the treaties that were between them. Roger made the excuse that these people were not subjects of his [of al-Ḥasan].[1]

The following died in this year:

Mujāhid al-Dīn Bahrūz al-Ghiyāthī. He was the dominant figure in Iraq for thirty years and more.[2]

Yarunqush al-Zakawī, lord of Isfahan. He was also a prefect in Iraq, who had been an Armenian eunuch servant of a certain merchant.

---

1 See Idris, *La Berbérie*, 350.

2 He died in Rajab/18 December–16 January 1146 in a hospice he had built on the Tigris bank (*Muntaẓam*, x, 117).

Emir Īldikiz, prefect of Baghdad.

Shaykh Abū Manṣūr Mawhūb ibn Aḥmad ibn al-Khiḍr al-Jawālīqī, the scholar of linguistics. He was born in Dhū'l-Ḥijja of the year 465 [8 August-5 September 1063] [**107**] and studied Arabic language with Abū Zakariyyā' al-Tabrīzī. He used to lead the prayers for al-Muqtafī, the Commander of the Faithful.[3]

Aḥmad ibn Muḥammad ibn al-Ḥasan ibn 'Alī ibn Aḥmad ibn Sulaymān, Abū Sa'īd ibn Abī'l-Faḍl al-Isfahānī. He was born in the year 463 [1070-71]. He transmitted a lot of Ḥadīth and followed the way of life of the early generations. He was assiduous in modelling his life on the *sunna* of the Prophet (may God's mercy be upon him).[4]

3 After seventeen years of study with Abū Zakariyyā', he followed him as professor of Arabic language at the Baghdad Niẓāmiyya for a while. He died 15 Muḥarram/8 July 1145 (*Muntaẓam*, x, 118).

4 *Muntaẓam*, x, 116, gives his *kunya* as Abū Sa'd and says that he died in Rabī' I/22 August-20 September 1145.

The Year 541 [1146-1147]

[**108**]

Account of the Franks' capture of western Tripoli

This year the Franks (God curse them) captured western Tripoli. This came about because Roger, king of Sicily, fitted out a great fleet and sent it to Tripoli, which the Franks surrounded by land and by sea on 3 Muḥarram [15 June 1146]. The defenders went forth to meet them and battle was engaged. The fighting between them lasted for three days.

When the third day came the Franks heard a great uproar in the city and the walls were denuded of defenders. This was because a very few days before the arrival of the Franks dissensions had broken out among the people of Tripoli. One group amongst them expelled the Banū Maṭrūḥ and appointed as their leader one of the Veiled Ones who had arrived, with a following, on his way to perform the Pilgrimage. They placed him in authority. After the Franks had begun the siege, the other faction restored the Banū Maṭrūḥ and fighting broke out between the two parties. The walls were left unmanned, so the Franks seized their opportunity, set up ladders and scaled the wall. After fierce fighting the Franks took the city by the sword which was followed by a blood-bath and seizure of women and property. Those who could flee did so and sought refuge with the Berbers and the Arabs. Later there was a proclamation that guaranteed security for all. All who had run away returned.

The Franks remained for six months until they had strengthened the walls and dug the city moat. When they withdrew they took hostages from the inhabitants, including the Banū Maṭrūḥ and the Veiled One. Later they sent the hostages back [**109**] and put a member of the Banū Maṭrūḥ in charge of the city, retaining his hostages alone. The situation in the city was regularised. The people of Sicily and the Byzantines were obliged to travel there and it quickly flourished and its affairs prospered.[1]

How Zankī besieged [Qal'at] Ja'bar and Fanak

During this year Atabeg Zankī marched to the fortress of Ja'bar which overlooks

---

[1] These events at Tripoli are rehearsed in Idris, *La Berbérie*, 350-52, and references there cited. The governor appointed was Abū Yaḥyā ibn Maṭrūḥ al-Tamīmī. 'Obliged to travel' (*ulzima ... bi'l-safar*) may be too strong. Idris speaks of an edict inviting the inhabitants of Sicily to emigrate.

the Euphrates. It was in the hands of the son of Sālim ibn Mālik al-'Uqaylī. Sultan Malikshāh had given it to his father when he took Aleppo from him, as we have already related.[2] Zankī besieged it and sent an army to the castle of Fanak,[3] which is in the vicinity of Jazīrat Ibn 'Umar, with two leagues between them. He besieged that too, its lord at that time being Emir Ḥusām al-Dīn al-Kurdī al-Bashnawī.

The reason was that, for motives of prudence and caution, Zankī did not wish there to be in the middle of his lands any place that was controlled by someone else. So he descended upon Qal'at Ja'bar and put it under siege. The defenders resisted him and, when some time had elapsed, he sent a message to the ruler by the hand of Emir Ḥassān al-Manbijī, because of the friendship between them both, proposing its surrender. He said to his envoy, 'You may guarantee on my part a large fief and plentiful money, if he agrees to surrender, but otherwise, say to him, "By God, I shall continue to press you until I take it by force, and then I shall not spare you. Who is there who will protect you from me?"'

Ḥassān climbed up into the castle and delivered his message, made him the promises and offered what he had been told. Nevertheless, the ruler refused to surrender, so Ḥassān said to him, 'He says to you, "Who will protect you from me?"' The reply was, 'He who protected you from Emir Balak will protect me from him.' Ḥassān returned and told Zankī of his refusal, without mentioning what else he had said. A few days later Zankī was killed.

The story of Ḥassān and Balak, the nephew of Īlghāzī, was that Ḥassān had been the lord [**110**] of Manbij and Balak besieged him very closely. One day while the fighting was in progress, Balak was hit by an arrow, shot by a person unknown, which killed him and thus delivered Ḥassān from the siege. This has been mentioned previously.[4] Those words [of Sālim's son] were fortuitously spoken.

When Atabeg Zankī was killed, his army, which was besieging the castle of Fanak, withdrew. Fanak has been held by the descendants of its then lord until this present time.[5] I have heard them say that they have been there about 300 years. They are sought out by all and sundry, for they possess good faith and strong cohesion, willing to take the hand of all who seek their protection and asylum, and

---

2 In 479/1086 Malikshāh took Aleppo from his brother Tutush. Sālim the Uqaylid was holding the citadel and surrendered it in return for Qal'at Ja'bar (see Richards, *Annals*, 225-6). The text here omits 'the son of', but the reading of Ms. Pococke 346, fol. 101a, has been followed (cf. also *Bāhir*, 73).

3 A strong castle of the Bashnawī Kurds on the Tigris about 10 miles upstream from Jazīrat ibn 'Umar (Yāqūt, iii, 920). See *EI*, 1st ed., ii, 1138, s.v. Finīk.

4 See above under the year 518/1124, but there Ḥassān (called al-Ba'labakkī) is a prisoner of Balak and not besieged in Manbij. According to a version of this passage in *Rawḍatayn*, i, 156 (quoting a lost *Life of Saladin* by Ibn Abī Ṭayy) it is a son of Ḥassān who tries to persuade the lord of Qal'at Ja'bar to surrender.

5 Here Ibn al-Athir means the time when he was writing, which, since the passage also appears in *Bāhir*, 73, is probably about 609/1212 or soon after.

never giving anyone up, whoever he may be.

Account of the killing of Atabeg ‘Imād al-Dīn Zankī and some biographical remarks

This year on 5 Rabī‘ II [14 September 1146] Atabeg and Martyr ‘Imād al-Dīn Zankī ibn Āqsunqur, lord of Mosul and Syria, was killed while he was besieging Qal‘at Ja‘bar, as we have mentioned already. Several of his mamlukes murdered him at night and fled to Qal‘at Ja‘bar. Those defending the place shouted out to the [besieging] troops to tell them of his murder and manifested their delight. His men entered his presence and found him at his last gasp.

My father told me on the authority of one of Zankī's close companions that he said:

> I went in to him immediately, while he was still alive. When he saw me, he thought that I was intending to kill him. He gestured to me with his index finger, appealing to me. I halted in awe of him and said, ‘My lord, who has done this to you?’ He was, however, unable to speak and gave up the ghost at that moment (God have mercy on him).

[My father][6] also said:

> He was a good-looking man, of a swarthy complexion and with pleasant eyes. His hair had turned **[111]** grey.[7] He was more than sixty years of age, for he was a young boy when his father was put to death, as we have related previously.[8] After his death he was buried at al-Raqqa.

He was held in great awe by his troops and his subjects and his political control was strong. No mighty subject was able to oppress the weak. His lands, before he conquered them, were in a ruinous state because of oppression, the many changes of governor and the proximity of the Franks. He developed them and they became busy and populous.

My father told me:

> I saw Mosul when most of it was ruined, in that a man could stand near the Quarter of the Drummers[9] and see the Old Mosque, the Market and Government House, because there was no building in between. Nobody was able to walk to the Old Mosque, unless he had someone with him to protect him, because it was so far from any habitation. Nowadays it is in the middle of a

---

6 See *Bāhir*, 76.

7 *Bāhir*, 76, adds: ‘[he was] tall, but not outstandingly so.’

8 Āqsunqur was killed in 487/1094. Zankī would have been about 10 years old.

9 i.e. *maḥallat al-ṭabbālīn*. It appears as *maḥallat al-ṭabbāliyya* in the N.W. part of the town in a map in Khāshi‘ al-Ma‘āḍidi, *Dawlat Banī ‘Uqayl fī'l-Mawṣil*, Baghdad, 1968.

built-up area and in all the parts mentioned there is no unused tract of land.

He also told me that Zankī came to Jazīrat [Ibn 'Umar] one wintertime. Emir 'Izz al-Dīn al-Dubaysī, one of his senior emirs, part of whose fief was the town of Daqūqa, entered and took over the house of a Jew. The Jew appealed to the Atabeg and reported his case to him. Zankī stared at al-Dubaysī who backed away, entered the town and brought out his baggage and his tents. My father said, 'I saw his mamlukes erecting his tents in the mud, having put straw on the ground to keep the mud away. The emir left the town and took up his quarters in his tents. Zankī's authority reached such a level.'

Mosul had been one of the least productive lands for fruit. In Zankī's days, and in those that followed, it became one of the most productive of fruit, aromatic plants and such like.

Zankī was also extremely protective, especially of the wives of the soldiers. He used to say, **[112]** 'If we had not guarded the wives of our soldiers by the fear we inspire, they would have been corrupted because their husbands are so frequently absent on campaigns.'

He was the bravest of God's creatures. As for the time before he became a ruler, it is enough to mention that he was present with Emir Mawdūd, the lord of Mosul, at Tiberias, which belonged to the Franks. He hurled a spear which reached the city gate and damaged it. He also attacked the citadel of 'Aqr al-Ḥumaydiyya, which is on a high mountain, and his spear-throw reached the wall. There were other similar feats. As for the period after he came to rule, his enemies surrounded his lands, all of whom were attacking them and wishing to seize them, but he was not content simply to protect them, with the result that no year passed without his taking part of their lands. The Caliph al-Mustarshid bi-Allāh was his neighbour in the region of Takrit and attacked Mosul and put it under siege. Next to him in the region of Shahrazūr and those parts was Sultan Mas'ūd. There was also Ibn Suqmān, lord of Khilāṭ, and Dā'ūd ibn Suqmān, lord of Ḥisn Kayfā, and the lord of Āmid and Mardin, and the Franks from the vicinity of Mardin to Damascus, and finally the rulers of Damascus itself. These realms encompassed his realm on all sides. He attacked now this one and now that, taking from this person and cajoling that one, until he seized from each one of his neighbours some tract of land. We have dealt fully with his exploits in our book, *al-Bāhir*, concerning the history of his reign and the reigns of his descendants. Reference should be made to that work.

Bibliographical References

Manuscript source

Ms. Pococke 346: Bodleian Ms. Pococke 346, 195 folios, completed Tuesday 7 Rajab 691/24 June 1292, covering the years 502–71/1108–76.

Primary sources

al-Abīwardī, *Dīwān*, ed. 'Umar As'ad, 2 vols., Damascus, 1974-5.

Ansāb: al-Sam'ānī, *Kitāb al-ansāb*, ed. Abd al-Rahman ibn Yahya et al., 13 vols., Hyderabad, 1962–82.

Bāhir: Ibn al-Athīr, *al-Ta'rīkh al-bāhir fī'l-dawla al-atābakiyya*, ed. A.A. Tolaymat, Cairo, 1963.

Bundārī: al-Fatḥ ibn 'Alī al-Bundārī, *Zubdat al-nuṣra wa-nukhbat al-'uṣra*, ed. M.Th. Houtsma, Leiden, 1889.

al-Fāriqī: Aḥmad ibn Yūsuf ibn al-Azraq al-Fāriqī, *Ta'rīkh al-Fāriqī*, ed. Badawi Awad, Cairo, 1379/1959.

Ibn Ḥamdīs, *Dīwān*: Ibn Ḥamdīs, *Dīwān*, ed. Ihsan Abbas, Beirut, 1960.

Ibn al-'Imrānī: Ibn al-'Imrānī, *al-Inbā' fī-ta'rīkh al-khulafā'*, ed. Qasim al-Samarrai, Leiden, 1973.

Ibn Muyassar: Muḥammad ibn 'Alī ibn Muyassar, *Akhbār Miṣr*, ed. Henri Massé, vol. viii, Cairo, 1919.

Ibn Qal.: Ibn al-Qalānisī, *Dhayl ta'rīkh Dimashq*, ed. H.F. Amedroz, Leyden, 1908.

Ibn Shaddād, *Damas*: 'Izz al-Dīn Ibn Shaddād, *La Description de Damas d'Ibn Šaddād*, ed. Sami Dahan, Damascus, 1956.

Ibn Shaddād, *Liban*: 'Izz al-Dīn Ibn Shaddād, *Liban, Jordanie, Palestine: Topographie historique d'Ibn Šaddād*, ed. Sami Dahan, Damascus, 1963.

Ibn Zuhr: Abū Marwān Ibn Zuhr, *Kitāb al-taysīr fī'l-mudāwāt wa'l-tadbīr*, ed. Michel al-Khuri, Damascus, 1403/1983.

Itti'āẓ: al-Maqrīzī, *Itti'āẓ al-ḥunafā' bi-akhbār al-a'imma al-faṭimiyyīn al-khulafā'*, ed. Jamal al-Din al-Shayyal, 3 vols., Cairo, 1967-73.

Kāmil: Ibn al-Athīr, *al-Kāmil fī'l-ta'rīkh*, 13 vols., Dār Ṣādir ed., Beirut, 1965–7.

Kāmil (Thornberg): C.J. Thornberg ed., *Ibn-el-Athiri Chronicon quod Perfectissimum Inscribitur*, 14 vols., Leiden, 1851–76.

Mir'āt al-Zamān: Sibṭ ibn al-Jawzī, *Mir'āt al-zamān*, ed. Ali Sevim, Ankara, 1968.

Mufarrij: Ibn Wāṣil, *Mufarrij al-kurūb fī akhbār Banī Ayyūb*, ed. Jamal al-Din al-

Shayyal et al., 5 vols., Cairo, 1953–77.
Muntaẓam: Ibn al-Jawzī, *Kitāb al-muntaẓam*, vols. v–x, Hyderabad, 1357–9/1938–40.
Nafḥ al-ṭīb: al-Maqarrī, *Nafḥ al-ṭīb min ghusn al-Andalus al-ratīb*, ed. Ihsan Abbas, 8 vols., Beirut, 1968.
al-Nuwayrī: al-Nuwayrī, *Nihāyat al-arab fī funūn al-adab*, 31 vols., Cairo 1923–98.
Rāwandī, *Rāḥat*: al-Rāwandī, *Raḥat al-ṣudūr wa-āyat al-surūr*, ed. Muḥammad Iqbāl, London, 1921.
Rawḍatayn: Abū Shāma, *Kitāb al-rawḍatayn fī akhbār al-dawlatayn*, ed. Ibrahim al-Zibaq, 5 vols., Beirut, 1418/1997.
Sibṭ ibn al-Jawzī: Sibṭ ibn al-Jawzī, *Mir'āt al-zamān*, vol. viii, Hyderabad, 1951.
Tijānī, *Riḥla*: 'Abd Allāh al-Tijānī, *Riḥlat al-Tijānī*, Tunis, 1378/1958.
Wāfī: al-Ṣafadī, *al-Wāfī bi'l-wafayāt*, ed. H. Ritter et al., 1931 – in progress.
Yāqūt: Shihāb al-Dīn Yāqūt al-Rūmī, *Kitāb mu'jam al-buldān*, ed. F. Wüstenfeld, 6 vols., Leipzig, 1866–70.
Yāqūt, *Irshād*: Yāqūt al-Rūmī, *Irshād al-arīb ilā ma'rifat al-adīb*, ed. D.S. Margoliouth, 7 vols., London, 1923–31.
Zubdat al-ḥalab: Kamāl al-Dīn Ibn al-'Adīm, *Zubdat al-ḥalab min ta'rīkh Ḥalab*, ed. Sami al-Dahhan, Damascus, 1954.

Primary material in translation

Eddé, *Description*: 'Izz al-Dīn Ibn Šaddād, *Description de la Syrie du Nord*, trad. Anne-Marie Eddé-Terrasse, Damascus, 1984.
Gibb, Damascus Chronicle: H.A.R. Gibb (trans.), *The Damascus Chronicle of the Crusades*, London, 1932.
Hillenbrand, *Muslim Principality*: Carole Hillenbrand, *A Muslim Principality in Crusader Times: the early Artuqid State*, Istanbul, 1990.
Juvainī, *History*: Juvaini, *The History of the World-Conqueror*, trans. John Andrew Boyle, 2 vols., Manchester University Press, 1958.
Matthew of Edessa, *Chronicle*: Matthew of Edessa, *Armenia and the Crusades Tenth to Twelfth Centuries: the Chronicle of Matthew of Edessa*, trans. A.E. Dostourian, Lanham, New York and London, 1993.
Recueil: Recueil des Historiens des Croisades, Historiens orientaux, ed. Reinaud, M. de Sacy et al., 5 vols., Paris, 1872–1906.
Richards, *Annals*: *The Annals of the Saljuq Turks: Selections from al-Kāmil fī'l-Ta'rīkh of 'Izz al-Dīn ibn al-Athīr*, trans. and annotated D.S. Richards, London and New York, 2002.
William of Tyre: William Archbishop of Tyre, *A History of Deeds done beyond the Sea*, trans. and annotated E.A. Babcock and A.C. Krey, 2 vols., New York, 1976.

Secondary material

Abun-Nasr, *Maghrib*: Jamil M. Abun-Nasr, *A History of the Maghri*b, Cambridge, 1975.

Adams, *Land behind Baghdad*: Robert McC. Adams, *Land behind Baghdad: a history of settlement on the Diyala Plains*, Chicago and London, 1965.

Allan, *Persian Metal etc.*: James W. Allan, *Persian Metal Technology 700-1300 AD*, London, 1979.

Alptekin, *Reign of Zangi*: Coşkun Alptekin, *The Reign of Zangi (521-541/1127-1146)*, Erzurum, 1978.

Asbridge, *Principality of Antioch*: Thomas S. Ashbridge, *The Creation of the Principality of Antioch 1097-1130*, Woodbridge, 2000.

Barthold, *Turkestan*: W. Barthold, *Turkestan down to the Mongol Invasion*, ed. C.E. Bosworth, 3rd ed., London, 1968.

Beckingham, 'The achievements of Prester John,' in Charles F. Beckingham and Bernard Hamilton, eds., *Prester John, the Mongols and the Ten Lost Tribes*, Aldershot, 1996, 1-22.

Biran, *Empire of the Qara Khitai*: Michal Biran, *The Empire of the Qara Khitai in Eurasian History: between China and the Islamic World*, Cambridge, 2005.

Bosworth, 'Dailamīs etc.': C.E. Bosworth, 'Dailamīs in Central Iran: the Kakūyids of Jibal and Yazd,' *Iran*, viii (1970), 73-95.

Bosworth, *Later Ghaznavids*: C.E. Bosworth, *The later Ghaznavids; splendour and decay. The dynasty in Afghanistan and Northern India 1040-1186*, Edinburgh, 1977.

Bosworth, *New Islamic Dynasties*: C.E. Bosworth, *The New Islamic Dynasties: Chronological and genealogical manual*, Edinburgh, 1996 (paperback 2004).

Bosworth, 'The Iranian world': C.E. Bosworth, 'The political and dynastic history of the Iranian world (A.D. 1000-1217),' in J.A. Boyle, *The Cambridge History of Iran*, vol. 5: *The Saljuq and Mongol Periods*, Cambridge, 1968, 1-202.

Cahen, 'Historiography': Claude Cahen, 'Historiography of the Seljuqid Period,' in Bernard Lewis and P. M. Holt eds., *Historians of the Middle East*, Oxford, 1962, 59-78.

Cahen, *Pre-Ottoman Turkey*: Claude Cahen, *Pre-Ottoman Turkey: a general survey of the material and spiritual culture and history c. 1071-1330*, trans. J. Jones-Williams, London, 1968.

Die Kernländer: Heinz Gaube and Thomas Leisten, *Die Kernländer des 'Abbāsidenreiches im 10./11.* Jh., Wiesbaden, 1994.

Dozy, *Supplément*: R. Dozy, *Supplément aux dictionnaires arabes*, 2 vols., Brill 1881, reprinted Beirut, 1968.

Eddé, 'Riḍwān': Anne-Marie Eddé, 'Riḍwān, Prince d'Alep de 1095 à 1113,' *Revue des études islamiques*, vol. liv, 1986, 101-25.

EI(2): *The Encyclopaedia of Islam*, eds. H.A.R. Gibb et al., 11 vols., 2nd ed., Leiden, 1960-2002.

Elisséeff: Nikita Elisséeff, *Nūr ad-Dīn. Un grand prince musulman de Syrie au temps des Croisades (511-569 H./1118-1174)*, 3 vols., Damascus, 1967.

Encyclopedia of Arabic Literature: Julie Scott Meisami and Paul Starkey eds., *Encyclopedia of Arabic Literature*, 2 vols., London and New York, 1998.

Fagnan: E. Fagnan, *Annales du Maghreb et de l'Espagne*, Algiers, 1901.

Forstner, *Das Wegenetz*: Martin Forstner, *Das Wegenetz des Zentralen Maghreb in islamischer Zeit: Ein Vergleich mit dem antiken Wegenetz*, Wiesbaden, 1979.

Gabrieli, *Arab Historians*: Francesco Gabrieli, *Arab Historians of the Crusades*, trans. E.J. Costello, London, 1969.

GAL: Carl Brockelmann, *Geschichte der arabischen Litteratur*, 2 vols. and 3 Supplement vols., Leiden, 1943-9.

Garsoïan, *Epic Histories*: *The Epic Histories attributed to P'awstos Buzand*, trans. Nina G. Garsoïan, Cambridge, Mass., 1989.

Hinz: Walther Hinz, *Islamische Masse und Gewichte*, Leiden/Köln, 1970.

Hopkins, *Medieval Muslim Government*: J.F.P. Hopkins, *Medieval Muslim Government in Barbary until the Sixth Century of the Hijra*, London, 1958.

Idris, *La Berbérie*: H.R. Idris, *La Berbérie orientale sous les Zīrīdes Xe-XIIe siècles*, 3 vols., Paris, 1962.

Imad, *Vizierate*: Leila S. al-Imad, *The Fatimid Vizierate, 969-1172*, Islamkundliche Untersuchungen, Band 133, Berlin, 1990.

Klausner: Carla L. Klausner, *The Seljuk Vezirate: a study of civil administration 1055-1194*, Cambridge, Mass., 1973.

Krawulsky: Dorothea Krawulsky, *Īrān - Das Reich der Īlḫāne: Eine topographisch-historische Studie*, Wiesbaden, 1978.

Lambton, *Continuity and Change*: Ann K.S. Lambton, *Continuity and Change in Medieval Persia: aspects of administrative, economic and social history, 11th-14th century*, Albany, N.Y., 1988.

Lambton, 'Reflections': Ann K.S. Lambton, 'Reflections on the *iqṭā*',' in G. Makdisi ed., *Arabic and Islamic Studies in Honor of Hamilton A.R. Gibb*, Leiden, 1965, 358-76.

Lassner, *Topography*: Jacob Lassner, *The Topography of Baghdad in the early Middle Ages*, Detroit, 1970.

Le Strange, *Baghdad*: G. Le Strange, *Baghdad during the Abbasid Caliphate*, Oxford, 1900.

Le Strange, *Caliphate*: G. Le Strange, *The Lands of the Eastern Caliphate*, Cambridge, 1930.

Le Strange, *Palestine*: G. Le Strange, *Palestine under the Moslems*, reprinted Beirut, 1965.

Maalouf, Amin, *The Crusades through Arab Eyes*, trans. Jon Rothschild, London, 1984.

Makdisi, *Ibn 'Aqīl*: George Makdisi, *Ibn 'Aqīl et la Résurgence de l'Islam traditionaliste au XIe siècle (Ve siècle de l'Hégire)*, Damascus, 1963.

Makdisi, 'Topography': George Makdisi, 'The topography of eleventh century

Baghdad: materials and notes (I and II),' *Arabica*, vi (1959), 178-97, 281-309.

Mayer, 'Angevins versus Normans': Hans E. Mayer, 'Angevins versus Normans: the New Men of King Fulk of Jerusalem,' *Proceedings of the American Philosophical Society*, cxxxiii, 1989, 1-25.

Mez, *Renaissance*: A. Mez, *Die Renaissance des Islams*, English trans. S.K. Bakhsh and D.S. Margoliouth, Patna, 1937.

Nowell, 'The historical Prester John': Charles E. Nowell, 'The historical Prester John,' *Speculum*, xxviii, 1953, 435-45.

Order of Assassins: Marshall G. S. Hodgson, *The Order of Assassins*, 's-Gravenhage, 1955.

Pelliot, *Notes on Marco Polo*: Paul Pelliot, *Notes on Marco Polo*, 3 vols., Paris, 1959-73.

Riant, 'L'invention de la sépulture etc.': Comte Riant, 'L'invention de la sépulture des patriarches Abraham, Isaac et Jacob à Hébron le 25 Juin 1119,' *Archives de l'Orient Latin*, ii, 1884, 411-21.

Richard, *Comté de Tripoli*: Jean Richard, *La comté de Tripoli sous la dynastie toulousaine (1192-1187)*, Paris, 1945.

Richards, 'Ibn al-Athīr': D.S. Richards, 'Ibn al-Athīr and the later parts of the *Kāmil*: a study of aims and methods,' in *Medieval Historical Writing in the Christian and Islamic Worlds*, ed. D.O. Morgan, London, 1982, 76-108.

Richards, 'Some consideration': D.S. Richards, 'Some consideration of Ibn al-Athīr's *al-Ta'rīkh al-Bāhir* and its relationship to the *Kāmil*,' in *Actas XVI Congreso UEAI*, ed. C. Vazquez de Benito and M.A. Manzano Rodriquez, Salamanca, 1995, 443-6.

Rosenthal, *Historiography*: Franz Rosenthal, *A History of Muslim Historiography*, Leiden, 1952 (second revised ed., 1968).

Runciman: Steven Runciman, *A History of the Crusades*, 3 vols., Cambridge, 1952.

Salmon, *Introduction*: Georges Salmon, *L'Introduction topographique à l'histoire de Bagdâdh*, Paris, 1904.

Sezgin: Fuat Sezgin, *Geschichte des arabischen Schrifttums*, 12 vols., Leiden, 1967-in progress.

Stevenson, *Crusaders*: W.B. Stevenson, *The Crusaders in the East*, Cambridge, 1907, reprinted Lebanon, 1958.

Vermeulen, 'Note sur les insignes': U. Vermeulen, 'Note sur les insignes royaux des Mamelouks,' in *Egypt and Syria in the Fatimid, Ayyubid and Mamluk Eras*, ed. U. Vermeulen and D. De Smet, Leuven, 1995, 355-61.

Wittfogel et al., *Chinese Society*: Karl A. Wittfogel and Fêng Chia-shêng, *History of Chinese Society: Liao (907-1125)*, Philadelphia, 1946.

Wright: W. Wright, *A Grammar of the Arabic Language*, 2 vols., third revised ed., Cambridge, 1955.

Index

The definite article (al-) is ignored for purposes of alphabetical order